The Hydra's Tale

Imagining Disgust

D1706461

Published by
The University of Alberta Press
Ring House 2
Edmonton, Alberta T6G 2E1

Printed in Canada   5   4   3   2   1
Copyright © The University of Alberta 2002
A volume in (*cuRRents*), an interdisciplinary series. Jonathan Hart, series editor.

NATIONAL LIBRARY OF CANADA CATALOGUING IN PUBLICATION DATA

Wilson, R. Rawdon.
  The hydra's tale

  Includes bibliographical references and index.
  ISBN 0-88864-368-3

  I. Aversion. I. Title.
BF575.A886W54 2002   152.4   C2001-910101-5

Printed and bound in Canada by Houghton Boston, Saskatoon, Saskatchewan.
Book design by Lara Minja.
Index prepared by Western Indexing.
Proofreading by Jill Fallis.
∞ Printed on acid-free paper.

Cover and frontispiece: Gustave Moreau, French 1826–1898, *Hercules and the Lernaean Hydra* (ca. 1876);
oil on canvas, 175.3 x 154 cm. Gift of Mrs. Eugene A. Davidson, 1964.231. Reproduction © The Art
Institute of Chicago. All rights reserved; used by permission.

The University of Alberta Press is committed to protecting our natural environment. As part of our
efforts, this book is printed on stock produced by New Leaf Paper: it contains 100% post-consumer
recycled fibres and is acid- and chlorine-free.

The University of Alberta Press acknowledges the financial support of the Government of Canada
through the Book Publishing Industry Development Program for its publishing activities. The
Press also gratefully acknowledges the support received for its program from the Canada Council
for the Arts.

for

Jonathan Locke Hart
and
Deirdre Susan E. Crandall

There is no morality, no knowledge and no hope; there is only
the consciousness of ourselves which drives us about the world
that, whether seen in a convex or a concave mirror, is always
but a vain and floating appearance.

w

... a trick worthy of human perverseness which,
after inventing an absurdity, endeavours to find for it a
pedigree of distinguished ancestors.

—*Joseph Conrad*

Contents

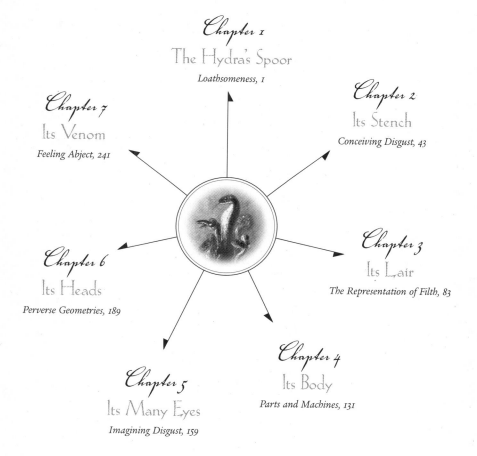

Introduction

Disgust seems like a commonplace human affect. All people feel it, although not for the same reasons. It can show up anywhere, in the midst of nearly any activity. It is easy to imagine, often in deeply loathsome,

nausea-causing scenes. Violent and copious vomiting, sudden incontinence, public excrement (at least in its mammalian instances), rot, putrefaction and stench all suggest experiences that would lead most human beings to feel disgust. For a book that sets out to study disgust, such scenes are at once obvious and almost too easy. Turn the problem of disgust around and look for the border cases: the scenarios in which disgust emerges abruptly from things that ought not to be disgusting or else marks the transformation of the attractive (or innocent) into its opposite and those moments, equally problematic, when things that have long been experienced as disgusting suddenly become acceptable, even desirable. These scenes will be more difficult to interpret but also more apt to focus the problem more clearly. In such moments, you will be looking not at open sewers or running rivulets of filth and gore but at the body's pulse or the constant flow and swish of its fluids. (And we are all, male and female, plain or lovely, hairy bags filled with fluids of varying viscosity.) Imagine a "thick white jam" that lisps, trickles and sticks until "there is nothing but gnarled knots of pale solid animal hair in the morning shower." That is how David Foster Wallace describes an adolescent boy observing his nocturnal emission in the morning.[1] Nothing there is particularly disgusting. Yet the author has clearly set out to evoke disgust. The character seems to feel disgust. You might almost smell the acrid stench of decaying sperm even though Wallace has made his character experience only a "clean sweet smell" that he cannot believe comes from anything made inside of himself.

For a book such as this one, the subject is everywhere and in everyone. And, although this book is not intended to be an exercise in gonzo cultural theory, the subject is both within and close to the author himself. I have long been interested in disgusting things. Sometimes I strike others as having a genuine enthusiasm, almost teen-age in its spontaneity, for slimy, deliquescent rot. More certainly, I take a writer's pleasure in metaphors, the imaginative constructions that actual disgusting things can make possible. And I have also, I believe, a scholar's interest in the what (or who), why, when and how of disgust. What is disgusting? Why, and under what conditions, do certain objects and acts become disgusting? How does it work upon you: upon your eyes, throat, viscera and imagination? I also have a writer's interest in how disgust has been represented. What are the images of disgust? How do disgusting images exert their power over viewers and readers? How are disgusting phenomena made sense of, used and transformed in our society? In part, my continuing interest in disgust may go back to having had a morally repressive middle-class upbringing, my mother (in particular) always finding things that I should not taste, touch or even see. It may also relate to my anti-repressive young adulthood. In a series of work experiences, largely intended to make my parents shudder, in such roles as a merchant seaman or a ringmaster for a small Australian circus, I encountered all manner of things—objects, acts, attitudes and practices—that I had never previously experienced. I learned to recognize the sight and smell of rotting fish in Manila, both intense enough to gag a maggot, the reeking odour of human ordure in the Australian bush and quite a few unhygienic practices in San Francisco. Most significantly, I learned that it is quite possible to eat food that once, under different circumstances, might have nauseated me with overflowing disgust.

Once, in the remote bush of Western Australia, I found the ground meat that I had intended to cook for dinner already fly-blown. It slithered with maggots, all performing their little humping crawl beneath the plastic covering. In a spasm of loathing, I threw the contaminated bundle into the rubbish, scurrying to wash my hands as quickly as I could. However, an experienced bushman rescued the package and showed me how to cook the meat using a long-handled frying pan over an open fire. By keeping one side of the skillet relatively cool, slanted downwards and hanging out over the fire, he tricked the maggots, desperate to continue their minimal existence, into crawling out of the meat onto the cool side. He then dumped them into the fire and presto! the meat was ready to eat, savoury if not entirely appetizing. (A bit later, I learned that many bushmen would simply cook up the maggots in fly-blown meat, devouring the ugly dish without qualms as just "protein.") For many people, such as my mother, the taboos that govern disgust reactions might still operate. A numbing sense of pollution would still make the meat impossible to eat. The maggots in the fly-blown meat might have vanished, but not the overpowering awareness that they had been there.

In many encounters, I learned that hunger and a radical change of circumstances, even if neither always nor forever, can weaken disgust and its supporting consciousness of contamination. In all such experiences, I would wonder how people managed to overcome disgust or how they learned to tolerate so easily what often struck me as deeply repulsive. Very early I had a strong sense that disgust was rigidly coded, given to us by our parents and our culture in unmistakable terms, but readily transformed as lifeworld conditions changed. This paradox doubles every manifestation of disgust. You can always ask about the powerful social forces that have brought it into being, its rigid and choking etiology, but you can also remark upon its unstable and variable nature, always subject to shifting conditions and values. Indeed, anyone who ignored this paradox would probably not write a very penetrating study. I also came to recognize that disgust was both a psycho-visceral and a moral term. A bigot's words can wound the spirit much as the sight of something deliquescent and sludge-like can torment the sight. Racism, sexism and homophobia, or any other form of identity chauvinism, all may invoke the sense of foulness and filth that leads to disgust and contamination. The Euro-American gesture of overtly refusing to shake another person's hand marks the moral disgust, disguised as physical disgust, that one person may experience in the presence of another. Even to touch a bigot might, for some people, invoke a loathing so strong that a personal sense of contamination would result. (The ways human beings disgust one another seem almost to be infinite.) Consider the complex doubleness involved. A bigot will assert that another human being disgusts him, no doubt alleging physical disgust (certain bodily characteristics, such and such acts or behaviours) that makes him wish to vomit, but his bigotry, on a moral level, should be deeply disgusting. It will cause others to turn away from him. The bigot's disgust will probably have been learned during childhood and adolescence, a rigid product of cultural training, but, however hateful and evidently intractable, it can be transformed. The person who experiences moral disgust at the bigot's nasty identity-jingoism might once have felt a similar kind of hatred. At least, that does seem often to happen, and it is the ideal hope behind much education, religion and literature: however deeply ingrained, human aversions can be modified, transformed and even wholly up-ended.

Like other European languages, English permits single words, "revulsion" and "loathing" as well as "disgust," to designate both physical and moral aberration. This makes disgust an extremely complex term, but, inescapably, it also makes it a deadly simple one. Disgust offers a ready-to-hand term of abuse which people at either end of a moral spectrum can hurl at each other. Calling another person "disgusting" may be a spontaneous response to bodily presence, either personal grooming or behaviour, but it may also be a ritual-practice incorporating distinct gestures of revulsion, a wrinkled nose and curled lip or even an extended palm-forward hand. Part of the fascination of disgust is its power to serve as an abusive term. It is not particularly vivid, scarcely as strong as quite a few Shakespearean terms, lacking imagistic depth, but yet capable of delivering insult and hurt. Few people, it seems, enjoy being called disgusting even if they are willing to own the loathed practices.

What disgusts is never stable, never irrevocably fixed and certain. It changes from culture to culture, and from time to time within a single culture. Furthermore, an individual person can pass through many phases in each of which what is disgusting will evoke very different responses, modifying from loathing to indifference, ambivalence and desire. In his *History of Shit*, Dominique Laporte tries to show that the history of human excrement is also the history of subjectivity.[2] Similarly, the history of disgust (if it were even possible to write) would reveal an overlapping, if not wholly coterminous, history of consciousness. Like consciousness, disgust is highly metamorphic. It undergoes constant alteration in focus and attention, like the bulges and bloats beneath the membrane of a ravenous pseudopod, as time and experience shift onwards. Oddly, the normal theories of disgust all seem to claim both constancy and fixedness.

There are several different theories to explain why certain objects and acts are disgusting, all of which cast at least a weak light, but they have all struck me as inadequate. Not worthless, and certainly not to be ignored, they are nonetheless too limited adequately to account for disgust's multi-faceted complexity. By and large, the theoretical models assume that once acquired, once fixed in consciousness, the disgusting must remain what it is or as it has been learned. Yet my personal experiences had shown me, over and over, that disgust did change, its well-marked boundaries did shift, and what one might once have learned to avoid could be accepted calmly, with detachment and equanimity even. Most strikingly, what had once been learned as disgusting, in the transformations of experience, could be (eagerly, hungrily even) yearned for. Thus one major issue that confronts any serious study of disgust must be the comparative inflexibility of the theoretical positions that have been used to explain an unstable, shifting human experience. I might like to begin this book by claiming, as William Ian Miller does, that disgust is a "roiling" subject, closely identified with all manner of bodily secretions and effluvia, for which, given its obviousness, the question of an explanatory theory must be either unimportant or easy.3 This is not the case. The question of theory dogs every step of a study of disgust.

Familiarity with disgust in art has re-enforced my personal experiences. Art, and perhaps especially literature and film, indicates that disgust has always been characterized by shape-shifting, never definitely fixed. In-the-world things that evoke powerful feelings of disgust, such as mutilated, dead and maggot-crawling bodies and stinking piles of excrement (perhaps again with an overburden of burrowing, slithering maggots), can be experienced as extremely aversive, disgusting in the extreme. Yet, with repeated contact, the same object can lose its capacity to stimulate disgust. Many common human occupations would not be possible, or comfortably performed, if it were not the case that initial disgust reactions can be overcome. It is difficult to imagine that doctors, paramedics, policemen, firemen, soldiers or workers in the sex trades could carry on their tasks easily if they had not overcome reactions, including the gag reflex that prompts vomiting, towards rotting and eviscerated bodies or, in so many ways, the public display of private slime. Transformed into a representation in literature or film, a disgusting thing or act may evoke quite different feelings, even including aesthetic pleasure. This is particularly the case with regard to horror films, or what is sometimes called "art-horror." Images of deliquescent and dismembered bodies keep some of the power to shock that actual bodies possess, under conditions of ruin and rot, but a concomitant effect (an intended effect, of course) is that of pleasure. I know that some people, Americans who loathe the NEH or people who find performance and avant-garde art disturbing (and who think that books, films, galleries and museums should be censored), either do not see or will not grant this point, but I think that it makes fundamental sense. Later in Chapter 3, I shall argue the distinction at some length and try to show that actual disgusting things and acts lack an aesthetic dimension while even "poor" art can cause a positive response, a sense of pleasure or even joy, that disgusting in-the-world things simply cannot create. Your reaction to participating in, or even just seeing, a golden shower would be, I suspect, quite different from reading a story or seeing a ballet about the same act.

Even casual observations suggest that disgusting acts and objects are both various and variable, shape-shifting and Protean to an extreme degree. It may strike some people's common sense that disgust is always pretty much the same and that some objects and acts are just "naturally" disgusting. This, empirical investigation shows, is not the case: disgust is multiple, plural and metamorphic. It is, to borrow a wonderfully apt term from Salman Rushdie, "hydravarious." I intend to examine the range and variety of this metamorphicity, but I want also to look squarely at the inadequacy of current theory to deal with disgust's extreme elasticity. Something must have gone wrong when a culturally diffused affect, by all empirical tests various and variable, can only be described by the available theoretical models as rigid, repetitive, unyielding and having, at best, only a few, limited uses (such as helping to maintain the moral order or as underlying the legal system). Theory's rigidity appears in several ways: arguing for a single cause, a single origin for the psycho-visceral responses that are experienced as disgust; claiming only a single cultural purpose or end; evincing a single object or type of object that is taken to be most, or essentially, disgusting; failing to examine any positive (whether exciting, playful or liberating) consequences for encounters with the disgusting. Writing on another topic, philosopher Mark Kingwell observes that it "is difficult to say anything intelligent about a subject that is at once so apparently clear and yet so resistant to explication."[4] Like happiness, disgust blares numerous warnings to an approaching scholar. Marked by obvious gagging and vomiting, accompanied by unmistakable sounds ("Yech!" "Yuck!"), disgust *seems* clear, but it both resists easy explication and prompts too many simplistic accounts. Little reveals the shortcomings of theory more clearly than the claim that disgust, at once so obvious and so intractable to analysis, is only one thing, has one chief purpose or only certain roles in culture, or that certain things (mammalian excrement, say, or corpse rot) are more essentially or necessarily disgusting than others. The study of disgust leads from a fascinating empirical investigation to an examination of theoretical models and how (and why) they work. It is a study in which bottoms and tops get thoroughly mingled.

Although I have been interested in disgust for a very long time, I had never written on the topic until recently. My academic interests in Shakespeare, Renaissance literature, theory and such syncretic problems as play and post-modernism kept me fully occupied. I may once have paused in the course of a scholarly paper to admire Spenser's account in *The Faerie Queene* of the human anus opening and closing (II, ix, 32–33), but I certainly did not take up the fascination of disgust as a scholarly problem. Eventually, I began to think seriously about the possibilities of the topic. It was evident from the beginning that both the vastness of the empirical subject area (everything and everyone *can be* disgusting, you as well as I) and the uncertainty of the theoretical models would pose difficulties. I knew that I would need to construct an argument to serve as the spine of a readable discussion and that I could not set out to write an encyclopedia even though the latter was exactly what the topic seemed to demand. An argument needs to be stream-lined and, if possible, elegant—the very opposite of an encyclopedia. Disgust is not a topic that lends itself readily to either precision or elegance. Hence this book will often show the untidiness of its subject matter: the roiling, hydravarious material that refuses simple categories, even though these are what theory seems most easily to solicit. I shall examine different theoretical models, move selectively across distinct areas of human experience and frequently cross the boundary between in-the-world things and their repre-sentations in art. Crossing boundaries of all kinds might strike you as the signature move of any serious study of disgust.

I decided to write this book on the very day (but before hearing) that news items from Milwaukee indicated that a new serial murderer had been revealed. Jeffrey Dahmer had killed at least eleven men (later known to be seventeen) in his apartment. He had cut them apart and taken photos of them in various stages of dismemberment. He also took video film. At least three heads were kept in his fridge. Male genitalia were kept in bottles. He had a vat of acid to dissolve flesh. All this struck me as profoundly disgusting. However, it was disgusting in rather intricate ways: I could imagine the scene and how I might react if, like an investigating policeman, I had to enter the apartment, perhaps catching a blasting whiff of the stench as I entered, and sort through the human ruins. I could also imagine the gross immorality of the acts: murder, dismemberment and canni-balism. A great deal of what I imagined was, as seems so often the case in cultural studies, how other people might have imagined the scene. It was, I thought, just the kind of unsimple human scene, full of transgression, evoking horror, crowded by numerous loathsome details (the male genitalia in bottles, say) that I would need for a study of disgust. Viewing the horror in Milwaukee from a wider scholarly perspective, Elliott Leyton, a Memorial University anthropologist and author of two books on serial killers, was reported to say it was "bog common." That seems to be the way with disgust: a more experienced, a broader or more disciplined perspective transforms both perception and judgement.

One way or another, Jeffrey Dahmer slipped out of this study. A little of this original interest shows up in Chapter 4, but most of my research into serial killers fell outside the eventual shape of the argument. This is not an occasion for regret. Properly to investigate the phenomenon of serial killers in American culture would require a book of its own. Indeed, Jeffrey Dahmer would demand a book on his own. Richard Tithecott's excellent study of Dahmer fulfills that need by delving deeply into the fundamental problems of the social construction and the culture roles of serial killers as well as the surrounding issues, in Dahmer's case, of homosexuality and cannibalism.[5]

Although "disgust" is not an especially vivid term, the experience itself gives rise to many striking images. Metaphors are never far from the topic. One Internet site gives more than two hundred metaphors for vomit, of which my favourites are "sidewalk pizza" and "Technicolor yawn." *The Hydra's Tale* turns repeatedly upon metaphors, seeking the images in art as well as in common language that highlight the disgusting, reveal the many difficulties that people have in dealing with their revulsions and open startling perspectives. My title evokes a monster from classical mythology who figures horrifically in one of the Labours of Herakles. The Hydra was a swamp creature, the granddaughter of the Medusa, known for her gut-wrenching stench as well as for her cephalic fecundity. The Hydra is Herakles' antagonist during his second Labour and (it is said) he has to hold his nose during combat. Robert Graves is no doubt correct when he argues that the Hydra's stench is a metonym, a mark of its habitation in the swamps at Lerna. However, her repulsive odour has other values as well. It figures in a long sequence of sensory horror that begins with the Medusa and ends on the island of Lemnos with the snake that bites Philoctetes. Stench underscores the vomit-inducing properties of all deliquescence and rot, even though odour in itself may not wholly explain why such existential conditions are experienced as disgusting. Blatant in her fecundity and stench, associated with rot (the swamp) and snake-like sinuosity (those many necks), a monster for whom wet slithering constitutes its most natural movement, the Hydra both recurs throughout this study as a *leitmotif* and rises over it as its most appropriate emblem.

Since the material of *The Hydra's Tale*, both empirical and theoretical, is Hydra-like, hydravarious in the extreme, but also sinuous to the point of slithering, an overview seems in order. Think of it as a road-map through difficult and unpredictable terrain. I have divided the book into seven chapters, each given either one of the Hydra's attributes or a body part as a directive metaphor. I have also begun each chapter with a short personal fiction, at once a kind of ficto-theory and a bio-fiction, turned to the purposes of scholarly discussion. I have not done this because I believe that my own encounters with disgust have been essentially more vivid than those that other people have had, but rather from a desire to distill conceptual analysis out of personal experience. Both the metaphoric chapter headings and the personal tales are intended to make the topic as graphic as possible and to engage the imagination (disgust's primary residence) vividly. Disgust is a highly personal affect (a spasm of nausea is so intensely yours alone), more so than pleasure or the perception of beauty. The latter two experiences can be easily discussed and can draw upon the study of aesthetics for validation, but disgust is difficult to articulate, its immediate vividness nearly impossible to convey. It may even lie, as philosopher Immanuel Kant argues, beneath representation, an experience, like the sublime in the opposite direction, that blunts expression and forbids generalization. And so it makes sense both to elicit its potential for striking metaphors and to embed the argument in my own experience.

Chapter 1, which establishes the problem of disgust and indicates the range of the intellectual disciplines that have contributed to understanding it, evokes the Hydra's spoor. It does this because Herakles has to track the Hydra before fighting it. (Even the Hydra's pawprints, it is said, were venomous and gut-churning.) Like the Hydra, disgust leaves an unmistakable spoor, but also one that is highly diffuse, full of misdirections and cross-trails. Chapter 1 tracks the problem of disgust, finding it in many aspects of human existence and on two distinct levels of reality, the physical and the moral. Furthermore, this chapter follows disgust through many disciplines. Anthropology, psychoanalysis, behavioural psychology, moral philosophy, cultural studies and literary criticism all have examined the significance of disgust. Above all, Chapter 1 examines the uses of disgust in shock art; from Frank Wedekind to G.G. Allin, and in bodily modifications, such as piercings and tattoos (taken here as small instances of street theatre). In each case, I come back to an overarching question: how is disgust imagined? What individual and cultural purposes are served when the mind imagines deliquescence, bodily effluvia and excreta? Disgust is not merely violent gagging and nausea; it is also the imagination of physical rot.

Chapter 2 explores the Hydra's lair. In this chapter, I examine five theoretical models that have been used to explain both disgust's what and why. As a metaphor, the lair suggests both the monster's home and her emergence. Our conceptual systems explain phenomena, but they also assign them diverse meanings: like distinct perceptual organs, each system experiences the world differently. Both the psycho-visceral response of disgust and the in-the-world disgusting things that elicit it will seem quite dissimilar from the standpoint of different conceptual models. For example, there is a moral-legal model according to which disgust is a powerful affect underlying social prohibitions. If certain actions were not inherently disgusting, the argument asserts, then laws and other kinds of negative sanctions would be either impossible or largely ineffective. Hence disgust is a primary, if not exclusive, foundation for both moral and legal behaviour. "Disgust," William Ian Miller writes, "is more than just the motivator of good taste; it marks out moral matters for which we can have no compromise ... its presence lets us know we are truly in the grip of the norm whose violation we are witnessing or imagining."[6] There are also models that attempt to explain the origins of disgust, the etiology of its coming into being, but ignore its socio-legal functions.

One explanatory model, giving an account of the origins of disgust, is based upon the principles of social construction. Another is founded in Freud's theory of ego defences. Although they are significantly different, both models trace disgust to the individual's early origins and to the process of socialization or social formation that begins from the moment of birth. These are both compelling models that make possible accounts of disgust as an affect shaped by an inevitable process of familial and cultural training. The social constructionist model allows for cultural variables: disgust will never be quite the same across cultural frontiers even though the nose may still wrinkle and the throat convulse. The psychoanalytic model tends more towards universalism, but it also provides, if you suppose that all human beings possess egos and that these develop and function in analogous ways, a serious account of how disgust enters into human life and what its purposes are. Neither the social constructionist nor the psychoanalytic model addresses the moral issues that disgust raises, and neither assigns disgust a role in founding legal systems. Psychoanalysis does place disgust, along with shame (both of which Freud thought to be "moral" affects because they regulate behaviour), at the basis of the repressive mechanisms, both individual and collective, that make human civilization possible. All three of these models, the moral, the social constructionist and the psychoanalytic, possess a built-in propensity to fix disgust and see it as inflexible and unyielding. Like acute but narrowly focussed perceptual organs, they make disgust visible but only in a deformed way, like a shadow figure or a caricature. They simply do not "see" disgust's many-headedness.

For this reason, I also examine two other theoretical models. One derives from Jean-Paul Sartre's foundational work in existentialist philosophy, *Being and Nothingness*, and has been widely diffused through its adaptation in Mary Douglas' *Purity and Danger*. This model stresses aberrant behaviour and the "sludgewards fall" of all existence.[7] That is, it immediately grasps an important factor in disgust's makeup that the moral and originary models ignore: the power of the human mind to imagine deliquescence and invent small narratives, whether of horror or loathing, to expand the immediate experience of disgust. In Sartre's account, disgust is always slime or the imagination of slime, an aberrant and ambiguous state. Adapted in Douglas' anthropological study, Sartre's formula for disgust receives the apothegmatic definition of "dirt out of place." In either case, Sartre's existentialism or Douglas' more explicitly phrased anthropology, disgust is invariably a matter of boundaries: a problem of slippage or transgression leading to anomalous, indeterminate states of being. The second term, transgression, leads directly into the fifth model.

Georges Bataille's writings provide a jolting insight into the potential uses of disgust. In experiencing disgust, you can take delight in what should offend you because that moment (in actual lifeworld situations as well as in reading or viewing) will expand your sense of life, push back the boundaries of your socialization and may even transform you. There are no limits to the possibilities of transgression; the worst conceivable crimes as well as comparatively mild boundary-hopping, such as participating in golden showers or engaging in coprophragy, can be acts beyond society's normal frontiers. Hence the fifth model returns to the question of morality, but it does so from a completely different perspective. Transgressions against established norms of disgust and loathing, perhaps even crimes, have the power to free the mind from its culturally conditioned repressions. "The grandest transgression of all," Richard Tithecott writes in his sustained reflection upon Jeffrey Dahmer, "is perhaps that which makes us forget what it was that was transgressed."[8] Bataille belongs to an honourable alternative tradition in French thinking (although Nietzsche must also be included) that reaches back, at least, to de Sade, including Baudelaire, Huysmans and Céline. It is a tradition of rebellion and self-acknowledgment, anti-repressive to its core. Gustave Flaubert's often-stated hatred for all manifestations of bourgeois values and morality, typically expressed in a militant irony verging on sarcasm, or the reactive hostility of the nineteenth-century avant-garde provide key examples. What Bataille argues, and it is a position that any scholarly study of disgust should consider, is very clear. Human life is circumscribed by repressive forces, most of which will be internalized through socialization, all of which control behaviour. Break these, or break out from their hold; become, in the phrase that Deleuze and Guattari have made famous, a "nomad." Having broken out from the striations of a repressive society, you may hike purposefully towards the fulfillment of your desires. Transgression, and in particular encounters with disgust, opens life, breaks society's repressive constraints and leads to a greater, more encompassing sense of self. It might even, in a strongly anti-Freudian manner, make you happy.

Throughout this study, usually well beneath the surface, Bataille and Sartre occupy dialectically opposed positions. They have much in common, not least the willingness to reflect repeatedly upon disgust, but I shall see them as generally expressing strikingly different positions. Transgressing social and religious boundaries in order to experience disgust is, for Bataille, a means of self-knowledge (of limitations) and, in some cases, transcendence. Sartre has a very explicit theory of disgust: it is an aberrant state, a transitional mode of being between two conditions, which he describes as *visqueux* (variously translated as "slimy" or "sticky"). However, Sartre also associates disgust with bad faith. A person who exists in bad faith is disgusting and may be characterized by his or her predilection for disgusting objects and acts. Thus in "The Childhood of a Leader" Lucien Fleurier grows up narcissistically obsessed by his body (which he smells and feels with exploratory fascination). At one point, he stares at some maggot-crawling dog excrement and fills his nostrils with a "forbidden, powerful odour, putrid and peaceful."[9] Lucien evolves through several mindsets, surrealism and anti-Semitism, for instance, eventually to become a Fascist, still anti-Semitic but now also a "patriotic" nationalist, and an industrial Boss. At each stage of this personal evolution, Lucien derives his sense of identity from the ideology that he has accepted and claims to believe. "Lucien thought, he was not a jellyfish, he did not belong to that humiliated race ... Lucien studied himself once more; he thought, 'I am Lucien! Somebody who can't stand Jews.'"[10] Lucien exists in bad faith, which in itself is morally disgusting, at once sham and slime, but his weakness and human insufficiency are marked throughout by his acceptance of, and participation in, the conventionally disgusting.

On the other hand, Bataille stresses the transformative potential of disgust. The experience of disgust turns out to be rather like contemplating the big toe: a conventional hierarchy, privileging the head and the upright stance, will be inverted and the big toe will be seen, finally, as an intricate, important bodily part.[11] Even Bataille's pornography ends on the note of transformation and triumph. His *Story of the Eye* ends with the narrator's discovery, "erectile with horror," of the missing eye in Simone's vagina, "gazing at me through tears of urine." Two hours later, he, Simone and Sir Edmund escape to Gibraltar, changing their personalities "at every leg of the journey." And at Gibraltar, they buy a yacht and sail forward "towards new adventures."[12] Disgust calls the imagination into play, but it does so in two distinct ways. It invokes small disgust scenarios, all of which are experienced vicariously and as personal displacements, in which images of rot and ruin unfold towards eventual catastrophe. It also gives rise to scenarios of transgression and, at least sometimes, self-revision.

Chapters 3 and 4 examine particular aspects of disgust, the nits, grit and slop of the phenomenon. Chapter 3 focusses on the distinction between actual disgusting objects and their on-stage (as it were) representations. I turn to several passages in modern literature that have struck many readers as disgusting or at the very least (in Judge Woolsey's famous comment upon *Ulysses*) "emetic." What I want to argue at this point is both straightforward and essential: a representation of filth can be as appalling as the object it represents, although not necessarily in the same way, but it may also cause aesthetic pleasure. Urinating on another human being sounds like an aggressive and tormenting act, and in times of war or personal combat it must be so, but as a sexual act between two consenting people it may not be. That is, once urinating upon another person has become sexual—a "golden shower," in other words—it may cease to be disgusting. From the outside, from the standpoint of moral disapprobation, the act may continue to seem extremely loathsome. Yet transformed into a work of literature, or into a dance, the golden shower might no longer seem disgusting at all, even to a stern moralist or even to a bigot, or it might seem no longer *only* disgusting. The argument from literature is just one move, although a significant one, in a more complex argument. Disgust changes, evoking shifting intensities of feeling, and the evidence for this is everywhere available even if the theoretical models are radically uncooperative.

In Chapter 4, I look closely at the way imagination takes "props" from the world to transform them into small, private disgust-worlds. This chapter continues the argument in the previous chapter, but it does so by looking at instances of human physical collapse and decay. The modalities of physical collapse are various, of course, but they are all, I argue, either instances of dismemberment or decomposition. The body falls sludgewards either by losing parts, by being broken and dismembered, or by changing shape, by undergoing a destructive metamorphosis. Hence the problem of prostheses or "cyber(body)parts" plays a central role in the discussion. Prostheses create a range of split consciousness, a series of possible subject positions between yearning for cybernetic enhancement (the "bionic" body) and disgust over the fall from a bodily ideal. I argue that the split consciousness that the possession of cyber(body)parts induces is closely related to, and exemplary of, self-disgust. In both Chapters 3 and 4, although I examine a number of disgusting phenomena, my focus is upon the powers of imagination and how disgust enters into private fictional worlds. One kind of disgust-world elaborates the self as the focal manifestation of loathing and revulsion. I have devoted Chapter 5 to the examination of the work of imagination in building small, but persistent, disgust-worlds. Think of it as a slight interruption in the argument, a kind of interlude perhaps, in which the analysis turns to a fundamental issue in the investigation of disgust that is not in itself normally disgusting: imagination.

Chapters 6 and 7 pursue the argument about disgust's metamorphicity, theory's rigidity and the imagination's suppleness under the rubrics of the Hydra's heads and its venom. Chapter 6 deals with, in H.P. Lovecraft's phrase, "perverse geometries." I take both horror and terror to embody, or else to reference, perverse geometries because each is the product of human intelligence and each is also anti-human (in its destructiveness and infliction of misery). Ideologies can be experienced as disgusting. For example, religions have consistently seen modernism (not technology as such but rather the principles of the Enlightenment carried forward as the basis for democratic government and civil policy) as the embodiment of moral decay, social rot and human depravity. On the level of representation, as "art-horror," say, disgust tends to function as a focussing device. It anticipates the monster, or the monstrous event, much as the Hydra's venomous tracks anticipated her lair in the swamps of Lerna. As a mode of representation, art-horror tends to utilize numerous disgust motifs to foreshadow what has yet to happen. On the other hand, terror always bursts upon the world, or upon the individual, causing disgusting things to appear (ripped, torn and eviscerated bodies, for example) like ripples around a central causative event. As representation, art-terror tends to ration disgust motifs, saving them for their radiating effect after the event which will have appeared abruptly, with nearly baroque theatricality. What I am concerned to show in Chapter 6 is the way in which even extremely abstract human constructions, such as an ideology or a moral system, can be experienced as disgusting. These abstract systems create the diverse effects of horror and terror and can be transformed into representations in which the disgusting motifs can also, because of the intelligence and skill required to create them, evoke a number of aesthetic responses, including suspense and surprise, admiration and pleasure. Thus Chapter 6 picks up the main theme of the previous two chapters, that imagination can appropriate in-the-world disgust and transform it. It carries this theme on into an analysis of two major genres of popular literature and film.

Finally, in Chapter 7, under the metaphor of the Hydra's venom, I conclude the discussion by closely examining the personal experience of self-disgust. This had formed a part of the discussion in Chapter 4 where I looked at the split in consciousness that can arise when a person acquires a prosthetic body part. However, there is an even stronger experience of self-disgust when your very being is called into question or has come to seem unworthy of either continued existence or membership in a human community. This strong version of self-disgust is known as abjection. The term "abject," which once meant only to be outcast or cast down, has been given a more incisive sense in recent cultural theory. The state of feeling yourself abject arises from something more corrosive, more painful to endure, than mere dismemberment or personal slippage (from some bodily ideal). Being abject is the condition of having been discarded, like excrement or a corpse, feeling this like venom in the veins, yet still clinging to a sense of personal identity. You may feel discarded (even excreted, perhaps) from your community, but still feel yourself. Chapter 7 considers the discussion of abjection in the works of Julia Kristeva and turns upon an extended analysis of Doris Lessing's magnificent 1962 novel *The Golden Notebook*. In this final chapter as in the previous ones, I am interested in the varieties of disgust and the limited, and very partial, capacity of different theoretical models to account for its existence as a human affect, its shiftiness and its multiple psychological and cultural uses. I also want to show that imagination plays a fundamental role in the condition of being abject. Abjection, I shall argue, invokes scenarios, ghastly intimate worlds in which the imagination incorporates various prejudicial stereotypes and uses them against itself to destroy the self's personhood.

Several of the topics I had originally planned to discuss have fallen by the way. Jeffrey Dahmer, although he seems to have towered above my initial reflections upon the topic, found little place in the finished book. My first research, partly because of my long interest in circuses, concerned freaks. I have been able to use some of this material, especially in Chapters 5 and 7, but most of it proved to be intractable within the argument that began to develop. I had a strong early interest in what are called "captive narratives," the records of Europeans, usually women, who had been captured by aborigines but eventually returned to their own cultures to tell the tale. Of this fascinating topic, nothing at all remains. In her splendid book on narratives by European women who had lived with North American natives, June Namias points out that the attitudes about what was disgusting changed radically from one century to another. "Colonial women," she writes, "were repulsed by native food; mid to late nineteenth-century women were repulsed by dirt. Their faintheartedness was matched by what they saw as their profound sexual mistreatment."[13] Namias' analysis would have tied into my interest in food, but this topic, too, became largely marginalized by the direction the argument took. Even more conscience-wrenching, I have not found the opportunity to pursue in any depth the relation of the disgusting to the sacred: the sense (in some cultures) that a boundary excludes in order to protect what lies behind from pollution. Behind the boundary, there will be a sacred area, the precincts of a deity or a religious tradition, that contains a *mysterium* projecting its "'numinous dread' or awe" upon all those who stand outside and are prohibited from crossing.[14] (The opposite sense of boundary, that it protects you, the potential crosser, from being polluted by materials behind it, constitutes the major focus of this study.) In the theory of the sacred, a taboo defends a sacred site or symbol from the corruption of ordinary touch. A personal tattoo might be said to work in this way: it marks off the bearer and creates a small territory of (in intention) inviolable personal experience. I shall have much to say about this sense of the inviolable which the disgusting pollutes, but it is not, I admit, a full, or even a satisfactory, discussion of the sacred. *The Hydra's Tale* could not be an encyclopedia, its most satisfying potential form, but rather it had to be an argument. Arguments are exclusive. They scant or completely exclude all manner of interesting material in the pursuit of restricted goals. My experience in writing this book proved to me once again, if further proof had been needed, that arguments determine their evidence: evidence always shows its provenance as argument's kidnapped child. ❧

1

The Hydra's Spoor

Loathsomeness

One autumn day in 1997, when a man threw me a wild apple, I thought of my father. The apple-throwing man had found a tree growing wild in the bush near the marina across from the Ladysmith harbour on Vancouver Island. There were several wormholes in the apple. But he, an old German from Kiel who kept his yacht in the marina, didn't seemed bothered by worms. And after all, I thought, wormholes are a part of the natural condition of fruit. When I was a child, we didn't mention worms much but simply ate around them. You had a choice: you could eat the worm for the protein (perhaps only to show your indifference to worms) or you could throw the apple away and look for another one. My father would have eaten the apple without pause, scarcely looking, indifferent to worms.

My father was an Apollonian individual. He dressed formally and spoke with precision. I remember him wearing a vest with a gold watch fob, prominently displaying his Phi Beta Kappa key, strung from buttonhole to pocket. He was a scholar who had taught at several important American universities, who had written books and helped to found scholarly journals. I grew up thinking of him as a stuffed-shirt type, rigidly governed by codes of etiquette and (senseless) duty. However, in one significant respect he was quite Dionysian: he was unconcerned how food looked, was prepared or was mistreated. Seeming barely to care how it tasted, he could eat nearly anything. I remember a fly falling into a dollop of mashed potatoes and, while my mother exclaimed in horror, my father forked it up and ate it calmly, without ostentation. "It is only protein," he observed evenly as my mother expostulated, disgust scrawled runically upon her face. At other times, I saw him eat flies that had fallen into drinks or mosquitoes that had landed near his mouth. A quick flick of his tongue and, with luck, a hapless bug would disappear into my father's Dionysian digestion. This indifference to food, at least when it served him to act this way (for at other times he enjoyed good food and sought out famous European restaurants), originated in his childhood growing up on ranches in west Texas, near the Mexican border, in the early part of the last century. As a child he had strangled chickens and turkeys, participated in butchering animals and lived roughly in many ways. Insects, especially flies, had been familiar companions at meals.

My friend Giancarlo was born in Naples and grew up there until he was a teenager. He remembers how his father, another Apollonian person, would recoil in disgust whenever a fly landed on a plate of food. His father would insist that the entire plate be served again, all the food on it replaced, before he could eat. A single disgusting object, a speck-like fly for instance, could contaminate the whole plate. It was necessary to begin over. Food for Giancarlo's father was clearly a special event bordered by taboos. It may even have been ritualized in his mind: a compulsive, reiterative desire to aesthetize food a certain way, giving it a definite shape and arrangement. For my father, it was the satisfaction of a biological urge, an opportunity for companionship, but not ritualized except in so far as the social occasion itself called for ritual behaviour.

I don't know how Giancarlo's father grew up or what pressures and constraints upon eating he experienced as a child (for all I know his extreme reaction to food contamination might have been an adult affectation), but I do know how my father grew up. His adult Dionysianism was only a transformation of childhood necessity. As an adult, he could re-invoke the exigencies of his early life whenever he wished to make a point. It allowed him to demonstrate that although a distinguished scholar, he was also a man of the people (as it were) and not squeamish like his wife and son. And perhaps Giancarlo's father also wished to make a statement. Behind the boundary of ritual taboos, there may have been an urge to impress others, his family or anyone else who might see him eat, that he was fastidious, a cultured man. Still, beneath their respective masks, they may also have experienced disgust differently. My father did not often express physical disgust, but he could, I knew well, feel deep disgust about the transgression of moral and legal categories. Giancarlo's father (and, of course, I am only supposing) may have experienced a more visceral disgust, a strong gorge-cracking reaction to all physical transgressions, all decay and slippage in the structure of appearances.

In western cultures, disgust is everywhere and touches everything. As a conceptual topic, an area for investigation, disgust is rather like play: any single thing may become an object of disgust, but it may not seem always so or always so in the same manner. The human world is full of things that look slimy, muck-crusted or mucoid, from one angle, but from another perspective may seem lovely, desirable or indifferent. It is crowded with things that seem to bulge and smudge, but, from another viewpoint, may also seem to possess a clean definiteness of line, a neat order. Each generation discovers new disgusting objects and acts. It forgets, other than in mockery and parody, many of the objects and acts that had been disgusting for the parental generation. Furthermore, there is a double-sidedness to disgust: from one perspective an object may cause nausea, or else an extreme moral revulsion; from another, it may seem attractive, exciting and even desirable. Early in Jean-Paul Sartre's novel *Nausea*, Antoine Roquentin remembers holding a pebble that disgusted him. He finds the pebble by the sea and picks it up: "It was a flat pebble, completely dry on one side, wet and muddy on the other. I held it by the edges, with my fingers wide apart to avoid getting them dirty."[1] The pebble is a small emblem of disgust. It is both filthy and clean. Turn it around, shift your perspective, and it will change from one aesthetic category to another. It may make your fingers dirty if you touch the wet, filthy side; it might also fill you with pleasure if you examine the dry, clean side. On that side you might see intricate patterns, the whorls and striations of crystals. Think of a human hair. Growing upon a head (especially if the head belongs to someone whom you love or who is otherwise desirable), the hair may be beautiful. (Even a body hair, if you desire the person, may be beautiful or, at least, very far from being disgusting.) But if you find it in your salad or, more revolting yet, in your soup, it may disturb you. It will not seem beautiful and it may even seem disgusting. If you find the same hair on the tip of your tongue, what will you feel? The pebble may also seem disgusting to Roquentin (who characteristically sees the world as dissolving, collapsing from integrity to slime, oozing with bad faith) because it has been contaminated: look at its clean side first and then see how mud has corrupted it. Its smooth, clean beauty has been polluted, lost.

The exploration of disgust, as I shall try to show, easily merges with other kinds of theoretical pursuits. If you think of the theory of disgust in the plural (as you might think of the theory of play), as a network of paths that will lead to a number of different explanatory models, paths that will lead away from a stinking object towards an aseptic conceptual structure, then you should be able to see the problem of disgust as an intensely harrowed field, criss-crossed by paths. How many paths? Some are very twisting, but are any straight? Viewed from above—the inevitable "meta" view of scholarship with its panning and panoramic shots—the network of paths might resemble a Hydra's head, twisting, writhing uncertainly, dangerous, endlessly replicating. This is also the view that Sartre, with his enormous genius for imagining how imagination might be re-imagined or seeing how one person's mind would be seen within another's, could imagine as pure distance, the god's-eye view of human detail.

> I look at the grey shimmering of Bouville at my feet. In the sun it looks like heaps of shells, of splinters of bone, of gravel. Lost in the midst of that debris, tiny fragments of glass or mica give little flashes from time to time. An hour from now, the trickles, the trenches, the thin furrows running between the shells will be streets, I shall be walking in those streets, between walls. Those little black dots which I can make out in the rue Boulibet—an hour from now I shall be one of them.[2]

There are many paths to follow. They start in all directions, winding, intertwining and criss-crossing, towards very different theoretical models. Some paths are perplexingly tangled (such as those, discussed in several places but primarily in Chapter 7, that lead through the theory of crowd behaviour to the analysis of self-disgust and abjection), labyrinthine or mandala-like, but all of them should be followed at least a little distance. In that sense, the problem of disgust recalls the analogously shifting, constantly altering problem of play.[3] Like play, disgust has both an empirical history, a body of relevant literature and a swarm of theoretical propositions surrounding it. Part of its fascination lies simply in its shifting qualities and in its resistance to facile summations.

This book must begin with a brief reflection on a noteworthy absence. Shakespeare, for all his dazzling lexicon, does not use the word *disgust* nor any of its cognates. The word enters the English language from the

French *dégout* and the Italian *disgusto* via Florio's English/Italian dictionary, *A Worlde of Words* (1598). The *Oxford English Dictionary* cites a medical use from 1611 as its first example where "disgust of stomacke" is used as an equivalent for "queasinesse." Originally, then, disgust is related to distaste or a lack of taste and, by extension, to anything that removes or prevents taste. A disgusting thing, an unidentifiable, shapeless, slimy lump served to you upon your dinner plate, might be disgusting in that it does not inspire your taste. In one of its most powerful senses, disgust names that which cannot be represented or which lies beneath the possibilities of representation. In that sense, it is the opposite of the sublime. What is sublime cannot be represented because it transcends the possibilities of representation. It is above the beautiful just as the disgusting is beneath the ugly. This is the philosophical use of disgust, and it remains a potent, if unidiomatic, sense.[4]

Disgust has come to have far wider meanings than untasty, tasteless or even foul or loathsome taste. *Disgust* is commonly used to register disapproval and disapprobation. It has become a moral term without losing its descriptive power to indicate objects in the world that are physically repulsive and loathsome. In modern English, disgust serves to identify acts and objects that are physically off-putting, such as crowd behaviour and other modes of human de-individuation in riots or the more extreme visual forms of hooliganism and gang violence as well as such unmistakable in-the-world items as putrefying flesh, vomit, excrement and pus. It also serves to indicate a moral judgement upon someone else's actions or beliefs. Thus disgust is closely tied to such moral concepts as disdain and contempt. William Ian Miller puts the connection neatly: "Disgust makes beauty and ugliness a matter of morals." Contempt and disgust, Miller adds, "do much salutary work."[5]

Disgust can serve to describe any conceptual system, whether a covert ideology or an overt theoretical model, that seems to corrupt human thinking or to have slipped from some supposed norm for rational conduct. *Disgusting* might well be the word of choice to describe bureaucracies, from big government to university administration, all of which seem inexorably (and always swiftly) to evolve a local administrative culture of unthoughtful, uncaring blockheads. (A local administrative culture of blockheadism manifests on the outside what is experienced within the bureaucracy as ecstasy: the power to look down on others, to demonstrate this power in many small transactions.)[6] Disgust also serves as a term to mark difference and, hence, distance. It is a tool, casual and unreflective, that one person uses simply to register that he or she is unlike someone else, disagrees with that other person and wishes to dissociate from the other's person, actions and beliefs. (Phrases such as "That's disgusting" or "You disgust me" probably add little to a theory of disgust, but they do indicate how the word, as distinct from the concept, has crept into the language of ordinary insult.) Disgust has become a commonplace word with a wide range of uses, both descriptive and metaphorical. In this book, I shall examine some of these uses, especially as they occur in literature and film. I am interested in both the range of physical uses, the sensation of gagging and vomiting that accompanies certain experiences, and also in the metaphorical uses of disgust, transformed into contempt, to register moral and aesthetic judgements. Disgust is a highly charged word, possessing both a history and a manifold of culturally specific uses, but it is also a conceptual problem from which a number of potentially engrossing paths open.

What does Shakespeare use in place of disgust? What words and descriptive phrases in Shakespeare does the later word disgust displace? Shakespeare employs an extremely concrete vocabulary. He uses words to signify very physical things and to evoke, correspondingly, very physical mental images. When you read Shakespeare you can infer a number of affects and any number of terms that are appropriate for judgemental descriptions, but such terms are not usually explicitly written. When you read *Julius Caesar*, for example, you might, thinking as a modern person, infer that the assassination of Caesar is disgusting. Dante found the act a monumental violation of trust and duty, loathsome and appalling if not precisely disgusting, and hence placed both Brutus and Cassius in the pit of hell, endlessly to be chewed by Satan in a disgusting cycle of consumption and defecation. There is a loathsome quality, both to their fates and to the environment to which they have been condemned, that indicates that, for Dante, their crime must have been imagined as disgusting in itself. Today, it is the messiness of the act, assassination, that might make an audience call it disgusting. The mob behaviour at the close of the third act of *Julius Caesar*, when Cinna the poet is physically torn apart for his "bad verses," is certainly disgusting in a contemporary sense. A modern viewer or reader might tend to associate images of human bodies being physically ripped apart with horror narratives, particularly in film. It is also very much an aspect of a modern person's experience of viewing war on television. From Vietnam through Bosnia to Chechnya, East Timor, and Afghanistan, TV viewers have watched while other people have been ripped apart and physically dismembered, or else they have observed in detail the mutilated bodies, hunched, splayed or curled, that measure the progress of ethnic hatred. In Shakespeare, from *Titus Andronicus* to *The Winter's Tale*, such scenes invoke compound affects, such as tragic pity, existential sorrow or comic retribution. If you read through Shakespeare looking for powerful affects, you will find them, but they will be only occasionally named as such. Semiotic inference has always been the dominant challenge in reading (or hearing) Shakespeare, both the most exciting reward and the steepest obstacle. Disgust is present, but it is never named.

Here is a striking example. In *Hamlet*, the Ghost tells Hamlet, "I find thee apt, / And duller shouldst thou be than the fat weed / That roots itself in ease on Lethe Wharf, / Wouldst thou not stir in this."[7] Of course the words are overdetermined and pluri-significant. However, they are also words charged with affects, with emotions that boil and bubble. It is not only the Ghost who speaks but also a father who speaks to his son—a dead father to a live son—and he is talking about the son's action, or failure to act, in the world. The "fat" describes Hamlet (and the question of his physical conditioning actually emerges in the play) and is combined with the image of a weed, part of the thin drizzle of filth that rains steadily upon the fictional world of *Hamlet*. There are many common and unpleasant associations with "fat": greasy, oily, ill-formed or slipped-from, ugly to eye and, under many conditions, nose. The weed "roots itself"—unbothered, untroubled, unconcerned—on Lethe Wharf. It is, on top of every other attribution, both a forgetful weed (or else forgotten) and linked to death. It is an ugly image. It is also emotionally charged. It suggests ugliness, failure, irresponsibility, deviation, perversion perhaps; it radically undercuts any heroic self-concept that Hamlet might have. It invokes shame. Nothing in the texts says this, but you can, validly I think, infer that shame is part of the message. Humiliation is close at hand. It may even be that self-disgust lies implicit in the message. Note the mood of the sentence. The Father-Ghost is speaking in the conditional: Hamlet *would* be duller than the fat, lazy, forgetful weed if he were not to "stir" on the Ghost's behalf. It is very much as if the Father-Ghost has created a small fictional world within the one that he and his son inhabit, the dark, claustral world of *Hamlet*, a world in which Hamlet would be very disgusting indeed, on a lower order than the weed itself, and then invited his son to imagine himself within that world. Yet nowhere in the words that establish this embedded world could you find "shame," "humiliation" or "disgust." These, inferences all, are among the rewards of reading the other words thoughtfully.

If you were to make a transcript of this discourse from *Hamlet*, even including a videotape of two actors performing the lines, and then sought to develop a "discourse analysis" of the kind that sociologists often create, a template of affect terms placed over the transcript to show the spirals of shame and anger, pride and shame, pride and humiliation, nothing would appear. Discourse analysis, Thomas J. Scheff writes in *Microsociology*, is a tool for observing the individual's lifeworld, a conceptual microscope involving verbatim texts, audio tapes and videotapes.[8] But the passage from *Hamlet* would reveal nothing but description: metaphorical description perhaps, classical in allusion, but not affect-charged. Yet that *is* what it is. The Ghost's sentence is packed with compound affects.

I think that this is what commonly happens in Shakespeare and, indeed, in most literature. An affect such as disgust is seldom named, no markers point directly towards it, but it can be felt. Lear's anger does not need to be named in order for it to be felt.[9] One of Shakespeare's very physical terms for moments of revulsion and loathing is "gorge." Shakespeare's gorge is not the throat so much as what might be contained within, or pass through, it. Holding Yorick's skull, Hamlet reflects that Yorick had borne him "on his back a thousand times, and now how abhorr'd in my imagination it is! my gorge rises at it."[10] A few lines later, Hamlet uses a word that King Lear, imagining (in madness) the female body, also uses when he feels disgust: holding Yorick's skull, but thinking of Alexander, Hamlet exclaims "pah!" The stench from the skull disgusts him in almost a medical sense. The word seems precisely chosen since you can hardly cry out "pah!" without narrowing the nose and pursing the mouth as if in vomiting. The image of the gorge rising suggests vomiting, or perhaps more precisely the moment just prior to vomiting when the throat seems crowded and full, the convulsive muscular spasms acute, the rising chyme rapid and irreversible. It is a strikingly concrete image from which it is possible to infer a physical, although only imaginary, feeling of disgust. Yorick in decay, his skull in Hamlet's hands, his rotted body in Hamlet's imagination, dissolves before the mind's eye, stinks in the mind's nose.

As a word, disgust works very differently than gorge. Once it enters the English language, it makes possible an abstract description that invokes a standard repertory of expressions and gestures. It is a formulaic word, attributing the semiotics of revulsion easily associated with eating and taste to all manner of objects and acts. When you read a novel written two centuries or so after Shakespeare, the word *disgust* may seem to repeat over and over again. It will seldom, if ever, indicate a physical revulsion. Dr.

Johnson finds the form of Milton's pastoral elegy *Lycidas* "easy, vulgar, and therefore disgusting" since it employs a stock of dead imagery and an "inherent improbability" that forces dissatisfaction upon the mind. I do not think that Johnson was made to vomit by reading *Lycidas* nor that he supposed reading it would endanger the physical well-being of readers. He may have meant that Milton's poem was not to his taste. However, I suspect a hidden moral judgement: *Lycidas* is not worth the intellectual attention that reading poetry requires. Johnson shows contempt for Milton and invites his readers to share in that contempt. No one, Johnson continues, "could have fancied that he read *Lycidas* with pleasure, had he not known its author."[11] (Already in the mid eighteenth century you can experience the literary person's moral judgement upon the study of literature as it is taught in universities.) In his 1755 *Dictionary of the English Language*, Johnson carefully distinguishes between the physical sense of "disgust," which is an "aversion of the palate from anything," and the moral sense, which is "ill-humour" and "malevolence" with respect to the manner of doing a thing. Johnson defines "disgustful," or as we would say today, disgusting, as the power of something either to "raise aversion in the stomach" or "to strike with dislike." I suppose that when Johnson read *Lycidas* he was struck with dislike, although it may not have actually raised aversion in his stomach. The next time you read *Middlemarch*, in many ways the central English novel of the nineteenth century, note the incidence of the word *disgust*. It is used more than forty times and does not once indicate physical revulsion. No character actually vomits in *Middlemarch*, but many experience conceptual disgust at ideas and manners. However, revulsion at another person's manners, at social behaviour in a general sense or even at ideas and conceptual schemata does not seem quite the same judgement as when you feel nauseated before filth or, nostrils clogged by stench, you turn vomiting from a sight that does not bear seeing or smelling. No character in *Middlemarch* has anything like Hamlet's experience of imagining death, the horror of the body's rot and the ghastly possibilities beyond pain, death and corruption in Yorick's reeking skull. Unlike Hamlet, the characters in *Middlemarch* do not infer the image of their own mortality from particular disgusting images (much like a dead spider steeped in wine and lying unswallowed at the bottom of a cup), their gorge rising while their mouths are distorted, racked even, by the violent "pahs" that they expel. For all their moral power, novels such as *Middlemarch* wholly lack a dimension that is commonplace in Shakespeare.

Since its introduction into English, *disgust* has become an abstract word, pointing at once in many directions, that performs multiple tasks in our language. If you believe that the English language since Shakespeare has become, in general, more abstract, less vivid, then the success of a word such as disgust will probably tell you a certain kind of story. It may seem rather like words such as *alcoholic* or *obese*, abstract and multi-purpose (a generic tool, like a Swiss Army knife), and not at all as graphic nor as vivacious, nor even as interesting, as (say) Shakespeare's "maltworm" and "gorbellied" with reference to Falstaff. We do not swear as vividly as Shakespeare's characters nor do we register the semiotics of revulsion (which we may well feel just as sharply) as diversely nor as intensely. William H. Gass, reflecting upon the empty-minded repetitiveness of modern English curses, observes that the swear words we use are simply uttered, no more than "phatic like the delivery of 'good morning', the wearing of evening clothes, giving of handshakes, painting of smiles, adding the complementary close." If you tried to avoid the pinched, gutless modern insult, all abstraction and stereotype, you might come up with something like one of Gass' own suggestions,

> may your cock continue life as a Canadian
> *or*
> may the houseflies winter over in your womb
> *or*
> may you be inhaled by your own asshole.

Such insults (even to think about, much less to use) would be exceedingly intricate, "like a purse full of chocolates and needles." Every word would have an internal purpose, like "a fugue."[12] Even if you could invent curses with Gass' flair, you probably would not receive the response that you would want from the person you had insulted. It would sound too strange, too unlike a normal curse, more like chocolates than needles. Shakespeare's characters could curse like that, but few others after (in or out of literature) could do so. Something has happened to the register of revulsion since Shakespeare that has left us with the serviceable, multi-tasked, but rather dull, "disgust." Today, burdened by the exigencies of politically correct language, all manner of abstract, impersonal phrases do the work of the more vivid language that Shakespeare could use. You might even prefer (taking an example from Robert Hughes) to call a fat corpse a "differently sized non-living person."[13]

I am fascinated by the network of metaphorical associations that stretch out from the concept of disgust in all directions. Sometimes it may seem as if it were a kind of mythological being, like a hidden chaos monster, with innumerable tentacles that grasp outwards in all directions, continuously growing and mutating, doubling and reshaping whenever one is destroyed. To begin with the most obvious, I shall start with what may be the only common factor to all instances of disgust: the human face. What do obvious, simple disgust objects have in common? Excrement may be disgusting, it may even be, as some experimental psychologists suggest, the universal *disgust-object* (although I, personally, doubt this), but so are certain ideas, conceptual schemata and ideologies. The varied uses of the word might seem to share little, neither appearance nor stench. What they do seem to have common is the sense of turning away, of feeling revolted at a repugnant object (the face twisted sideways, a hand raised, palm out, between the eyes and the loathsome thing), and it is, I think, one of the a few factors, perhaps the only one, linking all uses of the word. This link between uses is sometimes called the *disgust face*. Experimental psychologists seem to agree that, for one thing, the nostrils always narrow in disgust. The mouth also contorts, the lips twisting and even writhing, but this may be either a motion that closes the mouth (the lips mimicking the nares) or one that opens the mouth, pursing it with rounded but distended lips, as a readiness for vomiting.[14] Alas, the disgust face, though common, does not provide an accurate measure of disgustingness. In fact, there does not seem to be any "disgustometer" (to borrow a term from Monty Python) that will actually measure disgust or empirically establish its parameters.[15]

Furthermore, disgust seems always to be a question of boundaries. Only a scholar with the most universalizing view of disgust could carry on a discussion without raising the problem of boundaries. After all, a boundary surrounds every individual or, to put it another way, each individual is partly defined by the physical boundaries of his/her existence. Clifford Geertz observes wryly that the sense of foreignness "does not begin at the water's edge but at the skin's."[16] Many things seem disgusting only because they threaten the boundaries of individual personhood. They seem as if they might touch the skin, contaminating it by their mucoid or otherwise slimy condition, or even pass through it bringing the horrific possibility of personal dissolution. A boundary will also mark the sacred site of a taboo. A boundary can also be created to protect the group within. What happens behind a boundary, or within a group, may seem disgusting when viewed from without. It is difficult (though not impossible) to see how certain conceptual frameworks might seem disgusting even to those who accept, or even passionately hold, the conceptual system or model, but it is not at all difficult to see that others, not holding this particular scheme, might say that it is "disgusting." Outside the boundaries of the particular system or ideology, faces register their disgust easily. Even certain acts that might seem inescapably disgusting, such as eating excrement, will not seem so to members of a group, such as Sadians or people who enjoy roasted intestines fresh from the hunt, who regularly eat excrement in each other's presence. On either side of a boundary, facework can come into play.

Here, then, are two propositions with which to begin. *First*, disgust involves a certain expression which may be authentic but can be easily imitated. That is, whatever the definition of disgust, and whatever nexus of social connections it fits within, the face will constitute the primary evidence. *Second*, disgust involves the transgression of boundaries, either real or pretended. A person who does nothing different, who thoroughly "belongs" to a social group and who makes no mistakes, who is on all accounts "like," will never seem disgusting. These distinctions are, in Ross Chambers' phrase, "heuristic and of considerable fragility."[17] They will, I hope, gain both substance and many ramifications, as this discussion advances. To begin with, they show that the range of concerns touching upon the problem of disgust is very large. Disgust, which is both physical and moral, concrete and metaphorical, can also be a matter of simulation, of pretense and make-believe. It is as basic to human life as is desire: everything and anyone (you as well as I) may be experienced as disgusting under conditions in which boundaries break and things appear to slip towards slime or sludge. The world is a potential theatre for the untoward and the offensive. Socially marginal groups, such as Ranters or punks, may use disgust only to mark their own separation, their own distance from social or religious orthodoxy. Other groups, such as many avant-garde art movements or punk-style social nihilists, use disgust motifs to offend, either to effect change or to indicate the hopelessness of change. The use of disgust motifs in social interaction, although very different from their use in literature and art, can be extremely complex. For example, eighteenth-century Ranters used blasphemy as a means of arousing orthodox disgust in order to mark their own distinctness and distance, to mock the members of established religions and to show, as in theatre, how a truly free spirit, created so by an omnipotent God, should act.[18]

Within the boundaries that a particular culture establishes, what seems disgusting probably strikes the individual as naturally so. The psycho-visceral responses that human beings acquire from earliest childhood function as if they were innate or as if they were both completely and obviously what they had to be. Yet disgust is also a kind of behaviour learned in adulthood, a set of strategies both for survival and for domination. When one person expresses disgust, narrowing the nostrils, slitting the mouth open, twisting the lips, in view of another, she or he is making a judgement. The face will say (ever so plainly) that something or someone has fallen beneath human standards, is corrupted or otherwise unwholesome, and must be rejected. If the other person does not experience disgust equally, his face remaining composed and unwrinkled, then the judgement is doubly against him. His values or his hygiene have been poorly disciplined or have never existed at all. Disgust is a regulating affect, a method that societies promote to control individual behaviour, but it is also a bully's device for gaining control over others. Those who practice moral blackmail, or achieve their ends by intimidating others with moral judgements, understand both the versatility and the force of disgust. An affect that is at once an immediate reaction and also a managed response is worth thinking about.

The measureless range of things that can be disgusting to human beings argues against its instinctual basis. Psychologists often refer to the apparent universality of disgust and of universal disgust-objects, such as feces, but it is far from clear that there is an actual uniformity to the experience of disgust. Disgust comes in many shapes and in disparate intensities. Indeed, if you wanted to explore the scope of disgust as a universal affect, it might make more sense to investigate what anthropologists have said than to listen exclusively to psychologists.[19] An anthropologist acquaintance likes to tell a story (of the kind that all anthropologists have but do not always put into their published writings) of how, visiting among the Masai in Kenya, he was offered a calabash of fermented milk and blood which he found personally repugnant but drank, pretending pleasure. He drank slowly in sips through his teeth, finding the drink rather like a thick, sour malted milk, but his host noticed what he was doing and asked sharply, "Don't you like it?" He did, he said, but even as he spoke he saw that something was swimming in the calabash. In the gloomy interior of the skin tent, he could not make out what the object was, but he tried to pick it out. He only managed to push it down into the bottom of the drink, but his host also noticed this effort and evidently felt that his guest, though an anthropologist, was being too alien, too western perhaps, in his behaviour. He became noticeably unfriendly and in a few minutes snatched the calabash away and swallowed it in a single gulp, unidentified bug and all.[20] Later the Masai host expressed disgust, wrinkling his nose and twisting his lips, when he observed my friend cooking crabs that he had caught. A Somali interpreter, who also felt disgust at the sight of someone eating crabs, explained that in Kenya and in his own country people did not eat "spiders."[21] Tales such as this reveal not merely the diversity of disgust but also its deep-seated structuring. It also suggests the metamorphic nature of disgust, its continuous restructuring as learned behaviour. Stay with the Masai long enough and you may like fermented milk and blood, but you will surely cease to enjoy eating spider-like crabs.

Not only are human life and culture crowded with multifarious objects that appear to be disgusting, and which each member of a culture learns to experience as such, but the representation of the world in literature and art also swarms with disgusting images. The purpose of disgust motifs in literature does not necessarily correspond to the way they appear, and are used, in culture. They may be exaggerated and otherwise deformed, but most importantly disgust motifs in literature are given intelligible functions in fleshing out narrative, building characters and creating a distinctive thematic ambience, a topocosm that both encompasses and informs the fictional world itself. In literature, the crushing blankness (as it may seem) of ordinary life metamorphoses into lucid, often brilliant, extraordinariness. In *Ulysses*, James Joyce demonstrates that, for example, an ordinary bowel movement, taken at a regular time and in a predictable place (a back-yard privy), can be extraordinarily fascinating and narratively important. A disgusting in-the-world object, a small heap of putrescent mammalian filth, say, may become a symbol, a narrative linchpin, or a character's sudden epiphany. In his wonderful little book on excrement, *Merde*, Ralph A. Lewin distinguishes between coprology and scatology.[22] The former constitutes the study of actual, in-the-world excrement; the latter, the study of verbal (and imagistic) representations of excrement. In the course of my book, this distinction will be important. A study of disgust must clearly turn towards the varieties of actual excrement and the human responses that they evoke, but it must also take into account the varied human representations of excrement and their many cultural uses.[23]

Satire, in making militant comments upon the shortcomings of human life and culture, is the most obvious place to look for disgusting representations of filth.[24] Satire often turns upon the power of filth to disgust, embarrass and shame. In its strongest, Menippean, form, satire transforms repressed or discarded aspects of human life into comments, distorted enactments of lifeworld situations that are normally taken for granted. "The turd is the ultimate dead object," writes Kelly Anspaugh.[25] Comparisons between turds and human persons, or any human actions or institutions, will necessarily emphasize the inherent inertness, corruption or death-likeness of the living. The latter point can most clearly be shown by a consideration of how shock functions in literature and film. An aspect of all avant-garde art, as well as of communal and generational hostility, showing up graphically in modes of expression as different as propaganda and pop culture, high art and gutter coprolalia, shock projects the unmistakable purpose of infuriating or humiliating other people and, in particular, of disgusting them. Images that will evoke nausea serve to isolate a dominant culture (as retrograde, unimaginative and repressive), but also to solidify those who produce and appreciate the disgusting image as members of the new, united in their capacity to enjoy images of what had been, until their historical moment, only filth.

I want to be completely clear about the point I am making. It will run through this study, reappearing at crucial moments in the argument, but always lurking somewhere in the neighbourhood. *Disgust is a powerful, although rather mysterious, psycho-visceral affect.* It undergoes many metamorphoses as an individual grows older and experiences cultural and social changes. It is not rigid and psychologically fixed. Above all, disgust can be imitated. Hence, one important aspect of disgust is that it is a spontaneous reaction, but one that can be pretended, transformed into a deliberate, even theatrical display. In the first place, this can be seen in the facework associated with disgust. The "disgust face" seems quite real. Your nose will wrinkle, the nares will close, your mouth will twist when you confront a pile of putrescent filth. In the second place, that face can be easily imitated. You can make the same face when you observe behaviour you dislike or see a colleague you despise. This ability to pretend disgust leads off in many directions. It underlies important cultural phenomena such as scatological jokes and graffiti. Insulting squibs, mocking lampoons, biting travesties and small acts of street theatre, all performances of one kind or another, develop the possibilities of the human disgust reaction. More complex disgust scenarios can be developed in fine art, literature and film. That is, you can imagine disgust scenarios in different aesthetic modes. You can also imagine them as using disgusting phenomena as motifs to establish a scene, to support a theme or to help build a character. However, a whole painting or an entire narrative can be disgusting in itself: its motifs, characters, situations, themes and even its stylistic content may be linked together and made cohesive by a creative intelligence in order to nauseate, disgust and shock an audience. And all of this will be a make-believe version of that genuine, in-the-world spontaneous human reaction, the disgust face, to ugliness, stench and filth.

Consider *Hamlet* once more. Contemplating Yorick's skull, Hamlet stages a small performance in a theatre of shock. Holding the skull, he imagines the dead jester going, as a rotted body or as fleshless mannikin of bones, to a court lady to make her laugh. Tell her, Hamlet instructs the skull, that although she paint herself an inch thick, she must come "to this favour." Make her laugh at that, Hamlet adds. Seated in the audience to that tiny but horrifying theatre, you should see Yorick, a jester of "infinite wit" and "excellent fancy," enter the lady's room, display himself as he now is (lipless and chapfallen), point out the futility of cosmetics, indeed of all human defences against decay, and still execute his role as a court jester. He is a clown (of sorts), a merry madcap fool, whose genius had always been to make others laugh. Now he has only to overcome the handicap of his appearance or, to make the point even more strongly, to use his present condition as an instrument of comedy. After all, comedy, especially Shakespearean comedy, is largely built upon the conventions of reversal of expectation and incongruity. What could be more incongruous than a lady, in the act of applying her make-up, being made to laugh by a death's-head who has himself long since lost the flesh upon which he might have applied his jester's whiteface and rouge? The reversal of expectations is absolute. Whatever the lady might have expected—flattery, courtesy, pleasure—she receives only the emblem of her own death. And she will be made to laugh at this. It will be horrifying, even disgusting, since the lady may also feel her gorge rise at the ugliness and stench (and, like Hamlet, she may involuntarily exclaim "pah!"), but she will laugh.

What are the uses of shock? The motives for telling an aversive story are immensely varied: to baffle, disturb, insult, frighten or disgust the audience. A writer may wish to tell a story that disgusts, and which will be read with aversion (but like an unmoving victim staring into mythic snake's eyes, chilled with horror, fascinated until the end), simply to startle the audience out of its habitual complacency. Not every storyteller seeks misty eyes, a snuffling nose or even the sentimental radiance of a happy ending; not every fiction has been written to delight or to persuade. Some fiction, such as Samuel Beckett's novels in *The Trilology* (but especially *The Unnamable*) or David Lynch's 1977 film *Eraserhead*, represents bleak, self-contained worlds, wastelands and garbage worlds, in which everything, the smallest details and the characters' most minute traits, evokes a pervasive sensation of disgust and alienation. In such representations, disgust motifs work to establish the characters' sense of estrangement, of corrosive non-belonging. However, in much fiction, disgust motifs are used to offend, insult and shock. Imagine the aggressive, often hurtful, punchlines of many jokes. Such jokes are like violation or even a form of rape. Now imagine the pattern of the joke expanded over a longer narrative. You will find yourself imagining satire. At least in its militant forms, satire mocks ways of behaving and believing. It does this by developing representations of behaviour and belief that are grotesque, exaggerated towards a single trait or feature. (Swift's Yahoos, for example, are recognizable human beings deformed in the direction of human selfishness, greed and incorrigible filthiness. They hold and throw shit.) In classical literature, Old Comedy and Menippean satire both turn upon images of filth and disease, or upon situations in which the human characters experience debasement and reduction. In one form or another, shock art has always had an aesthetic role and a social purpose.

In Shakespeare, as well as in much other Renaissance writing, shocks are delivered in diverse guises, but they always have the function of reminding characters that their pretensions are weakly founded. Shakespeare's *Troilus and Cressida*, for instance, employs Menippean elements, both images (disease) and characters (Thersites) to reduce and mock the chivalric ideals of both honour and love. In an exchange with Ajax that begins the second act, Thersites supposes that Agamemnon might be a suppurating boil and draws from that conditional reflection the image of a "botchy core," an actual oozing, ulcerous boil to represent the Greek general. When Thersites draws attention to Agamemnon's corrupted body, that physical equivalent of the spiritual authority so often discussed during the Renaissance under the rubric of the "King's two bodies," he makes a comment upon the king's mind, purposes and nobility. Thersites reminds the audience that, if Agamemnon's body did actually parallel his spirit and his works (an ill-managed war running to disaster), then it *should* ooze and splatter pus. Agamemnon's body is said to be ill-fashioned (a "botchy" body) and disgusting, flawed and certainly botched, to match his ill-fashioned, and definitely botched, war. By extension, Thersites' words seem also to judge the whole Greek enterprise, all "those that war for a placket," ruled by empty, but destructive, chivalric ideals.[26] The images of decay, rot and disease counterpoint the high expressions of authority and honour among the generals and of love between the lovers with which the play begins. *Troilus* shocks in many ways, although primarily through the words of Thersites, but it does this for the purpose of mocking a number of widely accepted, long-held values of Shakespeare's time. It shocks beneath the banner of Menippean satire.

Shock art has had a long history. Artists have always wanted to change the world. Tracing the brief, intricate history of the Sex Pistols, Greil Marcus observes that John Lydon, the group's lead singer (who sang under the *nom de guerre* of Johnny Rotten), expressed in his angry word-like sounds the purpose "to make the world notice; to make the world doubt its most cherished and unexamined beliefs; to make the world pay for its crimes in the coin of nightmare."[27] (Like Shakespeare's Thersites, Johnny Rotten was a Menippean, but in-the-world, character.) Satire raises edifices upon the recognition that the world has gone wrong and followed mistaken paths, has been corrupted or else settled into mind-numbing conformity (or all of these). It can come as an overpowering revelation. Opposition to the world as it exists usually takes mild forms, such as grumbling or local sabotage (laziness, clever goldbricking, calling in sick or deliberate inefficiency), but in art the sense of being opposed, of feeling a fundamental oppositionality, takes the form of registering difference, often with stunning exaggeration.

Oppositional art usually entails mockery and satire, but the striking fact of being different is opposition's first move. Mockery follows close behind, nose to butt. One form of mockery is defamiliarization: the creation of art that hides, or even denies, meaning. When that happens, a conformist audience will have been mocked by forcing it to perceive that its aesthetic norms and habits of perception are inadequate for the avant-garde art it now confronts. The audience, Peter Bürger writes, responded to "the provocations of the Dadaists with blind fury."[28] Yet the Dadaists used only art, not bombs, to achieve their effects. They startled perception, but not the body. Dada "stood for a wholly eclectic freedom to experiment; it enshrined play as the highest human activity, and its main tool was chance."[29] If you played the Dada game, perceiving art objects as composed out of disjunctive bits rather than as organic wholes, you were also denying all the received opinion about art, all the conceptual sludge that society had come to believe about art. In effect, playing at Dada, you were cocking a snook.

However, Bürger wants to see the "principle of shock" in avant-garde art reflecting a necessary connection between the uses of defamiliarization and the intention to change society.[30] That intention certainly seems to recur in shock art, although not always as the primary motivation. Dada *is* more formal, more committed to aesthetic re-education than to social revolution, than punk or contemporary tag art in North American cities. The difference between Dada, or even surrealism, as artistic movements and punk, grunge and scumrock, or the entire category of "mondo" films, is the simple perception that the world as a whole, not merely its repulsive stratum of bourgeois culture, is loathsome, corrupted by its own stinking death rot. Punk represents a mode of shock performance, but it is one in which the entire audience is invited to share the experience of shocking others (parents, the authorities, all the "pod people," as Greil Marcus puts it) even if those others are not present. Their horrified, disgusted faces can be imagined. Outside the nightclub, in the world, "every gray public building came alive with secret messages of aggression, domination, malignancy," but the punk audience masters this vision of ugliness by acting it out:

> They were ugly. There were no mediations. A ten-inch safety pin cutting through a lower lip into a swastika tattooed onto a cheek was not a fashion statement; a fan forcing a finger down his throat, vomiting into his hands, then hurling the spew at the people onstage was spreading disease. An inch-thick nimbus of black mascara suggested death before it suggested anything else ... They were fat, anorexic, pockmocked, acned, stuttering, crippled, scarred, and damaged, and what their new decorations underlined was the failure already engraved in their faces.[31]

The history of shock art is radically dichotomous: on the one hand, there are the avant-garde elites, the targets of Bürger's analysis, who attempt to transform aesthetic consciousness by defamiliarizing art; on the other, there are socio-aesthetic movements, such as the punks whom Marcus discusses, who reject society as it is known by holding up its own symbolic image for anguished reflection. In each case, you can see how important facework is: the disgust face you make; the one you can imagine being made; even the ones that you hope others, or all, will make.

Each polarity, both the avant-garde elites and the socio-aesthetic movements, tells something important about how shock works. Each reveals an aspect of the complex intention that lies behind the act of shocking, by disgusting, other human beings. That "ultimate dead object," the human turd, has an intimate relationship both with shock and with satire. There are clear, and obvious, reasons for this. Excrement stinks "like" death (but only in imagination) and looks, in dark deliquescence, as many people might suppose a corpse to appear.[32] It is hidden away as a corpse will be, a bodily product that anticipates the object the body will become, and it is seen as the very antithesis of cleanliness, of the "clean and proper" body, that it is the purpose of toilet training to instill. Society, hiding bodily wastes and death, can be shocked by either excrement or death. The simplest, most straightforward act of shock is to display a human turd out of place, where it ought not to be.[33] Public display of excrement constitutes a violent shock in a society where excrement is systematically hidden or hastily flushed away. A highly symbolic act, public defecation reminds everyone who sees it that death, too, is a hidden, repressed end-product. It also reminds an audience of how many other things are hidden away, or even of the society's general repressiveness. The hypocrisy of a bourgeois culture, pretending that surfaces are reality (that the repressed content of the individual, and the collective, life does not even exist), has been fair game for artists who have ripped illusions to shreds.

This is the motivation behind Menippean satire.[34] Hypocrisy is a common motif in Renaissance drama, not merely comedy, and suggests an entire constellation of dramatic moves in Shakespeare. On one level, *Hamlet* concerns the hypocrisy by which secret intentions are hidden; on another, it is a major theme in the comedies and in the problem plays, especially *Timon of Athens*, *Troilus and Cressida* and *Measure for Measure*. Exposing hypocrisy, with sad or deadly consequences, is a motif that runs through all the tragedies, *Hamlet* and *King Lear* in particular. Making society's dirty secrets visible is Swift's signature (often in Menippean language) as it is, if less famously, in much eighteenth-century writing and, though somewhat muted, in some romantic art. But using a tangible human turd, actually defecating upon stage, is an act far different from showing the representation of excrement or introducing it obliquely by euphemism and sly comment (which is what happens in the "frank" eighteenth-century novel). Despite the long history of shock in art, it makes sense to think of it arising as a distinct mode from the late nineteenth century and developing countless styles, variations limited only by the imagination itself, throughout the twentieth.[35]

There seem to be two salient reasons for this explosion of shock as deliberate provocation, aimed at both aesthetic perception and at social attitudes. First, the presence of revolutionary social movements in European society, Marxist, anarchist, socialist and fascist, all seething together in combinations of affiliation and disaffiliation, alliances and warring tribes, made aesthetic revolution more obvious, even more "normal."[36] Second, the entire course of the nineteenth century could be measured against improving standards of hygiene, social decorum and seemliness. In many respects, this is the historical fact that counts most when considering the eruption of shock. In cities such as Paris that had been progressively deodorized, cleaned and made neat in thousands of ways the previous century could not have guessed, the sight and stench of excrement had more impact than it had before. It had gained a new symbolic force. Gustave Flaubert saw the value of excrement in mounting a challenge to the bourgeoisie's good manners. He was caustic, as he was also in denouncing received ideas, in calling for the overthrow of the new social codes that regulated the human body, repressed excrement and tried to outlaw stench: "Let diarrhea drip into your boots, piss out of the window, shout out 'shit', defecate in full view, fart hard, blow your cigar smoke into people's faces ... belch in people's faces."[37] From Flaubert's symbolic gestures, so unlikely in a previous century (when someone shouting out *"merde"* would probably have been giving a warning or advice on where not to step), it was only a short step to cabaret acts where performers defecated upon the stage and to literature that happily esteemed its excremental visions and cloacal obsessions.[38]

Even mild satire involves a measure of transgression. Attitudes, customs and prejudices (all of which establish psycho-cultural boundaries) have always been the common game of satire. Few things are more comic than observing a holder of unreasoned opinions being forced to see their consequences for the first time or being made to examine them (then learning, with surprise, that they have all along hung vaporously from a skyhook). Stronger versions of satire, such as Menippean, are fundamentally transgressive. They aim not merely to dart across boundaries but to break them open, to demolish them. Bakhtin argues that Menippean satire, with its methodical undermining of authority, its fecund creation of violent, disturbing voices to mock the easy monologic voice of governing elites and received opinion, was a precursor of the novel in that it provided a textual model for multi-voiced narrative (one voice playing against another, the unofficial against the official).[39] All art is, at least potentially, offensive; all art crosses some boundaries. However, in extreme modes, the boundary crossing can be very offensive. It may be transgressive to the point that it causes hurt, even destroys the person, practice or institution that has been its target. Granting that transgression has functioned traditionally as either a moral or a legal concept, I can now ask a distinctly modern question: what are its aesthetic purposes?

Leaving aside the obvious examples of narrative content (plot moves and character development, say) in which transgression occurs as a dimension of the story being told or of the scene being represented, transgression takes two fundamental forms. First, transgression is a formal, aesthetic concept. It describes what artists often do with respect to the existing norms of their art, the standard conventions by which problems have been solved. This is evident in movements such as Dada, which Hughes defines in terms of its playfulness, but it is also very much an aspect of all new art. Gérard Genette speaks of Marcel Proust's "decisive transgression" in developing new methods of characterization, methods that inaugurate the "limitless and indefinite space of modern literature."[40] When Shakespeare introduces an important Menippean character, Thersites, into the story of Troilus and Cressida for the first time in its long history of varied retellings, he is playing with both the available repertory of dramatic strategies for dealing with a heroic tale and the story matrix itself. He too inaugurates a new method of characterization that will have a powerful impact on the unfolding history of the novel; he gives the anti-hero a distinctive voice: a genuine counter-voice that barks and spits with devastating accuracy. *Hamlet* is transgressive in many ways; for example, Ophelia's telling of a story in the form of disconnected tag lines from different songs or in its sustained recursiveness, telling the same story over and over from the Ghost's analeptic *mise-en-scène* to Horatio's summary on the level of personifications. Above all, *Hamlet* is transgressive in the way it takes a revenge tragedy of blood, normally told in external, tracking-down-the-guilty manner (precisely as Shakespeare had told a revenge story in *Titus Andronicus*), and internalizes it, transforming it into a psychological drama. This kind of aesthetic transgression is heuristic and marks off the territory of significant art. It constitutes a basic level of the literary text's openness and creativity. Aesthetic transgressions are heuristic in being exploratory, playful in the Nietzschean sense of moving beyond boundaries in order to learn something new.[41] Such formal moves, as Hughes points out with respect to modernist art, can be deeply disturbing, even shocking. Uncomprehendingly, misunderstanding the purposes of these moves, a reader or viewer might feel much as the first audiences of Dada felt: disgusted.

Second, transgression refers to the way in which the content, more than the form, affects the audience. Transgressive art builds worlds and extends invitations to visit. It offers make-believe, but of a kind to make the participant sweat horror. As a mode of play, make-believe explores the conditions of life in non-actual worlds.[42] Converted to the uses of shock, make-believe transcribes actual life into deformed versions of itself. This may be quite elaborate (a performance, a fiction, an installation) or rather simple (a tattoo or a pin). Imagine an artist sitting for three weeks in a bathtub filled with black water. Each day "a piece of meat was put next to the tub and it kept rotting while he was starving. At the end of the action guests were invited to a meal of rotten food."[43] The viewers entered a world of gross contrasts and disparities (black water, starvation set against wasted food, rotten meat and eating) which, if it were not make-believe, would constitute torture equal to the things done to unwilling victims during the processes of juridical torture in countless, human societies. Even more extreme instances of disgust in performance art are easy to find. Any installation or performance by Hermann Nitsch would illustrate the Dionysian potential of theatrical events to shock. Long before he had founded the Orgies Mysteries Theatre in 1965, Nitsch had created actions that involved decaying animal corpses, skinned animals and naked human beings.

> The slaughtered animals were cut, crucified, trampled upon, hanged or similarly mistreated. Buckets of blood (with chemicals added to prevent coagulation) were spilled. Monstrances, crosses, chalices and other Christian cult objects were used to invoke the presence of the sacred in opposition to the profane. All this provoked public complaints and disturbances and the local police force often intervened.[44]

The combination of sacrificial animals, blood and other conventional tropes of rot, as well as the blasphemous use of religious objects would create a thick brew, offering opportunities for shock at different stages. In *Meat Joy* (Paris, 1964), Nitsch staged naked men and women interacting, "in a rather frenzied, Dionysian way," with hunks of "raw meat and carcasses of fish and chickens." They tore the chickens apart, smeared each other with blood and rolled about in an exhausting frenzy.[45] Nitsch argues that all his "actions," but especially the most recent, extended performances of the Orgies Mysteries Theater, are intended to re-introduce the spirit of the ancient cult of Dionysus into modern life, allowing "all fears and irrational complexes" to be acted out until a "higher and purer state of consciousness is reached."[46] (Nitsch's reasons for his art recall Pentheus, who was, if not the first, an early audience for, and an unwilling participant in, a shock theatre.) Performance art such as Nitsch's invokes imaginative worlds, usually to be entered from several points, that are so different from, and so opposed to, normal western culture that they almost *have to* shock. However, exposure to such art might also help to transform the viewer. *That* is always the secret bonus of a Dionysian experience. The complex intention behind shock art (to offend and to transform) shows up plainly in Nitsch's work, but it is also available in the punk performances that Marcus writes about, or even in a small, single-scene theatre such as an obscene or otherwise loathsome tattoo.

I want to briefly to underscore the phrase *single-scene theatre*. In many ways, that is one of the central concepts in this book. Disgust, I shall argue, plays out in the imagination. You can certainly imagine disgusting things on the largest scale: disasters and catastrophes, wars and plagues with all their myriad horrors, their baleful consequences of deliquescence, decay and rot. However, you may more easily imagine precise moments of disgust in which slime or sludge dominates. Imagining such moments, you will probably also imagine facework. Expressions of shock and disgust on another person's face are the stuff of comedy, but they can also constitute the vicarious experience of an act. It is not simply that a tattoo or a pierced body part may seem disgusting in themselves, but also that they evoke small imaginative scenarios (having it done, parading it, putting it on display, being seen, being confronted, etc.) in which disgust's facework has much to do. And thus the "ultimate dead object" has an indispensable role in shock. Imagining a turd or any symbolic equivalent, or imagining someone else encountering a turd, seems like one of the archetypal moments in the experience of disgust. At that moment, you are invited, in Hal Foster's phrase, to "touch the obscene object-gaze of the real."[47]

Much of what artists like Nitsch do with blood and animals' bodies displaces the effect of human excrement on stage. The impression of decay and deliquescent rot always points towards one of western society's core prohibitions: the revelation of feces. Günter Brus, an early associate of Nitsch, would perform dressed as a woman, slash himself until he was covered in blood, and then defecate on stage, finally eating his own excrement.[48] Art and feces have developed a synergistic relationship only because human excrement, through many years of loosening taboos, has retained its status of a prohibited space. Obituaries for Leigh Bowery, an Australian performance artist most famous for having been one of Lucien Freud's models, high-mindedly noted that he had taken enemas and then defecated upon his audiences.[49] Piero Manzoni's outrageous (or perhaps merely *outré*) act of tinning "his shit as if it were tuna" could not have had the effect that it did if the revelation of feces were not still taboo.[50] Manzoni signed and numbered the top of each can as an official act of authentication. They have, predictably, increased in value since.

Manzoni's act of self-transvaluation obliquely suggests (as an invitation to the collectors) the ultimate shock possible: publicly eating human feces (private acts of coprophagy, which I discuss in Chapter 3, are quite another matter). Günter Brus did this as a member of Nitsch's *Wiener Aktionismus* in the 1960s, but there are even more aggressive instances. The late G.G. Allin, self-described as the "sickest, most decadent rocker of all time," created a scumrock theatre far more alienated from, and more disgusting towards, ordinary repressive "pod" society than anything the Sex Pistols had imagined. "G.G. shits on the stage, laps it up, spits it out on the crowd, hitting rock journalists in the face with a taste of their own medicine."[51] Compared to Manzoni, or even Brus, this seems like an almost unimaginably aggressive act, but it is probably consistent with the aesthetics of a musician who wrote lyrics like "Outlaw Scumfuck" or "Kill and Fuck," not to forget "Rape and Torture." Asked how he managed to defecate regularly for each gig (something his fans came to expect, reacting with aggravation when they were denied), Allin replied, "I take in account my life and my mind spins, and the shit pretty much just comes out."[52] Scumrock represents one direction, and perhaps the furthermost possibility, of the punk movement Marcus describes. Loathing for a repressive, drab (because abstract, inescapably "mega") society, always invited to participate in the mockery-by-degradation of its chief values, may not have a conceivable endpoint beyond publicly defecating, eating the product and then spitting it out at the front-row audience. A scumrocker may not care about changing society, or even actively consider that end, but he or she can enjoy the act of insulting, by demonstrating his or her alienation from, and disgust towards, that society.

Another direction of punk is exemplified in so-called Gothic rock (the "new wave" music of groups such as The Cure and singers such as Robert Smith and Peter Gabriel in the mid 1980s and early '90s), in which the punk hatred for society is remodulated into malaise, alienation and an attenuated *weltzschmerz*. Gothic rock generally, but in particular such modes as grunge, displays the methodical popification of punk.[53] The "inch-thick nimbus of black mascara" might still suggest death, but only as a symbol of alienation, not as a personal expression of desire (for the wearer's own death or for her parents').[54] G.G. Allin stands out as the immoderate fulfillment of punk, even perhaps of the entire twentieth-century tradition of disgust art.[55]

The popularized necrophilia that permeates North American culture picks up many motifs from punk and from shock art in general. It is both an indication of how badly many people want to be seen as rejecting contemporary society (though not, perhaps, *actually* to reject it) and how easily disgust motifs can be assimilated. Disgust is a manageable affect and easily codified in art as symbolism having complex aesthetic purposes. The artist painting, singing or writing about disgust may not want the audience to vomit, or even to feel put off, but only to grasp the symbolic connections that link the art to a conceptual background.

In 1994, I saw the Jim Rose Circus Sideshow, a Seattle-based circus that emphasizes various disgust motifs and attracts its audience largely from university students and young punks or pseudo-punks.[56] The acts, which involved the simulation of torture, freaks (a geek who eats the glass fragments of broken light bulbs),[57] threats of death, all carried out in punk-style costumes, hid an important fact: they were either traditional circus acts or modifications of such acts. The audience desired disgust and was given the image of it. Of course, shock, once it has become just another motif, another way of dressing or acting, no longer shocks. Commodified, disgust can be comfortably consumed as pastiche. In part, this is what took place in the controversy surrounding the showing of the British exhibition *Sensation* at the Brooklyn Museum of Art in the autumn of 1999. The exhibition, which had shown in London and other European capitals, included works intended to shock, such as dead animals in sealed environments being buzzed by flies or Mark Quinn's bust, "Self," created from several litres of the artist's own blood in a refrigerated environment. The show was largely pastiche, most of the pieces having analogues in the previous work of other artists; the hostile reaction by New York politicians, especially Mayor Rudy Giuliani, was a kind of political pastiche as well.[58]

How does Hamlet shock *his* audiences? The secret of *Hamlet*, as well as of Hamlet, is surprise. Shock shocks most when it is most unexpected. Hamlet, of course, not only stages imaginatively the encounter between Yorick and the court lady but has already physically staged the Mousetrap in which Claudius is confronted by the shocking image of his own secret actions. (His actions in his three encounters with Rosencrantz and Guildenstern, or with Horatio and Marcellus after the first appearance of the Ghost, are extravagantly theatrical, intended to baffle if not to shock.) In *Hamlet*, everything happens for the first time or as if it had never happened before in the whole history of drama. This is a dramatic secret that Shakespeare understands well: if you want to shock an audience, you must make sure that they are unprepared. In *Titus Andronicus*, like *Hamlet* a "tragedy of blood" full of many gross and repugnant deeds, Titus stages a miniature theatre of horror when he invites Tamora to dinner, serves her own sons in a pie and then observes her reaction before killing her. (This was an ancient dramatic motif, of course, but Shakespeare reframes it by placing the emphasis upon Titus watching Tamora's face when she realizes what she has eaten.) Even in the comedies, shock plays many roles. In *Much Ado About Nothing,* the young aristocrats denounce Hero at her wedding, accusing her of shameless sexual behaviour that she can scarcely guess at, for the purpose of theatrically pricking what they take to be (wrongly) her pretense and arrogant make-believe. In *Cymbeline*, Jachimo stages a mental theatre of shock when he narrates to Posthumous the story of how he has seduced Imogen, playing upon Posthumous' fears of being made into a cuckold and his inherent misogyny, building up to the shocking conclusion when he describes a mole on Imogen's breast and reveals her bracelet (a prop in his little drama), which he claims that Imogen has given him. Posthumous can only stagger away, his worst fears realized, his pretensions shattered and his misogyny murderously activated. Although he must have seen Imogen's mole thousands of times, Jachimo has made him see it for the first time.

Modern shock art has been a way of disturbing smug, complacent and hypocritical audiences either by showing them what they find offensive (but the performers do not) or by representing their own bourgeois assumptions to them in a display of physical alternatives, scenes strikingly conceived to embody the very opposite of received values or the dominating ideology of the socio-cultural elite. As the two directions that punk has followed demonstrate, shock must always seek an act more disgusting than those previously seen. The other alternative is to become a style; that is, to become codified into ritual gestures of rejection, alienation and horror.

Shock art is like a lilliputian revolution. It ruthlessly grabs attention, cuts sharply to the viewer's or reader's established values, disgusts them, mocks them and implicitly proposes alternatives, often deeply transgressive. Shock art presents an extreme instance of what seems commonplace in more gradual terms. If you can learn how to control the urge to vomit, forcing those involuntary spasms back down your throat, then you will have learned how to modify either your natural instincts or your early training. I suspect that these modifications must be very common experiences since people are always acquiring new tastes and giving up old ones. Indeed, as Norbert Elias points out, the very processes of civilization demand that you *must* acquire new tastes, new responses, new habits. What you once found disgusting (peaches, say) you may learn to love (and now you have become a vegan). This process of personal re-education extends along the entire spectrum of human activity. One aspect of a genuine revolution in society is that affects will be transformed or restructured on both the individual and collective levels. New objects of disgust appear, and old ones vanish or are displaced into ordinariness. Every revolution, even a small one, transforms values. The downtrodden mock the former elites: there is a loud element of carnival in a revolution. When the killing is over, or between volleys and firefights, the class in revolt can enjoy the humiliation of the once powerful. Once the American Revolution had ended, monarchists became as repugnant as graverobbers. English-speaking Canada was largely populated by Tories fleeing the newly independent colonies where loyalty to the King had become a disgusting moral act. Northrop Frye observes, rather acidly, that a Canadian is simply an American who has rejected the Revolution. Those United Empire Loyalists greatly increased Canada's English-speaking population and forever set a certain political agenda. Their motivation for emigration had been both fear of reprisal and a sense that they had become disgusting within a non-monarchist, democratic perspective. After the Bolshevik Revolution in 1917, the ownership of property began to seem disgusting, and to have been a member of the rentier class would have marked one as loathsomely as a leper's bells had done in another age. After the French Revolution, all manner of social conditions changed. A more vigilant, socially aware consciousness led the inhabitants of Paris and other cities actively to seek social improvements. Excrement became a public issue.

Alain Corbin observes how in France, during the early years of the nineteenth century, fecal matter became "an irrefutable product of physiology" that the bourgeois society attempted to deny. Its implacable recurrence "haunted the imagination; it gainsaid attempts at decoproralization; it provided a link with organic life, as the traces of its immediate past ... Excrement now determined social perceptions."[59] The 1960s still seem a revolutionary period that transformed many values, turning some topsy-turvy, shattering the rectitude that surrounded others. Many things that had seemed disgusting ceased to seem that way. The '60s was also a romantic period.[60] For a short time (with still a few lingering eddies), North American values were transformed in the direction of both greater self-fulfillment and greater mutual reciprocity in human social exchange; the force of disgust as a social barrier between people or as a strategy for achieving distance was diminished. For the brief span that the '60s cultural revolution endured, people willingly learned the hard lessons of political revolutions, of certain demanding professions and of literature and art: disgust can be relearned and transformed.

A little thought should provide a great number of examples of disgust being unlearned or displaced laterally onto some new object during the 1960s. Young people learned to pass joints around and to drink from the same bottle or cup, or to live in communes with pit toilets, very much in disregard of the hygienic values of middle-class American society. For a number of reasons, human excrement became less of a disgust-object than experimental psychologists like to believe; certainly, it prompted some positive metaphors, as in "getting your shit together" for thinking constructively ahead. Sexual practices loosened up during the '60s, but for that to have happened, learned responses to sexual situations involving disgust had to be unlearned. Freud notes repeatedly that disgust, along with shame and "morality," restrains the polymorphous yearnings of the sexual appetite; but that restraint, as the sexual experience of the '60s shows, has to be autocratic.[61] Actions that had once been experienced as immediately disgusting, such as oral sex (which was still outlawed as sodomy by many American states), became acceptable, non-disgusting, even the indispensable vehicles of desire.

A study of disgust needs to investigate the functional interrelationships of social prohibitions and restrictions. Disgust can be, as Freud and many others have argued, a psycho-motor agent of social taboo, a personal police force that patrols the boundaries of social exclusion, censoring violations.

A study of disgust must examine both the idea of transgression and the multiple ways in which transgression operates within the context of cultural norms. It must acknowledge both the presence of deep and traditional forces that define pollution and contamination, and the social processes of re-education and professionalization. Moreover, a study of disgust must acknowledge the radical shifts between cultures which transform one culture's disgusting objects and acts into another culture's pleasures or, at least, the causes for bored shrugs. It should also examine the changes of what counts as disgusting from one period of time to another even within the same culture. Above all, a study of disgust must consider how and why the sense of disgust, always a deeply encoded yet inconsonant affect from early childhood, can undergo profound, and sometimes continuous, metamorphosis within an individual.

The standard theories of disgust and disgust-formation (which I discuss in Chapter 2) emphasize its intractable properties and cultural rigidity. They model disgust as a psycho-cultural phenomenon that exists behind strongly established psychological and/or culture-specific boundaries. They argue, or else assume, that these boundaries have been created in childhood during early socialization and remain effective (and powerful) barriers to new experience throughout life. They also predict that disgust, once formed, will always function in determinable ways, always a censor whose punishing strokes may be foreseen. Yet abundant and varied empirical evidence suggests that human beings learn and relearn disgust.

What was once sickeningly disgusting will, under the conditions of living through new experiences, cease to be so. Furthermore, a large number of human occupations and professions require that their members learn to overcome or manage their conditioned responses of disgust. You could hardly be an effective physician, dentist, policeman, plumber, soldier or anthropologist if you could not learn to manage your disgust. For this reason, a study of disgust should also explore some of the ways in which disgust is overcome, transformed or (at least) socially managed so that it is kept hidden or else displaced onto unfamiliar objects. Of course, the difference is very great between learning to manage your disgust, to keep it hidden or undisplayed through professional control, and transforming it into an entirely new set of responses directed towards a freshly reconstituted object-world. However, both argue against the comparative rigidity of the theoretical models.

Finally, a study such as this must also examine the positive uses of disgust. There are well-known culinary and sexual uses for conventionally disgusting materials and acts (some of which I discuss in Chapter 3), but the problem far exceeds particular behaviours such as, say, the ingestion of urine. What might be learned from a personal experience of disgust? The standard theories of disgust, whether psychoanalytic or social constructionist, would appear to say that you will learn only re-enforcement of your early social formation. Yet you will also, inevitably it might seem, learn something about your personal limitations. What causes you to vomit, in either the actual or the metaphorical sense, is worth knowing. Disgust will make your limits plain, but it may also show, as Bataille argues over and over, how inadequate are the intellectual models that explain the violence, the inherent wildness, of human experience. The varied empirical range of disgust demonstrates the extent to which intelligence produces waste products, conceptual refuse that fails, even when apparently most powerful, to accomplish its desire: the creation of rational models of experience. In nature's excessive game, Bataille writes,

> it makes no difference whether I exceed her or she exceeds herself in me (she is perhaps entirely excess of herself), but, in time, the excess will finally takes its place in the order of things (I will die at that moment).[62]

Disgusting phenomena force the mind to reflect upon its fundamental incapacity, its abstractness in the face all psycho-visceral encounters. Even though disgust can be an overwhelming affect, making the gorge crack, tormenting the mind and making it savage, it is also vitally reflexive. It causes the mind to take stock of itself. At that point, a final positive dimension of disgust begins to appear. In the experience of disgust it may be possible not simply to learn both your physical and conceptual limitations but to transcend yourself, to go beyond socially formed boundaries into the new and the previously unimagined. This is another point that Bataille, writing from within a tradition of thought that includes both de Sade and Nietzsche, makes repeatedly: in transgression, within the prohibited territory of the disgusting, it may be possible to discover new behaviour, new personal potential and even new conceptual models.

Disgust is not only a powerful affect in itself, but it also intersects with a number of other affects. Shame, humiliation, contempt, anxiety, dread, anger and hate all are implicated with one another. In his study of ascetics,

Gananath Obeyesekere reports how he observed a woman with matted hair, "flowing like the wind," dancing near the shrine at Kataragama in Sri Lanka and was reminded of Freud's paper on "Medusa's Head" which links the "fear of the Medusa to the terror of castration." It is possible, Obeyesekere reflected, that Medusa's snakes are "only matted locks." He then wrote in his field notes that "I had seen an ugly woman, her teeth stained with betel nut juice and bearing repulsive matted locks, dancing in ecstasy and adoration before the god." With unusual self-awareness, Obeyesekere observes that the question why he had been initially repelled by the dancing woman kept "haunting" him. Why had he been "rendered anxious by her disturbing presence?" He continues this line of analysis, raising two further questions outside the normal constraints of objective ethnographic writing. "Was it the anthropologist's own castration anxiety that provoked this reaction? Or was it the ordinary disgust of a fastidious scholar for something dirty and anomalous sticking out of her head?"[63]

To live as an anthropologist is to live within an ongoing revolution in human affects. A medical student or a young police officer will have to overcome initial disgust, arising in many situations (inserting one's finger, without sexual intent, into a stranger's anus, for example, or viewing eviscerated and dismembered human bodies) that their professions comprise, but they will have to do this only once, or only during an early period of professionalization. An anthropologist may have to do this over and over in a personal revolution that will have several areas of struggle, but no absolute end. Fully professionalized, the anthropologist, like the doctor, will know how to keep a calm expression, nostrils open, lips smiling.[64] Perhaps at those moments the face is also a false path, apparently leading to serenity, an absence of anxiety, whereas the professional actually experiences loathing and disgust. A revolution in personal selfhood would still be genuine even if the person has learned merely to manage his or her secret affects but has not been able to eradicate them. A genuine revolution transforms or restructures affects, but it does not necessarily destroy their memory. The old objects of disgust vanish and new ones take their place, but the shadows of the old may still play beneath the surface of self-consciousness. Ordinary life, although still ordinary, will swarm with (perhaps unrecognized) disgusting novelty.

The mere existence of anthropologists suggests that anyone, given sufficient motivation, can overcome disgust. There are many professions that require one to overcome previously learned disgust, but anthropology is a peculiarly diversified example. Many people travel and encounter objects and customs, particularly dealing with food and drink, that they find disgusting and with which they must deal in one way or another.[65] However, anthropologists are both intensive and extensive travellers: they stay long periods of time and they dig in; they try to learn a culture's structures from the inside as well as from the outside. An anthropologist has to overcome his or her disgust, to overcome it radically so that it will not show and even (perhaps) no longer exist at all, and must do this many different times.

As Obeyesekere indicates, the sight of something that causes disgust may also prompt anxiety. The object is there, in front of you perhaps, mushy, slimy, changing shape and colour, perhaps verging on sludge, and the sight may suggest that what caused it may still be nearby, or even that you may end up in a similarly degraded state. Worry about the cause enough and you may begin to experience dread. You may even, if the dread begins to merge into terror, begin to excrete, adding your own excrement to the ambience of the disgusting object in front of you. Terror produces diarrhea, but, as Martin Pops remarks, reflecting upon the scene in Aristophanes' *The Frogs* in which the god Dionysus voids in terror, "cortical thinking regards shitting in terror not as an instinctual response to which no obloquy attaches ... but as an act of cowardice unworthy of a god or man."[66] You will be shamed for having felt terror as a consequence of having felt disgust. On the other hand, if you enjoy the sight, or even touch the object for pleasure, then you may also feel shame. Transgression of the boundaries that separate a disgusting object or action from the normal world of human life can cause shame. If someone comes across you, down on your knees perhaps, touching and snuffling the disgusting object, even indulging your secret coprophagous desires, then that person will feel disgust, but it will be directed towards you, towards your act more than the disgust-object itself. And you will feel shame, even humiliation. Disgust holds open the possibility of being doubly shamed. Indeed, it holds open a third possibility: self-disgust. After having been shamed, the associations of the disgusting object may transfer to the person. Thus you may also, transferring the object's properties to yourself, experience yourself as disgusting. You may even feel abjection, the sense of having been cast away or to one side while still remaining consciously yourself. In the narrow sense of the abject that Julia Kristeva has popularized, the experience of abjection within yourself will be like seeing the borders collapse, the walls of the "fortified castle" breached, but it may also be "the precondition of narcissism," the source of intense literary creation from Dostoevsky, Proust, Joyce, Sartre and Céline to Patrick White, William Burroughs, Thomas Pynchon and Doris Lessing.[67] The path downwards may prove to be the path upwards.

Here is a parable about disgust.

In a university whose name I do not choose to remember, though here I will call it the University of Ultima Thule, the English Department advertises for a position in theory and postmodern literature. There are quite a few applicants, but one stands out. His record indicates brilliance and a promising future. He has already, as a graduate student, published in leading journals, and his thesis has been accepted for publication by a distinguished press. His references are wildly enthusiastic and promise the highest levels of professional achievement and success. Yet the selection committee is disturbed that each letter of reference concludes with comments urging them not to make quick judgements or to judge the candidate at first sight. Do not make his physical appearance the basis of your decision, one referee writes. When the selection committee finally meets the candidate, they can see why the referees have cautioned them. The young man has a tattoo of a spider on his forehead. He is cheerfully nonchalant about the uneasiness he inspires in the committee and, while they interview him with averted eyes, he brushes his hair back with his hand, making the spider even more conspicuous. In his interview he is as brilliant and every bit as promising as his referees had suggested, but when the committee asks him about his current research, he points to the spider and answers, "Carnivalesque emblems." Is he mad? or is he merely brashly imprudent? Does he get the job? Under what conditions would a selection committee hire him? If they will not hire him, why not?[68]

He will not get the job. I feel quite confident about that. Despite his brilliance, his achievements, his references, his horizon of publication, he will be rejected. The selection committee will say that he must be eccentric, perhaps mad, but they will actually think that he will prove disruptive. They will worry about student reactions. They will allege professional worries, fears for the future, scruples. Above all, they will fear the reaction of the university's central administration and *its* worries about political reaction, and the possible implications for its budget. The committee will ignore all the candidate's positive worth, including the very public commitment to his research. Down deep, each person on the selection committee will feel that the candidate is—or has done something—disgusting. The western taboo against tattoos on public skin will play a role in their rejection; perhaps there may even be a general impression that tattoos are degrading, a violation of both Leviticus and western civilization, and belong chiefly to a stigmatized, "spoiled" underclass. Even the image of the spider, though carnivalesque (but also a traditional symbol of genius), will elicit all the committee's negative associations with the entire class of the *Arachnida*.

A spider is an overdetermined and deeply provocative image. Consider the concrete image of disgust which Shakespeare creates out of a spider in *The Winter's Tale*:

> There may be in the cup
> A spider steep'd, and one may drink; depart,
> And yet partake no venom (for his knowledge
> Is not infected), but if one present
> Th' abhorr'd ingredient to his eye, make known
> How he hath drunk, he cracks his gorge, his sides,
> With violent hefts. I have drunk, and seen the spider.[69]

This is also another Shakespearean use of "gorge." Leontes has told himself a story, the story of his wife, Hermione, and her adulterous copulation with his best friend, Polixenes. He is devoured by jealousy. Leontes has seen (in his mind's eye) an image of horror. Listening to Shakespeare, I find it impossible to know precisely what it is about spiders that so disturbs Leontes, that might crack his gorge, filling his body with the violent hefts of vomiting. But I remember that Renaissance writers, the archive of classical literature intact, all its hybrid monsters and images of deformed humanity still available for allegory and the wonders of the new world freshly accessible, had an extensive repertory of horrifying and disgusting images to call upon. Yet Shakespeare gives Leontes the image of a spider: the eight legs, the round, hairy body (looking like a bulb or a bloated pustule), the central devouring mouth, the hunting and trapping associations, the implacability, the marvellous fecundity, the metaphoric connections with weaving, with labyrinths, with both skill and fragility. For European culture, a spider is a complex image with many associations. It exists behind many boundaries, as behind the many single strands of its web, but its emergence, from whatever angle, may be like an explosion, a bomb going off within the mind. You can scarcely make too much of such an image, nor easily read too much into it. Now what happens when the spider's image is upon the skin? What does the tattoo tell you about the person who has inscribed Arachne upon his body, transgressing several boundaries? How will the selection committee read the spider tattoo?

Rather than carnival, or genius, the committee may think about spiders' predatory eating practices. They may imagine the swollen, bulb-like body, the hairiness, the squatting stance of the eight legs, each bent upwards at the joint as if ready to spring, but they may not recall that the web, symbol of construction, of labyrinths and of infinity, had early in European mythology been linked to the skill of weaving.[70] (To weaving and thus to storytelling: Arachne not only weaves but tells ekphrastic tales, and it is these that so disturb Athena. The members of the committee, although thinking in stories, will not be thinking about stories.) Collectively, they will bear in mind many intricate thoughts, worm-like stalks stretching out towards many aspects of western civilization, but none of these will be comforting, none pleasing. Their imaginations may work as Leontes' does. If the young scholar understands that the committee has found his spider image disgusting, a stigma rather than a symbol of self-enhancement, and that he has been rejected for what he had done in an act of self-confidence and pride, then he may feel shame. Disgust and shame are mutually coupled.[71]

Conventional revulsion "imbues tattooing with significant power and appeal."[72] A tattoo can attract the gaze, fixing attention even while causing averted eyes, and inspire at once loathing, horror and fascination. It can be, perhaps commonly *is* in western culture, a poke-in-the-eye proclamation of social disaffiliation and/or re-affiliation. John Gray comments, "Nothing evokes that superior shudder, that anal-retentive cluck of civilized disapproval, quite like a tattoo."[73] Its material condition, a human skin, calls attention to itself, as a multiply sanctioned canvas or page, in a way that no other art form does. The material condition is unavoidable: it is an "organic canvas."[74] A tattoo carries many messages—affiliation, disaffiliation, exfiliation, re-affiliation, anger, alienation, empathy and (like the well-known knuckle tattoos) both hate and love—all of which can be "read," or semiotically decoded, within a given culture or group. Tattoos are often sexual in the message they communicate (and may always be read erotically, even if that is a misreading), telling stories of availability and prowess, of versatility and polymorphous adventure. Like scarification and piercings, tattoos are vehicles of sexual communication and "normal among many people, perhaps among *most* people" but until recently largely marginalized in western culture. Instead of body markings, western people have developed elaborate systems of fashion and cosmetics.[75] The design of a tattoo might be beautiful in itself, but once it is inked into a human skin it becomes, as Kant observes, a dependent form, to be judged in relation to another kind of beauty, free or self-subsisting, such as a human face itself. A wilful, energetic exercise in self-symbolization, a tattoo may suggest a sociopathic personality or merely a carnivalesque one. Erving Goffman refers to the class of "stigma symbols" that may display, perhaps quite deliberately, the subject's sense of "spoiled identity."[76] Until recently at least, a tattoo has been both an emblem, an image to be interpreted or read, and a stigma. It focusses definite socio-cultural boundaries. Across the boundary of a visible tattoo (and particularly on "public skin") exists someone whom universities probably will not hire, someone who appears disturbed, perhaps dangerous, alienated from normal society but also, it may be, a member of a sub-community of outlaws, deviants or sociopathic types, or even geniuses. Members of rock bands have typically "acquired tattoos as a feature of their neo-savage persona."[77]

Hence a tattoo poses an engrossing problem in interpretation: it will have textual features, even if these are quite minimal, and it will evoke a vast, indeterminate matrix of contextual associations. Very often the textual aspects of a tattoo indicate a story, a potential narrative, and seem to demand that the viewer fill in the gaps and make narrative sense of it.[78] A tattoo must be read much as any other minimal narrative text in paint or words. A reader has been given, as Peter J. Rabinowitz puts it, a "licence to fill."[79] Some minimal texts are more insistent, more clamorous in their demands to be filled, than others. Much depends on the nature of the boundaries that they focus, the range of contextual evidence and the interpretive models that they invoke. Some boundaries are more hostile, more difficult to cross, than others. (Leontes' spider exists across a boundary, corrupted conjugal love and infidelity, that he finds nearly unbearable to imagine.) Because it is drawn upon the organic canvas of the skin, a tattoo calls into the play of interpretation a large number of extra-textual categories that are not always brought into the reading process. Human skin is a problematic canvas. A much-tattooed member of the rock group Circus of Power laments, "Skin prejudice is the worst form of preju-dice."[80] In literature, then, a tattoo has often constituted a powerful element in characterization: an index that the reader may use to interpret the character in a number of overdetermined, extratextual ways. More recently, customized or "new wave" tattoos have been essentially private and usually more explicitly narrative, evoking, say, mythological contexts, not the sociopathology of modern life. However, the general impressions of spoiled identity and social stigma remain, making the reading of the stories that tattoos pose a provocative problem in narrative analysis.[81] The young man in my parable will not get the job and his brilliant career will have to be pursued outside of any university.

Given the plot and the thematic preoccupations of *The Winter's Tale*, Leontes may associate the image of a spider with women. Arachne, the young girl who had bested Athena in a weaving contest, became, as every Renaissance writer must have known, a spider. Arachne's fate, her body transformed into a spider's devouring centrality, her skills misappre-hended, engenders envy. Retelling the story, Spenser has Arachne herself poisoned by her own envy:

> Yet did she inly fret and felly burne,
> And all her blood to poysonous rancor turne. (*Muiopotmos* 343–44)

When I reflect upon Leontes' violent disgust, I also recall that the spider is one aspect of the Great Mother, the Terrible Mother in her role as weaver of destiny, the archetype of the witch and enchantress, and hence a source of dread as well as of loathing and disgust.[82]

Doris Lessing captures the potential horror of the spider image in having Anna Wulf, the protagonist of *The Golden Notebook*, at the moment of her deepest personal uncertainty and greatest psychic fragmentation, introject the misogynistic image of woman-as-spider and experience self-disgust: "My wet sticky centre seemed disgusting … I was gripped by my disgust."[83] I think that Shakespeare calls upon these associations, and indeed there are many more, in writing Leontes' soliloquy. That soliloquy may be more indirect, more distanced and shaped in metaphor, than Lessing's monologue, but it is not less evocative of the human consciousness of disgust.

Standing in the Prado viewing Titian's oil painting of *Danaë*, you will fall back on an understanding of Greek mythology, on other versions of the story in words (perhaps in paint as well), other ways of telling the same story, on variants along a spectrum of possible expression. The multiplex image of Titian's painting evokes an extended range of prior/possible tellings. A reading of the painting outside of its know(n)able story matrix would be quite feasible, and indeed the many uninformed summer visitors to the Prado must interpret it largely without its mythological matrix. They will do so by supplying a story of some kind, a personal matrix that reflects their own immediate culture or their own idiosyncratic sexual fantasies. (Danaë might become a sexually repressed young woman dreaming an erotic fusion of gold and a divine phallus, or else enjoying an actual sadomasochistic experience in which Titian's greedy servant might become either a procuress or an S/M technician. Titian's shower of symbolic gold might, then, become an actual golden shower.) From the standpoint of narrative analysis, there does not seem to be an unresolvable difficulty in admitting the existence of extremely minimal narrative forms, in either images or words. Literature can be thought of as a vast repertory of what Umberto Eco calls "intertexual frames," various and variable contexts for reading that make possible the labyrinthine replication of stories out of which further replication emerges. A single image, an emblem or even a few lines clustered together in skeletal representation, *can* tell a story, but only if a prior story matrix exists that can be recognized or imagined.

A recurring problem of narrative theory concerns the minimal nature of certain narratives. If we imagine a story with few incidents ("The king died, and then the queen died of grief," in E.M. Forster's famous example) that is told with only the most strictly necessary narrative development, showing bare temporal sequence and causation, then we can experience something close to a truly minimal narrative. Look about the world and note how many items in its vast inventory imply stories or suggest stories that could be told. The world seems partly constituted by its immense micro-narrativity. There have been, Roland Barthes remarks, "ever so many stories."[84] Thus, constructing a model of how minimal narratives work should be an important initial move for both theories of narrative and of culture.[85]

In this book, I shall hardly be able to talk about everything that can, or might, be disgusting. My objective is to create an argument, not an encyclopedia. Disgust, as William Ian Miller observes, is a "roiling" subject, vast, hydravarious and shape-shifting. However fine the net, much will elude capture. Often the discussion will concern ideas about disgust, those diverse theories and models that lie behind thinking. Furthermore, a great deal of what I have to say will actually concern the representations of disgust in literature and film rather than things themselves. I hope to show that there are disgusting images and texts just as there are disgusting things, but that these are fundamentally different experiences. By the final chapter I shall have made clear what kind of a phenomenon disgust is, why it is so important (and in so many ways) for the understanding of both art and culture and why no single theory actually explains it even though several theories do provide partial accounts. Disgust always appears doubly: from one angle, the disgusting thing may fill you with the urge to vomit, shivers of loathing tingling through your body; from another angle, the disgusting thing may actually seem attractive, hiding its loathsome side from view. Then it may begin to appear like the apple with a wormhole, both desirable and off-putting, attractive and repulsive.

This book will examine a number of situations in which a person places himself or herself across a cultural boundary and thus appears to become disgusting in the eyes of his or her community. (The reverse situation also occurs: a person may transgress a boundary and, in seeming to pollute the protected region, manifest him/herself as disgusting.) Throughout this book, I shall return to the question of theory and the different models that have been proposed to account for the phenomenon of disgust. Ultimately, I hope to show that they all have some bearing upon the problem of under-standing disgust, depending upon the question asked. For example, the model derived from Sartre's *Being and Nothingness* (and recurringly illus-trated by his fiction), holding disgust to be the consciousness of indeter-minate states of being and hence a major stimulus of the imagination, accomplishes a great deal of conceptual work, but it does little to explain the social purposes of disgust. The de Sadean position, so convincingly argued by Bataille, tells us many things about disgust and its potential to bring about self-knowledge and even self-transformation, but it has nothing to say about either morality or law, nothing to say about the terror of chaos or the (occasional) desirability of social order. A world of six billion self-transcending Titans might not be a happy one. My own position is that no account of disgust as either a psycho-visceral or socio-cultural phenom-enon will be adequate unless it incorporates a theory of the imagination and the human capacity both to create and to participate in fictional worlds. It is one of the most striking weaknesses of Miller's provocative study of disgust that he closes his discussion to art and literature and, in doing this, to imagination. Human life must always be imagined as being lived, in Beckettian phrase, astride the grave and that is just, as Pozzo observes, "how it is on this bitch of an earth."[86] Fleetingly, your lifeworld may seem solid (if it does at all): from the standpoint of a pluralistic theory of disgust, life is a process, infrequently broken by stray moments of light, characterized by muck, ooze and verminous sludge. The wormhole is the apple's most undeniable part. ❧

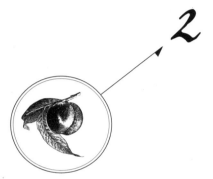

2

Its Stench

Conceiving Disgust

The memory is very distinct. My mother held a peach out to me. I can clearly remember how doubtful I was. Perhaps I had never seen one before. She put it on the kitchen table and cut it open in halves, dug out the pit and then sliced it into quarters. She put two quarters of the peach on a dish and handed it to me. I screamed.

I refused to touch the peach. I actually hated to look at it. It made me queasy just to see how yellow and wet it was. I was somewhere in the neighbourhood of four years old, not as young as three but not yet five. Old enough, you may say, to eat a peach. Or too young to experience disgust of something I had never seen before? The only certain thing is that from that moment and throughout my childhood peaches filled me with loathing and revulsion. I didn't like them and refused to eat them. And, I recall this clearly, it made me feel ill simply to look at one. This odd condition persisted until I was about seventeen. Then two friends were eating peaches out of a paper bag while we were in one's backyard shooting hoops. Suddenly, without giving it thought, I asked for a peach and bit into it deeply, tasting the sweet flavour, feeling the thick juice dribble around my lips and down my chin. I did not experience disgust. Since that moment, I have always enjoyed peaches.

What qualities did I see in peaches that made me loathe them so? It may have been the wet, slippery flesh. I have memories of other wet things, but none of any, except excrement and (sometimes) snot, that might have filled me with disgust. That hardly rules out the possibility. If you believe that strong affects, such as disgust, are formed within the family, or within the family as it reflects the surrounding culture, then you would want to find the familial assumptions that constructed my sense of disgust. That wouldn't mean that my parents told me to loathe wet and slimy things, but it might mean that certain "rules," from which I had extrapolated, had been laid down. I may actually have transferred onto the peach my loathing of excrement, conflating the colour of urine with the solidity of feces, seeking to preserve, just as my parents had taught me, my "clean and proper body." If you take a "systemic" approach to the early construction of phobias, then you might seek the contradictions in my family that caused me to find something slippery or indeterminate to be disgusting. The cultural rule that organic wetness and slime are off-putting, even disgusting, might never have been expressed in my family nor even made easily found (for a four-year-old boy), but still have had agency. In one view, that is how culture works: sending messages that no one observes being sent.

It may be that the peach's apparent lack of definite being frightened me. The slippery, juice-oozing flesh may have suggested an indefinite existence, an amorphous being lacking precise shape and definition, just at the time when I, as a four-year-old boy, was beginning to establish my own personal sense of existence. Jean-Paul Sartre thinks that disgust arises inevitably out of the perception of a mucoid world in which slime invokes essentially ambiguous states of being, indeterminate or caught between definite states. No doubt, I had become sensitive to slime. Successful toilet training would not have been more than a couple of years behind me. Besides inducing a revulsion for dirty and "don't touch" feces, this training may well have included other bodily effluvia, such as saliva and nasal mucus. My mother, I feel confident in saying, would have found human wetness unpleasant and the body distressingly soggy. No doubt, she would have done her best to bestow her aversions upon her son. Furthermore, I must have been unconsciously engaged in the "management" of my sexual, or phallic, being. I would have been busy, though deeply beneath the surface, far from my mother's eyes, establishing my boundaries, building up my ego defences. And so the peach, all yellow, wet and slimy, might well have struck me as a threat. Your sense of personal identity is fragile. No one needs to tell you this as an adult, since existence itself proclaims the fact from each situation and through every other form of being. For a child, a ripe peach, oozing and slimy, might serve as the emblem of human dissolution. Perhaps a little boy, scarcely older than a toddler, might see such things.

However, these are not the only available hypotheses. Two events had taken place in my life at just about the time that the peach disgusted me. One day when I was about four, I went out into our backyard to play. We lived in a cul-de-sac on the edge of a wet Pacific forest. (A year later, shortly after I turned five, I was actually kidnapped from that backyard by a man who stepped out of the woods and engaged me in conversation. But that's another tale.) The place teemed with small forms of life. I climbed part of the way up the fence and stayed there for several minutes, my hands grasping the picket top. Abruptly, I noticed that my hands, arms and even my neck were covered with tiny, freshly hatched brown spiderlings. I ran screaming inside and my mother bathed me in the tub. I have no doubts about this event. I remember it with maximum lucidity. Hardly bigger than pinheads, the baby spiders had crawled all over my upper body. There is no doubt that this experience gave me a definite phobia for spiders and, most likely, for all insects. Even today, I am unsettled by teeming insects. I draw back from their Hydra-like fecundity. Often when I see them in swarms, nests or hives, I experience a sharp loathing and the chill *frisson* of horrified disgust. Many years later, while fossicking about in a dark, filthy cupboard of a cheap flat in Sydney, I came upon a female cockroach, bloated with her eggs and surrounded by myriad tiny replicas of herself. I froze in horror. Shuddering and nearly gagging, I managed to find some insect spray. Relentlessly, I killed her and her family with far more spray than was actually necessary.

Could my experience with the tiny spiderlings, long before adult encounters with insect swarms and cockroach nests, already have made peaches disgusting? Possibly, but then it would have been more the peach's brown, fuzzy exterior than its yellow interior that put me off. Or else the peach's exiguous peel might have reminded me of my sense that my skin had been violated, the thin ego-covering invaded, by the swarming spiderlings. In either case, my fear and subsequent anxieties arising from my brush with the spider multitude would have been displaced upon the peach. The actual mechanism of displacement may be unclear, but you have to admit its possibility.

The second event was more personal and should appeal, as the basis for an hypothesis, to anyone with a inclination towards psychoanalysis. Shortly before the experience with the peach, and more or less about the time of the spiders, three little girls in the neighbourhood, a couple of years older than myself, persuaded me to undress for them so that they could see, and touch, my male organ. We did this in the forest just beyond my house. One of the girls volunteered to expose herself for my benefit. I had no sisters and so had never seen a girl naked before. I honestly do not recall any negative feelings about the little girl's vagina, but since it is a common feminist perception that men (even little boys) have negative associations with the female genitalia, I have to admit that I may have had such feelings, although only at an unconscious level. All that I ever consciously remembered was the vulva's shape. Did I touch her? It may be so, but, the image either repressed or non-existent, I cannot recall. If this led, by another process of unconscious displacement, to my aversion for the peach, then it might have been the wet, yellow flesh of the peach that aroused me. But what were the links? It would be many years before I would hear a woman invite me to participate in oral sex by saying, "Take a bite of the peach."

There is more to this story. My mother, with ever-alert maternal eyes, had seen us go into the woods and knew what we had been doing. She called the girls' mothers and complained that they had abused me. I don't know what else she may have said, but it must have been potent. Later I learned that the girls had been severely punished. The next day, long before I knew what had happened, they came rushing at me and pushed me off my tricycle, breaking my nose. I ran home, my nose flowing blood, and once again I was put into the tub to be washed. If the peach reminded me of my experience with female sexuality, it must have done so with an overlay of fear and embarrassment. This last hypothesis, although it does seem rather luminously psychoanalytic, draws a hint of confirmation from something that happened thirteen years later. Shortly before I happily ate the peach in my friend's backyard, I had engaged in cunnilingus for the first time. In the back seat of my father's Studebaker, I had performed this taboo act (at that time and that place) on my girlfriend. I had survived the act, and I had not vomited. I even enjoyed it, or at least I enjoyed the impression that she had enjoyed it. Let us suppose that my experience with the three little girls had filled me with fear and apprehension with respect to female sexuality, later represented by peaches. I was able to overcome this phobia by immersing myself in the root itself of the phobia, in an actual female sex organ. You could think of it as a bit of theatre-based therapy (self-administered) or as the acting out of a deeply founded phobia.

Still, this story told and the psychoanalytic implications drawn out, I much prefer the hypothesis based upon the invading swarm of spiderlings. The sense of self is always rather thin-skinned and open to violation. Invasion, violation, in the guise of needles and knives, may be terrifying, but, as countless horror films have shown, massified insects, in hives, nests or swarms, may be even more frightening, more invasive in their multitude. That, however, is a personal aversion, intense to the point of horror. A small boy's disgust over a ripe peach turns out to be a pretty torturous psychic phenomenon, open to several conflicting hypotheses, which, like all good stories, defies a simple, single, telling. Pulling on a single loose end, "how many silken scarves, like the tail of a kite so far away we cannot see it," might be drawn from experience's sleeve?[1] A boy's disgust shows that the experience of loathing and revulsion, of gagging and retching before an unviewable object, is not simple. It might even be a necessary precondition of desire. Thus Bataille observes that eroticism is a "closed book to us so long as we do not see man's beginning in the repugnance he felt for a nature that was filthy in his eyes."[2] The solution to my peach phobia that came when I was seventeen may have been erotic, but it would certainly have been less erotic if I had not so loathed peaches in the first place. Many things occur in even the most apparently simple experience of disgust. And many conflicting, but also overlapping, accounts of that disgust are in play.

Once disgust has ceased to appear merely the obverse of the naturally attractive—a spontaneously overpowering reaction to perverse deviations from the norm in either nature or society—it demands an explanation. Such a powerful affect, energizing both somatic and psychic systems while taking such varied shapes, cries out for a reasoned account. Throughout this book, I shall call upon five models to explain disgust. Although "model" is a conflicted term, capable of both great refinement and considerable obfuscation, I shall use it in a fairly simple and straightforward manner. By model, I mean what Max Black calls a "theoretical model": a way of *talking* that claims explanatory power.[3] All models seek to simplify experience in order to promote conceptualization. Thus a model adequate to provide an account of disgust in anything like its full scope must both simplify the astounding range of its manifestations and also supply a basis for identification and explanation. A model of disgust that failed to identify putrescent human feces or a deliquescent human corpse as potentially disgusting would not be a good model. In a strong formulation, a theoretical model might be called an axiomatic structure; that is, a more or less rigorous structure of definitions that leads directly to certain results.[4] In a weaker formulation, a theoretical model is only a number of propositions, in some kind of loose relationship to each other, that are assumed for the purposes of their explanatory powers. When we use a theoretical model, a known discourse is "extended to a new domain of application."[5] A fruitful model should possess predictive as well as identifying and explanatory power.[6]

By and large, I am interested in the explanatory depth of models, not their predictive reach. The five models I shall discuss have only a limited, or warped, predictive capacity with respect to disgust. They can fully explain disgust only by making assumptions or accepting postulates (a specific religious doctrine, say) that are outside common, or evident, experience; or else, like psychoanalysis, they have emerged from an initial examination of limited, culture-specific data. However, these five models seem to bear upon the primary domain of disgust in fruitful ways. They are all commonly understood and perform much more general conceptual work than merely to explain in-the-world disgust phenomena.

Of the five, only the fourth model, derived from Sartrean phenomenology, actually accounts for the diversity of disgust in human life, and even that model does not explain how disgust, deeply structured and very powerful, can be transformed into something else, displaced or unlearned. Perhaps only the fifth model, the de Sade/Bataille project for opening (to) experience and transforming the self, can adequately explain how disgust, which *seems* so ingrained, so deeply formed, can change so many times, and so profoundly, in an individual's life. Taken together, these five models, considered as a theoretical array, seem to cover the problem well. Even if not exhaustive, together they cast a widely flung net over the phenomena.

Furthermore, the experience of art, especially literature and film, contributes to an account of disgust's metamorphic properties. Art seems to show how possible it is to unlearn a conditioned response and to acquire new disgust-objects while holding them for only a short time. Throughout this book, I shall turn to the representations of disgusting and loathsome things, bearing always in mind the distinction between an actual thing and its representation, for enlightenment. Art draws out the disgusting properties of things, heightening their deliquescence and amorphousness, underscoring their deviations from socio-cultural norms; but it also demonstrates how readily such in-the-world things can become acceptable, the mere content of aesthetically pleasing forms.

Disgust weaves itself through all our conduct. Its web is unpleasant, winding itself around all manner of objects, proscribing certain acts, spreading like contamination through consciousness, limiting the scope of human life. In its unavoidable threads, you may find yourself, face contorted into the classic disgust grimace, beginning to throw up, or you may find yourself an object of disgust, someone else's mouth (pointing you-wards) pursing towards vomit. Yet it is also a web that transforms itself repeatedly. Sometimes when you think that you see it clearly, it isn't even there. A web, then, but one that is often illusory, often metamorphic.

Attempting to explain its origins as an affect, or to show how it works in the individual or in the culture, models of disgust all fail to account for its radical metamorphicity. For the most part, theoretical models routinize disgust: explaining it in the terms of knowable preconditions, fixing it behind determinable boundaries and constraining it into a stable, predictable affect. Since I am arguing that, within the same person or culture, disgust may assume manifold expressive shapes and possess varying intensities, a multiplicity that is endlessly replayed in representations, it makes sense to treat the theoretical accounts as both various and variable. As a topic for investigation, disgust clamorously demands that its theory be pluralistic.

First, some philosophers have found the idea of moral disgust highly seductive and have argued that disgust, as a strong repugnance to certain acts, constitutes a universal feature of the human "relationship to the rest of the world."[7] The definition of disgust assumes a normative formulation. In the absence of disgust, it can be argued, it would be difficult to see how any prohibition could work other than through the stark fear of punishment or disease. (The contemporary argument, so often heard in the United States, that AIDS and other diseases constitute a *punishment* expresses a culturally sanctioned strategy of avoidance.) In the absence of disgust, anything would be acceptable as behaviour and society, straining to contain the acceptability of all acts, would disintegrate, life within it becoming inevitably nasty, brutish and (most likely) short. William Ian Miller remarks that disgust "installs large chunks of the moral world at the core of our identity."[8] This captures the moral argument about disgust exactly. Human civilization and law rise upon an underlying human capacity to find certain kinds of acts fundamentally disgusting. Disgust is not simply a "moral sentiment," as Freud supposed, but also a proto-legal activity, a necessary condition for the legal system as well as for civilization itself. Disgust teaches you to keep certain things at a distance, to avoid contact and (hence) contamination, and that is, for civilization, an important lesson. "Disgust rules," the socially inscribed prohibitions of specific contacts and acts, evolve everywhere, and everywhere possess multiple socio-cultural purposes. Although it may seem that the moral-legal model is brutally simplistic and inflexible, a kind of riot police for enforcing the most inane middle-class morality, it actually works quite supply. It is possible for a moral judgement to point in more than one direction. It may work to repress certain specific behaviours, coprophagy or necrophilia, say, but it may also function as a brake on excessive prejudice. An extreme moralist, someone preaching brimstone and punishment for many particular transgressions, can also appear to be disgusting. Disgust can be a curb upon many different kinds of behaviour, including bias, prejudice and inequitable moral judgements. Prejudice, bias and bigotry, whether based upon ethnicity, race, language, gender or sexual preference, can seem overwhelmingly disgusting, a slimy fall from the norm of enlightened human behaviour. You may find the acts of a confirmed coprophagist to be disgusting, but you might also find disgusting a moralist's judgement that such a person should be publicly tortured and flayed alive. Miller observes that disgust is a democratic emotion that people low on a social scale can use effectively against those who stand higher. Democracy is a "grid of competing contempts, variously styled—but distinctly recognizable and perhaps even a necessary starting point for a minimally basic respect for persons."[9]

From the moral point of view, the multiplicity and elasticity of disgust rules matters less than their existence. However, formed, they need to exist. John Kekes remarks that

> The rules can be violated, but if their violations are widespread and lasting, civilization will be replaced by barbarism, and human welfare will stand in jeopardy ... [F]ear in disgust has the violation of moral taboos as its object. And it is reasonable to fear that because the widespread violation of moral taboos leads to the disintegration of society.[10]

Moralists are always inviting you to imagine a world where everything is possible, in which there could be no transgressions because all is permitted. In the absence of disgust, the argument might be, there would be either total barbarism or a society ruled solely by force, violence and terror. Disgust, although you may not like to think so, softens the harsh angles of a Hobbesian world.

The moral-legal model of revulsion shows, if little else, the ardent desire to make disgust universal, an essential or biological aversion. If universal, then the phenomenon of disgust would point the way towards a common morality, or at least a deep common framework among human beings which could provide a justification for the concept of a trans-historical natural law and an actual basis for positive law. Miller argues that disgust has many uses in human society (even if the disgusting has not); above all, disgust constitutes a moral weapon. Expressing disgust, you may be delivering a reprimand, a refusal or a rebuke. Most importantly, you will be making a judgement that an act has fallen beneath a standard or has ignored an accepted norm. It may be a complex judgement, but it will always be pointed towards the correction and regulation of other human behaviour. Disgust, Miller observes, "communicates rather better than most emotions."[11] Drawing upon David Hume and Adam Smith, he underscores the importance of observers in the world's moral economy. Citing from Smith's *Theory of Moral Sentiments*, Miller notes that even the "failure of the observer to sympathize constitutes his adverse judgment on the propriety of the behavior observed. And this failure of sympathy, depending on the exact nature of the impropriety, can end in disgust."[12] The "unsocial moral sentiments" actually make possible a moral society.

The moral-legal model of disgust is quite powerful, if rather one-eyed. Of course, I want to argue that each of the five models I shall discuss is distressingly one-eyed. They are certainly, taken singly, far from stereoscopic; taken together, they may create a partial stereopticon: a device that sees in depth, if still imperfectly. The power of the moral-legal model is twofold. On the one hand, it provides an account of how human beings manage to survive together in a "human" society (not altogether nasty and brutish yet not very forgiving either) and behave together in mostly predictable ways. On the other hand, it drives home a fundamental, if normally ignored, reflection. What would society resemble if nothing were disgusting or, more strongly, nothing *could be* disgusting? If that "unsocial sentiment" did not exist or were to evolve out of existence, what then? It might resemble nothing so much as an amorphous, shapeless struggle.[13] Miller writes,

> Disgust is more than just the motivator of good taste; it marks out moral matters for which we can have no compromise. Disgust signals our being appalled, signals the fact that we are paying more than lip-service; its presence lets us know we are truly in the grip of the norm whose violation we are witnessing or imagining. To articulate one's disgust is to do more than state a preference or simply reveal a sensation in our bodies. Even if we are only using the diction of disgust as a fashion of talking, that is, independent of the feeling, we are still stating most emphatically the belief that the norms being referenced by our expression of disgust should be the sort that hold us in their grip.[14]

This is a strong plea, not quite an argument at this point, for disgust as a necessary moral sentiment and even a proto-legal condition.

The moral-legal model leaves much out of account. It cannot directly deal with the problem of origins (why do only adult human beings, but neither animals nor small children, experience disgust?) without appealing to one or another religious doctrine. Nor can it deal with distribution. Many things that have no social content whatsoever are found by some people to be disgusting. (The peaches which I found disgusting as a child possessed no social content. My feeling of disgust was idiosyncratic in the extreme. Or was it?) A moral account of disgust cannot deal at all with transgressive art or with personal treks across social boundaries for self-fashioning or enlightenment. Indeed, it has difficulty in dealing with art and literature on any level. Miller finds art either irrelevant or counter-productive to his argument. Although he does discuss a few aspects of medieval literature, he treats most modern literature (George Orwell is the sole exception, and then only his essays, not his fiction) and all disgust-evoking, or transgressive, art as either irrelevant or "adolescent."[15] "Latter-day Platonists," one philosopher writes, insist that "the consumption of popular fiction can lead to personal moral degradation, to misogyny or misanthropy, and to a loss of sympathy and humanity."[16] It may seem odd, but one of the thorniest problems in every approach to disgust is precisely the distinction between disgusting things, whether objects or acts, and their representations. This extremely basic distinction, familiar to every student of aesthetics and art, attacks moral theorists from the flanks. It is difficult for them to handle and for the most part they, as "latter-day Platonists," have little wish to do so.

The problem of representation within the moral-legal model can be seen in a striking passage in Kekes' discussion. He distinguishes between a rather ordinary disgust, simple squeamishness, and the deep disgust that follows observing, or even contemplating, certain profoundly unacceptable acts. He writes,

> ... if some people, possessing a contemporary Western sensibility, are not disgusted in certain situations, then there must be some very special explanation of their failure in terms of repression, brutalization, pathological inattention, or the like. The experiences include eating feces, disemboweling a person, drinking pus, being splattered with someone's brain, the sight and smell of putrefying corpses, the spectacle of extreme torture, such as dismembering live humans with a chainsaw, or immersion in excrement.[17]

I would not wish to argue that these acts and sights are not deeply disgusting. However, some, such as "the sight and smell of putrefying corpses," are everyday experiences for soldiers and policemen, doctors and nurses, forensic scientists and undertakers (to name a few). This is one of the difficulties with the moral view of disgust: seeking trans-historical categories, it tends to universalize and to disallow exceptions. Furthermore, I think that it is important to observe that these acts do take place, occasionally as a general practice or as a matter of state policies with many political supporters, and (thus) cannot be universally disgusting. They also occur as representations. Millions of people living in western societies apparently enjoy seeing representations of all these acts, in horror films and fiction, even in documentaries that explore such practices when they are, or have been, state policy in various countries. A representation of an act is quite different from the act itself and stimulates, in the manner of art-horror, different responses.[18]

Kekes' list neither saturates nor demarcates the category of the disgusting. His list is arbitrary and, as exemplary instances in argument tend to be, *ad hoc*. The list does not distinguish between acts that you might perform and those that you might watch. Eating feces as an act is very different from watching it being done.[19] Watching extreme torture does not seem to be at all similar to the act of torturing someone or participating in another person's physical degradation. Seeing, smelling and touching, all second-hand participation in disgusting acts, can be overwhelmingly powerful, but is not quite the same as performing them. However, as I shall argue in Chapter 4, the accusation of taking part in something that is appalling (or, at best, sleazy) touches anyone who would even consent to watch.[20] Even more important, the experiences can all be accepted under certain conditions (as their representations commonly are in both entertainment and scholarship) and endured. Certain professions, such as medicine, plumbing, policing, military service and anthropology, require that their members all learn to witness and accept the sight of the very acts that both Kekes and Miller think show human brutalization, desensitization and diminishment. Without evidence, Kekes assumes that when people ("members of juries, triage nurses, the police, and attendants in mental hospitals," in his own examples) are required to witness disgusting acts, their "imagination subsequently preys upon them."[21] Indeed, this may happen, but it does not seem to be the rule, and the noteworthy occasions when it does occur hardly seem like a basis for making high-flying generalizations about the whole of human experience.

The moral-legal model does not adequately treat aesthetic questions and tends to ignore art and literature (other than to denounce them or else to promote simplistic versions of art as moral propaganda), stumbling clumsily over the problem of representation, but it does highlight the role of disgust in forming and proclaiming moral judgements. Above all, it forces you to ask, What would human life be like if disgust were either impossible or universally unlearned?

Second, it is possible to see disgust as a construction, like desire, that takes place during a process of socialization within a particular socio-cultural context.[22] A culture's values replicate themselves in the individual: values are encoded by forming institutions such as law, education and religion, and consequently function like encrypted strings of commands, determining surface manifestations. The human child, Bataille observes, is taken "out of the muck" as his/her parents strive to wipe out the traces of his/her natural origins.[23] Since Durkheim, social scientists, and more recently humanists, have seen human "nature" as a construction of socio-cultural technologies that determine (for individual experience) what seems to be the case. The process of socialization involves, as Peter L. Berger and Thomas Luckmann put it, the "three moments" of externalization, objectification and internalization. The individual "simultaneously" externalizes his or her own being and also internalizes "the social world."[24] Hence a dialectic exists between the individual and the society: each constructs the other. Society is actively constructed by individual human beings, but these have no existence, and certainly no worldview, independent of the society in which they have grown up. Thus there is a net-like quality to social worlds in which not only is everything in the world "woven" by interaction, but each individual internalizes, and in real sense *is*, the social world. Embodied in the individual as a set of behaviours, of values and judgements, even as encrypted commands, the social world will seem strong, fixed, inevitable. Slowly constructed during the entire childhood process of socialization, the individual's world possesses a "peculiar quality of firmness."[25] That firmness, if it actually exists, predicts that psycho-visceral affects, such as disgust, will function as entrenched and unyielding habit-grooves within a given social world. A fully socialized individual should exercise immense powers of recognition but have little or no capacity for re-cognition, for rethinking and even re-seeing familiar items in the world's jumble.[26] With no capacity to see freshly, a word such as *disgust* would seem to mean pretty much the same thing, within a given culture, whenever it is used.

Yet a word in context, Thomas J. Scheff writes, is "at least as complex as a strand of DNA." Within a social context, meanings "involve the enfolded intricacies of both the human brain and the social world."[27] Consider the problem of transgression once more. People who enjoy having their bodies transformed by tattoos or piercings, or who eat excrement, or who find pleasure in golden showers, are all pursuing deviant acts: acts that, within western society and even within many deviant sub-groups, strum jarringly along the "enfolded intricacies" of human interaction between brain and society. For example, there do seem to be people who like golden showers and who "take" them often, when chance or assignation permits. They are engaged in a deviant act; its deviance will of course be a product of the culture in which it occurs.[28] You may judge takers of golden showers to be deviant, but nonetheless you will have to admit that there are (perhaps a few, perhaps many) such people. For several reasons, concerning which you may speculate, they enjoy the provocations of *urolagnia*, the desire to witness someone else urinate, to urinate upon another person or to be themselves urinated upon.

Social formation creates the "fit" between brain and world. Desire and gender, to take only two concepts that currently receive a great deal of attention, can be seen as constructions since they cannot be the same outside the socio-cultural context in which they have emerged. Indeed, they cannot even be imagined as being what they are (or seem to be) in some other context.[29] Seen from the perspective of social construction, disgust is a culture-specific affect that does precise work in entrenching taboos, limiting pollution, defending the sacred and generally contributing to a culture's cohesiveness. Inverted, pried loose from the socio-cultural matrix that has made it possible, disgust can become a free weapon in the "politics of oppositionality," a motif in shock theatre, satirical literature and graffiti. Neither the thing nor the motif could have any force in opposition if it had not already existed to support society's dominant values. This is what Ross Chambers has in mind when he refers to the "law of oppositionality," which defines the change that is "generated *within* a system of power even as it works against it."[30] Thus the model of social construction has two correlative dimensions: one, the hegemonic, dictating voice of society, including its mechanisms for control; and two, the oppositional voice of rejection. Each defines itself against the other. Still, there is a fundamental problem in the social-constructionist model: the dynamic that creates opposition, permitting both prohibited objects and acts to assume shock purposes, remains largely uncertain. The difficulty with injecting cognitive dissonance into the constructionist model lies in the inherent instability of the equation. The constructionist dimension will be clear enough, the deeply worn grooves of your habits quite evident, but the elements of opposition and deviance always unclear. How, if the model of social construction is accepted, do deviance and resistance, or even oppositionality, come into existence? Where does transgressive art come from? What account can we give of Menippean or punk?

There are many loops and feedbacks in the process of socialization. For example, it would not be a sufficient critique of the social-constructionist model of disgust merely to point out that disgust, having been formed in early childhood, can be unlearned or regulated by internal management. It could always be claimed that distinct pockets or layers of counter-indications were present during socialization and have emerged in adulthood as positive values. A systemic view of the family, easily accommodated within the social-constructionist model, would hold that the divisions, contradictions and "double-bind" rules, function together as transmitters of clear, yet unclear, directions. Gregory Bateson's hypothesis of "schismogenesis," often taken as a central concept of systemic views of the family, suggests the method by which double, or confused, messages are sent in their doubleness but received as clearly instructive, single directives. During toilet training, for instance, the parental admonishments not to touch, or even (sometimes) not to look and certainly not to play, may have conveyed the message of importance and value. Having received messages in childhood that, though indirectly, over-esteemed feces, the adult, although never becoming a coprophage, may desire to look, even to play (if only in the sense of wilfully retaining and expelling stool), or may take a subversive pleasure in scatological jokes and tales. A well-trained child easily becomes an adult who might enjoy reading Joyce's *Ulysses* or Pynchon's *Gravity's Rainbow*, viewing Pasolini and Greenaway films, or even sitting in a front row to watch a scatological performance artist such as Leigh Bowery or G.G. Allin defecate and then, as in the case of Allin, refecate. The adult may continue to imagine human feces to be disgusting but still have learned sufficiently to manage the affect so as to enjoy it in certain contexts. Socialization is neither a simple nor an altogether straightforward process. Its incorrigible loopiness leaves us all mindful of indirections.

The social-constructionist model, other than in the hands of its most unreflective exponents, can certainly contain the possibility of opposition. Oppositionality is built into the very process by which values are shaped and inculcated. David F. Greenberg writes,

> social definitions of appropriate and inappropriate behavior are clear and consistent, with positive sanctions for conformity and negative ones for nonconformity, [then] virtually everyone will conform irrespective of genetic inheritance and, to a considerable extent, irrespective of personal psychology.[31]

Social facts, however, may seldom, if ever, be so unmistakable. Social life exhibits a great deal more multi-variance than any social definition, urging conformity, can touch or even approximate. What about the peach that so filled me with loathing as a child? A social-constructionist explanation might seek the rules that operated in my family. What had I been told to avoid or reject? Had I been told to avoid slime? No doubt, I had been taught to love my parents unconditionally even though they were, just as I was, obvious producers of slime. Clearly, many messages had been sent telling me to love myself even though I was to despise my body's excreta. This systemic account points directly back to my toilet training and whatever other collateral formation I had received in avoiding mucoid human effluvia such as snot and spit. It has little to say about the invading spiders and nothing to say concerning my early sexual encounter with the three neighbourhood girls. Yet those two hypotheses do seem potent accounts. I cannot altogether reject the explanation of my early response to the peach based on an extrapolation from early socialization centred around toilet training and the avoidance of slime, but I suspect it. I doubt its fullness.

Furthermore, the social-constructionist model can postulate but never conclusively demonstrate that there are *no* "essential" natures, biological drives or genetic predispositions.[32] In its strong, or radical, form, the model holds that the individual, social life and society are all products of the interactive process of externalization, objectification and internalization, with no true exceptions possible. Yet there is evidence from neurological and genetic research to suggest a biological basis for sexual orientation. There is also the evidence from history and ethnography that, although homosexuality (say) has been constructed differently, similar patterns of behaviour can be identified. Thus Greenberg observes that "the gender-crosser who engages in homosexual relations appears as a distinctive role in many cultures." While the hijra's place in modern India "is not exactly the same as that of the berdache among North American Indians, I believe that each would recognize the other as someone very much like himself," rather like the way that members of two Christian denominations might recognize their "common religious heritage, despite their doctrinal or liturgical differences."[33]

Conceptual struggles that turn upon the axiomatic nature of argument (assumptions made, conclusions derived) can never wholly or satisfactorily account for fundamentally diverse experience. Brought to bear upon the problem of disgust, the social-constructionist model seems to explain it well enough as the product of early socialization or as an encoding of values enacted within a number of formative institutions such as the family and the school. Once disgust's metamorphicity comes into discussion, the model must respond by creating loops as complex as an epicycle in

Ptolemaic astronomy. Desire may be built into the lessons of revulsion just as love may begin as a seed secretly buried within hate. This does not mean that the model is wrong, or even that it does not possess immense explanatory power, but it does indicate that it is inadequate fully to explain phenomena as labile as the world's many loathsome and disgusting things.[34]

The first and second models are in apparent conflict. The second model posits disparate realms that can only be explained in the flexible terms of socio-cultural relativity; the first, a larger area called "western" that even seems to escape that already-vast space in order to hightail towards universality. Neither model can be demonstrated conclusively and neither can call upon decisive empirical evidence in its support. For each, disgust creates a boundary case, an edge phenomenon, that the model has trouble explaining. They answer different, correlative but incommensurable, questions. The moral-legal model explains the purposes of disgust and why society needs a well-developed, even educated, sense of the disgusting; the constructionist model explains origins and causation. Yet both models can argue that each best *explains* the facts and that otherwise, without their explanatory power, things would make less, or no, sense. The moral-legal model cannot convincingly show how disgust and other affects come into existence and wear the myriad shapes that they do. The constructionist model, assuming that disgust must be culture-specific, has difficulty in accounting for the unmistakable similarities that all experiences of disgust manifest.

The nose seems always to narrow and crinkle. Nausea is always present, cracking the sides with vast hefts, or else waits in the throat to happen. Psychologists, who infer from precise but limited empirical data, assume both the universality of the disgust face and the experiential development of the affect. "The intensity of disgust," Angyal writes,

> increases with the degree of contact: vicinity, contact with the skin, mouth, ingestion. This series strongly suggests that the nucleus of the disgust reaction, the main threat against which disgust is directed, is the oral incorporation of certain substances.[35]

The insistence upon a universal, or primary, disgust-object, though it could scarcely be elicited from experiments nor even found in ethnographic writings, leads directly to highly general proositions about disgust. Noting Angyal's conviction that feces elicit "the most intense disgust response and are close to being a universal disgust," Fallon and Rozin conclude that "disgust for the putrid feces of humans or mammalian carnivores is virtually universal."[36] The modifiers "putrid" and "virtually" tell a great deal about the experimental psychologist's desire to speak within a scope much wider than the narrow experimental data warrants. The position that psychologists take is, in its simplest terms, both constructionist and universalizing tendencies aside, hard to deny: disgust is a learned response that is primarily founded, if it is founded anywhere in experience, in the human response to feces. Except under very special circumstances, few people willingly eat feces.[37] However, Miller seems quite wrong when he asserts, without evidential support, that coprophagy is "peculiar now to the insane."[38] It exists more widely, though for peculiar reasons, among human beings (and commonly among animals) than most moralists would care to admit. Disgust's metamorphicity begins to appear only after it has been narrowly learned.

Third, psychoanalytic theories provide a model of disgust formation on the level of the individual's psyche. Although there are several versions of psychoanalysis, Freud's being only the originary and exemplary model, they all share the conviction that human affects, the evidently spontaneous responses to all in-the-world things, originate in early experience and work mostly beneath the surface of consciousness like (in Freud's image) an iceberg.[39] Affects emerge from infantile sexual experience, from early familial conflict, from the multitudinous (and conflicting) messages that arrive blindly from the surrounding culture, though largely refocussed by the family environment, or from memories that have been broken into bits and pieces. Whatever the specific origin of the affects, they work unconsciously. They flow beneath the surface, springing from some early experience and then channelled in memory, but burst out into the open, often like pus from a suppurating boil, as bizarre physical excrescences of the unconscious.

Freud argues that disgust is a bridle upon the feral demands of the sexual drive and that it is learned during early stages in the development of a super-ego, particularly during the process of toilet training. It belongs fundamentally to, in Richard Wollheim's words, the "building-up of mental forces opposed to sexuality."[40] Although disgust has physical manifestations, primarily nausea and vomiting, it is, along with shame and morality, a mental phenomenon. Wollheim's phrase "building-up" strikes me as precisely right since disgust may be no more an instinct than shame. Even if all human beings experience disgust (and this is far from demonstrable), they do so for strikingly dissimilar reasons. Disgust is a formation that develops slowly through stages of infantile experience. The disgust reaction is "an ego mechanism which helps to counter libidinal drives."[41] Disgust arises, Freud observes to Fliess, with regard to "abandoned" sexual zones (i.e., the oral and anal cavities).[42] Freud seems to have thought that certain acts, such as licking excrement and necrophilia, must be universally disgusting. However, a glance at Bourke's *Scatalogic Rites*, published during the very early stages of Freud's career, would indicate that this cannot be the case.[43] As the sexual acts of cunnilingus and fellatio show, it seems obvious that what is counted as disgusting shifts radically from culture to culture and within a single culture over time. To make an important point once again: this is what revolutions, on both the collective and individual levels, unexceptionally accomplish. Jerome Neu observes with matter-of-fact lucidity that perverse practices, widespread and recurring in human culture, reveal that the claim that there are universally disgusting acts "is not true, and Freud should know better."[44]

The build-up of mental forces that can regulate the polymorphous demands of the sexual drive occurs early in the child's life and through a series of stages during which he or she acquires a rudimentary capacity to reject pleasure, if it is "wrong," in response to parental admonishment and punishment. What once gave pleasure will in adulthood be bound to arouse his resistance or his disgust. We are familiar with a trivial but instructive model of this change of mind. The same child who once eagerly sucked the milk from his mother's breast may a few years later display a strong dislike to drinking milk, which his upbringing has difficulties in overcoming. This dislike increases to disgust if a skin forms on the milk or the drink containing it. We cannot exclude the possibility, perhaps, that the skin conjures up a memory of the mother's breast, once so ardently desired. Between the two situations, however, there lies the experience of weaning, with its traumatic effects.[45]

However, it is once again chiefly toilet training that formalizes the development of disgust. The child learns to reject as dirty a product in which previously he or she had taken pleasure. This establishes a precise habit-groove that pervades adult life. The human person experiences disgust in dealing with matter and acts that ought, if there were an essential "nature" (as Freud seems to assume), to provide pleasure. The child's early pleasure in its bodily excreta, soon controlled by an inculcated disgust, projects the adult experience of sexual repression. (And hence the peach that so filled me with loathing as a child would be simply an extension of toilet training, a displaced piece of excrement. It would also remain, like other repressed objects of desire, a latent area of delight that might unexpectedly revivify at the right provocation.) Repression rules the unconscious and, by an imaginable (if not wholly reasonable) leap, all of human society. Its official police are the different reaction-formations such as disgust and shame.[46] Reaction-formations function below the level of consciousness, out of the light as it were, keeping buried those subterranean rivers that might, but must not, burst abruptly to the surface. Other experiences than toilet training can contribute to the development of the child's sense of disgust and shame. Early, and barely understood, sexual encounters play a role in building up both the "moral sentiments" and individual phobias. (Did my loathing of peaches stem from my unconscious conflation of the spiders and the neighbourhood girl's genitalia?) What happens in the unconscious is vast, complex and hard to analyze. As an hypothesis, the unconscious may provide a less than satisfactory account of such affects as disgust and shame, but it does underscore the basic point that they are not learned in school and do not arise from formal lessons.

Disgust also introduces, as a problem for psychoanalysis and as a puzzle in human life, the fundamental paradox that a mental reservation can control a visceral urge or, to reverse the polarities, that a bodily mechanism can be activated by a psycho-conceptual understanding. This problem, although it is typical of psychoanalysis, runs through virtually all theoretical discussions of disgust. Writing about Freud's analysis of hysteria, Ned Lukacher notes that there is "an epistemological break between the psychical and the physiological, a break that Freud's theory, which insists upon the continuity between these two orders of experience, refuses to acknowledge."[47] The dualism built into Freud's analysis of disgust (a distinctive instance of the unyielding mind/body problem) identifies a persistent difficulty in developing theoretical models for disgust. This difficulty is illustrated by the dual work, both physical and moral, that *disgust* has performed in the English language since the eighteenth century and Dr. Johnson's dictionary. How do you bring together the two sides of a psycho-visceral affect in order to explain its origins and functions? Freud never resolves this problem, but he does make it unmistakable.

The analysis of disgust as a reaction-formation constitutes the primary version of the great Freudian monomyth that human persons achieve civilization, both individually and collectively, by learning to reject early pleasures. Freud's late work *Civilization and Its Discontents* (1930) stands as the elegant but gloomy coda to this monomyth. Civilization behaves towards sexuality more or less as a colonial government does towards a people it has subjected: "Fear of a revolt by the suppressed elements drives [the colonial power] to stricter precautionary measures."[48]

For all psychoanalytic theories, disgust is a regulating or policing affect, a "moral sentiment" as Freud said, but one that helps to establish, as well as to regulate, whatever moral-legal order exists. Translated into the Lacanian terms which Kristeva employs, disgust becomes an element in the symbolic order, a modulation of the Father's voice (as it were), that establishes the boundaries that define the abject within which, and according to which, the Real can be imagined. (The peach incarnated for me my boundaries, the protective shell that my Ego had already begun to create, as an abrupt, unexpected but already wholly historicized, image of the Real as I understood it.) It is no less a regulating affect. Slavoj Žižek, writing specifically about sadism, gives the Lacanian position a lapidary formulation: dark desires, for pain or for disgusting behaviour, are at work "... in the obscene, superego underside that necessarily redoubles and accompanies, as its shadow, the 'public' Law."[49] Imagination forms the Real, giving it a syntax, a body even, that it does not in itself possess. When the Real speaks to the subject, or "interpellates" it, it does so in the language of the Imaginary, in its choreographed associations of images and image sequences. However, the Imaginary follows instructions that it receives from the Symbolic Order, the psyche's dimension of signification and conceptual insistence, which may have been entered originally from any number of angles. Lacanian psychoanalysis, like its Freudian prototype, postulates a level of cultural contact, a trans-subjective area of contact and exchange. In this area, the inner/outer space of the trans-subject, disgust shapes experience, but also regulates it. Despite its internal diversity, the psychoanalytic model makes clear that human persons pay a large price, in neuroses and discontent, for having learned to reject themselves. Walking upright, or sitting to defecate, exacts a cost that can never be fully paid.[50]

Fourth, it has struck some thinkers that the common factor in all instances of disgust, both physical and moral, is the process of dissolution itself, the slimewards progression of organic matter. This might seem like another essentialist project, but it actually argues only for a necessary condition: *if* you are going to experience disgust, you must first have perceived something (on some order of reality) that disturbs you, that reminds you of the fragility of your existence, that is anomalous and that corresponds to slime. Imagine that you have neglected a plate of food. Perhaps you were talking, or left the table to make love, or went out to see a film. The food begins to turn liquid. It metamorphoses into muck. At what point do you begin to lose your appetite? Suppose the food is Italian sausages. Merely in allowing the sausages to cool, you also allow them to slip from one category to another. They sink from a category of desire (succulent, spicy-smelling, the hot fat glistening brightly in the candlelight) to one of disgust (fat-congealed, turd-like, a heap of brown worms slithering into muck). A dog or a hungry person with no Apollonian categories to inhibit appetite would still find the sausages good to eat. Disgust arises when something is seen to have slipped into a disapprobative category: to have fallen within the boundaries of the prohibited, the taboo, the loathed. Behind those boundaries, everything shows decay, rot, sliminess; things lack the sturdiness, the categorical definitiveness of the approbative. Slime suggests something that is a sickening colour, perhaps has a stench and feels repugnant to touch, but the theoretical issue is more abstract: what now is slime was once something else that has degenerated. Slime is disgusting because it is uncertain, a phase in the dissolution of existence. And it may remind you, as you peer beyond those boundaries, of gnawingly personal associations with slime, such as snot, shit and death.

This fourth model of disgust derives from Jean-Paul Sartre's analysis of viscosity in *Being and Nothingness*, although its most current version is that which Mary Douglas has advanced, particularly in *Purity and Danger*.[51] Sliminess, Sartre argues, invokes "a host of human and moral" characteristics: "A handshake, a smile, a thought, a feeling can be slimy."[52] (The doubleness of the term, at once physical and moral, that marks all discussions of disgust, is present here as well.) The slimy "reveals itself as essentially anomalous because its fluidity exists in slow motion; there is a sticky thickness in its liquidity; it represents in itself a dawning triumph of the solid over the liquid ... Slime is the agony of water."[53] The sensation of a solid melting or of a liquid solidifying, both behaving aberrantly, can make a rather powerful mental impression. Roquentin seems to have precisely this kind of experience when he notices the pebble that is filthy on one side but clean on the other. It is a transitional border thing: a double object prompting a double response. His whole experience of life in Bouville is of this kind. Things slip from their accepted categories or else solidify into new ones or into none at all (like the famous root of the chestnut tree that causes Roquentin to feel an access of nausea). The *patronne* of the café Rendez-vous des Cheminots with whom he has casual intercourse has a very similar effect upon him. "She disgusts me slightly," he writes in his journal. She is too white, she smells like a baby, she performs sexual acts in a perfunctory manner. As he toys "absent-mindedly with her sex under the bedclothes," Roquentin imagines

> a little garden with low, wide-spreading trees from which huge hairy leaves were hanging. Ants were running about every-where, centipedes and moths. There were some even more horrible animals: their bodies were made of slices of toast such as you put under roast pigeons; they were walking sideways with crab-like legs. The broad leaves were black with animals. Behind the cacti and the Barbary fig trees, the Velleda of the municipal park was pointing to her sex. "This park smells of vomit," I shouted.[54]

The nausea that haunts Roquentin arises from his experience of the world as slimy, mucoid, filled with both double- and semi-objects. He perceives a "nightmarish and universal proliferation."[55] The proliferation of insect life, even more than the phantasmagoric creatures, suggests the absence of human order. In this respect, Roquentin's vision recalls the famous opening scene of Luis Buñuel's 1930 film *L'Age d'Or*, in which numerous scorpions crawl, fight and copulate, showing the force of libido within a basically antisocial instinct (precisely the point about human beings that the film proceeds to demonstrate).[56] The *patronne*, with whom Roquentin routinely copulates, is only one among many in a world full of such objects. Although Sartre's thinking on the subject of slime (of aberrant and amor-phous states of being) seems to derive from the tradition of phenomenological philosophy, it also owes a great deal to the French literary tradition, the Sadean mode of seeking deviance, dissolution and transgression. Thus Baudelaire captures the sensation of a solid deliquescing when he writes in "Les Métamorphoses du vampire" that the vampiric woman he imagines is, after making love, no more than "une outre aux flancs gluants, toute pleine de pus!" (a slimy wineskin filled with pus). Pus (one of Kekes' examples) seems like an extremely powerful instance of slime, and one privileged in both horror and decadent literature, since it is the body itself, transformed by infection, flowing in thick ooze.[57]

Slime and ooze show the shakiness and drift of things. Imagine a loved one's skull dissolving in your hands, or that person's blood growing thick around your fingers. (Here you enter the province of horror, a narrative domain that is as visual as it is conceptual, across the borders of which exist experiences too appalling to contemplate, too compelling to ignore.) A vast archive of images, showing decay, rot, dissolution and putrefaction everywhere, can flash before the mind's eye when the hand touches, or the eyes see, ooze and muck. In Sartre's "mucoid object-world," slimy things recall and exemplify each other.[58] In the very apprehension of the slimy there is, Sartre observes, "a gluey substance, compromising and without equilibrium, like the haunting memory of a metamorphosis."[59] Disgust arises in the mind (but often in the throat as well) when the slippage of things, apparently "without equilibrium," becomes evident. The capacity to perceive slippage and slime may be a function of the individual's socialization or toilet training. It is reasonable to suppose that the categories that can be seen dissolving will have been constructed in the first instance by the relevant formative institutions in the individual's culture. Sartre's argument does not preclude this provenance nor indeed the entire social-constructionist position. It goes far beyond it, easily absorbing it along the way, and holds that disgust arises when slime, whether a deliquescence or a thickening of things, enters into experience. Disgust is located in the imagination, an affect energized by the perception of slime as its necessary condition, whatever first made that slime recognizable. Yet this perception, acting within the imagination, is an objective recognition of in-the-world qualities "which exercise their effects on us."[60]

Mary Douglas' enlargement of Sartre's argument brings her knowledge of ethnography, her own fieldwork and that of other anthropologists, into the analysis of slime. Dirt, she argues, like everything else in human culture, expresses a hidden symbolic system. Dirt is matter that is out of place. It is "never a unique, isolated event. Where there is dirt there is system. Dirt is the by-product of a systematic ordering and classification of matter."[61] Pollution occurs when matter that has been classified in the functioning system as dirt slides over into the categories of the clean, or at least the non-dirt. Filth contaminates.[62] Douglas can thus argue that certain experiences evoke disgust because they manifest category slippage and breakdown. Imagine that you are travelling in a crowded minivan across the mountains between Mexico City and Acapulco. As the minivan winds down a mountain, a large woman sitting next to you begins to vomit. This might be upsetting, but not in your case particularly disgusting since you know that all human beings will vomit on occasion and that motion sickness is an understandable cause of vomiting. Embarrassed by her very public sickness, the woman attempts to minimize her condition by vomiting into her hands. You may note this act and feel a great deal of empathy for her since you yourself, similarly caught, would probably do much the same. However, having thrown up into her hands, the woman realizes that she has no place to put the vomit. Perhaps she looks around hastily, peering at the floor or at the window which is one or two people away from her, but there is no help for her: she is sitting between you and another person, her cupped hands filled with her vomit, and there is no available place for its disposal. Then she puts her head down into her hands and begins to eat her vomit. Since you are sitting immediately next to her, you can easily tell that her eating combines lapping and sucking actions. For the first time, you begin to experience nausea yourself. It was not the understandable act of vomiting that makes you sick, but the totally unacceptable way of disposing of the vomit. The woman's vomit is more fully out of place at this moment than it had been in the initial vomiting.[63]

The abominations cited in Leviticus involve animals that do not belong clearly to one category or another: they are conceptually "sticky." "The underlying principle of cleanness in animals," Douglas writes, "is that they shall conform fully to their class." If they fail to conform fully, then they are imperfect members of their class and may be seen to "confound the general scheme of the world."[64] This proposition can be generalized to cover all human experience: what class of actions does vomit belong to (what is its *place*) and how should it be disposed? Once out of place, vomit also confounds the "general scheme" of things. Sartre's analysis of sliminess as a philosophical problem provides, in the hands of an anthropologist, a very powerful account for the human experience of disgust, contamination and pollution. It applies to everyone (a proposition with which Sartre would surely have agreed), there being no "special distinction between primitives and moderns" on this score, and everyone will know some things that are anomalous, not belonging clearly to known categories, tending slimewards.[65]

Freud's analysis of disgust as a reaction-formation that helps control the possibilities for sexual perversion, largely (if not wholly) connected with the rejection of feces during toilet training, falls easily within an analysis of anomalous states and category slippage. The learned behaviour that transforms excrement into filth (keeping it from being a plaything) also makes the anus, as an "abandoned" and hence prohibited zone, attractive. In the grips of physical desire even excrement can become, for some people anyway, an aphrodisiac. Despite the dictatorial category of filth, humans seem to find the anus fascinating. (Edmund Spenser, staid and serious in reputation at least, found the human anus remarkable.)[66] The second and third models may be seen as constricted versions of the more powerful Sartre-Douglas model with its psycho-cultural sweep. We learn how to identify deliquescence, and to invest it with symbolic weight and significance, which leads to the creation of our domineering reaction-formations. Even the first model with its insistence on disgust as a moral category, a basis for the disapprobation that (it is claimed) makes civilization possible, could operate within a conceptual framework that held disgust to result from the perception of slippage in the world or of dirt falling outside its culturally assigned place.

Still, there are problems, unexplained areas, that the fourth model, for all its inclusive strength, fails to settle. What is the etiology of disgust? How does it arise? How is it shaped (if not actually constructed) by society and family? Why, since the perception of slimy semi-objects is indescribably varied, do the observable aspects of the disgust reaction often seem to be so similar, even between different cultures? What happens in the mind when one observes an anomalous object or someone performing acts outside their normal place? What corresponds to the perception of slime? Sartre puts an emphasis on the inwardness of the experience. It is impossible, he argues, "to derive the value of the psychic symbolism 'slimy' from the brute quality of the *this* and equally impossible to project the meaning of the *this* in terms of a knowledge of psychic attitudes."[67] The things themselves, both objects and acts, are undeniably material, but the psychic response ("our repulsion, our hates, our sympathies, our attractions") are otherwise: active, vigorously associative, inclusive. The built-in tendency towards essentialism or towards a universally applicable definition of disgust is as strong as it is obvious. Do all human imaginations actually work like this? Can you make such general assumptions about a human faculty? The Sartrean model shows weaknesses similar to the other models. It can answer a few important questions about disgust, but not all. There are a number of questions it answers well, but the others are locked out, condemned to lurk shadowily on the outskirts of analysis.

It may be that there will always be more questions than can be answered. However, a conceptual model has rather different obligations than an individual person. You may not feel like inquiring after the etiology of disgust, nor how it is to be imagined, nor yet what its moral purposes may be. A conceptual model that claims to be able to give an account of disgust should be able to deal with more questions, even some that clearly go against its grain. In part, this is why I have insisted all along that no single conceptual model fully explains disgust. An array of models can at least make plain the range of questions that could be asked. Consider Shakespeare's Leontes once more. When Leontes imagines a spider in the bottom of his cup, "steeped" in wine, and feels disgust cracking his gorge, the reader is asked to imagine an intricate network of associations, both fantastic and factual, narrative and iconic, suddenly actualized within his mind. Like Herakles, Leontes follows a spoor, but it is within his own mind, a self-told fiction. His jealousy, his narrative fantasies about Hermione's infidelity, his bubbling misogyny, his anguish over the apparent failure of his childhood bonding with his best friend constitute the traces. They all seethe together in his mind, and all are symbolized by the image of the drowned spider that is, but might not have been, seen. Massively overdetermined, the image of a spider haunts the memory, the mind's depths and recesses, as powerfully as it dominates the bottom of Leontes' cup. This is the way that the implications of a problematic experience reshape themselves as analytic questions. My argument in this book is that every example of disgust, fully to be understood, should be treated like Leontes' imaginary spider at the bottom of his imaginary cup. Look for its conceptual implications, its bright nimbus of associations, like a silk scarf waiting to be pulled.

In Douglas' discussion, Sartre's emphasis upon the interiority of the experience is overlooked for a exterior, more straightforward analysis. "Sticky" describes a logical state of categories, much as terms such as "inclusive" and "exclusive" or "clear" and "fuzzy" do. It is located outside personal experience on the level of cultural system. While there is a steady creep in the constructionist and Freudian models from the personal experience of disgust to generalizations concerning the exterior relations between subject and object, neither Sartre's nor the moral-legal models can be said to "creep" since they begin with generalizations and proceed, deductively, to cases. What is needed is an explanation for the mental landscapes of disgust. How do you imagine disgust? How will you account for its radical shape-shifting? How will you be able to use your personal experience of disgust productively? Could you, as Bataille suggests, actually confront yourself through your experience of disgust?

Fifth, the last query leads directly to a consideration of the fifth model. The examination of theoretical models for disgust turns back in a full circle. The fifth model is also a moral, though not a legal, model of aberrant, transgressive and conventionally slimy behaviour. The position that moralists, such as Kekes and Miller, argue claims that there is a deep, significant purpose for human disgust. It regulates behaviour, limits excess and makes human social life bearable. The fifth model argues that such a regulated and delimited society is scarcely worth living within. It stunts human potential, racking the person into a deformed caricature of human life, and imposes restrictive boundaries on human experience. In this view, you will have been trained, formed and limited by many social agencies, all of them working to bind your joys and desires if not exactly with thorns at least with conventions, rules and law. You will have been given a social consciousness, a personal censor, a superego, a deeply encoded fear of transgression or at least habits so rigidly conditioned that they will seem "natural" (which is to say, unbreakable). You will not have been told how to enjoy yourself fully or how to realize your latent desires. Indeed, you will have grown up within an "arborescent" system, a logical tree-like social structure dominated by a conceptual taproot (of some ideological kind), that will have stratified and regulated all your libidinous potential.[68]

The recognition that human life, having to pay the cost of civilization, is burdened by a dense (almost impossibly complex) system of repression has led many thinkers to seek ways of escape. Once you understand that you have been born into a massively repressive system, striated and impacted, embracing you so closely that it seems nearly like a second skin, what should you do? Of course, like most human beings you may never reach this understanding. The repressive system will fit so snugly that you may mistake it for nature itself, a second nature even more than a second skin, and hence entirely miss all the many ways it constricts you. Having understood the force of social repression, you may also decide that your best move will be to live with it, accepting repression, as both moralists and Freudian analysts urge, as simply the price you must pay for social stability and protection. Civilization, they will insistently tell you, rises upon, and continues to depend upon, repression. Outrageous behaviour will be both immoral and anti-social; indeed, it will work to destroy the society that contains it. If you both understand and reject the repressive mechanisms that surround you, then you will confront the usual range of options. You may learn better to accept the repressive mechanisms your community supports. You may learn to live in the interstices of society, following hidden practices or joining a secret community. You might even join a revolutionary movement dedicated to changing society and, you might hope, loosening the repressive system. What the moralists of the fifth model tell you is more personal and, it may turn out, far more dangerous. They urge you to know your repressions, the aspects of the total social system that you have incorporated from the earliest moments of your existence, and then to act deliberately against them. Cross the boundaries that they establish. That is, the moralists will say that you should explore the possibilities of transgression as a step towards self-knowledge and freedom. The moralists of the first model, such as William Ian Miller and John Kekes, will urge you to accept social repressiveness and not to transgress in the name of civilization; those of the fifth will exhort you to transgress actively in the name of happiness.

As I argued in Chapter 1, an important purpose of all shock art is to puncture conformity's protective balloon. Transgression is a strong, upsetting way of making someone else, hidden within the protective covering of social conformity, face both the absurdity of any particular social habit and the sad recognition of how much has been missed. Behind all performance art, all theatrical shock, whether in a small circus or a large rock concert, there lies the sad story of wasted life. How much intelligence, affective experience and potential creativity is lost through the regulations, the brutal smothering, of social conformity? Now what happens when you turn transgression against yourself, crossing the established boundaries of your own person? It is not only a question of ingestion, swallowing objects (drugs, say, or human secretions) that have been prohibited, but also of acts, of performing in forbidden ways. You can see immediately that this kind of personal transgression could be given two quite opposite interpretations. A moralist, such as Kekes, might find it a sign of corruption, of wasting a particular kind of potential for cooperative action within a community, or of a rather pathetic process of self-ruination. A moralist of the fifth model might see only the exercise of freedom in those personally transgressive acts, a breaking loose from an arbitrary, but always pernicious, system of repression. Such a moralist might also see an admirable experiment in self-exploration. Know yourself, the Socratic adage instructs; it can be expanded to include know your boundaries, know how to cross them and know what you may become.

The fifth model has a long philosophic and literary tradition, always functioning as a counter-voice to society's dominant versions of itself. It has run along beneath the surface of western civilization, a minority position but an agent of change, usually mocking, occasionally strident and always revolutionary. It holds up the ideal of an (literally) upset society, one that has been inverted, turned upside down and shaken, so that its repressed content can emerge. It is difficult to pin down the scope of this tradition.[69] Of course, you would want to include the Marquis de Sade, but for all his vivid and unforgettable images of transgressive behaviour, he is only a central figure in a way of thinking about human society that goes far back into classical times. The subtitle of Roger Shattuck's investigation of "forbidden knowledge" accurately identifies this tradition, even if it does not exhaust it: *From Prometheus to Pornography*.[70] De Sade is certainly a part of this tradition (and Shattuck gives "The Divine Marquis" extensive discussion), but it must also include Menippus, whom Shattuck ignores, Rabelais (also ignored) and the countlessly varied displays of unofficial popular culture. It should be clear that this minority position in western civilization takes two forms: actual in-the-world transgressions, in which cultural boundaries are physically crossed; and mimetic transgressions, in which representations, in works of art, reach beyond repressive boundaries in order to mock, hurt or even destroy those who smugly inhabit the protected territories. This rather sweeping distinction follows Ralph A. Lewin's between coprology and scatology, which I discussed in Chapter 1. Eating excrement or indulging in golden showers, for example, are both highly transgressive acts, but it makes a huge difference whether these are actually performed or merely represented. In either case, such acts will be disgusting to many people, but they should not be confused.

One important aspect of the tradition of advocating transgression or of acting out prohibited or taboo cultural materials lies in the possibility of using disgust motifs as engines of mockery. In a broad usage of the term, this is scatology, disgusting, painful to watch, even hurtful, but still make-believe. You can see many in-the-world objects, such as putrescence and human excreta, that are separated off from normal social interactions by clearly defined boundaries. In effect, they are taboo. You can also see that their representations are likely to be disturbing, even disgusting, and will have powerful uses in shock and satire. This correspondence lies at the heart of Menippean discourse. Menippean satire is always bodily specific, precisely attentive to human effluvia and disease. It is also highly intelligent ("witty," in an old sense), a conscious exploitation of analogy and metaphor. When the images of disease and excrement appear in Menippean discourse, you can feel confident that they represent a deliberate, conscious choice. In his study of Menippean discourse, Garry Sherbert stresses its intellectual content. "Menippean satire," he writes, "attacks moral or aesthetic constraints by praising and, indeed, practising the improper and exuberant forms of wit that the learned deem as false."[71] Thus Menippean discourse can be said to engage in a radical demystification from which nothing at all is exempt; it breaks up, in Northrop Frye's words, "the lumber of stereotypes, fossilized beliefs, superstitious terrors, crank theories, pedantic dogmatisms, oppressive fashions" and everything else that exercises social repression.[72] Although always intellectual, as Sherbert argues, it is also physical, bodily, grotesque and focussed upon (what would be taken as) human filth.

In the first chapter, I briefly discussed Shakespeare's *Troilus and Cressida* in order to emphasize the bodily elements in Menippean discourse. Consider it once more. Known for his bodily ugliness in Homer, Shakespeare's Thersites, still lacking in "handsomeness," speaks an ugly discourse that ferrets out, highlights and exaggerates the ugliness in others. When he first appears, exchanging verbal abuse with Ajax, Thersites draws attention to the king's body, that physical correlation to spiritual authority so much discussed in Renaissance political theory under the rubric of the "King's two bodies":

> Agamemnon—how if he had boils, full, all over, generally?
> ...
> And those boils did run—say so—did not the general run then?
> ...
> Were not that a botchy core?
> ...
> Then would come some matter from him ... (II.I.2–9)

Imagining Agamemnon's body covered with pustulant boils, the pus oozing and leaking "matter," rather takes the mind away from the heroic conception of the noble body. Thersites' first lines anticipate his discourse as a whole: biting, harsh, counter-factual, always turned towards the rotting, stinking, oozing human body. Menippean discourse, wherever it is found, is always like this: rich in disgusting imagery and difficult ideas, physical and intellectual at once, mocking and unceremonious. It is powerfully scatological, but it may often carry the force of actual, psycho-visceral disgust.

A literary and philosophical tradition lies behind the fifth model, but it is not altogether clear. It seems less a written history than a written-about history. Roger Shattuck's study examines the history of transgressive art in so far as it has represented characters seeking, as the title indicates, forbidden knowledge. His interest is much more in Faust than in Menippus. Peter Sloterdijk's history of Kynicism (which he opposes to Cynicism, the conscious acceptance of the postulates of a repressive society even while fully understanding the critique which would expose them) includes Menippus, at least in the person of his follower Lucian, but excludes most of the historical material that interests Shattuck, although he does include Mephistopheles within the "Cabinet of Cynics." Greil Marcus' *Lipstick Traces* examines punk in the larger context of European anarchism and shock art, but has no interest in the deeper historical rhizomes of the tradition.[73] M.M. Bakhtin provides something like a history of the Euro-American counter-voice, but only over the course of several different studies. However, it is to Bakhtin that you must go for anything like an overview. Bakhtin argues that Menippean discourse evolved from the polyglot marketplaces of classical cities, the exotic voices of distant cultures making themselves at home in mercantile centres, and became in time the complex travesty (parodic, mocking and always irreverent) of medieval comedy. The novel, Bakhtin thinks, evolved from the many-voicedness of Menippean discourse and carnival. The multiple voices, the distinct dialects and sociolects in Menippean led Bakhtin to locate Menippean discourse precursively in the early history of the novel.[74] Incorporating different voices makes both Menippean and carnival creative forces for travesty, rich in mockery and insult, typically characterized by scatological and other disgust motifs drawn from, in Bakhtin's words, the "lower bodily strata."[75] Bakhtin's concept of carnival, the mocking, travesty-performing exuberance in the play of masks and role-inversions, suggests a point where the two dimensions of the fifth model actually conjoin. A carnival is both literary, a problem in representation, and an actual social event involving physical actions.

It should be clear that the fifth model, unlike the moral-legal model to which it corresponds, covers both social and aesthetic experience, both in-the-world things and their representations, both coprology and scatology. To be sure, the moral-legal model can point to a large body of literature and art, moral fables, say, or the nineteenth-century bourgeois novel, which supports the position that a regulated, even policed, society is necessary to stave off the horrors of human appetence. What the fifth model claims is rather more powerful: art can be exploratory, like an intelligent life itself, and the representation of transgression can be as instructive as, though distinct from, the actual act. A transgression across prohibited boundaries can occur in both your own lifeworld and in the art you create or consume. Although the fifth model may seem most powerful in urging exploratory forays across actual boundaries, it also allows for the force of art both to shock and to transform. Seeking out disgust, striving for shocking new experiences that will both evoke and deny deeply encoded disgust reactions, is as much an act of conscious self-transformation as learning how to over-come your gag reflex or your long-habituated disgust reaction in the pres-ence of putrescence. It is a process that occurs both on the level of disgusting things and on that of disgusting representations. If, for example, a person invokes disgust motifs as revolutionary weapons (to dismiss, to hurt, symbolically to kill others: parents, rulers, cultural elites), then a very complex process, carefully stage-managed for public effect, of imagining the world will be taking place. The individual may wish to register his or her loathing for certain others or else to display, perhaps as a challenge or else as an insult, his or her own spoiled identity, the culturally marked stigma, that he or she bears. Or, even more complexly, the transgressive individual may wish, as Bataille urges, to see the world in a different light, as a foun-dation for new, Dionysian experience and deliberately set out to embrace disgust in order to relearn the world, to *re-cognize* it freshly.

Considered as a program to free the individual or to revitalize society, the fifth model argues against constraints generally, but in particular against the "rules" that delimit behaviour, restrict action and prescribe narrow possibilities for pleasure. For this reason, the Marquis de Sade occupies a central position in the tradition of transgression. He imagines scenes in which men, and sometimes women, attempt to cross all boundaries.

Reflecting on de Sade's writing as a potential instrument for the liberation of women, Angela Carter writes, "if we could restore the context of the world to the embraces of these shadows, then, perhaps we could utilize their activities to obtain a fresh perception of the world and, in some sense, transform it."[76] Every taboo is broken in de Sade with deliberate intelligence and careful purpose. Nothing occurs that is merely accidental. It is easy for a reader to overlook the intelligence of de Sade's characters. For example, the agents of transgression in *The 120 Days of Sodom*, the "Libertines," are entirely conscious of their actions. What they seek out, what they actually do, is always conscious, purposeful and subject to reflection. All of de Sade's libertines abuse their victims (or their acolytes) not because they have been themselves sexually abused, which would be a contemporary understanding, but because they want to do what they do and have considered their actions thoughtfully. They have a will to enjoy, but it is far from instinctive and it is always intellectualized. Sexual abuse is, in Sadean terms, an acquired taste of the intelligentsia. Žižek observes that the Sadean will to enjoy is thoroughly pure, "ethical in the strictest Kantian sense." And it is, he adds, the "exemplary case of a pure, nonpathological desire."[77] When you elect to abuse another person, a Sadean dictum might run, do so only for the most conscious ends and act neither lightly nor instinctively, but with an acute intelligence.

Bataille suggests an important element for any theory of disgust. He thinks differently about human existence, or at least he thinks provocatively from within the minority position that I have been discussing, but always with the recognition that man has an "incessant vision of himself."[78] For Bataille, the problem is how to free up, how to open towards new possibilities and along new trajectories, the range of this unending visioning and re-visioning. For this reason, de Sade is central to Bataille's thinking, as the mighty opposite standing against both repression and conformity.[79] Writing about Bataille's pornography, *The Story of the Eye*, Carter observes that he puts "pornography squarely in the service of blasphemy. Transgression, outrage, sacrilege, liberation of the senses through erotic frenzy, and the symbolic murder of God."[80] Whatever else, Bataille's writing constitutes an adventure, as daring as it is clamorous, against all Apollonian constraints. And indeed, the world may be seen as encrusted with categories, stiff with its Apollonian carapace, such that both freedom and self-knowledge are made possible through, and only through, transgression. This is the scope of Bataille's "antiproject," the program to "undo man" and, as well, all utopian, humanistic and rationalistic systems.[81] In his essay "The Big Toe," to take a simple but brilliantly clear example, Bataille argues that the head displaces the lower body in western thinking. It is a displacement that must be registered as a loss. Men have a "secret horror" of their feet, but this horror stands for the pervasive horror of all lower bodily functions, both excretory and reproductive. (And yet, Bataille argues, parts of the upper body, such as a "gaping mouth," are objectively far uglier, more "monstrous.") The big toe, intricate, physically important and ignored, provides Bataille with a synecdoche for lower body ellipsis in western discourse.[82] From the perspective of a craftily Apollonian world (tightly made, narrowly edged), the Dionysian realm appears only as transgression, a despised assault upon the rules of a well-ordered state, but it also opens the pathways to self-discovery.

Disgust has the role not merely of establishing boundaries and of marking out tabooed areas of experiences but of opening up a vast number of pathways for personal exploration. The de Sadean method of choosing an act that is known to be prohibited and then performing it might strike most people, even those who would like to expand their personal horizons, as rather too confrontational. The fifth model is long on theoretical objectives, but short on procedures and methods. Of course, you might survey the prohibitions of your society and then, in the de Sadean way, choose one that seems particularly taboo and set out to break it, either in private or else among a few like-minded comrades. In the tradition of shock theatre, you might even choose to perform it, or more likely its mimetic representation, square in the teeth of those whom it will most offend. A more exact, and more end-pointed, method would be found in the writings of Deleuze and Guattari. Take stock of your desires, not the array of taboos that enclose you, and then set out to satisfy them. In a striated society, compacted with constraints, regulations and prohibitions (usually with penalties attached), finding a means to your desire may not be easy. Once you have identified your desire(s), you can construct a specific means for reaching that destination across all the strata of society. That means will be like a machine, or an assemblage of conceptual and imagistic tools, which you may employ to bear you to where you desire to go. Literature and other representations may help you in that goal, but it will not be the same as experiencing your in-the-world desire.[83] If the fifth model has its most eloquent voice in Bataille, its clearest conception of method lies in Deleuze and Guattari.[84]

There are other possible theories of disgust. It might be that disgust is only a mental phenomenon, a corrupting way of seeing things that only the human mind, in its terrible sickness, inflicts upon an innocent reality. Once cured, in a more evolved society, say, the world would become "natural," as it is for small children and animals, and all things would seem attractive in themselves. Disgust might also be understood as everything that is not divine or, alternatively, as whatever crosses, polluting and spreading filth, the boundaries that mark out the precincts of the divine. However, the five models that I have discussed seem to be most central to the discussion. Indeed, the additional theories of disgust could all be subsumed into one or more of the five. No single model fully explains the power, range and meta-morphicity of disgust, but each casts a great deal of light on the problem. It is not altogether clear how five such models, each directing a searchlight upon the problem's darkness, can be employed together. I have left open the possibility of a serial array which would allow each model to be used in turn until something like a full account was available. The effect of using such a serial array would be additive: each lesson following upon the previous one, until something like a full, or even clear, picture emerges. It would also be possible to use one or more of the models together in a compound explanatory strategy. You would then ask a number of different, apparently unrelated questions, but always the ones that each model makes possible: What are the social uses of disgust? Where does it come from and what has made it possible? How does it shape our lives? How is it imagined? What, if any, untraditional activities does it make possible? They might all be asked in an integrated fashion, each touching upon an area for exploration that the others neglect. In that case, you would have a synchronic, not a serial, array. Its purposes would remain much the same. It would constitute an effort to raise most, if not all, of the question that the phenomenon prompts and to do so in a genuinely open, non-dogmatic way.[85]

My chief concern in this chapter has been to highlight the complexity of the topic. Looking at five distinct explanatory models should have made this complexity plain. Each model seems to bring to light different aspects of disgust phenomena and each ignores important aspects that another model will accentuate. The fifth, or transgressive, model shows how encounters with the disgusting can become paths to self-knowledge, and in so doing it also demonstrates how constrained and rule-bound normal human life unhappily is; but it completely fails to take into account the abuse of, and pain to, other human beings that a self-centered boundary crossing may cause. Despite Žižek's optimistic assertion that the de Sadean will to enjoy is ethically "pure," it rather seems to be anti-Kantian in that it urges you to act as if everyone else were a means, a object in your field of pleasure and self-discovery. On the other hand, the moral-legal model fails to allow for self-discovery and seems promiscuously to accept restrictions and social constraints of all kinds. It accepts and hardens a deeply conservative view of human society. Worse yet, it cannot deal competently with the difference between things and their representations. (The fifth model, it might seem, deals better with representations and their Menippean uses than it does with lifeworld situations.) The array of five models focusses the inadequacy of normal explanatory accounts. So much is going on that no single model ever works in a fully satisfactory way.

In the first chapter I argued that disgust involves a certain expression that may be authentic but can be easily imitated. Whatever the definition of disgust, and no matter what nexus of social connections it fits within, facework will constitute the primary evidence. I also claimed that disgust involves the transgression of boundaries, either real or assumed. Now it is possible to see that specific accounts of disgust turn upon these two propositions. Disgust is always, no matter what other claims are made, a question of boundaries, either those that you cross or those boundaries that you experience as having been crossed. Touching a deliquescent object, whether a rotting animal corpse or only a decaying cucumber, can thrill you with disgust, but being rubbed or penetrated by such an object, or perhaps having its putrescent juices squeezed upon you, would be even worse. All the models of disgust that I have examined in this chapter acknowledge the importance of human facework, although the moral-legal model has difficulty in making room for make-believe. Facework is very much a part of this account.

In closing this chapter, I want to return to the experience of the peach and the unbearable disgust I experienced at its sight and continued to experience whenever I saw a peach for at least thirteen years. I think now that at the age of four I was quite able to understand many things and to imagine things that were not. When my mother held out the two quarters of sliced peach and I screamed, I must have imagined something, something else that the peach represented or otherwise indicated. I was caught in the grips of an authentic disgust experience in which something unexpected, often very negligible and inconsequential, breaks open with startling force to disclose something else that is no longer present. Each disgusting in-the-world thing as well as each disgusting motif in literature, film or art can be read as a path into a fictional world. In most cases, such motifs will create a network of paths leading to the same fictional world, or to different regions within it. However, even if the motif is singular, a kind of world, small but provocative, will open up to the interpretive imagination.[86] When I saw the peach and screamed, what might I have been imagining?

I have no doubt that the peach startled and shocked me because it disclosed something about reality that I was either unprepared to grasp or unable to confront (again?). Moments of true disgust when the throat gags and fills with chyme, acute spasms of revulsion passing through the mind and consciousness seeming to wither, tell us secrets about reality. Such moments reveal the unexpected depths of existence. This is the case, I think, no matter which explanatory model you bring to bear. The imagination snaps into play and you begin to see, or even inhabit, a tiny fictional world in which loathsome things occur. Here a strong paradox about disgust becomes evident. The experience of disgust strikes you as powerful, always a startlingly unexpected disclosure of reality, but it is also an experience that is imagined through familiar or analogous experience, imagined in terms of mental boilerplate, stock images, clichés and stereotypes. Race- and gender-based stereotypes, for example, promote disgust and encourage the person who believes in such stereotypes to imagine small disgust-worlds into which other human beings have been abstracted to play parts.[87] Other stereotypes may evoke other kinds of disgust: bad habits, impure actions, coarse behaviour, gross mannerisms. They are ways of seeing, modes of perception and experience, but neither the thing itself nor an accurate depiction. In the case of my experience with the peach, I suspect that it simply evoked unpleasant previous experience, most likely with excrement and other bodily effluvia, but it may also have reminded me of the thousands of tiny spiders that had invaded my body not long before. Today, when I try hard, I can nearly imagine the peach dissolving into countless tiny spiders like an image out of Dali. Perhaps, to give credit to the third model, I also imagined the girl's vulva or conflated its remembered image with that of the spiderlings, but I am much less certain about this. Still, despite present-day uncertainties, I think it makes sense to say that a person as young as four can imagine and that he or she will do so with the available staples of mental imagery.

Still, the lesson that I most want to derive from the tale of the peach is the rich complexity of the disgust experience as it shimmers deceptively, like a silken scarf, before the mind's eye. ✲

L Its
Lair

The Representation of Filth

**Nineteen** years can be a mature age. You will have learned how to do certain things, to accept commitments and to behave responsibly towards others. When I was nineteen I did not often behave maturely. For the past half year, I had been working as a merchant seaman. I was green in mind, but I had read philosophy and French literature during my single year at university. I also knew a bit (hardly more) about history and political theory. Though brightly callow, depthless, I absurdly thought that I was sophisticated. Perhaps I had some reasons for thinking so. I had sailed out of San Francisco for half a year or so, and I had seen a number of Asian cities. And I had continued to read during all this time. No doubt, I had been misled by the narrowness and simplicity of my experience into this fantasy of sophistication. My sexual experiences had all been unshaped, happenings in a green mist, like sudden dream-shoots in a green world. I had an inadequate understanding of many little things. I had never given serious thought to disgust, although I had experienced disgust, quite powerfully at times (beginning with the sliced peach my mother had attempted to give me). Nineteen is a wonderful age for fantasy, but an unlikely one for introspection.

One night in San Francisco, I met an attractive red-haired woman. I had been drinking with two shipmates in an upscale lounge off Lombard Street west of Van Ness. The woman smiled at me as I sauntered back from the men's room to the lounge. I responded as swiftly as an eyebrow arching or an eyelid opening. I stopped, bent down close to her ear and whispered that she was beautiful, the most beautiful woman I had seen since I had got back from Japan. (Thus I managed to advertise my false romantic life.) She was certainly pretty. Years later, I still remember her as lithe and seductive, having perky breasts, a long, intelligent face and large, sparkling green eyes that could glisten doubtfully. Almost instantly, she had engaged my fantasies. A few minutes after we had begun talking, we decided to leave together. I waved goodbye to my friends who chortled lubriciously at my good luck while she spoke *sotto voce* to her girlfriend who gazed at me quizzically. When I actually had her out in the street, hand in hand, heading somewhere, I abruptly realized how little I knew about San Francisco. After a bit of discussion, we went to Chinatown and found a place that she knew. She took the task of ordering for me. Wonton, spicy shrimp, squid in black beans and garlic, chicken in nuts of some kind (cashews, of course, but I didn't know that then). I talked endlessly about being a seaman, about literature, about myself. She said little but played with my feet and caressed my knees under the table. She asked if I liked women. Did I like to love women? Did I want to love her? I kept saying that yes, of course yes, yes I loved love, yes. Did I have limits? she asked, her green eyes shimmering. I replied urgently that I had no limits. I was limitless, my passion was boundless, my drives unquenchable: limits were only the wretched anxieties of the bourgeoisie.

At the time, eating a good Chinese meal and talking about love and sexual possibilities, I actually thought very little about her. Her name was Georgie, a nickname for Georgia Lee. She was an artist, and she taught art at a local high school. I have always remembered some patch of conversation when we talked about frames and framing prints. Did I understand how important frames were? she asked. But most of the details of her life slip my memory. Georgie's apartment was on Russian Hill, north of Nob Hill, on Green Street. Years later I walked through the Russian Hill neighbourhood looking for her apartment but couldn't find it. I paused for a few minutes at the corner of Green and Leavenworth contemplating one of the best views in San Francisco, Alcatraz Island down the steep hill looking very much like an image in old-fashioned stereoscope. I couldn't find her apartment, although it was likely that it had been torn down to make room for several new high-rises. I did remember that her apartment had looked very lived in, a vivid expression of individual human life.

In her apartment her own paintings and reproductions of other works hung on all the walls. I looked at prints of Chagall, Dufy, Klee and Miró.

There were also reproductions (or copies, perhaps) of Odilon Redon's paintings. When, years afterwards, I came upon Redon's *Sibyl* in the Walker Art Center in Minneapolis, Georgie flooded back, her apartment off Hyde springing up around me, pervading the museum. She had books, too, mostly art histories and surveys, but there was also some anthropology and modern history.

I learned that she was twenty-five, six years older than myself, and that she had been born in Seattle not far from my own birthplace. Our paths had crossed momentarily, never intersecting again, having spun out very differently from very similar physical birth-points. The difference in our ages meant that our memories were quite unlike: Georgie remembered shops and museums, the university, but all I could recall were water and evergreen trees, ferry boats and drawbridges, islands, harbours and lakes. A brilliant image of Mount Rainier, breaking through clouds with the sunlight behind it, loomed over my memory. Georgie remembered it more as a familiar landmark. Still, we both carried tatters of fog in our hair and wet sunsets in our hearts.

She made me a drink, a sticky concoction called a Singapore Sling (strictly for adolescents, in that time, of that place) that I had specifically requested. She had not giggled as she made it, nor smiled knowingly. Then we sat talking irresolutely about art. I persistently interjected comments about novels I had read. Finally, we began the exploratory process of having sex together, or "making love" as I might have said at the time. We settled down together on a dark-green calico couch, kissing and touching tentatively, but she engaged in delaying tactics, keeping her legs pressed closely together, crossed at the ankles. The delaying tactics were, of course, familiar to me since they had been standard moves in my rather narrow sexual experience.

I had not yet advanced far when I felt an urgent need to urinate. All the liquids I had drunk that night had rivered their way to my bladder. I got up to go to the toilet, saying something disingenuous like "I'm going to miss you" or "Wait for me, darling, I shall return with infinite desire." But Georgie followed me into the bathroom. I was surprised, but I was also familiar with the sexual associations of urination. The "place of excrement," at least insofar as that meant urination, was exciting and watching the Other pee, as I had grown up understanding sex, was a fairly common stop on the way to actual copulation.

I was not ashamed to have Georgie watch me urinate and I would have enjoyed watching her if that became part of the situation. I had seen other women urinate and I had always found the experience, though not necessary to arousal, definitely exciting. (More musical than a male's rather crashing performance I might have said then, thinking of my favourite modern author.) Five years before, when I was fourteen, I had peeked through some bushes to watch my girlfriend pee while we had been on a romantic stroll through a local park. I found the female squatting position charming, endearing even, not especially "earthbound" (as Camille Paglia puts it),[1] and delicately thrilling. I might not have been so compliant, or so excited, if it ever became a matter of defecation. I had never watched a woman defecate and had never wanted to. *Urolagnia*, though not its more robust comrade, had always been a potential frolicker in the stiffly managed routines of sex. So I expected Georgie to stand beside me and watch me urinate and then perhaps to sit on the toilet while I, kneeling in lust, watched her. Instead, she reached down and took my penis in her the fingers of her right hand and pinched the glans. "Not yet," she whispered. "Don't pee yet." Then, still holding my penis, she began wriggling out of her slip and panties, and with her left hand reached behind and unhooked her bra. Leading me by my penis, she edged over to the bathtub. Slowly, languidly perhaps (that's how I would remember the moment), she slid down into the tub, opening her legs for the first time, and said, "Do it on me."

I had heard of golden showers, but I has never quite believed in them. It was rather like the very different, but semiotically linked, act of eating excrement: I had heard about it, but it was totally outside my immediate experience. I had not yet explored the interrelationship between sex and disgust. "Piss on me," Georgie murmured huskily from the tub. I gaped and felt queasy. I said stupid things like "You don't *really* want me to, do you?" or "You won't like that, I better not." But Georgie knew exactly what she wanted. She wanted a man to urinate upon her. She insisted. And the situation, afterwards graphically incised upon my memory, seemed to demand that I do just that.

I looked down upon her. She had very small breasts (no longer quite as pert as they had seemed earlier, shrunken perhaps in experience's cold light) and a thin clump of long, curling red hair around her vagina. I aimed at this flaming tuft, as if it were a target, and began to urinate directly onto it. Immediately, Georgie commanded me to widen my range. "Don't do it all there. Pee on me everywhere." I moved the direction of the stream up to her bellybutton, her breasts and along her neck and shoulders. I could not bring himself to urinate upon her face. As my urine slowed, I brought the stream, now an exhausted dribble, back down to her vagina, the final drops falling upon her knees and feet. Georgie seemed very happy. Could she pee on me? she asked. "That's not necessary," I said foolishly. I led her by the hand, naked and wet, back to the green couch. Taking her back to the couch, wet but drying, was simply an absurd thing to do, as ill-mannered as insensitive. But I couldn't think clearly at the moment. No doubt, I should have let her urinate on me and then have taken another shower, in water, with her. That would have been the right way to incorporate excremental pleasures among the many steps of sexuality. But I was inordinately upset by the real-life experience of a golden shower. I felt a deep disgust over the act. At the door to the bathroom, I had begun to gag, controlling my vomit only with difficulty. My participation in Georgie's fantasy had lessened me.

Back on the couch, I discovered that I had lost all sexual yearning. Georgie's breasts no longer excited me. Her vagina was too wet, slippery from my urine, and everything about her depressed me. I very much wanted to leave and make my way back to the ship. At nineteen, I was completely impotent. Georgie must have realized that her desire for a golden shower had disgusted me. When I mumbled that I had to get back to the ship for the four a.m. watch (a lie), she said nothing to stop me from going. I slunk out of her apartment.

I felt a great deal of shame when I left. Georgie's perfunctory, embarrassed farewell suggested that she too felt shame. It had been a sexual adventure that has gone stupidly wrong. There had been no romance at all, no romantic archetypes had been in play, but only a wintry misadventure in human absurdity. In time, I was able to make out the important lesson that sexual pleasure takes diverse shapes and rises upon any number of practices, not all of which receive bourgeois, nor Apollonian, sanction. However, in the moment I learned an even more important lesson: that shame and disgust are intimately linked, coupled in a bawdy, carnivalesque dance. I felt shame, but only after I had experienced disgust. When I had begun to gag leaving the bathroom, I had not yet felt shame. That came a few moments later when we were sitting once again on the couch. I had done something, an act that would have made my bourgeois mother physically ill even to hear about. It had been an act that, in the terms of my childhood training, was unclean, improper, dirty. Georgie may have felt shame first, upon recognizing my hesitation, even before the surprise of my impotence. Then she would have experienced self-disgust, a corrosive sense of having been made abject. My hesitancy, my lack of wholehearted participation, my momentary gagging, my impotence, all would have combined together as a harsh judgement upon her, to create self-disgust. She must have felt as if a stranger had caught her out in a private act of something (almost) universally taboo.

A bit later, perhaps a couple of days, after I had taken time to reflect upon the secret *pas de deux* with Georgie and had tried to make sense out of it, I experienced another kind of shame and even self-disgust. In my extravagant creation of a romantic self-image, I had certainly told her that I had no reservations about sex. Sitting in the Chinese restaurant, pushing against her feet and having my knees squeezed between hers, I had tried to make her believe that I was a sophisticated, accomplished lover who recognized no sexual boundaries. I had bragged without knowing what I was bragging about, or in the least regard understanding the moral consequences of speaking to another human being in duplicitous ways. There had been neither honesty nor actual sophistication in *that* persona; no undisclosed shard of my being was being fashioned then, no projection of an ideal conception, but only a confident falsity for the single purpose of screwing Georgie. I had led her to believe that whatever she desired I would be happy, because mutually excited, to perform. I had no idea what, in the real world of other people's fantasies, this might entail.

And Georgia Lee? In the future, looking back, I would romanticize *her*. I would imagine her as an artist who found her creativity in transgressing the boundaries of sexual experience. She was in the de Sadean tradition, a Dionysian artist, perhaps a secret reader of George Bataille, pursuing always the obverse connotations of her own name (Arcadian and idyllic), trying to live her life without measure, without limitations. In perverse experience, along the obscure paths that are liberating to follow, through the limit cases beyond which lies abhorrence, the deliquescent domain of the disgusting, creativity might be found. Look for it, the de Sadean mind advises, look for it in the Dionysian, not within the Apollonian.[2] Break the boundaries, symbolic but seared into the unconscious like brands; explore, and see then how the fingers, the tongue, the whole body, will explode into flames. Overcome your horror, nuzzle Medusa's hair and hear the many little tongues whisper the possibilities of creation. I would have Georgie on my mind for all the years to come. I would fantasize that, had I been different, had I not broken her creative dance, she might have painted, later that night or the next day, a picture that never found life: a loosed, unbound tongue of fire.

The next morning, when my shipmates asked about her, I deceitfully said that she had been great, juicy in so many ways and so forth. My dishonest tongue wagged clumsily with falsehoods and shame. Mostly what I actually remembered was her sparse red pubic hair slick with my urine. I did not like the memory, but I was stuck with it. It would grow upon me.

What were the lessons from this misadventure? I had already learned that disgust is complex and characterized by uncountable personal variations. I knew that it could come suddenly as you stepped unwittingly across a boundary or were abruptly struck by something hurtling across your own. Eventually I would learn that you could overcome disgust and thereafter never feel it again in any similar situation. What I had not understood before is that two people, collaborating to perform a mutual act, create a dynamic, a view of life and a scope for action within it, utterly different from their single inclinations. I learned that the appearance of disgust functions like a judgement. Georgie had felt judged by my gagging, by a man engaged with her in a sexual exchange who manifested disgust. Observing both her and eventually my own shame, I also learned that it follows disgust like an obsequious bootlicker. Above all, I learned that dishonesty and wilful deception (what I had told Georgie at the restaurant) and conscious deceit (what I told my shipmates) could be profoundly disgusting. Insofar as disgust is a moral term, then, it seldom functions more meaningfully than in judging human deceit and dishonesty. Moralists have a point when they see such misleading and ensnaring actions as kinds of filth.

There are many kinds of filth. Blasphemy, racism and sexism, to cite three examples that strike many people coldly to the heart, are types of filth whose representations run paracursively throughout the history of literature.[3] Invisible at close range, many conditions, such as "the scandal of power that ruins our sleep," become disgusting in the perspective of distance.[4] Even, at an opposite extreme, to take a minor image from the Marquis de Sade, the "blackish and fetid scum Nature deposits" between the toes and which "with a little encouragement easily gathers there" is a kind of filth. Although toe jam may be a minor kind of filth, the act of sucking it, which de Sade describes at length, surely constitutes a filthy act, and an act on a different order of loathsomeness than the comparatively innocuous excrement that is its pleasurable aim.[5]

In any such case, from blasphemy to sucking toe jam, the experience of watching filth enacted may prove disgusting. The person performing the act may not feel disgust, at least for its duration (although later its memory may cause shame and self-disgust), but to see it done can be like witnessing an abomination. A boundary suddenly exists beyond which revolting, nefandous and even barely imaginable acts are taking place. It may seem that previously definite categories of behaviour have begun to deliquesce, things and human identity now metamorphosing into muck. However, two distinct levels of disgust are involved. First, there is the object, the slimy thing itself, such as racism, deceit or toe jam; second, there is the act, the slime-like behaviour, such as hating others, lying or sucking toe jam. The object is physical; the act, moral. The two, as Sartre's fiction shows over and over, are intimately intertwined. In either case, you may respond by enacting the disgust face: your nose will narrow, your mouth contort. But notice how the simple example from de Sade introduces important distinctions. Even if restricted to physical manifestations, disgust is not a uniform affect, always causing the same reaction or the same intensity of response. A merely conceptual disgustometer (the only kind currently available) shows heterogeneity and universal variance. Certain disgusting objects are not, in themselves, very disgusting. Urine probably strikes most people as less disgusting than human stool. And toe jam, of course, is not really very disgusting at all, unless you set out to make it so by licking it. Context is, if not always everything, important: urinating upon another person is an aggressively insulting act, and it may be done as a deliberate violence in order to create disgust and inflict shame, but among warriors or athletes celebrating the end of a campaign, or among lovers, it may seem only playful or tender, the very opposite of disgusting. In my first experience of a golden shower, Georgie had not proposed that I undertake a naturally or indisputably disgusting act; it was only that I had experienced it that way. Innumerable things can be disgusting, but none of them are so without the mediation of the imagination. When you glimpse a disgusting thing or view the unviewable, you will imagine yourself in a little world in which you have been momentarily transformed. Looking at Georgie in the tub, I knew that I was being asked to cross a prohibited boundary. Urinating upon her, I knew both that I had crossed that boundary and that I was myself contaminated, polluted by her pollution. In that momentary world of my imagination, I had become less, diminished, the target of reprimand and scorn. Now I can hardly find that little imaginative world when I look for it, but then it was very imposing.

The measureless range of things that can be disgusting among human beings argues against both its instinctual basis and the reification of any single thing as *the* disgust-object.[6] Neither necessity nor tribal law quite accounts for the wide diversity of things that human beings find disgusting. A great deal of the literature of empirical psychologists refers to the apparent universality of disgust and of universal disgust-objects, such as feces, but it is not clear that there is an actual uniformity to the experience of disgust. It comes in diverse shapes and intensities. The domain of the disgusting is as various as all the imagination's dark musings.

As I argued in the previous chapter, an appeal to early training and social formation explains a great deal about disgust. It accounts for the very negative response most people might have to a golden shower. However, it does not explain why some people might desire such an experience, or even why others might participate (tolerating though not desiring) if asked warmly enough. Nor does it go much distance to show why the representation of something disgusting, such as a golden shower or an act of excretion, may not be disgusting at all. The moral and psychological models for disgust suppose that in-the-world disgust is the same as its representations. These models postulate that to account for an actual disgusting object or act is either the same as, or else the first step towards, giving an account of a representation, the real-world thing both determining and exhausting the aesthetic. Approaching the topic from the direction of a moral-legal model, you might easily suppose that all the questions are the same, that textual disgust will prompt the same questions as in-the-world disgust. However, textual and aesthetic disgust in general seem to raise quite different sets of questions.7

The presence of nausea provides an inexact measurement of an object's disgustingness. The psychological studies of disgust often suggest that nausea is a routine concomitant of perceiving disgusting objects, but it seems clear that nausea is experienced in stages and with different degrees of intensity. First there is queasiness in the stomach; next there may be gagging; finally there may come the act of vomiting. Furthermore, repeated contact with disgusting objects and acts can make them less so. It might seem that such contacts desensitize. This is the position that some moral philosophers, such as John Kekes, argue: the experience of disgusting objects and acts will be desensitizing and diminishing. Miller comments upon the "definitional absurdity of calling the aversive attractive."8 Yet this is precisely what seems to happen: what has been, and will still seem, aversive now becomes attractive. Furthermore, the experience of art convincingly shows that the "aversive," even if its in-the-world being remains as it has always been perceived, can be very attractive.

Certain acts, no matter what physical object is involved, can be extremely disgusting. In any disgusting event, the contents of the event can be analyzed as a problem in boundaries: their creation, their maintenance and their crossing. How do such boundaries arise? What is their social purpose? How are they kept viable and active? Under what conditions can they be crossed? What happens when someone is seen to have transgressed them? What are the available sanctions? Are boundaries only, or no more than, a number of social codes? Actions taken, or imagined in make-believe, in direct opposition to a social code, strike at the security of boundaries. As I tried to show in the previous chapter, there are several possible accounts of the origins of socio-cultural boundaries. Even if you want to accept the social-constructionist model, you may find it rather slippery, dangling from unexamined assumptions and occluding difficult questions.

People on the safe side of boundaries may feel disgust, but those on the outside, consciously engaged in shock tactics, will already have taken that disgust into account. Its presence, and the fact that it might be aroused even to the point of destructive revulsion, may be the most important motivation for the shock action in the first place. Punk modalities, such as hairstyles, facial piercings, tattoos and discordant fashions, all aim, as Greil Marcus points out, to taunt authority by enacting shocking performances of prohibited behaviour. In literature, Menippean satire aims violently at social boundaries that seem repressive, corrupt or hypocritical. Carnival exists primarily, and perhaps exclusively, as an occasion to challenge boundaries. Laughter, the spirit of carnival, Bakhtin argues, explodes when boundaries are pierced, dissolved, aggressively crossed or shown to be absurd, illusory fictions. Laughter may be particularly explosive when the defenders of boundaries are shown to be hypocrites. Although social boundaries seem to provide security, a safe zone for private opinion and bias, the other side always pushes against them, breaking across their defences. Even the very rational oppositionality that Ross Chambers has in mind will both incite disgust and potentially modify the boundaries it mocks.

Like codes in general, sanctions are shifty things and slip through time and place. There is another factor to consider. For any disgusting event, it will be possible for an observer to make the disgust face. Indeed, the disgust face, the visible sign of disapprobation and rejection, is itself one possible sanction. Yet it is important to bear in mind that the face may be simulated. Social boundaries exist in the imagination more than on streets or in buildings. (Signs that warn against certain actions, or even laws that prohibit and punish them, serve primarily to energize the imagination of those who dwell on the safe side.) Imagine a reader who is a secret sucker of toe jam, or perhaps even an eater of more disgusting forms of excrement. That person may "make a face" if asked to read de Sade's *The 120 Days of Sodom*, but the face will be a pretense, a little scenario of make-believe. How will anyone know the difference? Writers on disgust, such as Miller, often try to deny the make-believe potential of the disgust face, but it seems to stand out as one of the many ways that human beings register distaste and dislike. It is, I think, as confrontational as it is obvious. A person may display actual disgust with the face but also pretend disgust using the precisely same symbolic markers.

The parable of the two fathers with which I began the first chapter suggests an important point about human conduct. Disgust is a powerful affect, working on both the physical and moral plane, but it is extremely various in expression. It may be easily faked. Julia Kristeva comments that the abject, a narrowed category of disgust, constituted in post-Lacanian psychoanalysis, is a "composite of judgment and affect," a "twisted braid" of affects and thoughts.[9] Elizabeth Grosz expands the image of the twisted braid into the more complex image of a Möbius strip, the "torsion or pivot around which the subject is generated."[10] A powerful affect, but tempered by mind's chimerical scope, disgust takes myriad, unpredictable forms. Psychologists may agree that the nostrils narrow and crinkle, but that may be the only physical concomitant that everyone shares who feels disgust.[11] Its ideational (or judgemental) dimensions are as various as the mind itself. You can sometimes observe another person experiencing disgust. Pay attention if the opportunity arises since you may have before you both a mirror of your own possible responses and, more importantly, a demonstration of a reaction so complex that it might stand for the human condition itself. Imagine a young parent, up to his elbows in excrement, changing a child's diapers for the first time; or a person feeling a lover suddenly vomit upon her legs and feet; or anyone coming abruptly upon another person on his or her knees happily snuffling fresh dog feces. In any of those instances, if you could see them from a secret vantage, you might perceive an immediate reaction, without exaggeration or controlled gestures. Making the same observation from a public standpoint, face to face as it were, you might never know the precise degree to which the disgust face has been imitated or enhanced.

Now imagine a scene in which a senior academic comes upon a junior colleague, whom he does not like or admire, while she is showing affection to a friend. Imagine them sitting upon a bench in a campus quadrangle, holding hands or even gently embracing, but nonetheless talking seriously with one another about intellectual topics. The senior colleague wrinkles his nostrils, twists his upper lip inwards and upwards towards his nose. He is registering disgust for the young academic's behaviour, a disgust that may well be a displacement of a feeling that he has more constantly for her work, her theoretical position in their discipline or her professional comportment within their department. Do you believe him? Does it not seem quite likely that he is displaying a theatrical personal judgement, not unconsciously showing an immediate reaction? His disgust, which you can see so plainly, matching in all visible respects the facial criteria (the "elicitors") that psychologists claim identify the presence of disgust, has been simulated. He will be managing his facial expressions in order to make a point. How will you, observing but unobserved, know whether the classical expression of disgust on his face is immediate and genuine, or mediate and false? The hostile academic will not pretend to vomit, but he might do so. That would be only the next step in an acted-out performance of showing disgust. The primal and ultimate rejection is "the retch."[12]

The difference between this hypothetical situation and those I gave first involving direct contact with feces or vomit is that disgust has been transformed into a moral response. Moral disgust, an extension to the dimension of conceptual and metaphoric experience, must be possible. Philosophers observe it and seem, some of them anyway, to believe in it. "Deep disgust," John Kekes writes, "is a visceral reaction to the violation of a moral taboo."[13] Alas for the rigour of moral inference, even deep disgust can be simulated. It is an action that a person might play. When you observe another person experiencing disgust, you may be seeing an uncontrollable physical response to an object or an action, but you may also be seeing, even at the same time, a managed display of judgement and rejection. Once the make-believe dimension of disgust has been recognized, it will be possible to see that even actual, gut-wrenching disgust can be enhanced, made convincingly theatrical, in order to emphasize the moment.

Another person's face is like a pathway that you are invited to enter: a network of paths, a nexus or web. Facework, to borrow Erving Goffman's term, comments upon and punctuates action. Almost "all acts involving others," Goffman writes, "are modified, prescriptively or proscriptively, by considerations of face."[14] Facework is metadiscursive; it helps to interpret signs. Or, to put the matter more elegantly, facework is the dynamic of expressions that are exchanged in human intercourse, discursive and otherwise, and each single expression is a sign that aids, or pretends to aid, in the interpretation of other signs. An extreme version of facework can be seen any evening in North America merely by watching TV news. Newsreaders learn to match the words they are reading with various facial moves. These include the full range of possible eyebrow, cheek, mouth and lip movements, all employed expressively to add significance. The anchorperson's baroque facework is intended to function as a semiotic ledger in which the words of the news have been overscored. This TV facework is largely illusory. For the most part there is no genuine correspondence between the words read and the elaborate metadiscursive register. A little girl has been run over by her father's tractor in Iowa, a Canadian politician seems to be dying from the ravages of flesh-eating bacteria, or a man in Texas has been executed even though everyone knew that he was innocent, but the anchorperson raises an eyebrow as if posing a question, perhaps showing incredulity, or else pushes her or his mouth into a meaningless pout. Even a little close examination reveals that it is acting, facework in play only. Facework acts like a prop in a small game of make-believe.

Facework is often misleading, often illusory (though seldom as baroquely textured as the TV news), and imposes false readings, distorted interpretations. It can be metadiscursive in much the same way that Iago's silences and self-musings are in his conversations with Othello. Confronting the deceptive facial web, you follow a path that the face has marked out and discover the values that lie behind expressions. Smiles are paths that open to admiration, friendliness, warmth and love. Slightly modified, tightened or chilled, they lead to scorn. Snarls lead to interior landscapes, lit by blood-red suns and streaked by jagged lightning flashes, in which ferocity rules. A face wrinkled in disgust offers a path leading directly to a mental world in which everything takes on the dark colours of putrid decay, a world swarming with rot-clogged stenches and glimpses of dissolution, and which makes possible an inner experience of negative judgement, contempt and rejection. The narrowed nostrils of disgust, the slitted or pursed mouth, the contorted lips, the tensed facial muscles, the slowly blinking eyes, all point inwards towards repugnance and loathing. The mind responds to its environment much like a body turning away, eyes averted, a hand poised between seeing and seen, revolted. This can also be contempt: a deftly managed display of the disgust face in order to make a moral point. Contempt is a psycho-intellectual affect, building upon or even taking for granted actual disgust, an exercise in pretense and theatre, but inescapably real.

The human face is an instance of evidence pointing along a path towards an unknown, though anticipated, object. The object has not been seen, but it can be predicted by what it has left behind. It is rather like following the spoor of an animal that you have not yet seen or a monster that you dread but are determined to expose. Evidential fragments of a whole that has not yet been exposed begin to indicate a presence. Foreseen only in outline, anticipated in the mind's eye, this presence begins to acquire a shape through the evidence that points towards it. In literature, faces are always important. Normally, you are required either to see or to imagine them. In film and in drama they are physical manifestations of the action that an audience can see and interpret. Certain actors, Lon Chaney to cite a famous instance, become known for their faces and are given roles that seem to call for their face, their repertory of faces.[15] The visible face can be read and even stored in memory as an aid in future interpretations.[16] However, even in narrative fiction, faces are extremely important. Readers are constantly being asked to imagine human faces in certain specific situations. Comedy could hardly be imagined at all unless one were able to see, in the mind's eye, a human face with its diacritical marks of surprise, shock, astonishment, woe or wonder. A great deal of the comic effect generated by a convention such as reversing a character's expectations comes from being able to see, or to imagine, that face. That, I suppose, is why the pies thrown in the silent films made during the "golden age" of comedy were invariably either cream or meringue. A nose, eyebrows raised sharply, a broken arc of mouth, isolated parts of the face, fragmentary expressions, could be seen through the slipping meringue registering the character's shock. And, of course, the disgust face, so formulaic, so easily made, runs through the history of film as it does much literature, especially in such sub-types as the novel of manners and the moral novel. It also plays an important role in horror fiction. It registers, and helps to interpret, the spoor along the trail that will lead, either in the climax or just beyond closure, to the monster's lair.

Consider for a moment the facework of shame that at first glance seems quite distant from, even if psychologically linked to, disgust. The face of shame reveals a person who, by being made an object of disgust, now feels mortification. I have already claimed that disgust and shame are affective partners in a complex dance: usually accompanied by self-disgust, shame arises when a person sees that his or her identity, individual or collective, has fallen behind one of the boundaries that isolate disgust (and hence slipped from an ego-ideal that is, often, culturally sanctioned as well), prompting the reaction of mortification, self-accusation and regret that constitutes shame. Now imagine their relationship as a dance of faces, or of masks. Shame may be a face drawn tight, pale and withdrawing, or it may be a blushing face, reddened by disgrace. Crestfallen, downcast, hangdog, dejected, shamefaced, heartsick, even such plain words as down, low and blue, are all terms you can use to describe the face when it registers shame.[17]

What about the face of embarrassment? What relationship does it bear to shame? If shame constitutes a "generic class name for a whole family of emotions," then embarrassment can easily be located within a conceptual home.[18] Anyone can experience embarrassment and most people have, I suspect, felt it often. Take it as an affect that anticipates shame. You may feel shame beginning to grow upon you even in the midst of an embarrassing moment or, perhaps more commonly, you may experience shame in the memory of an embarrassing experience. Suppose that you lose control of your bowels in a public situation, or, more likely, you begin to suspect that you may do so. You are "caught short" or suddenly in the most urgent exigencies of diarrhea. The situation is wrong. You are (so to speak) "out of place" or soon will be. If you were in the privacy of a lavatory, or even in Leopold Bloom's garden-corner jakes, there would be no reason to feel embarrassment. However, you are in a crowded public meeting, giving your weekly seminar, at church, in your bank manager's office, and the sensation of loosening bowels is abruptly very powerful. This is an embarrassing situation and may well prove to be the occasion for shame. The dynamic is still the same as I have already suggested: you become an object of disgust (as you would likely become if perceived to have befouled yourself in the bank manager's office, in a crowded meeting or during a seminar) and you feel shame, perhaps accentuated by the shame-dealing expressions and words of others who perceive what has happened.[19] Indeed, embarrassment is much more common than the rather extreme case I have just invented would indicate.[20] Erving Goffman observes that, in Anglo-American-Canadian society at least, "there seems to be no social encounter which cannot become embarrassing to one or more of its participants, giving rise to what is sometimes called an incident or false note."[21] Embarrassment only adds an intermediary stage: the uneasy apprehension that you will become, or are about to become, disgusting in the eyes of others. Here is how Goffman describes the face of embarrassment, a face that you can easily recognize and which everyone must imagine in reading comedy or novels of manners:

An individual may recognize extreme embarrassment in others and even in himself by the objective signs of emotional disturbance: blushing, fumbling, stuttering, an unusually low- or high-pitched voice, quavering speech or breaking of the voice, sweating, blanching, blinking, tremor of the hand, hesitating or vacillating movement, absent-mindedness, and malapropisms ... There are also symptoms of a subjective kind: constriction of the diaphragm, a feeling of wobbliness, consciousness of strained and unnatural gestures, a dazed sensation, dryness of the mouth, and tenseness of the muscles. In cases of mild discomfiture these visible and invisible flusterings occur but in less perceptible form.[22]

These are the signs that visibly indicate the presence of unease, the flustered and flustering state of self-awareness (harbingers of personal dissolution) that heralds the temporary transformation of a person into an object of disgust. Such signs, paths leading to inner worlds of affects, are the materials that literature builds upon. Writers must know how to employ them in characterization, actors to represent them, and readers to imagine them. Both disgust and its surrounding constellation of affects (humiliation, shame, contempt, hate, for example) may seem to appear in a disordered, even chaotic, manner in the actual world, however strictly a line of causation might be retrospectively traced back to a point of origin. In literature such affects appear in ordered sequences, within a narrative design. The argument that disgust functions differently in horror and terror (which I shall make in Chapter 6) or appears differently sequenced in those different modes, does not, of course, claim that in-the-world horror and terror (anymore than shame or humiliation) must be experienced as they are in literature. The human face is fundamental to the literary experience, but, as a textual representation, it is often rather like a choreographed masque: stylized, baroque, a succession of character-masks in a single dance.

Up to this point in my argument, it has been possible to see that an investigation of disgust starts from the recognition that first, disgust is an immediate and powerful affect with at least some basis in early conditioning and the childhood acquisition of social codes; second, it can be learned, unlearned and relearned, either as a voluntary or involuntary response to new experiences; and third, it can also be managed and deployed strategically, even simulated and played out as make-believe, in order to create shocking contrasts and effects, like a bluebird tattooed beneath pubic hair.[23] Although my argument has been very abstract (and will become so again), it allows for all manner of examples, instances from literature, film and the world at large: metaphors, parables and fables that specify the problem. Hence, for the moment I want to follow a particularizing path.

Urinating on another person is not normally a friendly act. Any bodily fluid spewed or spat upon another person without permission, or against desire, constitutes a profound insult. Urinating upon another person might be the concomitant of ethnic or gender violence, the final indignity given to close a process of degradation and pain. Chilled by dread and loathing at the prospect, you might expect to be pissed upon on a battlefield, in the street during a riot or after a rumble, or in jail. You would expect to have been defeated, beaten, raped or killed before it would happen. It would constitute a symbolic hurt, an indignity, like someone spitting in your face, that could not easily be erased.[24] Being urinated upon could never be a congenial experience and no one in his or her right mind would seek it out. Even our language demonstrates that piss is undesirable: "Piss off!" and "Piss on it" show contempt, the recognition of unworth. Yet being urinated upon can be a desired experience and some people, right-minded enough in other respects, do yearn for it. In the tale with which I began this chapter, Georgie was an intelligent, creative woman who easily attracted other people to her, but she desired to feel the stream of another person's urine upon her. There was, I think now, nothing wrong with her other than a kinky desire.

Imagine a golden shower. Imagine a much longed-for person's urine gushing upon your chest and neck, or along your stomach and thighs, flooding your genital area. It is warm as it strikes you, hitting with a force that jars without hurting. Perhaps it will remind you of a parent playing the hose upon you when you were a child: you were laughing and skipping delightedly into the stream's path. It solicits all your senses. As it wets your body, hissing gently with contact, reeking slightly, golden or citrine, even tasting salty and bittersweet in your mouth as stray drops splatter your lips or else cascade into it, perhaps eddying up your nostrils, you will find yourself drawn imaginatively into your partner's body, into its hidden spaces.[25]

The idea of a golden shower luridly poses the problem of disgust. It isn't an experience that most people would want. Probably most people wouldn't even want to watch.[26] Certain acts, like certain objects, are abhorrent to see, hear, touch, taste or smell. They violate the socialized conditions of perception for at least one sense, often for all of them. Anyone may have had the disgusting experience of seeing or smelling something that is unpleasant, has gone off or is simply in the wrong place for easy perception. Such acts and objects are off one's experiential limits. But why? What is it that makes the nostrils tighten, the throat clench and vomit rise? Think about the experience of a golden shower.

What is it about a golden shower that is so repulsive? [27] It cannot be the presence of urine in itself. You may not much like urine, but it is so common, so much a part of all human experience, that it could not be, for most people, the cause of deep, throat-convulsing disgust. People can learn to drink urine, and under emergency conditions will do so more or less cheerfully. Soldiers have often been forced to drink urine in desert conditions in order to survive. In Shakespeare's *Antony and Cleopatra*, Octavius remembers how Antony, after having been defeated at Modena, "dids't drink the stale of horses" even though he had been "daintily brought up."[28] If a golden shower causes disgust, it cannot be merely that it involves urinating. More likely, the disgusting quality of golden showers lies wholly in the social inappropriateness of the act. Two people urinate in each other's company, a common enough experience, and do so not only with but upon each other. Above all, they do it to enhance sexual pleasure. That's the rub. The act is out of place, performed incorrectly in a situation (sex, love) that normal social discourse doesn't admit may be modified in this way. No matter what physical object is involved, certain acts can be extremely disgusting simply because they are performed in the wrong place or with the wrong intention (a more complex notion).

My disturbing experience with the red-haired Georgie taught me the immense rigidity of boundaries at first crossing. At the time I did not ask where the boundaries had come from or how they had been instilled in me, but I sensed that they were there. Moreover, it had been clear that the boundaries were mine only. I could see, plainly enough, that the idea of one person urinating upon another did not constitute a boundary for her. In fact, a golden shower must have been a familiar, perhaps even a common, experience for Georgie. All the difficulties of crossing that boundary were mine alone, until I began to gag. And then they had become hers as well. At that point I brought shame into the scene. Indirectly, I had shamed her. Although it was not a simple process, it didn't take long for me to feel shame at the way I had treated her. We never saw each other again, but we had entered into a recursive loop.[29] Later, I began to fantasize Georgie and invent scenarios in which I had blocked her creative potential. Then I could feel shame for several quite different reasons: my deceit, my unmanly failure to control my emotions (allowing my gag reflex to show), my having shamed her, my having told fibs about her to my shipmates and my having obtruded upon her artistic talent. Then my shame began to metamorphose into guilt. The realization that I had shamed her, and then the two-step emergence of shame and guilt, took some time to register. Once it did, I became obsessed by complex memories of my sad little tryst. I have had Georgie on my mind ever since.[30]

What kind of an experience is a golden shower? There are many other socio-cultural boundaries that it might be painful to cross, or even to observe being crossed. These are boundaries that, while social in their regime, are also visceral and involve bodily excreta. Thus, watching a golden shower might be rather like seeing someone take his food from the table and retire to the toilet in order to eat, undisturbed, in (as it were) privacy. Then you would be able to observe several boundaries being transgressed at once: do not take food away from the table, especially when you are a guest at another person's home; do not eat in the toilet; do not mix your different levels of effluvia and excreta (saliva and urine, say); do not expose your toilet habits to strangers. Imagine a plate of food, a piece of cake, say, or a delicious pecan pie. Nothing disgusting there. There is, however, a person at the table who prefers to eat it as a dog or a raccoon might, nose down, tongue flicking outwards, in close proximity to the food. Suppose this is done in public, even at your very own dinner table. A definite boundary that prescribes the relation of the mouth to food in a public place will have been crossed. Now imagine the same plate of food which you will have just served to a guest. But your guest gets up, taking the plate of cake or pie, and heads towards the lavatory to eat it there in personal comfort. A boundary that separates places for eating from places for excretion will have been crossed. These examples are simple and far from unimaginable, but they show clearly how an action, the manner of doing something, can be disgusting even when the object itself is not. Ways of eating, even more than what is eaten, seem to touch an in(de)finite number of sore spots.

In Luis Buñuel's *The Phantom of Liberty*, the famous "shit-together" scene begins as an embedded narrative in which a lecturer on human mores before a group of police cadets refers to a personal experience to illustrate the point that mores, like laws, are always changing. Two couples, a young woman and a child gather together for an evening at the table. However, they have been invited to excrete together, not to eat. The table is set with six pink ceramic toilets instead of chairs. The young woman settles upon her toilet, lifting her skirts delicately, and the men drop their trousers more coarsely. They discuss the vast amounts of excrement that human beings produce each day (twelve million tons, it is claimed). They also express nausea at the mention of food. The lecturer at the police academy recounts how, in a recent visit to Madrid, he had been sickened by the smells of food. The little girl announces that she is hungry and her mother shushes her as if, at another table, she had announced that she had to pee (she should not use such words as "hunger" while at the table). The lecturer finishes, flushes the toilet, and asks to be excused. He gets up from the table and in a hushed voice asks the maid where to find the dining room. She whispers that it is down the hall. When he gets there, it is a small private room with a fold-down table. He summons his meal by pressing a buzzer and it arrives on a dumb waiter—a plate and a bottle of wine. He begins to eat without preliminaries and with no manners (in private, manners are what you want them to be). Later, the young woman also leaves the table and knocks politely on the door of the eating-room. Visibly disturbed in the act of eating, the man calls out that it is "occupied." The young woman, embarrassed and flustered, apologizes and turns away, walking thoughtfully down the hallway.[31] The police lecturer's tale can be viewed as a fable, an objective hypothesis, of cultural transformation. Given the human history of cultural revolution and upheaval, such a change can be imagined as taking place, at least among small groups of revolutionary intellectuals. However, Buñuel's fable also shows the metamorphicity of disgust through changes in mores. Hunger, food and eating have become disgusting in Buñuel's embedded fictional world, relegated to a private sphere of action.

What happens when someone is seen to have transgressed socially encoded boundaries? (For instance, the person who prefers to eat your pecan pie while sitting contemplatively on your toilet.) What are the available sanctions? Well, you will never invite this person again. You will let other friends and colleagues know about this behaviour. The human mind seems always to have been fertile in inventing sanctions. Whenever you tell this story, you may enact the disgust face. How does this facework, which the guilty eater will neither see nor suspect, constitute a sanction? Facework is a code, social as well as semiotic, that will inflect your story, drawing moral judgements from your listeners. It is rather like writing marginalia along the borders of a text. Your guest will have been transformed into a character in a fiction, but a character that, whenever retold, must always endure the author's stout stroke along the margins.

Are boundaries no more than a number of social codes? Clearly, they seem also to involve the body and all the manifestations of its private slime, as well as the personal memories of bodily experiences. People are sometimes said to have visceral reactions; that is, they experience a sudden, overpowering queasiness, gagging and an urge to vomit in the face of some act or object that they perceive as loathsome. Calling a reaction "visceral" identifies it as being abrupt, spontaneous and overpowering. John Kekes' claim that disgusting situations elicit visceral reactions seems, insofar as it goes, correct enough. "To say that we are sickened by them is not a metaphor," he writes; "we are nauseated, our guts heave, we tremble, our hearts race, we both sweat and shiver, we cannot control our physical responses, or control them only with great effort."[32] Physical disgust is not usually under voluntary control: it can be suppressed, but far less easily activated. What the guts appear to do, squirm, convulse and upheave, may be only what they commonly do given a certain stimulus. From the social-constructionist perspective, an act of vomiting would be as formed, as much a definite habit-groove, as a regular bowel movement.[33] A healthy peristalsis is (so to speak) a matter of conditioning, an image, as Leopold Bloom reflects while sitting on his garden jakes, of life itself.

Joyce's *Ulysses* contains a number of descriptions of human excretion, but it is not, I suppose, scatological in any marked way. It is difficult today to imagine anyone reading *Ulysses* for pornography, although this is, it seems, how it was once read both by those seeking thrills and by those finding only the "disgust of the original philistines."[34] The Calypso chapter, the chapter that introduces Leopold Bloom, in which Bloom begins his day by defecating in a privy in the garden of his house, indicates how complex an act defecation may be once it has been transformed into a textual representation:

> He kicked open the crazy door of the jakes. Better be careful not to get trousers dirty for the funeral. He went in, bowing his head under the lintel. Leaving the door ajar, amid the stench of mouldy limewash and stale cobwebs he undid his braces .... Asquat on the cuckstool he folded out his paper turning its pages over on his bared knees. Something new and easy. No great hurry. Keep it a bit. Our prize titbit. *Matcham's Masterstroke.* Written by Mr Philip Beaufoy, Playgoers' club, London. Payment at the rate of one guinea a column has been made to the writer. Three and a half. Three pounds three. Three pounds thirteen and six. Quietly he read, restraining himself, the first column and, yielding but resisting, began the second. Midway, his last resistance yielding, he allowed his bowels to ease themselves quietly as he read, reading still patiently, that slight constipation

of yesterday quite gone. Hope it's not too big bring on piles again. No, just right. So. Ah! Costive one tabloid of cascara sagrada. Life might be so. It did not move or touch him but it was something quick and neat. Print anything now. Silly season. He read on, seated calm above his own rising smell ... He tore away half the prize story and wiped himself with it. Then he girded up his trousers, braced and buttoned himself. He pulled back the jerky shaky door of the jakes and came forth from the gloom into the air.[35]

I first read *Ulysses* when I was eighteen. The scatological interests of adolescence still alive in my mind, I was struck by this passage, and by the startlingly graphic description of a man playing with his stool, yielding and resisting, and finally yielding. I read the passage out loud to a friend, a young man perhaps a year or two older than I, and it made him sick. He gagged and was barely able to control his vomit. Well, you will say, that is mild stuff, not in the same league of scatology as, say, the Marquis de Sade, Thomas Pynchon or even David Foster Wallace. It is just Joyce following his naturalistic conventions, representing a bowel movement because there must be one. That is how, in a costive Irish society of one hundred years ago, the day would have begun. And, of course, I must agree. It *is* mild. And it is perhaps an aspect of the novel that led Judge John M. Woolsey, in the famous 1933 district court decision allowing *Ulysses* to be published in the United States, to assert in his verdict that the novel was not aphrodisiac, but that it was "somewhat emetic."[36] I don't find the appeal to Joyce's naturalistic conventions, if these truly exist, to exhaust the interesting questions. Nor do I find explanations based upon his supposed immature desire to shock or to indulge a puerile imagination of much interest. If Joyce was intrigued by excrement, perhaps more by urination than by defecation, as his biographers claim, then I can only say, so what?

What interests me is the way Joyce writes this simple passage describing a bowel movement as a way to originate his character, Leopold Bloom. It introduces a trait, anality, that will emerge during the novel's development as a significant characteristic. Bloom is always fascinated by bodily functions and aspects. He is associated with what Bakhtin calls the "lower bodily stratum."[37] Bloom eats "with relish the inner organs of beasts and fowls," but most of all he likes "grilled mutton kidneys which gave to his palate a fine tang of faintly scented urine."[38] Ellmann observes how in *The Portrait of the Artist as a Young Man* Joyce compares Stephen's soul to a flower, while in *Ulysses* he uses the image of a flower to describe Bloom's penis.[39] Bloom is always associated with bodily functions, with stinks, with unwashed underwear, with decay and dissolution. He is the image of a human person trying, not wholly successfully, to transcend excrement, to rise above *dreck*. As he walks through Dublin all that famous day, he carries a bar of soap in his pocket. Now *that* interests me. Eventually, the reader learns that he sleeps head-to-bum with Molly. He draws satisfaction from the "adipose posterior female hemispheres, redolent of milk and honey and of excretory sanguine and seminal warmth, reminiscent of secular families of curves of amplitude, insusceptible of moods of impression or of contrarieties of expression, expressive of mute immutable mature animality."[40] When he crawls silently into bed with the sleeping Molly, placing his face against her buttocks, he "kissed the plump mellow yellow smellow melons of her rump, on each plump melonous hemisphere, in their mellow yellow furrow, with obscure prolonged provocative melonsmellonous osculation."[41] The passage that I cited from the Calypso episode links Bloom to all his other interests, his fascinations even, with the "lower bodily stratum." Joyce's textual description of Bloom's defecation is a fundamental act of characterization. Italian essayist Aldo Buzzi, writing on Gorgonzola cheese, remarks that the stinks emitting from a human being's rear-end are, in a sommelier's lingo, like "an intoxicating bouquet of roses and Parma violets" and he goes on to add that the human buttocks, because of their round form and their "inscrutable mixture of the human and the divine, can be considered one of the most convincing proofs of the existence of God, certainly more convincing than the ontological argument of Saint Anselm."[42] Perhaps Bloom must be imagined as experiencing his lifeworld in terms such as these. Bloom's enjoyment of his flawless peristalsis reflects the deeply conditioned human longing for easy, smooth and pleasant bowel movements, but it also suggests a model ("Life might be so") for happy life. The single private act, in which Bloom finds so much pleasure, reflects a private, but nonetheless entire, worldview.

There are also thematic links as well: Bloom is reading a newspaper, from which he eventually tears a piece to wipe himself, and that looks ahead both to his job in the world (he sells advertising space) and to Stephen's more intellectual concerns with newspapers. Furthermore, he reads fiction, a prize-winning newspaper story, which is just the kind of literature that Bloom, in some real sense a very literary man, likes to read. He sits above his own rising stench "reading analytically the prize story in *Tidbits*," Fred Radford remarks, while reconciling the Apollonian and the Dionysian "in an act of practical criticism" when he tears the page in half to wipe himself.[43] The words are charged with their dual directions. Take "titbit." It is a column in the paper. It might refer to Bloom's stool or to his apprehension of it. And it clearly has a sexual significance that is appropriate for the dreaming, secretive lover who is also a cuckold. The line, "It did not move or touch him but it was something quick and neat," has a double significance both to the story Bloom is reading and to the act he is performing. This is simply how Bloom's mind works, not Stephen's, and not necessarily Joyce's either. And, clearly, all the quantification must count for something. Bloom estimates how much Mr. Beaufoy might have been paid for his story at the rate of a guinea a column. It is a very Bloomian concern. It might even call to mind Freud's equation of feces with money. An anal person likes to collect, it is sometimes said, to retain and to keep. Money is the abstract mode of collection. "The king was in his counting-house," Bloom thinks while sitting on his cuckstool.

Now I want to return to Georgie once more. The examples from Buñuel and Joyce suggest a double point. They bring out, more vividly than any merely personal example, the force of boundaries and the strong loathing, emetic at the very least, that transgression can cause. Even to read Joyce's description of Bloom's morning bowel movement has been, and might still be, overwhelmingly aversive for many readers. However, the examples from Buñuel and Joyce also show that fictional accounts of disgust work on the mind differently than in-the-world encounters with disgusting things. They raise more and different questions which have the effect of making a literary account of disgust both more complex and more symbolic. Bloom's act of defecation occurs only once and it does so within a vast net of symbolic associations. It helps to establish character and it links ahead to the bar of soap in his pocket and Bloom's characteristic anality. You can see that the questions to be asked are very different from those that an actual bowel movement could prompt. A representation in literature or art is surrounded by an intricate nexus of questions quite different in scope from an actual thing. As a consequence, it is embedded in an entirely different epistemological field. Still, it is hard to convince some people that representations are different from the actual things for which they stand. Latter-day Platonists, such as Miller and Kekes, like to collapse the distinction either because they cannot see it or because it fits their arguments to do so. Other people, including ordinary North Americans who hate the NEH or the Brooklyn Museum of Art for having mounted the *Sensation* exhibition, often seem to loathe representations even more than their in-the-world counterparts. I find this puzzling, but it can be explained as an extra fury over someone else's deliberate provocation, an act chosen to offend as opposed to an offensive act.[44] My argument in this book depends in part upon making distinction.

Despite its apparent spontaneity, the gut reaction to disgust shows as much social training as excretion.[45] It is the human way of recognizing something that, long ago but seldom far away, was put into a category on the other side of a boundary as something not to touch, not to taste, probably not even to look upon. Then, during that ideal time upon which so many humans look back fondly, the child (which was you) received training in recognizing boundaries, in acquiring social formation, in fashioning a magnificent, serviceable-in-all-weathers superego. Once you had this in place, you were able to identify all kinds of things, both objects and acts, that you could reject, even despise and scorn. You would have achieved the great human conquest of growing into adulthood: an ability to hate everything your parents, as well as your relatives and peers, hate. Above all, you were probably taught to identify your own waste products as filth, neither to play with nor to treasure, from which the eyes should be averted. These products were made to disappear in a flush of water or a long plummet, like a hangman's sad drop, into darkness. This seems to make excrement, in particular feces, the core experience of disgust. Thinking of the early training that human children receive in rejecting their own waste, Julia Kristeva reifies feces, along with menstrual blood, into the fundamental instance of the abject: always the wet, putrescent, overdetermined substance of primal repression.

> No, as in true theater, without makeup or masks, refuse and corpses *show me* what I permanently thrust aside in order to live. These bodily fluids, this defilement, this shit are what life withstands, hardly and with difficulty, on the part of death. There, I am at the border of my condition as a living being. My body extricates itself, as being alive, from that border.[46]

A human corpse is the utmost in abjection. It evades the entire human apparatus for regulation, whether we call this symbolic or simply Apollonian, to point out how frail actually the borders of human identity are. Elizabeth Grosz puts the problem of the rigid but frail human boundaries with great clarity: "The child, and the semiotic/biological raw materials it brings with it, are born into an already existing symbolic/linguistic system; such pre-existent systems of signification are necessary for the subject's constitution as a subject, with the body's registration as its own, and an access to speech and symbolization."[47] You can feel called by what has been expelled, what has been named as abject, drawn even to the sight of corpses. What is abject can call out in a clamorous voice. Thus the relation between the self and abject may be seen as dialectical. The experience is at once degrading and potentially creative. This is the experience that Patrick White traverses so often in his novels.[48] It is what Bataille means when he writes about the importance of living one's life without limitation, without measure.

I think that it should be clear that in my absurd encounter with Georgie, the moment in which I almost vomited revealed an immense amount about my social formation. It was not merely the novelty of the situation, but the certain consciousness that I had crossed a border into a forbidden realm. It may even be, though I cannot recall, that I heard my mother's regulating and controlling voice in my mind's ear. It is also true that the territory of the abject, the no-place of expulsion and rejection, was quite evident. It is possible that Georgie may have normally thought of herself as abject because of her secret pleasure in having men urinate upon her. It is more certain that by gagging and then rejecting her, I had shunted her off into the corrosive territory of the abject. Even a very short encounter with disgust, a brief misadventure or a quick glance at something you would have preferred not to have seen, opens up the immense complexity of the problem.

Consider the problem of the golden shower once more. You may think that it would be an appalling idea, a degrading and diminishing act. If you think that then you will likely also think that I did the right thing in declining to participate fully and that my mature memories, romanticizing Georgie for her transgressiveness, are foolish. Yet there are occasions when a golden shower might be acceptable, although it would not be called by that name. One person might urinate into another's mouth in an emergency situation when, no water anywhere available, the companion has become weak with thirst and appears to be dying. Urine will keep you alive in desert conditions and while normally each person prefers his or her own, another person's, even a horse's (as Mark Antony learned) or a dog's, will do quite as well. Until recently, doctors tasted their patients' urine as a diagnostic tool (a sweet tang will reveal one type of diabetes), though they seldom nibbled upon their patients' stool. Imagine yourself with a few companions alone upon a plain during war. Someone notices that clouds of chlorine gas are billowing towards you. You discover with dismay that you have no gas masks. Then you remember that the ammonia in urine might be a counteragent for chlorine and you rip a piece of material from your shirt and urinate upon it. Your companions are unbelieving, already prepared to die, but they follow your lead.

> The rest of the men were waiting numbly, holding torn pieces of cloth in their hands—staring at Robert with their mouths open. "What are we s'posed to do?" one of them asked. "These won't save us. Not if it's chlorine."
> "Piss on them," said Robert.
> "Unh?"
> "PISS ON THEM!!!"[49]

If one of the others, nearly dead with fear, has already voided his bladder or experiences a locking of sphincter muscles, a frozen bladder incapable of even dribbling, then you will place the piece of cloth over this person's face and urinate upon it. This will be a brilliant solution to a deadly problem. You will never refer to this moment as a golden shower.

The problem of textual representation strikes even closer to the key issue: not every golden shower will be disgusting. The anecdote with which I began this chapter may describe a disgusting act. However, the anecdote's textual disgust is neither wet nor stinking, and it should cause only a mild unease. If you felt sensations, stickiness or liquid warmth turning chilly on your skin, these were optional, triumphs of your reading skills. Furthermore, there were a large number of questions that you might have asked about the story that you could never ask about any in-the-world equivalent: questions about purpose, function, allusiveness, tropes and style. Take style as an instance. You might ask questions about corporeal style(s) when watching two actual people performing a golden shower together. Perhaps you thought that you saw one person strut or the other cringe. Or you may have seen other indications of aggression or vulnerability. These would be body styles chosen for the act, and very likely they would be conventional mannerisms that each partner had rehearsed many times before. Even so, these ways of acting during the performance would be neither the first nor the most important aspect of the performance. In the textual representation, style is first and may be nearly everything. That is simply how stories are told: with style, good or bad, effective or ineffective. Texts prompt very different questions than the actual events they seem to represent. There are many questions, most of the best ones in fact, to be asked of textual representations that you simply would never think to ask (because it would be silly or wrongheaded) about actual-world things.

This distinction seems fairly basic to the study of aesthetic experience. No one can say quite what it is that Leontes feels when he imagines a drowned spider, steeped in wine, lying at the bottom of his cup. Yet it is clear enough that he imagines it to be equivalent to what he also imagines to have been his wife's adultery with his best friend, a sight that, like the scandalous mental image of Hermione spreading her legs for Polixenes' sexual pleasure, would create overpowering disgust. The "abhorr'd ingredient" would "crack his gorge" and rake his sides with violent hefts.[50] Reading *The Winter's Tale*, you may have a sense of Leontes' emotions, disgust coursing through his body, his mind bent downwards like a head in vomiting, but the passage is not itself disgusting. Take a stronger instance. Here are five stanzas from Baudelaire's poem "Une Charogne" (a corpse), in which a man reminds a woman how they had once seen a dead body "by the roadside" and then goes on to instruct her that she may expect to look much the same one day.

> Her legs flexed in the air like a courtesan,
>   Burning and sweating venomously,
> Calmly exposed its belly, ironic and wan,
>   Clamorous with foul ecstasy.
>
> The sun bore down upon this rottenness
>   As if to roast it with gold fire,
> And render back to nature her own largesse
>   A hundredfold of her desire.
>
> Heaven observed the vaunting carcass there
>   Blooming with the richness of a flower;
> And that almighty stink which corpses wear
>   Choked you with sleepy power!
>
> The flies swarmed on the putrid vulva, then
>   A black and tumbling rout would seethe
> Of maggots, thick like a torrent in a glen,
>   Over those rags that lived and seemed to breathe.
>
> They darted down and rose up like a wave
>   Or buzzed impetuously as before;
> One would have thought the corpse was held a slave
>   To living by the life it bore![51]

William H. Gass links this poetic description to "Hamlet's little speech to Yorick's skull" and to Rilke's reflections upon his mother's genitalia, and to one of his own short stories, "In The Heart of The Heart of The Country."[52] The point is evident: disgusting events, things too ghastly to contemplate easily, can be represented with delicacy, even beauty, far from a visceral affect such as disgust. And when disgust is not, or no longer, visceral, what is it?

I want now to return to one of my examples in the first chapter. *Hamlet* is a play that is almost extravagantly rich in literary examples, as illustrative of Shakespeare's narrative techniques as of his dramatic genius.[53] As a fictional world, it is full of paradoxes and crossed paths. Furthermore, the world of *Hamlet* is drenched by all manner of filth. It represents, in Maynard Mack's phrase, a "dirty-minded world of murder, incest, lust, adultery" and is full of images of disease (physical and mental), decay, rot and dissolution.[54] There are several images of poison, supporting the more general pattern of disease, and many of moral dissolution. Laertes refers to the "sickness in my heart," while Gertrude seems convinced that Hamlet's problem is his diseased wit. Even the people of Denmark are said to be "thick and unwholesome in their thoughts."[55] In this context, the "fat weed that roots itself in ease on Lethe wharf" demands an even more complex reading than I first gave. The phrase shames Hamlet, although only in the conditional mood, but it does so by linking him to his father's fate: death, the afterlife journey for which a wharf is not a bad image, the journey into the "undiscovered country from whose bourne / No traveller returns," rot, decay, bodily transformation and forgetfulness, or rather perhaps the condition of having been forgotten, and the profound sense that there are horrors, things truly nefandous, that cannot be spoken, cannot be known in life. What does a weed feed upon, there rooting itself lazily on Lethe wharf, in order to grow fat? Imagine the bodies of the dead, or better, imagine their spilling life, like a cornucopia for vermin, worms and weeds. The shameful weed, or the conditionally shamed son, feeds upon the transformed body of the father. The father's body, penetrated by the "leprous distillment" which curded, "like eager droppings into milk," his "wholesome blood," becomes barked about, "most lazar-like," with a "vile and loathsome crust" covering all his "smooth body." The transformations of the human body, the father's, Polonius' ("a certain convocation of politic worms are e'en at it"), Yorick's, Ophelia's, eventually the son's, constitute one of the play's paracursive motifs. Not the only one, not even the most important perhaps, but one with tentacles that twist outwards through the text, blighting every other consideration, every image. What happens to the person, bodily and spiritually, in death? How can a living person become a weed upon the dead? How does life feed upon death? How does a person, Hamlet, say, come to appear "like life in excrement" as Gertrude ambiguously observes when her son's hair seems to move at the sight of his father?

Hamlet's fictional world is a continuous representation of filth, but it might be difficult to see this. Too much else is happening, including Shakespeare's dazzling language and his sense of tragic form. If you were to ask a group of readers or viewers to discuss the ugliness, the filth, the "dirty-minded world" of *Hamlet*, you might be disappointed. They might prefer to remember only the beauty of the words, the power of the action, the stunning complexity of characterization. When I remember *Hamlet*, I recall most clearly the web of questions, the piling of questions upon questions, even the repetition of the key word "question." *Hamlet*, to cite Maynard Mack once again, is "a play in the interrogative mood."[56] The nearly five hundred questions, the many complex questions where a single interrogation mark governs a series of questions, all create an interrogative web, a web of blinding diversity and variance. *Hamlet* is a dramatic action written largely in the hermeneutic code, in Roland Barthes' phrase, the code of enigmas.[57] I remember Shakespeare's intellectual energy, not his images of filth. But these are also present and must be understood to see his energies. *Hamlet* concerns ugliness, filth of many kinds, but it is not itself ugly.

The representation of filth is not filth. Put so simply, that assertion sounds weak, almost anemic. I have put the proposition so baldly because I want to make my central point reiteratively. Reiteration is often disgusting, even a kind of horror, as anyone knows who has watched the mechanical unfolding of gothic conventions in horror films, but it is a double horror: at once, the appalling experience of flatness and level extension across a murk-shrouded wasteland and, as well, the unsettling experience of fecundity. Borges once created a fictional world, known as Uqbar, in which religious leaders have prohibited both mirrors and copulation on the grounds that the multiplication of human persons is abominable. What is a disgusting abomination in Uqbar is not one outside the fiction that has made it possible. That brings me, circuitously but with deliberation, to the allusion in this book's title: the Hydra.

The Hydra is the monster whom Herakles kills during his second Labour. She lives in the swamps at Lerna in Argos and is noteworthy for having numerous heads. Accounts vary, occasionally giving the Hydra as many as fifty heads (and corresponding necks), but I shall assume, for the purposes of this discussion, a simpler version that gives her only nine heads and necks. Some accounts say that one of the heads is made of gold and is immortal, but that, too, is irrelevant for my purposes. Like other fictional monsters, the Hydra can be made to symbolize many things, only a few of which are relevant to this argument. She recalls, in quite complex ways, many other monsters.[58] Later in this chapter and again in Chapter 6, I shall briefly compare her to Spenser's indeterminate monster, the Blatant Beast. But first I want to meet the Hydra from a distance, and coming from a sharp angle. Imagine the island of Lemnos sometime during the Trojan War. The only person living on it is a hero who possesses a wonderful bow and many deadly arrows. The bow never misses and the arrows always kill. The hero's name is Philoctetes. Why does he live alone on an island killing birds to eat when there is a war going on? What has become of his heroism? The answer is strange. Philoctetes has been abandoned at the start of the war by his heroic comrades. He has been abandoned because he bears a wound that will not heal and which stinks so disgustingly that his comrades cannot stand to smell it. On his way to offer sacrifice, Philoctetes was bitten on his foot by a snake. The wound would not heal, festered, period-ically throbbed, burst with dark blood and, above all, stank. The stench was so appalling that Agamemnon and the other heroes felt compelled to leave him behind. Much later, the Greeks learned that Philoctetes' wonderful bow, the bow that never misses, would be necessary for the conquest of Troy and so they sent Odysseus and Neoptolemos, Achilles' son, back to Lemnos to bring Philoctetes and his bow, by whatever means, back to Troy.

Neoptolemos is also known as Pyrrhus and, in *Hamlet*, Shakespeare imag-ines Pyrrhus, now victorious, storming the inner rooms of Troy, "Roasted with wrath and fire, / And thus o'er-sized with coagulate gore, / With eyes like carbuncles, the hellish Pyrrhus / Old grandsire Priam seeks."[59] However, in Sophocles' play, Neoptolemos, although dedicated to the destruction of Troy, is a hero's son capable of feeling compassion. He feels it for Philoctetes and even worries if he is doing right in deceiving the wounded hero. Everything about Philoctetes' wound is disgusting: in Sophocles' version of the story, Neoptolemos, approaching the cave where Philoctetes lives, lets out a cry of disgust when he sees rags, "stiff with matter ... pus," that have been left out to dry.[60] Later, Philoctetes falls writhing upon the ground, in the throes of agony from his wound, and the blood pours out. Now this is all of the story of Philoctetes that I need, but there is much more. There is a dialectic of shame and disgust, and a powerful transfer of disgust affects when Neoptolemos eventually feels self-disgust at having deceived Philoctetes, but all that I need for my argument is the image of the snake-bitten wound, stinking disgustingly, that will not heal.

What does Philoctetes have to do with the Hydra? On one level, the connection is simple. Philoctetes received his wonderful bow from Herakles as a gift for having been willing to light the pyre on Mount Oeta that would burn Herakles and allow him to ascend among the gods (although perhaps only as a doorkeeper). The arrows that come with the bow are inevitably deadly because Herakles dipped them in the Hydra's blood after he killed her. On another level, the connection is more complex. The Hydra's blood is venomous and her breath stinks. In his fight with her, Herakles has to keep his nostrils squeezed closed, fighting constantly without breathing, in order to endure her proximity. She is a monster of fecundity and her heads doubly regrow each time that Herakles lops one off.[61] (His nephew Iolaus finally sears each neck with a burning torch, cauterizing the wound, before the fresh heads can grow.) When I imagine Herakles fighting the Hydra, I suppose that he carried a *harpe*, the curved short sword that Perseus also uses, which would have been an ideal weapon for lopping heads.[62] After he kills her, Herakles dips his arrows in her venomous blood, but with deadly consequences for himself. When he kills Nessus, the centaur, with one of the arrows, Nessus duplicitously advises Herakles' wife to keep some of his blood as a love potion. When Deianira rubs Nessus' blood into a shirt, she kills Herakles. And it is at this point, writhing in the agony of the Hydra's poisoned blood, that Herakles needs a comrade to light the pyre that will bring him a quick death and a metamorphosis into godhood. Hence, looking again at Philoctetes, it is possible to see a connection between his disgusting wound and the disgusting blood that so very indirectly causes the wound. The snake that bites him on the foot on his way to offer sacrifice also recalls the Hydra's serpentine necks. Furthermore, the Hydra is the daughter of Echidna, a sea-snake who was herself the daughter of Poseidon and Medusa. At the time when she conceived Echidna, Medusa was still beautiful; she was transformed into her mythic ugliness by Athena only afterwards as a punishment for having copulated with Poseidon in one of Athena's temples. Still, it is difficult to ignore the continuity in descent from Medusa, with her head of snake-hairs, to Echidna, to Hydra to the snake that bites Philoctetes.

On this level of connection, Philoctetes is linked to the Hydra by guilt and retribution. His wound gives off a disgusting stench to remind others that, if not strictly *because*, his mentor, Herakles, killed the Hydra. Justice and fairness are not, of course, an issue: only connection counts. However, if the Hydra's blood flows somehow in the veins of the snake that bites

Philoctetes, then so must Medusa's. And that, I think, is precisely the point. Disgust in literature is often highly symbolic; no longer visceral, it takes on the resinous, clotted flesh of metaphor. In literature, disgust embodies many other textual functions that would be utterly alien to any in-the-world disgusting object or act. Thus no writer actually represents (or could represent) the stench of Philoctetes' wound, but a close reader should see that it is also the Hydra's stinking foulness. It is easier to imagine the connection than the actual stench. Here is the sequence of connections: Herakles' heir, Philoctetes, his companion and his comrade, the man who lit his pyre and to whom he has given Apollo's bow, is bitten by a snake. The bite first makes the intended sacrifice impossible; second, it prevents Philoctetes from reaching Troy and thus prevents him from realizing his heroic destiny; third, it causes him to live as an outcast, the "eyesore of the gods"; fourth, it makes him, in his festering, suppurating, stinking wound-edness, an object of disgust; and fifth, it makes him feel shame, actually to live in shame, in the consciousness of shame.[63]

Philoctetes has been feminized. He has been given a wound that, through an act of symbolic displacement, represents female menstruation. He has been feminized (by the gods perhaps, or merely by the female connection that runs from Medusa to the snake) so that he must seem repugnant in his male comrades' eyes. Male revulsion at the female reproductive system, and in particular menstruation, is widespread throughout human culture. This revulsion, which is often fear as well, takes the form of pollution and contamination taboos, prohibitions and restrictions such as cultural rules that might forbid a menstruating woman the privilege of cooking for her husband or of poking the fire. These taboos vary immensely, as Mary Douglas observes, "from place to place."[64] Traditional peoples often believe that men who inadvertently touch or otherwise physically contact a menstruating woman will experience enervation or actual sickness.[65] In western society, menstrual taboos are informal and usually amount to little more in public than warnings about flushing sanitary napkins down toilets. However, women normally maintain secrecy about their menstrual practices either because they think that they should or because they fear aversive reactions from men.

> Oh! menstruating woman, thou'rt a fiend
> From whom all nature should be closely screened.[66]

In Doris Lessing's *The Golden Notebook*, Anna Wulf begins one of the most important days in her life by concealing her tampons under a handkerchief in her handbag.[67] The most overt operation of implicit taboos regarding menstruation, and perhaps explaining Anna Wulf's self-imposed furtiveness, lies in male commentary, in the form of misogynistic jokes and putdowns. Disgust and loathing expressed in the form of jokes constitutes a fundamental dimension of racial, sexual and gender hatred. A misogynistic discourse supplies the ready materials (an archive of stereotypes and clichés) for the creation of small fictional worlds in which women will act as freaks, monsters or death-dealers. Although it would be possible to cite many examples from popular (male) humour, it should be sufficient merely to recall the passage in William Faulkner's *Light in August* in which the adolescent Joe Christmas beats a black girl who has been supplying sex to a group of white youths, then kills a sheep to wash himself in the mystery of its blood.[68] Shortly afterwards, another adolescent, speaking from the depths of male ignorance, explains menstruation as "something that happens to them once a month." The narrator observes that

> he drew a picture, physical, actual, to be discerned by the sense of smell and even of sight. It moved them: the temporary and abject helplessness of that which tantalized and frustrated desire; the smooth and superior shape in which volition dwelled doomed to be at stated and inescapable intervals, victims of periodical filth.[69]

The male imagination seems always to have been fertile in dysphemistic re-imaginings of the female body and its reproductive cycles. Philoctetes' fate merely reshapes that imagination on the level of myth.

Commenting upon Kristeva's coupling of excrement and menstrual blood, Elizabeth Grosz observes that menstruation "marks womanhood" as outside itself, a "paradoxical entity, on the very border between infancy and adulthood, nature and culture, subject and object, rational being and irrational animal." She continues,

> the representation of female sexuality as an uncontainable flow, as seepage associated with what is unclean, coupled with the idea of female sexuality as a vessel, a container, a home empty or lacking in itself but fillable from the outside, has enabled men to associate women with infection, with disease,

with the idea of festering putrefaction, no longer contained simply in female genitals but at any or all points of the female body.[70]

Philoctetes bears the Hydra's curse.

That connection has had a long life in literature. Stench is one attribute of monsterhood and often clogs the nose, while choking the throat, of readers who choose to enter the fictional worlds of horror. The usual concomitant of decay and physical corruption, stench signifies both the body's natural leakage and its final collapse into death-rot. I do not know whether Shakespeare was thinking of these connections when he created the character of Pyrrhus, but it is the "whiff" of his sword, the "whiff and wind," that knocks Priam to the ground. I am more confident that Spenser knew the tale and incorporates some of the Hydra's attributes into his characterization of the Blatant Beast. That monster also stinks, carrying gobbets of rotting flesh between its many teeth, and, above all, it inflicts wounds that do not heal, wounds that last far beyond the instant of biting. Fictional monsters leave a definite spoor. One property of this spoor is likely to be a disgusting stench.

Now think of the Hydra once more. Imagine all those necks writhing, like Herakles in his death agony or like Philoctetes in the throes of his wound. Her necks twist and contort. Her mouths are certainly open, trying to bite, their teeth as yellow as turpentine, blood leaking outwards over her loveless, reptilian lips. And the mouths also emit a stench, their disgusting breath. As Herakles severs a head, two new ones grow, erupting quickly from the bleeding neck wound like a bursting boil. Seen this way, from the hero's perspective, the Hydra resembles a subaqueous forest, each stalk of which is a tumescent enemy, loathsome and frightening. However, seen from above, from the "meta" view (the literary view with its panning and panoramic shots), the Hydra resembles a knot of snakes. She is like her grandmother, Medusa, writhing in turmoil, appalling to behold. Imagine a labyrinth of snakes. The paths open and shut, deceptively, dangerously, with molluscan finality. Frozen in motion for an instant, the Hydra resembles an aerial view of a mandala. It is that precartographic view that I evoked at the beginning of my first chapter with reference to Sartre's novel *Nausea*: the mandala map of paths, of ways that twist outwards from centre to circumference, from text to scholarly account. The Hydra offers me an image of my subject, but also of my method. She represents the hidden connections, the secret pathways, by which literary texts are linked.

Furthermore, she represents a model of how the attentive reader might read: in hyperplayful exploration of the paths that branch outwards from the text.

I have stalked the Hydra long enough. I shall return to her, and to her grandmother, Medusa, but for now that path can twist shut. As a mythological beast, making many appearances in literature and leaving many literary children (such as Spenser's Blatant Beast), the Hydra shows, perhaps even more clearly than Bloom's morning bowel movement, how textual connections are made. Little in Philoctetes' persistent and stinking wound corresponds to the way wounds behave in the actual world. However, the wound does tell us much about how the significance of corporeal features, such as infected cuts or poison blood, is determined in literature. Philoctetes has a textual wound, rather as Bloom enjoys a textual peristalsis, that can be largely accounted for in terms of its symbolic associations. If I had to make my distinction between an actual object or act and its representation hang upon a single argument, it would be just this: *disgusting representations are surrounded by, and embedded within, a nexus of associations, either symbolic or analogic, all of which can be discovered even if they are not immediately evident.* You can ask different questions about disgust in literature and art than you can about actual disgusting things, although many questions overlap.

I have reached the point where I must confront the central problem of this chapter, the representation of disgust, on an even more fundamental level. What does it mean to eat shit? How does the representation of coprophagy differ from the in-the-world act?

Coprophagy certainly exists in the world. Despite William Ian Miller's confident assertion that it is limited to the insane, it clearly exists far more widely than that. For one thing, it very much forms a part of shock and performance art. It is important to insist that not all coprophagy is sexual: some is performative, some penal, some culinary. Acts of public defecation, even including coprophagy, do occur in shock theatre. In those circumstances, it constitutes a statement, a calculated provocation against straight society or a public affirmation of the distance the audience (and the performer) have travelled from the acknowledged sources of repression in their families or social conditioning. Insofar as coprophagy is penal it may occur as a technique in torture, in hazing or as simple bullying in schoolyards or back alleys. Immersing victims in tubs of excrement has always been a method of torture. In Latin America it is known as the *pileta* (the little basin or baptismal font) and was a standard method of punishment under General Pinochet's regime.[71] In the *Inferno*, Dante imagines flatterers and seducers to be languishing eternally in a huge pool of human excrement. As a kind of food, excrement is relatively common. Lewin, in his discussion of refecation among certain animals, observes that excrement is unnecessary to the diet of human beings and is normally deprecated.[72] No doubt that is true, but it is the exceptions that matter. Many peoples in the world eat excrement, either as a dietary addition or even as a delicacy. If you like to eat tripe, animal intestines, but do not wash them first, then you will have eaten excrement. (Unless you believe in a kind of magic by which excrement becomes what it is only upon being passed through the colon and exuded from the body, but remains food until then.) Roasted caribou tripe may well taste wonderful, but it is a coprophagous dish. People have often been forced to eat excrement, theirs or another's, as an act of punishment or retribution, a bullying humiliation inflicted by a stronger person upon a weaker.[73] In that sense, eating excrement is rather like being spat or urinated upon as an upshot of aggression and violence.

Sexual coprophagy strikes many people as peculiarly disgusting, even people who might, though carelessness or a sense of culinary adventure, occasionally eat uncleaned tripe. It is seldom if ever the dominant practice in a community. When it is practised, it must be a solitary pleasure or, at most, an act shared between a very few people of similar tastes. Taken as a sexual perversion, coprophagy could have several explanations, more or less complex. It might be taken as showing a "bad" nature, a natural disposition to veer away from the good. It could be seen as a desire to punish one's self, to construct humiliation, in the manner of masochism generally because of some traumatic and repressed experience. And it could be seen as a consequence of anal fixation, a failure in toilet training or the residue of childhood desires to enjoy excretory stinks and play with one of the body's creative toys. Freud refers to the "coprophilic pleasure in smelling which has disappeared owing to repression." He analyses foot fetishism as a substitute for excrement play. "It is only dirty and evil-smelling feet," he writes, "that become sexual objects."[74] Remember that de Sade's toe-jam-sucking libertines always prefer the dirtiest feet possible:

> "Pray remove your shoes," says he. Louise, who had been explicitly enjoined to wear the same stockings and slippers for a month, offers the Marquis a foot that would have made a man of less fine discrimination puke straight off; but, as I say, that foot's very filth and nauseous quality was precisely what our

nobleman cherished most. He catches it up, kisses with fervour, with his mouth he spreads each toe, one after the other, with his tongue he gathers from each space, and gathers with incomparable enthusiasm, the blackish and fetid scum that Nature deposits there ...[75]

However, as Freud also writes, the foot "represents a woman's penis, the absence of which is deeply felt." Thus, following an analysis that is best seen in his case study of "Little Hans," the desire to swallow excrement, displacing the intermediate desire to incorporate a foot into oneself, manifests an inner need to reassure oneself that the penis can grow back or, perhaps, be rediscovered. In that analysis, coprophagy would be driven by castration fears.

I cite Freud only to show that there are many actual-world accounts of eating excrement. Most, perhaps all, stress psychic needs that are either uncommon or experienced with uncommon intensity. Thinking back to the five models that I discussed in the second chapter, it is possible to say that coprophagy is disgusting because first, it undercuts the power of a human community to conduct its affairs in a sensitive and positive manner, without having been desensitized or morally diminished by unsavoury, probably unhygienic practices; second, it violates established cultural norms and constitutes a practice for which there is no public encouragement, but for which there may be very public sanctions; third, it regresses, in Freud's words, to the pleasure that was once taken in "abandoned" erogenous zones and is unhealthy, in a psychological sense, because it stands in the way of adult maturity which is adaptation (which is also repression); and fourth, it is aberrant behaviour, falling outside of a number of possible categories, and will be perceived as slimy or sticky in the sense that it will be difficult to categorize.[76] The slimewards tendencies of the human psyche are nowhere more vividly seen, one might claim, than in the desire to eat excrement. The fifth model might suggest a more positive use for coprophagy. The scatological representation of eating excrement has an obvious place in Menippean satire. The actual in-the-world act of eating excrement might play a role in deliberate cultural transgression. It is much more difficult, though not impossible, to understand how coprophagy might serve a program of personal development and transcendence. Since nothing more elicits the stern prohibitions of human repression, it is at least possible to imagine excrement-eating as a violent step out from under the iron nets of repression.

As I indicated at the end of the second chapter, I think that the Sartre-Douglas model, though incomplete, does an adequate job of accounting for disgust. Slime suggests, profoundly, the world's shakiness and transience. Imagine once more a loved one's skull dissolving to mush in your hands, or that person's blood turning into thick, verminous sludge about your fingers. At such moments it would be as if the world had lost its coherence and stability. It would be as if chaos had come again. Being forced to eat excrement, or even to watch it consumed, might test your capacity to believe in your own existence, or the world's. This hardly means that coprophagy cannot exist or that it has no socio-cultural uses.

As excrement itself is the metamorphosis of food, the sifted-out and discarded *excreta* of the body, so excrement-eating might seem like the metamorphosis of other human capacities: memory, sexual appetite, adventurousness, transgressiveness. One admires the hero struggling against the stench-oozing Hydra. Why not admire him or her transgressing, even overcoming, cultural constraints upon pleasure? The answer to "why not?" seems present in the Sartre-Douglas model. Coprophagy strikes most people as aberrant, slime-like and revolting because it is impossible to find a positive category for it (leaving aside cultural practices of punishment, retribution, medicine and cuisine), other than pure transgressiveness. It seems to exist for no *good* reason. It does not exceed the Dionysian (since nothing can do that), but it may show the possible limits to transgression. A life lived "without measure" might have to draw back from some few things, admitting a touch of Ariel into Caliban's realm. Even as an aspect of shock performance, enacted from within an alternative or avant-garde subculture, it is almost too extreme, and certainly too self-hurtful, to work. The most minimal norms of hygiene will always be against it.77

In literature and film, coprophagy may exist for excellent reasons. It can serve quite a few very reasonable textual purposes. The fictional world may require it. It may be consistent with characterization—not all characters in literature are likeable nor are meant to be so—or with the fictional context. What kind of thing or experience is a fictional world that it could require, and make acceptable, an act such as coprography?78 What would a fictional world in which filth dominates be like? Imagine a world without sunlight, a claustral world of darkness and decay through which all manner of filth falls like a drizzling rain. Nothing much good happens there, other than the human mind itself for "there is nothing either good or bad, but thinking makes it so." If you can imagine such a world, then you can also imagine the world of *Hamlet*. And, as I have already claimed, a great deal happens in that world of filth that is not filth. Throughout the action, there is an upward curving line that rises above the conditions of its world. Filth and dreck can be transcended. And it may be that often their chief purpose in literature is, precisely, to be transcended.

In both literature and film, disgust motifs are used in significantly different ways in the creation of horror- and terror-worlds. For example, in a horror tale, a face will show, as a kind of displaced symbolism, the anticipated monster. Slime-coated teeth, narrow needle teeth, cat's eyes, rotting corpses, deliquescent heaps of malodorous putridity, all point, as anticipatory evidence, towards something else, something Other. This kind of sequence is what Stephen King has in mind when he refers to the "clockwork" of a horror tale and its qualities of a dance, a "moving, rhythmic search."[79] Horror's dominant affects are anxiety and dread (the "creeps," in King's phrase). However, in a terror tale, the face gives nothing away. The exterior is calm and placid. There are no traces, no symbols to read, no anticipatory evidence of dissolution and collapse. A terror-world is one that calls out for investigation. Conspiracies belong to it much as festivities and carnival belong to certain comic worlds. Paranoia will be, with terror itself, its principal affect. Unlike horror, terror is seldom intimate. It is a question of events happening abruptly, of events falling upon one without warning or bursting into the present from somewhere unknown. Terror is secretive and hidden. It is unexpected. Terror, Salman Rushdie observes, "is a reverse form of intervention."[80] It is the opposite of massive police formations or army groups storming ashore, storming buildings, storming lairs. Terror is always an abrupt action proceeding from a system, an organization, a cell, that has objectives and has elected to accomplish these through sudden violence. It is as abrupt, say, as the beginning of Rushdie's *The Satanic Verses* in which two men fall from a plane over the coast of England after it has been destroyed by a terrorist bomb.

Rushdie's novel plays off terrorist actions against the experience of state control and "dictation." The novel begins with an abrupt terrorist act, the bombing of an Air India plane over the English Channel. The two main characters, Gibreel and Saladin, fall to earth singing Indian pop songs. It is a sudden and surprising opening, at once terrorist and surrealist (calling to mind the intimate historical connection between revolutionary and avant-garde movements), leading into the novel's key metaphor of involuntary metamorphosis. Behind that abrupt beginning there is a terrorist action. The *Bostan*, flight AI–420, has been commandeered by Sikh terrorists who hold it on a remote oasis for more than a hundred days. The passengers regard the terrorists with the "obsessive attention paid to a cobra" and exist unhappily in terror (not in horror), waiting for the unreasonable system that has trapped them to explode in fury. Rushdie gives the terrorists a profound sense of purpose and dedication. When the terrorists appear to lose heart, their leader, Tavleen, stands before the passengers, "like a stewardess demonstrating safety procedures," and lifts up

> the loose black djellabah that was her only garment and stood before them naked, so that they could all see the arsenal of her body, the grenades like extra breasts nestling in her cleavage, the gelignite taped around her thighs .... Then she slipped her robe back on and spoke in a faint oceanic voice. "When a great idea comes into the world, a great cause, certain crucial questions are asked of it," she murmured. "History asks us: what manner of cause are we? Are we uncompromising, absolute, strong or will we show ourselves to be timeservers, who compromise, trim and yield?" Her body had provided the answer.[81]

The tight dance between the state and the terror that constitutes resistance has here the choreography of a ballet. And it is entirely literary. The episode, though gripping and wonderfully evocative, has little to do with actual smashed metal, eviscerated guts and charred flesh.

Terror is as sudden as the death of Rajiv Gandhi, foreseen only in the terrorist's last-minute smile or in the "speeding balls of deadly light" at the instant of death.[82] Terror is the violence of calm surfaces that unexpectedly erupt. Thought of as a problem in human faces, terror requires a face that gives nothing away. Only the mind behind the face, not the face itself, is evil. Writing of contemporary terrorism, the kind of terrorism that has selected Rushdie for transnational execution, Cynthia Ozick writes that the terrorism of "our time" is "stone-deaf to reason."[83] Whereas horror is often irrational, terror is rational, being always a question of plans, strategies and conspiracies.[84] It may even be excessively rational, but it is deaf, stone-deaf, to any competing claims for rationality.[85]

A terror-world has something to do with the aesthetic creation of shock. It has more development, and plot will play a significant role. It is as arti-factual as shock and its effects are calculated, not to kill people nor to force states into capitulation, but only to cause certain definite feelings in its readers or viewers. In a terror-world coprophagy could be important, either as torture or as punishment. Its very eccentricity might serve to highlight the arbitrariness of the fictional world itself. A description of a character eating excrement is likely to burst upon the reader, at once unexpected and undesired, like an explosion. For the purposes of my argument, I have been imagining the experience of a terror-world from the perspective of the characters, not primarily that of a reader. However, it is simple enough to think as a reader. Then the shock of abrupt and loathsome actions falls upon you directly, not vicariously as in your imagining of a character's experience.

Consider the following description of excrement-eating from a modern terror novel. The novel is *Gravity's Rainbow*. It is a novel that allows its readers some access to the controlling systems, but not a complete access. In the end, a reader will see only that there are many overlapping and interlocking systems and that these are, in some sense, equivalent to the real-world systems of late, or third-phase, capitalism: that mode of multinational capitalism that, Jameson argues and Pynchon shows, possesses interconnections so dense, so complicated, that they can only be imaged in the architecture of a computer chip.[86] The characters within Pynchon's novel understand more or less of the international controlling systems, but usually they understand very little. I call *Gravity's Rainbow* a terror novel (although it is many other things besides) because it concerns systems, the power of unknown masters of systems to intrude upon the lives of people, corrupting and destroying them. In *Gravity's Rainbow*, systems fit into other systems, subsumed into higher and higher organizations of control. These overlapping systems of control constitute synecdoches for the modern Terror State. *Gravity's Rainbow* is a novel about the powers of "Them" and how easily, and secretly, "They" control whoever is within their systems. It is a novel about godgames, but it is also about terror. The coprophagy occurs suddenly in the novel between the beautiful Dutch double-agent, Katje, and the British spy master, Brigadier Pudding:

> ... he glances quickly over at the bottles on the table, the plates, soiled with juices of meat, Hollandaise, bits of gristle and bone ... Her shadow covers his face and upper torso, her leather boots creak softly as thigh and abdominal muscles move, and then in a rush she begins to piss. He opens his mouth to catch the stream, choking, trying to keep swallowing, feeling warm urine dribble out the corners of his mouth and down his neck and shoulders, submerged in the hissing storm. When she's done he licks the last few drops from his lips. More cling, golden clear, to the glossy hairs of her quim. Her face, looming

between her bare breasts, is smooth as steel ... Now her intestines whine softly, and she feels shit begin to slide down and out. He kneels with his arms up holding the rich cape. A dark turd appears out the crevice, out of the absolute darkness between her white buttocks. He spreads his knees, awkwardly, until he can feel the leather of her boots. He leans forward to surround the hot turd with his lips, sucking on it tenderly, licking along its lower side.[87]

Nothing in *Gravity's Rainbow* has anticipated this act and it does not anticipate anything else. It bursts upon the narrative. It is one of many powerfully evocative moments in the novel. The episode of excrement-eating, as well as the containing narrative and the putative fictional world, is, in Brian Edwards' words, "radically decentering."[88] Norms, standards, even expectations, are brutally thrust off-centre by this act of coprophagy. When the act is over, its shock passed, it leaves an after-image, a faint glow like foxfire. Thereafter the Freudian monomyth seems to hang over the narrative, flickering like the foxfire light of decay and putrescence. The reader will hardly forget that civilization, the technology of the Rocket-state, the City Dactylic, mounts upon the repressed human body.[89] It is not shallowly theatrical in the manner of *The 120 Days of Sodom* on the paracinematic mental stage of which one character will gobble another's excrement without implications. In de Sade's work, the arrangements that bring two people together in coprophagous acts are complicated, involving procuresses and pimps, and reflect the economic power of a self-absorbed aristocracy, but they are also mechanical. In Pynchon, the libido has been bound by vast, though secretive, internalized systems of external control.

In *Gravity's Rainbow* every image, implicit with significance, connects with multiple other images. Brigadier Pudding, veteran, military hero and now intelligence officer, eats excrement because it reminds him of death on the battlefield, of war, of Passchendaele. He smells death, "mixed with the mud, and the putrefaction of corpses," in Katje's excrement, and she reminds him of the spirit of death, Domina Nocturna, whom he first met on the battlefields of the Great War. The associations are dense and impacted. In *The Great War and Modern Memory*, Paul Fussell calls Brigadier Pudding's coprophagy the paradigm of the wasteland: guilt, humiliation, excrement, sterility all combine in the "style of classic English pornographic fiction of the grossly masochistic type, the only style, Pynchon implies, adequate to memories of the Great War." It was a war characterized in memory by stench: of trenches stinking of excrement, of human decay and of death-rot. A character in John Fowles' novel *The Magus* remembers the Great War as stench: "mephitic stench."[90] The scene of excrement-eating is, Fussell writes, a "fantastic scene" that is at once "disgusting, ennobling, and touching."[91] It is a shocking and fantastic scene, but it is not merely (or simply) disgusting. A vast corpus of associations spans the scene. Furthermore, neither Katje nor Brigadier Pudding are free agents in this act of coprophagy. Their liaison has been arranged by Pointsman, the Pavlovian psychologist who masterminds the unconventional programs of English psychological warfare (although that national limitation falsifies his role). The Dutch double-agent and the English spy master are both playing roles (Pudding's beneath the level of consciousness) in a godgame whose master is an expert in human conditioning. The coprophagy is one instance among many in which systems overlap in an intricate godgame, the ultimate *magister ludi* of which is, simply, "Them."

When an image of disgust comes into one's perception, the mind begins to fit it into a fictional world, a whole of which the motif must be taken as an exemplary part. For example, each member of the selection committee that will reject the young man with the spider-tattoo on his forehead, whom I introduced in the parable in Chapter 1, begins to imagine a fictional world, not quite the actual world in which they all exist, that the young man will dominate with his vile acts. His presence will inject an element of degradation, of sleaze and corruption, slime into the university. (Someone reading the parable might easily think that the members of the committee, in their smug priggishness and inability to take risks, are morally disgusting. Who would want to teach in such an environment, among such colleagues? The parable discovers a small, unpleasant fictional world.) However, it is not merely such overtly transgressive acts as wearing a tattoo on public skin that work in this manner. The far more disgusting act of excrement-eating in *Gravity's Rainbow* indicates a world of blunt shocks and grossly repugnant deeds. Its shocks will emerge abruptly from a systematic mechanism, the godgame-like conceptual systems of the novel's world, that cannot be known but can be guessed, inferred from narrative hints. By contrast, the disgust motifs in a fictional horror-world build incrementally towards an anticipated monster or monstrous event whose presence will be sensed almost from one's first entrance into the world. In each of the cases I have examined in this chapter—Bloom on his cuckstool, Philoctetes and the Hydra, Brigadier Pudding eating Katje's excrement—the disgusting act, a representation of what might happen in the actual world, has possessed vast, complex connections with other textual events and characters. In art and literature, disgust functions quite differently from in-the-world disgust. It embeds itself in the imagination on a distinct symbolic order.

Finally, I want to return to the tale with which I began this chapter. The idea of a golden shower, let alone the image, would be enough to disgust many people. It would certainly have turned my mother's stomach. I knew even as I was engaged in the act that I had crossed a definite moral boundary. I wished that I had not crossed it and it nearly, but not quite, caused me to vomit. It was a powerful moment, full of psychological consequences, that I have never forgotten. Now suppose that I have received a commission to compose a new ballet. Remembering my encounter with Georgie, I decide to write a ballet called *L'Averse dorée*. Modeling my music on Delibes, I may even decide to call it *La Douce averse dorée*, allowing for plenty of tinkle and splatter. More likely, since this will be a postmodern ballet, I will simply quote Delibes and the body of the music, splintered and dismembered like a tortured human body, will be highly dissonant in order to represent the cognitive dissonance of the ballet's hero. I will work into the music an hallucinatory motif, a "falling glissando of disgust."[92] My commission will permit me to hire the world's best dancers and I will open my new ballet in Washington at the Kennedy Center or in Sydney at the Opera House. Imagine the enthusiasm in the audience. Great music (my own), magnificent choreography, the finest ballerina in the North America dancing the role of Georgie, and a splendid stage, all at the service of my imagination. Critics will call the ballet audacious or even bold. It will be a triumph. No one will confuse my representation of a golden shower with any actual event that might have taken place once or ever. If the word "disgust" arises at all, it will be with respect to the spiritual transcendence inherent in the performance. A critic writing in *The New Yorker* will refer to Bataille, quote from Patrick White's *Voss* or from *The Twyborn Affair*, and observe that the way down has so often, in literature and art, proved to be the way up. No one will assert that either my ballet or myself has been disgusting. Everyone will have understood that *La Douce averse dorée* has been an aesthetic experience, a work of art, and not an actual golden shower.

My solution to the problem of disgust's radical metamorphicity should begin to appear. I am arguing first, that disgust can be simulated, both in actual life and in literature as representation; it can be imitated on the face (as contempt or personal theatre) and it can be transformed, as representation, into high art; second, that the boundaries that locate disgusting objects and acts, that constitute "dirt out of place," can be crossed repeatedly, both learned and unlearned; third, that disgust engages the imagination to envision small, often quite minimal, fictional worlds ("disgust-worlds" in which loathsomeness dominates); and finally, that the operations of disgust, though open to analysis from several directions and to several kinds of disciplinary taxonomy, cannot be fully accounted for without the reference to the experience of art, and in particular literature. This experience is radically distinct from in-the-world disgust, in the sense that the affects it generates are different and the questions that you need to ask will be unlike those you would ask about non-textual disgust; but it also focusses the experience of the world. A brilliant image, in whatever aesthetic mode, will be like strong light that highlights features otherwise hard to see. For example, Menippean discourse, always as intellectual as it is vulgar, with its reliance upon the "lower bodily strata," brings the world into a clear perspective: all hypocrisy, whether trumpery or woserism, exposed.

The theory that disgust is a conditioned response that takes place in the imagination, a reaction to the perception of slime or to the potential for slime, the slimewards degeneration of things, also accounts for the ubiquity of disgust as a moral judgement.[93] The word *slime* constitutes an instance of the larger problem of disgust. It describes the ambiguous, indeterminate state of experiences that are common in human life. It can become a category for delivering moral verdicts. Even though it massively shunts the word into the dimension of conceptual and metaphoric experience, moral disgust must be possible. Some philosophers actually claim to observe it and seem to believe in it. Slime can also describe a logical state of categories, much as terms like "inclusive" and "exclusive" or "clear" and "fuzzy" do. In a very real sense, slime is located beyond an individual's personal experience within the realm of a culture's systems. Slime, both moral and logical, can be easily borrowed from one cultural domain into another. However, what the world seems to show most unmistakably is a shifting, manifold nest of experiences in which all manner of things can be disgusting, but no single thing is always so or always so for the same reasons. Slime is only an instance, and not a very comprehensive one at that, of disgust's metamorphicity. It would highlight and partially focus the experience of a golden shower, but it would not exhaust it. It might frame Georgie, in both life and art, but it would not explain her. Looked at in terms of the hypothetical experiences of literature, no theoretical model quite grasps firmly the slippery problem of disgust. None succeeds in showing the violence of the disgust some people might feel for other people engaged in golden showers, nor why some people can enjoy such experiences nor why many others, though feeling revulsion for the in-the-world act, might applaud it as an aesthetic representation.[94]

A golden shower would be dirt out of place and, even more powerfully, dirt injected into a place, the site of love, where (given the romantic, religious and even legal sanctions of western morality, at once labyrinthine and hypocritical) it would not seem to belong. It would make love itself slimy, a deliquescent puddle of what previously had been ideals. My ballet, *La Douce averse dorée*, will be received warmly only because it will have transformed the disgusting act into aesthetic form. It will discover a new place for the repulsive golden shower, recuperating it on a high order of experience. The critic who will praise it in *The New Yorker* will surely cite Willie Pringle's words in *Voss*: "The blowfly on its bed of offal is but a variation of the rainbow. Common forms are continually breaking into brilliant shapes. If we will explore them."[95] That seems to be what art is so fundamentally about. Georgie exists more fully as a character than as an actual flesh-and-bone woman. She always has. ✽

4

Its Body

Parts and Machines

For several years, between my late teens and my early twenties, I rode motorcycles. I made a number of long trips, through mountains and along sea coasts, often to extremely beautiful places, but my clearest memories return to ugly moments. What I always recall most precisely is a brief moment when I badly hurt myself. My next clearest memory evokes a moment when I nearly killed myself.

In the first instance, my bike, a 750-cc Triumph, spun out of control and hurled me, catapult-like, into a front yard. I tore the ligaments of my left knee, an injury that his remained with me through the years. Today a gimpy knee is my most tangible souvenir of my motorcycle adventures, just as the moment of the accident is, in memory, their most vivid experience. When it happened, the pain was intense. It felt as if a searing knife's-blade had slit through my knee. It was rather like a tooth-ache, deep inside, inaccessible other than as feeling, but more intense than an abscess, more real than any imaginable pleasure. All the usual clichés for describing pain—acute, hot, piercing, raw, searing, sharp—would have worked in that moment, but none of them would have been adequate. I recovered consciousness, under-standing immediately that I had severely hurt myself, picking myself up from the yard in which I had landed even as a woman, in a miracle of serendipitous presence, came out of her house offering me a cup of tea. A young man in a military sailor's uniform seemed prepared to give me first aid. I distinctly remember his dark-blue uniform with white trim and a thin row of campaign badges across his left pectoral. The woman who brought me tea was wearing a simple off-white frock with a pink floral pattern. The lawn had been freshly cut and as I came back to consciousness my nose flooded with the smell of mown grass.

I got to my feet, my knee feeling weak and floppy, pain gnawing it like fire or lime, righted my bike and rode to the hospital. Every time I had to use my leg, depressing the brake pedal or steadying the bike at stop-lights, the intense pain returned. When I parked the bike and walked into the emergency room, the pain was like hot tongs gripping the bone.

The time when I nearly killed myself occurred riding down the Wasatch mountains into Salt Lake City. It was after midnight and I had lost my lights. They had simply snapped off when I had hit a bump. "Hail! Lucas, Prince of Darkness," I had murmured to myself. That mock invocation, a self-deprecatory witticism known to all riders of English motorcycles at that time, underscored the utter unreliability of the manufacturer of magneto-based lighting systems. Instead of stopping and waiting out the night under a tree, I nestled the bike into the wake of a Greyhound bus, using its lights to find my way. This stupid, bonehead stratagem actually worked for about thirty miles. Then the bus abruptly disappeared around a curve, leaving me in total blackness at a speed not far under a hundred miles an hour. (Since I couldn't see the speedometer, I never knew how fast I had been going.) I followed the direction of the bus into invisibility and then, drawing upon a power of intuition that I didn't know I possessed, I saw that the blackness immediately in front of me seemed darker than that to my right. I turned, leaning hard into the curve as if I could see it, knowing that if this move was a mistake I would hurtle off into the night air two or three thousand feet above the bottom. And then I leant deeply back to my left, once more intuitively following the corkscrew road I could not see. I did survive that night ride, finally making my way into Salt Lake City by riding on the shoulder using an ordinary flashlight for illumination. I recall that experience largely in terms of the surging fear I felt. It was not essentially the fear of death that frightened me, though that was certainly present, but the particular fear of being hurt in excruciatingly terrible ways. Even as I shot blindly around the invisible curve, I could imagine my bones breaking, my face being smashed and ripped apart, my eyes gouged out or peeled and sliced open like juice-filled grapes, my ribs cracked and sticking out through my split and ruptured sternum or else driven backwards into my wetly bubbling lungs. I felt the bones in my legs break and, degloved from their flesh under the pressure of falling against rock, actually explode into splinters like eggshells struck by a hammer. Vividly, in the night's nearly total darkness, I saw myself as a paraplegic, my legs either dismembered or paralyzed. Even as I was leaning my bike into absolute darkness, I watched myself play a role in an unscripted mental theatre. It was my instinctive fear of pain, not death, that evoked this theatre and later etched the experience into my memory. I saw myself ripped apart, broken and dismembered. Today, some forty years later, I can fully recall the strips of asphalt across the pavement, the faint scattering of stars above a high cloud cover, the flickering shapes of pine trees. The feathery, drooping pine branches would break into light fifty or so feet in front and then fade rapidly into darkness as the bus passed and I approached. I can also recall the contents of the mental scene that I played at that moment, re-imagining my terrible imagination.

Pain enhances memory. Nothing remains as clearly present, nor so readily evocable, as an experience that has been accompanied by intense pain. There is a paradox hidden in this assertion. Pain also dulls the imagination. It cuts the body off from communication, blocking narrative. "What happened?" is hardly a good question to someone who has been hurt. The answer, if there is one at all, likely will be blurred. Words will be dropped, sounds slushed and sentence structure deformed. Elaine Scarry argues that physical pain "does not simply resist language but actively destroys it, bringing about an immediate reversion to a state anterior to language, to the sounds and cries a human being makes before language is learned." The attempt to "de-objectify" pain, as may occur in therapy or during treatment for survivors of torture and trauma, is not easy, Scarry thinks, but always a "project laden with practical and ethical consequences."[1] Yet, pain is also, as Nietzsche observes, a powerful mnemotechnic. Evoked long after the event, a remembered pain can function as a powerful searchlight. In the case of my little adventure in the Wasatch mountains, the anticipation of pain prompted my imagination and has made acute the memory of both the event and of how my imagination worked.

The theory of fictional worlds explains a great deal about the power of disgust to capture the imagination. Dismemberment and death both engage the imagination in small fictional scenarios, at once disturbing and brief. The image of the human body slipping towards dissolution, verging on deliquescence and corpse-rot, constitutes one of the imagination's reference points. The obsession with death, the pervasive necrophilia, both in horror fiction and in actual-world phenomena such as murder and execution, throughout North American culture shows the ability of the idea of death, not only nor necessarily your own, to bore deep into the mind and to engage imaginative reconstructions. There is something about another person's violent dissolution that fascinates the mind's eye. This may reflect a universal human empathy with other people who are experiencing inevitable finality or, perhaps equally, it may reflect the hidden sense of triumph (which cynics always suspect) at someone else's misfortune. The crowds that gather outside prisons in the United States when an execution occurs indicate that the contemplation of another's painful death can take place without commiseration or even rudimentary sympathy. Issues of justice, retribution and revenge are certainly involved when condemned criminals are executed, but the passion of the prison crowds, the intensity of their enthusiasm, shows that more than juridical distance is at work.

What in the spectacle of death engages the imagination? I want to argue two points about the contemplation of death. First, a fictional world is created when another person dies in a way in which it is possible for the spectator both to imagine the dying person's situation and also to imagine an alternative scenario in which he or she undergoes the same experience. That is, the fictional worlds of death engage others both as observers and as participants. Second, as a bodily experience, death is a dissolution (the traditional metaphor) that has two distinct paths. It may be a straightforward decomposition in which body parts break down and lose their functions, sliding the body sludgewards more or less swiftly; or else it may be a progressive (swift or gradual) transformation.[2] In the latter case, death is a metamorphosis in which the body changes from one state into a series of different states, each subsequent one evoking a further degree of loathsomeness. You could imagine the sequence like a morphed image in a horror film: the smooth face begins to distend, the lips curl back and the incisors lengthen and sharpen into points, hair sprouts all over, growing long and tangled, while the eyes sink back into their bulging sockets and may even gleam, like foxfire, with the phosphorescence of decay.

Projected from the individual imagination, decomposition and metamorphosis play important roles in literature and film. Horror fiction, for example, is largely about what happens to human bodies under the stress of extraordinary forces. Much traditional horror fiction concerns the breaking down of the body into parts or the removal and recombination of parts. Mary Shelly's *Frankenstein* and H.G. Wells' *The Island of Dr. Moreau* both hinge upon the separability of body parts from an original organism and their potential to be re-used, even re-integrated, in novel combinations to create a new organism. Tobe Hooper's 1974 film *The Texas Chainsaw Massacre* (probably inspired by the actual-world murders of Ed Gein, a Wisconsin serial killer) embodies a mild version of the loathsomeness of the body's decomposition into parts.[3] What was the Russian serial killer Andrei Chikatilo thinking about when he dismembered his victims, cutting out their hearts and stomachs, chopping off fingers, noses and genitals and then eating them? He seems to have been giving himself the imaginary experience of actually having performed "a real sex act."[4] On the other hand, metamorphosis also evokes disgust and horror. The dissolution of things that Sartre discusses and places at the centre of the imagination's activity, the slipping motion from one condition to another, lies at the heart of much horror fiction. It is the basis for the abominations around which vampire stories unfold. Even more obviously, but less interestingly, metamorphosis is the governing principle of all werewolf stories. "The human identity and the wolf identity," Noël Carroll writes, "are not fused, but, so to speak, sequenced."[5] It must be imagined as a sequence in which minute changes occur rapidly to produce an effect that horrifies partly because of what now appears (a wolfman, a vampire's fangs) and partly because of what has been lost, a human form and identity. By contrast, Ovid's notion of human change in the *Metamorphoses* entails a systematic potential for transformation built by divine law into the fabric of existence. The gods regulate life (an individual metamorphosis manifests the agency of the gods and is done either for punishment or for reward) and determine the body's fate. It is this regulatory perspective on change that has dominated western writers, such as Spenser, who have written within Ovid's long shadow. However, the metamorphoses of horror fiction reflect a natural, a more purely Sartrean, sense of change. It is only the inevitable, entropic pattern of substances to lose their shape and definiteness. Horror fiction and film merely speed up the process. Imagine a time-lapse montage of a dead body: the loss of shape through bloating, the slippage of visible features, the collapse of form, the appearance of vermin, the transformation into sludge, and (perhaps) the eventual scraps of desiccated and rotted flesh clinging to bleached bone.[6] *That* seems close to the essence of contemporary horror fiction.

When you consider the cheering crowds outside an American prison at the time of an execution, you can suppose that their imaginations have been engaged by the mental image of pain and helplessness in the hands of implacable force and by the captivating image of human metamorphosis.[7] The body writhes in a grotesque parody of death throes or else grows preternaturally rigid (in electrocution), changes colour, froths, leaks and stinks. An executed body would certainly seem to be disgusting, and it can be experienced as horrifying. Because of the condemned person's crime and the legal distancing that coldly positions his or her fate, it may be that an execution is easier to imagine, easier to reconstruct as a vicarious experience, than would be a friend or loved one's death. Perhaps for many people it is even fun. The paracursive necrophilia that runs through North American culture shows, I think, that fictional worldhood—the ability to imagine an alternative existence both as an observer and as a participant— is very much a function of in-the-world situations, not only of literary texts and films. Executions pose a complex problem in audience response in which the imagination is engaged and clearly plays out private scenarios. There are two sides to this problem. There are, indeed, the crowds that contribute a ghoulish, or perhaps sadistic, dimension to many American executions, but even more significantly there are many people, perhaps millions, who would like to watch executions if they were available on TV. The difference between the two groups is quantitative, not qualitative. Consider the first person who was ever electrocuted.

William Kemmler was executed at Auburn Prison in the state of New York in a comfortable lying-down position. The execution had been preceded by a great deal of public controversy. Americans wanted a clean, modern (that is, "scientific") way of killing criminals, something better than hanging with its notoriously unpredictable results (ranging from slow strangulation to decapitation), something up-to-date and appropriate for a new civilization. Recent developments in electricity had suggested a means that would be quick, clean and humane. Five years before Kemmler's death, New York had established a commission to explore "electrical alternatives" to hanging.[8] Experiments had been conducted with animals as small as chickens and as large as horses. In Albany, at the request of the commission, the man conducting the experiments, Harold Brown, electrocuted an orangutan. In what should have been a premonition of the future, the animal's hair caught fire. Electrocuted people have always literally burned. The metaphors for electrocution, "burning" and "frying," have a hard, empirical basis. (Opponents of electrocution like to claim that the condemned person is actually cooked.[9] The body temperature rises sharply, the internal organs fail, the hair burns, swirls of smoke mount from the scalp, and the execution room fills with a pungent stench.) Kemmler's body showed purple mottling on the face, neck, arms and hands. The electrode on his head had burnt into his scalp.[10] The autopsy reports indicated that Kemmler had been cooked, several regions of skin, muscles and brain carbonized.[11] Electrocution had proved itself to be, like all other forms of execution, messy, squalid and disgusting.

The reports of Kemmler's death indicate that no one had foreseen that an execution by an "electrical alternative" would be, in its way, as disturbing as any other kind. In its extensive coverage of the execution, the *New York Times* observed that Kemmler had died under "the most revolting circumstances" and called the execution "so terrible that the word fails to convey the idea."[12] Not only were there procedural hitches (Kemmler did not die at once and, the warden having had to restart the dynamo, a second electrical surge had to be administered) but the rigidity of the body was horrifying. Kemmler wore a leather cap rather like the football helmets worn in the 1890s, from under which the witness could observe a "slimy ooze" that drooped from his mouth and "ran slowly down the beard and onto the gray vest."[13] Only gushing blood, which was an ordinary concomitant of beheadings and judicial torture, and a not-infrequent consequence of hanging, was missing. In its place was the stench of burning flesh and hair. For the future, there would be the possibility that the eyes might melt and that fat might boil through the skin to drip from the ends of the dying person's rigidly extended fingers. Instead of the hanged person's "writhings," there would be the unnaturally rigid body, jolting forward and straining against the straps with each fresh surge, its fingers pointing stiffly at the audience. And, unavoidably, there would be the additional stench of the dying person's bowels opening, the reflexive defecation and urination. Executions, even clean ones, stink.

It may seem strange that the first execution "team" gathered to kill a man by electricity (among the twenty-six witnesses, there were eleven doctors present) did not grasp that killing a human body is never "clean," never actually humane. (A proposition that is not the same as claiming that no executions are worse than others, more brutal, cruel and *in*humane.) The men who gathered together on August 6, 1890 were true Victorians. They believed in science and human progress. They believed in the experimental method and in a progressive course of experimentation leading inevitably to improved technologies. When they considered Kemmler, they must have remembered that experiments had been carried out over a period of five years. They believed they were advancing humanity's cause. Pictures from that moment indicate a number of gentlemen in frock coats, looking serious and grave, like so many scientists and technicians supervising an experiment. They show Kemmler wearing the helmet, reclining on something rather like a beach chair, his hands crossed contemplatively over his stomach, and his feet (still with shoes) resting upon an adjustable trestle. He appears to be waiting quietly for the experiment to begin. Reports say that he chatted amicably, discussing the experiment's methodology, with his humane executioners. He was said to have "kept up his pluck in a wonderful way."[14] No doubt, all the participants in the experiment, other than Kemmler himself, were startled, even perplexed, to find themselves disgusted.

Who would want to see an execution? Could there be pleasure in seeing another human person being caused pain, his or her body distorted, convulsed, writhing or rigid as bone, perhaps (as in lethal gassing) turning purple or red, the hair and flesh burning, the eyeballs popping out upon the dying person's cheeks or else melting? The fingernails dropping off? The blood gushing "from every orifice"?[15] Once an execution by electrocution has been completed, the sheer messiness of the procedure becomes more evident. Fred A. Leuchter, a manufacturer of execution equipment, observes that the

> execution team's job of unstrapping the dead man from the chair is often repugnant, as they have to tug and push at the body. There is always suppuration from the third-degree burns on the head and leg, and in some cases the "cooked" flesh comes away from the body when touched.[16]

Would anyone actually wish to see this human suffering or, more dreadful even, the condemned person's anticipation of suffering, the hysterical supplications and fruitless cries for help, the spectacle of the person being dragged roughly towards death? (William Kemmler proved to be the rare, though certainly not unknown, kind of person who shows no fear and behaves cooperatively in every detail.) The answers to these questions seem to be: plenty, evidently and yes.

Public executions have usually been good entertainment. Crowds gather and hucksters sell sweets and drinks. There is good humour and gaiety. Elizabethan and Jacobean executions, often as ingenious as they were brutal (employing several forms of death to kill a single person), extended the crowd's pleasure by forcing the condemned to walk from Newgate to

Tyburn, often two men shackled together by the ankles hobbling along in the "Newgate walk." On November 13, 1849, Charles Dickens sat all night at a window to observe the double hanging of Frederick and Marie Manning in the morning. He was struck by the "atrocious bearing, looks and language of the assembled spectators":

> When I came upon the scene at midnight the shrillness of the cries and howls that were raised from time to time, denoting they came from a concourse of boys and girls already assembled in the best places, made my blood run cold. As the night went on screeching, laughing, and the yelling in strong chorus of the parodies of negro melodies with the substitution of Mrs. Manning for Susannah were added to these .... Fighting, faintings, whistlings, imitations of Punch, brutal jokes, tumultuous demonstrations of indecent delight when swooning women were dragged out of the crowd by the police with their dresses disordered, gave a new zest to the general entertainment.[17]

The last public execution in the US was a hanging in Indiana in 1936. Old newsreels show a man completely covered by a knee-reaching white death shroud with two eyeholes cut raggedly in it so that he might see the event. He stands on a raised platform beneath a gallows with a noose slung around his neck. He is entirely surrounded by a human sea. Then a large, swag-bellied man in suit and vest, looking at a pocket watch, makes a quick gesture and the condemned man is given what seems to be a "short drop" and the crowd breaks into cheers, waving their hats in celebration. Turn to any point in history and it will be the case that some people like to watch other people being killed. There seems, sadly, to be nothing special in this desire. The human condition embraces brutal entertainment.[18]

Today, executions (in the US: no other western country imposes capital punishment) are carried out in privacy, away from crowds and public jubilation, before a small audience of officials, reporters and the victim's relatives. Who in a western country would even want to watch an execution? The answer is still the same: plenty. When an execution takes place in the US, crowds assemble outside the prison. A few people will stand vigil in silent protest against state murder and the barbarism of the entire procedure. A much larger group will gather to whoop and yell slogans, often religious in tone, to celebrate the condemned person's imminent death. When Ted

Bundy was electrocuted in Florida, the crowd shouted "Burn, Bundy, burn" and generally behaved as a carnival mob might. When the hearse carrying Bundy's corpse left the prison, the mob broke into wild cheers. A photograph in the *New York Times* shows a young man outside San Quentin prison on the night that Robert Alton Harris was executed by cyanide gas.[19] He stands next to a placard with an inscription from Exodus 21:24 urging an eye for an eye, a life for a life. His face is twisted into a shouting grimace and his right hand is raised as if cheering a team on to victory. Of course, one may only speculate as to what goes on in the minds of people who stand all night in front of a prison to cheer an event that they cannot see. Leaving aside the pervasive "religious right" in American society and the dominating redneck ideology, either of which would lead some people to believe that the state has an obligation to seek retribution and thus to take some pleasure in seeing the state fulfil its duty, it seems reasonable to suppose that they imagine themselves into the death chamber among the select group of invited witnesses. What you cannot see, you can pleasurably imagine. Small fictional worlds in which a human body undergoes radical transmutation are being staged. On cold nights outside American prisons, the mind's eye dilates with the scene of death's metamorphoses.

In the spring of 1991, the San Francisco PBS television station KQED brought a suit against the warden of San Quentin prison, Daniel Vasquez. KQED sought to compel Vasquez to admit TV cameras during the execution of Robert Alton Harris. The trial lasted for more than two months, during which time many strange, half-baked, ill-thought-through and, above all, sentimental and sanctimonious arguments were heard. The moral argument that watching an execution, especially on TV, would corrupt and diminish the personality of the viewer was central. Wendy Lesser's 1993 inquiry into murder, *Pictures at an Execution*, turns pivotally upon the KQED suit. Lesser frames it as the problem of "sleaze." Wouldn't it be disgustingly sleazy to watch, even to want to watch, an execution? Ultimately, Judge Robert Schnacke found in favour of the warden and San Quentin prison.[20] Of that trial, Lesser writes,

> It set our concerns about individual dignity and privacy, even for an individual who had been convicted of murder, against the public's right to know. It posited spectacle versus procedure, excess versus restraint, bloodthirsty revenge versus bureaucratic enforcement of justice, sleaze versus highmindedness. It mixed up everything from bad taste to moral depravity,

from empathetic concern to sentimental illusion, from fear and disgust to curiosity and hilarity; and it did so in a way that had no easy answers.[21]

A great number of issues were involved, but largely they came down to the "right to know" on the one hand and the importance of decorum and decency on the other. The lawyers for KQED argued from assertions that Chief Justice Burger of the US Supreme Court had made in 1980, in *Richmond Newspapers Inc. v. Commonwealth of Virginia*, that the "crucial prophylactic aspects of the administration of justice cannot function in the dark; no community catharsis can occur if justice is 'done in a corner [or] in any covert manner'."[22] Needless to say, nothing in Burger's statement leads to a conclusion that would force open executions to the public or to the TV networks. California law requires, as do the laws of other American states, that witnesses be present: "they are there not just to ensure that the deed is actually done, and without excessive harshness, but to represent and embody the wider public in whose name the execution is being carried out."[23] (They are not asked to imagine the scene, only to see it, but as the reported comments from witnesses of the Kemmler execution, and many subsequent ones, show, they do, indeed, imagine.) In *KQED v. Vasquez*, the state primarily argued the overriding importance of security. A TV camera-person, it was said, might disturb the procedure or even provide an opportunity for the condemned man to grab a weapon. Seeing an execution on TV, it was even claimed, "might cause riot and retribution" both inside and outside the prison.[24] Beneath that specious argument, there lurked, more significantly, the questions of taste, decorum and decency—that is, the disgusting properties of an execution were implicitly acknowledged. Although he spoke of the presence of cameras as posing a security risk, Vasquez seems to have been more concerned that "they were tactless—in short, because they represented an extreme of bad taste."[25] Invoking the larger issue of public attitudes towards disgusting phenomena, this is clearly a valid point and ought to run loudly through American culture— but it doesn't.

The ethical argument, for or against public executions, slides inexorably into "an aesthetic and phenomenological argument."[26] An execution is a methodical step-by-step process, with many possibilities for delay (fewer for acceleration) and intervention. Lesser quotes Robert Alton Harris, reflecting on his impending execution, that "[t]his is something well planned, well thought out."[27] It is much more like ritual sacrifice than theatre, although theatrical elements (not least of which are the theatre-like execution chamber, master of ceremonies, cast and audience) invariably surround the act. The ritualized elements in an execution must once have had the purpose, as Michel Foucault makes plain, of impressing upon a large public audience the solemnity of the occasion and the majesty of the monarch.[28] Execution resembles both a game (in which play, although highly complex, is biassed against the condemned person) and a machine. The latter metaphor reveals what must be most appalling about human execution (and what might be the most disturbing element in watching one performed): first, the implacable and inexorable process, from which compassion and mercy have been deleted; second, the transformation that it works upon all the human agents, other than the condemned person, making them distant, indifferent machine parts, like transistors or cogs; and third, the near-total depersonalization of the condemned person.[29]

Lesser identifies two ethical problems that quickly slip into the aesthetic category. First, she suggests that the desire to witness an execution must be similar to the desire to see murder committed (though she also argues that the actual experiences are different) in that there is inevitably a "killer inside us." If everyone is capable of murder, then everyone is able to contemplate the act of killing from both sides, in identification with both the victim and the killer. (The hypothesis that it is possible to find pleasure in the imagination, and in imagining acts and worlds that cannot be seen, takes added strength from this proposition since it allows for the possibility of imagining both, or all, sides of any act, however appalling or degrading.) It is possible to "identify with" both wretched victim and the brutal, merciless killer, although, she observes, this is never entirely "predictable."[30] Writing of the film version of Thomas Harris' novel *The Silence of the Lambs*, Lesser remarks that it

> plays on our fears of people like Hannibal Lecter, but it also plays on our even deeper sympathies with them; and the movie so revels in Hannibal's increasingly theatrical antics that poor Jame [the primary serial killer in the story] becomes almost a sideshow, his crimes reduced to providing the necessary but rather perfunctory denouement.[31]

Lesser does not suppose that the capacity to feel "even deeper sympathies" for characters like Hannibal Lecter is exclusively male. Writing of Harris' earlier novel, *Red Dragon*, and Michael Mann's 1986 film *Manhunter* that was

made from it, she observes that "we are all, men and women, asked to identify with the strangely appealing though strikingly repellent killer."
Reading, she observes, "brings things in through the eyes, and words enable
us to create sickening mental pictures."[32] Other critics commenting on *The
Silence of the Lambs* have not taken such a gender-neutral stance. Suzette
Henke, for instance, thinks that an interest in the film (and by extension,
the novel) must be a male-specific perversity: "Aesthetic revulsion may,
indeed, offer contemporary society a powerful form of psychosexual
catharsis. But how many of us actually feel moved to gestures of apocalyptic
laughter in the face of Hannibal Lecter?"[33] Only male viewers and readers, it
would appear. However, Lesser thinks that reading books, like viewing
films, engages the imagination in ways that are neither distinctively male
nor female, including the creation of pleasure from "feeling the anxiety of
guilt, especially when it is someone else's guilt and can be sloughed off at
will."[34] It would be a "moral disease or an aesthetic affectation" to confuse
victim and killer, but the human imagination seems able to play both sides
of the field.[35] Horror is "always partly personal."[36] In an execution, the
drama, and hence the possibilities for imaginative play, is extraordinarily
scrambled: the killer has become a victim without ceasing to be a killer
while the executioners are killers enlisted on the side of the murdered
victim, at once killers and surrogate victims. In that tangle, there are many
opportunities for the imagination. Those carnivalians roaring and
yahooing outside a prison on execution night may well imagine themselves
into the execution chamber, but they do so in multiplex ways.

Second, watching an execution would entail what Lesser calls the "sleaze
factor." Plenty of people might like to witness an execution (as they always
have), but what would it do to them? Would they be able to watch, as
Turgenev did when invited to witness an execution by guillotine of the notorious murderer, Tropmann, in Paris, with "a steadiness infused with all the
flinchings of a decent moral disgust?"[37] It might turn out to be shoddy
public policy, in a culture already torn by excessive violence, to promote TV
executions. Moral philosophers, such as John Kekes, claim that watching
degrading events must, by a kind of contagion, degrade the witness. The self
will be lessened, the mind coarsened, as if a constricting, shrinking force
were to grip the person, forcing the head downwards, diminishing his or her
moral scope. Kekes' argument, as I insisted in Chapter 2, flies in the face of
the diversity of human cultural practices and totally ignores the common
ability to relearn disgust and to acquire (at least) the discipline of managing
affects. It does, however, point to experiences that many people claim to have

had. The first contact with an execution can be sickening, perhaps dimin-ishing. (Soldiers detailed unwillingly to firing squads often vomit after-wards. The execution "teams" at American prisons are always volunteers.) Dickens felt sickened at having witnessed the execution of the Mannings, but he also felt that the crowd itself was degraded, diminished caricatures of human people. Lesser observes that "the whole course of the *KQED v. Vasquez* case, both within and outside the courtroom," was coloured by the question of motive.[38] What kind of TV station would want to broadcast an execution? Who would watch? If "plenty," what will that tell us about the state of American society? What about reruns? Wouldn't there eventually have to be (a question Lesser does not raise) anthologies, popular magazine shows, in which different executions were gathered together?[39]

The moral claim is that watching an execution on TV would constitute sleaze: it would diminish the viewer and society as a whole. But is this the case? This dimension of the argument rubs against the grain of the previous proposition that the human imagination is versatile, capable of multiplex investments. Discussing Mailer's 1979 novelistic account of Gary Gilmore's life and execution, *The Executioner's Song*, Lesser observes that it is

> the spectators, not the participants, who convert an execution
> into a sporting event, and their interest is not so much in the
> competition as in the final results. Theirs is the spectatorship
> not of football but of foxhunting or bullfighting or (to recall
> Mailer's presidential recommendation) gladiatorial games.[40]

Yet the case has already been made that such "spectatorship" is grounded on the capacity to imagine grim mental scenarios and to do so on both sides of the killer/victim, life/death chasm.[41] Why would it be sleazy to watch Robert Alton Harris being killed, but not a condemned person from Nigeria? Lesser's reply would partly (at least) call upon the powers of narra-tive to provide context. However, this does not fully answer the question. It seems only to say that the execution of someone you know, or know about, would be harder to bear, since it would have narrative context, than the execution of someone you do not know. Sleaze would cling to the observer if the condemned person is known, has context or can be imagined in human perspective. It is a strange, elitist argument. The argument from sleaze—degradation, diminishment, lessening—seems more appropriate for someone, such as a moral philosopher, who can grant the imagination neither its plasticity nor its scope. An execution would be squalid, but it does not follow that watching it would be sleazy.[42]

Deaths by electrocution or by cyanide gas seem like especially vivid examples of bodily metamorphosis. The horrific fascination of the human body's swift transformation, the multiple small changes occurring rapidly as if in time-lapse photography, prompts scenes that the imagination can grasp greedily. On the other hand, decomposition occupies a large, varied spectrum. The lopping of the human body into pieces certainly does have a role as a method of execution and juridical torture in many cultures (and historically in many more).43 Robert G. Ingersoll, addressing the New York State Bar Association in 1890, a few months before William Kemmler was electrocuted, summed up the history of torture as a record of pain and degradation inflicted by the powerful on the powerless:

> They were broken on the wheel—their joints dislocated on the rack. They were suspended by their legs and arms, while immense weights were placed upon their breasts. Their flesh was burned and torn with hot irons. They were roasted at slow fires. They were buried alive—given to wild beasts—molten lead was poured in their ears—their eyelids were cut off and the wretches placed with their faces toward the sun—others were securely bound, so that they could move neither hand nor foot, and over their stomachs were placed inverted bowls; under these bowls rats were confined; on top of the bowls were heaped coals of fire, so that the rats in their efforts to escape would gnaw into the bowels of the victims. They were staked out on the sands of the sea, to be drowned by the slowly rising tide—and every means by which human nature can be overcome slowly, painfully and terribly, was conceived and carried into execution.44

No doubt, the human body undergoing radical decomposition, whether in surgery or in execution, can be imagined with much the same gusto that analogous scenes of metamorphosis in American death chambers evoke. Visions of torture have always been popularly engrossing (this is an aspect of the contemporary fascination with the Nazi experience) and reoccur in literature from (say) Webster's *The Duchess of Malfi*, in gothic novels, in *fin-de-siècle* decadence and in recent novels depicting the acts of serial killers. "Torture in fact," David B. Morris writes, "is a highly developed, if obscene, contemporary art."45

I want now to consider a different dimension of the body-into-parts dissolution. There is an intimate, and evolving, connection between the human body and machines. The generic "machine" can be an "impersonal artifact for generating and multiplying force" in torture, producing and intensifying pain; yet it can also be a potentially beneficent tool to supplement the human body.[46] Increasingly, it has become possible to supplement the body with prosthetic parts. In these cases, a more or less complex machine is appended to the body and functions as an original body part. In this sense, the process of decomposition proceeds by means of replacement and supplementation. A body part will be lost, or perhaps lopped off because it has become dysfunctional, but it will be replaced by a new part, a small machine, that will do the same bio-physical work. And may even do it better.

Although any single prosthetic part might be called a cyberpart or, perhaps, a "cyber(body)part," the name most commonly used to describe the hybrid form produced by integrating a machine into the human body is "cyborg."[47] The concept of a cyborg focusses the ambivalence concerning body parts and the potential decomposition of the body. The notion of intactness, or of "being intact," pervades much thinking about the human body. The very concept of being intact would seem to locate, always already, any prosthesis within a consciousness of ambivalence. Intactness, as part of the body myth that constructs human thinking about the body, is a function of the process of socialization. That is, the second, or social-constructionist, model which I discussed in Chapter 2 provides the strongest account of why human beings commonly think of themselves as having intact bodies or, sadly and regretfully, as having bodies no longer intact, requiring prosthetic supplementation. The consciousness of being intact, promoted by most orthodox religions, seems like a small but very important part (a mytheme, in effect) of the overall mythology about the body that is learned during socialization. The same consciousness of mythic integrity can also make tattoos and body piercings objects of revulsion or ambivalence. The sheer terror of being invaded by insects, or the personal disgust at urinating upon another person, indicates how strongly, even at an early age, the sense of integrated selfhood is founded. The vivid fear of dismemberment and mutilation reveals how profoundly this sense, even if it is only a fiction, activates the imagination, filling consciousness with scenes of horror. If the self is a "fortified castle" (to use Kristeva's image), it is also one that may be scaled at every point.[48]

A cyber(body)part, although necessary and perhaps wonderful to have, given the mutilated alternative, can cause ambivalence, even an actual sense of loathing and disgust. If it does cause disgust, this would be only a small, personal instance of the feeling of disgust that machines often cause. They arouse disgust for several reasons (their soullessness, their implacability), but primarily because they do not have anything that corresponds to the human sense of an integrated identity, corporeal intactness. Machines are assemblages, and when they are integrated into the body they will always seem to mark a process of disintegration: at once belonging and not belonging.

The initial uses of the term "cyborg" to signify an "artificially extended homeostatic control system functioning unconsciously" reflect an optimistic conviction that technology can, and will, expand merely organic potential.[49] Artificial body parts will serve as obedient and beneficial tools. D.S. Halacy, Jr., whose early study of cyborgs attempts to outline all possible uses and environments, observes that a "hybrid human may well be a forerunner of the men of the future."[50] The optimistic view that prostheses are generally servile and availing carries over into the discussion of hybrid body forms, man plus integrated tool, and cyborgs. Two 1970s TV programs, *The Six Million Dollar Man* and its spin-off *The Bionic Woman*, splendidly capture the eye-bulging, mouth-gaping yearning for cyborgian evolution.[51] Subsequent reflection upon the possibilities of hybrid bodies has opened a rather darker perspective. A cyborg, such as the Bionic Woman, who possesses legs that will enable her to run faster than a car or leap over houses or who has acquired ears that allow her to hear faint sounds at immense distances, might not prove always to be a friend or even a good neighbour. There seems little doubt that there will be, perhaps rather soon, cognitive prostheses, neural implants that will possess countless functions. In his 1999 film *eXisTenZ*, David Cronenberg invents a world in which prosthetic imaginations are possible.[52] When this level of cognitive enhancement has been achieved, the phrase "cognitive dissonance" will acquire an entirely new meaning. There will be unnamed types of schizophrenia afflicting the human mind and as yet unguessed modes of paraphilia. Recent science-fiction stresses the dark side, the undecidables and double binds, of cyborgian potential in which modified humanoids, such as the *Star Trek* Borg, pose terrifying threats. It has been doing this for the very best reasons.

The 1980s literary movement cyberpunk shows a further development in the attitude towards cyber(body)parts. It has concentrated on the interface between human beings and machines, but also on the edge aspects of life within technological "systems," the modern, or near-future, techno-states. Although William Gibson's *Neuromancer* is the paradigmatic cyberpunk text, the definition of the movement includes a wide range of body-machine interfaces.[53] For example, cyberpunk fiction largely deals with marginalized people engaged in struggle with some oppressive government, paternalistic corporation or other overriding system (in the manner of Pynchon). These systems will be enhanced by various technologies, in particular information storing and retrieval systems, often including brain implants or other prosthetic supplements and genetically engineered body parts. There is, thus, a strong freedom-fighter, or resistance, aspect to much cyberpunk. It can certainly be explained in terms of developments in science fiction, always responsive to advances in technology, but it is also obvious that Pynchon, especially the dark, future-brooding *Gravity's Rainbow*, shadows over the movement as a whole.

More powerfully yet, a line of analysis has developed in which the "cyborg" provides a metaphor for the discursive codes that program our biological existence. The argument often seems to have a particular focus upon the condition of women in a patriarchal world since (it is claimed) the historical discourse of men encodes the female body. The discourse of man, Gayatri Spivak writes with unmistakable undertones of Roland Barthes, is "the metaphor of woman."[54] That is, women have had to accept men's language but have used it obliquely, as metaphoric code, to express their own distinct experience. However, the actual application of the cyborg analogy encompasses both genders. Both women and men must exist within an inherited, trans-individual discourse. Even if that discourse is identified as male, or as patriarchal, it is nonetheless relentlessly imposed upon single individuals, most of whom will participate in it unthinkingly, but some, uneasily. It is part of the cyberpunk version of reality to see human beings existing within vast systems of control exercised through mega-corporations, through faceless, hypercomplex organizations more or less as Pynchon imagines "Them" in *Gravity's Rainbow* or as Jameson supposes third-phase capitalism to have the unrepresentable multiplexity of a computer chip. From a feminist perspective, the cyborg analogy has been revelatory. Donna Haraway observes, "Language is the effect of articulation, and so are bodies."[55] We are all chimeras, she argues, theorized and fabricated hybrids of machines and organism; in short, we are cyborgs. The cyborg is our ontology; it gives us our politics. The cyborg is a condensed image of both imagination and material reality, the two joined centers structuring any possibility of historical transformation.[56]

If knowledge brings freedom, as so many philosophers have supposed, then knowing how consciousness has been constructed in cyborgian fashion should bring the freedom to revise these constraints. Thus Haraway argues that women, existing within "the integrated circuit" of patriarchal domination, can reconstruct, creating a new cyborg (but not becoming a non-cyborg), their own consciousness. If we "learn how to read these webs of power and social life, we might learn new couplings, new coalitions."[57]

Cyborgs register the strongest position currently available with regard to cyber(body)parts.[58] The prostheses that I have in mind, such as hearts or penile implants, will not transform you into a cyborg, but they will be enough to breathe life into the divided consciousness that machines create. They are "cyber" in the sense that they entail vast but unseen technological systems (of innovation, experimentation, applications, development, production, marketing, medical installation and monitoring) and will, in a limited sense, compose a "cybernetic organism, a hybrid of machine and organism."[59] Still, they will not actually allow you fully to become a cyborg, an integrated being whose technological amplifications will be superior to the biological parts they replace. Your prostheses will only supplement your body with respect to dysfunctional parts, such as an incorrigibly flaccid heart or penis, but not usually exceed their normal optimum performance. (Of course, a prosthetic arm might be stronger or a penile implant more reliably tumescent.) Only on the level of metaphor (which is where Haraway's argument takes place) is it possible to think of yourself as fully a cyborg. Nonetheless, you may still yearn for technological enhancement and yet experience disgust at the alien presence within your body. What is the threat from machines? Why do they inspire such compound affects as, among many others, yearning-disgust?

People do certainly experience disgust in the presence of machines, and they often pretend to do so.[60] Not everyone likes, or can like, machines. Nonetheless, machines exert a double-edged attraction: it is possible both to loathe and to desire a machine (or at least what it may offer). As a literary movement, cyberpunk (rather like art-horror) revels in a "surrealist perspective" that displays the "deformation and destruction, the resurrection and reformation" of human existence.[61] Even if people do not actually experience visceral disgust, they may wish to do so and feel that they should pretend to express it for public scrutiny. Why do machines give rise to disgust? Why *should* they? Many machines, from syringes to nuclear bombs, are destructive, and all machines, however apparently benign, can be used carelessly or inappropriately to create unintended destructive effects. Writers, J.G. Ballard and Thomas Pynchon among them, have been able to imagine the potential of machines, in their most horrifying modalities, to inflict pain, anxiety and death. Ballard's *Crash*, for example, describes a bleak urban techno-landscape in which proliferating automobile crashes, with the concomitant incidence of pain, mutilation, scarring and death, totally dominate the world. It is a de-eroticized landscape in which, paradoxically, the possibilities of eroticism re-emerge from the human carnage of machine violence. The sexual aspects of the human body fit, over and over again, against and into the various parts of automobiles.[62] "The deviant technology of the car-crash," Ballard writes,

> provided the sanction for any perverse act. For the first time, a benevolent psychopathology beckoned towards us, enshrined in the tens of thousands of vehicles moving down the highways, in the giant jetliners lifting over our heads, in the most humble machined structures and commercial laminates.[63]

Crash invests (perhaps explaining its continuing cult status) the alienating urban bleakness with a "vision of transcendent sex and violence."[64]

Ballard's vision of human-machine intercourse, of human persons modified by and into machines is already present in Pynchon's 1961 novel *V*. The novel follows the search for a mysterious woman who seems to prolong herself through time by gradually replacing body parts with prostheses. Late in the novel, the narrator remarks that "V. by this time was a remarkably scattered concept."[65] V.'s transformation is paralleled by other characters who undergo plastic surgery and who have prostheses implanted or appended to their bodies. *V.* is a novel about the desire for, the maintenance of and the consequences of cyber(body)parts. Even Ballard's fascination with the manikins used in simulating automobile accidents shows up as a motif in *V.* SHOCK ("synthetic human object, casualty kinematic's") was a "marvelous manikin."

[I]ts flesh was molded of foam vinyl, its skin vinyl plastisol, its hair a wig, its eyes cosmetic-plastic, its teeth ... the same kind of dentures worn today by 19 per cent of the American population, most of them respectable. Inside were a blood reservoir in the thorax, a blood pump in the midsection and a nickel-cadmium battery power supply in the abdomen. The control panel, at the side of the chest, had toggles and rheostat controls for venous and arterial bleeding, pulse rate, and even respiration rate, when a sucking chest wound was involved. In the latter case plastic lungs provided the necessary suction and bubbling. They were controlled by an air pump in the abdomen, with the motor's cooling vent located in the crotch. An injury of the sexual organs could still be stimulated by an attachable moulage, but then this blocked the cooling vent. SHOCK could not therefore have a sucking chest wound and mutilated sexual organs simultaneously.[66]

Like Ballard, Pynchon traces a complex fable of the mutual human and machine destiny. Both novels exemplify what Jameson calls "schizophrenic fragmentation."[67] Machines are frightening as well as desirable, sources of disgust and loathing but also of yearning and private mythologizing. The gradual transformation into a machine, an actual cyborg, may turn out to be an eventual fact (as so many writers of science-fiction have supposed), but it is already a deeply rooted component of contemporary myth. In fables such as Ballard's and Pynchon's, little seems more evident than the double-sided power of machines to attract and to disgust.

Cyborgs have appeared repeatedly in science-fiction films of the past thirty years.[68] They may be distinguished by the degree of connection and re-integration that their prosthetic parts have achieved. My glasses, for instance, are scarcely connected to my body at all, but a penile implant, if I were to acquire one someday, would be intimately (as it were) a part. In Paul Verhoeven's 1987 *Robocop*, the transformation of the dead, or almost dead, policeman into a cyborg requires the elimination of most of his body other than his face and brain. One executive of the corporation that is manufacturing the cyborg exclaims, when he learns that the doctors have saved one of the policeman's arms, that the objective is "total prosthesis" and orders the arm amputated. (It is never made clear how much body Murphy retains other than his brain, which has been modified by the implantation of a programmable chip. He eats a baby food-like pap that oozes from a machine next to his chair-bed, but a metal shaft driven into the area above his heart does not harm him. He certainly has only prosthetic appendages.) *Robocop* is particularly interesting because it contrasts Murphy, the cyborg cop, to an android. The android is called "Ed 209" (signifying "Enforcement Droid 209") and is squat, ungainly, clumsy and given to malfunctions. It has too many "glitches." (Although quite deadly, it comes across as a *comic* representation of a human being.) Later, the cyborg outwits the android and wins a shoot-out. This plays to the human chauvinism that assumes "we" *are* better than machines and that a good cyborg, simply because it retains elements of a human brain, will out-think, and so outperform, a good android any time.

Three key propositions are relevant to an account of human-machine interactions. First, machines are implacable; they are "soulless" in an old, Cartesian lingo. Second, they are composed of parts, lacking organic integrity, at once depersonalized and depersonalizing. In effect, machines possess the same attributes as do execution teams and the processes, or "protocols," of execution (which create metaphorical machines). Third, propositions one and two suggest that the qualities attributed to machines, causing so much fear, loathing and desire, reside like templates in human consciousness. This is not the same as claiming that the human mind contains an archetype of the machine. Rather, it points to basic anxieties, which can be identified empirically, concerning difference and otherness.[69] Not only are machines threats to human individuation, but they lack that individuation themselves since they appear to be assemblages with operating systems, all of which can be removed, enhanced or replaced. Our collective development towards cyborg status, or any degree of hybrid prosthetic existence, is certain to prove unsettling.

The opposition between a human who can experience many affects, including compassion and mercy, and a machine that feels nothing is very old. Descartes refers to animals as machines because they have, he thinks, no souls. Legends return again and again to the merciless, implacable hunger of animals, wolves for example, or, even more horrifically, of insects.[70] Alfred Hitchcock's 1963 film *The Birds* builds explicitly upon the birds' unswerving, remorseless attack. In the tradition of horror, lacking a soul, such as a golem or a zombie, or the being fashioned from necrotic body parts in the manner of Dr. Frankenstein's creation, means that the creature will be incapable of compassion and will be deaf to your pleas. Machines inspire a similar response. If you find yourself caught in a machine, an assembly line, for example, as Charlie Chaplin's character does in *Modern Times*, experiencing the "irony of a bashed ego who has got caught up in the clockwork,"[71] you will not expect it to stop simply because you cry out that it should. Robots, androids and cyborgs all can create genuine horror effects in part because they can be supposed to behave soullessly and hence act without pity or compassion. The Borg in *Star Trek* or, on a less technologically advanced plane, the Daleks in *Dr. Who* (they retain a humanoid brain inside their machine bodies whereas the Cybermen, in the same BBC series, appear to be entirely android), all evoke horror because they act without human-like feelings.

The second proposition may be even more important. Machines are composed out of parts. They may be assembled, disassembled and reassembled. They are open to modifications or "retoolings." The very idea of being given new parts is only slightly less horrible than the corresponding idea of losing parts. Your right eye might fall out or your genitalia drop off, but, appalling as that would be, contemplating a technological replacement would not be an altogether satisfying compensation and might even constitute another source of horror. A machine both sheds parts and acquires new ones easily. The human perspective seems to insist upon organic integrity as the only desirable norm. Of course, a machine will have integrity, but that will exist only on a cyber level. (It is my computer's operating system that gives it unity and without which it would be, less or more, only a collection of bits. That is, one part functions as a super-set of the others.) It is the hidden system of conceptual rhizomes that constructs integrity for a machine, but that systematic net, invisible to most eyes, is so different from organic integration that it might, once perceived, only create more horror.

The image of a being composed out of parts, any single one of which might be replaced or simply removed, has had an evocative place in horror fiction and film. Pynchon's character, V., may be the most literary hybrid creature, but she is not the best known. Several film cyborgs have undoubtedly reached larger audiences than V. Robocop, having spawned several sequels, is so well known as nearly to stand for the entire category. However, hybrid creatures, or beings who have achieved (or been compelled to accept) nearly "total prosthesis," run through modern horror literature. Furthermore, the perception of organic parts separated from their former being or of inorganic and organic parts linked together to create a bio-machine, seems to cause disgust as well as horror. That puts the problem of human prostheses into focus. Consider the interconnection between parts, whether being composed of or being dissolved into, and disgust.

The disgust that decomposing body parts, separated or rotting, can cause, and which performs so effectively as a convention in horror fiction and film, indicates one dimension of consciousness: the complex awareness of prostheses. The classics of horror fiction fragment the human body or underscore single parts for effect. The "nameless metahuman" in Mary Shelly's *Frankenstein* is composed from distinct cadaverous parts (an aspect of the tale of which much is made in all the film versions).[72] One of the most instructive examples is H.G. Wells' *The Island of Dr. Moreau*, an allegory of vivisection and plastic surgery, in which human shapes (twisted or otherwise not quite right) are surgically constructed by bodily modification of animals and the supplementation of different animal parts. Wells' narrator, Charles Edward Prendick, experiences a "quivering disgust" in the presence of Dr. Moreau's creatures once he begins to grasp the island's secret:

> Imagine yourself surrounded by all the most horrible cripples and maniacs it is possible to conceive, and you may understand a little of my feelings with these grotesque caricatures of humanity about me.[73]

An appended body part not only recalls the previous, now missing, organic part, but actively calls into question the body's integrity. A prosthesis, however hopeful and henceforward-yearning, is also, like pain, a mnemotechnic. It evokes a consciousness of dis-integration (which may be either, or both, historical or fictional). For that reason, a hybrid body poses a disturbing dilemma: would you (or anyone) choose to have yourself enhanced by the addition of superior prosthetic parts when that process, however it begins, must dis-integrate your body, dissolving its boundaries, and batter down the "fortified castle" of your identity?

The experience of a split consciousness is captured in an exemplary fashion in Verhoeven's *Robocop*. The action of *Robocop* is set in a near-future, trash-culture Detroit which has been compared to the Los Angeles world of Ridley Scott's 1982 film *Blade Runner*.[74] Verhoeven's Detroit is not overpopulated, but it is in the hands of criminal gangs that are run by large corporations (invoking the mega-corporations of cyberpunk paranoia). In this Detroit, the police have been privatized by the corporation that supplies arms to the army. It also seems to have direct ties with the underworld. Murphy, heroically outnumbered and outgunned, is murderously shot by a pack of degenerate criminals. However, the arms-supply corporation also has another plan, which involves reconstructing a dead cop into a cyborg. A hint is given that secret plans have been made to transfer good cops to a dangerous precinct so that they will be killed and can then be reconstructed. Murphy is the fall-guy. His new existence as a cyborg begins with blurred vision and coded messages flashed onto a flat screen within his visor. "The screen flickers to life as technicians reconstruct [the dead cop's] body, piecing it together with steel [actually, the film is explicit that the robocop will be made of titanium] and microchips, giving the viewer a brief perspective of a cyborg coming to life."[75] The convention of showing the world through the cyborg's eyes complete with typed designations and commands, although familiar from other films (such as *The Terminator* and *Terminator 2*), entrains what becomes an important subtext in the film: the cyborg has been given a new consciousness, but he struggles to regain his old human self-awareness. Robocop is "part-toy, part macho-metaphor, an instrument of mechanical overkill." Lumbering like "another Golem," he is said to be curiously unappealing: when the whole face is "unmasked, drastically increasing the chances of eradication by even the most ineffectual opposition, the clumsiness of the whole venture, a cobbled assembly of bolts, circuitry and flesh, looks even more bizarre."[76] The subtext, however, which unmasking him from within his cyborgian skull-helmet and visor helps to establish, clearly poses the appealing futurity of the cyborg. With his implanted chip, the robocop has what his makers believe to be a restricted cyborg's consciousness. However, one night, sleeping in his chair-bed (which has been assigned to him as a "home"), he abruptly begins to dream. As his struggle to regain his human memories develops, he begins to recall specific images of his past life. At one point, he even visits the old house where he had once lived with his wife (now moved away) and a son whom he had taught how to twirl a pistol (a trick that, as a cyborg, he still remembers). Accessing the police department's computer files, he identifies himself as the dead cop, Murphy. Subsequently, he begins to ripen a peculiarly human sense of revenge. At the film's conclusion, he is called "Murphy" and responds with a thin smile of pleasure, "Thank you, sir." Among the many cyborg films, none captures so well what would have to be the cyborg's divided consciousness, the sense of being (now) an improved artifact and of having been (then) a fully human person. *Robocop* may be viewed as an allegory of the prosthetic consciousness.

That consciousness is always split. Even a prosthesis as comparatively straightforward as my glasses fills me with doubleness. If someday I were to have a cornea transplant, then I might sense an even more profound split. The eye itself would have become a mnemotechnic to remind me of the dead person whose eyes I now partly bear. If in some future technology, functional prosthetic eyes are possible, then a different, but even more profound split will haunt me. Of course, to refer to a "split" or a "double-ness" in consciousness is to speak metaphorically, characterizing consciousness as a space, an extended area or zone. I do not feel apologetic about my metaphors. The history of western concepts of consciousness has been exclusively a history of metaphorical thinking in which spatial values have been attributed to minds. Whether you think of consciousness as a light (the sun of common Renaissance analogy, whether pre- or post-Copernican, the *lumens naturae* of Cartesian philosophy or the sparkling light bulb of comic strips), a patriarchal helmsman or pilot (a metaphor dear to Renaissance poets and moralists alike), a mirror (or even a mirror-like *tabula rasa*) or, in the postmodern fashion, a nexus (a neural net, a computer web or the "architecture" of a chip), your discourse will invoke spatial metaphors. Freud's analysis of consciousness as a series of distinct functions, moving upwards from id to superego, actually constructs a narrow tower. This tower imperiously summons into use further metaphors of light, reflection, a helmsman (the superego) and a nexus of commands (a censor, a system of repression): it is monumentally spatial in all its nooks, branches and layers.[77] My metaphorical splitting of consciousness neither adds nor subtracts from this long tradition of metaphors. You may pick your favorite metaphor and imagine a further division (a shift in degrees of refractivity, a modulation on the surface of the mirror, two helmsmen—two rudders, at least—or a duplex chain of commands within the nexus) in which it will be possible both to yearn for enhancement and also, remembering what you had once been and your physical need that necessitates this desired supplement, feel disgust at your bodily transformation. Imagined as a place, a nutshell, a room or a tower, consciousness is always already a metaphoric space.

Consciousness serves as a theatre in which the imagination plays out all kinds of scenarios. Some of these are happy, pleasant or pleasure-filled. Some may be green worlds in which idyllic love overcomes all threats and creates happiness for all (or nearly all); some may be ideal worlds in which talent and virtue triumph. The imagination is multi-dimensional and highly flexible. Its limits are difficult to fix other than through tautology (imagination is what can be imagined). However, many of its worlds are nasty places, where horror and terror, loathing and fear dominate. Among the nastier places where the imagination leads are disgust-worlds. These may come into being around any disgusting item, a deliquescent object or morally degraded act, but a great many of them seem to concern what can happen to the human body. The metamorphoses of the body and its decomposition into parts, or even smaller bits, are primary material for the imagination. You can imagine a small fictional world in which the body begins to sink irreversibly towards its inevitable sludge, or one in which the body is cut, lopped, sliced or minced. Following the enticements of your imagination, you will always have two very different trajectories before you. In one, you can imagine, with terror, your own body undergoing painful and humiliating transformations. In the other, you can imagine, with horror, all this happening to another person. When I rode my motorcycle in almost total blackness around mountain curves in Utah, I could clearly imagine a small, terrifying world in which, having survived my plummet, I would be radically changed, body parts both lost and rendered dysfunctional. Today, that world is more clearly present in my memory than the actual one I rode through.

I have examined two exemplary situations, freely granting that the actual inventory of similar situations would be vast, in which the imagination is engaged by the bodily fate of human existence. The first, the scene of execution, shows that the violent transformation of the body in deliberate, and often retributive, killing draws the eyes of others, even total strangers, towards the envisioning of another's death. The second, the process of replacing bodily parts with prosthetic substitutes, shows that the gradual transformation of the body by cyber parts splits the consciousness into hopeful expectation and shame, into yearning and loathing. As themes for the imagination, even as discrete motifs in carefully unfolded imaginative worlds, both situations restate variations upon the idea of human frailty. The integrated fortress of the self can be easily split apart, severed into pieces, transformed or destroyed. From the standpoint of a horror-world, or existence itself, the human body confronts daily the death by a thousand bites, and does so in myriad forms.

In both cases, decomposition or metamorphosis, the imagination creates theatrical scenarios in which the contrasting possibilities may be played through. Small but fascinating fictional worlds emerge in which the body's paths towards dissolution and finality are envisioned. This, I think, was the single most important lesson from my ugly moments on motorcycles: even suffering considerable pain, or anticipating extreme pain on what seemed to be the actual edge of death, I was able to invoke my imagination to envision my own dissolution, more vividly than my actual death, in a theatrical fictional world of bodily decomposition and pain. I will develop the idea of the split consciousness, divided by the double role of prosthetic parts, further in the final chapter. In the next chapter I want to analyze what disgust-worlds look like and how they perform within consciousness. ✽

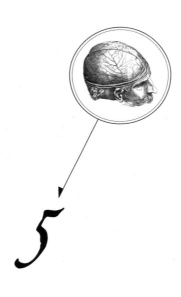

5

Its Many Eyes

Imagining Disgust

In the summer of 1993, I took a train from Toronto to Ottawa. I met a man on that trip whom I will call the Sports Bore. He was a dispiriting person in that he had only one topic for conversation. He solved the problem of speaking to a fellow human being by delivering monologues in the flat, nasal twang of southeastern Ontario. These monologues were entirely about professional sports and, even then, only about sports played by Toronto teams. Talking to such a person, unless you share the obsession and can override his monologues by those of your own, squashes the spirit, numbs the mind, freezes the voice. The Sports Bore, a man of seventy-five or so, lived for sports; they were his only texts. But he was not limited to one sport: he talked baseball, hockey, football, even basketball. On the other hand, he only talked the sports of one place: Toronto. I had met him half an hour before in the first-class lounge for Via Rail as I waited for the train to Ottawa. Wasn't that an indignity, he had asked, Gretzky not getting a penalty in the game with Los Angeles? And the Kings' goalie, Hrudey, what did I think of him? I had ducked and backpedalled. I didn't know much about it. I hadn't seen the game. The Sports Bore didn't take hints. He shifted on to football, the prospects of the Argonauts, quarterbacks and management. I could see that he lived and breathed Toronto sports, about which I knew very little.

On the train, the Sports Bore sat down in the seat across the aisle from me and one ahead. I felt chill with apprehension when I saw him take a seat across from me, nothing but a slight twist of his body required to pin me down, to monologue against my mutters and sighs, all the way to Ottawa. It would be like a banker insisting on talking investments to a pauper, only the desire for monologue on a privileged subject driving the engine of discourse. I was about to be invited, or perhaps kidnapped, into the monotonous worlds of his imagination. But I had luck that day.

Directly in front of me four seats had been reserved for the wife of the Governor General of Canada. Across the aisle from her, but one row ahead, another four seats had been reserved for her two aides, a young man with her attaché case chained to his wrist and a Canadian naval officer who wore enough yellow braid over his blue uniform to spur the envy of a Bolivian Admiral of the Fleet. The Sports Bore found it easier to talk to the young men in front of him than to me. And so Ontario's Precambrian shield swept by me, pine forests and lakes, as if I were light-years from Toronto's sports, not simply a single aisle. Ignored by the Sports Bore in his intense desire to talk about Toronto sports, past, present and to come, I read a recent novel about metamorphosis and bifurcated fictional worlds all the way to Ottawa. Occasionally, I caught a few words, a sentence or two. (The two young men tried to keep him at bay, as I had done in the waiting room by mutterings and disavowals, by speaking in French, but he saw through, or simply ignored, that favourite disguise of Canadian bureaucrats.) He would recall specific plays, mistakes and triumphs in different games. The wonderful successes of the Blue Jays, the failures of the Argonauts, the Maple Leafs in quest of a Stanley Cup, names of players, managers, owners, future and past, possible and actual, all ran together in his on-flowing voice. He didn't seem to discriminate among sports. In his mind, they were all aspects of a challenge that Toronto was playing with the rest of the continent. He was already imagining the future NBA basketball franchise and trying to suppose how the Raptors might rank in its first year as an expansion team.

Sports, Toronto sports, filled his mind and were his single issue. (The Governor General's wife also read a book, her head turned on the seat towards the window and away from sports.) The young men, trying to fend off the Sports Bore with French, looked desperate and miserably frustrated, though in the Ottawa station they smiled, shook his hand and told him, in English, how much they had enjoyed meeting him. Bureaucrats, I thought, are as predictable as bores, speaking a supine discourse on a single plane. Some days, in certain moods, you might even call them both disgusting.

I learned something important from the Sports Bore. Contemplating him, I began to see that his obsession was a way of living as well as thinking, a form of life, in effect. He was playing athletic games in his mind. Leaping and whirling within that phantasmagoria, the different sports flowed together to constitute a single game. The fragmentary, disjunctive way he had of spinning from one anecdote to another, of speaking about different sports at different historical moments as if they were all being played at once revealed a kind of mental play that was very different from merely replaying a single game or a number of separate plays within a game. His disconnected shards of different games played at different times had the consistency of a lived experience. He inhabited a world in which professional sports, Toronto's sports past, present and future, were played out continuously like small skirmishes upon a single field of battle. Sports were real for him in a way that they may not be for every person, even a fan. Toronto sports constituted a complex fictional world for him. He inhabited it as a good reader might a narrative. He was an observer, perhaps vicariously a participant-observer, of Toronto's sports as if he were standing on a castle's battlement watching the tangled unfolding of siege warfare.

Other people have also discovered how to live largely, if not exclusively, in fictional worlds that they have built from fragments of their professions, pastimes or paranoias. Academics often build fictional worlds out of their ambitions and resentments, out of committees, courses and competitions. University administrators build worlds out of paperwork and power lunches. In general, bureaucrats build fictional worlds out of the lives of those they manage: "a million bureaucrats," Thomas Pynchon writes, "are diligently plotting death and some of them even know it."[1] No doubt, there are people, perhaps more than a few, who inhabit fictional worlds wholly composed out of the "mucoid object-world" that Camille Paglia finds in reading Sartre's *Nausea*. I think that it is possible that very personal fictional worlds built out of disgust, or out of all one's personal objects of revulsion and loathing, can exist. People dominated by, say, race or gender disgust, or driven by hidden sources of misogyny or homophobia, may well inhabit worlds in which scenarios built upon these corrosive mindsets play out continuously, being modified in detail as the actual world outside the play-world, at once stimulating and delimiting, provides fruitful props. I would not be surprised to learn that living in worlds of obsessive disgust, constituting everyone else as transgressive or abject, may be for some a source of pleasure. Certainly, it seems that some people do enjoy inhabiting the worlds of shock art in which disgust, or some sequence of disgust motifs, gives those worlds most of the shape they have. A fictional world built upon the perception of shock art—excrement, the ingestion of filth, vomit, torture, degradation and, at the extreme, death—would have to be, I think, both obsessive and narrow, as repetitive as a compulsion. Fans who followed G.G. Allin, listened to his music, went to his gigs or today buy the video of his funeral (during which the coffin was opened and the corpse shot up with heroin) live in fictional worlds built upon transgression and (by straight norms) disgust motifs of many kinds. Like other fictional worlds, such as that the Sports Bore had created for himself, a G.G. Allin world is also cramped, defining itself by exclusion. All the possibilities of the actual world, all of its many versions, shrivel away, reduced in scope to the transgressiveness of Allin defecating on stage, his style of punk music, the potential violence of his followers. (Many of Allin's fans found him hateful, but they were fascinated by him and his music-making much as they might have been by a terrible car wreck. He was, as was once said of Sid Vicious, a "wonderful disaster.") That such fictional worlds are demonstrably possible indicates that equivalent worlds, built upon actual or in-the-world details, might well be habitable. Pornography, one current argument holds, creates disgusting fictional worlds that may be inhabited with pleasure, but only on the supposition of a prior actual world that actively contains gender-disgust.[2]

The problem of how disgust-worlds come into existence and how they are imagined presupposes another issue, one I have already raised. Do fictional worlds arise only from fiction? Are they only as large as a narrative is long? I have been arguing that such worlds of the imagination do emerge, directly in most cases and without much mediation, from the texture of experience itself. I began the last chapter with a story about my own experience in riding motorcycles. Even as I hurtled down a mountain highway in nearly complete darkness, and at a speed that ought to have been (if Elaine Scarry were right) mind-numbingly dangerous in the situation, I was able vividly to imagine my body torn open and dismembered. In the fleeting seconds of navigating my motorcycle around a mountain curve in darkness, I was able to create a minimal fictional world of great intensity. It did not last long and its range was acutely narrow, but it was both sharp and memorable.

In this chapter, I want to consider how minimal narratives create their effects. I am not as interested in the general theory of minimal narratives as I am in the particular workings of those small disgust-worlds that spring up suddenly, and often nauseatingly, at the prompting of immediate in-the-world things. When this occurs, it makes sense to claim that private fictional worlds, engaging the imagination and partially directing it, have come into existence. To direct my discussion, I have chosen to focus upon the concept of tattoos, which I introduced in Chapter 1. A tattoo is a double experience: at once a small work of art and a class of image that has traditionally evoked at least moral disgust. In some cases, a tattoo could even cause physical disgust, either because of the nature of the image or because of its physical location (the face, say) or its bodily excessiveness.[3] The young scholar with the spider tattooed on his forehead fills the selection committee with moral loathing, but you can suppose that some members of the committee also experience physical disgust. In that case, the young man has crossed several socio-cultural boundaries, and the effect of the image (a spider) and the location of the tattoo (the forehead) have pretty much driven out aesthetic considerations. However excellent the artwork in the tattoo, its physical properties will evoke disgust on different levels. Thinking about a tattoo, you can see how its material conditions as much as, or perhaps even more in many cases, its aesthetic content can cause disgust. The very fact that a tattoo's canvas is the human skin makes it quite a different matter than, say, graffiti. Often disgust arises as much from the material conditions of expression, as in the human skin of tattoos, as it does from the content. Some of the paths that a reading of a tattoo may open up for the imagination have to do with the skin itself.

A discourse that delimits the possibilities for sense-making, culture imposes the rules for "reading" another person's skin. Thus tattoos may strike western viewers as both violations and threats. While they can establish boundaries that demarcate the "normal" from the spoiled, the transgressive and the disgusting, they also funnel the eye, drawing attention complexly both towards the content of the image and to its presence on another person's skin. The person may seem to have stigmatized him- or herself, violating prohibitions as least as old as Leviticus. Yet at the same time the tattoo may achieve something visually exciting. Tattoos are invariably intensive: they manifest complex individual lifeworlds in which a number of definite choices have been taken. Tattoos evoke symbolic associations. They display the significance of private moves within the scope of a controlling cultural discourse. Above all, they hint at larger stories, the possibilities of full narrative expression, in a complicated interaction between material conditions and viewer.[4]

One of Flannery O'Connor's stories recounts a man's difficult choice of a back tattoo and the hostile reception it earns him at home. In "Parker's Back," O'Connor points directly towards the explosive potential of emblematic, narratively suggestive tattoos: "It was as if the panther and the lion and the serpents and the eagles and the hawks had penetrated his skin and lived inside him in a raging warfare."⁵ Her character, who acquires a new tattoo whenever he feels particularly insignificant or especially alienated from the world, has had the image of a Byzantine Christ, as if figured in coloured mosaic tile, tattooed onto his back in a vain effort to win the affection of his strict gospel wife. The potential self-transcendence of a tattoo, in contrast to its ordinary down-to-earthness (it is only human skin, after all), has seldom been captured so vividly. O.E. Parker's back tattoo links together the problem of alienation and self-transcendence. His personal feeling of emptiness and flatness, his sense of the world's coldness and his desire to win his wife's love, even to rise above his condition, are displaced into the image he has had tattooed on his back. Parker has acquired what Erving Goffman calls a "prestige symbol" (as opposed to a stigma symbol, such as a jailhouse tattoo), a symbol that will identify him as being associated with God and personally aligned with his wife's religious beliefs. All of his tattoos have been aimed at correcting his feeling of alienation and his awareness that, even in his wife's eyes, he lacks "respect and regard"; but his back tattoo of Christ is a special, magnificent if entirely failing, effort to achieve some kind of transcendence.⁶

I draw my primary evidence for the interpretations of tattoos from Martin Scorsese's 1992 film *Cape Fear*. Neither the previous film version of *Cape Fear* nor the John D. MacDonald novel, on which both films are based, use tattoos to characterize the villain, Max Cady. Scorsese introduces the element of tattoos into the characterization of a pre-existing story; hence it makes sense to ask what this adds to telling the story and what effects it achieves. When I view a tattoo, I place it, not merely consciously, within a larger matrix of narrative experience to which it alludes. Everything that I have read and heard becomes a tool for interpretation.⁷ Considered as a narrative problem only, and leaving aside such important issues as social stigma, "spoiled identity" and the voluntary affiliation to marginalized social groups (such as punks or hardcore bikers), the semiotics of tattoos leads to much the same formal accounts, explanations and models as do other minimal narrative modes such as ekphrases, Homeric similes and puppet shows.⁸

You can make sense out of minimal narrative texts by considering them as the starting points from which different paths, directions of understanding and personal expression open. I use the term "path" to name these lines that open from texts, even the most minimal, to prompt exploration.[9] I shall try to avoid the impediments of unnecessary concreteness by saying simply that the paths I have in mind are paths-in-play: sequences of interpretive choices that open up variously depending on the limitations imposed by rules and by the skills of the player. A path is a line of potential play that unfolds according to the choices the player makes. It is not a *Holzweg* (at least not as Heidegger uses that term), although lines of play, ways of a certain nature, may open through symbolic forests. As I shall use the term, a path is close to what Derrida means when he writes *cheminer*. It is everything that "goes in the direction of the step," but it is also all that goes up the chimney.[10] A path-in-play explores possibilities and takes pleasure in doing so even when, realized, these possibilities would entail defeat. The path-in-play as reading also involves both excitement (in the process) and the prospect of unpleasantness (in the product). A negative scenario, dark or painful, may always reward the paths one has chosen to follow in exploring a literary text.

One aspect of play is the metonymic combination of moves according to rules. It does not matter whether the rules are random, as in aleatory games where chance determines moves, or purposefully directed, as in the model of constitutive rules that Bernard Suits has argued in *The Grasshopper*.[11] However, a great deal does depend upon whether the rules are known or not. As Ross Chambers argues, there exists a "rules/moves complex" in which either polarity may be more clearly known than the other.[12] In human culture, unlike the experience of certain games, it often seems that the rules are unknown although the moves are explicitly prescribed and just as explicitly sanctioned. The individual's recognition of what certain moves entail leads to transgression. The absence of clarity concerning the rules, which may lie hidden deep within "discourse," leads to the human condition of splitness awareness. Human subjectivity may be said to seek "to grasp the mediations through which the moves that constitute its own search are produced."[13] "Seeking to grasp" sharply formulates the lusory attitude that underlies all play, that provokes the player on to the paths he or she will follow, and that proposes the destination, or the *adestination*, that lies ahead.

That there are destinations, or their illusions, points to another aspect of play: the exploration of possibilities. In this second sense, in strict opposition to the metonymic combination of moves according to rules, play is heuristic, always a pushing towards the undiscovered and unformulated, a sequence of explanatory hypotheses, of fresh accounts. Playfully, you may reach towards something previously unseen, however momentarily, in developing sequences, paths-in-play, that always seem new. Mihai Spariosu observes that play, "because of its amphibolous nature," is, like art, ideally suited to take on mediating roles between antinomies.[14] Play is both a discipline (unfolding within its constitutive rules) and an escape from discipline; it "transcends not only all disciplines, but also all discipline."[15] These exploratory sequences are "paths": there may be a large number of them, they may be followed, they may be full of surprises, they may turn out to be deadends leading nowhere or (more painfully) they may lead where the player would much prefer not to visit. In the engagement of the imagination that one may call (following Kendall Walton's already-blazed path) "make-believe," there are negative scenarios to be imagined that a reader might, often enough, happily forego.[16] All the little make-believe fictional worlds that make your experience of the world so interesting and that raise perception beyond itself into realms of alternatives are acts of the imagination, swift mental responses to the world's stimulation that draws upon prior cultural experience. They all emerge from autonomous mental acts that are, as Edward S. Casey argues, both independent of, and unreducible to, perception.[17] Although many theories of the imagination privilege voluntary acts or, in the Romantic posture, hold that the imagination is both autonomous and voluntary, at the height of a mental hierarchy of disparate acts, I want to argue that it is often involuntary and always a supplement to, enhancing or reconfiguring, experience.[18]

Having made this statement of methodology and at least partially defined "fictional world," I want to return to tattoos. A tattoo may be either a symbolic emblem or a scene from a larger narrative; that is, a tattoo may suggest either a hidden realm of values or an inferrable story matrix (or both). Traditional tattoos, whether of the "poke-and-joke" type or by a tattooist with claims to art, are usually emblematic.[19] "Vow" tattoos can scarcely be described in any other way since they purposefully invoke an absent person and an otherwise invisible relationship. Anchors or death's-heads, like the crosses that medieval knights are said to have had tattooed on their foreheads to indicate that they had seen Jerusalem, are essentially emblematic. A person who has had the words "hard" and "luck" or the letters AFFA (another popular "stigma" tattoo in North America) tattooed across the fingers, usually above the knuckles, will be sending a very concrete message to anyone in the position to read the words.[20] The elements of shock theatre can be seen in even a very small emblematic tattoo which may attempt both to embody the person's values or private relationships and to outrage "the sensuous smugness of conformity."[21] One American artist describes her tattoos as "totem figures" which, although no doubt technically incorrect, captures the emblematic spirit.[22] Perhaps the majority of traditional tattoos, in particular "jailhouse," scratched or poke-and-joke types, are carnivalesque in that they challenge the viewer to understand hidden values, to feel revulsion in so doing but also to see himself as weak, vulnerable and ill-prepared for reality. A tattoo of a spider nestled in the corner of an eye, its web spreading downwards, could scarcely be intended to win friends or to seduce lovers. (Of course, in a punk scene, an eye-spider might be genuinely aphrodisiac.) It is a mode of personal graffiti that probably suggests, and will certainly be read as suggesting, a number of sociopathic values, such as alienation, disdain, outrage and hate. As an emblem suggesting values to be inferred, it is a more powerful image than even the death's-head on a biker's arm.[23]

A carnivalesque emblem will pose a number of exploratory paths to be followed, although it may hint at unpleasantness to be found. The young man's tattoo in my parable may suggest the eighteenth-century symbol of genius, but it may also signify the predatory eating habits of *Arachnida*. The selection committee will foresee both destinations, among others, and so, even with averted eyes, they will begin to play along at least two paths, testing their progress by the responses that the young scholar makes. (Too much arrogance, the slightest hint of male charmlessness or plain surliness, too many quick answers, and they will place him among the *Arachnida*.) Narrative tattoos, common in "new-wave" tattooing, pose a nexus of paths to be followed towards a story that can be imagined in a full narrative expression. Suppose that a person has tattooed on his or her right shoulder the picture of an ancient trireme with a man waving farewell to a woman who, with tears and distress, leans from a tower's window or, perhaps, raises her body from a funeral pyre. Clearly a story of some kind is suggested. It is certainly a culturally embedded narrative, although not every viewer will have heard it, that has been told over and over again. Eventually, an uncovered path might lead the viewer to the story of Dido and Aeneas. The symbolic values will seem to vary according to gender. A man who has this crucial scene from the story of Aeneas tattooed on his shoulder might very well wish to indicate his attitude towards women or his self-conception as a heartless lover or even, evoking two story matrices at once, as a ruthless type of Don Juan. A woman might wish to inscribe her contempt for men or even her personal sense of victimhood.

In Scorsese's *Cape Fear*, the avenging criminal, Max Cady, has crude jail-house tattoos on his arms. In the source novel, John D. MacDonald's understanding of Cady is that he is "big and fast and in good shape,"[24] but he is untattooed. The tattoos are Scorsese's innovation, a layer of characterization superadded to his sources that makes the narrative discourse far more complex than it had been before. Scorsese has used the representations of tattoos in other films, such as his 1988 film *The Last Temptation of Christ*, but never so intensively as an aspect of characterization.[25] Phrases and vow-like images are tattooed on Cady's forearms. The effect is powerful. It suggests both the "spoiled identity" that Goffman analyzes and a system of values. Cady's tattoos on the front of his body are carnivalesque emblems. They challenge the viewer to play through a number of paths towards an exploration of values that may prove to be up-setting, even disgusting. In this respect, FTW and poke-and-joke tattoos, whether jail-house or underclass, work much as shock art has always done: a strategy to transgress, even to disgust, in order to question conventional, straight values and to make the bearer's (or artist's) own work stand out as a counter-statement.

Max Cady's back bears a carnivalesque figure of justice: scales hang from the tree of Justice, as in "normal" iconography, but the scale weighs a knife against a book.[26] The knife outweighs the book. Back tattoos are always both very private and attention-grabbing. They are often flagrant (a back tattoo of a Japanese dragon's head, chosen by a young American man for the single purpose of frightening other people, in Bob Brooks' *Tattoo* comes to mind), but they are also the tattoos most likely to make aesthetic claims. Immediately upon seeing Cady's back tattoo, a nexus of paths opens for exploration. Certain values are suggested: a mocking (Menippean, in effect) attitude towards justice, a view that the law, represented by the book, has not worked (which is Cady's fundamental complaint) and may not be capable of working, and a clear indication that everything associated with knives—violence, blood and personal vengeance—counts for more. However, other paths lead towards two interconnected, but distinct stories. First, the viewer is invited to explore the situation in which the tattoo was acquired. It is clearly "jailhouse" (crude, black lines only: an effect that suggests pins and ordinary ink or soot), but unlike those on the front of his body, Cady could not have done it himself. Hence a story emerges from the tattoo that tells of his years in prison, someone else willing to execute the tattoo, hours in a cell while another convict scratches and pricks his back to place there a picture that will both represent his disgust for, and scorn of, the existing legal system and his conviction that only personal vengeance, seen as violent and bloody, can achieve true justice. Cady has exchanged pain for self-symbolization. The tattoo also invites the viewer to imagine another, much larger story in which justice always fails. Along this path, where many narrative modes might be encountered, justice is only words and cannot stand up against violence. In Cady's tale, it is up to the individual to look after personal interests; Justice cannot help.

A quick glance at almost any tattoo magazine will demonstrate that back tattoos are both more intricate and more integrated. It will also indicate that tattooed persons take more pride in their back tattoos than in other, frontal or leg and arm, tattoos. Full-body tattoos are seldom wholly integrated in western culture. In western society, most full-body tattoos are random, drawn at different times, and non-integrated. (Japanese tattoos, because they are commonly mythological, are often highly integrated: but it is the recognizable *story* that creates the integration.) Thus a back tattoo actually functions differently from, and indeed in opposition to, full-body tattooing. Kathy Acker's back tattoos, a stylized Japanese shark, swimming from left shoulder to right flank, and chrysanthemums across the right shoulder, have become famous and exemplify the explosive flair of back tattoos.[27] A back tattoo opens up an extensive matrix, in which many possible actions are performed and subordinate characters can be imagined, for imaginative exploration.

The results of exploratory play may not be altogether what the player might wish. There is a sense in which the paths of a minimal narrative may be followed unwillingly. Implications, often in the form of stereotypes or other cultural scripts, may simply click into connection. The imagination draws on a vast archive of images, some of which are programmed to act as instructions, out of which it fashions its private scenarios and hidden worlds. This archive is the imaginary.[28] The imaginary "discloses itself in interplay with its activators," but it is not the same as either the intention to imagine or the experience that is being imagined.[29] However, an imaginary is a malleable structuring force, ever shifting with education and experience. It promotes recognition and shifts, losing or acquiring images, with re-cognition. This explains why pollution, the personal experience of a given disgust that makes its way from one object to another, is at once so fiercely assertive but also so bizarre, as in a faded memory, once its power has been overcome. Looking back on the sources of pollution you once recognized, you may feel as if you were viewing the ruins of an ancient and nearly forgotten city beneath the sea.

Many of the experiences I have discussed in this book, both personal and taken as *exempla* from literature and film, have had about them the distinctive whiff of pollution. The maggots that infested the ground meat I had intended for dinner clearly polluted it. (And even when they had been driven out and killed, I continued to think of the meat as having been polluted.) Similarly, Giancarlo's father must have had an exceptionally strong sense of personal pollution (which my own father evidently lacked) when he would throw away an entire plate of food only because a single fly had touched it. My sad encounter with Georgie made me feel sleazy and may even have polluted me. My own mistreatment of her, and the lies I told about her later, made me considerably more sleazy, even in my own eyes, and may well have acted like a pollutant. Bad encounters with food (finding a maggot in your food or a worm in your apple) and with sex (being asked to do what you do not like to do) typically contaminate. A single piece of rotten or taboo food, its image lodged within your personal imaginary like a shred of filth between your teeth, will not simply pollute the act of eating but also fill the mind with loathing, sending cold shivers through your gut or a "falling glissando of disgust" racing downwards along your spine, perhaps even making your gorge crack.[30] Paradoxically, such experiences of pollution, although felt intensely in the moment, are usually passing and may often lead to revised consciousness in which those particular pollutants never again appear, or never with their initial strength.[31] Disgust, as I have argued, is highly metamorphic and nowhere is this more clearly seen than in the changing (fading and undergoing transformation) images of what pollutes.

Both your cultural imaginary, which you share so obviously with others, and your personal imaginary of hoarded negative images will work to provoke the sense of having been polluted. Touch an object, allow yourself to be brushed lightly or merely see it, if its image lies stored in your imaginary as a marked pollutant, and you may feel all the sensations of being invaded by filth, your frail ego defences smashed. A mental image is imposed on an object such that all the image's negative markers come into play. Sartre emphasizes the voluntary character of this transaction; that is, your private effort to bridge the distance between yourself and an absent object. My sense is that the claims of your imaginary are often uncalled upon. They are rough, exigent interpellations. The imaginary is both a psychological taskmaster and imagination's wildcard. Your mother told you that bugs are dirty and not to put them in your mouth, and now bugs make you squeamish and their slightest contact with your food would make it utterly inedible. Something very similar happens when the feeling of sleaze, a weak form of pollution, arises. If you see or do something that makes you feel sleazy, it will be because some prohibition, no doubt acquired during your social formation, has attached to some image that someone gave you. Wendy Lesser's discussion of the sleazy character of watching executions seems to invoke unexamined assumptions, taught during her middle-class up-bringing in North America, about respect for other human beings, privacy and the ugliness of gawking.[32] In the ongoing metamorphoses of the imaginary, sleaze is probably more vulnerable to transformation and excision than pollution.

The paths of a minimal narrative, followed and elaborated in imagination, may be disgusting, or ideologically unacceptable, or in many ways negative. The unviewable is always one possible destination. Consider once more O'Connor's story "Parker's Back." In O'Connor's narrative, Parker's pious wife, Sarah Ruth, thrashes him across the back with her broom and drives him from the house. Once she actually recognizes what it represents, she sees the tattoo as idolatrous, literally unviewable. Thus, following Chambers' distinction, Sarah Ruth recognizes in the tattoo what Parker has already, albeit delusively, re-cognized. In Scorsese's film, the tattoo on Cady's back explicitly represents both values and a story that his victim, a lawyer, could not happily accept. If understood, it would undermine everything for which his life and profession stand. It challenges the viewer, as all minimal narratives must do if they are to be read, and it invites heuristic play. The rewards of play—a certain state of imagination, an ability to contemplate a story matrix and ultimately the ability to imagine a fictional world—are frequently disturbing.

Minimal narratives can often generate maximal narrative effects.[33] How this happens seems like a difficult question that falls within another discussion's scope: one that could explain how imagination works in general. An adequate theory of play must either assume or generate on its own an account of how the imagination can envision make-believe and hold steadily before the mind's eye alternatives to reality. Imagination is the realm of plural world-versions. A theory of reading must also embody an account of the imagination. The theory of reading according to which the act of reading is seen as exploratory (choosing its object out of a matrix of common possibilities) and which moves ahead according to culturally inscribed "rules," such as those for notice, signification, configuration and coherence, may be, I think, assimilated to a general theory of play. In the end, both theories must call upon, assert or fashion anew, some larger, more powerful theory of imagination and imagining.[34]

A limited model of exploratory play (playfulness here understood as entering into a sequence of steps, which can be formulated as either a series of moves or as a series of explanatory hypotheses) can be used to account for the success of minimal narratives in engaging their audiences. Like all other modes of exploratory play, including both philosophical and scientific, narrative play leads to a state of imagination in which the possibilities of a minimal expression, whether an ekphrasis or a tattoo, are suddenly perceived in their potential fullness. This imaginative depth may be described as a pattern of make-believe in which the bare indices of the narrative expression have functioned, in Kendall Walton's term, as "props." The Sports Bore, the exemplary character with whom I introduced this chapter, clearly possessed an active imagination in which he took from Toronto's professional sports teams the props for a continuous world of make-believe. Literary texts, including such minimal expressions as tattoos, are games of make-believe built out of the props that the world, or one of its versions, has provided.[35] The make-believe scenarios that result from exploratory play may be either positive or negative. Both O'Connor and Scorsese create minimal narratives, embedded within the larger discourse of the containing narrative, the end-product of which is disturbingly negative (at least it is within the larger fictional world in which the narrative appears). O'Connor does not indicate what Sarah Ruth's strict gospel revulsion at idolatry leads her to see in her husband's new back tattoo, but it must be imagined as dark, deformed, horrible, perhaps as satanic. (Here the theory of horror doubly folds into the problem of reading a tattoo: first, in terms of the character's perceptions; second, as the reader's path to those character-restricted perceptions.) Both narratives, expressed in back tattoos, exemplify how many paths, crossing over one another and intersecting at many points, lead away from minimal narrative expressions to the experience of fictional worlds. The paths of play head quickly, if diversely, towards the fullness of imagination.

A fictional world need not be perceived as a whole. It can be experienced, as it normally is in postmodern fiction, through its discrete parts. Indeed, a fictional world may emerge into being as a coherent object of imagination in the fashion of a puzzle (connect the dots), a paragram or dreamwork. Quite a few postmodern narratives, structurally disrupted (snares, gaps, misdirections, objective hypotheses, discontinuities, embedded alternatives) but nonetheless cleidoic, would demonstrate that a fictional world does not have to develop sequentially. It may emerge, with relative coherence, out of a vertically stacked mosaic of parts. The model to bear in mind is that kind of electronic writing known as hypertext. In hypertext a large number, actually in(de)finite, of paths lead from a central point to relevant source materials, to analogous texts, to commentary, to factual illustrations, and so forth. Hypertext writing leads from a single point (a screen, a virtual text, say, or an initial web of icons, all of which will represent a complex of text chunks connected by links) in many directions, to many disparate but convergent points.[36] Hypertext constitutes the formal problematization of texts by computer access. Discussing the possibility of writing philosophy in a hypertext format, David Kolb observes that hypertext

> looks like a natural for the attempt to show that any presumed overall structure, narrative or philosophical, argumentative or dialectical, works within a larger field that it does not control. Hypertext's endless possibilities for recombination and reuse should facilitate the creation of texts in which the narrative or philosophical line is self-consciously reinscribed within, yet does not dominate, the space of the text.[37]

In a hypertext format, there will be no single, no stable, textual version, but only paths and a corresponding number of "virtual" (screen) texts. The text is de-centred, but any individual reader can choose a fresh, if temporary, centre from which countless paths will start. George Landow writes, "One experiences hypertext as an infinitely de-centerable and re-centerable system" in which the text becomes a "directory document that one can employ to orient oneself and to decide where to go next."[38] Even in a hypertext environment, something far more extreme and radically de-centred than any postmodern narrative told under linear constraints, a fictional world would emerge. At least, various world-versions, bearing family resemblances, would be possible.

Even under linear constraints, the paragramatic condition of many fictional worlds can be dazzling. Vladimir Nabokov's postmodern (or proto-postmodern) *Pale Fire* provides an excellent example. Nabokov's novel consists of a 999-line poem in heroic couplets by John Shade, an American poet and university teacher with a modest international reputation. The poem "Pale Fire" apparently would have had a concluding thousandth line except that Shade was murdered shortly before he could write it. The poem has an *apparatus criticus* of more than two hundred pages of scholarly commentary. The commentary is written by Shade's neighbour and colleague at Wordsmith College, Charles Kinbote, who may or may not be the exiled king of a "distant northern land" known as Zembla. The novel also has a foreword by Kinbote, an epigraph from Boswell (to be thought of as chosen by Shade, Kinbote or Nabokov, depending upon the position it is given) and an index. As would be the case with any scholarly work (but not, normally, a novel), the reader may begin at several different points, not necessarily at the "Foreword," even with the index. If, for instance, a reader begins by scanning the index and stops at the word *Kolbaltana*, suggesting a place or region characterized by its blue colour (not silver-grey since blue, associated with glass and mirrors, is a motif that runs through the narrative), he will discover the following annotation:

> A once fashionable mountain resort near the ruins of some old barracks now a cold and desolate spot of difficult access and no importance but still remembered in military families and forest castles, not in the text.[39]

If Kobaltana is not "in the text," where is it? What ontological status does it have? Christopher Nash observes how characters (such as Pnin, Lolita, Murphy, Malone) are often mentioned in *Pale Fire* but do not appear in its pages. They do, evidently, appear in other books and "the very flat, 'matter-of-fact' quality of the allusions confers a kind of 'objective, external' existence on the central figures of those other works of fiction."[40] One lesson from the study of minimalism is that neither characters nor places can be reduced to the indications that, as necessary conditions, make them possible to imagine. The lesson from hypertext is that these indications may appear in any possible sequence and combination. Existing only in Kinbote's note, Kobaltana may take on flesh in the reader's imagination, becoming, with its ruined barracks, mountain desolation and continued viability in the memories of "military families and forest castles," a deeply romantic place that is, though "not in the text," wholly consistent with Kinbote's spatial fantasies and distinctly imaginable. Minimal aspects of *Pale Fire*, such as Kobaltana, manifest, like Chinese boxes or Russian dolls, the difficulties of "the innovative structure of the whole."[41]

An analogy, if one were needed, could be found in *Hamlet* in the way that the Player King's and Hamlet's mutual account of the death of Priam in their version of Aeneas' "Tale to Dido" works or in the way that Ophelia's mad songs evoke small but highly distinct narratives. Aeneas' "Tale to Dido" breaks into the action of *Hamlet* in an extremely exact manner, shifting the focus of the action to the distant elsewhen and elsewhere of

Troy; but once attention has been transferred, then, like a bubble suspended in shadows, it becomes enveloped within a surrounding story matrix. It is, to borrow a phrase from Roman Ingarden, as if a beam of light illuminated a part of a region, while everything else "disappears in an indeterminate cloud but is still there in its indeterminacy."[42] The story matrix, the shadowy, indeterminate cloud of potential narrative, is the "Matter of Troy," the tentacular accounts of Bronze Age heroes, the nested networks of legendary materials. The fifty-seven lines of the narrative are a shard of, or perhaps a small peephole into, the vast story of Troy. Every schoolboy knew well the matter of Troy which, Levin writes, "Caxton had popularized, which English ballads celebrated, which poets and artists could draw upon as freely as the matter of England itself."[43] A vast number of fictional objects, not solely characters, immigrate into the apparently restricted narrative of Troy's final moments, crowding it with the significance of other tales.[44] If Ilium has been evoked, then its parts, even if not designated, are in some sense implied. Entirely new paths, like innumerable question-quests, make their demands. Outside the narrative's immediate foreground, obscure yet available to recognition, are Pergamum, the Scaen Gate and the Simoïs; Achilles, left within the indeterminate cloud of the story matrix, exerts a ghostly presence over Pyrrhus' revenge. Direct lines of access open up allowing readers and auditors to cross over from Elsinore into a distinctly different place, the dark claustral scene in Priam's palace, and from there innumerable lines open towards a larger fictional world. The problem of minimalness seems acute at this point: how much is actually required, once a fictional world has been constituted, to re-evoke it from within an alien discourse? Both Aeneas' "Tale to Dido" and the startlingly brief allusion to Kobaltana in *Pale Fire* demonstrate Thomas Pavel's proposition that world-complexity depends far less upon the length of a text than the disposition of interior semiotic domains.[45] Aeneas' tale, only very incompletely retold in Hamlet's and the Player King's ensemble performance, displays, like the allusion to Kobaltana, the maximal potential worldhood of a minimal text. You can easily imagine other maximal worlds in *Hamlet*, evoked by the most minimal textual suggestions. What is the world behind the "fat weed" that roots itself along Lethe wharf? Or that behind the "convocation" of worms that, even now, is eating Polonious?

Now that I have returned once again to the world of *Hamlet*, claiming once more that it is dark and problematic, ruled by what Roland Barthes called the "hermeneutic code," the code of enigmas, I think that I have reached a point where it will make sense to give a brief account of what I mean by the term "world," which I have used so often throughout this book but which until now I have left only sketchily defined. I take a fictional world to be an imagined space in which a number of actions or events, at least one, can take place. More strictly, certain actions and events can be imagined as taking place. The text provides "indices" (deictics, names, descriptive phrases) which possess a prop-like function in starting the mind along a path of world construction. (I have been arguing since the first chapter that the actual world itself also provides props, both things and people, for the imagination to use in building fictional entities.) It seems like a good idea to distinguish between the imagined spatial, or spatial and temporal, properties of the world and what takes place within it. Hence, people who think about fictional worlds, such as Seymour Chatman, often draw a distinction between "existents," the setting and the characters on the one hand, and the events or actions on the other hand. A fictional world, Doreen Maitre argues, is rather like an hypothesis in that you invent or imagine it in order to see what will happen with it, what sense it will make. Both hypotheses and worlds draw upon the power of the human mind to suppose alternative accounts. Imagination, Maitre observes, posits "non-actual states of affairs, it enables us to consider what alternative states of affairs *could* be the case."[46] Some fictional worlds seem to depend more closely upon the actual world than do others: they may seem to cling, like a thin mist, over the actual world's body. Others seem more radically alternative, supposing existents (flying horses or time-travel machines) or events (the birth of dragons in fireclouds or the exploration of the galaxy at speeds faster than the speed of light) for which there would seem to be no in-the-world grounding. What all these worlds have in common is a potential to be imagined in hearing, viewing or reading. When they are imagined, they have, or seem to have, cohesion. They make sense and often have a profound impact upon those who enter them. What interests me are the very different ways in which fictional worlds do hang together. A horror-world, for example, seems very different from a comic-pastoral world in which everything works out well enough, the characters kiss and marry, and no one drinks hot blood or rips flesh apart. If you were to enter a fictional world the dominant effects of which were horrific, you would probably soon understand that you had not reached a pastoral world. You would not need the absence of shepherds and shepherdesses (replaced, it might be, by rustic rednecks with chainsaws) to tell you that had missed a comic destination. What you actually saw there would be sufficient to tell you worlds. The monster's traces, the disgusting spoor, would be all around you, for one thing, and the faces of the characters you met would be drawn in anxiety, or twisted in loathing, for another.

One reason for talking about fictional worlds is to place a primary emphasis upon affects: feelings are available within fictional worlds, both among the characters and, vicariously, for the reader or viewer, although these may be experienced quite differently from in-the-world affects. In some fictional worlds, the feelings of disgust and horror may be very powerful. They may even be experienced as actual, but with an intense or delimiting focus. (In the actual world, I may feel disgust or horror even while feeling something else. I might run away from something horrifying, but even so feel the stone in my shoe and the rain on my face.) An enumeration of a fictional world's disgusting features will certainly tell you something about it or allow you to classify it, but the more genuine problem is how these features work in the reading or viewing experience. For that, there must be some account, even if only preliminary, of the imagination. Not so much how it works, but, rather, what its capacities are. The dimension of the imagination that most interests me in this chapter is its capacity to generate worldhood. Here is a small fictional world to reflect upon.

> The beach, wide and bleakly wet, is strewn with driftwood. The sky is overcast, and dispiriting gusts of rain occasionally blow in from the sea. The surf is splendid, though. It rolls in regularly, no choppiness and no apparent rips, at more or less the right height for good bodysurfing. A few people duck into the surf, dancing on their toes, their bodies turned sideways to the breaking waves, and then retreat quickly. The water feels every bit as cold as it looks and the only surfers, far out on boards, wear wet suits. Yet it is a beautiful vista. Sunlight frequently breaks through the overcast. The waves are a glorious dark blue, almost gun-metal in richness. This blueness stands in sharp contrast to the rich green of the pine forests that enclose the beach. Huge rocks a short ways off the beach at one end, veils of white foam surging around them, pines struggling upwards from each crevice, make the whole scene, like a late Flemish landscape, hauntingly beautiful.
>
> A dog runs enthusiastically into the surf, in full canine vigour. It looks like a golden retriever, the darker, more russet-coloured type, but, its hair matted wet and dark from the sea, it is impossible to be certain. The dog runs out into the first

line of breakers, plunges through and then rides the next breaking wave onto the sand. It is body surfing and clearly as happy as a puppy in a warm basket. Somewhere on the beach, or out past several rows of breakers in a full-body wet suit, the dog's master, his head poking seal-like towards the beach, may be watching. But right now the dog is alone, surfing for its own pleasure, just being a dog at play. Another dog, this one more like a border collie mongrel, comes up to the edge of water, keeping a few steps back from the quick fingers of foam while it watches the first dog play. It holds a short stick, obviously a piece of driftwood, in its mouth. When the first dog has ridden a breaker onto the sand, it sees the stick-holding collie and leaves the water. They exchange looks. Then they circle each other sniffing. The unusual stink of salt water, its pelt like seaweed, must have given the golden retriever a startling, unusual stench. Now the collie offers its stick. Clearly, it wants to play. It shakes its head from side to side and then, with a vigorous neck twist, throws the stick just past the surfing dog's head. The collie watches the surfing dog intently and barks twice encouragingly. The golden retriever turns to consider the stick. After a moment's reflection, it picks the stick up and holds it for a few seconds. The collie watches hopefully. And then the golden retriever lets the stick fall. It darts back into the surf, but turns to watch the collie. It, too, makes two or three sharp, suggestive barks. Now the collie stands at the edge of the water, ripples of foam edging around its paws, and observes the surfing dog observe it. It rushes out into the water, finds itself swamped in the breaking wave, and retreats back to the sand. The golden retriever watches for a second or two and then dives through a wave into the trough. While it waits to catch the next wave, the collie takes one last look and then trots off down the beach.

What kind of a fictional world was that? A world in which dogs want to play but find themselves separated by their antinomic senses of game? Was it a semiotically simple world? Only: a beach, a pair of dogs, the impossible-to-extirpate canine urge to play, an odd incompatibility? Or was it an allegory? About human beings in *their* play? Was it about, as you must have surmised, the imagination? If it was an allegory, would that make the fictional world itself (because open to double reading) more complex? These are a few of the questions that swarm, like an expanding galaxy, around the problem of fictional worlds.

One straightforward but important distinction creates an immense amount of white-water turbulence in all scholarly discussions of fictional worldhood. Some fictional worlds are extremely simple and little goes on in them, or if a lot goes on, it is all much the same. They are built from the same blocks. Other fictional worlds are much more complex and much more goes on in them. They are more difficult to read, more strain is exerted upon your diminished capacities to attend, and they may be more fun. (Opinions vary considerably on this last point.) This has nothing to do with either the length of their narrative expression or with their supposed proximity to the actual world which they may imitate, mimic, distort, deform, displace or even replace. A very cluttered fictional world, presented in a long narrative, can be quite simple; a truncated fictional world, presented in a short narrative, can be extremely complex. Thus Pavel remarks that Borges' story "The Approach to Al'Mutasim" can invoke a world more extended than, in his example, a novel such as Proust's *Remembrance of Things Past*.[47] Clearly, if this is the case, it is not so because more existents and events crowd the pages of Borges' narrative. If it is so, it will be because more different kinds of things happen in Borges. The problem can be simplified by appealing to what Pavel calls "semiotic domains." A list of all possible words used to designate snow and sleet, even if this were to include borrowed words from other languages, such as Aleut, Inuit or Na-Dené, would not make a fictional world especially complex. However, a list of distinct kinds of words, each pointing to a distinctly different category of object and action, might help to create a complex fictional world. Diversity, not repetition, seems to be the key strategy: layers of significance, not puddles of similar signification, achieve this effect in world-building.

To make this point clear, I shall take my example from the kind of contemporary writing that is known as minimalism, or sometimes "dirty realism" or, disparagingly, "brand-name" realism.[48] It achieves its effects by burrowing into apparently simple fictional worlds in which more or less the same kinds of characters and the same kinds of events recur. Bill Buford, then the editor of *Granta*, once defined dirty realism as the exploration of the underbelly of society. An underbelly—unless you happen to inhabit one—is a fairly homogenous place, rather like what is shared in common by all the Hopper paintings in existence.[49] Take a story by Raymond Carver, the much-revered master of minimalism. The story is called "So Much Water So Close to Home." Here, in a nutshell, is what happens in Carver's story.

> Four men go fishing in a remote mountain river. They find the body of a young woman floating in the water. When their fishing trip is over they report the body to the police. The wife of one of the men is upset at their insensitivity in waiting to report the body. She begins to sympathize with the dead woman. Her antagonism to her husband grows. They feel mutually alienated. The wife seems to accuse the man of complicity in the crime.

Claire, the wife of one of the men who has gone on the fishing trip, narrates "So Much Water So Close to Home." It begins at the breakfast table the morning after the men have returned from fishing. The trip to the Naches River, discovering the young woman's body, the fishing camp and what the men did there, calling the police and returning home are all supplied in the narrator's voice after the narrative has begun. Later, Claire steps outside the immediate content of the story she is telling to narrate her childhood ("There was a girl who had a mother and father ... who moved as if in a dream through grade school and high school and then, in a year or two, into secretarial school"), the couple's courtship and marriage.[50] Carver's fiction is expanded by this retrospective narration even as its chronology is broken. Claire recounts the incidents of the fishing trip and the events that immediately followed (newspaper stories, angry telephone calls, the discovery of the dead woman's identity) so that the story is entirely her narration, wholly her reconstruction of events.

Claire puts an unmistakably personal touch upon the events she narrates. From the opening paragraph, it is apparent that she sees her husband as a distant, unsympathetic being, now alienated from her by irreconcilable differences. "Something has come between us though he would like me to believe otherwise."[51] That something is the knowledge that her husband continued to fish while the dead woman floated nearby in the river. Her feelings swiftly become evident. She resents her husband's indifference and, as she thinks, callousness in allowing the woman to remain in the water while he fished. It is unquestionably a disgusting act. She feels polluted by her husband's indifference. Violence, rape and murder are disgusting, but so is indifference to those acts. Claire begins to associate him with a general sense of oppressiveness and insensitivity. (Disgust, in the mode of moral outrage, is very strong in the story.) Then Claire remembers that he had made love to her upon returning from the trip, without mentioning the dead woman, and experiences a more physical revulsion: "I looked at his hands, the broad fingers, knuckles covered with hair, moving, lighting a cigarette now, fingers that had moved over me, into me last night."[52]

Claire's aversion, her profound alienation from, and disgust at, her husband's body, recalls Sartre's character Antoine Roquentin, for whom the physical properties of the world become alien, loathsome excrescences. Claire easily believes the worst concerning her husband (whether or not he deserves the harshness of her judgements is left an open inference), even associating him with the crime. Carver's narrative provides a strong fictional instance of contamination. A single disgusting object or act can pollute many others. In the final sentence of the narrative, Claire exclaims, "For God's sake, Stuart, she was only a child."[53] Claire projects upon her husband aversive feelings that she has for all men. At one point in her narrative, she remembers two brothers who had killed a girl whom she knew in high school, cut off her head and thrown her into a river.[54] Stuart becomes a target for her generalized resentment and, focussed by his supposed insensitivity in the matter of allowing the woman to continue floating, androphobia. Her various comments and her long drive over a mountain range to attend the woman's funeral indicate her increasing sympathy with the dead woman and alienation from her husband. The reader can, of course, take the narrator's account as authentic, but it is also possible to play through the voice to another version in which the husband, though easily baffled and not particularly thoughtful with regard to the implications of his actions, may be seen as well-meaning, certainly innocent of an actual crime, and genuinely caring towards his wife.

Carver's "So Much Water So Close to Home" evokes a fictional world that is narratively complex. Although it is relatively circumscribed in its place (rivers and mountains surround the unnamed town; no character travels more than a hundred miles from home) and contains few characters, the range of human feelings and actions is extensive. Characters experience feelings of affection, empathy, love and many kinds of desire (for sex, community and understanding); they also feel dislike, revulsion, disgust and hatred. In the background of the narrative, characters commit rape and murder; in the foreground, they feel both passionate identification with, and apathy towards, victims—a closeness that verges upon madness and an emotional remoteness that might suggest complicity. Yearning for both the past and the future, characters reach out to one another and strike each other back. On a first reading, it may seem that male characters are apathetic but capable of violence; women, passionate but easily victimized. However, this initial reaction misses Carver's textual indications that ambiguity surrounds human feelings and that intentions can never be directly inferred. A reader may conclude that Stuart does feel love as well as desire for his wife even though, in his frustration, he occasionally speaks to her with shocking violence:

> And then I am lifted up and then falling. I sit on the floor looking up at him and my neck hurts and my skirt is over my knees. He leans down and says, "You go to hell then, do you hear, bitch? I hope your cunt drops off before I touch it again." He sobs once and I realize he can't help it, he can't help himself either. I feel a rush of pity for him as he heads for the living room.[55]

The reader must infer whether she feels pity for his (male) violence or for his frustration. During her drive over the mountains to the young woman's funeral, Claire is followed by a man in a pick-up truck. When she drives off the road to wait, he turns around, comes back and knocks on the window of her car which she has rolled up. Evidently, she fears that he may be violent, perhaps a rapist. However, given the narrative situation, it is more likely that he is only worried about her and would like to help. Nonetheless, she asserts that he "looks at my breasts and legs" and that his eyes "linger on my legs."[56] Both the intention of the one character and the accuracy of the other's account are uncertain.

The fictional world of "So Much Water So Close to Home" is, borrowing Pavel's phrase, divided into distinct semiotic domains. The male characters inhabit one domain; the female, the other. However, the boundaries between them, despite their surface clarity, are quite fuzzy. The fictional world of the narrative appears very differently depending upon whether the reader reads from the point of view of the female narrator or from that of her focalized male characters. The question that the male characters pose (are they essentially violent or merely inarticulate?) hangs suspended, unanswered, at the narrative's close. The fictional world of Carver's narrative is intricate: a double world with uncertain interaction across its borders. It is a world built upon feelings and perceptions, not upon geography or descriptions. It achieves this complexity despite its succinctness, its concentration upon a few events and its repetitive use of the idiom of domestic life. It achieves this even though it has a single narrative voice and that voice is evidently prejudiced against the other character and the narrative's central events, the fishing trip and its ghastly consequences. However, instead of internal contradiction (with a concomitant loss of clarity and narrative authority), the result is consistency and cohesion. "So Much Water So Close to Home" generates an astounding coherence.[57] If you think of another version of this story, Robert Altman's use of Carver's fiction as a basis for his 1993 film *Short Cuts*, the point should be clear. Altman introduces Claire as a professional clown. She is first seen wearing a clown suit and last seen sitting with Stuart in a hot tub with two acquaintances, all of whom she has made up in clown faces. There seems to be a possibility of reconciliation in Altman's film that does not exist in Carver's story.[58] In both cases, relatively simple materials lead to complex worlds, but Carver's tale, though it involves less detail and fewer specifics, strikes me as almost unimaginably varied, infolded and multi-layered. Altman's *Short Cuts*, by contrast, uses far more visual detail (simply in being a film) and yet flattens the story potential into a single homogenized, if still interesting, domain. The imagination builds worlds out of specific items, but also out of the differences, the fissures and lines of distinction, between the semiotic domains that envelop those specifics.

The promising young man in the parable that I introduced in the first chapter exists in a simple fictional world. It is a world in which boundaries, unlike those in Carver's "So Much Water So Close to Home," have been incised with exactitude. He will not be appointed to a position at the University of Ultima Thule. He will have to pursue his brilliant career outside of academic institutions. His spider tattoo will have engaged too many negative associations among the members of the selection committee. They will suppose either that he is inherently disgusting or that he will cause disgusting acts to be performed. Although they are interviewing him in an academic context, they may actually think of him as they might a performance artist, as a monologist in a small theatre of shock. When boundaries dissolve, whatever they have kept securely in place can get loose and roam. Dirt out of place may indicate many things, but primarily it may suggest that the *place* itself no longer exists. Unbounded, dirt will range and may turn monstrous. The young man may not follow other culturally embedded prohibitions; he may be capable of anything. Even his own personal identity, for the enhancement of which he chose to have the spider tattooed upon his forehead, may seem to be uncertain, like a rotting heap of something putrid. Of course, the members of the selection committee will not allow these feelings to show. They will keep stone-faced about their true responses. They will ask him questions about his work, courses he might teach, his future research. In due course, the chair of the committee will thank him for having applied, congratulate him on his brilliant research and tell him that they will let him know. They will not let him know that they have been thinking about slime.

For this reason, the Sports Bore is a hyper-parabolic figure. He shows how easily, and with what pleasure, you may create small fictional worlds out of the actual-world materials that daily life offers. Standing on his battlements overlooking Toronto as local warriors defend him against intrusions from foreign lands, he may be happy. When I think about him now, he hardly seems very different, though far more benign, from the yahooing carnivalians who gather in front of American prisons on the nights of execution. The Sports Bore also makes plain how divided, how split into disjunctive spheres, human consciousness may be. On the train to Ottawa, he bodily followed a private purpose, a task or duty perhaps, which he seemed to have organized satisfactorily, but in his mind he played over different games that Toronto teams had played. He seemed to play them over separately but also seemed to fuse them together into a compound world in which history had been flattened, made depthless. If his consciousness was divided (and I suppose it to have been so), it was split along the fissures that different fictional worlds have made possible. He took in-the-world materials and reconstructed them into make-believe, and the way he did this demonstrates the labyrinthine paths to the body's mythic existence.

No materials in the world are more readily available for the imagination's play than the body. It is the cardinal, and most clamorous, prop. You may even imagine the body as the original hypertext, or at least its natural model. Touch the body at any point, stroke any appendage or tug any excrescence, and a mosaic of alternatives, worlds stacked vertically upon one another like a pull-down menu, will crowd your mind. Loathsome and terrible diseases may afflict you (is that numb wart-like growth on your forefinger the first sign of leprosy?); hideous, wretchedly unviewable consequences may fall upon you (will that persistent, rumbling congestion in your lungs become a death-rattle?). The single point upon your body that you touch, playing it like a kazoo in your imagination, may evoke very complex states of affairs.[59] Small, private disgust-worlds will explode about the body, like constellations of foxfire and death rot.

In the next chapter I will examine disgust-worlds that assume the full range of disgust responses and employ them as plot devices to build or maintain suspense. These are the worlds of horror and terror in literature and film. Before arriving in that murky territory, I want to summarize my argument up to this point.

Disgust is fundamentally a problem in crossing boundaries. The first, and most difficult, boundaries are those associated with the body. These boundaries exist in culture, reinscribed in human psychology, as a result of both prohibitions and habitual aversions that have been constructed during the process of social formation (the details of which are open to argument and may be more or less collective). It may be difficult to say precisely why, and out of what specific formation, a particular disgust response has arisen, but there seems to be no genuine evidence for claiming that disgust is either a natural or a universal response. Everyone, even the most solitudinous, is surrounded by cultural scripts which both limit and direct experience. Disgust is made available by many diverse scripts, but these are primarily aimed at the preservation and control of the body. All people may feel disgust, but they do so in very different ways, and under very different conditions. Appeals to universality, always falling far short of conviction, overleap the evidence.

Although disgust is extremely diverse, both "roiling" and "hydravarious," all manifestations of physical disgust seem to involve deliquescence, rot, stench and other signs of indeterminate or transitional states of being. There are a number of physical concomitants to disgust (such as the disgust face and vomiting) which are variously shaped in different cultures and at different times. For example, disgust may be more readily associated with the ingestion of food in some places and at some times, but with sexual practices in others. There are often powerful secondary affects, such as shame or horror, associated with disgust. Disgust, and all of its secondary affects, can be a product of make-believe. This is especially evident in the use of disgust to register moral disapprobation and outrage. However physical, disgust can be translated into a mental response, into an act of moral judgement. Hence moral disgust responses, such as contempt or disdain, are best thought of as psycho-intellectual affects that build upon physical disgust (as outrage builds upon anger or nostalgia upon simple homesickness) but are not identical. The make-believe versions of disgust that operate in moral judgements and in a more extended manner in the acting-out of psycho-intellectual affects, such as contempt, point towards what often seems to be an autonomous disgust-realm. Representations of disgust in art, literature and film, while both showing and evoking disgust, are not themselves disgusting or not in the same way that the objects and acts they represent would be. Representations of disgust fit into their contexts, their local environments, quite differently than actual disgusting things fit into the world. Anyone can carry out a number of simple personal experiments to demonstrate that the questions he or she might ask of a representation are very different from, and far more directed towards purely aesthetic issues such as symbolism and coherence, than are the questions he or she might ask of any in-the-world disgusting thing.

Once aesthetic disgust, operating in the realm of representations, has been clearly distinguished from actual disgust, it is possible to turn back to the initial problem of physical disgust and ask a new set of questions. Where does disgust happen? Is it primarily a physical response? A spasm in the guts? A sequences of small convulsions in the throat? An overpowering feeling of nausea which might include not only gut-churning and gagging but also a pervasive sense of physical weakness, anxiety and dread? Is it more than these physical symptoms? If so, where would you look for a disgust experience that underlies, either helping to construct or else reinforcing, physical disgust's varied symptomology?

I have tried to show that it makes sense to say that disgust's primary place is in the mind or, more precisely, in the imagination. In the imagination, countless scenarios, often brief and largely without much detail, occasionally long and intricate, are played out daily in response to stimuli from the world. The world is a vast room of props for the fictional worlds that the imagination creates.[60] A disgust-world is not formally unlike all the other worlds that come into being within the imagination. Its nauseous content, all its mucoid details, will be characterized by "dark" sensations, such as loathing, revulsion, anxiety, horror and even dread. Certain objects in the world, chosen by perception according to previous experience, including whatever has gone into social formation, call attention upon themselves and become props for the imagination. A tattoo, for example, stands out as a problematic visual experience, functioning both as a thing and as a representation. It calls the imagination into play in order to make sense of it, to place it in context, to give reasons, but also to interpret it as a work of art might be. For some people, such as my mother, a tattoo might lead into a world so dark that it could cause physical disgust, but for others it might lead only to a fictional world where the meaning of the tattoo's content would be played out at a distance, almost indifferently. Aesthetic distance (or "psychical distance") can be a factor in actual-world interpretation just as it is in the case of representations. However, even for those who have mastered aesthetic distance, certain in-the-world prompts may be overwhelming. When I saw a man with a spider tattooed in the corner of his right eye, the web trailing down beneath his shirt collar, I experienced a sharp sense that things were not right, as if the world had suddenly clouded over, and I distinctly felt an incipient horror, much anxiety and definite, unmistakable loathing. I feared having closer contact with him and I feared what he might do.

Up to this point, I have tried to show that disgust is far from simple, never a self-evident affect, and open to several disparate accounts. Above all, I have argued that disgust and the representation of disgust are distinct, if mutually reinforcing, mental events. Their common link is the imagination itself which underlies all experiences of disgust. Although many versions of the imagination claim that it is autonomous, even that it transcends experience, capable of recreating the world in a free and untrammelled manner, I have argued that it exists, does both constructive and interpretative work (in the form of small disgust scenarios and fictional worlds) and also helps in recreating the world in outside-the-mind representations such as art, film and fiction. Imagination may be free, as Romantics claim, or else tied to determinate cultural scripts, but it is in either case demonstrably both constructive and pervasive. ✸

6

H^{Its}eads

Perverse Geometries

The Calico Cat was located up against the Illinois Central tracks near 54th Street in South Chicago. Physically it wasn't far, a few blocks at most, from where I lived. Intellectually, it was several galaxies away. For one thing, it was entirely an African-American bar; no whites would have gone there at that time. A white university student would have been doubly out of place. He would attract comment, probably insult, at least hostile questions, and even perhaps violence. I went into the Calico Cat only once.

I went in with my roommate of that time, a graduate student in biochemistry. He had insisted that we go, his Marxist, or pseudo-Marxist, principles urging him always to display tolerance in an ill-balanced world. He had to demonstrate, as he habitually did, that he was not a racist, not a bourgeois pig, but a man ruled solely by principles of human equality, brotherhood and working-class solidarity. Those principles were strong enough to carry him forward into considerable danger, like a inexperienced surfer choosing a wave too big only to be dumped, twisting helplessly in the combing surf, onto rocks. My own principles weren't much different, although (had I been asked) I would have said that I had inherited them directly from the Enlightenment. My friend would have seen himself marching in a revolutionary army of 1917, but I would have remembered the original ideology of the French Revolution, before the guillotine had bloodied things. And so, against my strong objections, bowing to accusations that I was either a racist or an elitist snob, or both, I followed him into the Calico Cat.

Entering the Calico Cat was a bit like dropping into an alien bar, like the one in *Star Wars* or its several imitations in forgotten episodes of *Star Trek*. Nothing was familiar. The music was strange and everyone stared at us. We edged up to the bar and ordered beers. Probably I ordered a bottle of Miller's High Life. At the time in the United States, I usually drank a brew from New Jersey, Ballantine Ale, drawn to the dark-green glass of its bottle, or else an imported beer, but the Calico Cat would not have had such fripperies. It must have been Miller's, a light, frothy, tasteless lager. I stood silently against the bar, not talking to anyone and deeply resenting my friend's arrogance. He had immediately begun a conversation with a large black man in an army uniform, a sergeant from the nearby Fifth Army Headquarters. I paid no attention to their conversation, doing my best to keep my head down and not arouse anyone's interest in me. Suddenly, I heard a crash very close, the sound of a bottle smashing. The sergeant had broken a beer bottle against the counter's edge and was flourishing it in my friend's face. "You want it high, I give it to you low," he screamed, waving the jagged neck of the bottle at his antagonist's face and then at his groin. "You want it low, I give you it high." And he jabbed it upwards again at the face. I was terrified, but that was little compared to what my friend must have felt. Everyone in the Calico Cat stood by silently, staring, waiting to see him slashed.

I managed to get my friend out of the Calico Cat without hurt other than to his psyche. He had wet his pants in fear. As far as I could make things out later, he had given the sergeant an injection of vulgar Marxism. He might even have tried to convince him that his "class" interests lay in joining the Party. He and I had often argued over the question of race in Marxist analysis. I had never found his version of Marxism convincing in its cartoonish vulgarities, which were all that I encountered at that time, on questions of race, ethnicity, language or gender. The argument always seemed to be that those interests were not authentic and ought to be abandoned in the promotion of internationalism. I remember that I especially disliked his insistence that ideology was merely, or specifically, a class concept. (I didn't like that formulation then, and I don't much like it now, even with all the Althusserian refinement it has received since.) For him, class was the only concept that possessed analytic force; the rest was all mythology. When a Marxist talked to a black man about his class interests, or his consciousness as a black man, it was really a kind of double talk. That night at the Calico Cat, the black sergeant had rejected the Marxist analysis of his "class" situation. He might have taken it as arrogant coming from a white man, or as inadequate to the overwhelming injustices that black people had endured at the hands of whites. He might even have seen my friend's words as a threat to his position in the United States Army. Perhaps he was a patriot who thought that he was being suborned to treason.

When the sergeant broke off the neck of his beer bottle, I was quite aware of what he was doing. I already knew how easily one man can take exception to what another has said. And I knew, with considerable clarity, how quickly unexpected violence may erupt over you. Three years before the episode with my roommate, I had experienced a similar explosion in Las Vegas. I had driven down from San Francisco with another friend, a shipmate in any event. He was someone with whom I thought I got along well. We had been together on three voyages to Japan. Once we had gone up to Tokyo from Yokohama to explore what we had heard would be the more sophisticated nightlife there. Among the many things we had done together had been a visit to a place known as the Bacchus Club, a cabaret frequented by western diplomats and officers from the different European militaries. (This was, I remember, the final year of the Korean War.) In the Bacchus Club we had discussed Plato and the world's uneasy future. There had been a number of erotic dancers whom we had largely ignored in the intensity of our conversation. At one point a young girl had emerged with nothing on but a cluster of grapes. She had offered these to different men who pinched off one or two and would invariably attempt to touch her sexually. We had both waved her on, to the hissing of the club's patrons. Finally, a British major had grabbed her by the buttocks and eaten through the grapes in a single, ravenous slurp. A bit later a girl appeared wearing nothing but a single long pin from a game of quoits fastened in the phallic position. She gave a rope ring to each patron, but no one could actually hook the ring on the pin. When she offered it to me, I took it and threw it wrist-flicking in a quick sidearm motion, irritated at having my conversation interrupted. Perfectly thrust, it rammed squarely up against the base of the pin with a resounding thwack. The patrons all roared approval. Then the girl flung herself onto my lap. There must have been an expectation that I would do something interesting, at least fondle her breasts. However, I was so discombobulated that all I did was to spill a glass of scotch down her front, rocks and all. She squealed, leapt up and fled. My friend and I went back to our discussion of philosophy. Joseph Conrad would have understood our desire to talk in preference to the Bacchus Club's erotic pleasures. There was a time for everything. There would be an opportunity for geishas later, after philosophy. With that kind of shared experience behind us, you would think that we would have been deep, trusting friends. Friends for life, not just for a voyage or two.

But in a squalid tavern in Las Vegas, long before it had metamorphosed into its contemporary world-of-fantasy appearance, when the Flamingo Hotel was the still the classiest place in town, he took exception to something I had said. Instantly, he broke a bottle on the edge of a table and lunged at me with the jagged neck held straight ahead like a Roman short sword. He screamed, "I'll cut your guts out!" I back-stepped, filled with terror and disbelief. It was precisely the kind of abrupt explosion of energy, fuelled by rage, that you might see in a bad Kung Fu movie, but without any of the concomitant skills. My friend, a strong but unathletic man, could only charge forward, thrusting the broken bottle towards me, his eyes glassed over with hate, his mouth slobbering. I stepped aside, grabbed his wrist, pivoted and pushed his head down onto another table. The tavern had grown silent, just as the Calico Cat did three years later, except for the couple at the table who, splashed with beer, were cursing us both. The spectacle of violence is rivetting, no doubt, but oddly so. (In the spring of 1999 when NATO was pounding Yugoslavia to bits, people, including myself, watched TV with a similar stupefied fascination. It must run in Old Adam's blood.)

As I forced my friend's head down with my right hand, with my left I twisted his wrist until the bottle's neck fell out of his grip. Then, holding him in a Japanese strangle-hold that I had learned years before, my right knee in the small of his back, I sweet-talked him into calm. It all took only a few seconds and today I can't remember what I said to cool him down any better than I can recall what I had said that had set him off. It had all been explosive, crazy, macho perhaps and, even if explicable in some abstract way, unexplainable. The other people in the tavern watched in fascinated silence, but also gleefully, just as the patrons in the Calico Cat would do. A bartender had come around in front, but he didn't offer to help. Once my friend had quieted down, everyone went back to their drinks, conversations or shuffleboard. The bartender warned us to "tone things down." And then it seemed we were both good friends again. Yet that moment of extreme violence had been genuine. I might have been killed.

I wouldn't suppose that anything like that would usually happen in even very rough bars. But it could. The noisy, moderately drunk men in almost any bar or pub, to whom you might well seem a pathetic alien creature, all know how to break the neck off a beer bottle. They could do it quickly and neatly against the edge of the counter or a table, in order to obtain an instant deadly weapon. That knowledge is part of male culture. If you haven't seen it before, then such abrupt volcanoes, spewing pent-up magma and hard little rocks of hate, might startle you. Once you have seen it, you know what to do: avoid it, flee if you can.

In February 1997, in Valparaíso, Chile's second largest city and a tough working-class seaport, I stepped into a small bar near the Plaza Sotomayor, an area dominated by the navy. There are always lots of military sailors and longshoremen. Chatting away with a couple of men in my quite serviceable but influent Spanish, I inadvertently got into an argument with one of them when he took exception to something I had said concerning General Augusto Pinochet. I knew that Valparaíso was Pinochet's home, but I also knew very well that it was a strongly proletarian place, just south of and connected to the upper-class resort town of Viña del Mar, which had suffered a great deal under the dictatorship. I think I said, carefully and with caution, that General Pinochet's economic policies seemed to have been partially successful, but there may have been some other issue in play. The man may have been annoyed at the opacity of all gringos or frustrated by my spattering, bookish and peninsular Spanish, or driven by something I could never have guessed. In any event, he grabbed his bottle (*Escudo*, ironic for the context) and I knew, with instantaneous clarity, what he planned to do. In the briefest of moments, I snatched up my Tilly hat, wrapped it around my left hand while I held my own unbroken bottle of *Escudo* in my right. Clenching the hat from inside, making it serve as a shield, I began backing towards the door. Everyone became utterly silent, watching to see an old gringo cut to pieces. However, the man only shrugged and turned away. It seemed like a very sudden, last-minute decision, but he didn't break the neck off his bottle of *Escudo*. I felt absolutely certain that up until the moment in which he turned away, he had intended to break the bottle and use it to attack me. I left as fast as I could and no one tried to stop me. Later, I reflected that the act of wrapping my Tilly hat around my fist might have reminded him of the Argentinian custom of fighting with a knife in one hand while the other arm, shield-like, is protected by a rolled poncho. He might, just possibly, have attributed to me more knowledge (and hence skill) than I actually possessed. I experienced a tiny tingle of pleasure from supposing that I had, however briefly, stepped into the mythical world of Argentinian gauchos and Chileno *huasos*, the world that Borges evokes so wondrously in "The South." In the moment, however, I had felt only fear. I took the first taxi I could hail back to my hotel in Viña.

These episodes of abrupt, apparently spontaneous violence indicate an important distinction between horror and terror. Horror is a slow, gathering action, everything moving, with anxiety or dread, towards an inevitable conclusion which you will anticipate coming like a revelation. Terror is abrupt, coming without evident preparation, never giving you the chance to feel anxiety or apprehension, its unexpected conclusion striking you like an explosion. Translated into representations, into kinds of narrative, horror and terror constitute antithetical varieties of aesthetic experience. The three episodes of sudden violence that I have recounted were evidently moments of terror. Nothing had led up to them and they were mind-freezingly abrupt. If I were to tell them in a literary manner, I would want to draw attention to the unsuspecting confidence of the man who is about to confront the violence. I might make much of the disgusting aspects or the moment such as the distorted faces, the slobber and spit flying from the mouth of the enraged man, and the slivers of glass crunching like beetles under foot. I would want to emphasize what is already present in the stories as I told them: the breath-held silence of everyone watching. Watching terror explode or horror unfold, you tend to become still, holding your breath or breathing shallowly in (vicarious) fear, while you watch dreading, but still expecting, a murderous outcome. The phrase "waiting with bated breath" means something. In the dead stillness of anticipation the mind may hear the chirr and crack of unlit pyres.

The sense of disgust can be extremely important to both horror and terror, but it works in quite different ways. Dispersed into a number of distinct motifs in a narrative, disgust will function both in single episodes, increasing the growing impression of apprehension or else causing gasps, forcing the mind's eye to blink, and as a dimension of the whole. There are fictional worlds in which disgust dominates much as starlight and love do in others. Certain narratives will leave the impression that they are essentially disgusting even if this is far from the whole story.

In horror, disgust motifs appear gradually, like a faint spoor, and increase as the moment of maximum horror, the revelation of the monster or some other cataclysm, nears. In terror, things occur quickly, without apparent preparation, and, from the victim's perspective, seem to happen irrationally, as if the earth had opened or the air caught fire. In terror narratives, if some act or thing is disgusting, it will also break into the narrative suddenly, without warning. Or else the sudden act itself may appear as disgusting: a quick and loathsome sight that torments the vision even as it may threaten the body. Both in life and as a narrative strategy, terror occurs abruptly, erupting violently upon the unprepared, unready consciousness. In William Blake's words, terror has the "Human Form Divine" for disguise. It is difficult to prepare for what such a disguise might hide. The scene of coprophagy in Pynchon's *Gravity's Rainbow* exemplifies the unanticipated abruptness of terrorism.[1] Not only does the act explode within the narrative as an unprepared assault upon the reader, but it must also be understood as an act involving the intersection of two fantasies, two systems of fantastic desire, Brigadier Pudding's and Pointsman's (for whose desire Katje is merely an instrument, an agent). Like all terrorism, the coprophagy in *Gravity's Rainbow* is a manifestation of a godgame, an indirect demonstration of an intelligence whose plans are unknown, even unknowable, to its victims.

Either as deliberate acts of terrorism or as random and inexplicable violence, the actions that cause terror proceed from systems of thinking that are unknown, even unrecognized. Resistance arises from the intersection of contrasting belief systems.[2] The person engaged in resistance not only stands against "power and its depredations,"[3] but also stands for (something). A belief system functions like, and may even be congruent with, an ideology, but it can also be idiosyncratic, "minoritarian" in Deleuze's and Guattari's phrase. A controlling power proclaims itself (in edicts, laws, *fatwas*, propaganda, allegorical literature) as, and in an effort to promote, a majority consciousness. The majoritarian, Deleuze and Guattari write, is a homogenous and constant system (which is to say, repressive) whereas the minoritarian, always a subsystem, is a creative potential to become the Other.[4] From the outside, the struggle between a state system and a personal conviction may seem like arabesques buzzing between an insect and a hand, but, since personal conviction *can* modify the controlling system, another metaphor is needed. Think of them as contradictory geometries that overlay each other. Each geometry, the individual and the supra-individual, will be bent upon drawing, redrawing or erasing possible striations. Each will strike the other as perverse. Such perverse geometries are the realm of both horror and terror narratives. Behind the murderous acts, so precisely indicated by disgust motifs and images, lie systems of ideas.

In order to make this point as vividly as possible, I am going to invent a small fictional world, a representation less of terror than of ideology, but one in which the disgusting plays out daily in its inhabitants' minds and where terror is an ordinary expression. This world is called QueAng-QueAng and it is nowhere and everywhere. It is not on any map: as Herman Melville says of another place, "true places never are."

> A speculative traveller from an antique land tells the following tale. Did you know, he asks, that the people of QueAng-QueAng drink the eyeballs of living animals using a slender metal straw? The trick, that only practice can teach, is to pierce the eyeball through the iris to the exact centre and then drink the vitreous gel in many tiny sips. In QueAng-QueAng, they also execute blasphemers in a similar manner. The community kneel and angrily pierce the condemned person's body with their metal straws. When the execution has been finished nothing much is left but skin and bones. These dry in the desert air until, withered and empty, they blow away into the bleached horizon. The condemned, like husks, are soon forgotten. You hardly know how to respond. The people of QueAng-QueAng may exist beyond understanding. You may try to remember Montaigne, but he offers scant help. Finally, you may decide that, no matter what, QueAng-QueAng is not a place to visit. The traveller only advises that you should leave the people of QueAng-QueAng to their private intensities.

It is impossible to understand the people of QueAng-QueAng since their motivations are secret and their acts spring from an ideological system that is mysterious, though explicit in ascribing perversity to others. Whatever they do will appear in the mode of terror. Thus the question of Salman Rushdie has seemed until very recently, and continues so even today, deeply disturbing precisely because in his case the people of QueAng-QueAng decided to force their intensities upon the entire world. It was as if they had boarded an airbus and flown to London (but really to all places in the world), carrying their slender metal straws in their flight bags, and sought out Rushdie for execution according to their custom, but piously ignoring London's.

Rushdie's 1987 novel *The Satanic Verses* embodies several different senses of the term "perverse geometries." Taken as an abstract conceptual system, an ideology in some sense, a perverse geometry distorts reality in vicious ways and transforms others into objects of disgust. Yet it is itself also an object of disgust, viewed as having deformed both reality and the human mind. In *The Satanic Verses*, the fanatical Imam promulgates an intolerant and death-yearning revolutionary doctrine. The new religion, Submission, might appear from outside its belief system to be perverse since it is inflexible, intolerant and anti-diversity. The British social system, especially with respect to its policies towards foreigners, people who are physically distinct from "normal" British subjects, also appears as a deforming and perverse ideology. The novel itself has been seen by most Muslims, and many others as well, as a perverse distortion of Islam. When it caused riots in the late 1980s and was publicly burnt, it was understood not as a work of fiction, or as a nexus of metaphors, but as a deforming and perverse *view* of Islam. On the other hand, the huge mobs, the obvious fury and intensity, the refusal to examine what the novel actually said, struck many in the west as a perverse distortion of human intelligence.

I am using the phrase "perverse geometries" to indicate the horror and terror of conceptual systems. An ideology, a belief, a theory or a complex system of thought may strike those who do not share it as horrible, a perverse deformation of "normal" (that is, their own) human thinking. In this sense, a disgusting conceptual system, although inherently abstract and unphysical, other than in its representations, causes loathing and revulsion much as any other disgusting object or act. It will appear to be a deformation of, an obvious twisting away from, some accepted standard. A decomposed or metamorphic body may arouse disgust merely because it falls short of some normal standard of the human body (whole, integrated). Even the most basic instance of a disgusting object, a pile of mammalian feces, say, evokes disgust because its mere presence violates a boundary (what should not be seen) and may also suggest the corporeal deliquescence of living things. Hence an alien conceptual system, an ideology that you find abhorrent or a religion whose chief tenets you must (with violent loathing) reject, can cause disgust much as the sight of something out of place or else deliquescent might do.

I am also using the phrase "perverse geometry" because it is associated with H.P. Lovecraft, the American master of both horror and terror. In a Lovecraft tale, landscapes are often out of kilter, twisted or malformed in definite ways. That is, they are highly symbolic, indicative of the action to follow, but also in themselves disturbing. Physical deformations, even when they do not symbolize corresponding intellectual distortions, are always taken as potentially threatening and actually disgusting. In horror fiction, a sense of perverse thinking, like a barely seen landscape, may contribute to the growing impression of an impending revelation too horrible to contemplate undisturbed. Even a monster, deformed or otherwise grotesque, may also embody an alien set of values and a loathsome way of feeling. That is, a monster may stand for something outside of itself even as an agent in a terror-fiction does. In horror, there will be an alien intellectual ambiance through which a faint but increasing spoor will lead towards some monstrous revelation; in terror, the monstrous act will suddenly and explosively burst. In both kinds of fiction a perverse geometry, an alien landscape (of ideas) or a conceptual machine for destroying a prior belief system, poses the problem of containment. The source of the threat must be destroyed. In a terror-fiction, the action is often construed as a battle between opposing belief systems, each intent upon the destruction of the other. (A terrorist is an agent of a belief system acting, in its interest, against another such system.) In-the-world containment, although it can manifest itself as war or repression, usually takes the form of censorship. It is an evident, if not always observed, point about disgust that it is inseparable from censorship. What is disgusting is excluded from view, or at least from public contemplation. Aesthetic forms such as shock theatre, pornography or "emetic" fiction (Joyce's *Ulysses*, for instance) frequently give rise to calls for censorship. In overtly repressive societies, such texts will be blocked, deleted or otherwise censored. Even in open societies, a public demand for censorship may lead to civil unrest.

Hence the question of Salman Rushdie's *The Satanic Verses* poses an interesting problem for this study because it focusses the opposed claims of censorship and freedom of expression with rare clarity. Rushdie's novel raises an important question for a study of disgust since what is disgusting has so often been subjected to censorship. What is perverse, it will be said, ought not to be represented. Should writers be executed for having given offence? Should the offence count more sternly if it has been given to members of a world religion? Should it count for less (or perhaps for nothing at all) if it is given "only" as a representation, in the form of fiction? Should the offended citizens of one country be able to condemn the offender even if he lives, a free person, as the citizen of another country? How should the inhabitants of a largely secular world understand the "crime" of blasphemy? Can an act of violence that must be seen as terrorism in one place actually constitute justice in another? These are only some of the difficult issues, as slippery as they are impassioned, that surround the Rushdie question. Any fool, Paul Theroux writes, "can see that the Ayatollah's *fatwa* is barbarous and ignorant." And, reflecting on the failure of western nations to influence Iran, he comments, "How disgusting to see that so far the intimidation of fanatics has worked." Anger flashing in each word, Theroux writes that on a personal level,

> people are muddled or uninterested; on an official and governmental level, the response has been weak and cowardly; on a religious level, the Muslims have either been supine or vindictive.[5]

Anyone who thinks about such matters as literature, free expression, the nature of liberty and the requirements of justice, or even the commingling of diverse peoples in a pluralistic society, should take an interest in Rushdie. And anyone who thinks about the problem of disgust as a whole, as more than squirming maggots and the stench of excrement, will find the interwoven issues of the loathsomeness of belief systems, the threats they pose and the calls for their repression and censorship worth a long, penetrating look.

Above all, the Rushdie affair makes clear how easy it is to hate another person for his or her commitments, beliefs or ideas.[6] A belief system, whether fully understood or not, can be experienced as disgusting. Because disgusting, it may also be the occasion for hate. The enraged response to *The Satanic Verses* in Muslim countries (and in India where rage has been an instrument of governmental policy) and the Iranian *fatwa* against Rushdie show how a book can easily plummet beyond the boundaries that mark off the disgusting, delimiting action and expression, from the ideologically correct "world." Rushdie's predicament, to have become a public target of religious terrorism and consequently to have "vanished into the front page," has made several things clear.[7] It has shown that blasphemy, which may be in "a persistent vegetative state in America, and in a state of suspended animation in Great Britain," can still energize large numbers of religious people.[8] Amir Taheri, an Iranian journalist and biographer of the Ayatollah Khomeini, observes that the "very idea of using the prophet Muhammad as a character in a novel is painful to many Muslims." He adds that Islam considers "a wide variety of topics as permanently closed."[9] A fiction such as *The Satanic Verses* can be read, Jamel Eddine Bencheikh writes, as "a major attack" on Islam simply because Islam is "an order that gives a significance to prophecy and fixes limits to the writing about it." In Muslim countries, Bencheikh adds, "fiction is not fictive." It can only speak of realities "that leave no room for any criticism."[10]

The charge of blasphemy against *The Satanic Verses* masks several different issues. David Lawton puts the accusation into perspective: it identifies Rushdie's offence to a cultural community, to a religious outlook on human life, upon a number of common values and a shared (if closed) tradition, but it does not offend Islam itself, nor yet God.[11] For fundamentalist Muslims, Rushdie's novel has been perceived (that is, sensed, not read) as a perverse geometry: a belief system, a conceptual frame, that is so warped that it can only be experienced as disgusting. For many westerners, those at least who support a writer's right to free expression or who love Rushdie's novel, the fundamentalist reaction has seemed itself perverse, an abstract notion of prohibition traced upon a work of fiction.

Imagination is a powerful, if perplexing, human capacity: it disturbs ideological fundamentalists, no matter what their dogma. The charge of blasphemy against Rushdie does not address theological doctrine, nor even his religious convictions, so much as it marks a community's reaction to his representation of it. *The Satanic Verses* rewrites the representation of that community, picking up direction from Nietzsche, "according to the laws of simulacra and polyglot, multivocal schizophrenia."[12] God appears in the novel only as an ordinary human person, balding, wearing glasses and with dandruff on his collar: in true metafictional manner, the author himself.[13] If he can be said to appear at all, the Prophet exists only as a character in a "Bombay theological" envisioned through an actor's, Gibreel Farishta's, vividly filmic, but distorting, imagination. The novel reads as an overlayering of simulacra, of images replicating in a series of distorting mirrors, that denies a definite source for its representations. Moroccan writer Nadia Tazi notes that what Muslims find impossible to forgive is Rushdie's apparent "withdrawing from the *Umma*; his refusing to be one whom the community forms; his maintaining of a singularity on the margins of that fraternity; and his challenging of the basic meanings on which it is based."[14] All that play, the inescapable metafiction, may indeed seem to constitute a "singularity," and even a withdrawal from a community that denies such modes of play. As Lawton argues, blasphemy is "an exchange transaction."[15] Once given, the offense spreads throughout a much larger cultural community that engages in countermeasures, seeking cancellation or retribution.[16] Censorship attempts to protect a community from hurt.

The international controversy over *The Satanic Verses* raises other questions as well. How weak, vacillating and ignominious will politicians in a democratic society appear when confronted by an international objection driven by religious and third-world passion? (The answer: disgustingly so.)

What are the limitations upon fiction in an open society? To what extent should a democratic society respect the sensitivities of religious people? Of people in other countries? Of third-world immigrants in their own midst? Should limitations on free expression, if any, extend to censorship? The mere question ought to make your flesh crawl. With Miltonic undertones, Rushdie remarks that free speech "is life itself."[17] Leaving the option of censorship aside, then, what *would be* the best response to religious outrage within a pluralistic society? How should other writers treat a writer who has been singled out for execution because of what he has written? What should readers, students and teachers of literature have done in 1988 and since, in response to the *fatwa* against Rushdie? The *fatwa* has tested the foundations of more than a few western shibboleths.[18]

Western politicians looked weak, sadly pusillanimous, during the early days of the *fatwa*. British politicians often had ridings with large Muslim populations to placate, and other local reasons to temporize.[19] Julian Barnes notes that, had the Rushdie affair been a novel, British readers would have complained about the "postmodern loops." In the United Kingdom, there have been too many subplots for local taste:

> minority communities, their rights, vulnerability, and leader-
> ship; electoral votes, and M.P.s' fear of losing their seats; trade,
> and the potential loss of overseas customers; racism and
> antiracism; the intelligentsia's lack of political muscle; victim-
> blaming (disguised as the academic thesis "Hero or Anti-Hero?");
> plus, finally, the eternal national quest for a quiet time.[20]

Many writers early recognized the implications. Nadine Gordimer, who knew about both censorship and tyranny, clearly perceived the "religious thuggery" involved and its appeal to the "unchanging principle of censorship, which was and is and always will be to harness the word to the tyrant's chariot."[21] Rushdie stands for, even in the minds of many Muslims, the resistance to tyranny and the internal terrorism of certain states against their own citizens. He is, Edward W. Said says, "everyone who dares to speak out against power, to say that we are entitled to think and express forbidden thoughts, to argue for democracy and freedom of opinion." He is "the *intifada* of the imagination."[22]

In their respective studies of blasphemy, both Leonard Levy and David Lawton each refer to the 1887 New Jersey trial in which Charles B. Reynolds was charged with blasphemous misreadings of the Bible.[23] Levy gives a detailed analysis of the trial and Robert G. Ingersoll's magnificent defence of Reynolds. Lawton quotes the concluding remarks from Ingersoll's summation to the jury, and also takes them for an epigraph to his book as a whole: "What we want," Ingersoll urged, "is intellectual hospitality. Let the world talk." (This would also make a good epigraph for the Rushdie affair.) However, in an essay on Thomas Paine, Ingersoll also notes that religion "always looks back."[24] An orthodox religious person, Ingersoll observes, neither forgets nor learns, neither advances nor recedes. An orthodox religious person is "a living fossil embedded in that rock called faith." When the orthodox believer has power, heresy, entailing torture and death, is "the most terrible and formidable of words."[25] Talk is neither always easy, nor always fruitful.[26]

Alas, QueAng-QueAng does not cherish talk. Perhaps it may be true, as Nadia Tazi writes, that *The Satanic Verses* cannot be killed. It will live or die on its own, going its adventurous way and always encountering "mutations, and festivals of the spirit."[27] That would be the most optimistic outlook for Rushdie's novel, or for any work subjected to the terrors of censorship. In QueAng-QueAng the possibilities are bleak.

> In QueAng-QueAng, the people do not like to read. The traveller reports that once they did enjoy reading and that in that time they had many books, beautifully written and produced, which they esteemed. Centuries ago, he says, they learned to forget how to read. Reading, they believe, always raises problems that cannot be solved or that have various solutions. One of their wise men taught them to tell stories from strings. They take many lengths of coloured string and braid them into patterns that they have learned to interpret. These narrative nets are colourful and often very intricate. Bright tints twist together in dazzling sequences. The inhabitants of QueAng-QueAng know by heart every possible sequence and can always say what it means. Foreigners cannot understand these patterns, even when they have studied the techniques for string-writing. The fundamental rule, which foreigners have much trouble understanding, insists that all patterns must finish at the same point. All the patterns possible in braiding strings lead to a thick knot of black string. Sometimes the string-writer will use a piece of dark glass or an unpolished pebble. The effect is the same. The patterns of string are

spliced into the knot or tied to the piece of glass. The inhabitants of QueAng-QueAng say that this shows that all problems have the same solution. All their stories are meaningful only because there is, forever and inalterably, a single story.

A perverse geometry is a belief system seen from the outside, from an alien distance. It will be seen to twist the world, to distort and deform what has been accepted as reality. Its explanations and the accounts that it makes possible will be falsehoods, lies intended to corrupt. When Iranians, and other devout Muslims, call the United States the "Great Satan," they have in mind not solely a memory of how it supported the Shah and defended the Peacock Throne, but also a belief system—modernism—that it seems to represent. They do not see that system as American citizens might (democracy, pluralism, freedom), or as a refugee from tyranny might.[28] In that sense, the character of the Great Satan merely follows fairly ordinary conventions for creating personifications: strip the character down to those essential traits that will represent a concept or a set of interlocking concepts. Typically, as seen in TV coverage of many anti-American demonstrations, the Great Satan wears an Uncle Sam suit and has long teeth (to represent the greed of capitalism), blood on teeth and fingers, a tail and other deformed body parts. The figure embodies the twisting of the world which the American belief system is felt to perform. When participants in different belief systems experience each other as perverse, or as abstract schemata that pervert, the opposition reflects irreconcilable difference. In that sense, the disgust that belief systems evoke may be more entrenched, less easy to eradicate or manage, than physical disgust. You might find it simpler to learn how to eat new foods, to eat in different ways (with your fingers, say) or to adopt never-imagined toilet practices than to tolerate a genuinely alien set of concepts. Modernism is a good test case. It touches almost everyone, as fact or as desire, and affects human life nearly everywhere. Modernism may have brought better technologies, superior medicine and anti-repressive entertainment (in ever more diverse forms and media), but it has not been universally loved.[29]

Early in Mary Gordon's novel *The Company of Women*, an episode occurs that points up the interconnection between modernism and disgust for an orthodox religious mind. Father Cyprian, a priest much concerned with the conduct of life, takes Felicitas, a young girl who has demonstrated a precocious talent for piety, to visit a farm. Felicitas has made the mistake of saying that she imagines that heaven will smell like a springtime field in up-state New York, filled with the scents of new grass and wild flowers. In anger at this attribution of physical experience to heaven, Father Cyprian takes her to the farm to "show this young lady the differences in manures. She says she is interested in perfumes." Very much a hardscrabble operation, the farm is "filth and death and heaviness in every limb that made no action possible."

> "This is cow shit," said Father Cyprian, pulling a handful of brown dirt. "It has a warmer, meatier aroma."
> "Chicken shit," he said, stooping for a yellow handful, "is a higher smell. More pungent, more bouquet."[30]

Father Cyprian then takes Felicitas to experience pig manure. He takes her by the hand and she feels "against her palms the dust of the manure liquefying into stinking mud."

> "Pig shit," he said, "is slimy and green, and among connoisseurs, it is considered the most aromatic. This is because pigs eat garbage, like the mind of modern man."
> He pulled her over to the pigpen. She could feel her stomach rise against her, something firm let go. She vomited a clear brown pool against the pigpen, clear because she had fasted for communion.[31]

Father Cyprian tells Felicitas that he doesn't want her to be poisoned by "the sentimental claptrap that passes for religion in this age." She must understand that "the spirit is life eternal, not the smell of grasses."[32] Shortly after this scene, the reader learns that Father Cyprian hates the "whole sewer of the modern world, the great dark stink of it." He wears his priesthood "like a cloak cut big to hide the body."[33] The lesson in the discrimination of animal excrement has been executed in order to stamp out any childish sentimentality about religion and spiritual values, but it has also been intended as a laboratory experiment in modernism. The modern world, modernism and materialism should all stink like pig shit in the nose of the pious.

Modernism has always had several meanings. In an important sense, it is not especially modern at all, but only a new name for an old direction. The roots of modernism lie in the Enlightenment: in the doctrines of liberty, fraternity, equality, justice for all, the free pursuit of knowledge and the method of critique to expose the hidden assumptions and secret ideologies of authority.34 Thus, all attacks on modernism have a target that is not in itself obviously "modern." (And so the attacks upon it are, as such, centuries old.) Leszek Kolakowski observes that modernity is "not modern, but clearly the clashes about modernity are more prominent in some civilizations than in others and never have they been as acute as in our time."35 For the purposes of this discussion, modernism has two rather different meanings. First, it is a rubric to designate twentieth-century movements in literature and art (a turning away from inherited conventions, an eagerness for formal experiment, a preoccupation with the "new," such as machines, and with representing interior states of consciousness, all shocking in their ways). Second, modernism has meant both the attempt to redefine orthodoxy by the light of pluralistic and innovative thinking and also the secular materialism (with its full panoply of Enlightenment ideals of pluralism, scientific discovery and social amelioration) that has come to dominate western civilization.

Joyce's *Ulysses* is a fairly obvious example of a modernist text because it not only turns away from the narrative conventions of the nineteenth-century novel, such as lucid characterization, clear plot lines and no-loose-strings endings, to play with the possibilities of style, from pastiche to stream of consciousness; but also because it imagines a fictional world that is contemporary without illusions. The world of *Ulysses* is dreary, pervaded by alienation and crowded with inherited deceptions (religious, nationalistic, aesthetic) that are systematically exposed. Its two main characters, Stephen and Leopold, feel themselves alienated, albeit for different reasons, and look for escapes from their radical apartness. Leopold Bloom concentrates on his body, seeking happiness in a healthy peristalsis, and imagines his world in coarse bodily images; when, in the Circe chapter, he imagines metamorphosis, it is towards transsexual exposure (he lacks confidence in the body that obsesses him) and degradation. Furthermore, it is world in which disgust motifs abound. Like *Hamlet*, the world of *Ulysses* crawls with images that define both individual and collective experience: excrement, stains, stenches, worms, decay and rot. Unlike *Hamlet*, it is without spiritual, though pointing the way towards aesthetic, transcendence. Stephen may go to Paris, but not to heaven; lines of modern poetry sound in his mind's ear, but not the songs of angels.

The precise meaning that modernism has had for the Catholic church (but taking it as a stand-in for all orthodoxies) turns much more upon the second sense of the term, although the first meaning is certainly contaminated by the second. It is worth considering. What is called the "modern world," Pius IX is reported to have said, is "simply Freemasonry."[36] When Father Cyprian associates pig manure with "the mind of modern man" and the "whole sewer of the modern world," he seems to be thinking about the world's materialism or even, as Pope Leo XIII had said in his 1899 apostolic letter, *Testem Benevolentiae*, "Americanism."[37] A reader may even imagine him as remembering the Oath Against Modernism that he swore while still a candidate for the priesthood. The oath contains several propositions intended to reinforce the young priest's resistance to secularism and inter-faith tolerance. Above all, it proclaims the intellectual content of religious faith as a "real assent of the intellect to truth by hearing from an external source."[38] When Father Cyprian cautions Felicitas against sentimentality and against being "womanish" (to substitute external marks of devotion, such as carrying "pastel holy cards and stitched novena booklets," for intellectual attention), he seems to have very much in mind the antimodernist rejection of nineteenth-century accounts of religion, stemming from the theological writings of Friedrich Schleiermacher, as blind feeling (an "opiate," even) or an up-welling from the unconscious.[39]

Within the Catholic church, modernism, as a "synthesis of all heresies," came to signify an ideological orientation that was antagonistic to ecclesiastical authority.[40] Pope Pius IX developed his *Syllabus of Errors* (1864) to combat the ingrained fallacies of modernism that had sunk deeply into the fabric of modern life (in Europe and North America, at least) and tended, Pius IX thought, to undermine legitimate authority.[41] Modernist thinkers urged changes in Catholic doctrine to bring this more in agreement with modern thought even if this was at "the expense of radically changing the church's essence." Modernism called for freedom and equality for all people, including women, under the constitution of multi-ethnic states, the emancipation of scientific research from church dogma, located the divine as an immanent presence and denied the supernatural as an object of knowledge.[42] In 1907, Pope Pius X published the decree *Lamentabili Sane* and the encyclical *Pascendi Dominici Gregis,* both of which identified the errors of modernism, locating them in "epistemological agnosticism and religious immanentism."[43] The influence of several philosophical positions, most of them Protestant in origin, lay behind modernism.[44] In a sense, the Catholic battle within its own ranks seems like a continuation of the Counter-Reformation on a new front.

Catholics experienced modernism as a perverse geometry because it attacked traditional positions, urged the importance of recent Protestant theology over and against the church's own tradition of deductive scholastic, or neo-Thomistic, argument, militantly separated feeling from intelligence and sought to limit the church's authority on matters of private conscience and the pursuit of scientific knowledge. It claimed—or seemed to claim—to overlay the world, like a new geometry, assigning new significance to old features and entirely new values where they had not previously existed. Father Cyprian has all of this in mind when he seeks to break Felicitas' affection for the merely natural world. He has a larger sense of modernism in mind as well. He may think, as Pope Leo XIII did, that American Catholics will be "affected by the spirit of the times despite themselves."[45] The modern world's attributes crowd the individual very closely. Secularism, materialism, sentimentalism, not to forget liberal tolerance, all jostle each person, however devout, away from tradition, away from the verticality of authority into horizontal mush, the modern world's sewer, "the great dark stink of it." Father Cyprian tries to show Felicitas many things in the deceptively simple, but actually overdetermined, analogy of pig shit.

Similarly, the Muslim reaction to Rushdie's *The Satanic Verses* reflects an extremely complex set of oppositions. It is an opposition that bears many resemblances to the Catholic rejection of modernism and even the "modern" world itself. It would seem that, however narrowly focussed the public rhetoric, no one should accept that charge of blasphemy as the sum of the matter. The very ferocity of the opposition might suggest that much is involved that may not meet the eye. Many westerners have found both excessive and irrational the outrage that Muslims expressed after February 14, 1989, the day that the Ayatollah Khomeini pronounced the *fatwa* calling for Rushdie's execution. On the other hand, many Muslims find western surprise and incomprehension disturbing, one sign (among others) of materialism and the degradation of spiritual values in western civilization. Mughram Al-Ghamdi's reaction to *The Satanic Verses* might seem, in the context of the *fatwa*, to be a typical response. Writing for the United Kingdom Committee on Islamic Affairs, Al-Ghamdi called *The Satanic Verses* "blasphemous" and "filthily abusive." It is, he wrote, the "most offensive, filthy and abusive book ever written by any hostile enemy of Islam and deserves to be condemned in the strongest possible way."[46] Non-Muslims may find such an expression of outrage to be itself outrageous, a product of narrow and fanatical thinking, a vile misreading of Rushdie's fiction. *The Satanic Verses* is not truly blasphemous and far from filthy. Writing with the moderation of a legal historian, Leonard Levy comments that the novel's language is "street-smart," but it is "definitely not an obscene book, surely not in the disputed passages, Muslim assertions notwithstanding."[47] A non-Muslim might suspect that many deeply encoded cultural values, not only the sense of a supreme being's majesty, have been offended.[48]

Rushdie's "blasphemy" focussed Muslim hatred of the west and of its perceived irreligion. The attack on *The Satanic Verses* was a single battle, a terrorist assault behind the enemy lines, on western materialism which was understood as a terrible perversion of revealed truth. Khomeini made this clear in a radio address on February 23, 1989, when he observed that God had wanted *The Satanic Verses* published so that "the world of conceit, arrogance and barbarism would bare its true face in its long-held enmity to Islam ...."[49] The arrogance of the materialistic (but also pluralistic) west, seems to be much more an issue than the putative blasphemy of Rushdie's novel. Like the pig shit in Mary Gordon's novel, Rushdie's *The Satanic Verses* functions, in Muslim eyes, as a complex, overdetermined symbol of a perverse geometry that is believed to have traversed human society as a whole and remains potentially capable of penetrating and deforming every cultural expression.

Some Muslims have expressed the conviction that the *fatwa* was only a single clash in a much wider war. (This is Rushdie's own view.) Amir Taheri observes that Khomeini's motives were "not entirely religious." After having experienced several setbacks, international humiliations and domestic failures, he had been looking for an issue "to stir the imagination of the poor and illiterate masses."[50] Writing of the "spirit of innovation" as well as the tradition of "tolerance and respect for the opinions of others" that characterized both the European Enlightenment and the "Arab-Muslim patrimony," Khédija Ben Mahmoud Cherif observes that contemporary Muslim societies "clearly suffer a form of amnesia with regard to this aspect of their own traditions; they have turned their backs on this part of our patrimony, just as they have turned their backs on the now universal legacy of the rights of man."[51] Against that legacy (if indeed it existed), there is, as Aziz Al-Azmeh puts it, the "new and totally 'super-Islamized'" Islam, the very "fantasies" that Rushdie explodes in *The Satanic Verses*.[52] Zhor Ben Chamsi, a Moroccan psychoanalyst, refers to the *fatwa* as being itself a "blasphemy," a product of "our contemporary sclerosis."[53] Chamsi's comments are close to Rushdie's own argument that Islam, in denying "redescriptions," shuts down the imagination. The profound sense (and hope) that there is another Islam, closer to tradition and the "patrimony," than Khomeini's super-Islam, an Islam that respects diversity and difference, runs through the writings of many Muslim commentators on the Rushdie affair. Bencheikh declares that there "certainly does exist an open, fraternal, compassionate, and generous Islamic tradition that not even the furious howling of today's hyenas can succeed in silencing."[54] For most western readers, *The Satanic Verses* is a novel, possibly a great one, that creates a complex fictional world; for Muslims, it seems to have functioned as a prosthetic imagination that demands its own rejection. The promises of modernity (or the attractions of a coherent theory of modernism) and the heritage of the Enlightenment, both of which play major roles in *The Satanic Verses,* have had no resonance among its Muslim readers.

Blasphemy may seem to be an archaic charge, but it is a verbal act that can still knock many people roughly in the heart. Levy makes plain the extent to which, in Great Britain, the accusation against Rushdie immediately cohered with a national debate over the validity of blasphemy laws.[55] It struck sensitive nerves within the Anglican church, for example, and the Ayatollah Khomeini found warm supporters there.[56] As a perverse geometry, warping the world from the ways it has been fixed by given religious discourse, blasphemy can hurt the believer deeply and give massive offense. It is also, and always, an offense more complex, hidden from surface inspection, than a simple insult to a supreme being. Both Levy and Lawton treat the charge of blasphemy as an injustice disguised within the garb of legal right. Lawton concludes that he has yet to find a single case that was not either vexatious or tyrannical, or else punished "people who should have been helped."[57]

Members of the eighteenth-century Ranter movement, in which sincere men and women claimed the truth of conscience's "inner light" in order to act disruptively, even scandalously, were systematically treated as blasphemers. They wished to mark their opposition to religious orthodoxy and repression (which seemed to deny Christ's teachings), but their sexual openness, excess and subversion of social codes were read as particularly disgusting blasphemy. "When orthodoxy sees libertinism," Lawton writes, "it sees both blasphemy and sexual deviance."[58] Even more bitingly, Levy concludes that "the feculent odor of persecution for the cause of conscience" has not yet dissipated.[59] The Iranian *fatwa* may be said to stink feculently in western noses.[60] The debate generated by the Rushdie affair tears directly into the heart of western pluralism: how to respect the sensitivities of minority religious groups without allowing them to dominate, or even to modify, social commitments (painfully achieved) to tolerance and freedom of expression. What the centuries have taught, Levy writes, "should not be abandoned out of respect for a minority religion or the feelings of its believers, any more than out of respect for a majority religion or the feelings of *its* believers."[61] Lawton observes that fundamentalism "offers a false identity, a spurious recoding of the many as one."[62] Few events, short of war or revolution, could be more destabilizing to a pluralistic democracy than such a recoding whereby a minority voice, intolerant and unyielding, transforms its religious ideology into a discursive hegemony over the majority. Whatever blasphemy once meant, in terms of civil order and social dominance, it now carries other possibilities and poses other problems.

Can a conceptual structure actually evoke physical disgust? Did modernism actually cause Pius IX to vomit? When Felicitas vomits at the stench of pig manure, Father Cyprian wants her to believe that she should also vomit at the "great dark stink" of modernism. Do devout Muslims actually vomit over *The Satanic Verses*? Mughram Al-Ghamdi may think that Rushdie's novel is the most "filthy and abusive" book ever written by an enemy of Islam, but did it cause him to vomit? Putting the issue this simply makes it appear as if all conceptual disgust would have to be hypocritical, a matter of crinkling the nose and making the disgust face to display a negative judgement. However, it is necessary to remember that disgust is a psycho-visceral affect, striking the mind as well as the guts. An overwhelming feeling of psychological disgust, whether or not accompanied by visceral twinges and an actual vomiting, must be possible. Father Cyprian experiences disgust when he thinks about modernism, sincerely taking pig excrement as an accurate analogy, but he does not vomit.[63] A perverse geometry evokes disgust as a mental and psychological response even without visceral accompaniment. The disgust that rises in reaction to a conceptual structure, an ideology or a belief system, is very close to a condition of pure horror: a fear verging on dread of what may happen, of a source of pollution not yet fully understood. Indeed, the shifting boundary between horror and terror, the slow spoor-tracking and the abrupt invasion, is perhaps nowhere more clearly seen than in the way the human mind thinks about ideological perversity. A perverse geometry can strike horror into the heart, casting forward small signs of its presence, but it can also invade consciousness with the explosive force of a bottle breaking.

Disgust motifs play significant roles in both horror and terror fiction. They do this in specific, and quite dissimilar, ways. However, the mere presence of disgusting objects does not necessarily signify either horror or terror. Disgust-objects define the fictional worlds in which they appear, and these may not be worlds in which anything violent occurs. You could, for instance, imagine hopeless worlds, bleakly without promise, or worlds in which the sheer inevitability of decay and death dominates. You might even, if you set your mind to the task, invent a fictional world, like one that David Foster Wallace imagines in his *Brief Interviews with Hideous Men*, in which all the details, each fictional fact, reeks of "flatus and tussis and meaty splats. Defecation, egestion, extrusion, dejection, purgation, voidance. The unmistakable rumble of the toilet paper dispensers."[64] The fictional world of a Samuel Beckett novel, in contrast, typically teems with things, acts and people that might seem disgusting (because showing decay, degeneration or degradation), but the narrative objective is not to introduce a phantasmagoria of disgust. It is only to show the ineradicable bleakness of human life, its bare desolation, or how a solitary person, without support or precise goals, may continue moving forward even without knowing where he is going, even if he can no longer walk.

David Lynch's 1977 film *Eraserhead* shows plainly the difference between a simple disgust-world and a disgust-horror-world. It is, Stuart Samuels remarks, "one of the strangest films ever made."[65] The soundtrack, which hisses and pounds, corresponds to the film's "dreary industrial landscape."[66] The world is as pervasively bleak as that of, say, Sartre's *Nausea*, Beckett's *Unnamable* or Pynchon's *Gravity's Rainbow*. Henry walks awkwardly across the industrial landscape, the noise of locomotives roaring near at hand, and over piles of slag, to accept an invitation to dinner from Mary, his former girlfriend. In her house, the grandmother sits catatonically in the kitchen, the mother alternately abuses Henry and snuggles into his neck, and Mary scurries about the house, obviously worried about something. At the dinner, Mary's father, a retired plumber, asks Henry to carve the small "manmade" chickens which begin to pump congealed blood, rather like sewer sludge, with an up-and-down piston motion of the drumsticks. It turns out that Mary has given birth, but the doctors are not certain "if it is a baby." The baby turns out to be monstrous in appearance, though not in action. It looks raw, almost skinless, and its lidless eyes are open in the sides of its skull. "From one angle," Paul M. Sammon observes, "it resembles a bandage-swathed penis-and-scrotum, from another a weird cross between a giant spermatozoa and a skinned, limbless lamb."[67] It never stops crying and distresses Mary acutely. At one point, while the two parents are lying in bed together, Mary appears to excrete, or else give birth to, numerous slug-like worms which Henry "delivers" and throws against the wall with loud, wet plops. Eventually, Mary goes home to sleep and Henry kills the baby with a pair of scissors. He cuts its swaddling cloths and exposes an unformed viscera, open to sight. After he has stabbed it, the baby begins to excrete huge quantities of feces resembling porridge. *Eraserhead* clearly creates a disgust-world, equivalent in its distinctive manner to those of Beckett, Pynchon and Sartre. These are all worlds in which the disgust motifs help to build a sense of alienation and of being distanced within a world that is the representation of modern bleakness and comfortlessness, images of modern wastelands if not quite of modernity itself. The fictional world of Burroughs' *Naked Lunch*, slithering with deliquescent and hallucinatory beings, also resembles *Eraserhead* in employing disgust motifs to invoke alienation, not horror.

The point can be made simply: disgust motifs in literature and film serve other ends than the creation of horror, although that is indeed a frequent objective. Like the novels I have mentioned, *Eraserhead* creates a world of alienation and anomie, a world in which the main character passes through his life without significant affect, almost ataraxically. Like other alienation-worlds, *Nausea* for example, *Eraserhead* is an interior world, centrally psychological in focus, that concerns disintegration.[68] The "baby," though it looks monstrous, does not seem to be a monster since its only act is to exist (and cry) in a world from which it too, like its father, is alienated.[69]

The role of the (actual-world) freaks in Tod Browning's 1932 film *Freaks* indicates how deformity, or interstitial status, does not necessarily invoke horror. Though deformed, they are too sympathetic, too morally honest, to be actual monsters. (Only Cleopatra, the aerialist, seems like a monster, and she has been a moral monster long before she is transformed into the "chicken lady.") In *Nausea*, Bouville is also a dreary, "suffocating" landscape, contorted by its commercial monomania, crowded with disgust motifs of several kinds, but it does not point to horror (other than the metaphorical horror of bad faith). Like *Eraserhead*, it is an affectless world in which the dominant feelings are separation, alienation and anomie. In a world such as Bouville, pervaded by bad faith in all manner of grotesque forms, these responses might seem no more than rational and (like Menippean satire) only intelligent rejoinders to falseness. *Gravity's Rainbow* suggests an even more unmistakable example. None of the disgust, not even Brigadier Pudding's coprophagy, contributes to the development of a full horror-world, although there are certainly moments of intermittent horror (mostly waiting and dread). The disgust motifs in the novel do, because events happen abruptly and out of some underlying system of causation, evoke a fairly deep sense of terror. On the other hand, toilets and excretion create running motifs, building a flat world of alienation, throughout the novel. There is even a toilet ship, the *Rücksichtslos*:

> Shit, now, is the color of white folks are afraid of. Shit is the presence of death, not some abstract-arty character with a scythe, but the still and rotting corpse itself inside the whiteman's warm and private own *asshole*, which is getting pretty intimate.[70]

Disgusting food, including Katje's excrement of course, shows up everywhere in Pynchon's narrative.

> "Oh, I don't know," Roger elaborately casual, "I can't seem to find any *snot soup* on the menu ..."
> "Yeah, I could've done with some of that *pus pudding*, myself. Think there'll be any of that?"
> "No, but there might be a scum soufflé!" cries Roger, "with a side of *menstrual marmelade*!"

In a swift sequence, there are allusions to "smegma stew," "scab sandwiches," "discharge dumplings," "barf bouillon," "toe jam" and many other similar culinary aberrations. The sequence ends with a reference to "pimple pie with filth frosting."[71] None of Pynchon's extravagant use of disgust motifs actually adds up to horror. There are no obvious monsters (other than the Rocket itself). There is no spoor that leads anywhere (other than to the Rocket's bunker), but only the appalling world itself. What Pynchon's disgust motifs do show is the flat, dreary and suffocating atmosphere of the Zone and, by extension, the modern western world of international technologies. Represented by its complex and death-dealing technologies, the world has become in itself a perverse geometry. That bleak image includes everyone, denying opposition and flattening out sides.

Roman Polanski's 1965 film *Repulsion* presents a more difficult, border-line case. Crowded with disgust motifs that point to madness, it may also be (depending upon whether you think there is a monster revealed in the final frame) a horror-world.[72] It is certainly a world in which alienation suffuses everything. The film opens with a close-up shot of a woman's eye, the lashes crusted with mascara. (The eye figures significantly throughout the film.) The eye in the close-up belongs to Carol, played by Catherine Deneuve, and as she becomes increasingly demented, there are several shots of her eyes, often looking like black holes in her skull. She stares, looks moody, broods while working (as a cosmetician) and peers at her food. Above all, she seems to be remembering. There are a great number of disgust motifs in the film that are used to support the general theme that repulsion, a deep aversion to objects in the world, functions as a symptom for madness. As Carol goes mad, the walls begin to crack. Male hands reach out from the walls and fondle her breasts (from behind). Carol's sister has planned to cook a rabbit, but leaves with her lover for Italy before she can cook it. The rabbit remains, skinned but uncooked, to rot and gather flies. (Some critics have thought that the "baby" in *Eraserhead* quotes this skinned rabbit.) At one point, Carol takes the rabbit's head in her purse to work (where a co-worker sees it in her purse and feels a repulsion of her own). When a young man kisses her (much against her will), she leaps from his car, rushes into the apartment building and, while riding up in the lift, rubs her mouth with the heel of her palm. Then she vigorously brushes her teeth. *Repulsion*'s world is deliquescent and muck-crusted. However, its single most dominant theme is that present repulsion reflects past experience. The experience of aversion and disgust for in-the-world objects manifests the return of repressed memories. It is a film, and a fictional world, that calls unmistakably for the third theoretical model, the psychoanalytic account of disgust, to lend it interpretation.

The final shot of the film is another close-up: this time of a "family photo" that has been sitting throughout the film on a cabinet. The camera zooms in on the photo and it is possible to see a man, his face partly obscured by a shadow, slightly to one side and behind the family group. A young girl with long blonde hair (obviously Carol as a girl) can be made out staring slantwise out of the corners of her eyes at the man. Finally, the camera reaching maximum zoom, the girl can be seen to peer intently at the man, even grimly. From her eyes, it is clear that she does not like him. You can infer that the man in the photo is the uncle who has been mentioned earlier in the film. The film seems to leave only a single inference: the man in the photo is Carol's uncle and he has sexually abused her when she was a girl. (The viewer knows that it is her uncle because, in the depth of her madness, she has told her employer that she has missed work because her "uncle" has paid her a visit.) Given the specificity of her hallucinations (men walk out of walls and through locked doors and rape her from behind), the uncle must have raped her *a tergo*. The associations with Freud's Wolfman are richly multiplex. Still, the most profound connections are with the eye. The opening scene explicitly quotes the eyeball scene in Dali's and Buñuel's film, *Chien Andalou*, in which a woman's eyeball is slashed with a razor.[73] The film concerns repulsion, but especially the repulsion that women may feel for men, and the particular repulsion that the shadow cast by early traumatic events may cause in adult life. Just before the camera zooms in on the family photo, it pans over a collection of bric-a-brac on the shelves and furniture in the living room. It is obviously a collection of mementos of the sisters' girlhoods. The camera passes over a large clock and the audience hears it ticking. The clock might remind the viewer that repulsion is a function of memory and memory occurs in time. Carol's repulsion externalizes her memory (she feels alienated from anything that reminds her of her uncle and of her past experience) and works like a shadow cast over her life. Thus *Repulsion* can be viewed as a film of alienation employing frequent disgust motifs in order to underscore Carol's sense of isolation, her incapacity to relate positively and her overwhelming anomie. However, if you think that the man in the photo is her uncle, and that he has raped and abused her (the film insists upon the *a tergo* position), then you may infer that he is a moral monster, a minor avatar of the monsterhood that Patrick Bateman, the psychopathic narrator of Bret Easton Ellis' *American Psycho*, represents more fully. The final zoom shot discloses the monster whose presence you have vaguely sensed.[74] Viewed from this angle, *Repulsion* is a psychological drama that verges into horror by employing a single classic horror convention (the revealed, or almost-revealed, monster behind the door towards which a spoor has led); viewed from another angle, it is a film, like *Eraserhead*, that represents the disturbing consequences of alienation.

I have made this detour, examining the use of disgust in representing alienation, to make explicit the multiple uses of disgust in creating very diverse fictional worlds. There certainly can be disgust-worlds, such as *Eraserhead* or Beckett's *The Unnamable*, in which the dominant affect is alienation: distance, coldness and dissociation combining to build repellant worlds in which each character follows out an irremediably lonely existence.

In such fictional worlds, disgust motifs underscore the overpowering sense of the world's bleakness and the characters' dissociation from this world as well as the distance between them. In an alienation-world, a disgusting object, the fat worms that Mary appears to excrete in *Eraserhead* or the skinned rabbit in Polanski's *Repulsion*, will serve to represent all manner of dissociation as well as helplessness, isolation and pervasive non-belonging.[75] Such motifs work very differently in horror.

In horror (or "art-horror"), disgust motifs register, and help to interpret, the signs along the trail that will lead, in final moments, to the monster's lair. The fictional worlds created in horror narratives are unusually open: facework most often means what it seems to mean; expressions actually register, as metadiscursive commentary, the feelings that characters have in reaction to the world's sights. (In fictional worlds dominated by alienation, facework is usually closed, resisting interpretation, brooding, puzzled and puzzling.) In acts of displaced symbolism, faces show the anticipated monster. Here is a sylleptic world of horror mapped by the sequence of affects that are registered within it:

> 1) little things seem slightly wrong, the ordinary economy of the world has gone awry, and this is marked by faces that show curiosity or puzzlement; 2) certain things begin to appear that are sticky, slimy or deliquescent, and faces begin to show disgust; 3) small and intermittent frights occur, tiny shocks or puny bogeys, and faces begin to show fear; 4) a pattern begins to emerge, a sense of connection between events, and faces register this as anxiety; this may become actual dread as the story unfolds; 5) the monster, or monstrous event, will take place (if it does not, if it is narratively withheld, its impact will still be felt), and faces will flow into the expression of horror.

In most horror narratives, the elements of the sequence will overlap as the affects crowd each other and combine. Both fear and disgust play roles in horror narratives; however, they have different intensities. As William Ian Miller observes, pure "fear decays much more rapidly than the slow-decaying, always lingering disgust."[76] Disgust, lingering like a cloacal stench over a varied scene, will invade the other affects, combining with them to form compound affects such as "disgust-fear" or "disgust-anxiety." By contrast, terror narratives keep their monsters secret until it is time for them to erupt upon the action. In terror, faces give little away.

Faces are almost always significant in literature and in horror; as in comedy, they are usually essential. If you cannot see them, then you must imagine them. The disgust-face is central to the experience of horror. As a reader or viewer, you must imagine the character's face as he or she climbs the stairs towards the shut door at the top, observing the small telltale signs along the way. In a film, the facework will be obvious, perhaps too obvious. In either case, the facework, especially the twisted disgust face, is inescapable. The face is an instance of evidence pointing along a path towards an unknown, though anticipated, object. In no form of literature does this seem more the case than in horror. The object has not been seen, but it can be partially predicted by what it has left behind. Little bits of evidence, evidential fragments of a whole that has not yet been exposed, begin to indicate a presence. Foreseen only in outline, though anticipated in the mind's eye, this presence begins to acquire a shape through the evidence that points towards it.

Now imagine Herakles tracking the Hydra. He may be on foot or else in the chariot that stories say his nephew, Iolaus, drove. As he comes closer to Argos and the swamps of Lerna where the Hydra lives, he can begin to smell the monster. The spoor's stench is appalling. Herakles' face begins to wrinkle, and his nose moves rather like a rabbit's. He knows, too, that even the Hydra's breath, from each of her nine heads, stinks, that it will provoke nausea. Her fecundity, her heads regrowing and (in some tales) doubling, actually hides her destructiveness: a chaos monster, the Hydra's apparent creativity and capacity for renewal masks the principle of dissolution that she incarnates. Perhaps even at an early stage in the hunt Herakles can foresee that, to kill the Hydra, he will have to hold his nostrils closed, never allowing himself to inhale. He can begin to see the Hydra vividly in his mind's eye and imagine the struggle between them solely from the spoor. When Herakles begins his Labour, the close interrelationship between monsters and disgust is forced upon him. During his struggle with the Hydra, Herakles does hold his breath, his nostrils and mouth tightly clamped shut, knowing now first-hand that each of the Hydra's nine heads exhales a rank, miasmal stench.[77] The Hydra's blood is also venomous, and once Herakles has killed her, he dips arrows in her spilling blood, knowing it to be an incurable poison. All the stenches and poisons that are associated with the Hydra simply forecast her natural deadliness, represented most memorably by her having poisonous blood. As the later fate of Philoctetes, with his disgusting wound (transformed into an "eyesore" of the gods), shows, this deadliness aims directly at the core of the male hero's purposes, his role and social identity, even, his ego-ideal. Herakles knows this very well. His mind will have foreseen the Hydra long before he reaches Lerna. He will have taken the spoor's stench as partial evidence for creating a world in his imagination.

Horror illustrates the paradigm of spoor-tracking. Anyone who has entered a fictional world in which the dominant experience is horror will begin to observe the presence of a monster (who may look quite human, only its mind deformed) by an intensifying trail of clues, traces and hints that leads to the monster's lair.[78] The effect of horror in narrative does not depend on actually revealing the monster (although this may happen in some horror narratives, and many low-budget films), but rather upon creating the anticipation, the outline and untested image in the mind's eye. Within that image swarm the affects of anxiety and loathing.[79] In a horror-world, the characters first experience diffuse anxiety (although this may be preceded by puzzlement and active curiosity), underscored by sudden qualms and lingering worries. This diffuse anxiety rapidly acquires an admixture of disgust. Suppose that this compound, "anxiety-disgust," is possible in fiction, even if you think that it does not exist outside of literature or that you have never experienced it. Now try to imagine what happens to it in a horror-world. It sharpens and narrows in focus as the outlines of the monster, or anticipated horror, begin to take shape. At least in most well-conducted horror-worlds, "anxiety-disgust" narrows acutely, through a sequence of isolated frights, into trepidation. Ultimately, disgust transfers from a compound with anxiety to one with fear, and then, perhaps, to one with horror. At that point, the character should show indications of tension and worry: shallow breathing, increased heart rate, sweating, dryness of mouth, weakness and trembling. The face will be bloodless and drawn, the flesh may dissolve into many tiny wrinkles (feeling as if it were "crawling"), the skin over the skull has tightened and drawn close like an ill-fitting cap, and the hair may move "like life in excrement."

Now imagine the mythic horror-world that Medusa inhabits. Transformed by Athena into something loathsome, given a face more ugly than the human imagination can envision and a head of snakes in place of hair, Medusa petrifies with fright everyone who sees her. That is an easy metaphor for a horror-world, but in Medusa's case it is literal: struck by her petrific visage, gazers turn to stone. Helped by Athena, the hero Perseus can look upon her only indirectly by seeing her face reflected on the surface of a polished bronze shield. He succeeds in cutting off Medusa's head with a *harpe* that Hermes has given him, and from her blood spring, immediately, a winged horse and an armed warrior, the Hydra's uncles. The Medusa's tale makes a few important points about the world of horror. First, the monster, in this case Medusa, is anticipated in all her petrifying frightfulness. Her reputation precedes her, and the hero takes precautions. Second, the monster is so frightful that it can only be looked upon indirectly. Perseus' polished bronze shield may be taken as micro-emblem for the method of horror universally: seen indirectly, obscured, hidden, never-to-be-seen, the monster exercises a conceptual presence over its world. Third, the monster can only be approached with anxiety. Perseus worries, and the gods worry with him, about Medusa's power. Perseus' story has a happy ending (for everyone but Medusa), which is not the case with all horror narratives; but the threat has always been present, anxiety the condition of mind. "Men's minds are wild," Horatio says at the end of *Hamlet*, and that may stand for the way minds usually seem in the worlds of horror.

In horror, the world seems to collapse, to have broken down (in the sense of having escaped its normal conceptual categories) and begun a descent into chaos. It is the latter especially, the slimewards slippage, away from both the ideal and the ordinary, that makes the mind wild. And one aspect of being "wild," of being profoundly distraught, is the anxiety of not knowing quite what to expect, not knowing in advance what the monster can or will prove capable of doing. Suspense is the usual experience of an audience or a reader while following through the unfolding of a horror-world, but it is also what the characters feel, the intellectual dimension of their anxiety. Transformed by monsterhood, the world may seem unsteady, an anxious place, or no longer a place at all. In such an ambiguous world, you may even find the monster nearly as attractive as loathsome; the hero may find himself loving that which he must kill.[80]

Thinking about the tale of Perseus and Medusa, Freud interpreted Medusa's snake-crowned head as the boy-child's image of the castrated woman. The snakes are exaggerated images of female pubic hair. In this reading, Medusa's head symbolizes (that is, constitutes a representation of) the female genitalia. Barbara Creed writes that, if we accept Freud's equation between Medusa's snake-hair and female genitalia, "we can see that the Medusan myth is mediated by a narrative about the *difference* of female sexuality as a difference which is grounded in monstrousness and which invokes castration anxiety in the male spectator."[81] Later in her discussion, Creed points out that Freud seems to have assumed that the boy-child's first sight of a naked woman would have to be his mother, and not a sister or a playmate. If he had thought more about the possibilities of play, then he might not have given the mature woman such an important role in shaping the boy's unconscious. He might also have seen, Creed remarks, that there is a significant distinction between fearing a woman as the premonitory image of what might happen to him, the source of all his anxiety, and fearing a woman as the potential doer of the deed, a potential castrator.[82] Horror fiction, she argues, is crowded with images of castrating women, vampires and lamia, but that is a more specific, and far more narrative, role than Freud's static icon of male trepidation. Creed's discussion shows that while horror films do, indeed, show images of women as castrated, symbolic vehicles for male anxiety, they are more often dominated by active female figures that threaten castration, and often perform it as well. Thus she rethinks Freud on the image of Medusa's head.

> With her head of writhing snakes, huge mouth, lolling tongue and boar's tusks, the Medusa is also regarded by historians of myth as particularly nasty version of the *vagina dentata* ....
> Freud's interpretation masks the active, terrifying aspects of the female genitals—the fact that they might castrate. The Medusa's entire visage is alive with images of toothed vaginas, poised and waiting to strike. No wonder her male victims were rooted to the spot with fear.[83]

I think that Medusa's head, both in Freud's discussion and in Creed's revisionary analysis, focusses the significance of anxiety in horror-worlds. Gananath Obeyesekere recalls how seeing a woman with matted hair, "flowing like the wind," reminded him of Freud's paper on the Medusa and disturbed him with thoughts of castration.[84] This anxiety is paradigmatic for horror-worlds.

The anticipation of the monster, closely bonded with "anxiety-disgust," constitutes the basic narrative convention of H.P. Lovecraft's horror fiction: he creates worlds in which the monster's spoor becomes increasingly unmistakable but in which the monster itself is never directly seen. (Sometimes, as in "The Call of Cthulhu," Lovecraft partially describes the monster, but only indirectly as the narrator pieces together fragments of the story long after the event.[85]) One of Lovecraft's signature moves in

creating a fictional horror-world is to describe imbalanced, disproportionate, asymmetrical landscapes. The "geometry of the place was all
wrong," the narrator of "The Call of Cthulhu" observes as he recreates
another person's experience. A Lovecraftian world is likely to be one dominated by perverse geometries that are unmistakably physical.[86] In one of
Borges' short stories, actually dedicated to Lovecraft, the narrator is driven
mad merely by seeing the furniture that belongs to the unseen monster.[87]
In such worlds a path opens, or, more likely, begins to emerge out of a
number of possible paths, leading to a door behind which a monster lurks.
In the reduced scope of a gothic horror-world, one could say that the reader
is asked to climb a number of steps towards a closet door. The door of the
closet, as Stephen King puts it, is never opened. Nothing, King writes, is "so
frightening as what's behind the closed door." And, he adds, what is
"behind the door or lurking at the top of the stairs is never as frightening
as the door or the staircase itself."[88] In a horror-world, faces mostly tell the
unpleasant truth.

The face is also deceptive. Thus a snarl may seem to point towards a
blood-red sun but actually hide a thick mist of fear. Dread can be imagined
as an affect in others to mask its presence in oneself. A person's crimson,
blood-suffused face may seem to display bashfulness or even shame, but it
may also mask sexual appetite. (Think of all those Petrarchan poets in the
Renaissance who described themselves as blushing in the presence of the
woman they loved, but who indirectly describe their tumescent desire for
real or for imagined women.) The crinkled expression of disgust may mask
a desire to impose oneself as distant from, or superior to, an action, an
event, a moral or philosophical position. As I have been arguing since the
first chapter, disgust can be a physical metaphor for moral judgement. That
is what happens when people wrinkle their noses at food that they think is
beneath their social or cultural class, or that seems to violate their self-
imposed diets. It is the vegetarian's overt response to the offer of meat; the
fruitarian's to the offer of vegetables. It is what happens when one person
observes behaviour that he or she disapproves. A person simply begins to
contort his or her face into the well-known paths that lead to the feeling of
disgust. The face reacts to certain words, to propositions, as if they were
slime-drenched objects, dissolving and deliquescent *traces*. But the face can
also hide the mind's purposes. It can create false, deadend paths that only
seem to lead where they point. In that distinction lies the basis for distinguishing between horror and terror. Consider *Hamlet* once more.

In *Hamlet*, Claudius' face points away from the truth. It seems to show a correct world of genuine brotherly grief and avuncular affection. However you imagine Claudius' face (and it must be imagined), whether as shifting, duplicitous, deceitful, greasy, leering or even rigidly self-contained, it is a face crowded with signs. Each facial sign is a snare, pointing away, almost convincingly, from the world (of *Hamlet*) as it actually exists towards a false world in which Hamlet has nothing to fear, no dangers to run. Thus Claudius builds an inset, but false, fictional world for Hamlet, much as the Ghost creates another embedded world, the conditional shame-world that Hamlet must prove untrue, into which Hamlet may step. Shakespeare's plays and narrative poems (such as *The Rape of Lucrece*) abound with embedded worlds which characters are invited to accept as actual but which are both deceptive and dangerous. The dramatic action discloses their false-hood and either the folly of a character in having believed them or else the jeopardy he or she has run.[89] The misleading face is a recurring convention in Shakespeare. In *Othello*, Iago's face is not smooth and without signs, but rather the expressions on his face, the signs he permits to be seen, all lead in wrong directions. Richard III smiles and seems warm, loving at times, but he is always a villain, and his face, at least until the final scene in which he must confront the ghosts of those he has killed, always misleads. In *Cymbeline*, Jachimo misleads, his face showing many emotions, none of which actually reveals his mind, to both Imogen and Posthumous. The list would be long. The problem is constant: faces are not blank, never inno-cent, but rather point the paths to alternative worlds.

Think about *Hamlet*. The world of *Hamlet* seems crowded with voices and faces that mislead. It is a world of rumours, lies and elaborately told false narratives.[90] It is also a world of seductive, illusory facework. The pattern is established by the opening lines when the two sentinels, Bernardo and Francisco, peer into the darkness asking questions. Everyone in the play peers into darkness, so to speak, and asks questions. All those questions seem to be asked in darkness, addressed to faces that lie. (The darkness functions as a symbol for the human face and, in a sense, is another human face.) Rosencrantz and Guildenstern present deceptive faces to Hamlet, but he returns the favour with an even more deceptive face. Hamlet makes many faces which are as impenetrable as the document he seals with the Danish seal that he wears as a signet ring: the document by which he sends Claudius' courtier-spies to their sudden deaths, "Not shriving time allow'd." If you try to imagine the world of *Hamlet*, you must always try to see the darkness in which events take place, the impenetrability of misleading signs. Whose face could you trust in that world? Ophelia's in her madness, perhaps; Hamlet's when he sees the Ghost or at the end when he dies. Perhaps Fortinbras' when he first sees the quarry of dead bodies. Horatio, since he seems honest and is a narrator, may tell the truth and his face may not mislead. A student of literature soon understands that faces are important and that, when they cannot be seen on the screen or on the stage, they must be imagined. Facework lies at the heart of literature; or perhaps to say it better, it rides upon that core's visible rind.

The faces in a horror-world should all display the traces of horror, the loathsome anticipations of a monster. All those slimy, mucoid and deli-quescent objects pointing the track to the monster's lair simply repeat the basic proposition that disgust and fear conjoin to promote horror. Everyone who encounters the carefully displayed spoor of the monster will experience anxiety and fear. In the best horror narratives, there is more involved. Think of an easy example: Stephen King's *The Shining*, or even Stanley Kubrick's 1980 film version, in which the young father's ambition to write a novel and his frustrated parental rage against his son constitute layers of significance, paths leading off into different alternatives for action. Even King's setting, a haunted hotel, introduces diversity, since a hotel, like a Renaissance memory palace, contains a diversity of rooms, each of which will have had a distinct history and will seem like an independent world of its own.[91]

Facework is always Janus-faced and double-dealing. To raise the perspective to the meta-level once more, facework may indicate the nature of the fictional world. What kinds of faces predominate? How dishonest, misleading and false are they? How many faces, or how much diverse face-work, can a fictional world contain? The distinction between horror and terror shows the way towards the answers.

Imagine a path without spoor. There are no traces of an unseen presence, no hints of the monster to appear. But that monster can, and will some-times, make itself known. It will burst suddenly upon experience without anticipatory hints. It moves by stealth and sudden violence. If the path is through a fictional world, then the narrative holds back the indications of the monster. What is to come, what will happen, waits to erupt, spoorless, upon the imagination. This is how terror differs from horror, in actual life as well as in fiction. "Terror," Isabel Allende remarks, is "a black cloth that is always over us."[92] In horror there is a path to follow, usually incremental in its display of evidence; but in terror there is no marked path, although there may well be a radial and apparently random distribution of signs, such as disgust-objects and abjection, that suggest a presence.

In terror, there may be anticipation, an unnamed dread and diffuse anxiety as you wait for *something* to happen, to explode upon you with unexpected violence, rupturing your defences, those frail boundaries; but there will not be, at least for the character-victims, a definite path to follow. Although you may think of terrorism as fundamentally political, ideology embodied in a deed, it can operate in any sphere of human life. It is a way of dealing hurt or death, not itself a political program, although it often serves such programs. A serial killer, who may be motivated by nothing other than a personal desire or compulsion, is an agent of terror.[93] In either case, horror or terror, you are invited to enter a fictional world and to experience it from within. In the one, the nature of the world is made appallingly evident early in your explorations; in the other, it is kept hidden, furtive and stealthy, waiting as a surprise both for the characters and, at least sometimes, for yourself as a reader-participant. On a small scale, terror is the abrupt, unexpected explosion of violence, surrounded by stillness, that comes when a bottle is broken into a weapon.

Horror and disgust, intimately joined, reflect each other as conclusion and evidence; terror and disgust, as apparently random correlatives. Characters in horror narratives loathe having to make physical contact with the monster. In fiction, one has to imagine a fundamental convention of horror that can be shown extravagantly in film: fear and disgust, as Noël Carroll puts it, are "etched on the characters' features":

> Within the context of the horror narrative, the monsters are identified as impure and unclean. They are putrid or moldering things, or they hail from oozing places, or they are made of dead or rotting flesh, or chemical waste, or are associated with vermin, disease, or crawling things. They are not only quite dangerous but they also make one's skin creep. Characters regard them not only with fear but with loathing, with a combination of terror and disgust.[94]

The traces that indicate the existence of an unseen monster drip, leak or ooze. Everything along the path founders towards muck and slime. These dissolving traces point ahead to the central fact of horror. The monster, or the monstrous event, that you begin to anticipate will constitute an assault upon your integrity. Boundaries turn liquid in horror. The integrity of the individual (secure behind its defences of being and identity) slips and begins to sink into self-loss and abjection. Humanity is most touching, Georges Bataille writes, when "the horror of night" transforms human beings into rubbish.[95]

Horror films often stress the monster's liquidness, its decaying moistness. By simple displacement, the monster may be associated with liquid. It may arise from a swamp, like the Hydra, or emerge from a dark lagoon. Arthur Machen's 1894 novel *The Great God Pan* obsessively returns to the late-Victorian scientific model of protoplasm, a wetness from which beings emerge and back into which they dissolve. In Machen's novel protoplasm has the symbolic function of displaced liquidness. Another form that symbolic wetness in horror-worlds may take is unlikely and unexpected wetness. Take, for example, the wall of flowing blood that begins Kubrick's film version of *The Shining*: it is shown to the audience and then reappears later in the film. Although it is supposed to be imagined as an aspect of the small boy's clairvoyance, it is given in the film to everyone. It is anticipatory, narratively proleptic. Lots of blood and, behind the blood, decay and rot will characterize the film's world. Other aspects of the action—a hotel where the previous winter the caretaker had committed suicide, a boiler that doesn't work well and may be dangerous, suggestions of occurrences that are difficult to understand, the main character's psychic decay, eventually ghosts and noises—all point to something horrific.[96] Writing of the scene in King's *Carrie* when the young girl's first menstrual period begins while she is taking a shower, Leslie Fiedler observes that "the combination of blood, running water and sanitary plumbing has a special appeal for contemporary movie fans."[97] It is the basic appeal of horror: the call of wetness and slime, the twisted braid of the body's integrity and dissolution which fascinates (as do all abject materials) and puzzles the mind.

Representations of decay, rot, deliquescence, all things that tend slimewards, are the basic building blocks in the creation of a horror-world. They recur so often in horror films, even when not precisely necessary to the action, that you can scarcely think about the properties of horror-worlds without beginning with the indications of slime. Consider one exemplary instance. In David Cronenberg's 1979 film *The Brood*, images of injured bodies begin to appear almost from the first moments. A man with debilitating Oedipal fixations displays his torso to a psychotherapist in front of an audience. They are acting out the man's unresolved difficulties, expressed in violent rage, with his father. The torso is covered with bruises, apparently self-inflicted. Later, the hero, whose wife is undergoing treatment with the same psychotherapist, sees similar bruises and marks on his young daughter's body. Disgust and anxiety build together. Still later, the hero encounters a former patient of the doctor who displays cancerous tumours growing on his neck, which he claims the doctor caused by opening psychosomatic outlets for his rage. All this anticipates the film's end-point of horror: the wife, under treatment for her rage, begins to produce half-formed human monsters who kill the people in the world whom she most hates—her parents, her child's teacher, eventually the doctor himself. In the final scene, the monster is actually revealed. It is the wife, bearing an external womb, a bloody and purple pod, rather like a slime-covered eggplant, from which the brood of her rage spring. This monstrous oviform womb hangs between her legs, growing from her lower body, like a repulsive tumor or a deformed scrotum. As her husband watches, a new child is born and she licks the blood from it with evident pleasure. The husband expresses disgust (which has always struck me as a rather straightforward emotion to feel at this point) and the wife reads his face. "I disgust you," she exclaims with petulant recognition. Barbara Creed interprets this passage in the film as evidence that the husband feels disgust "at her maternal, mothering functions. Nola as archetypal Queen Bee, as woman in her reproductive role, repulses man."[98] However, Nola, the wife, is obviously deformed, her external pod more like an insect's ovisac than a woman's womb, and the husband reacts to her deformity (and its lethal uses) directly, and only indirectly to her archetypal female-ness. To prevent her from willing more of her brood into action and to protect his daughter who is with her "siblings" at this moment, the husband now strangles her. *The Brood* is unusual in that the monster is actually seen clearly and is so morbidly misogynistic. In the film's terms (within *its* fictional world, that is), strangling the woman seems like a good thing to do. The woman who breeds half-formed monsters from an egg-like bag, growing like a genital appendage, a bloody and bleeding ovisac, clearly recalls Medusa and other female monsters whose deformed and horrifying genitalia (or, as Creed argues, their bodily equivalents) frighten male characters. Nola functions as both a monstrous womb and as a castrating mother. She is only one more, though complexly overdetermined, female figure from the male imagination, at once dangerous and a premonition of a dreaded destiny, that swarms through the history of horror literature. She is very much what Creed thinks of as the "monstrous-feminine," but treated wholly without sympathy so that her death must be understood (within that fictional world) as a positive benefit.

Cronenberg's film is a highly instructive exception to the Lovecraftian rule that monsters are most effective when not shown. *The Brood* records, with unforgettable lucidity, the way in which early indications point towards the final narrative monstrosity. Of course, it might be argued that the Lovecraftian rule works only in fiction, not in film. The demand for the visual, as well as the compulsion to use special effects once they are available, makes film horror a very different genre from literary horror.[99] However, it is important to bear in mind that Lovecraft's method of writing horror fiction, emphasizing suspense over wonder, is innovative and not universal. It is also Stephen King's way of writing horror in which there are steady rhythms, "interconnecting and intersecting," of motifs building towards a partially explained cataclysm.[100] It was not the traditional way of depicting monsters when wonder seemed like the prime literary effect, not suspense. Edmund Spenser's disparate monsters are always *seen*, always the scrutinized objects of moral attention. The Hydra, the archetypal monster of this book, must be imagined in all her wondrous multiplicity and loathsomeness in order that the danger of Herakles' Labour may be understood.

Because of the genre's emphasis upon explicit images, horror films are rich in examples of wetness and dissolution. Humankind's irreversible fall into rot and muck has been imagined, directly and in multifarious symbolic displacements, in countless horror films. In *Alien, Aliens* and *Alien3* and *Alien Resurrection,* the xenomorphic monsters drip liquid from their mouths in improbable ways. At one point in Ridley Scott's 1979 film *Alien*, a crew member, just before being killed by the xenomorph, encounters what seems to be water dripping from the ceiling of the overheated spacecraft and relaxes in it, as if enjoying a cool shower. Improbably, the water turns out to be slime that constantly drips from the xenomorph's mouth, beslobbering and making more ghastly, the teeth. (The character then reappears, already wrapped in web-like secretions, as a host-incubator in the alien's reproductive cycle.) The association with slime is more fundamentally established in the stages of the alien's developmental phases. It is a "Linnean nightmare, defying every natural law of evolution; by turns bivalve, crustacean, reptilian, and humanoid." At different moments, it behaves like a snake, an arthropod and, in depositing its larval forms in another species, a wasp.[101] The xenomorph is also machine-like, both a digestive and a reproductive machine, but also evolved (or designed) to resemble a non-biological machine: hard, shiny, metallic in texture, sleek, aerodynamic in shape. Its existence destroys human categories as, but more certainly than, do the "abominations" in Leviticus that Douglas analyses.

In all four *Alien* films, there are androids characterized by slime-coated inner parts. This is particularly significant in Ridley Scott's *Alien* where the android, or "synthetic humanoid," Ash, is hostile, a servant of the ship's computer ("Mother") and the remote Company. However, it is not Ash's nastiness that is in question, but that of the monstrous life-forms. In the subsequent three films, other androids also leak thick, viscous liquids.[102] In *Alien3*, only the android's head remains, still functioning to read encoded data, but it has been "blinded" in its left eye, now transformed into a wall-eyed blankness leaking mucous around the edges. One cheek has been torn into a flap of flabby "flesh." There is no reason why an android should have wet parts except as displaced symbolism. The androids' unnecessarily wet inner parts merely hint at the very different alien beings that threaten the crew. (You have only to remember Commander Data in *Star Trek—The Next Generation* to realize that an android should have neat, clean electronic parts. If nothing else, an android would be internally tidy.) The slime in the *Alien* films points indirectly to the true objects of horror, the monstrous xenomorphs. They drip liquid, their mouths and teeth slimy, because that shows what their purpose is: to dissolve their human opponents, to break down personal integrity, to transform them into mere feeding sources in the chrysalis stage of their "nightmare" growth cycle. Everything about the *Alien* films, and the xenomorphs in particular, seems to exemplify the model of disgust found in Sartre's *Being and Nothingness*: slime, ambiguity, categorical unsteadiness, deliquescence and dissolution.[103] The androids' wet body parts provide, as displaced symbolism, further evidence along the way.

Though it is almost universally the least admired of the films, David Fincher's 1992 *Alien3* makes absolutely clear the process of creating an incremental trail of disgust-objects in building a horror-world. An emergency escape vehicle falls into the ocean of a prison-colony planet. The prison colony is inhabited by only a few fanatically religious criminals, all of whom have committed abominable crimes. Fog, steam and bits of decaying equipment pervade the *mise-en-scène*. The convicts appear beaten and bedraggled, their shaven heads glisten in the humid atmosphere, the back of their heads are tattooed with bar codes (the only detail, it is rumoured, that survives in the film from William Gibson's rejected screenplay) and they exude their worn-down hopelessness. They compose only a "pilot-light" in their prison colony. An autopsy is performed on a child who has died aboard the crashed emergency vehicle, to see "what" might be inside her. There is a quick montage of shots showing a doctor's tools, blood swirling down a drain, the look of pain on Ripley's face, now very bruised, one eye blackened. Bishop, or Bishop 341-B, the synthetic humanoid from the previous film, is shown in a ruinous condition, leaking and experiencing techno-rot. A dog barks at the entrance of the spacecraft and is later shown displaying the signs of an agitated animal in distress. Later still, while the human characters are not watching, an alien imago tears loose from the dog's body. The newly born xenomorph, unseen by the human characters, stretches itself as if preparing for action; its head is like a nacelle on a racing motorcycle, emphasizing the alien's bio-mechanical, machine-like horridness. Then the xenomorph's sloughed-off skin from its larval phase is discovered. A convict is shown with a single black tear, raised like a boil, tattooed beneath his right eye. The xenomorph approaches Ripley and appears to snuggle up against her, showing what might be taken as affection. At that point, it will be clear that the worst of all possible scenarios has actually occurred: Ripley herself, unknowing, is carrying a pupa; indeed it is later identified as a queen, an "egg-layer." The path to the final conflict with the alien xenomorph unfolds slowly, but with complete clarity, each step of the way marked by unmistakable disgust motifs.

It is not until *Alien3* that the true nature of the horror is clearly seen: not the monstrous xenomorphic bio-machines, killing and dissolving human persons, but the awareness that one has become, like a spider captured by a wasp, a mere breeding chrysalis for an appalling pupa, identity dissolved along with integrity in the full awareness of consciousness. The actual flame of horror would be not the experience of being killed or even of being eaten as such but the sensation of being fully conscious of being devoured implacably from within. As Ripley falls, lying prone, calm and evidently relaxed, into the space above the vat of molten lead, she "gives birth" to an adult imago of the alien xenomorph. That is, the xenomorph, which the audience has already learned will be a queen, an "egg-layer," bursts through Ripley's abdomen, tearing its way implacably into life. At that point, you become fully aware of what has been hinted in the previous two films: the absolute horror of the xenomorphs is not that they kill, but that they transform their victims into food. In becoming a host, incidentally wrapped in slimy webs, for the alien's pupal stage, the victim has full consciousness and will be aware that he or she has lost identity as a human person and has become simply food. The victim endures the additional horror of being conscious of his or her own complete abjection, cast out from all human belonging, available only for reincorporation within an alien life-form. The young boy in *Aliens*, seen still alive in the xenomorph's breeding chamber, almost completely obscured by webs, pleads to the "colonial marine" who finds him, "Kill me." It is not only being torn apart, being killed or being eaten that Ripley avoids in leaping, back forwards, into the molten lead, but the consciousness of her own abjectness.

French director Jean-Pierre Jeunet's 1997 *Alien Resurrection* (his first American film) plays off the previous three films, utilizing the established image of the alien xenomorph with its metallic skullbrow, second head within its mouth and blood capable of dissolving metals. However, Jeunet introduces two new lines of horror and disgust both connected with Ripley herself. Ripley has been cloned from a small blood sample two hundred years after her death on the prison planet. She is herself but not herself, an exact replica with inexplicable memories. She is also the result of a series of failed experiments that were successful only on the eighth attempt. (Early in the film, shortly after she has been cloned and the alien creature surgically removed from her body, Ripley notices a stylish figure 8 tattooed on her left forearm.) At one point on the science vessel in remote, "unregulated" space she enters a room where the various failed versions of herself have been kept in large bottles or vials. She confronts, as does the audience, a number of grotesquely deformed "miscarriages" of herself. The second line of new horror makes Ripley contain the genetic material of the alien monster which she has carried as a host. It was only to extract the alien being, a queen or egg-layer as had been made clear in the previous film, that the scientists had gone to the trouble to clone her. The alien genetic strain seems to have permeated Ripley's body, interweaving with her own DNA, giving her both extra-human strength and agility as well as the alien metal-dissolving blood. In *Alien Resurrection*, Ripley becomes both the hero and a monster herself. She is a departure from the normal human standard for bodily ability, but also, as a trans-genetic clone, a monstrous hybrid. Hence the possibilities for disgust are much more diverse in *Alien Resurrection* than in the previous films. In particular, it plays upon the contemporary edginess about cloning and other genetic interventions into "normal" human existence.

In all four *Alien* films there are two perverse geometries at work. In the first place, the alien creatures represent a consistent way of behaving, even though nothing is ever said about their "culture" or power of conceptualization, which is intrinsically loathsome, at least from the human viewpoint.[104] In the best tradition of science-fiction aliens, they are ravenous, implacable and inimical. Their bizarre reproductive cycle involves living hosts to incubate their pupae. One of the more gruesome plot moves in *Alien Resurrection* is for the military to import living human beings, in "stasis," onto the science station to serve as hosts for the pupae of the queen alien that has been cloned along with Ripley. In the second place, each of the *Alien* films adopts as a narrative premise the existence of a powerful, controlling bureaucracy striving, against all human interests, to capture and "domesticate" the alien creatures. In the first three films, it is the "Company," a private corporation, that seeks to make a profit from the alien creatures at the expense of the human race; in the fourth film, it is a public corporation, the "United Military," that, with an identical indifference to human well-being and blinkered stupidity concerning the alien xenomorphs' destructive potential, seeks the creatures for military and police purposes. In all four films, it is possible to experience moral disgust at the shortsightedness and indifference of the distant bureaucracy and to feel it as a perverse geometry, twisted against the interests of the human species it claims to represent. In Chapter 1, I argued that bureaucracies, comprehensive but abstract systems of human control, can be disgusting. Few works of recent literature or film make this point more forcefully than the four *Alien* films.

In contrast to horror, terror is the experience of unanticipated degradation. When actual humans, living in actual in-the-world terror situations, describe their lives, they often say that it is "degrading." It is degrading to be compelled to wait for something to happen to you suddenly that you will not understand and for which no justification will be given, other than general propositions, slogans and war cries.[105] Beneath the calm surface of life, plans will have been worked out, purposes and strategies will have been rationally evolved, but the potential victim of terror will know nothing of this and may not even suspect its possibility. Within the terrorist's mind, or the mind of terror perhaps, everything is cold and precise. You will not realize it yet, but you will have been abducted into that mind, transformed into a role to play. It is a role that is based on a sliver of your being, a fragment of your personality, perhaps no more than the nationality that you are taken to represent, but it will fit into the theatrical design that the terror-monster will have created for you. In terror you will play, perhaps unknowingly, certainly uncomprehendingly, a role that is based on yourself but is not yourself. You will play this role upon a stage that has been created in the mind of the terrorist. It is a stage empty except for the roles that have been created. Horror is lush with evidence; terror, spare as a torturer's interrogation. The terrorist himself will be like a puppet master, or a director, who not only creates the stage, the roles and the design, but also directs the action. The terrorist imagines a fictional world in which his victims will be characters. In terror, the victims become actors in the terrorist's mental theatre, transformed into characters within an alien fictional world. The terrorist will be the *magister ludi* of a godgame.

Thus, terror-fiction often takes the form of a godgame: that is, a game-like situation in which one character (the terrorist) has created a network of illusions within which to trap another character.[106] Nothing points towards this action other than the action itself. As a narrative mode, terror normally invokes a high degree of intelligence and strategic planning. In a horror-world, a monster may be entirely inarticulate and capable of only slow and clumsy moves. A terror-world usually assumes an intelligent, deeply plotting agent behind its abrupt explosions. Just as serial killers are usually assumed to be more intelligent, both more imaginative and more strategic, than mass murders, so terror narratives evoke fictional worlds in which intelligence is much more a factor than in horror. In terror, nothing "just happens" or seems only to follow an instinct to kill, and nothing corresponds to the often shapeless, blob-like monster at the head of the stairs. The godgame always assumes a directing, playful intelligence, although in terror it will most likely be malevolent and pitiless. For this reason, ideology usually plays an important role in terror. The monster in horror may stand for values or indicate a system of feeling very different from the human ideal, but the perverse geometry it represents will be a problem in inference and interpretation.

When disgust motifs appear in terror-fiction, they do not mark a monster's spoor. They appear abruptly, as shocks, not as anticipations, epiphanic not paragenetic. Of course, I am speaking now primarily from the vantage of a character within a terror-based fictional world. The characters know little, understand little and experience the affects that correspond to ignorance: fear, anxiety, paranoia and shock. On the other hand, a reader will often possess the advantage over the characters (and over the inhabitants of any actual-world terror situation) in that he or she may know what constitutes the organizing systems, understand and anticipate the violence. The distinction between the character's perspective and the reader's privileged overview plays an important role in much terror-fiction. (In *The Satanic Verses*, Rushdie makes the experience of terror as abrupt for his readers as for his characters, but it is not necessary for art-terror to be written in this way.) Very powerful narrative effects are possible when a narrative incorporates the distinction between what reader and characters each know. In *The Silence of the Lambs* and his earlier novel *Red Dragon*, Thomas Harris tells the narrative from both the point of view of the characters and from that of the police. Once the reader has been given access to the evidence and the thought processes of the police, it is possible to experience both the terror that characters feel and the intellectual challenge that the police confront.

Red Dragon is particularly interesting on this point since, having kept the distinction throughout the narrative, it collapses in the final scene when Francis Dolarhyde, a particularly intelligent serial killer, is allowed to attack, in an act of pure revenge, the family of the FBI agent who has previously identified him. Having experienced both the pleasures of intellectual challenge and the terror of the victims, the reader must suddenly abandon the cerebral perspective of the narrative and experience terror on the same level as the surprised victim. In his 1986 film *Manhunter*, Michael Mann pares down the terror action of *Red Dragon* in order to make it conform more closely to the parameters of a standard horror film. Dolarhyde is much less present in the film, nothing is said concerning his hare-lip, and he is largely unsympathetic.[107] Mann strips the character of the interiority that Harris had carefully created for him. The result is a horror narrative in which Dolarhyde degenerates into a rather simple monster. He is given a series of monster-appropriate acts, his motivation and not the trail he leaves is important, and his final death actually quotes the deaths of other monsters (such as King Kong) in its stalked, entrapped and bloody finality.[108]

Terror as a narrative and dramatic form (that is, to adapt Noël Carroll's way of talking, "art-terror") differs from horror in two fundamental ways, both of which I have already indicated. First, acts within a terror-world happen suddenly and, at least from the victim's perspective, without warning. The manifestations of terror will come with the startling abruptness of a bottle being broken. There is no spoor to follow in a terror-world. Second, terror erupts into the fictional world, but it does so from the unseen foundation of an underlying conceptual system. In horror, a monster may be demented, mindless or, like the xenomorphs in the *Alien* films, possess a truly alien, unfathomable mind (as well as a truly unknowable, fundamentally uninferrable culture). It may be unhuman, deformed, hybrid or even, like the typical Lovecraftian monster, unimaginable. What matters is that it should cause anxiety and dread among the characters who inhabit its world. In the end, it may be disclosed, or nearly so, and then destroyed. In terror, there are no monsters other than the human mind and its creatures. Occasionally, a technological destructor, itself a product of the underlying system of terror, may act something like a monster in a horror-world. Thus the rocket in Pynchon's *Gravity's Rainbow* possesses certain horror characteristics: it leaves a spoor in the damage it causes (though this is randomly distributed in a radial pattern, apparently tracing Tyrone Slothrop's sexual conquests), it must be tracked and it is ultimately located in an underground labyrinth. However, it does not act independently (like a good horror monster) since it must be designed, built, maintained and fired within a system that has many other ways of killing its victims. It is also overdetermined, embodying many themes within the novel, in a way that the normal monomaniacal monster never functions. If there is a monster in *Gravity's Rainbow*, it is the Rocket-state itself, the *racketenstadt* in some future version of which a computer technology will structure all human activity. Everything is "trans-observable" in the world of *Gravity's Rainbow*, pointing beyond itself and leading uncertainly towards "Them" and "Their" systems. Paranoia plays an important, and often noted, role in all terror novels. It is, as Rushdie puts it, a "prerequisite of survival" for the exile or the alienated loner.[109] Paranoia (the sense that there is something to know that cannot be known) seems like an appropriate psycho-conceptual affect for a terror-world just as anxiety and dread are the pervasive affects of a horror-world.

Manhunter demonstrates how a relatively complex terror narrative, involving deep motivations and actions on diverse strata, can be simplified, refocussed and degraded. However, Harris' *Red Dragon* shows how, taken as problems in perspective, horror and terror may co-exist within a single narrative. Dolarhyde may be a lone terrorist, unconnected with any terrorist organization, but Harris gives him an explicit personal belief system, based upon an idiolectic theory of self-transcendence and "Becoming," that provides the underlying foundation for his acts. The Tamil and Sikh women in Rushdie's "Chekov and Zulu" and his *The Satanic Verses* share an prerequisite trait for terrorists: they possess certainty (eyes turning inward in righteous contemplation), act uncompromisingly and can smile in the face of death.[110] The Imam in *The Satanic Verses*, who hates secularism and modernism, watches his followers in Desh walk slowly into death and thinks that it is love. "They love me for my habit of smashing clocks," he tells Gibreel. Human beings who turn away from God lose love, certainty and the sense of "boundless time." Hence the Imam's first act after the revolution will be to smash the clocks, even to expunge the word *clock* from the dictionary, and to create an "Untime."[111] Certainty about the cause for which the terrorist will kill and perhaps die is an absolute condition: the terrorist must behave as if he or she were already dead.[112] Although terrorists occur frequently in his fiction, always characterized with understanding, Rushdie also knows that terror states exist and act upon their citizens with the same abrupt, unreasoning violence. In *Midnight's Children*, the Indian government, personified in the figure of the Widow (Mrs. Gandhi), acts in terroristic ways towards the gifted children of Indian independence. It kidnaps them, holds them secretly in a prison, desexes them (Saleem has his gonads removed) and destroys their special talents. *Shame* treats Pakistan as a consistent terror state, consumed with its collective sense of religious purity and righteousness, that acts both arbitrarily and violently towards its own citizens. All the examples from Rushdie show that a terror state is not only dictatorial but also, in Ross Chambers' phrase, dictates. To live within its power is to live under dictation in a regime that constructs itself allegorically.[113] An official discourse, in which your part will be pre-inscribed, will tell you who you are and how you should behave.

In *The Satanic Verses*, the terror state has several shapes. It is there in the Imam's vision, it takes incipient form in Mahound's transformation of Jahila, city of ignorance and sand that becomes a city of certainty, and it can be seen dying in the Empress Ayesha's final violence while being born in the unswerving religious faith of the peasant Ayesha. However, the United Kingdom is also redescribed as a partial terror state. The metamorphosis that Saladin Chamcha undergoes, into a hairy goat-like Satan figure, represents the power of the British state to describe, and thus transform, its immigrants.[114] Shortly after his "macabre demoniasis" begins, Saladin is arrested by immigration officers who bewilder him by treating his metamorphosis as if it were "the most banal and familiar matter they could imagine." When he begins to excrete goat pellets in the back of the police Black Maria, one officer observes, "You're all the same. Can't expect animals to observe civilized standards. Eh?" He then puts his hand behind Saladin's neck and forces "his head down towards the pellet-littered floor," compelling Saladin to eat his own excrement.[115] Saladin's demoniasis is only what the officers expect and what, it seems, they have witnessed many times before. When he demands that the police check their computer to confirm his identity as an English citizen and a member of Actors' Equity ("My name is Salahuddin Chamchawala, professional name Saladin Chamcha"), one police officer replies, "Look at yourself. You're a fucking Packy billy. Sally who?—What kind of name is that for an Englishman?"[116] The redescriptions have been dictated by the British state's consensual ideology and, unhappily for the immigrants, they stick.

Taken to a detention centre, Saladin discovers that there are many dark-skinned immigrants there who have metamorphosed into bizarre shapes. Someone who appears to be a manticore explains how it is done. The English simply describe them: "That's all. They have the power of description, and we succumb to the pictures they construct."[117] Escaping from the detention centre, Saladin glimpses

> beings he could never have imagined, men and women, who were also partially plants, or giant insects, or even, on occasion, built partly of brick and stone; there were men with rhinoceros horns instead of noses and women with necks as long as any giraffe.[118]

You could hardly find a better example of "dictation"; that is, the power of a terror state to impose its discourse upon individuals.

Yet it is obvious that Rushdie does not mean that the United Kingdom is committed to terrorism in the same way that the Imam, the empire of Desh or Mahound's new theocracy are. Rather, he seems to have in mind something close to Isabel Allende's proposition that terror is a "capacity" of the human mind that is present in the world. As capacities, terror and the terroristic resistance that it breeds are both possible in different degrees. Dance and counter-dance of perverse geometries: they are ways of seeing that make the world conform to an ideology or belief system. From the outside, alien ideologies appear to twist the world into deformed shapes. Disgust rises in the mind, if only infrequently in the throat, at the recognition of the ways in which the world has been skewed from its "natural" order. Terror and terrorism manifest the toilet training of the mind: the compulsion to flush the Other into non-existence, or into a realm of repressed abjects. They also constitute the theatrical reach of the mind into everyone's life who disagrees or even seems not fully to support the ruling ideological system.[119] This is why terror plays out in the world very much as a godgame. Rushdie's characters are always playing in such games.

QueAng-QueAng has a coastline, a littoral of land that runs along the sea from one point on the map to another, but it has no beaches. It does not have beaches because the people of QueAng-QueAng have no concept of play. Hence they have no room in their lives for swimming, or for picnics, or for sunbathing, or for surfing. The people of QueAng-QueAng say that they are serious and do not lead their lives for fun. Fishermen draw their boats upon the sand and women often look for anemone in tidal pools from which they make dark, sullen dyes. No one goes to the sea to swim. They tell foreigners who ask that it would be frivolous to waste time swimming or playing in the surf. On certain days when the sky is empty of everything but light, the sun burning with red ferocity, young theological students may hire a carriage that will be drawn by peasants over the sand. The carriages are black and completely sealed. Inside, there is neither light nor air. The young men have themselves pulled at great speed along the sand, from one headland to another, and back. They do this only to demonstrate that there are no beaches in QueAng-QueAng.

The real reason there are no beaches, writes one traveller who knows QueAng-QueAng well, is that no one has ever imagined a beach before or what could be done on one. The people of QueAng-QueAng do not have a word in their language for fun. The only word that even begins to translate *play* applies only to the flighty actions of puppies and very small children. Believing in conformity, they do not easily tolerate deviance. People dress alike. They always tell the same stories. They weave patterns that are different, but somehow always the same. There are only a few patterns in life, they say, and these are all one pattern. Even if God were to be seen playing in the surf, the people of QueAng-QueAng would not emulate Him.

QueAng-QueAng's inflexible intensity has often disturbed others. It is difficult to negotiate with a people who have only a single story, who cannot fail to be right and who reject the larger world with animosity and disgust. Grasping the massive weapon of their intolerance, their closed fist has been able to strike into distant places, even into open societies where the citizens do play, recognize fun and enjoy beaches. Living in these societies there are many exiles from QueAng-QueAng, men and women who have fled repression to seek an openness in which imagination and play would be possible. Some exiles from QueAng-QueAng have been killed, others threatened with death. The playfulness in their words, disrupting the national seriousness and overwriting the single story in which QueAng-QueAng believes, has condemned them. The hand of QueAng-QueAng reaches out suddenly, no warnings given, and strikes.

In this chapter, I have examined one of the most difficult senses of disgust. I have argued that conceptual structures, alien value systems and ideologies, can often inspire disgust. These abstract conceptual structures can be experienced as perverse geometries. The disgust that is experienced in confronting strange or foreign conceptual structures is, in the first place, moral, the familiar masking of the face as physical disgust to show contempt, but it is also intellectual. Sometimes when talking to a true believer, if you pose an antithetical conviction, even as a bare hypothesis, you may see disgust pass like a thin spasm through his or her mind.[120] Although there would be as many examples as there are belief systems, I argue that it is modernism that, whatever technological improvements to life and aesthetic freedoms it has brought, strikes many religious people as a whiff of the devil's excrement might. Modernism is too materialistic, too "American," too now-oriented, to please the mind of those who believe deeply in spiritual values or in a "better place." The Muslim attack on *The Satanic Verses* shows the intense disgust that believers can feel about modernism.

In the next chapter, I shall consider what happens when disgust turns inwards upon the self. Then the individual, self-aware and still independent, falls rapidly towards the mucoid condition of sludge that lies behind the boundaries that define disgust. As I have argued throughout, disgust is an extremely powerful affect that can find its metamorphic expression in the world's every aspect, but when it is turned inwards, to become the emotional context of self-awareness, it will be like acid. A vast, complex set of metaphors, crowded with images of inward gnawing, of corrosive contamination and of being devoured, is available to describe the sense of self-disgust. The image from the *Alien* films of being gnawed or eaten from within while serving as a host-incubator, is only one, but a powerful one, for the sense of inward decay and dissolution that accompanies self-disgust. Self-disgust is a transformation of consciousness analogous to having one's blood replaced by vitriol: inward burning and dissolution flowing through all the channels of personal existence. Yet as scarifying as self-disgust may be, there may exist an even more corrosive personal image. The condition of being abject, of having fallen into abjection, involves not only the sense of self-disgust but also that of feeling disgusting in the eyes of others, of having been cast off, discarded like waste, and individually isolated as an object of loathing and nauseous revulsion. ❀

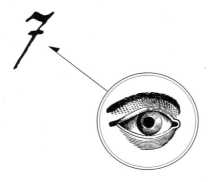

V^{Its}enom

Feeling Abject

The most unhappy man I ever knew was a brilliant student of philosophy. When I first met him, we were both in a tavern near the University. He was alone at the bar, but a mutual friend introduced us and we ended up spending a late evening talking through an endless series of ancient difficulties. He smoked constantly, a habit that even then I found repulsive, but it seemed so much a part of his character that I barely noticed. Sometime before midnight, I was astounded to see him take a lit cigarette and grind it out against the back of his left hand. As I got to know him better, I learned that he had scars from cigarette burns up and down both arms. The inside of his mouth was often cut from broken glass. He would bite the rim off a beer glass and hold the jagged shards in his mouth as blood pooled behind his tightly squeezed lips. Then he might spit it out on the floor, blood and glass together. He said, and I believed him, that he really wanted to swallow the glass and that he did, against bodily habit and disposition, sometimes succeed. I never knew another man so sad.

It didn't take me long to understand that he felt a deep uncertainty and a lack of confidence about many things, including existence and himself. Today, it would probably be easier to smoke out the root of the problem: abuse, sexual trauma and perhaps a failed repression of tormenting memories. At that time, although I certainly knew that many people had been sexually abused in their childhood, I assumed that everyone could bear up and carry on. My new friend didn't bear up well at all. Something gnawed at him savagely. Several times I tried to discover the reasons for his self-hurtful behaviour, always approaching the issue indirectly. ("Tell me about growing up in Texas?" "What was your worst experience?" etc.) On two or three occasions, I asked him directly to change his behaviour simply as a matter of hygiene and self-preservation. He always said that he would, but then I would have to watch as he stubbed out cigarettes on his skin. He was like an alcoholic who promises to quit but never can, because his craving overpowers him. Addicted to suffering and pain, my friend clung to his personal regime of punishment and retribution.

I lived alone at that time. I had a rather dingy room a few blocks from the university in an old building that was known affectionately to students as "Firstein's Flophouse." It was both cheap and convenient, a magnet for students in the humanities. One morning, shortly before five, I woke up to the sound of faint knocking at my door. It was my new friend, stinking in a wretchedly unwashed condition, reeking of stale beer and bleeding from the corners of his mouth. He was curled up on the floor against the door, weeping and whimpering faintly like a man who has been tortured to the point of near death. I brought him into my room and made him some instant coffee on a hotplate. I tried to persuade him to shower, but he wouldn't take his clothes off. I did manage to talk him into rinsing his mouth out with an antiseptic wash. The problem that always seemed to drive him to self-punishment was, he had tried to make me believe, a terrible sense that he was unloved. There would usually be a girl in the background, someone I would never meet, who had just dumped him. "I'm worthless," he would sob between philosophical disquisitions, his beer slopping over as he would gesticulate with his glass in hand. What he usually said was, "I ain't worth shit." By the time he showed up at my door that morning, I had understood that his difficulties with girls masked some other, far deeper problem. It was that submerged region of darkness that I would sometimes try to reach with my ineffectual questions.

After he had rinsed his mouth and spat out the last threads of blood, I suggested that we go for a walk. We walked down 57th Street, under the Illinois Central viaduct and out to the shores of Lake Michigan. It was still very early in the morning, no later than six-thirty, but the traffic was already heavy along the lake. There was a small peninsula, a tiny thumb of land sticking out into the lake where I often walked when I was writing term papers. I steered us out to the end of the point so that we could contemplate the cityscape stretching north towards the Loop and Navy Pier. We sat on a large rock almost against the edge of the water. Suddenly, he leaned his head into my shoulder, sobbing. I felt tense, but I let him keep his head pressed against me. I did not put my arm around him, but I did pat his nearest shoulder encouragingly. This was a moment of confession.

I was never certain what had brought on the weeping, slobbering self-revelation. Probably the need to tell someone had been building up within him. Today he would be seeing a therapist, but I never heard the least suggestion that he was receiving psychological counselling of any kind. On the two or three occasions that we talked about such matters, he had expressed the philosopher's scorn for Freud and psychoanalysis. He was a man, terribly hurt by something in his past, who had no resources other than his own. That morning by the lake, he abruptly welled over because I had acted like a friend. I had looked after him on more than one occasion, and that morning I had actually welcomed him in an almost brotherly manner.

He had been sexually abused. From the age of eight or so, his father had anally sodomized him on a regular basis. I might have guessed that he had been abused, but the knowledge that it had been his father struck me like a blow to the head. Through his sobs, he told me that he had never been able to escape his father and that his mother, although she must have known what was happening, did nothing to help. What was worse was that his father had often given him to an uncle for sex. He had been like a rent boy that his father had kept in the house for casual sex. No one ever offered to help or ever tried to advise him. His terrible fate was never discussed or even mentioned in his home. Now, grown into adulthood, he had left his family behind, escaped the dark pit that was Texas, as he said, and established that he was, or could be, a brilliant student in a difficult subject. He believed that he would never be happy until he went back to Texas and murdered his father. He was in the fork of a decision: he could ease his memory by killing his father or he could go on to earn a PhD in philosophy. Later, I realized that a third option was the most likely. He would continue on his self-tormenting course until, nothing resolved, no solutions ever found, he killed himself or went mad. Today if I were to meet him again, I expect that he would be living on the street in Chicago or San Francisco. He would be truly cast out.

After that spring, I never saw my friend again. A few years later, he learned my address and wrote to me in Australia wanting to know this or that, but saying nothing about his bad memories, his self-loathing, the confession at the lake or his wish to kill his father. I wrote back, but I never heard from him after that. He was the first man I had ever known who admitted to having been sexually abused. I had known women who kept dark secrets about their childhoods and who would intimate that terrible things that had been done to them. They would never say explicitly what had happened, but I could tell, from hints or coded allusions, that they had experienced horrors. My friend was the first man who had spoken about his abuse, and even the terse tale that he told had been slow in coming, obviously very hard for him to articulate. He was, I believe, the first person I ever met who was deeply, and perhaps irremediably, abject.

All the contemporary clichés about sexual abuse come into play when I try to recall him. He had been abused, his natural trust in his parents had been violated, he had been traumatized, he had been transformed into an object. He possessed a long string of painful memories that, it seems, he had been unable to repress. And these memories made him feel worthless, unloved and unlovable, cast off from both his family and society. All these haunting memories, and all the intensely negative affects that surrounded them, circled around one fact and one body part. His anus had been raped, but raped not merely in the narrow contemporary sense of exacting non-consensual sex from another person: he had been raped in the older sense of having been carried off, of having been kidnapped. His anus had been subjected to violent, undesired sexual intromission, but it had also been kidnapped, alienated from his sense of his own personhood. Unlike the phallus, a highly social bodily appendage, the anus, Guy Hocquenghem observes, is "essentially private."[1] Social formation, centring around toilet training, hides the anus from public scrutiny, denies its pleasure-giving possibilities and concentrates it upon its excremental function. Although much happens during intimacy that is never made public, including several varieties of anal sexuality, the anus is not usually a topic for public discussion. It does seem to be, in western cultures at least, an "essentially private" bodily part. Of all the many cyber(body)parts that you might imagine, a colostomy bag would be, I suspect, the least acceptable and the most difficult to endure. My friend had been stripped of this privacy, which no doubt, in a classic double bind, he had also been taught to preserve. Having been anally raped many times over a number of years had exposed his hidden anus to a terrible public knowledge, but it had also, paradoxically, transformed him into a boy whose anus was the most important thing about him. He had become morbidly conscious of his anus, both that it was a potential area for sexual pleasure (which could be commanded against his will) and that it had been taken away from him, made public in an extremely painful way.[2] He was experiencing, I know now, deep and corrosive abjection. The world opened before him, like a Beckett novel, in narrow vistas of existential bleakness.

Against the figure of the abject person, you have to set all those whom you have met who seem to experience no self-consciousness at all. Rather than having their self-consciousness stink in their minds like a rotting corpse, they seem hardly aware of their own existence (other than as a self-satisfied pleasure). They do not feel self-disgust, certainly not abjection, and they do not mind acting in disgusting ways. Like so many other aspects of the study of disgust, the problem of consciousness occupies an unmistakable highpoint. An abject person, such as my friend in Chicago, experiences an intense, overwhelming self-consciousness. You could say that an abject person lives in a fictional world, given over entirely to modes of victimization and punishment, in which he or she acts as a participant-observer. His opposite, the unself-conscious person who easily performs private acts publicly, inhabits no fictional worlds at all, except (like the Sports Bore, for instance) those which are wholly objective and contain only other people. In order to put the abject person into perspective, consider someone who so lacks self-consciousness that normally disgusting acts would be as ordinary as breathing or swallowing.

In early 1999, riding the bus to the seaside resort of Lorne on Australia's south coast, a beautiful young man sat in front of me. He was one of those splendid human beings, male or female, who can only be described as gorgeous. His magnificent Celtic face, high forehead, curving eyebrows, sharply defined cheeks and green eyes (rarities, a Spanish proverb asserts, like dukes and kings) held my attention. He also stank, badly. He was in his early twenties and probably, from his looks (trimmed but tousled hair, a rugby shirt), coming from school, most likely Deakin University in Geelong. His stench might have indicated that he had just left a gym or come from an Australian Rules game hurriedly without showering, or it might have suggested that he had just been having sex with someone. His rancid stench might just have included whiffs of dried sperm and vaginal juices. However, it struck me as more like the stale body odour of a person who seldom washes than that of someone coming unshowered from vigorous activity.

Stench is relative to the environment in which you smell it. My friend in Chicago often stank, and the morning he crawled up to my door his stench from drink and self-neglect had been appalling; but he was always aware that his body was repulsive in the noses of others. Stench was a part of his self-image. In a third-world country, I would hardly have noticed human body odour since everyone, normally unwashed, would have one. In Australia, where cleanliness and all the other modalities of modern hygiene are easily available, a stale, acrid stench most likely reveals a decision to go unclean. There are many reasons why a person might choose to stink. A loathing of water might be one; an active punk ideology another. The young man's decision to stink publicly might have shown an escape from family repression or just a personal choice to reject all repression, at whatever level, insofar as it can be seen to be as embodied in social mores. It would then be an instance of an individual seeking what Isaiah Berlin called "negative liberty," the freedom to act as one wishes, independent of restraint or hindrance. Having perceived himself as repressed, as constrained by a parental sense of hygiene or a generalized social sense of deportment, a young man might assert his liberty by choosing to stink. It might even have been a deliberate act of transgression, negative liberty subordinated to an active program of anti-repressive self-transformation. At the time, I doubted that hypothesis.

After a few minutes, the young man, who could not have known that I was observing him from behind, dipped his head under the high-collar of his rugby shirt and sniffed his left armpit. He did this more than once before I left the bus at Lorne, leaving him to carry on, now unobserved, to Apollo Bay. A man travelling on a bus in Bolivia between two small towns would probably not bother to sniff his armpits. All armpits would be much the same, ill-smelling but imperceptibly so. If a man riding a rural bus in Bolivia were to sniff himself, it would only be out of concern for what the gringo riding next to him might think. Observing the young man smelling his own bodily stench, I had to conclude that something more than negative liberty was in play. It seemed such an unstudied action, as innocent as a dog licking his genitals, that I had to suppose either a perversion, a compulsive physical expression of narcissism or an almost total lack of personal awareness of his body in space. Surrounded by other people, he acted oblivious of social norms. He was so absorbed in his own body, in his private narcissism made public, that he could not imagine that another person might observe him and note his behaviour. (Or care much if they did, I would guess.) Many people are fundamentally unaware of their physical scatter, their expulsive detritus, the many varied matters of their encroachment upon others, but some few are even unaware of their own persons in collective space. Their stenches, although lovingly sniffed, are unmeasured and unregarded.

One thing was certain: he was not, at least on the only evidence I had, what Australians call an "ocker." Ockers are performative; they act in calculatedly disgusting ways precisely in order to offend. They are like actors in an individual shock theatre, playing to small, unwilling audiences. An ocker's behaviour resembles the public actions of punk in unmistakable ways. It is an acting-out of the observer's dread and anxiety. It seeks to evoke disgust in order to demonstrate the paltriness of the observer's resistance: "This is what you dread; see what it shows you about yourself." Once, many years ago in Cowes, on Philip Island in Australia, I observed two young men in their late twenties, both dressed in suits and wearing ties, order spaghetti Bolognaise. When the spaghetti arrived, they ate it with their hands. Both hands. In fistfuls and by the strand. They may always have eaten in this manner, but it struck me as likely that they were responding to my presence in the restaurant. An obviously middle-class foreigner, studiously reading a book while eating my dinner, I was the right target for ocker behaviour. I did find the spectacle faintly loathsome, but I didn't flee, call loudly for my bill or evince any outward signs of disgust. The young men had targeted my conventional inhibitions about eating and table manners, but had not quite succeeded. The aimed-for spot had not been as tender as they had supposed.

The self-sniffer on the bus was not, then, really an ocker. He was too drawn up in himself, too absorbed and oblivious, and entirely non-performative. Nor was he what Australians refer to as a "dag."[3] He reminded me rather sharply of an experience I had in Argentina while staying in Mar del Plata, the largest seaside resort in the country. I was sitting on the terrace of a restaurant on the beach near the casino when a young woman came up to my table begging for money. She had an attractive face and a strong upper body, but her legs were crippled. She supported herself on canes, the kind that fit over the wrist and act like crutches. I had no change at that moment so I waved her away, but I decided that I would look for her after I had paid my bill to give her some small coins. When I stood up from the table eventually, I did look for her. I saw her about thirty feet away leaning back against a wall. She was picking her nose in an utterly unself-conscious way and leisurely eating her snot. I did not give her any money.

People act against conventions, making themselves disgusting. This may happen merely because they have crossed borders, geographical or social, and are ignorant of different mores or unaware how shocking their own familiar habits may seem. (Australians often seem to find strange accents in English disgusting: my own flat or intrusive R sounds, for example. You can observe a person's eyes bug, his nose crinkle and his lips pucker, rather as if he had unwittingly sucked upon a rotten prune, even as you speak to him.) It may also happen because, like punks or other nihilists (such as ockers), they want to act out their rejection of normal values. This usually follows an indirect course. People act disgustingly because they wish to force upon a shocked audience either the repressed urges of that audience or else their own judgement upon its values. In such moments, disgusting behaviour effects a grotesque transformation of hypocritically under-articulated values into something like their true character. Yet it is also possible for people to act disgustingly, within their own cultures, in purely unconscious ways. The young woman in Mar del Plata and the young man on the bus in Australia were not trying to shock or even disturb me, or anyone, but only enjoying their bodies, or their bodily effluvia. Such unconscious behaviour can arise from ignorance (the simple-minded may eat their own feces, for example), narcissism or the cultivated exercise of negative liberty. It might even be deliberately transgressive in the de Sadean sense. I concluded that the young Argentinian woman was ignorant; the Australian man, narcissistic. My friend in Chicago had been abject, neither ignorant nor narcissistic, but, indeed, their mordant opposite.

The human body is multiplexly split. I do not mean only that it has appendages or even that it creates the appearance of bilateral symmetry (until it has been split open), but rather that in consciousness, as an object of thought or as the subject of one or another conceptual system, the human body is experienced as a battleground, an area of conflicting themes.[4] You can imagine this battleground in many ways. In a straight-forward manner, it could be envisioned with the body reproduced as an image framed by words and arrows that identify parts and their functions. In a surrealist fabrication, the body opens like a cabinet to reveal the products and tools it employs in consumption. Phantasmagorically, the body morphs through a series of variations to show itself at different stages (or in different fantasies) of composition or decomposition. It can be imagined as actually split, like Italo Calvino's Cloven Viscount, or symbolically so, the shadow-side of consciousness darkening the face or else filling it with uneasy dreams. In Barbara Kruger's 1989 silk-screen photo of a woman's face, a line divides the face vertically along the bridge of the nose. On the left side, she stares ahead (intent, perhaps a bit grim), but on the right, a negative image, the intentness has been smoothed over in a softening gloom that is outside of the face itself. The right eye becomes a piercing flash of light or a mysterious hole bored deep into the skull. The image is bordered in red and has a message written in three parts, white letters on red background, that reads, top to bottom, "Your body is a battleground."[5]

The apprehension of the body as split, divided or in fragments not only can be imagined in different ways but has very different consequences both for understanding and for practical action. Marking the body in a highly visible manner, a tattoo must be interpreted (or "read") to make sense of it. It is a more complex marking than either scarification or piercing since it both conveys more significance than these other modes of bodily mutilation and reveals a more intricate intention. The design must be chosen, out of possibilities nearly as wide as those of all visual art (the tattooist's "flash" only hints at what can be done), and it must be inscribed slowly, often in phases. Thus, as I have already argued, tattoos are privileged as bodily markings, both more complex and more ineradicable than piercings.[6] Moreover, all tattoos create one dominant effect: they mark the body into separate places, transforming it into areas or zones. The potential significance of each zone is important, but the act of division, splitting the body into discrete areas, precedes that significance and is usually perceived first.[7] The differentiated areas inscribed by visible markings on the body point towards a possible *Spaltung* in the person's sense of identity, a division that may be written upon the psyche as well as upon the body. In this sense, the perception of a tattoo upon another person may evoke the issues of "spoiled identity" that Goffman discusses. One aspect of a multiplex intention may be to exhibit to the world an inner awareness of fragmentation and personal disintegration. Perceived in that way, a tattoo, like the jailhouse inscriptions on Max Cady's back in *Cape Fear*, flags a dangerous psychic state, a potential for violence. A person who sees himself as split and has taken deliberate and unmistakable steps to register this for the world might wish to impose an analogous fragmentation upon others. A human corpse, as Kristeva notes, is the ultimate instance of the abject: it is also a rather final act of division, of splitting one thing from another. Death, Norbert Elias writes, is "a problem of the living."[8]

In this chapter, I want to examine the most personal of all disgust-worlds: the private world of self-disgust or self-loathing. Ugly fictional worlds play out in which the self-loathing person may imagine him/herself in a variety of punishing or humiliating scenarios. My friend in Chicago once told me that he often dreamed he had died and his body was being cut apart by an anatomy class at the medical school. These dreams were, he thought, signs that he could still be "good for something," still able to possess worth. An ugly personal world of self-loathing reflects a bodily split that is intensely, perhaps unbearably, intimate, a split in which "good" and "bad" parts are isolated from each other. However, I want most to distinguish the inner sense of feeling oneself another object among many disgusting objects, a single point in a general field of disgust, from, in contrast, the inner sense of feeling oneself abject, cast apart and away. Throughout this book, I have emphasized the diverse array of both objects and acts that have been, or might be called, disgusting. I have stressed over and over again what seems to be an irreducible aspect of experiencing disgust: that it can be relearned, either effectively suppressed or else displaced entirely onto some new object. Up until this point, I have largely concentrated on the ways in which individuals experience disgust within a socio-cultural context. Disgust seems to be, and in the history of literature must be imagined as, an individual problem within some larger setting. Some people experience disgust more quickly, and some more forcefully, than others. Some people give occasion for disgust in others, and are themselves the cause of disgust, quite readily. A scum rocker, such as G.G. Allin, probably strikes most people as disgusting (he certainly wanted to strike you that way); but among his fans, and generally among punk audiences, who anticipated, perhaps yearned for, his violence and taboo-breaking, he seemed wonderful, glorious even.

In most of what I have said so far, I have pursued a model of a person who stands behind a boundary that marks certain objects or acts as disgusting or who, knowingly or unknowingly, crosses over such a boundary. Of course, taken only as a problem in representation, disgust will dominate, simply as a matter of course, exceptional fictions in which the world is pervasively a disgust-world and the characters who inhabit it live according to its terms: Beckett's characters, for instance, do not cross boundaries because such demarcations exist only for the reader or not at all. Their worlds are uniformly bleak, consistently without either joy or transcendence. David Lynch's character Henry in *Eraserhead* does not cross boundaries since, in his world, there are none. His dreams, his relationship, his food, his child, each aspect of his life, is, rather like the world of Beckett's *The Unnamable*, consistently grim and desolate.[9] The entire world, including Henry himself (who, after all, stabs his "child" to death), might be seen as disgusting, but within that world there are no divisions, no boundaries. It is more common for fictional worlds to contain internal boundaries that split it into distinct zones of disgusting and non-disgusting acts. Brigadier Pudding in *Gravity's Rainbow*, for instance, crosses a well-marked and highly illuminated boundary when he eats Katje's excrement, but he may not know what he is doing or be fully conscious of its significance. Pynchon is silent on this point, but he does let his readers know that Brigadier Pudding has been conditioned by past experience and manipulated by experimental psychologists. In Sartre's *Nausea*, Roquentin exists behind a self-constructed boundary that radically separates him from Bouville and all its commercial fussiness, but he has constructed it for himself out of the material of his personal alienation. Roquentin knows clearly that the world he experiences as disgusting is so because of who, and how, he has become. J.G. Ballard's *Crash* depicts techno-copulation, the intimate association of machines and sexual pleasure, as transgressive, but it is also a fictional world in which nearly everyone desires this transgression. The consciousness of boundaries exists entirely in the way the narrator (who is known as "Ballard") recognizes the potential destructiveness, as well as the excitement, of techno-sex.

I have treated disgust as, by and large, a question of boundaries, always an edge experience: that, but not this; them, but not us; you, but not me. Of course, this treatment may seem like the classical perspective on human cultural interaction, rather old hat, a discarded or repudiated "depth" model.[10] Still, even if it seems to make more sense to think of people as printed circuits, or as nodes or relays within a larger system of communication, as mere reflecting surfaces or as unconsciously structured by a symbolic system (an "ideology") that is class or gender based, it does usually seem *as if* one stood along the edge of boundaries, witnessing culturally sanctioned disgusting objects and acts across that edge, and either rejected or desired whatever stands on the other side. And certainly the history of western literature and film has accepted the depth model, the model of the individual as a conscious member of, yet distinct from, the culture in which he or she exists. Shakespeare's Leontes experiences disgust at the thought of Hermione's adultery with his best friend, but he does not appear to think of this as a communal system of information exchange. It is very personal, "deep" in the old sense, as it is for Hamlet when, contemplating Yorick's skull, he, too, experiences disgust. Hamlet feels his gorge rise when he considers the lipless skull, where once lips had hung that he had kissed, "I know not how oft," and his imagination runs immediately, in a characteristic manner, to historical, metaphysical, cosmic and comic speculations. Quite unmistakably, he seems to take Yorick's skull personally.

What happens when disgust moves inside and you begin to think of yourself as disgusting, as cast aside from the sane, integrated world of health and symbolic order? What happens when you begin to think of yourself as abject? The experience may be uncertain: both a hateful degradation and a potentially transcendent moment; a way down that leads to a way up. Often in modern literature the experience of degradation, of having entered the domain of the disgusting or of having become oneself disgusting (a "heap of rubbish," in Bataille's phrase), proves to be a liberating moment. Self-knowledge comes from testing yourself in extreme experiences, from discovering the limit cases that strip away the Apollonian carapace, the body armour of cultural rules that may seem to protect you but perhaps only hides or obscures your true self. Beckett's characters, for example, exist outside Apollonian encrustations, with neither the protection nor the hope that these bring, while Patrick White's characters often live secret lives, managing an Apollonian persona like a carnival domino. One of the most popular cult films of the 1970s, Phillipe de Broca's 1967 *King of Hearts*, tells the story of a soldier in World War One, a member of a Scottish regiment, who abandons the war in order to cast his lot with the inmates of an insane asylum.[11] The Great War was so futile, so degrading, so profoundly disgusting in so many ways that *only* Apollonian prohibitions made it possible. Men had to believe that it was proper, and even sweet, to die for their countries in mud and filth. When they stopped seeing the world that way, then an insane asylum would appear sane.

For many novelists, the moment of abjection has also seemed to be the moment of self-revelation. Patrick White, for example, returns over and over again to the moment of transcendence when the experience of disgust leads to knowledge, or the intimate sense of abjection opens a path to self-realization. In White's *Voss*, Willie Pringle, newly returned from studying art in Paris (it is the middle of the nineteenth century) and fascinated by the "grey of mediocrity, the blue of frustration," remarks to a group of astonished nineteenth-century Sydneysiders that the "blowfly on its bed of offal is but a variation of the rainbow."[12] There must be ways of seeing, whether painterly or punk, that allow the eye to peer beyond all social boundaries, even into the nominally disgusting and, more profoundly disturbing, the abject. Other of White's novels, such as *The Vivisector* and *The Twyborn Affair*, explore the persistent human problem of self-disgust and abjection. The main character in *The Twyborn Affair*, Eddie (but also Eudoxia and Eadith), experiences himself as a woman in a man's body. He can live successfully as a woman, but he never loses the anguished sense of his imperfection. He finds himself to be disgusting, and he has a keen eye for whatever seems disgusting in the world about him. Living as a young woman in France just prior to the Great War, he is almost happy, but futureless, if not hopeless;

living as a man in Australia after the war, he is raped, humiliated and degraded; living again as a woman in London just before the beginning of World War Two, he protects himself as a rule-conscious madame of an elegant brothel. Protected, he is nonetheless empty, still seeing himself as hopeless, unfulfilled, abject. Killed in a German bombing raid, he is left "little more than a white smile in a skin as rough and red as a brick."[13] Eddie is typical of the many limit-case characters that White creates, torn between worlds, existing behind boundaries while pretending to be on the other side. In limit-cases, you may discover yourself, or at least the Dionysian shadow-image of yourself, but never within the Apollonian constraints of, in Bataille's words, a "negative morality" that matches the "servile need of a constraint."[14] As a cultural boundary, disgust can constitute either a threat or a protection (a servile constraint that you may need); but it can also take shape as a moment of self-transcendence. Consider *Hamlet* once more.

Hamlet's self-appraisal after he has seen the Player King weep for a fiction he has seen performed, a contrast in registering affect that Hamlet calls "monstrous," reveals a negative and biting judgement. For a prince to call himself a "rogue and peasant slave" must show a negative self-accounting, a fall or shortcoming from an ideal standard. He calls himself an "ass" and compares himself to a "drab" or a "stallion" who, "like a whore must unpack my heart with words."[15] It probably would not be necessary for a reader/viewer to understand Hamlet's words as registering actual self-disgust, though self-disgust would be appropriate to the world of *Hamlet* in which so much is disgusting, deeply and inescapably loathsome. Hamlet's words may only establish a number of relevant analogies. Still, some readers of the play express considerable confidence in stating baldly that Hamlet feels self-disgust. In his recent study of character in Shakespeare, Imtiaz Habib writes that Hamlet "seethes with repulsion and disgust."[16] Camille Paglia also reads Hamlet as a character experiencing self-disgust. Hamlet, she writes, "as all sons of mothers, is bloated with 'this too too solid flesh'." She sees his first soliloquy moving with a "hidden chthonian logic" from

> suicidal self-disgust to thoughts of the world as 'an unweeded garden,' overgrown by 'things rank and gross in nature,' and ends in lurid visualization of his mother's sex life amid rumpled 'incestuous sheets,' sweaty soiled rags, both swaddling and shroud, mother nature's bindings of birth and death.[17]

The play, she adds, is "filled with bad smells." Although Paglia would seem to support my argument, I do not actually think that it is necessary to read Hamlet as experiencing self-disgust. Even the self-accusatory words in the soliloquy in the second act need not be taken as a self-analysis of disgust and loathing. However, I do think that one must understand Hamlet at this point, and indeed until the end of Act IV, Scene iv, when he reflects upon the significance of Fortinbras' projected invasion of Poland, as having introjected some aspects of the fictional world that he inhabits.

What critics sometimes call "images," or even "image patterns," are also fictional objects within a fictional world upon which the characters, the native inhabitants of that world, draw. Let us suppose that Hamlet feels only shame, an affect on the road to, but not quite fully arrived at, the point when a person might see himself as disgusting. The case of Hamlet shows what powerful fictional effects, both narrative and dramatic, can be gained when a character turns inwards and experiences itself negatively. It also shows the interrelationship between character and world in much fiction. The character's mind draws on the world it inhabits for its shape and self-definition. That mind reflects its own world, not the extra-textual lifeworld of the author or, if it does, it does so only at a sharply oblique angle. To cite another canonical example, Gulliver's ultimate misanthropy, preferring horses to humans, his stable to his house, may or may not indicate Jonathan Swift's personal misanthropy. However, it certainly does appear as the conclusion, the final mental state in a sequence of such states, to Gulliver's experiences of the human self diminished, its pretensions and ideals made ridiculous, among the Lilliputians; of the human body magnified, all its blemishes made large, among the Brobdingnagians; of the human mind parodied, its weakest proclivities manifested systematically, among the Laputians and Lagodians; and of the human person itself made vile, reduced to excrement-throwing, shamelessness and greed among the Yahoos.[18] His experience within his own world has taught Gulliver his misanthropy and has led him to feel physical disgust in the presence of other human persons, including his own family.

The body falls into its own matter and into disgust. Its degeneration and disintegration begin early and continue late (as a rotting corpse, as ashes). No consideration of the "lived body" should fail to take into account the experience of an actual body's disintegration. There are two ways to put the problem of disintegration into perspective. First, there are human bodies that have not quite achieved "normal" development. Although lacking the specific evocative power it once possessed when sideshows toured throughout North America, *freak* is still a word to reckon with. Even in the loose contemporary sense of a person who behaves in ways that are outside the bounds of ordinary conduct, a moral rather than a physical significance, a freak is someone whose disintegration has preceded development. The failure of the body is measured against some communal standard, real or imagined, that postulates an image of a human person's full, normal development. Second, there are bodies that have reached development, perhaps even helped to promote the flowering of a personal ego-ideal, but then failed in particular functions. In this second case, once-sound body parts have to be replaced. Disintegration is piecemeal, but nonetheless painful, an active source of self-disgust.

Both conditions exemplify the processes that I discussed in Chapter 4, metamorphosis and decomposition. While losing a body part and acquiring a prosthetic substitute in its place is a clear instance of decomposition, having an undeveloped or deformed physical condition may not seem like a case of metamorphosis since, by definition, a freak would be someone whose development has stopped or deviated at an early stage from the fetus' normal developmental sequence, not undergone change. However, this common-sense view underlooks the capacity of imagination to create scenarios that reinvent the world. The traditional lore of freaks, in sideshows and permanent collections such as P.T. Barnum's "American Museum," always held out two distinct possibilities: you might, but for God's grace, have looked this way yourself; you may still, luck or providence dealing you dark cards, look this way. There is something archetypal about freaks, pointing to large questions about human nature, identity, social roles and destiny. They prompt imaginary worlds and complex scenarios. In any event, it is the archetypal that Leslie Fiedler explores in his *Freaks*. The true freak, Fiedler observes,

> stirs both supernatural terror and natural sympathy, since, unlike the fabulous monsters, he is one of us, the human child of human parents, however altered by forces we do not quite understand into something mythic and mysterious, as no mere cripple ever is.

The freak challenges conventional boundaries "between male and female, sexed and sexless, animal and human, large and small, self and other, and consequently between reality and illusion, experience and fantasy, fact and myth."[19] The mental theatre in which disgust scenarios play out will be open to the possibility of mutation. You may imagine a world in which you might have been, or one in which you may still be, a freak. You may mutate, find yourself transformed by accident or disease or even by punishment. In all these situations, it will be possible to imagine a metamorphosis as a process that still unfolds. Metamorphosis is a process that is always with us, even when it seems not to be.

Tod Browning's 1932 film *Freaks*, censored and banned (in the United Kingdom) for years, brilliantly captures the equivocal two-sidedness of freaks: at once like and unlike those who pay to see them; at once sympathetic and disturbing. Browning's direction is masterful. Working together in a small tenting circus, the freaks are shown to form a tightly knit community. (By definition, as indicated in the inter-title commentary at the beginning of the film, freaks are outside of a community, viewed by the "norms" as monsters.) Within the film, the normal circus performers, such as Cleopatra, the beautiful but immoral aerialist, and Hercules, the strong man, constantly express their disgust for the freaks but are clearly themselves not members of a community. They are, like all bigots, at once exploitative and hypocritical. Hence the physical disgust they pretend to register at the freaks is offset by the moral disgust the audience is asked to feel about them. The first indication of disgust within the film occurs in the initial framing incident when a woman turns away, screaming, from a pit in which there is something frightening. The barker hedges the pit's contents in mystery. Then a cut-away shows Cleopatra on a trapeze. In the film's conclusion, Cleopatra becomes the most disgusting of all the freaks, or at least the only one who evokes an actual scream. The camera reveals what had been hidden at first: it is Cleopatra metamorphosed, reduced to a torso, squeaking unintelligibly in a bird-like chatter, and apparently covered with feathers.[20] It is as vivid an instance of metamorphosis, if surgical rather than divine, as those in Ovid.[21]

Fiedler observes that the "finale is so atrocious and contrived that it risks breaking the illusion completely."[22] It is also very powerful. After all, Cleopatra has become, by surgical intervention, a mutant. Yet if you wanted a single image, out of all the vast archive of literary representation, for either an unwilled metamorphosis or an abject person, you could hardly do better than the image of the beautiful and haughty Cleopatra transformed into a Chicken Woman. The film demonstrates the point that the existence of in-the-world freaks makes the disturbing impact of metamorphosis troublingly real. You can always imagine a fictional world in which undergoing metamorphosis, even becoming a freak, is held out as one of your lifeworld's unfolding possibilities.

Decomposition occurs in many ways, including death by torture (which I discussed in Chapter 4). However, the failure of a specific body part, because personal and so continuously an object of consciousness, focusses the body's fall into disgust in an especially acute form. A replacement body part is known as a prosthesis. What do prostheses tell you about the disintegration of the body or of its splitting and fragmenting condition? When they fail, the body's parts, (ordinarily so silent within the illusion of their "whole") scream their presence. When they are replaced, they grumble unnervingly in a new tongue. In having a prosthesis, I experience a split consciousness. When I put on my glasses or my contact lenses, I can see more clearly. I also correct a defect in my vision. At some point in the future, it may be possible to have prosthetic eyes. Contact lenses and glasses will seem primitive then; no longer commonplace, they will be difficult to find even for a person who can remember their use. I may wear a "visor," like commander La Forge in *Star Trek—The Next Generation*, or else possess a cybernetic eyeball. For the moment, I will imagine my prosthetic eyeball to be fully functional, unlike the one that Pynchon imagines in his parable of plastic surgery and bodily metamorphosis, *V.*

> As the distance between them gradually diminished Mondaugen saw that her left eye was artificial: she, noticing his curiosity, obligingly removed the eye and held it out to him in the hollow of her hand. A bubble blown translucent, its "white" would show up when in the socket as a half-lit sea green. A fine network of nearly microscopic fractures covered its surface. Inside were the delicately-wrought wheels, springs, ratchets of a watch, wound by a gold key which Fräulein Meroving wore on a slender chain round her neck. Darker green and flecks of gold had been fused into twelve vaguely zodiacal shapes, placed annular on the surface of the bubble to represent the iris and also the face of the watch.[23]

Pynchon's myth-inscribed eyeball is important to this discussion, but at this early point I want to imagine a future prosthetic eyeball that actually functions, enabling me to see. Still, even with ordinary in-the-world glasses, my consciousness is modified. It is not merely that I can see better, but also that an aspect of my being has been put behind me, if never out of mind. Nearly every human body part, other than the brain and the nervous system, can be replaced prosthetically. (However, in the case of the eyes and the testicles, the prostheses are only cosmetic. Undoubtedly, this situation will change.) Even on the threshold of a full-scale Cyber Age, the multiplicity of the human body seems astounding. Stephen Hawking is a good example of that multiplicity. Because he uses a voice prosthesis, his vocal presence would be electronic whether you were standing next to him or on Mars. His voice in China or Australia, on Mars or in a space station, would remain what it is. You could never be certain where his edges were. Multiplicity is another way of not being sure where people's edges are, where their identity begins and ends.[24] My prostheses elevate me to a higher plane of fulfillment, or a more ideal conception of myself, but they also remind me of how I have slipped from the plane that I have previously occupied. They attribute to me a multiplicity that I had not planned. They blur edges even while refining capacity.

Your body seems always to be dissolving, failing in one way or another, needing supplements. You feed it vitamins and healthy food and, as one part after another begins to fail, you discuss with various doctors the possibilities of replacement. For instance, the knee that I injured at seventeen in a motorcycle accident has been replaced by one made from hard acrylic and held to the bone by a titanium stud. I will someday have other parts replaced with either artificial parts or with transplanted body parts from someone else (but which someday may be grown in incubator animals, such as pigs). If my kidneys begin to fail, I can make use of a collective prosthetic kidney, called a dialysis machine, that I will share with other people in a similar condition. When my penis begins to dysfunction, if it does (and common male experience assures me that, most predictably, it will sadly do just that), my personal physician will refer me to a urologist who will recommend a penile implant which will actually improve my normal performance by making me permanently virile.

Always a "phantasmatic" body part, my penis will have been modified towards enhanced performance.[25] The implant may simply extend my penis so that it will never be entirely flaccid, always sufficiently turgid for action, or it may involve a small hydraulic mechanism that will permit me to pump my penis into tumescence simply by squeezing a tiny plastic reservoir that the urologist will have tucked away within my scrotum, like a third testicle. The bio-mechanical expansions of my natural potential may so please me that I might return to the urologist and ask for a cosmetic phalloplasty in order to have my penis sculpted into a more attractive shape. Once I have had that operation, my penis will have been lengthened (by cutting the suspensory ligaments that join it to the pubic bone) and thickened (by the liposuction of fat from my buttocks or abdomen) and I will seem, to my own mind at least, irresistibly bionic. (A person might also undergo neovaginoplasty, for cosmetic or transsexual purposes. I do not know if such a procedure would be experienced as bionic.[26]) If I do not like these possibilities (a permanently semi-erect penis will be conspicuous, especially when swimming, and the hydraulic mechanism may break, probably will in fact, leaving me with a piece of ruined machinery in my scrotum, a tiny replica of an abandoned industrial site), then the doctor can prescribe injections of prostaglandin, Phentolamine, papaverine or some other chemical or hormonal fluid.[27] I will then prick a syringe into the corpora cavernosa (left or right, depending upon the hand I use) and inject myself. This will leave me with a magnificent erection that will last for two or three hours, or (I would hope) long after ejaculation. It may also leave me with an embarrassing case of priapism, but, always optimistic in these matters, I will hope not. It may even be that something as apparently simple as Viagra will do the trick. Viagra acts like a chemical prothesis just as surely as does prostaglandin. The simplicity of its delivery (swallowing) masks its genuine prosthetic nature. In all of these instances, I will have been improved. In each, I will also have been diminished. Each prosthetic modification also marks the distance I will have travelled from my original physical condition.[28] Even as I approach a new ideal, bionic standard, I will be slipping below the natural bodily standard that I inherited and watched develop during its social formation.

The human body interacts with machines in many ways. Many of these ways are obvious, but none are ever simple. Some kind of system will always be presupposed. The simplest machine floats on the surface of numerous hidden systems, networks of connections and conceptual overlap. A machine that no longer functions or that has either lost or never had a purpose will seem, as Heidegger expresses it, "conspicuous." It will become equipment that is in "un-readiness-to-hand."[29] I draw from Heidegger's proposition the corollary that machines are only seen "fully" when, no longer in use, they cannot be seen fully. It may well be the case that machines are so omnipresent in the western technological environment that they are also invisible in the sense that they seldom attract attention, becoming visible, as David Porush argues, "only when resurrected by fear" or by metaphor in the abrupt shock of defamiliarization.[30] However, this seems far less important than the invisibility of their hidden systems. While they are still functioning, the extended systems that make machines possible are largely out of sight, too complex to be seen easily. Still functioning, a machine is a node, an expression of unseen rhizomes; no longer functioning, it becomes conspicuous, a thing in the world that can be seen but not understood. The most obvious example would be the use of tools. Philosophical optimists like to observe that human beings are toolmakers (rather than, say, predators or destroyers): "Toolmaking man learned," one such optimist writes, opening a proposition after which any fact from human history might follow.[31] There have been many tools and there will be many more, not all of which have suggested reasons for joyous hope. The strongest form of the toolmaking argument would hold that the human mind can constitute an interface with everything in the cosmos, including all physical laws, to create tools. In *that* proposition, there is neither woe nor wonder, only fascination.

Imagine a human ancestor picking up a stone with which to crack a shell or a nut, or using a twig to winkle out marrow from an already-gnawed bone. Another one, perhaps gimpy from combat with a mastodon, has discovered he could use a fallen branch to improve his walking. The branch actually performs much the same work as my prosthetic knee, supporting rather than replacing. Both ancient tools are elementary prosthetic devices: they enhance the body, increasing its force and range, but both are possible only because underlying systems of bio-mechanics, activated by cultural objectives, bring them into use. Today, resting in a glass case in a museum, both ancient devices would be conspicuous, surrounded by their sheer visibility and uprooted from their original cultural domains, with only the museum's documentation to provide a partial, but highly artificial, re-enrooting. You may see small chip marks in the stone, for example, and the documentation will explain that these show that a piece of hard stone, perhaps flint, had been used to rough-hew it. The documentation will scarcely reanimate the system of discovery, trade and craftsmanship that once obtained and fully shaped the smashing-stone. All tools, as all machines, slip into conspicuous meaninglessness once they have been severed from their operating systems. What documentation could fully make sense of or re-embed the "mountain of leather prostheses and wooden limbs" that you can see on display at Auschwitz?[32]

The modes of body-machine interaction are supplementary. Of course, a machine may kill you or cause you devastating injury. So far as machines are concerned, the world offers a million ways to die. Every technology carries its dark twin or, hidden within its total implicature, a death-system capable of destroying you. Science-fiction returns obsessively to scenarios in which computers break their programmatic limitations and attempt to seize control, or androids go wrong and claim their independence or seek, as the "replicants" do in Ridley Scott's 1982 film *Blade Runner*, extended and enhanced "life." In a favourite narrative motif of *Star Trek—The Next Generation*, hyper-complex machines (such as starships) evolve life. Evolved from a machine but no longer merely a machine, the new life form may be exploratory and curious (exhibiting, as in *Star Trek*, what human beings suppose to be prime human attributes) or malign as is the car in Stephen King's *Christine*. Even my glasses, products of a benign technology in common use, might shatter in an accident and create a glass shard that could drive into my brain, making optometry wholly irrelevant. Any consideration of prostheses has to take into account their potential failure and even the conditions under which they might go wrong or turn against their users. An awareness of machines always includes, as Porush observes, a dimension of fear. There is also an element of potential disappointment, fear's most intimate radical: the prosthesis may not work, may work inadequately or may entail unwanted consequences. However, I am primarily interested in prosthetic consciousness as a reflexive awareness of supplementation. What happens within the mind once an exotic mechanical part, reflecting an unseen technological system entirely alien to all your previous bodily processes, has been joined (whether integrated or merely appended) to your body?

The argument begins with two distinctions. First, all machines are both hard and soft. There will always be a system of instructions, of operating commands, such as a program. Hardware and software invite themselves as metaphors: "at one level or another one always needs both in any machine."[33] This may seem obvious, but it is so only because a tool uprooted from context, an *ur*-tool, such as the smashing-stone in the display case, conspicuously has no system, no accessible software. The difference between a functioning and non-functioning tool is precisely the presence or absence of operating commands, its system or culturally understood rhizomes. It is also within the operating system that problems arise, the "undecidables and double binds" that often make machines appear to be schizophrenic.[34] Those science-fiction scenarios that emphasize the turning or going "wrong" of machines, from simple to hyper-complex, play upon the potential schizophrenia, the sudden undecidables and abrupt double-binds, within the hidden operating system, the software.

Second, a prosthesis is not an android. An android, existing in the contemporary world only in the crude prototypical form of drone robots even though written deeply into our cultural mythology, is a self-contained artificial life-form. A prosthesis is a part, a supplement to a human body, and not, however complexly integrated, self-contained. (It would be an interesting problem for a science-fiction writer whether an android *could have* a prosthesis since each replacement part, even if it enhanced previous levels of task accomplishment, would be fully consolidated within the android's cyberbody.[35]) As I have used the term, a prosthesis is an artificial body part that supplements or replaces a genetic body part, but a part that implies, and to some degree continues to function under, an operating system different from the body's organic processes. Hence a prosthesis marks an intersection between two systems, two underlying networks of rhizomes, technological and organic.

Any cyber(body)part may degrade in either of its two intersecting systems. A prosthesis may fail either as a replacement for a diseased body part or as a machine. Either of the two intersecting systems may fail either through further disease and death, or through mechanical degradation. In both cases, the hopeful fantasies of replacement will have been destroyed. You may experience horror as you observe the manifestations of failure, additional disgusting evidence of the human body's disintegration and deliquescent collapse. You may also experience terror as you contemplate the abrupt dysfunction of your special cyber(body)part, its weakness with respect to random glitches or simple wearing out. Horror and terror, as I argued in Chapter 6, seem to move from the world towards the mind, slowly abrading or suddenly bursting upon consciousness, and both may be enclosed within the mind, working against personal identity.

There are many kinds of imaginative disgust scenarios, but abjection—a private world that extends self-disgust—is in many ways the most corrosive. Because the consciousness of being abject may be ambiguous, at once a loathed and a desired state, it could be potentially fructifying, a source of creative transcendence. That is, it could amount to a consciousness of a border experience, a path that opens beyond ordinary human routine in much the way that Bataille and others have described transgression. "The experience of abjection arises from an indistinction between self and other," Juliana De Nooy writes, "a blurring of the limits between inside and outside."[36] Because it does blur boundaries, and does arise from an "indistinction" which is felt even if it is not easily made clear, abjection calls all manner of ideas about identity and place into question.

My friend in Chicago must have felt as if he had been blurred. His entire existence had become a painful smudge, the past so powerful in the present, intentions running at such cross-purposes; but above all, he had lost his sense of himself as distinct and whole. Although I have been employing the example of prosthetics, or cyber(body)parts, which spark consciousness to remember the body's unmodified state even when they are most successful and corrode the conscious sense of well-being and wholeness when they fail, I actually want to make a larger point. All bodily failures, including the alienation of mythological parts in rape, can inspire self-disgust. Abjection can follow, nose to arse, as inevitably as the monster in art-horror slowly emerges from its own spoor. My friend had lost his exclusive proprietorship of his own anus, which his father and uncle had raped. As a consequence, he had been hurled downwards into unhappiness, self-destruction and abjection. If, at an early age, he had lost his anus through surgical intervention and had been given a prosthetic anus (a colostomy bag, say), he might have been able to face existence much differently. Fewer of the mythological associations encompassing his anus would have been evoked. Consider the following fable.

> On Zwffzwss, a distant planet, the inhabitants are perfectly spherical. Their bodies are uniformly filled with a stable gaseous substance. They need do nothing to replenish this substance, since their bodies simply ingest energy from the atmosphere, and they feel no necessity to excrete. Indeed, their bodies have no openings for either ingestion or excretion. Their anecdotal history indicates that their ancestors may once have had appendages, but this is uncertain. Now they think things. They have evolved capacities, telepathy and telekinesis, for instance, to act at distances. They can roll and hover, but mostly they communicate thoughts. If they desire something, they cause it to move towards them. They can even think things into existence. Their lives are comfortable, full and rounded.

One day their powerful sensors tell them that spacecraft filled with human beings are approaching. The knowledge that human beings possess appendages, limbs used for fetching and carrying, voices to communicate thought, fascinates them, filling them with confused mixtures of horror and desire. They hover softly above the ground quivering with anticipation. How do these appendages work, they wonder. Are they a kind of magic? A wise inhabitant explains the concepts of levers and soundwaves. The cognitive networks of Zwffzwss flutter with excitement. Can these beings actually carry objects back and forth? Can they make things? Do they really hear and listen to each other? Does this mean that they are not limited to thinking? That they don't have to think things into existence? The mind of Zwffzwss trembles. Human beings do not have to think.

Conquest is easy when the inhabitants desire it. Zwffzwss falls to human force. Colonies are established. The inhabitants are employed to supply low-cost telecommunications. They make cost-efficient tools for construction. They are cheap to keep alive since they synthesize nutriments from the atmosphere. They are wonderfully clean since they never excrete. Human life flourishes, but at the expense of the original inhabitants. They have been transformed into machines, servo-mechanisms. They are not allowed to hover or roll freely. They have become abject slaves on their own planet. And then one day someone wonders: What if we thought them out of existence? Or thought them home again? Or caused their spacecraft to disintegrate? And then they would be our slaves. (But Zwffzwss had never needed slaves before.) The networks, softly whispering to escape human surveillance, consider the possibilities. Suppose it doesn't work? Suppose they come back, even more hostile? What will we do without them? Who will organize us and give us purpose? Small murmurs in the collective thinking keep saying, Let us try. Let us try. And the suggestion becomes louder. It is now a serious meditation. It becomes a plea. An argument. A command. Let us try.

Could the inhabitants of Zwffzwss experience abjection? They have neither orifices nor parts. They do not eat and they do not excrete. So far as you can tell from the fable, they would have no bodily effluvia at all. They cannot be penetrated, though they can be kidnapped and colonized. Can they be made abject? Could they even feel self-disgust? The answer is found in the common factor linking the loss of body parts (whether are not they are eventually supplemented) and the alienation of body parts. Both conditions involve losing control over your own parts and both act upon consciousness as a burning brand upon flesh. You can never forget what you have lost, nor ever successfully re-imagine yourself as unshrunken. The inhabitants of Zwffzwss have lost their proprietorship over themselves. They have been colonized.[37] Victims of racism, gender or sexual-orientation discrimination can all be transformed into, if indeed they have not been born into, human abjects. The governing discourse of their places in the world will have made them indistinct, their identity blurred. And thus the inhabitants of Zwffzwss may feel abjection in the sense that their identity has been compromised and blurred. Colonization works against the spirit as sexual violation does against the body. My friend who had been raped as a child, and who had lost the exclusive control over his anus even while having his sense of self-being reduced to it, experienced a corrosive self-disgust. He saw himself as one among the world's many disgusting things. However, he also saw himself in an even more degraded condition. When he wept in my arms, he must have seen himself as being abject. That is, he imagined himself cast out, thrown away by his society and transformed into human waste, like excrement or a corpse. He had always to negotiate his life with the lucid apprehension of himself as worthless but still human. The abject, because it is transgressive and disruptive, always "out of place" but always self-consciously so, can break the conceptual constraints, the symbolic or Apollonian laws that constitute it. The truly abject person will be so far outside normal cultural boundaries that he or she may actually appear transcendent, saintly or hermetic. My friend did often strike me as a man possessing a high-order understanding, even an inhuman kind of knowledge, and as someone standing numinously to the side of the world's on-goingness. On the other hand, self-disgust passively inhabits a place within those symbolic and Apollonian boundaries: a pre-determined, submissive and regulated place. It is possible to feel both conditions at once (which, I am convinced, my friend did), although the relation between the two concepts is clearly intransitive. You may experience self-disgust without abjection, but the reverse condition seems wholly impossible.

The contrasting condition to self-disgust helps to focus and clarify the concept. I have already introduced the young man who likes to make his private stench public and the young woman who likes to eat her own snot. These are instances of human self-exposure, occasions for the disgust of others, but not instances of an existence that is felt as disgusting or abject. The element of self-consciousness is entirely lacking. Now consider self-disgust's opposite and antitype. Think of how disgusting, yet how very unself-conscious, mass behaviour can be. At the opposite extreme from self-disgust there is the experience of crowds, of people who lose their self-awareness entirely, swallowed within collective behaviour.

A crowd can be very frightening and it is, when seen exclusively from the outside, potentially disgusting. Indeed, any kind of mass behaviour, when seen from the outside, is likely to seem disgusting. Human identity will have dissolved into a collective form of action. Warfare seems like the paradigm case: individuals having abandoned their normal morality, having become swallowed and digested into a collective identity, will perform all acts of killing and mutilation. Nearly any memoir of warfare, from Thucydides to Paul Fussell, will record the perception of individual decay, of slipping and oozing into collective mass actions. Nation states, tribes, gangs, armies, warring factions, hooligans, bureaucracies all may seem, if you are not yourself among the collective, both disgusting and frightening. Nationalism, which sometimes seems like such a charismatic word, describes what almost everyone in a postcolonial age takes for granted: the right of a "nation" (either a group of ethnically similar people or a political entity composed of several such "peoples") to self-determination and self-defence. Yet the other face of nationalism is violence, the assumption of a right to violate and subjugate others, and the unquestioning participation in triumphant group actions. In the extreme case, people swallowed up in a collective action may participate in genocide against those outside of their collective consciousness. Michael Ignatieff writes that nationalism is "centrally concerned to define the conditions under which force or violence is justified, in a people's defence, when their right of self-determination is threatened or denied."[38] Nationalistic violence, such as ethnic cleansing, mob chanting and military massacres, even of a fairly humdrum kind, even seen from outside on TV as the mere simulacrum of violence, frequently appalls. The disgust you feel over the images of a massacre, the burnt and mutilated bodies, splayed in undignified positions or huddled helplessly against implacable violence, may inspire both physical and moral disgust. Television news reports often warn that the "following report contains scenes that may be disturbing to some viewers." The disturbance TV producers have in mind is disgust, not fear. However, the disgust that you feel, both physical and moral, for the image of a massacre touches more than the wretched victims. It also reaches outwards towards the indications of the mass collective behind the grossly disturbing action.

The responsible mass collective itself also prompts disgust: the sense that they are, in some genuine way, "mindless," collective automata acting like dehumanized machines.[39] Its members have lost or given up their individual identity for a collective one, and in the process they may seem to have undergone deliquescence, to have slid towards muck. Even very minor instances of crowd behaviour, a mob of sports fans (a vast distance from war or tribal hatred) celebrating after a victory, will strike the outsider as disturbing, potentially violent, a single dangerous entity moving in collective mindlessness. Not only will the members of a crowd have given up their individual identities, swept away in the mass contamination of de-individuating, but also they may acquire a powerful sense of unity, even cohesiveness. A crowd may feel itself drawn tightly together because of a common exuberance, as the fans or supporters do in sporting crowds, or else a common purpose, or the illusion of one, as in religious crowds. Salman Rushdie brilliantly captures the intensity, and singleness of purpose, in a mass religious movement when he has Gibreel Farishta, the mad actor in *The Satanic Verses*, observe from the air the steady march of a crowd into the firing machine guns of a tyrant's palace guard.[40] A crowd's cohesiveness may take on the further intensity of feeling persecuted, of being attacked by everyone who is not a member or does not share its singleness. Persecution increases intensity and reinforces the unitary sense of collective purpose.[41]

A crowd represents the opposite of personal self-disgust. It is unreflective and, once in motion, unhesitant, relentless, implacable. Self-disgust, whatever else, is intensely reflective and a cause of hesitancy. Whether on TV or in actual life, seeing a crowd move, often as purposefully as mindlessly, can be a disturbing experience. It is so chiefly because of the sense that everyone, each participant in the mass action, has given up his or her identity and with it all moral agency. Elias Canetti, whose *Crowds and Power* undertakes a probing analysis of crowd behaviour with a particular interest in how religions employ mass human action, writes that any crowd manifests four characteristics: first, it always wants to grow; second, within the crowd there is equality; third, it loves density; fourth, it needs a direction. It continues to exist, Canetti adds, only so long as it has an unachieved goal. Only that endpoint keeps it from disintegration.[42] In Canetti's analysis, the crowd's swallowing, homogenizing, thickening movement towards someone or some place makes it what it is: the antithesis of individual caution, responsibility and empathy. This is what is meant when someone says that crowd behaviour is "irrational." All disgusting behaviour can be bracketed between extreme poles: on the one hand, self-disgust, the inward gnawing of personal loathing, the actual crystallization of self into agonizing consciousness; on the other, dissolution of self, the absorption of personal identity into a larger, collective identity as a de-individuating crowd or mob action.

Bill Buford describes crowd behaviour in intimate detail in *Among the Thugs,* his study of English football hooligans. He travelled with Manchester United supporters, even into violent overseas excursions, and participated in some of their riots. He compares the exhilaration of being in a crowd to crossing a boundary which makes possible an incineration of self-consciousness, of obliterating "our sense of the personal, of individuality, of being an individual in any way."[43] It is, he says (with an echo of Bataille), like religious or sexual ecstasy, or like the experience of drugs. "Nothingness is what you find there." And, he continues, writing out of personal memories, "Violence is one of the most intensely lived experiences and, for those capable of giving themselves over to it, is one of the most intense pleasures."[44] Later, describing English hooligan violence in Sardinia, during which he was severely beaten by Italian police, he claims that he was "appalled" by the violence and the way the English crowd carelessly hurt innocent by-standers.[45] By his own account, however, he must have stepped momentarily outside the crowd in order to feel this: being "appalled" is not a judgement one can make while within the dense, impacted territory of crowd behaviour.

If a crowd can be characterized as "irrational" or even as "mindless," then self-disgust must be described as among the most intensely mindful, certainly the most conscious, of all human experiences. The nagging awareness of a prosthesis, especially when it has failed, or fails to do what you had hoped it would, aches like a suppurating boil. The brooding contemplation of a stolen or alienated body part may stab like broken glass in the gut. Furthermore, in the abject state, the boundaries of the actual world become etched within the mind, a network of acid-incised edges, conduits flowing with poison. A crowd may seem abject, but no member of a crowd could ever think himself or herself, while still within the crowd, abject.

I have made this brief trip into the theory of crowds in order to focus more clearly my main topic in this chapter: self-disgust and abjection. Human beings experience disgust within a socio-cultural context. Yet disgust seems to be, and in the history of literature must be imagined as, an individual problem. To be abject is an acutely individual problem. (Although it is possible to imagine abject groups in the sense that they are outsiders, despised or even persecuted, who register their collective identity as abject. However, unless the deviant group feel themselves to be abject and experience themselves as ambiguously double-sided, they will not be abject in the way that individuals, dwelling within their consciousness, feel themselves to be.) The distinction between self-disgust and abjection cannot be made in any very simple and straightforward manner. It must be seen as rather like that between the convexity and the concavity of a curved line. Each depends upon the other and each, except in thought, is inseparable from the other. Self-disgust is a possible, though certainly undesirable, state of mind in which you may think of yourself as an object, among others, of revulsion and loathing in the world. To experience self-disgust, disgust itself must be already a constitutive element in the world's make-up, clinging like a rancid ooze to its raw shapes. At such moments, you might even make the classic disgust face, about yourself. On the other hand, abjection invokes a personal experience of disgust in which you will be unable to admit that what has been called disgusting is actually merely that. The sense of touching the abject, or of being yourself abject, is never fully categorical and definitive. Further paths open from the experience of abjection. The abject is "what of the body falls away from it while remaining irreducible to the subject/object and inside/outside oppositions. The abject necessarily partakes of both polarized terms but cannot be clearly identified with either."[46]

In the contemporary use of the term, "abject" often seems to describe a permanent condition. Writers seem to assume that being abject is a state into which you are born, like race, ethnicity, sexual preference or gender, and which you can hardly abandon or transform. This ontological conservatism arises in part from Kristeva's insistence that the menses, and expelled menstrual blood, constitute one of the primary categories of the abject. The human mourning, deeply, violently and corrosively, for objects once intimate parts of the self that have been lost (or, more accurately, lost through expulsion), and have "always already been lost," runs through most aspects of existence.[47] In her *Shattered Subjects*, Suzette Henke adopts this position throughout. Discussing New Zealand writer Janet Frame, Henke notes Frame's difficulties as an adolescent and young woman with menstrual hygiene (destroying the signs of "female corporality by symbolically burying them [sanitary pads] in the cemetery") and specifically adopting Kristeva's "theoretical association" between the menses and abjection.[48] It must serve certain cultural and gender analyses to insist upon the permanence of abjection (you would then be abject in much the same way that you are a certain race, ethnicity or gender), but it seems like a weak position to hold. I have consistently argued that disgust is metamorphic, subject to transformation and displacement. Abjection, although a radically vitriolic form of disgust, also changes and undergoes conceptual shift. It is possible, I think, to feel abject in one respect but not in all; it is also possible to experience abjection only for a time, perhaps even a short one. My friend in Chicago felt himself to be abject because of what had been done to him as a child, but he was not abject in all respects. He was a brilliant student of philosophy, capable of both wit and slashing analysis, and he may well have gone on to star in his profession. Even if he did not, I cannot imagine him without his intelligence, wit and steadiness of conceptual focus.

There is a powerful, exemplary episode of self-disgust evolving into abjection in Doris Lessing's novel *The Golden Notebook*. The episode describes the novel's central character, Anna Wulf, falling steeply into an abyss of abject self-loathing and negative self-accounting.[49] The experience of disgust, self-disgust and abjectness is central to the novel; it is one pivot upon which the narrative turns.[50] It leads into a fictional world in which characters draw back from certain experiences, from each other and even from themselves. That fictional world demands that every reader imagine everywhere the averted face or the hand thrust between experience and perception. In the world of *The Golden Notebook*, characters are disturbed by what they see and by how they see themselves. They register disgust at the world's chaos and transgressions, turning away from or trying not to see the evidence of fragmentation, decay and deliquescence. Even nature is experienced in terms of inordinateness, incontinence and chaos:

> As soon as we turned off the main road on to the sand track
> we had to walk slowly and carefully, because this morning
> after the heavy rain there was a festival of insects. Everything
> seemed to riot and crawl. Over the low grasses a million white

butterflies with greenish white wings hovered and lurched. They were all white, but of different sizes. That morning a single species had hatched or sprung or crawled from their chrysalises, and were celebrating their freedom. And on the grass itself, and all over the road were a certain species of brightly-coloured grasshopper, in couples. There were millions of them too.[51]

In *The Golden Notebook* many things are, like the tree root that Roquentin experiences in Sartre's *Nausea*, excessive: eluding (or even breaking) conceptual categories, overflowing. Anna Wulf's character development begins in the perception of universal fragmentation in which everything is "cracking up," moves through different reflections upon the dissolving, unstable condition of western civilization and reaches a climatic point in which she sees herself as, spider-like, slipping from normal human categories into becoming an object of self-disgust. Her eventual climb back into normalcy ascends from self-disgust to self-acceptance. Anna experiences unmistakable abjection, but she does so only as a temporary, or conditional, state. Throughout, the novel is concerned with problems of fragmentation and disintegration. Structurally, it is broken up and intercut in many different ways, both formal and substantive. The notebooks, for example, are formal divisions, breaking up narrative movement and forcing a continuous reconsideration, but they also introduce variants of the action, setting up difficult contrasts between what happens in the "Free Women" sections and what is said to have happened in the notebooks. (Does Tommy marry an activist student from Oxford? Does he attempt suicide? In what/which reading is he blind?) "Free Women," depending upon how you read the novel, is either a frame, a traditional narrative convention for containing the main action which takes place in the notebooks, or it is the product of the notebooks, made possible by them (though markedly boiled down and variously transformed) and explicitly activated by the "Golden Notebook" itself. Throughout, and in any possible reading, self-disgust is not only a recurring theme but also an incremental force within the novel.

Anna has had a difficult time in maintaining a positive sense of herself. Many experiences, particularly with men, have undercut her and have given her a repertory of negative images to play against herself. She sees the world as endlessly subdivided and fragmented. She also sees herself as fragmentary, playing multiple self-conscious roles. After all, she is a woman of her times and so she, inevitably it might seem, embodies chaos and disorder.

She dreams of fragmentation, of disintegration and chaos. A malicious figure of spite, "something anarchistic and uncontrollable, something destructive," troubles her dreams.[52] This malicious figure, usually perceived as an old man or even as a dancing old man, often appears to be present in the actual in-the-world people whom she meets. Sometimes she even perceives it in herself. Her notebooks, which continuously reflect both her inability and her ability to write, record episode after episode in which she must play one role or another: a woman, mother, friend, lover, analysand in Jungian therapy, communist, Old Red and writer (herself a postcolonial ex-colonial) who has written of colonial racism and love across both race and class boundaries and who, although she can privately transform her personal experience into fiction, cannot commit herself to public expression. The men in her life have exercised a fundamentally abrasive influence. At worst, they have been controlling, indifferent, negative, undermining and degrading; at best, ataraxic. She remembers how one lover had described his wife:

> I remembered Nelson telling me how sometimes he looked at his wife's body and hated it for its femaleness; he hated it because of the hair in the armpits and around the crotch. Sometimes, he said, he saw his wife as a sort of spider, all clutching arms and legs around a hairy central devouring mouth. I sat on my bed and I looked at my thin white arms, and at my breasts. My wet sticky centre seemed disgusting, and when I saw my breasts all I could think of was how they were when they were full of milk, and instead of this being pleasurable, it was revolting. This feeling of being alien to my own body caused my head to swim, until I anchored myself, clutching out for something, to the thought that what I was experiencing was not *my* thought at all.[53]

The spider is not Anna's own thought. It is borrowed from the discourse of men. At the nethermost point in a process of mental disintegration, Anna thinks of herself as existing in a "fug of stale self-disgust." It is as if she herself had become an object in the world or even a place, since "fug" is a spatial as well as an olfactory term. With its connotations of both stench and stuffiness, a closed room suffused by noisome stinks, "fug" might take us back to the accounts of the Great War that emphasize, in nauseating detail, the stinks of the trenches, the wasteland of decay, putrefaction and death. A "mephitic stench," perhaps, but one that is located within the self, a personal and intensely private world of fetor and rot. The usual angle of perception in registering disgust has been radically shifted. Only Anna can experience her own disgust. From outside, she might appear distracted, split and divided in her lifeworld (keeping different notebooks, subdividing and cancelling them, writing in different handwritings, pinning newspaper clippings on the walls, feeling herself fragmented into distinct roles, and so forth), but she would not seem disgusting. She has done nothing disgusting, nor said anything that another person could judge to be disgusting. Her disgust is her intense personal experience of herself.

In the "Free Women" sections of the novel (the third-person novella in five discontinuous sections that may be read as intercut by the self-conscious and reflexive notebooks or as arising out of the notebooks, as a final distillation of their experience), Anna decides to evict two gay roomers in her flat, Ivor and Ronnie. Ivor is a paying tenant, a young man who has lived with Anna for quite a long time, but Ronnie, his lover, has moved in without asking Anna's permission and pays no rent at all. He lives in Anna's flat only because she is too sympathetic to ask him to leave. Things now seem out of hand, and she has decided to ask both young men to move out. In the scene that prepares this decision, the word *disgust* recurs several times. She finds Ronnie in the bathroom using her facial lotion and carries on a conversation with him in which he attempts to talk to her as if he were another woman. (Her disgust for him is repeatedly registered.) A few minutes later, returning from seeing that her daughter is comfortably in bed, she passes the room that Ivor and Ronnie share, the door purposefully left open so that she can hear them act out a misogynistic routine.

> Anna took her bath and went upstairs to see if Janet was settled for the night. The door into the young men's room stood open. Anna was surprised, knowing that they knew she came upstairs at this time every night to see Janet. Then she realized it was open on purpose. She heard: "Fat buttocky cows..." That was Ivor's voice, and he added an obscene noise. Then Ronnie's voice: "Sagging sweaty breasts ..." And he made the sound of vomiting.[54]

Ivor's and Ronnie's little routine, another fictional world in miniature (rather like the conditional shame-world that the Ghost creates for Hamlet), reflects deep disgust towards women. Mocking women in extreme physical images, making physically manifest the categories in which they would place her, their mode is evidently Menippean. The language is grotesque, bodily and degrading. Ronnie's mocking sounds of vomiting must be taken, like facework, as comic superscriptions that inscribe second-order semiotic significance. They encode the sense of ultimate rejection.

Anna seems threatened from many angles, not least from the men in her life. As Henke observes of Janet Frame, gender is "a cultural performance that she is unable to master."[55] Misogynistic images expressing male disgust with the female body pervade *The Golden Notebook*. The men in Lessing's novel might all have learned about female sexuality more or less as Joe Christmas does in Faulkner's *Light in August*. Even the images that Anna employs to record herself to herself have been taken from the language of men. She invents a world the materials of which she has found in what men, both lovers and strangers, have said. In the passage in which she thinks of herself as a spider, Anna is living within a fictional world she has created for herself out of misogynistic and anti-female motifs embedded in her culture. Within *The Golden Notebook*, these motifs find reinforcement in the fragmentary, splintered male perception of female anatomical difference in which menstruation, seen only as bloodstain or stench, stands for the whole reproductive system. In this alternative world of introjected male perceptions and judgements, the image of a spider is still overdetermined, as it always seems to be, but here it has been narrowed to signify simply femaleness. Now the spider represents only the degraded, and disgusting, male perception of the female body.

In this perspective, female anatomical difference may be, to cite Paglia once more, only a "mucoid swamp" constituted by "fishy female jellies, the dead weight of Medusan paralysis."[56] It is a world that frightens men; or, at least, both Lessing and Paglia seem to agree that men find it frightening. (Cronenberg's *The Brood* graphically captures the presumed male repugnance when confronted with the female reproductive system and its mysterious fecundity.) Grosz puts the issue of male fears, or male aversions, into its cultural context:

> Can it be that in the West, in our time, the female body has been constructed not only as a lack or absence but with more complexity, as a leaking, uncontrollable, seeping liquid; as formless flow; as viscosity, entrapping, secreting; as lacking not so much or simply the phallus but self-containment— not a cracked or porous vessel, like a leaking ship, but a

formlessness that engulfs all form, a disorder that threatens all order? ... My hypothesis is that women's corporeality is inscribed as a mode of seepage.[57]

This female world of viscosity and seepage is, Paglia remarks, alluding to Sartre, "Dionysus' swamp, the fleshy muck of the generative matrix." And there, she adds, "Apollo's solar torch is put out."[58] Even if it were nothing else, disgust would be an Apollonian response to the Dionysian. If, as I have claimed more than once in this book, disgust marks the way to the Dionysian, as one path to follow, it is only a trick of perspective. Disgust may seem to be the condition of the Dionysian, but it is so only from the outside.[59]

Anna experiences herself as abject. As the term is currently used, *abject* points to a related, but different, experience than mere self-disgust: it is at once more narrow and more profound. In an older and precursive sense, abject meant only "cast off" or "cast down" or even simply "downcast" (in the sense of feeling unworthy because one has been excluded, left out, or not permitted to belong). The *Oxford English Dictionary* traces it back to the fifteenth century where Lydgate employs it. Shakespeare uses *abject* as an adjective at least ten times, as a noun a single time and once, in *Titus Andronicus*, as an adverb. In *Richard III*, Gloucester observes to his brother Clarence, soon to be drowned in a cask of wine, that "We are the Queen's abjects, and must obey."[60] That is the single use as a noun. As an adjective, abject has several interesting uses. In *Troilus and Cressida*, Ulysses exclaims to the sulking, ill-tempered Achilles, "Nature, what things there are / Most abject in regard, and dear in use."[61] In *2 Henry VI*, Shakespeare uses it twice, once to mean, very precisely and unmistakably, unworthy, cast down if not downcast, when Suffolk exclaims, "O that I were a god, to shoot forth thunder / Upon these paltry, servile, abject drudges!"[62] It is an old word in the English language, and an older word in other languages, but in recent usage, abject has taken on a very precise meaning. Kristeva defines abject as a highly conceptual term that marks the condition of subjectivity and language, but also marks the edges of an abyss that threatens always to suck the subject into its disintegrating power. Kristeva's analysis of the abject has given it explicit significance for the present moment, and it is that sense that, as do both Henke and Grosz, I have borne in mind throughout this book. There is a creative dimension in abjection that Shakespeare did not recognize. Kristeva locates the "birth of narcissism" in the consciousness of being abject, or of having wilfully crossed a boundary into a domain that has been marked as abject. It is clear that the transgressive model I discussed in

Chapter 2 is much in play in Kristeva's analysis. Desiring the abject breaks down that Apollonian order which always seems to promise more than it can deliver. Creativity bursts from the Dionysian, the opening to which may be the "birth of narcissism" or, at least, the moment after the birth.

Lessing does not use the words *abject* and *abjection* in the Kristevan sense, of course, since in 1962, when she wrote *The Golden Notebook*, and even in 1971, when she wrote her famous preface, abjection still meant what it had for Shakespeare, cast down or simply downcast, lacking both social status and the freedom to act independently. Thus, it may seem that I am proposing an aggressively retrospective reading. And, to be sure, that is precisely what I am doing. *The Golden Notebook* concerns, in part, the struggle to overcome the "fug of stale self-disgust," the mental projection-room in which experience is recast in the introjected terms of male misogyny. However, there is a path for Anna to follow that will lead out of the fug, out of her negative self-accounting. As so often seems the case, the way upward begins in the way down. At the lowest depths, a person may discover the upwards way. Because there is a way up in *The Golden Notebook*, away from the introjected private world of self-disgust and loathing, it makes sense to reconsider Anna Wulf's predicament in terms of the concept of abjection. Lessing's novel shows the twisted braid, the Möbius strip, of the human body with elegant clarity.

What constitutes the Kristevan abject? How does it differ from the Shakespearean? In the first place, the abject is no longer merely that which has been cast aside or cast down. When Richard III, punning on the normal sense of "subject," remarks that he and his brother Clarence are "the Queen's abjects," he seems to mean only that they are outside of her good grace, excluded from her good intentions. In Kristeva's understanding of the term, the abject follows the paths of bodily expulsion. In its most primitive sense, the abject is dirt "out of place," dirt that has been expelled from the body but still calls back to the body as to a lost home. Grosz, observes that, for Kristeva, what is excluded "can never be fully obliterated but hovers at the borders of our existence, threatening the apparently settled unity of the subject with disruption and possible dissolution."[63] Of course, many functions of the body produce abject materials: tears, sweat, sperm and smegma, for example, or dandruff, nail parings and toe jam; but for Kristeva the primary, constitutive expulsions are excrement and menstrual blood. "Neither tears nor sperm," Kristeva writes, although they belong to the borders of the body, have any polluting value ... Excrement and its equivalents (decay, infection, disease, corpse, etc.) stand for the danger to identity that comes from without: the ego threatened by the non-ego, society threatened by its outside, life by death. Menstrual blood, on the contrary, stands for the danger issuing from within female identity (social or sexual); it threatens the relationship between the sexes within a social aggregate and, through internalization, the identity of each sex in the face of sexual difference.[64]

Excrement and menstrual blood are, according to Kristeva, the most massively sanctioned of the body's outpourings. Considering them, you can begin to see what, in any given place or time, the actual Apollonian order demands. If you think of all the cultural constraints upon both excretion and menstruation, you can begin to grasp what Kristeva has in mind. (You may also see how wrongheaded William Ian Miller is in supposing that the anus is "democratic" while the mouth, encoded by countless taboos governing ingestion, is mythological.) Imagine a person who feels free to have bowel movements on the public streets or a woman who ignores hygiene during menstruation and allows herself to bleed freely. What would happen to them? You may also see how uncertainly the boundary stands between them, active sources of expelled matter, and yourself. The abject, Grosz writes, attests to "the impossibility of clear borders, lines of demarcation or divisions between the proper and the improper, the clean and the unclean, order and disorder," all the partitions that the symbolic, or Apollonian, order forces upon its subjects.[65] If the abject matter is a corpse, the "ultimate" abjectness or (in Stephen King's phrase) "the really big casino," it is possible to observe both the complex psychological system of repulsion, of turning away from the corpse or of moving it quickly out of sight (and smell) and also the socio-cultural systems for keeping it in memory, as the object of religious ceremony and meditation, or as the matter for political, historical and cultural apotheosis.[66]

The abject is *atopic* in that it has no proper place: once outside the body, it marks the boundaries of the self. *That* is not me, you learn to say, but yet it still seems to be yourself. When experimental psychologists attempt to elevate human (or mammalian) feces into the universal object, they have a point. Despite the shady essentialism, or questionable biologism, of the project, feces does force its double-sidedness upon many, if not all, people.[67]

Neither smegma nor toe jam create quite the same compound affects: desire-loathing or longing-revulsion. The force of the abject lies in its double-edgedness. As always in questions of disgust, the abject seems a problem in boundaries, but ones that possess two clear and unmistakable sides. The expelled may seem to be beyond a boundary and to have become a not-me, but it is also within the boundary as a still-me. The expelled, the rejected not-me, continues to call; it is a *me* that still proclaims itself and can exert its fascination. You may often experience "an attack of itchy squeamishness" when you desire to touch what repels you.[68] In one sense, Kristeva's understanding of the abject recalls Freud's observations on excrement and the process of toilet training. What is abject is a part of the human person, but a part that must be denied and finally abandoned as a source of sexual pleasure. But as repressed content, excrement can return, in highly displaced forms, to disturb your peace of mind. (Neuroses, as Freud thinks, are the price you pay for civilization.) Everything that is thrust—or flushed—away returns. It will only have been sent on its *away*.

In another, and even more important, sense, Kristeva's understanding of the abject points towards a dialectic between the self and repressive powers far more sweeping and rigorous than even the parental restrictions that guide toilet training and promote the development of the superego. These powers, whether you call them symbolic or Apollonian, reside in language and enforce control, discipline and law. You may feel called by what has been expelled, what has been named as abject. Thus the relation between the self and abject is dialectical. The experience is at once degrading and potentially creative. This is what Bataille means when he writes about the importance of living one's life without measure, without limitation. Bataille finds the possibility of transcendence even in the spectacle of human torture (which, no doubt, is always an example of "deep disgust"), and the more horrible the death, the more degrading the torture, the more closely Bataille seems to have interrogated the victim's eyes. The abject constitutes a double-edged experience, an ambiguous fusion of degradation and creativity. Writing the abject, writing about what the Apollonian order has designated as perverse, will be an ambiguous experience. Yet it will discover the capacity to "soften" the superego, to reveal what must normally be repressed. Subject and object "push each other away, collapse, and start again—inseparable, contaminated, condemned, at the boundary of what is assimilable, thinkable: abject." Great modern literature "unfolds over that terrain ...."[69] Put another way, literature begins with the first thrust across the Apollonian boundaries.[70]

For Anna Wulf, the way upwards begins soon after when she invents another fictional world and another man, Saul Green. (Saul emerges out of the narrative materials that all her experiences with men throughout her life have given her, and disappears into a scanty trace, summed up in writerly abbreviation as "Milt," in the final "Free Women" section.) Saul allows Anna to explore her potential for re-integration.[71] He is an American who is in London, as were so many other Americans at that time in history, in order to avoid the investigations of the House Un-American Activities Committee and the pervading McCarthyite spirit of the times. Like Anna, he experiences alienation, fragmentation and an incapacity to commit himself to public authorship. He seems uncertain, even disoriented, easily hurt, skittish and afraid, and he cannot "sleep alone." The intense relationship that develops, full of mutual antagonism and mutual dependence, allows Anna to discover within herself a capacity for re-integration. Saul becomes the introjected mental projectionist in her imagination who shows her episodes from her life, small fragments of her actual lifeworld's experience. In the world that she inhabits with Saul she is able to discover how to bring pieces together into an individuated whole. In this reading, Saul and Anna are "crazy, lunatic, mad—what you will." They "'break down' into each other, into other people, break through the false patterns they have made of their pasts, the patterns and formulas they have made to shore up themselves and each other."[72] They recognize each other in themselves, and each gives to the other both the theme and a first sentence for a novel.[73] The inner "Golden Notebook" actually seems to be written by both of them, the boundaries between them dissolved, their identities interpenetrated. In this reading both Anna and Saul, because of, and through, their relationship, manage to overcome personal anxiety and alienation, succeed in achieving a significant measure of individuation and learn how to express themselves publicly once more. The world's disgust, which is always both vast and pervasive, is put into the perspective of writerly distance. Self-disgust disappears along with fragmentation.

On the surface it seems that Anna's process of disintegration follows the Sartre-Douglas model, her identity dissolving and sinking, but Lessing suggests a more complex understanding. Disgust breeds within the mind's powers to imagine worlds and invent stories. What happens with Anna Wulf indicates what must happen often as disgust undergoes abrupt metamorphoses. The imagination accepts disgust motifs as bits, discrete pieces to work from, and creates worlds, perhaps very partial and incomplete, in which it can watch, as a secret observer or as an active participant, negative scenarios unfold. Anna watches herself, and she knows both *why* she experiences self-disgust and *from where* the images of negative self-accounting have come. Her own unremitting writerly self-awareness helps her to find the path upwards even while being swamped by debilitating self-disgust. At this moment in the narrative, Anna is the position in which so many characters in Patrick White novels find themselves immediately prior to self-discovery or creative transcendence. She is in a position that Bataille might have seen as energizing, as opening towards self-knowledge and perhaps even wisdom.

Now, bearing Kristeva in mind, what happens when I read Anna's "fug of stale self-disgust" as revealing her personal sense of being abject? Reading Anna's predicament as more than self-disgust, I can understand her consciousness of herself not only as one additional disgusting object in a world that is crowded with such object but as revealing the workings of abjection. That "fug," that cramped place in Anna's own mind, has emerged specifically out of her experience of herself as a woman. I think there are no other satisfactory ways to read Lessing's novel on this point. Not only has Anna introjected male images (controlling, hysterical, a spider), at once dismissive and hostile, but she has been painfully self-conscious about her body. I take this to be largely what Lessing means in the 1971 "Preface" when she observes that part of the novel, but only a part, had been its depiction of the "sex-war," or what we might today rather call the gender war, between men and women. Anna has an intense self-consciousness of herself as a physical person, but that perception is already, and has always been, conditioned by male attitudes, male expectations. It is not simply a matter of Anna having overheard the misogynistic pantomime between Ivor and Ronnie or of remembering, in a downcast mood, how Nelson had likened his wife's body to a spider's, but of her whole self-consciousness.

In the entry in the "blue notebook" for September 17th, 1954, an entry that is later said to be cancelled, scored through and rejected, Anna writes about the break-up of her relationship with Michael, her lover for the previous five years, and her rejection of the Communist party. It is an important day in her life—a lover abandons her and she abandons her political commitment—and it begins in anger. Michael insists upon having sexual intercourse in the morning when they awake. Anna is already tense listening for the sounds of her daughter, Janet, waking. She feels resentment towards Michael. Her resentment is "like a raging poison."[74] But she comments in the notebook that, as she had learned in the most self-conscious of all her public activities, psychoanalysis, the resentment, "the anger, is impersonal." It is the disease of "women in our time."[75] It is the final time that she and Michael will copulate. As she prepares for the day, making breakfast for Michael, sending Janet off to school, dressing for her voluntary job at the Communist party press, she discovers, with a bit of a shock, that her menstrual period has begun. She begins to feel irritable because, she writes, the feelings of tiredness and irritability accompany her periods. That is, irritability seems to be a habit, a regular mental response to her body, but not necessarily a causal effect. She asks herself if she should even keep an entry in her notebook for this day (which will become, after all, one of the most important days in her life) and then decides that "the instinctive feelings of shame and modesty" are dishonest, not emotions for a writer. And so the blue notebook continues:

> I stuff my vagina with the tampon of cotton wool, and am already on my way downstairs, when I remember I've forgotten to take a supply of tampons with me. I am late. I roll tampons into my handbag, concealing them under a handkerchief, feeling more and more irritable.[76]

Once again, the dance between disgust and shame takes place. A slow chore-ography unfolds before the mind's eye. Just before going out the door, Anna waters her plants. "The leaves sparkle with water. The dark earth smells of damp growth." I infer that the image of the dark earth smelling of "damp growth" is not an iconic accident. The creative force of the plants contrasts vividly with the sterility of Anna's self-image at this moment. Taking a phrase from Angela Carter, one might suspect that there is "a subtext of fertility" in play.[77] The shame Anna feels about her period—which she notes she should not feel, not as a writer, but clearly does feel since she seeks to hide her tampons—reflects her awareness of the world about her and of the world's possible reactions. Throughout the day, working in an office with two men, she worries obsessively about her body, about her stench, about detectable evidence of her menstrual period. She washes herself with what might seem a nearly neurotic compulsiveness.[78] At the office she argues against publishing a book that has been submitted for publication: a flat, tame, optimistic piece of Communist hack writing. "It all comes out of myth," Anna writes. This, I think, constitutes one of the important themes in *The Golden Notebook* as a whole: so much in human life comes out of, and retreats back into, myth of one kind or another. The entry in the blue note-book for this day has concerned myths of several kinds, not least one aspect of a painfully complex myth about the female body that may exist in the discourse of men, but certainly must also reflect, if not entirely arise from, a symbolic, deeply Apollonian, dimension in culture. In contrast to the workings of that dark myth, Lessing offers the image of sparkling light and damp growth.

Sartre speaks of the imagination and the association of different images each with its correlative affects. He stops just short of describing (and Douglas entirely ignores) the powers of the human imagination to create worlds out of small bits of evidence. Imaginative worlds arise upon shards and fragments. From a single worm-bitten apple, you might easily build a world crowded with disgusting motifs: a disgust-world characterized by mucoid objects and loathsome acts. In fiction, a sparse array of deictics and descriptive phrases may provide a mechanism for the imagination to build worlds far thicker, more solid and more richly characterized than the thin narrative indices themselves. Seeing something disgusting in the actual world, a spider tattoo or excrement, prompts the imagination to envision deliquescence, a vast, interior galaxy of dissolving, muck-inhabited private fictional worlds. It calls into question all assumptions about identity, the Other and the Self. Once Anna Wulf has absorbed, or introjected, enough images of women from the standard male imaginary, she begins to lose control over her own identity. The chaos that she so easily finds in the world about her restates the chaos within her. Disgust is such a powerful affect because, as its fellowship with horror suggests, it invokes worlds in which it would be appalling, though necessary, to live.

The perception of disgust drives wedges through consciousness, splitting it into diverse spheres. This consciousness, as I have argued, can be split in many ways. However, the lines of rupture seem to follow most readily those body parts that have acquired, within a particular culture, definite mythic associations. Consider the eyes. The eyes, like the genitalia, are one of those encrusted body parts that are massively inscribed by citations, tentacularly mythological. The eye is connected to the powers of gods to see, to keep an eye on humankind, to overlook, to be omniscient. Apollo is an "eye-god," but so are they all to one degree or another. Mythological stories "always lie at the foundation of something."[79] The prosthetic eye in Pynchon's *V.*

cannot see, but it evokes the mythological spectrum associated with sight: the colours of sky and sea, the passage of time, the zodiac's symbolic categories. In myths both space and time precede human sight and consciousness. The vision of sky and days comes later than the things themselves. Even my glasses, though highly desirable in providing me with the corrected vision for which I yearn, invade my consciousness at a key point: my symbol-making capacity.

Consider the genitalia. If my prosthesis is to be a penile implant, then the invasion of my consciousness will be even more devastating. More than eyes even, the human genitalia, male and female, are entwined with myth. They are excitingly phantasmatic.[80] What happens to Semele, tricked by Hera, consumed by the force of Zeus' flame-hooded phallus, that "bolt which none can escape," pricks out the geography of human fate.[81] Hierogamy, Calasso writes, was how the gods chose to communicate at the beginnings of human time: "an invasion, of body and mind, which were thus impregnated with the superabundance of the divine."[82] Western mythology and lore are crowded with stories of how genitalia destroy and save, burn, bite and soothe, become weapons or havens. In myths, the gods are often more androgynous than their human playthings; for example, after Semele's death, Zeus rescues the embryo of Dionysus from her charred embers and sews him into a prosthetic womb that he opens within his thigh "till the months for which his mother should have carried him were fulfilled."[83] The human penis plays such a large and varied role in myth, legend and fiction that it makes sense, following Lacan, to distinguish the bit of bodily flesh and gristle, the penis itself, from the mythological phallus which is both "the idealization and the symbolization of anatomy."[84] The mythological phallus, huge but versatile, has always been the yardstick by which mortal men have measured their own potential: "Having a prominent penis is one of the primary characteristics that defines human males."[85] Hence long before the development of phalloplasty as a set of surgical procedures, men have tried to enhance the performance of the penis, edging it towards ideal phallushood. Pearls or steel balls, among other items, can be placed beneath the skin to increase friction or rings may be used to elongate the scrotum. More commonly, rings can be used to pierce the penis and scrotum in a variety of ways for either adornment or performance (or, longingly, for both).[86] Women can wear labial or clitoral rings, but nothing in female body piercings seems quite to correspond to such legendary male practices as the "Prince Albert," a Victorian "dressing ring" pierced through the urethra at the base of the penis' head, which is used by men (in the Prince's own manner) to secure the penis, either left or right, when wearing "crotch-binding trousers" and to keep the foreskin (if any) "sweet-smelling."[87] All of these practices are prosthetic in that they seek to supplement and enhance the penis. It might seem that they reshape the penis into a cyber(body)part only to satisfy yearning, but they are also, as are all prostheses, mnemo-technics.[88] The vast mythological entanglements that enmesh the penis make it inescapable: the penis cleaves the mind between the desire for enhancement and the disgust at slippage. An implant will represent both enhancement and dysfunction.

The penis is only a synecdoche for the male body as a whole. The mytho-logical web entangles the whole body and each of its parts, even the most hidden.[89] As myth, the body interpellates consciousness clamorously. When I contemplate my glasses or my artificial knee, or imagine the possibilities of a future penile implant, I experience a sharp split in my consciousness. I may enjoy my enhanced capacity to see and walk or I may yearn for, in tumescent daydreams, a godlike phallicity, but I cannot escape remem-bering myself as I once was (or should have been) in historical time. I may then feel disgust, even sharp twinges of shame, at my bodily modifications as well as for my personal deficiencies, my indeterminate fall from a now-lost ego ideal. In extreme cases, as when my university friend would contemplate what had been done to him, or how he had lost control over his anus, consciousness may consider itself abject.

Consciousness, it seems, cannot be fully commanded. It recognizes the body's failures (its slippages and blurrings) and may recognize the new condition as diminished (even though enhanced), disgusting, even abject. Like Stephen Hawking's prosthetic voice, the very multiplicity of my cyber-enhanced body blurs the edges of my being, deleting the intuition of integrity which I still remember and for which I may also yearn. My pros-theses constitute a nexus, harmonized by my mind's proactive interface, of distinct systems. I will become a cyborg, if only an absurd and inadequate one, when I bring together both a cyber system (a widely diffused structure of technological rhizomes) and a bodily system (a narrowly concentrated process of physiological capacities, memories and mythology), forcing them to cohabit within my consciousness. *That* consciousness, at once encompassing and split, will hold the diverse systems together, like howling winds from hostile poles.

Even the spherical inhabitants of Zwffzwss, in my parable, experience self-disgust. Judged against the physically more efficient human bio-mechanism, they see themselves as inept and clumsy, confined within their power to think. Although they never excrete, and hence are never confronted with bodily wastes that they must both reject and admire, the Zwffzwssians may experience abjection. They can see how far they have fallen and how their bodies are mocked and humiliated. They have become both servo-mechanisms and freaks within a society reconstituted by their human masters. It is as if they themselves were waste products, large and absurd turds in the human scale of things. Their fate suggests that the abrading experience of feeling yourself abject, lying always so close to the heart, may have less to do with the double-sided link between consciousness and waste products, such as feces or menstrual blood (or even smegma and toe jam), than with the awareness of self-loss and diminishment. In that sense, Anna Wulf, imagining herself trapped in a spider-world of alien values, seems to exemplify the basic dilemma of Zwffzwss: to think yourself in terms of hostile values, whether race- or gender-based, is to accept an invitation into a fictional world, unfriendly to your own being and utterly hostile to all generous imaginings, the construction materials of which have been provided by an invading force. In true colonial spirit, you will be required to do the building yourself.

Tightly bound to disgust in all cases, shame has a particularly ineradicable hold upon self-disgust and abjection. The dance of shame occurs most implacably within those hostile fictional worlds, such as the conditional world that the Ghost creates for Hamlet, that are created out of your perceived (or claimed) faults and shortcomings. Anna Wulf is most within the grip of mythological forces when she most feels shame. These mythological pressures, expressed from within a male imaginary, characterized by negative images and gender-hostile jokes, lend Anna her abject self-image.[90] Happily, she regains a positive view of herself, but while the alien image rules her imagination, shame acts as an enforcer.

My friend in Chicago was less happy. His negative self-image, heavily reinforced by shame, seemed to constitute a permanent condition. He would always be, even if he managed to live into old age, a boy whose anus had been raped. In his mind's eye, he would remain, through all the vicissitudes of his future life, a boy whose anus had been alienated by the person who should most have kept it safe. He would always be a boy reduced to his anus but who had also lost control over it, and hence himself. Both Anna and my friend exemplify the Kristevan concept of abjection. Both experience themselves with self-disgust, seeing themselves as items within a disgusting world, and both move from that unpleasant self-image to the even more corrosive sense of themselves as degraded beyond help, filled with shame, needing punishment. (Depression and the overwhelming sense of chaos for Anna; cigarette burns and broken glass for my friend.) Lessing's novel conveys a hopeful message in that it shows abjection as a temporary, and curable, condition. In-the-world existence, like the normal theory of the abject, may occasionally carry a more brutal comment: once you have lost control over a part of your body, all the more so if it is phantasmatic and mythologically encrusted, you may never fully climb back up from the abyss of abjection. The gnawing monster within may have found a home and, unhappily, remain your life-long companion. Yet, if the theory of the abject has predictive value, you may be able to transmute the devastating sense of abjection into art, like gold out of sludge. That positive thought lies at the core of the Kristevan theory of the abject: modern literature in particular has repeatedly, in the work of many different writers, traversed the territory of the abject.[91] Perhaps I should think of my old friend in Chicago as having transformed his painful experience into art. If I were to meet him on the streets in Chicago or San Francisco today, he might pull from his coat pocket a notebook, filled with stories and poems as corruscating as they (surely) would be corrosive. ✳

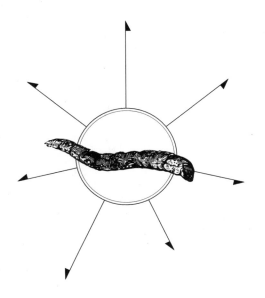

Conclusion • *The Hydra on a Pin*

A few years ago in Paris, I took a bus from the Louvre to the fourteenth *arrondissement* where I was staying with friends. The bus ride crossed over the Île de la Cité and continued along the Boulevard St-Michel. This route took

the bus very near the Sorbonne, and it was packed with university students. students. When I had boarded the bus, I had taken one of the single seats at the front, facing towards the rear. Across from me, almost knee to knee, a young woman, obviously a student, sat reading Merleau-Ponty. A single quick glance informed me that she was reading his posthumous *The Visible and the Invisible*. Her short, black duffel coat was open, exposing a beige wool sweater. Inadvertently, I noticed her body. I did not (I swear!) gaze upon her, but I registered her physical presence. Her breasts were pointed and high, but not large. Her face was pretty, though not beautiful, with sharp features, almost, I reflected, a *museau*. When she had grown older her face, I coldly supposed, would rupture into plagihedral surfaces. The distinct planes would thicken and sharply angle away from each other. She would begin to look like one of Cézanne's women. The 1890s paintings of Madame Cézanne, *Woman with a Coffeepot* or *Mme. Cézanne with her hair let down*, suggest what her face might look like one day: clotted, precipitous, disparate. I remembered the 1895 *Nude*, with its shadowed scalene head, the dark, adze-like nose that restates the black pubic delta. Nothing else could as accurately forecast her bodily dissolution. Although it may seem odd, I had taken the title of her book as a clue to my imagination. I had begun to imagine her as a now-invisible, older, far less attractive woman.

When the young woman left the bus at the Luxembourg Gardens, I slid across into her vacated seat, seeking the frontwards view. Instantly, settling into the thick plastic seat, I felt the vestigial warmth of her body. Had I felt this warmth on a toilet seat, one of the cylindrical shithouses along St-German-des-Prés, for example, my imagination would not have flared so ardently. The plastic bus seat was almost flesh-like, reminding me of buttocks or love handles, beneath my own body's pressure. Right away I understood that the warmth I felt had seeped from the young woman's anal and vaginal cavities. It was a trace of her living body, now gone into the Gardens or down the Boul' Mich. If she had known that I, the silent foreigner with the analytic glance, was feeling her body's warmth, even evoking in my mind's eye the corporeal spaces from which it had leaked, would she have felt shame? Could this invisible invasion of her person have signified anything at all? How would she have responded to the knowledge that she, a student at the Sorbonne, a reader of Merleau-Ponty, a woman with a rich and complex private life, had been metamorphosed into a trace? What would she have thought had she known that even as she left the bus a tiny, unobserved particle of her being, left behind and unremarked, was being transmuted into the stuff of a stranger's imagination?

What is the reality of a trace? How much being does it possess? What uses does it have? How much can you make of it? Even while still on the bus, I recalled Derrida's argument that the etymology of a word contains the spectrum of its previous common meanings, a history of traces, the reality of which is always present even if ignored. The traces of opposed meanings contaminate the concept that seeks to replace it, permeating its membrane of significance, cluttering the wishful clarity of its intention. (There are so many senses to "disgust" that the mind begins to stagger beneath its weight and appalling fecundity.) Little is clean, sharp and isolated; much is murky, fuzzy and contaminated.

Still, the trace is a powerful advocate for lost presence. From a trace as insignificant as fading bodily warmth on a plastic seat, the imagination can construct an entire person, exposing her in secret moments of vulnerability. Vast structures, intricate architectures and expansive cities take shape out of the tiniest shard, the merest fragment of sense or an obscure memory. As the bus passed the entrance to the Catacombs, I found myself wondering at a trace's cognitive force. Then I remembered how different dogs whom I have known had seemed able to sniff a whole dog into existence. By a mechanism that I can not grasp, but perhaps more concretely imaginative than my own, a dog selectively sniffs the piss-fragrant traces that other dogs have left behind. From these fading remnants of canine being, the dog begins to imagine whole other dogs, no longer present. The dog responds with excitement or uninterest as if to a representation, to a re-presented presence. The trace constitutes the irreducible building-block of all signification. Visible meaning seeps out from invisible constellations of ephemeral, endlessly permutable scraps.

Well, perhaps I was, in that moment, too quick to pin down meaning. I had been struck, even in the instant in which it happened, by the swiftness, the almost instantaneous opening into an unknown world, with which my imagination had transmuted a glimpse of a young woman's body and the fading sensation of her body's heat into an erotic scenario. I had not solicited it to perform this task. It had simply happened, as swiftly as a blink of the mind's eye. The imagination quickly picks up existence's scattered bits and makes stories of them. These stories may be as stripped down as a scenario, only the major characters and a bare sequence of episodes, but they often wait in the imagination for development and expansion. I would like to assert confidently that I have never thought again about the young woman on the bus in Paris, but it would not be true. For a long time I did not think about her; in fact, she was so inconsequential in my thinking that I never even turned her into an anecdote to tell my friends. A fleeting encounter, the kind that fills your life in a large city but also leaves it nearly empty, she simply did not matter. She never crossed my mind. Then one day more than a year later, I was in San Francisco. I planned to meet some friends for dinner at the Huntington Hotel on Nob Hill which, late in the afternoon, left me with the choice of taking the cable car from Fisherman's Wharf or walking. I decided to walk up Hyde Street to Nob Hill, which meant that I would inevitably have to walk over Russian Hill and cross Green Street on my way. Exactly in the moment, with amazing suddenness, when I began to cross Green Street, I remembered Georgia Lee with whom I had experienced such a dismal sexual encounter forty years before (my personal tale for Chapter 3). Without wishing to, I evoked in my mind the entire wretched experience. I even walked a couple of blocks east on Green in an effort to find where Georgie had lived. I walked as far as Jones Street, but too much time had passed and in any case it had been nighttime when I had seen her apartment. There were several relatively new apartment buildings, anyone of which might have displaced the old house where Georgia Lee's apartment had been. One, on the corner of Green and Jones streets, looked particularly guilty. Many of the houses and small apartments that had once lined the street had been torn down, and I could see that all traces of Georgie had disappeared. I couldn't find her apartment and so I quickly turned back to Hyde Street to continue my climb. For some reason, I changed my mind and, turning around once more, continued along Green to the long stairway that leads down to Taylor Street. At the bottom of the first flight of steps, surrounded by the trees that line the stairway, I paused briefly in the shade of a thick bush and the higher branches of an oak tree. A young power runner, wearing a Princeton baseball cap, charged up the stairs, a tawny ponytail swinging behind her. And suddenly I remembered the young woman in Paris. In my imagination, I saw her distinctly lying in a tub, her legs bent open. She looked up with wide dark eyes and begged me to urinate upon her. Most oddly, in my imagination, I instantly recognized her as Monique, the name of a French woman I had briefly dated as an undergraduate. She was "Monique," but she was physically, clearly and without mistake, the anonymous young woman on the bus in Paris. The association was very powerful, but it was also startling and strange. Monique and I, when we had known each other so many years before, had never practised eccentric sex in any way.

I did not encourage this fantasy, and I did not like it. I was even a bit shocked to have her occupying a place in my imagination. As soon as I had imagined her naked body, I had known who she was. Where had she come from? How was it possible after such a lapse of time for my imagination suddenly to evoke her and, in the same moment, both to transpose her with Georgie and identify her with Monique? Since then I have tried not to remember her. It doesn't seem right that such a brief, utterly ephemeral contact should have left traces with long-lasting imaginative consequences. The entire episode, fleeting as it was and absurd in remembrance, now seems quite ugly, filthy and even degrading. I had done nothing to solicit it, nor did I desire the image when it abruptly slithered into my consciousness, but there it was, crisp and sharp. As I stood on the steps leading down to Taylor Street, I experienced my imaginatively recast memory as several degrees more intense than sleazy. I felt it acutely as disgusting. Merely the fleeting image of "Monique," lying in the tub begging me to urinate upon her, had made me feel unclean. I did not enjoy that moment of recognition and even now I dislike thinking about it.

I *do* think about how my imagination worked in that short moment on Green Street and during the even shorter moment on the bus in Paris. It seems like a treacherous and disturbing capacity. However, my quick recognition of the young woman in Paris does sketch out the imagination's secret ways: swiftly, abruptly even, often uncontrollably, building with double-quick transformations coherent fictional worlds out of the actual world's pieces. The point is not that the imagination seems always uncontrollable (though it often is), but that, whether or not it has been invited, it constructs worlds that stand as alternatives to the one you actually inhabit. Quite consciously, I often return to my self-punishing friend in Chicago and to the sliced peach my mother gave me when I was four. These experiences, as well as my small adventures on motorcycles and as a sailor, come back repeatedly, frequently without being urged, enhanced and fully developed (with many variations) in my imagination. What happens in such moments is that the imagination builds small fictional worlds to account for, or else transform, immediate experience.

All the world's myriad parts can prompt the imagination into world-building, and each of these parts can then function as a prop in the new creation. Some things seem, more than others, to spur the imagination forwards. Love, sexual appetite, violence, heroism, even intelligence and beauty, are all particularly active in prompting the imagination. No doubt, certain cultures shape the imagination in advance, channelling its capacities and selecting the world-bits most appropriate to serve as prompts. The ancient Romans may well have found it as easy to build imaginative worlds that selected out acts of piety as it was for them to imagine worlds filled with unconstrained sexuality and extreme violence. I am certain that Australians build worlds around beaches and surf. Canadians, as Margaret Atwood pointed out long ago, like to imagine winter storms and other natural hardships. Americans, I suspect, may like to build fictional worlds out of the varied evidence for world power and dominance. (Such world-building may be easily transferred to scenarios about professional sports or conflicts with drug-dealers and other criminals.) Some in-the-world things seem constant, even granted cultural shaping, and infinitely recurring. Love and death are two such; disgust is still another. Throughout this book, I have attempted to show how many kinds of things evoke the disgust response and how varied it is. Disgust-worlds can be small, though disturbingly powerful, and they arise out of all manner of materials.

I chose the figure of the Hydra, a mythological creature known for dwelling in a swamp and for her appalling stench (miasmal exhalations in every sense) as well as for her grotesque fecundity, to provide the overarching symbol for this study. The Hydra, a monster with diverse parts, suggests an important aspect of the phenomenology of disgust. Disgust is highly multifarious, "roiling" (as William Ian Miller likes to say) and hydravarious, but it is also analyzable into distinct conceptual categories.

I have approached the topic in terms of its separate categories, its unmistakable partability, and I have done so using some of the Hydra's diverse members as symbolic rubrics. This method may have struck some readers as fanciful or even unnecessarily whimsical. However, *Hydra* has been a book about the uses of the imagination and the mind's capacity to build fictional worlds out of reality's shards. I have repeatedly turned away from the evidence for disgust in the actual world to representations of disgust. (Although, as I have insisted more than once and tried determinedly to show, actual disgust is a fascinating subject that challenges both sophisticated theories and unexamined preconceptions.) Readers who have stayed with my argument will have understood that I have been more interested in the representations of disgust than the in-the-world disgust phenomena themselves. My interest in the representations of disgust arose in part from my observation that writers on the topic of disgust have either ignored representations or conflated them with the actual experience. Considered in these terms, a touch of fancy may well seem appropriate: the Hydra's potential for symbols and her varied gift of metaphors.

In the first chapter, I tried to show, under the image of the monster's spoor, that the range of actual things that may evoke a disgust response is staggeringly large but still connected by a few characteristics. Considered only as a psycho-visceral affect, disgust may involve gagging and nausea. As a moral response to experience, a psycho-intellectual affect, disgust involves distance and superiority. It may well be the case that all disgust, as experimental psychologists have demonstrated, involves certain predictable facial gestures. Furthermore, all disgust involves a problem in the negotiation of boundaries. Disgust always marks a border that leads away from the well-regulated territory of socialized existence. And even if moral loathsomeness does not necessarily invoke the disgust face, that face can be pretended. Disgust is a wonderfully actable affect. This allowed me to introduce a point that would eventually become a key block in my argument. Disgust can be represented, in the actual world and in literature, and its representations are not the same as its in-the-world reality. Certain art forms, such as shock theatre, incorporate vivid disgust motifs and often act out the actual disgust responses that people, such as members of the audience, might have away from the theatre. Shock theatre is representation, but a particularly immediate and concrete type. Thinking about it helped to establish the argument and to prepare the way for more complex forms of representation.

In the second chapter, I explored the Hydra's lair, the conceptual models that human beings have used to make sense out of disgust. It is a powerful, often an overwhelming, affect and so it is reasonable to suppose that it must possess a lucid and adequate theory. Yet this, I argued, is far from the case. Nothing could be more wrong than the naïve and unexamined assumption that disgust is a "natural" response, but even vastly more subtle accounts fall short of the problem's complexity. All the theories that claim to give accounts of disgust create simple, or at least single-minded, models. Clearly, I find these different models inadequate though not completely wrong. Each contributes some understanding to the problem of disgust and can claim a place in an overall account. I argued that an array of theoretical models would best serve my purposes in analyzing disgust. Any single model would offer an explanation, but only at the cost of reducing the phenomenon to something less than its complexity and of ignoring vast amounts of relevant evidence.

Above all in Chapter 2, I tried to make the case that no available model of disgust could deal satisfactorily with its obvious, and empirically ascertainable, metamorphicity. Not only is disgust more than one thing, or one kind of behaviour, it never remains what it has been or seems to have been. For this reason, I tried to break the mindlock that constricts thinking about disgust. Don't say that disgust is moral prohibition, taboo or even dirt out of place. Don't feel satisfied with a genetic account, identifying the social or psychological origins of an individual's sense of disgust, or even with a more sophisticated explanation based on assumptions about how the imagination works. Don't even believe that you have got to the truth when you have learned that it is possible to transgress boundaries and to use your own disgust response to free yourself from social repression so that, wandering like a purposeful nomad across unstriated space, you may discover your previously unrealized potential. Instead, accept the diversity, working on so many distinct levels, and see how many aspects of the whole are revealed by each theoretical model. Although my discussion has been centrally focussed upon disgust, it is clear that the variousness of the phenomena and the inadequacy of distinct models shows how other human affects should be approached. Everything human is more intricate than any single theory can adequately handle. Behind even the simplest image (of disgust or desire, hate or love), you may hear unlit pyres crackling and chirring in your mind's ear.

In the remaining four chapters, I explored different aspects of disgust, but always in terms of the individual's imaginative capacity to create fictional worlds. (Chapter 5 was specifically devoted to the task of making the concept of a fictional world clear.) Representations of disgust can appear in labyrinthine, and otherwise undisgusting, works of literature and art, but they also come into existence as immediate responses, at once vivid and simple, to the observation of deliquescence, especially the varied collapse of the human body, in the actual world. I argued that disgust is one of the indications of how the mind engages the world: disgusting things (however they came to be disgusting) are grasped in the imagination and transformed into scenarios that are the skeletons of fictional worlds. Such disgust-worlds may be appalling, but they are different from the thing itself. This proposition lay at the heart of Chapter 3. Disgusting experiences, such as cophrophagy or golden showers, may be more or less disgusting as representations, but they will certainly be different. In a fictional world, disgust ties into other parts of the world, lending coherence, building certain themes, helping to develop characters or anticipating the denouement, in ways that quite unlike the relation of disgusting things to the actual world. In Chapter 6, I examined a number of fictional worlds, particularly those created within art-horror and terror, in which disgust motifs are systematically organized precisely to contribute to aesthetic form, not the transcription of reality. In such worlds it will be the appalling nature of an ideology, or other belief system, that will be disgusting, a perverse geometry of the human mind.

In both Chapters 4 and 7, I explored some of the ways in which the human body decays and begins to lose wholeness and integrity. The most painful disgust-worlds emerge from the contemplation of your own body. The body may undergo metamorphosis or be lopped and severed into parts (many of which can now be replaced), but in either case the process may be viewed as disgusting. No fictional worlds seem more difficult to endure, nor more ghastly in their content, than the imagination's building of corrosive visions of personal abjection. In an abject world, you might easily imagine yourself as without value, as both degraded and worthless, and even envision yourself as a spider. In such a fictional world you might feel yourself not merely cast out but also open to trampling and hideous forms of subjection. The analysis of fictional worlds that arise when the body is injured, malfunctions or seems worthless (because of personal experience or else the coded instructions from society) returns the argument to the initial proposition that disgust invariably involves the crossing of boundaries. The most immediate and evocative boundaries are always those inscribed on the body itself. The body is multiplexly split (always already partable), and each separable part can become a region for distinct experience and powerful, often highly negative, feeling. In opposition to theoretical models that claim disgust is objective, a matter of moral and legal prohibition, or otherwise claim that it is invariable, a standard product of similar processes of social formation, I have argued that disgust is both personal and variable, endlessly metamorphic. It centres upon the body, but flowers in the imagination.

The study of disgust shows both how various and metamorphic it is as an affect, the shape and range of the world's filth always undergoing transmutation; but it also shows how corrosively it works in the imagination, in those small, personal worlds that the mind experiences as explosions or wastelands. Small disgust-worlds emerge from ordinary experience, taking in-the-world things as props, but their play is regulated by cultural imaginaries, the stereotypes and clichés, the learned slogans of human socialization. The world seems always to be erupting into incandescent alternative versions of itself. It is as if everything possessed virtual fireworks displays, hidden in the mind's recesses or along an interface with the world's abundance, that lie in waiting for prompts to activate them. Nothing has been more important in this study than the sense that disgust is an unstable affect, constantly subject to change, and that it can be internalized as self-disgust and abjection. No theory of disgust would be adequate if it could not account for disgust's volatile metamorphicity. Disgust's variousness prompts many reflections: it cannot be fully isolated from other human experience; it shows up, often in strange guises, where you might least expect it; it challenges theory and the mind's model-building powers; it shifts provocatively across many boundaries (that might once have appeared to be as solidly fixed as mountain ranges); it solicits the imagination in often bizarre ways and gives rise to deep self-reflection; it changes radically and can be modified deliberately (following either new tasks or desires); it can be incorporated into life as the basis for transgression; above all, it may be transformed into literature and art. Disgust may be a changing dark shadow-image of human life, but it is a blackness that can be enjoyed and one that can be tamed into a very personal war-machine. Always an intimate-while-shifting experience, it pollutes the bright froth of human existence like a small maggot-slithering turd within a saucer of champagne. Disgust highlights the ravenous worm's body in human fun. ✳

Recognitions

Books always carry their secret histories. They send out, drawing

their life from, rhizomes that stretch far away into the soil of other books,

of films and paintings, and of conversations that (may now) seem largely

forgotten. *The Hydra's Tale* has drawn its life from many sources, some of
which, if not all, have been hinted at in the subtextual dungeon of documentation and recorded in the better-lit bibliography. Disgust is also an
extremely personal emotion. I have used a number of intimate anecdotes,
small tales from life, to illustrate the scope of my subject. I have written in
this way in order to show, but also to admit, that my interest in disgust is
deeply my own: the loathsomeness of peaches, brown spiderlings, golden
showers, motorcycle accidents, the sudden violence of broken bottles and
the dreary consequences of sexual abuse have all contributed to my sense
that disgust is a shocking but daily affect, as profound as it is always-
shifting. It is an affect that is deeply *labile* in every sense of that word.

I owe many people thanks for the advice, suggestions and help. My friend
and colleague of many years, Edward J. Milowicki, with whom I have co-
authored several articles, has helped me significantly over the years in
refining my thinking on the problem of character in literature and on the
shape of Menippean discourse. I have acknowledged Ed's advice previously
in other bits like this one, but I have never publicly stated that I admire, and
always learn from, his intelligence, wit and scholarship. I need particularly
to thank him for having invited me to Mills College to present a paper on
body parts that was, in effect, the initial version of Chapter 4. Imre

Salusinszky invited me to Newcastle University where I presented an early version of Chapter 3. His observations have always been as provocative as they have been sharp. Morten Kyndrup arranged to have me invited to the University of Aarhus where I presented a short series of four lectures on disgust, including an early exploration of the theoretical issues discussed in Chapter 2, to the Center for Kulturforskning. Brian Edwards, who has long been both a friend and a colleague, invited me to Deakin University where I addressed several lectures to the Deakin Literary Society on the general topic of disgust. Brian had previously invited me to guest-edit a special issue of the journal *Mattoid* (no. 48, 1994) on disgust and that experience enabled me to work out many nagging problems. The many contributors to that issue of *Mattoid*, including Kelly Anspaugh, Liz Day, Brian Edwards, Frances Devlin-Glass, Fred Radford, Wilm Robertson, Suzette Henke, Jason Kapalka, Clive Probyn, Alan Roughley, Lois Parkinson Zamora and Benzi Zhang, all deserve my deeply felt expressions of gratitude. The English Department of the University of Alberta invited me to deliver the annual Edmund Kemper Broadus Lectures on aspects of the theory of disgust. In that venue, I gave four lectures that constituted a proleptic overview of this book. To everyone involved in these invitations, and to all who listened patiently and asked questions afterwards, I owe sincere debts of gratitude. The English Department also allowed me to teach a seminar on disgust at an early stage in my research and that experience was at once stimulating and instructive. Hence I should like to recognize the contributions of all the students in English 694 to my thinking: Wayne Defehr, Jane Haslett, Shazia Rahman, Christopher Rechner, Mari Sasano, Leslie Vermeer, Sherryl Vint, Susanne Weber and Christopher Wiebe.

Jonathan Locke Hart and Deirdre Susan E. Crandall, to both of whom *The Hydra's Tale* is dedicated, each gave me invaluable (though quite different) advice and help in the writing and preparation of this book. Sally Ito and Jason Kapalka aided me immensely as research assistants. Jason, a witty and exploratory research assistant, also conducted an interview on disgust with three anthropologists for the special "Disgust Issue" of *Mattoid*. And for that contribution, he deserves a double measure of thanks. Many friends and colleagues made suggestions and offered advice along the (often torturous) path to publication. To all of them, I offer in exchange my warmest thanks: Chris Bullock, Dianne Chisholm, Patricia Demers, Bruce A. Forsyth, Robyn Gardner, Uri Margolin, Tana Polansky Mauer, Sandra Morris, Lars-Henrik Schmidt, Garry Sherbert, Elena Siemens, Lynn Weinlos and Paco Wilson. At the difficult juncture when I began major revisions, Reynolds Smith made important, and ultimately far-reaching, suggestions. The editor of *The Hydra's Tale*, the patient and instructive Leslie Vermeer, deserves a special word of thanks. I owe sincere gratitude to the Social Sciences and Humanities Research Council of Canada who aided me immensely with a research grant in the initial stages of my research.

Several parts of *The Hydra's Tale* have appeared previously, usually in rather different versions. The discussion of tattoos first appeared, in much different form, in "Tattoos: Play and Interpretation," *Textual Studies in Canada* 3 (1993). I first used the personal anecdote concerning golden showers that begins Chapter 3 in the "Introduction" to the "Disgust Issue" of *Mattoid*. That essay, "Nuzzling Medusa's Hair: Or, What Perseus Failed to Notice," also constituted an early version of the discussion of Bataille's idea of self-transformation through excess and transgression that figures significantly in Chapters 2 and 3. The discussion of prostheses and body-part replacement in Chapters 4 and 7 first appeared as "Cyber(body)parts: Prosthetic Consciousness," in *Body & Society* 1, nos. 3–4 (1995); reprinted in *Cyberspace, Cyberbodies, Cyberpunk: Cultures of Technological Embodiment*, eds. Mike Featherstone and Roger Burrows (Sage Publications, 1995). Aspects of the analysis of terror and terrorism in Chapter 6 first appeared in my essay, "Graffiti Become Terror: The Idea of Resistance," in the *Canadian Review of Comparative Literature* 22, no. 2 (June/juin 1995). Discussions of the problem of literary "character" and of fictional worldhood that dominate Chapter 5 (but appear throughout this book) can be found in my co-authored (with Edward Milowicki) essays, "Ovid's Shadow: Character and Characterization in Early Modern Literature," *Neohelicon* 22, no. 1 (1995) and "Ovid Through Shakespeare: The Divided Self," *Poetics Today* 16, no. 2 (1995). A reader interested in pursuing further the discussion of Menippean discourse should look for Ed Milowicki's and my co-authored essay, "A Measure for Menippean Discourse: The Example of Shakespeare," *Poetics Today* 23, no. 2 (2002). I first discussed the Hydra herself as a mythological figure in "The Hydra's Spoor" in *HEAT* 2 (1996). Several of the metables, including all three in chapter 5 that deal with the idiosyncrasies of QueAng–QueAng, appeared in *Boundaries, and other fictions* (University of Alberta Press, 1999). Oblique and disguised, many of the themes of this book appear in that collection of short fiction in (as it were) drag. ✻

Notes

Introduction

1   Wallace, pp. 5-6. The study of disgust, bearing especially in mind its role in the imagination, begins appropriately with an image that takes something ordinary (a boy's
semen) and transforms it into a scene of ugliness and disgust. I might re-imagine the
same scene and see only the glorious white froth of meerschaum or meringue. Or what
about William H. Gass' description of the way Aphrodite "slipped ashore on the
calcified splash of her father's balls"? (*Habitations*, p. 114).

2   Although everywhere implied, the point is actually made by Rodolphe el-Khoury
in his introduction to Laporte's book (p. viii).

3   Miller, p. 18. His study, Miller writes, begins "amid the darkest matter where disgust
arises from the fetid zone of what I call life soup, the roiling stuff of eating, defecation,
fornication, generation, death, rot, and regeneration." Sharply put, you may say,
though surely such a study might well begin in the imagination that has been prepared
for its encounters by socio-cultural formation.

4   Kingwell, p. 6.

5   On Dahmer, see Tithecott.

6   Miller, p. 194.

7   I take the evocative "sludgewards" from the title ("Disgust: Being's Sludgewards Fall")
of Robertson's review of Miller's book.

8   Tithicott, p. 173.

9   Sartre, "The Childhood of a Leader," in *Intimacy*, p. 137.

10   Sartre, pp. 215-16.

11   Bataille, "The Big Toe," in *Visions of Excess*, pp. 20-23.

12   Bataille, *Story of the Eye*, p. 67.

13   Namias, p. 100.

14   Otto, p. 16.

Chapter 1 ❧ The Hydra's Spoor

1   Sartre, *Nausea*, p. 10. A disgusting or a playful object will be alike in the way they vary with perspective: turn each around a bit and the one side may seem pretty, the other, programmatic.

2   Sartre, p. 224. Compare: "But what exactly is my superiority over men? Superiority of position, nothing more: I have placed myself above the human within me and I study it. That's why I always liked the towers of Notre-Dame, the platforms in the Eiffel Tower, the Sacré-Coeur, my seventh floor on the Rue Delambre. These are excellent symbols" ("Erostratus," in *Intimacy*, p. 110). Sartre's shadow falls heavily across this book. I have begun by citing from his fiction partly to anticipate this presence (which will make itself evident largely on the level of theory).

3   I speak in personal terms because I have always had an interest in play and the theory(s) of play. I wrote a book on the subject and the intimation of *that* book hangs over this one like carnival smoke. See *In Palamedes' Shadow*.

4   The discussion of disgust as an absence of taste, or as a violation of taste, was a common topos of eighteenth-century philosophy and aesthetics. The central argument lies in Immanuel Kant's *Critique of Judgment* (1790). The problem of representability has never been abandoned in philosophy. Recently, Italian philosopher Mario Perniola has published a study in the aesthetics of disgust.

5   William Ian Miller, pp. 200, 202. However, Miller treats contempt and disgust as distinct affects, though clearly related, each separately supporting the moral and legal order. The argument in this book will be that contempt is a psycho-intellectual affect while disgust is psycho-visceral. Contempt builds upon disgust, and presupposes its existence, much as outrage builds upon rage, or love upon desire.

6   Administrative "ecstasy" is Michael R. Katz's translation of Fyodor Dostoevsky's *administrativniy vostorg*. No doubt, a sense of "vortex" also informs the word. In *Devils*, Stepan Trofimovich uses the phrase to describe the extreme pleasure "some insignificant nonentity" experiences when newly appointed to a position of power however minor (Dostoevsky, p. 58). It is a question of being able to demonstrate power over another, whether this is selling tickets, issuing tax forms or answering inquiries about a university's internal procedures. From the outside, this behaviour will seem to be "disgusting," even loathsome.

7   *Hamlet*, 1.5.32–34; *The Riverside Shakespeare*, p. 1149.

8   Scheff, p. 27.

9   Lear's wrath *is* named early in the play, but it is simultaneously distanced by the metaphor which contains the word. Lear exclaims, "Peace Kent! / Come not between the dragon and his wrath" (1.1.121–22; *The Riverside Shakespeare*, p. 1256). Lear's wrath is highly complex. It is not simply rage, but also outrage, at once spontaneous and theatrical. The dialogue between Regan and Goneril that ends the first scene might seem to provide substance to the noun *wrath* but they speak in general terms about his

weakness, the "infirmity of his age," his rashness and his "infirm and choleric years." In the context, Goneril's use of "choleric" suggests rather more petulance than wrath. The burden of their dialogue is the charge that he has "ever but slenderly known himself." The possibility of semiotic inference is not bound to the precise words used. By the end of the first scene, an idea of "Lear" has begun to emerge that is compound and multi-affectual. He would not seem to be "humoral" in any important sense. I discuss the problem of character and characterization in Shakespeare in my *Shakespearean Narrative*, especially in Chapter 5.

10   *Hamlet*, 5.1.185–88; *The Riverside Shakespeare*, p. 1179.

11   Johnson, vol. 7, pp. 121, 120.

12   Gass, *On Being Blue*, p. 52.

13   Hughes, *Culture of Complaint*, p. 20. Hughes argues that a strident political correctness has flattened out, by making too abstract and non-specific, American English. He does not observe that this process has been underway for more than two centuries. Dr. Johnson's double definition of *disgust* already points towards the vapid moralism of much modern English (at least as it is used by the middle classes or, much the same thing, when it is used decorously). You might say that the language has become less crude, and hence less disgusting, since Shakespeare, but it is neither more precise nor more vivid. Its very abstractness could easily be the cause of disgust in someone who could feel the language. Language's explosiveness should be like stumbling upon a glistening white turd or finding frass in your breakfast cereal.

14   In registering the affect of disgust, human facework can be remarkably labile (see Rozin et al., "Varieties of Disgust Faces and the Structure of Disgust"). It is worth noting that Miller does not cite this article. He draws extensively upon Rozin's work, but overlooks his work on the "disgust face." This is doubly strange since Miller also cites the sociologist Erving Goffman frequently. Goffman discusses the social uses of facial expressions, or what he prefers to call it "facework," in his fascinating *Interaction Ritual*. Miller does show some interest in facial expression, though he refers only to Charles Darwin and the seventeenth-century French artist Charles Le Brun, not the more relevant work in psychology and sociology (Miller, p. 295 n. 18). Recent work in affective neuroscience has attempted to show that specific affects can be correlated with specific areas of the brain. (An experimental subject wears a cap of numerous separate electrodes while being shown stimulating pictures.) Results have shown that a person will blink after a burst of white noise made while looking at a picture. When the picture has shown disgusting content, the experimental subject will blink "harder and longer" (Kaufman). Hence the "disgust face" might also include a subsequent blink after the nose has wrinkled and closed. Later in this study, I shall argue, against Miller, that there is a social phenomenon of "make-believe" disgust, theatrical displays imitating visceral disgust which are created for the purpose of making unmistakable moral judgements. Miller ignores the theatricality of make-believe disgust, preferring to treat psycho-intellectual affects, such as contempt and disdain, as if they were simply visceral. In his *Dangerous Emotions*, Alphonso Lingis discusses faces or (in Goffman's term) facework in emotional exchanges (see especially his Chapter 3).

15   The term "disgustometer" is used in the Monty Python skit "Party Political Broadcast" during which the question of the Most Awful Family in Britain arises (Chapman, p. 330).

16   Geertz, "The Uses of Diversity," p. 112.

17   Chambers, *Room For Maneuver*, p. 12.

18   Both David Lawton and Leonard Levy discuss the charges of blasphemy brought against various Ranters in the late seventeenth and early eighteenth centuries (Lawton, pp. 25–36; Levy, pp. 136–67). Both writers have considerable sympathy for the antinomian Ranters, but little for the society that accused and condemned them. Levy sees the Ranter phenomenon as an instance of pure antinomianism, but expressed in such "blatantly offensive" terms, so intentionally determined to shock, that it could not be ignored (p. 137). The "extravagant flouting of normative conduct" reflected Ranter conviction that "normative principles were no longer right and authoritative" (p. 147). They set out to disturb their society, using religion, the "universal language" of their age (p. 146), and succeeded. Lawton sees Ranterism as a discursive struggle carried out against the entrenched discourse of authority. Ranters carnivalized discourse, including biblical texts and decrees of parliament, and the charge of blasphemy is merely the "vicious way that the discourse kicks back at its user" (p. 73). The Ranter phenomenon constitutes a particularly nasty battle in the long history of class warfare in which discourse, the striking arm of ideology, seems always to have been a bloody entanglement of weapons. Ranter disgust struggled bravely, but ineffectively, against Anglican repression. Lawton's dazzling analysis of blasphemy constantly recurs to the main point: blasphemy "functions in opposition to fundamentalism or monoculturism among those who would be anomalous" whereas the official charge of blasphemy works to insure the marginality of the blasphemers; blasphemy is a discursive "means of marking territory" (p. 46). I shall return to the problem of blasphemy in Chapter 6.

19   Like many other professions, medicine or police work, say, anthropology requires that its members learn to overcome initial disgust reactions. However, anthropologists seldom discuss the matter. One suspects that it must constitute one of the important aspects of their professionalization, including early self-selection out by young graduate students who begin to realize what will be asked of them. Hence ethnographic reports must often give a simplified account of culture, rather like a literary one, in which cultural details that might seem disgusting, or strongly aversive, are left out or minimalized. For an interesting interview with anthropologists on the topic of disgust and early professionalization, see Kapalka. One of the most fascinating examples of disgust within the anthropological community concerns Turnbull's *The Mountain People*. Turnbull, an experienced anthropologist undertaking fieldwork for the fifth time, found his subjects, the Ik of northeastern Uganda, to be disgusting. Their apparent lack of mutual cooperation and respect, their selfishness, their harsh treatment of their own children, their eating habits as well as their personal hygiene, all caused Turnbull to react negatively. Writing of an Ik woman who was said to have gone mad and who preferred being in jail to living in her community, Turnbull writes that "Nangoli, I think, was the last Ik who was human" (p. 271). Even within the context of Turnbull's unsympathetic discussion of the Ik, this seems like an extraordinary statement for an anthropologist to have made. Reading *The Mountain People*, it seems clear

that Turnbull found them disgusting on both their personal and their collective levels. In what appears to have been a great breach of professionalism, he concluded his research by recommending, to the government of Uganda, that the Ik be broken up into small groups and absorbed into other tribes, effectively eradicated. Other anthropologists reacted with anger, outrage and even enraged disgust. Frederick Barth accused Turnbull of having advocated "culturecide" as well as of having engaged in "vituperation against the Ik" (Barth, p. 102; see also, Peter J. Wilson and others with Colin M. Turnbull's "Reply" in *Current Anthropology*). Not all anthropologists accused Turnbull of having advocated culturecide, but all who wrote on the topic thought that he had failed to consider the adaptive strategies of a culture, such as the Ik's, that was experiencing famine. Turnbull's reaction to the Ik, "his people" after all, continues to invoke very strong responses. In 1993, Alex de Waal recalled the incident and added that the Ik had asked other anthropologists how they might sue Turnbull for libel. I would like to know whether they succeeded.

20   The drink aside, the very mixing of blood and milk would probably strike many western people as relatively disgusting in itself. The famous "Mondo" (and pseudo-snuff) film *Faces of Death* has a short early scene (following a shot of a shrunken head and preceding another shot of a woman cutting the head off a chicken) of Masai tribesmen bleeding cattle, mixing blood and milk, and butchering a cow. *Faces of Death* contains footage of all kinds of death, human and animal. The very fact that it is narrated by "Dr. Francis B. Gross" indicates that its mostly young audiences seek it out for false shock effects, or shock as play. Many of the scenes are thought to have been faked. Even so it is banned in many places (Rice, p. 156).

21   The anecdote belongs to Gary Tunnell and is partly retold in Kapalka's interview.

22   Lewin, pp. xiv–xv. Scatology implies symbolic or representational intent. Coprolalia, also the use of words signifying filth, indicates an involuntary display of tics, echolalia and uncontrollable obscenities. Merely to mouth words such as "shit" or "turd" without an intention to shock (or at least to represent), as a sufferer from Tourette's syndrome might do, would not constitute scatology. In this book, I am interested in scatology, not coprolalia.

23   It is a striking weakness in Miller's *The Anatomy of Disgust* that he ignores scatology, or the representation of disgusting things. When he does talk about disgust in art, he tends to conflate representations with in-the-world things, scatology with coprology, or else to dismiss scatology as "teenage" verbal behaviour. (I would grant that many teenagers are natural Menippeans, but it hardly follows that all Menippean satire is "teenage." Shakespeare's *Troilus and Cressida* is about as "adult" as you might find.) This absence seems to correlate with his disinclination to discuss make-believe disgust in human actions. The nearly infinite ways in which human beings register moral loathing (and find each other mutually disgusting) through simulated facework and gestures plays no part in his study. Indeed, imagination generally plays only a slight role in his analysis of disgust. W.R. Robertson observes that Miller "writes as a lawyer" and seems to have built up his argument from his conclusion "that disgust and contempt function as moral sentiments to maintain social harmony and public order. Lawyers like to say that the one who frames the issues will win the case; Miller has clearly framed the

issues. The exclusionary argument positions certain issues as primary: necessary moves in a discourse planned to make a strong case, and to conclude without surprise, that disgust and contempt are important enforcers of social hierarchy" (p. 218).

24 Looking through a book such as Spinrad's *The Re/Search Guide to Bodily Fluids*, you can take a rapid course in the variety of disgusting materials, and the corresponding motifs for insults, jokes and narrative, that arise from a single source: the human body's effluvia and excreta.

25 Anspaugh, "'Bung Goes The Enemay'," p. 226. Anspaugh also notes the long literary association between satire and shit (p. 225). Compare Anspaugh's observation on the satirical function of turds with Gass' comment that "the primal and still ultimate rejection is the retch" (*Habitations*, p. 135). The power of very physical images to satirize, or otherwise comment upon, ideas lies at the heart of Menippean satire.

26 *Troilus and Cressida*, II.I.I-9; 2.3.20; *The Riverside Shakespeare*, pp. 459, 463. Thersites' exchange with Ajax, opening the second act, begins the process of undercutting the chivalric ideals, honour and love, that Shakespeare had introduced in the first act. The hollowness of these ideals attracts Shakespeare's interest in many plays (and in the narrative poems), but nowhere else, not even in *Timon of Athens*, does he uses Menippean characterization and devices so enthusiastically. There are Menippean elements in other plays, *Hamlet* and *Measure for Measure* (for instance), but *Troilus and Cressida* stands out for its pervasive satiric, and even excremental, vision. For a discussion of Menippean elements in Shakespeare's *Troilus*, see Wilson and Milowicki, pp. 129-44, 234-40.

27 Marcus, p. 17. Marcus also observes that nihilism "can find a voice in art, but never satisfaction" (p. 9). The history of shock art, like that of the avant-garde in general, reveals only ephemeral triumphs.

28 Bürger, p. 80. The line of Bürger's argument sees avant-gardist artists as reacting against smug, conformist bourgeois audiences of the early twentieth-century in Europe. Thus he takes shock art to be culture-dependent and, fundamentally, aesthetic in purpose. The art that Bürger discusses achieves its purposes by denying its wholeness and integrity, or by displaying disparate parts that seem to bear no organic relationship to the whole. Shock art has other dimensions, including both content and meaning. Some shock art flaunts its meaning in order to disturb its audiences on the level of psycho-visceral response. When a scumrock singer, such as G.G. Allin, defecates upon the stage, it is not to deny or hide meaning, but rather to blazon meaning, reminding his audiences how disgusting someone else (parents, say, or "authority") would find this act. That is, it draws the audience into an avant-gardist elite.

29 Hughes, *The Shock of the New*, p. 61. Hughes quotes Jean Arp ("the most gifted of the Zurich Dadas") that the Dadaists turned to art because they had been repelled "by the slaughterhouse of the world war." Hughes' interpretation of Dada takes it back to Friedrich Schiller's proposition in the fifteenth letter of *On the Aesthetic Education of Man*. There, Schiller argues that only in play is man fully himself. Schiller's argument that play is central to human development has had an unbroken line of followers. In the next chapter, I shall discuss Georges Bataille's insistence upon transgression, upon crossing the boundaries of the prohibited, as a mode of Schilleresque play. Hughes'

interpretation takes Dada out of the sphere of social revolution, where it is sometimes placed, to reposition it within that of formal art alone. The shock of Dada was only the defamiliarization of the work of art and its aim was to re-educate bourgeois aesthetic taste. In his novella *The Childhood of a Leader*, Sartre makes plain the degree to which an aesthetic revolution can be merely conventional: the character of Achille Bergère represents surrealism, but entirely on a level of received opinion and second-hand gestures. The main character, Lucien Fleurier, acquires surrealism under Bergère's tutelage as he does all other ways of thinking, from capitalism to anti-Semitism, as mere convention, external relationship and bad faith.

30   Bürger, p. 18. Bürger observes that shock constitutes a "radicalization" of the normal aesthetic techniques of defamiliarization. Victor Shklovsky, for instance, chose to illustrate the techniques of defamiliarization through reference to *Don Quixote* and *Tristram Shandy*, not the avant-gardist art of his own period.

31   Marcus, pp. 73–74. Marcus idealizes the Sex Pistols and, indeed, the whole sleazoid punk movement, making them bear more cultural weight than is reasonable, but he gets right the sense that the audience participated in the shock and was an integral part of it. He also seems correct in claiming that punks had seen clearly the no-future society populated by "zombie counterpersons, shoppers, bureaucrats" into which they had been born. They had "heard the news" (p. 75) and it was desolating. Julien Temple's 1999 documentary of the Sex Pistols, *The Filth and The Fury*, reveals that the infamous language which resulted in their being banned in the UK, was weak, and rather childish, by today's robust standards. However, it also demonstrates that their attitude, their mindset, in effect, was deeply hostile to authority. Considered carefully, Temple's documentary supports Marcus's thesis.

32   Marcus reproduces, as a marginal note, a photograph that purports to represent the corpse of Rosa Luxemburg after it had been fished from a Berlin canal in 1919 (p. 117). If any analogy were sought, it would have to be that of a piece of human excrement. No doubt, the analogy must have been perfectly clear to Marcus. The photographic representation of human corpses has not been widely discussed. For a brief but incisive account, see Georgieff.

33   Spinrad's questionnaire reveals that only forty-six of his respondents would even answer the question, "Do you like to watch it go down after a flush?" Of these, only twenty-eight percent said that they did. This might indicate the pervasive hold of early toilet training in American culture. Many cultures, as anyone who has travelled in the north of Europe knows, distinguish between public and private excrement. Spinrad's respondents, more than half of whom refused to answer the question, seem to show considerable hesitation even in the matter of private excrement (p. 13).

34   The Menippean tradition is not only long but extremely varied (Eugene P. Kirk; see also Sherbert). For an acute but easily digestible scholarly introduction to the Menippean, see Branham's and Kinney's edition of Petronius' *Satyrica* (pp. xiii–xxvi). For a discussion of Sherbert's theories, see Milowicki, "The Quest for Genre."

35 Hughes observes that the "idea that the *avant-garde* and the bourgeoisie were natural enemies is one of the least useful myths of modernism." (*The Shock of the New*, p. 373). This might strike the literary scholar as a bit precious. Of course, the bourgeoisie provided most of the audience for painting, a great deal of it for literature and some of the audience for cabaret and performance art, but the notion that complicity (in buying the product) cancels antagonism seems simplistic. The literary audiences that read Joyce, Miller, Céline, Burroughs and Pynchon, and today writers such as David Foster Wallace, Bret Easton Ellis, Will Self or Matthew Klam, have been both pleased and revolted by what they have read. Hughes (as does Miller) misses entirely the point that Bataille makes over and over again: self-exposure to filth will be exciting as transgression, but it may also be self-enhancing.

36 Bürger sees Europe's revolutionary background as fundamentally Marxist. Marcus sees the same background as primarily anarchist. I try to see it as turmoil in which one movement gains momentum only to lose it to another. Revolution was needed, but whose was it to be? To what ends? With what limitations? In such social turbulence, Dada might have seemed rather cautious, even a displacement. Even after 1917, anarchism was far from finished (playing, for instance, a major role in the Spanish civil war). In 1999, during the protests in Seattle against the policies of multinational corporations, embodied in the World Trade Organization, anarchists sem to have spearheaded the action (David Samuels). In an anarchist worldview, repression, with its inevitable regulation and social codification, is always the enemy. It can be fought with oppositional graffiti, jokes or other marginal forms of writing back. It can also be fought on the level of political resistance with a terrorist's "gesture." For a discussion of Chambers' distinction between opposition and resistance, see Wilson, "Graffiti Become Terror."

37 This is Flaubert's advice to his friend Ernest Chevalier on March 15, 1842 (Flaubert Correspondences 1: 97), cited in Corbin, p. 219. Feces played an important role in Flaubert's "Rabelaisian schoolboy verbal revolt; he even referred to it in the polite formulas with which he ended his correspondence, although its potentially scandalous effect was diminished by the involvement of his male correspondents in the same game" (Corbin, p. 219). Corbin magnificently subtitles the section in which he discusses Flaubert's appropriation of excrement as a revolutionary aesthetic in a deodorized Paris the "Libertinage of the Nose" (pp. 218–21). It is worth observing that Dominique Laporte dedicates the *History of Shit* to Flaubert "for the beautiful explanation."

38 "Cloacal obsession" is H.G. Wells' phrase to describe Joyce's writing in *A Portrait of The Artist as a Young Man*. His review appeared in the *Nation* on February 24, 1917; it is reprinted in Deming, pp. 86–88. In his "Powers of Ordure," Anspaugh demonstrates the even more accurate bearing of the phrase on Joyce's later fiction, including *Finnegans Wake*. Wells was certainly "right" (as Richard Ellmann notes), but the point ought to be that Joyce was within, smack in, a modern tradition (including Flaubert, though hardly beginning with him) that reflects the freshly acquired symbolic potency of human excrement in a hygienic and deodorized world.

39   Bakhtin, *Problems of Dostoevsky's Poetics*, pp. 107–22. Bakhtin also links Menippean to the Socratic dialogue as modes of discourse that seek truth "counterposed to *official monologism*, which pretends to *possess a ready-made truth*" (p. 110). Another connection looks ahead to medieval carnival and the exuberance of laughter. Carnival was founded upon "laughter and the laughing word" to which "almost everything was permitted" (*The Diologic Imagination*, p. 72). Carnival was always, Bakhtin argues, the "laughter of the people," triumphant but also "mocking, deriding" (*Rabelais and His World*, p. 4). For a discussion of laughter and the concept of carnival, see McKenna. Menippean satire looked towards the Socratic dialogue because its objective was truth, but ahead to carnival laughter because its mode was laughter through mockery and derision. A history of shock art would have to include carnival, but it should begin with Menippus. For a study of satire that considers Bakhtin's theories, see Peto. On the relationship of Menippean to the Cynic School, and in particular the charismatic figure of Diogenes of Sinope, see Sloterdijk, especially Chapters 5 to 7.

40   Genette, pp. 168, 259. I discuss transgression as a primarily narrative concept elsewhere. See *In Palamedes' Shadow*, pp. 29–34.

41   For a discussion of heuristic play within a tradition begun by Nietzsche, see Spariosu, *Dionysus Reborn*. Spariosu's discussion reaches from Hans Vaihinger's notion of scientific fictions to Paul Feyerabend's proposals for an anarchistic epistemology, but the central figure is Nietzsche and the idea of exploratory play. Edwards, writing from (significantly) within a Nietzschean/ Derridean framework, locates play's "enabling factor" in the "principle or energy and difference" (p. 70). See also Spariosu's *The Wreath of Wild Olive*.

42   Walton defines make-believe as games founded upon "one species of imaginative activity; specifically, they are exercises of the imagination involving *props*." Representational works of art are, in Walton's thinking, "continuous" with children's games of make-believe (pp. 12, 11). In a children's game, a bush or a stone might be a prop, but in an adult game of make-believe a dramatic production or a novel would be props. In shock theatre, an actor defecating upon the stage, rubbing his crotch, breaking something (his guitar, say) or sticking pins through his cheeks and lips would all be props to help the audience imagine a certain kind of world. Roger Caillois identifies "mimicry" as one of the four basic categories of play (along with *agôn*, *alea*, and *ilinx*—competition, chance and vertigo), presupposing a closed, imaginary "universe." The rule of a game of mimicry consists, he writes, "in the actor's fascinating the spectator, while avoiding an error that might lead the spectator to break the spell" (pp. 19, 23). (For a discussion of Caillois' theories, see Edwards, pp. 20–21.) What Walton adds to Caillois' analysis is the recognition that make-believe can be far more extensive than theatre, or even all formal games of make-believe, and invade every aspect of human life. The punk movement that Marcus celebrates created many small, disgusting fictional worlds both in nightclubs and on the streets. As make-believe, shock is radically transgressive because it crosses boundaries that appear to divide fiction from life, cabaret from street. Even a tattoo, glimpsed hurriedly and at an angle, could invite you into a small world that you would prefer not to have visited.

43 The artist was Stuart Brisley and the venue for his performance was a museum in Stockholm in the 1970s (Kirchner, p. 73). Kirchner makes the obvious connection with Kafka's story, "The Hunger Artist." Notice how shock enters into the experience of Brisley's Menippean art at multiple angles, right up until the final invitation to share (as in a communal feast) the rotten meat.

44 Kirchner, p. 76. Nitsch's "actions" have become more elaborate, but the germ of them all can be seen in this description of an early experiment. It would be possible to find many examples of recent shock performance art in which everything is done, including eating feces, just so long as it is known to be taboo. In that sense, I take Nitsch to be a synecdoche for performance art in general. However, it is worth noting the existence of the Tokyo Shock Boys who toured Australia while I was there. One member lets a scorpion walk around inside his mouth, others, in classic geek fashion, drink various undrinkable liquids (such as dishwashing detergent), and one member sucks milk up through his nose and then squirts it out through his eyes (Bendeich, p. D2). It is difficult to suppose that anyone would ever watch performance art of this type unless he or she found the acts disgusting (and horrifying), but also thought that the transgressions were stimulating, exciting, perhaps liberating.

45 McEvilley, p. 72.

46 Kirchner, p. 79. Kirchner observes that photographs of Nitsch's performances are often more shocking than the performances themselves since people who look at the photographs "assume that the event was real" (p. 79). Representations of filth, if they are recognized as representations, do not produce the same effects as actual-world events. However, I owe to Lars-Henrik Schmidt, Aarhus University, the provocative point that representations may be *more* disgusting than in-the-world objects since they are often more vivid, more focussed and erase the world's "noise." I discuss this problem further in Chapter 3.

47 Foster, p. 157.

48 McEvilley, p. 73.

49 "His last public performance, at the Freedom Theatre in December [1994], involved generous amounts of blood, piss, shit and vomit. As he said himself, he loved to cause a stink whenever possible" (Burston and Swindells, p. 21). Burston and Swindells do not comment upon the morality of expelling, while dying of AIDS, bodily fluids upon an audience. No doubt, the only possible answer would be to say that punk, and its latter-day derivatives, are nothing if not transvaluative. Bowery's most enduring monument, impossible within the fleeting scope of performance art, will be as a model in Lucien Freud's painting.

50 Martin Pops, p. 37. Pops describes Manzoni as "my favorite *merdista*." He claims that Salvador Dali glazed his own turds into artworks. Pops indicates some of the conceptual background for this extreme, perhaps carnivalesque, act of making art out of the body's wastes: Duchamp's 1917 *Fountain* and, above all, Charles Marie Huysman's 1884 novel *À rebours* (translated, in 1959, as *Against Nature*) in which the protagonist, Des Esseintes, discovers "the last aberration from the natural that could be committed" (p. 39). There is a fascinating history to the uses of human feces in art. As Bürger says of the avant-garde, no one should "confuse the theory of a given field with a description of the way it presents itself. A theory of the novel is not a history of the novel, a theory of the avant-garde no history of the European avant-garde movements" (p. l). (On the cultural history of shit, its many uses and disguises, see LaPorte.) Compared to the deeply shocking uses of actual human feces in performance art or even the representation of feces in literature and film, the corresponding aesthetic uses of urine must seem comparatively mild. The immense controversy surrounding Andres Serrano's *Piss Christ* (1987), in which a crucifix is immersed in urine, stems from the act of (perceived) sacrilege, the transgression of the boundaries that protect the sacred, not from the inherently disgusting nature of human urine.

51   Parfrey, "G.G. Allin," p. 45. A fan who was present at Allin's final concert, describes the gig as follows: "GG started his show the usual way, with whisky, X-Lax, & lord only knows what other control substances :-) After a while, GG gets wild & starts doing his thing — the clothes come off & he's shitting all over the stage! He picks up his turds & throws them into the audience. What he doesn't throw into the crowd he EATS himself!!! At that point something snaps. GG, covered with sweat/whisky/shit, flips & runs out into the audience attacking everyone." Theodore Kleinman (*alt.punk*). Allin then ran out into the street, still attacking people, and disappeared. He was found the next morning OD'd on heroin. Some reports claim that at his funeral Allin's fans ripped open the coffin and attempted to inject his corpse with heroin.

52   Parfey, "G.G. Allin," p. 46. Allin's fans were devoted and, like Allin himself, "scummy and proud." A fan writes: "You know, some of us loved GG's work and were sad when he died ... GG changed the face of punk rock forever, like it or not. The number of people/bands he influenced is immense, and if you like any kind of punk rock, chances are some of your favorite bands learned quite a bit from GG!" (Edward Hirsch).

53   With acute narrative insight, Bret Easton Ellis makes Patrick Bateman, his psychotic narrating character in *American Psycho*, a devotee of gothic rock, new wave and Peter Gabriel. However, Bateman enjoys hearing this music only on CDs. This deft touch in characterization underscores his alienation from life, his remoteness from all aesthetic experience (other than as collection) and his affinity with a music intended to embody cultural estrangement. It also shows how attenuated, and distantly removed from its punk origins, the popified new wave became. Tanner points out the general triumph of simulacra over reality in the novel. "Throughout *Psycho*," she writes, "traces of sentience are overwhelmed by representations that present the human body as a set of veins, internal organs, or bones that respond to pressure, heat, or electricity in various ways" (p. 99). In this sense, Bateman's preference for CDs over live music is only a single, out of a coherent nexus, character trait. In Mary Harron's 2000 film version of *American Psycho*, Patrick Bateman (played by Christian Bale) listens to CDs constantly, earphones almost glued to his ears. The soundtrack to the film, a medley of 1980s pop music, suits Bateman well.

54   Punk, at least the kind the history of which Marcus writes, has become widely diffused. It is a set of gestures, a number of mannerisms. It is a fashion, a style and a way of drawing cartoons nearly as much as a way of making music. In London, it is still possible to see "punks" (if a purple Mohawk, a lip pin or a nose stud makes a punk) as a part of the tourist scene. Popular histories have been written for thrill/grunge-seeking tourists.

55   It is worth noting that the twentieth-century art that has received the most denunciation has been formal, avant-garde art of the kind Bürger's argument pivots upon. The Nazi attack on "degenerate art" was concentrated upon formal attributes. In 1993, the Los Angeles County Museum of Art held an exhibition on "degenerate art" which, though many works contained shocking images (Dix's paintings of the Great War, for example), fundamentally explored the formalist experimentations in (what one now calls) modern art. See Barron et al.

56   Actually, I saw the Jim Rose Circus twice in 1994. I first went to see it when it played at the University of Alberta to an audience (except for myself and a colleague) exclusively made up of high-school and university students, mostly in punk drag. A little over two months later, on July 31, I stumbled upon it playing to a pub audience in Coogee, an ocean-side eastern suburb of Sydney, Australia. The acts were a bit grosser, less curtailed by regulations (Mr. Lifto, a fakir who lifts objects by pins piercing his flesh, no longer hid his *coup de foudre*, lifting a heavy weight with the tip of his penis, behind a backlit sheet), but the circus was still basically simulation and (good circus) fakery. Nothing actually took place even remotely equivalent to a G.G. Allin act, but both audiences seemed happy to pretend that it had. Chainsaws were used extensively (reminding its tuned-in audiences of a popular horror film motif), but they were kept on neutral and could not have hurt anyone. When the performers rushed out into the audience carrying their roaring chainsaws, they were restaging a traditional clown routine, the chainsaws substituting for flappers and rattles. the Jim Rose Circus, though packaged as a disgusting experience, punk in some sense, is in fact an excellent circus with traditional acts. It is possible to acquire a video of the Jim Rose Circus Sideshow performing at the Moore Theater, Seattle, Washington on February 5, 1993 (C & P Productions, Inc.).

57   In the Australian performance and on the video, the geek, "Mr. Enigma," also ate maggots and small bugs. This dimension of the act was prohibited in Edmonton because of by-laws protecting animals (including maggots) against cruelty.

58   *Sensation: Young British Artists from the Saatchi Collection.* When the exhibition was shown in London at the Royal Academy, it was a bit controversial. The US response was as predictable as it was political; that is, like the art itself, it was a kind of pastiche (Schjedahl). Shortly after the official denunciation of the *Sensation* show in New York, the Australian National Gallery in Canberra cancelled the exhibition. Australian commentators believed that the New York politics had invaded their country and excessively influenced the gallery's conservative board (*Sydney Morning Herald*, November 29, 1999). Interestingly, at the time that *Sensation* was becoming a political sensation, the Canadian artist Tamara Zeta Sanowar-Makhan had her work, "Ultra-Maxi Priest," a robe constructed from feminine hygiene products, banned from exhibition in Ontario

(Deirdre Kelly). Art shows are often controversial, occasionally banned, but that does not mean that they have actually shocked anyone or that they have done so in proportion to the expressed outrage.

59 Corbin, p. 144. Deodorization became one of the important social issues in France throughout the nineteenth century. Its origin lay in the heightened public consciousness that the Revolution had bequeathed to the French middle class. Whenever you spray deodorant under your arms, think of yourself as a child of the Revolution, not merely of Madison Avenue. For a discussion of the growth of the sewer system in Paris during the nineteenth century, and the fascination it exerted over French intellectuals, such as Victor Hugo, see Radford.

60 Camille Paglia has insisted repeatedly that the '60s was both a revolutionary and a romantic period. (As were, one might add, the 1790s in France.) In an essay-memoir on Milton Kessler, she writes of the "pure Romanticism of the Sixties." She remembers it as a time marked by its energy and its liberation of human life from the moral constraints of the previous generation. She also thinks of the sixties as a failed revolution (*Sex, Art, and American Culture*, pp. 130-1, 294-5).

61 Disgust is a defence mechanism, along with shame, morality, horror and pain, that "protects us" from certain sexual aims. The sexual drive is difficult to master; evidently, mastering it requires powerful weapons. Disgust is one such weapon and, in Freud's view (perhaps because it involves vomiting), extremely powerful. For example, Freud observes that bringing the mucous membranes of the lips together in kissing is not a perversion, but that bringing the mucous membranes of the lips into contact with the partner's genitals *is* a perversion. "Those who condemn the other practices [cunnilingus and fellatio] as being perversions, are giving way to an unmistakable feeling of *disgust*, which protects them from accepting sexual aims of that kind." Freud then notes an obvious but important truth: the limits of such disgust are "often purely conventional." He gives the instance of a man wishing to kiss a girl's lips passionately while being disgusted at the idea of using her toothbrush though "there are no grounds for supposing that his own oral cavity, for which he feels no disgust, is any cleaner than the girl's" (Freud, "The Sexual Aberrations," pp. 151-52). Freud is always interesting on disgust. In Chapter 2, I discuss further his theory of the formation of disgust in childhood experience.

62 Bataille, *The Impossible*, p. 160.

63 Obeyesekere, pp. 6-7. Obeyesekere explicitly notes that he remembered Freud's paper "Medusa's Head" in which "he links the fear of Medusa to the terror of castration" (p. 6). I shall discuss the Medusa (after all, the Hydra's grandmother) later in Chapters 3 and 5 with a special attention to Freud's notion that the female genitalia excite fear in men because they evoke fears associated with male castration. I will also discuss Creed's revisionary analysis of Freud on this point in her *The Monstrous Feminine*.

64 Once settled down into a professional life, the difficulties of fieldwork over (at least for a time), the experience of disgust will become anecdotal, material for lighthearted professional conversation. Jean Dibernardi observes how she was "at a dinner once where we just went around the table telling stories of the worst bathrooms we'd ever seen, just one story after another. It's most often just funny. I had a friend who worked

in a tribal village in northern Thailand, where the rule was, there were no toilets—you just went out into the bush. And this pig would follow them out there, you know, because pigs eat excrement. It was very efficient recycling" (Kapalka, p. 171). On the differences between an anthropologist's fieldwork and his/her institutional work and life, see Geertz, *Works and Lives*. Geertz confronts head-on the distinctions between the tourist, the ordinary traveller and the anthropologist.

65   From Herodotus (at least), travellers have commented upon how disgusting the habits of other peoples seem. Having walked through public areas for excretion or eaten food that is too greasy, too spicy or too rotten will cause most western travellers to wax venomously hostile in their anecdotes. Travel can also, if only rarely, bring home how disgusting your own habits may seem. A number of years ago, travelling from Sydney to Panama on a French ship that carried passengers and copra (desiccated coconut), I visited Port Villa (before it became simply Villa) in Vanuatu. It was then a small tropical port in the New Hebrides governed in condominium by the United Kingdom and France. I went ashore with a few English friends to find a Vietnamese restaurant. To our shock, we were refused service in the first two that we visited. As the only member of the group who spoke French, I was asked to find out why restaurants that were only partially full would refuse service to travellers. A pretty teenage Vietnamese girl explained to me that it was because Europeans stank. We had innocently walked into the stereotypical oriental aversion for European body odours (thought to arise from the heavy consumption of meat). We had become, clearly enough that we were each shamefully aware of the fact, mere objects of disgust.

66   Pops, p. 59. Pops cites Simeons (p. 89) on the terror-response of involuntary shitting in human beings and in animals.

67   The first four are Kristeva's examples (pp. 53, 13–18).

68   I owe the expression "carnivalesque emblem" to Gary Sherbert, whose work on Menippean satire and genre theory has engaged me at several points. Guy Trebay mentions a young man in the L.A. punk scene with a "large blackwidow spider on his forehead." He goes on to note that "even among the heavily inked, facial markings are considered radical gestures" (Trebay). The face is the most public of all "public skin," possessing more sanctions, aesthetic, religious and social, than one could easily list. Kant's example of the contradiction between a "free" and a "dependent" beauty is, precisely, a tattoo on a human face. According to Kant, the design of a tattoo might be beautiful in itself, but once it is inked into a human skin it becomes, he observes, a dependent form, to be judged in relation to another kind of beauty, free or self-subsisting, such as a human face itself (Kant, p. 73.) A facial tattoo is, in western culture at least, a fundamental, indeed outrageous, method for making a statement. As Trebay's anecdote suggests, and against the grain of my parable, a facial tattoo, in particular one of an object as popularly loathsome as an image of spider, would normally constitute a gesture of self-distancing, a voluntary move to incorporate the bearer within an outlaw sub-group or to deny his/her membership in straight society. A facial tattoo would seem to exhibit "spoiled identity" in very forceful manner (Goffman, *Stigma*). Rephrasing Goffman in Kristeva's terms, one could say that spoiled identity is the deliberate (even ponderous) acting out of narcissistic *jouissance* in a person's own abject state.

69 *The Winter's Tale*, 2.1.39–45; *The Riverside Shakespeare*, p. 1576.

70 Chavalier and Gheerbrant, pp. 60–62.

71 Perhaps shame and disgust are not equal partners in their dance. Disgust may lead, shame follow. Freud, as I shall note later, links the two as co-partners in restraining the sexual drive. Anyone interested in exploring the partnership between disgust and shame should read Salman Rushdie's *Shame*. Rushdie makes clear the distinction between individual and collective shame. The same distinction must hold for disgust: in some worlds, such as that which Rushdie creates, an entire family might be shamed because of a single individual's disgusting presence or acts; a family, or even a nation, may come to seem disgusting, but its shame felt only by a single member who has escaped the collective tribalism.

72 Sanders, p. 58.

73 Gray, p. 11.

74 Sanders, p. 135.

75 "Instead of elaborate body painting, we have lipstick and eyeshadow. (Red lips like red vulva, eyes big and dark in arousal.) We have lingerie, neckties, tight jeans, high heels, anorexia and liposuction" (Tisdale, p. 113). Although scarification, branding and piercing (or other forms of bodily modification other than tattooing) do not figure largely in this book, they do, clearly and with great emphasis, represent the general problem of disgust. (For a discussion of body piercing, see Malloy.) A recent feminist film brilliantly captures the enthusiasm with which previously marginalised, or prohibited, practices of bodily modification can be embraced. See Leslie Asako Gladsjö, *Stigmata: The Transfigured Body* (1992) [27 minutes]. The film shows several varieties of bodily modification, including branding. There are interviews with several women who tattoo and incise bodies. In voice-over, Kathy Acker comments provocatively. She equates sexuality with play and suggests a way of reading voluntary bodily mutilation that the film only partly supports: that the women who seek mutilation are actually playing, exploring the possibilities of their own bodies (and of their own capacity to endure pain). One woman is shown having her labia pierced by multiple rings. She screams in bloodcurdling ways, but also seems happy about it. Other women are shown having tattoos on buttocks, brandings, cuttings (a fish is incised on a woman's back and the artist keeps a blood image on paper for her collection), and stapling. The staples are excruciating—the young woman screams and appears to be dazed by physical pain—but are used, exultantly, to hang ornaments upon. A tattooist insists that this is how women "regain their power" or "regain their sexuality." The emergence of piercing, scarification and branding as modes of sexual exploration, or even of personal heuristics, parallels the more evident explosion of tattoos as cherished personal markings among groups of people, middle-class and professional, who would not have considered the practice only a few years ago. Holding a minority position on this issue, John Gray denies that the "new wave" movement in tattooing has actually occurred: "Rumors of imminent respectability have been chasing the tattoo for a century. When respectable people acquire tattoos, and they do, it's not because the practice has become respectable: it's because the recipient wishes inwardly to be *not* respectable, seeking out acts of private outrage that won't adversely affect the career path" (p. 15).

However, a great deal of evidence, from San Francisco, from London and many other places, suggests that Gray (sticking perhaps too closely to Vancouver) has missed something important. DeMello does not share Gray's provincialism. She refers explicitly to the "Tattoo Renaissance" (p. 137). Tattoos, she observes, "can now represent spirituality, a connection to the earth, an instinctive drive, or a connection to the primitive" (p. 190; on tattoos as agencies of self-transformation, see pp. 143–51).

76   Goffman, *Stigma*, pp. 43–45.

77   Gray, p. 119. Often it will be the "persona" only that is tattooed. The stigma symbols that performers flaunt often must be symbols in play only, public intimations of the make-believe world that they create. If you learned that the much-tattooed lead guitarist (say) of a particularly "neo-savage" group read Heidegger in the evenings (instead of doing drugs), you might be surprised, but not *that* surprised.

78   The most obvious conventions for embedding smaller narratives in traditional, pre-novel narrative are extended, or Homeric, similes and ekphrases. Both embed distinct places, times and narrative agents within a larger narrative context. That is, they evoke, with only minimal narrative elaboration, other, often both distant and dissimilar, fictional worlds. Ekphrasis, a narrative convention the history of which stretches back to Homer and forwards from him, through the Renaissance, to the modern novel with its descriptions of photos, films and TV, provides a paradigmatic instance. Achilles' shield (*Iliad* XVIII), or Aeneas' (*Aeneid* VIII), carry embossed scenes that, in being described, point towards other fictional worlds that can be recognized as such. Aeneas' shield, for example, parallels the ekphrastic murals that Virgil describes in Book I: the murals evoke analeptic scenes from the Trojan War while the shield carries proleptic devices that call to mind the subsequent history of Rome. In English literature, the most famous ekphrases are probably those in Spenser's *The Faerie Queene*, Shakespeare's *The Rape of Lucrece*, and Keats' *Ode on a Grecian Urn*. All share the common convention of describing a work of art (tapestry, painting or urn), in some sense pictorial, that the imagination can transform into something larger, more fully visualized. Cribbing from a famous episode in *Don Quixote* (II: 26), I like to call this narrative phenomenon the "paradox of the puppet show." A puppet show, like an Elizabethan dumbshow, will be realistically primitive, its narrative elaboration, in plot, setting and characterization, will be quite minimal. Furthermore, the inadequacy of the props, whether actors or scenery, will offer little help to the imagination. The conventions will be perceptibly bare. Nonetheless, as Don Quixote's adventure with Master Peter's puppet show indicates, such literature can be powerfully evocative. The experience of minimalness, as readers or viewers are caught up within the illusion of primitive textual forms, can be overwhelming. The most minimal narrative can, it seems, entrap an audience. A tattoo is only another mode of narrative minimalness. In a work of literature, or in a film such as Scorsese's *Cape Fear*, the representation of a tattoo functions as does an ekphrasis in traditional literature.

79   Rabinowitz, pp. 148–54. Tattoos are certainly not the only mode of emblematic narrative, but they do constitute a particularly striking instance. Pictures of all kinds, cartoons or Renaissance frescos, tell stories; they do so, in part at least, because they can evoke recognizable story matrices. In that respect, a tattoo is similar to any other likeness: an image to be interpreted, a challenge to the reader's intelligence and knowledge.

80 Stern and Stern, p. 283.

81 There is an important distinction between traditional transgressive tattooing (nearly always stigma symbols) and new wave "customized" tattoos. Looking at back issues of *Outlaw Biker's Tattoo Revue Specials* might make the distinction clear since the mix of tattoos represented covers a wide spectrum. The Sterns do a good job of indicating the bad taste, indeed the appalling vulgarity, of much transgressive tattooing. (However, I disagree with them, as I do with John Gray, that the movement away from such tattoos was a "fad" that "faded" away in the 1970s and early '80s. On this point, I accept DeMello's analysis.) Their account of the annual Am Jam Tattoo Expo in Schenectady, New York, should cause almost anyone's gorge to crack. An early scene in Bob Brooks' 1981 film *Tattoo*, showing a corpulent young man having a spread-open vagina tattooed onto his shaven left armpit, captures the vulgar dimension of ordinary transgressive tattooing. Matthew Gwyther's photo-article in the London *Observer Magazine* provides evidence that art-tattoos are doing well, innovative and often quite beautiful, in the United Kingdom. Most of the tattoos reproduced in Grognard and Lazi are customized and demonstrate personal commitments. Gwyther also indirectly reveals that tattooists may now have names such as "Ian of Reading" (recalling a medieval craftsman) rather than, say, Fat Rick, Sailor Jerry or Hanky Panky. My interests are primarily focussed upon new wave tattoos because they are voluntary and private (usually reflected upon and carefully chosen) symbols of self-enhancement. Diane Ackerman refers to people who have tattoos as having adorned themselves "with magic emblems the Altimira of the flesh." She refers to a collection of some three hundred human skins, all bearing the tattoos of masters, that Tokyo University owns and comments that to enter "this chamber of skins must fill one with shock and wonder" (*A Natural History*, p. 100). Personal experience tells me that many people are extremely proud of their tattoos and have chosen them with care. For an instructive anthropological study (accepting the Foucauldian principle that only the presence of an established discourse makes a "community" possible) of the people who constitute the "tattoo community," see DeMello.

82 Neumann, pp. 177, 223.

83 Lessing, p. 532. I discuss male gender prejudice, as the basis for transforming women into pleasurable disgust-objects, in Chapter 3 and Doris Lessing's novel, as a representation of the slide from self-disgust into abjection, in Chapter 7.

84 Barthes, p. 3. The world's pervasive micro-narrativity that Barthes sees everywhere cannot be easily grasped. Every tattoo, even quite abstract ones, tells more than one story.

85 The analysis of minimal narratives takes two forms. First, there is the effort, empirically unlimited, to *find* minimal narratives and to collect them. They can be amusing, puzzling even, and perhaps paradoxical. Second, narrative theorists have occasionally undertaken the quest to locate a narrative that would be co-extensive with its own story. In such a narrative the story's narremes, its kernel events, would be told in chronological order, its characters and aspects of its setting reduced to simple deictics and bare agential functions. On the second point, see Umberto Eco's discussion of Alphonse Allais' "A Very Parisian Drama" (pp. 200–60, 263–66). Eco analyses how close a narrative may come to this zero degree of difference and yet how impossible it is to collapse fully the distance: the problem of minimal expansion (or maximal collapse) reveals the distance between story and narrative. Two basic propositions in recent narrative theory hold: 1) that narratives may be *very* minimal and that micro-narrativity is everywhere to be heard in human culture; 2) that the difference between a story and its narrative expression can never be fully collapsed. Pavel argues (correctly I think) that small narratives (measured neither in quantity of words nor in length of time indicated, but in numbers of distinct events and characters) may be more *complex* than vastly expanded ones (pp. 94–95). Colombo's *Worlds in Small* anthologizes 104 minimal narratives, one of which is (leaving out its necessary title) only a single letter long, but the scope of possible collection would be limited only by the constrictions, if any, upon the human imagination.

86   Beckett, *Waiting for Godot*, p. 25.

Chapter 2 ❧ Its Stench

1   Gass, *Habitations*, p. 121. Gass has Freud in mind. I have slightly bent his words for calculated advantage.

2   Bataille, "Cleanliness Prohibitions," p. 70.

3   Black, pp. 228–34.

4   Diesing, p. 31.

5   Black, p. 229. Black lists five conditions for the use of a theoretical model: 1) there is an original field of investigation in which some facts have been established; 2) a need is felt "for further scientific mastery of the original domain"; 3) some entities belonging to a "relatively unproblematic, more familiar, or better-organized secondary domain" are described; 4) there are available explicit or implicit rules of correlation for translating propositions about the secondary domain into statements about the original domain; 5) inferences made in the secondary domain are translated by means of the rules of correlation and checked against what is known in the original domain. Disgust would be the original domain while moral philosophy, social theory, psychoanalysis and Sartrean phenomenology constitute secondary domains available for theoretical modelling. The theory of fictional worldhood which I invoke to account for a primary domain of disgust motifs that call out for interpretation, such as tattoos, is itself dependent upon two secondary domains: the theory of play and the theory of the imagination (neither of which I attempt to develop fully in this book).

6   On the function of models developed for the social sciences, including prediction, see Diesing, pp. 108–14. David F. Greenberg observes that the "broader the scope of predictions, and the greater their accuracy, the more satisfactory a classification system will seem." He then adds that, using this criterion, "our contemporary system of classifying someone as either homosexual or heterosexual on the basis of his or her past sexual history leaves a good deal to be desired" (p. 491).

7   Kekes, p. 436.; the phrase "the seductiveness of moral disgust" is Michael Ignatieff's. There are moments, faced with ethnic cleansing or the extravagant brutalities of tribalism, when it might seem inevitable to settle for a moral judgement rather than make the effort to understand.

8   Miller, p. 251.

9   Miller, p. 237. Miller assumes that contempt is very similar to disgust, at the very least a "cousin." As I have already noted, the argument in this book will show that contempt is a psycho-intellectual affect building upon disgust much as outrage does upon more anger. It is also a very actable, or make-believe affect. That is a point that Miller either denies or ignores.

10   Kekes, pp. 436–37. Kekes bases much of discussion around this point on Devlin's *The Enforcement of Morals*. The first edition of Lord Devlin's book was highly controversial; the second edition includes rejoinders to his critics. The controversy is reviewed in Mitchell.

11   Miller, p. 194.

12   Miller, p. 188.

13   Much has been said about the disgusting "tribalism" of recent ethnic wars, such as Rwanda, Bosnia, Kosovo, East Timor, Sierra Leone and Afghanistan. The genocidal wars in Bosnia and Rwanda resemble on a collective scale the unrestrained acts of madness. East Timor, under Indonesian misrule, was positively Hobbesian. Sierra Leone, in mid 2000, exceeded Hobbes' imagination. I shall make no effort to discuss any of the recent writing on nationalism, tribalism and genocide, but I shall cite one instance of the United Nations following a deliberate strategy of displaying theatrical disgust. It may stand as a synecdoche. In October 1999, the official news agency of the interim government of Kosovo, Kosovarpress, published an article denouncing two Kosovar newspapermen as "pro-Serb vampires." The same article went on to accuse them of being mafiosi, of having committed unpunished criminal acts and of actually delivering "water to the arch-criminal Milosevic's mill." The United Nations officials, understanding that these accusations were virtually public calls for execution, adopted a policy of refusing to deal with the interim government for a short, punitive period. "'We didn't take calls, denied meetings to register our disgust,' said one UN official" (Finn).

14   Miller, p. 194.

15   Miller treats the corresponding theoretical positions with disdain as mere "academic celebrations." It is clear, I think, that he has no interest in either art or literature and finds the idea of transgression, whether in literature or personal life, to be upsetting to his own moral-legal argument. It may be for that reason alone that he systematically conflates in-the-world things and their representations. Kekes believes that disgust has not been "much discussed in philosophical literature, or, indeed, anywhere else" (p. 431). He observes that there is no entry under "disgust" in the various reference works that philosophers consult. However, if he had looked into the reference works that psychologists consult, he would have found many entries. In literature, the case is fuzzier: disgust shows up in a great deal of literature, indirectly as a part of the setting

or directly as a character's reaction within its fictional world, but the study of literature has not had much to say about disgust either as a human affect or as a literary motif. Discussions of this neglected topic can be found in several places; see Anspaugh, Gass, Pops, and Rushdy.

16 Catherine Wilson, p. 183.

17 Kekes, p. 433. People who "do not feel disgust at the sort of experiences listed above are in some sense diminished. They have been de-sensitized, brutalized, hardened in a way that sets them apart for the rest of us" (p. 334). The experience of diminishment, or of sensing oneself as having been diminished, constitutes an important problem. Clearly, those who hate pornography and violence in TV or film also argue that certain experiences, on the level of *representation*, will de-sensitize, brutalize and diminish. I would want to argue (against censorship) that such *fictional* experiences are indispensable in learning both what occurs in the world and how to manage affects, such as disgust or desire, and do not, in modifying your understanding of affects, necessarily harden or diminish anyone. Hence the problem of disgust immediately points us towards a fundamental distinction in aesthetics and literary theory: a representation of a thing-in-the-world either is the same (in the sense of having the same properties and of raising the same questions) as the thing represented or it is not. Moralists, such as Miller, Kekes or the Mayor of New York, who hate transgressive art, always prefer to deny the distinction.

18 I shall return to Kekes's notion of deep disgust and his list of disgusting experiences later in the course of discussing the relation between disgust and horror. I leave to one side Kant's argument in the third *Critique* that disgust is, like the sublime in the opposite direction, unrepresentable. Objects and acts that are disgusting, such as human coprophagy, can be (in some sense) represented; it is not certain that the same emotions that would accompany the perception of in-the-world disgusting objects can be represented. Certainly, analogous affects can be. The study of play indicates that there can be play emotions, or emotions that simulate the actual world but only in attenuated forms during play, or even, as in make-believe, played emotions. Derrida comments upon Kant's argument that what is disgusting is "non-transcendentalisable" and "non-idealisable" (Derrida, "Economimesis," especially p. 22). Kristeva accepts Kant's argument and positions the abject in opposition to the sublime. "The abject," she writes, "is edged with the sublime. It is not the same moment on the journey, but the same subject and speech bring them into being" (p. 11). I argue only that *all* representation is different from the thing represented, involving different rhizomes and different sets of questions, but that this difference neither precludes affective response nor prevents learning from the representation. The mind may inhabit many analogical worlds at one time and clearly observe how they bear upon one another. Perniola's *Disgusti* shows that the argument set by Kant continues to engage philosophers.

19 The lighthearted and irreverent respondents to Spinrad's questionnaire do not indicate whether they would wish to eat excrement. It is one thing to talk about, even to read about, human excrement, but quite another to eat it. Surprisingly, for a book that tries to touch all bases (even "coprolite," or fossilized feces), Spinrad's study ignores coprophagy.

20   Feitlowitz shows how the torture, murder and disappearances of the "dirty war" in Argentina became, many years later, a kind of theatre, an oral and written literature that was performed nightly on Argentinian TV, as former torturers seized their day on television. The transformation of secret horror into national representations of horror began when a former naval captain, Adolfo Scilingo, described his role, and the role of the infamous Navy Mechanics School, in the dirty war. He was followed on TV by actual torturers. Feitlowitz captures neatly the whole problem of torture and its representations when she asks, "How even to distinguish such fine gradations of horror?" (p. 209). Conroy makes the point that in any society certain classes of people are considered to be "torturable" and that the legal system, whether judges or juries, will inevitably side with the perpetrators, not the victims (p. 251). In Argentina, the torturable classes included left-leaning people, students and members of labour unions, and even those who simply knew, or were related to, such "acceptable" candidates for torture. For complex reasons, which Feitowitz analyses, they also included Jews (see Timerman). Conroy also explores the divided consciousness of torturers. The best way to punish a torturer, a victim of torture in the former Rhodesia told him, "is not with hatred. If you want to torture a torturer, he said, you do it with love" (p. 176).

21   Kekes, p. 435. Kekes walks a narrow line in his argument in that he seems to claim that he is talking within a context constituted by "contemporary Western sensibility," but his argument repeatedly crosses this frontier and hightails for universality. It makes sense for a philosopher in the Kantian tradition to assert, foregoing evidence, moral propositions that hold for all people. Time and again, discussions of disgust, whether among psychoanalysts, psychologists or philosophers, reveal a profound desire to speak universally. Some social scientists, less intimidated by potential charges of essentialism or biologism, argue unabashedly for the universals in human experience. Brown remarks that the normal skepticism among anthropologists about generalizations constitutes a neglect of human universals and "is the entrenched legacy of an 'era of particularism' in which the observation that something *doesn't* occur among the Bongo Bongo counted as a major contribution to anthropology" (p. 1). Brown links disgust to a particular facial expression which, like some others, is "recognized everywhere" (p. 134). Referring to the research of psychologists, such as Rozin, into the "disgust face" (which would be "recognized everywhere"), Paul Stoller probably expresses a more typical anthropological attitude when he says, "I react negatively to people making claims for universal affect. Okay, say disgust is a universal affect. What does that tell us? Not much. It's sort of like saying marriage is universal. What does *that* tell us?" And Jean Dibernardi adds, "I have a hard time believing in a universal facial expression of disgust" (Kapalka, p. 184).

22   On the construction of desire, see Belsey, *Desire* and *Shakespeare*.

23   Bataille, "Sexuality and Dejecta," p. 63.

24   Berger and Luckmann, p. 129. I have no interest in raising fundamental objections to the principles of social construction. As an explanatory account, it fails to deal adequately with the multitudinous properties of disgust. However, it does answer a number of important questions about the origins and development of affects. The true problems with social construction arise less with its accounts of psycho-socio-cultural behaviours, such as affects and stereotypes, but with its attempts to explain away, or to unmask, science. The claim that physics is as relative, as much a product of human limitations and prejudice, as religion seems to dash far in front of the evidence or even the possibility of a genuinely conclusive argument. On the other hand, the out-and-out rejection of social construction on the grounds, say, that it is "relativistic" does away, perhaps a bit hurriedly, with a number of powerful socio-cultural accounts. For a discussion of the philosophical issues implicit in the social constructionist position and methodology, see Hacking. Hacking argues that Berger and Luckmann do not claim that nothing "can exist unless it is socially constructed" (p. 25). But do they allow that things can be *known* other than through processes of social construction? Hacking wishes to combat strong social constructionist views that would hold that nothing, not even the laws of physics, can exist other than as social constructions. Everything, including Mars and the taste of honey, might have been other than they are. The extreme positions that some social constructionists take puzzle philosophers. Thus to argue that gender is a social construction while sex is a biological given makes a great deal of sense. It is quite a different argument to hold, as do certain radical social comstructionists, that sex itself is a construction or that bodies, distinguished from their learned gestures and behaviours, are constructions. The argument that sciences, even the "hardest" of these, are social constructions, always inventing, never actually discovering, disturbs the mind in a way that the claims for gender does not. If you claim that the "world" is a construct while the "earth" is not, you will make considerable sense. Once you begin claiming that the earth, too, is a social construct, you have engaged in a much more contentious, difficult-to-prove argument. Hacking observes neatly that "social construct" and "real," the two poles of his argument, "do seem terribly at odds with each other" (p. 101).

25   Berger and Luckmann, p. 135.

26   Ross Chambers makes the distinction between recognition and re-cognition ("Rules and Moves"). Recognition is possible because the discourse you inhabit, both the total body of cultural rules and the specific rules that govern a particular type of discourse, actually establish your perception; re-cognition is possible when the experience of the pre-existing discourse allows you the room to manoeuvre. It is difficult, I think, to suppose an interpretive move, or an explanatory hypothesis, that is not contained, at least in its parts, within a prior discourse. It is even more difficult to suppose a fresh move, or an original explanation, that does not move to the margins of, or seek to elude as far as possible, the prior discourse. Like an obscure and scarcely comprehended body of rules, discourse makes possible the moves that a reader can play. If the distinction between recognition and re-cognition seems riddling, it may be solved by a distribution of significance: the universal rules for reading belong to discourse, but they are actualized as moves in the pragmatics of the reader's lifeworld. Recognition, then, emerges from the rules of discourse; re-cognition, from the moves that one, as reader/viewer, can make. Holding this distinction in mind, it will be possible to see disgust both as a general phenomenon of culture in which a spectrum of discursive "rules," functioning like strategic boundary-markers and sanctions (for having crossed over), determine recognition and as an individual practice in which "moves," playing out like tactical decisions that are at once within and against the rules, determine

re-cognition. Disgust is a psycho-visceral, but also a cultural, phenomenon. It is always split between overarching prohibitions and individual reactions (which may incorporate disgust's apparent obverse, desire). The latter seem to register largely on the scale of little in-the-world things, small acts and discrete objects, or else of distinctive motifs. Reading the small and the miniature constitutes a focal problem for a theory of disgust.

27 Scheff, p. 27. Scheff may have had in mind Geertz's phrase "webs of significance." Such semiotic webs underlie cultural meaning (Geertz, *The Interpretation of Culture*, p. 5).

28 It would be easy to imagine a culture in which golden showers were taken as matters of ritual, either as a religious practice or as an initiation into a secret, but officially acknowledged, association. That is, it is possible to imagine a culture the symbolic universe of which allowed a place for golden showers. Berger and Luckmann observe that "monopolistic" societies, such as most western societies have been with regard to sexual practices until quite recently, presuppose considerable "social-structural stability." It is difficult to introduce deviant sexual practices into such a society, but much less hard to maintain them within a "deviant" subculture. "Traditional definitions of reality," they write, "inhibit change" (p. 122). However, it is possible to imagine a culture, western or Euro-American, in which alternative sexual practices underwent a shift in descriptive labelling and became "normal." The history of modern revolutionary movements, Berger and Luckmann write, "affords many illustrations of the transformation of revolutionary intellectuals into 'official' legitimators following the victory of such movements" (p. 127). Furthermore, supposedly deviant acts, such as drinking urine or engaging in golden showers, commonly take place as a matter of hazing and initiation (or building *esprit de corps*) in athletic and military groups. After triumphs, sports teams often express their exuberance by urinating upon one another. (I have been told, but have not witnessed the act, that communal urination after victories is typical among rugby teams.) You can see the now-ritual opening of champagne bottles and dousing one another with bubbly froth as a simple displacement or else a self-censoring of a traditional practice for the purposes of TV. In January 1995, the Canadian Airborne Regiment, an elite commando unit, was exposed to contempt when a video depicting initiation rites was given to the news media. The regiment had already been disgraced for racist behaviour and for having tortured and killed a teenage boy while on duty in Somalia. The video showed more racist acts (the regiment's only black member was shown being led about on a leash like a dog with the phrase "I love the KKK" scrawled in human feces upon his back). The video also revealed that the regiment's initiation rites included "mutual urination" as well as eating vomit, feces and urine. Soldiers ate bread that had been soaked in urine. Canada's defence minister at the time, David Collenette, announced that he had been both "incensed and disgusted" by the video (Sallot).

29 Gender is a particularly fascinating concept. Clearly, it does important conceptual work. The crowded shelves of many bookstores, packed with books dealing in different ways with gender, indicate that such is the common view: gender *is* an important concept. It is the analytic tool that dismantles mystification about sex and sexual nature. It has been one of the triumphs of feminist theory to demystify sexual difference. Little that might once have appeared natural, from alphabets to international zoögraphics, remains so; sexual difference, thanks to feminist theory, now seems as

unnatural, as purely artifactual, as (say) fashion, cuisine or landscape gardening. Gender identity, it is now assumed, is only a construction that has been built up methodically, in each child's consciousness (the voice of hegemonic discourse buzzing in the mind's ear) by culturally sanctioned discursive practices. It is important to recognize the "falsifying metaphysical nature" of socially constructed gender identities since, if for no other reason, nothing new can begin while the old is still accepted as natural or commonsense (Moi, *Sexual/Textual Politics*, p. 13). "In patriarchal societies," Weedon writes, "we cannot escape the implications of femininity. Everything we do signifies compliance or resistance to dominant norms of what it is to be a woman" (pp. 86–87). Butler puts the issue squarely when she writes, "The production of sex *as* the prediscursive ought to be understood as the effect of the apparatus of cultural construction designated by *gender*" (*Gender Trouble*, p. 7). It is important to note the essay, "The Technology of Gender," that opens Teresa de Lauretis' *Technologies of Gender* (pp. 1–30). "Technology," a term indebted to Foucault, signifies the discursive practices in culture that, in some sense, make cyborgs of its members. I shall discuss the concept of a cyborg throughout, but especially in Chapters 4 and 7.

30   Chambers, *Room For Maneuver*, p. xvii.

31   David F. Greenberg, p. 487.

32   "Social construction" is a term that has been, as Ian Hacking argues, overused (p. 3). John Boswell remarks how the doctrinal struggle between social constructionists and essentialists marks a latter-day skirmish in a conflict that is "as old as Plato and as modern as cladism" (p. 90). He associates the two sides with the long, impassioned debate in medieval philosophy between "realists" and "nominalists" over the ontological status of universals. Nominalists (who held that words, not things, exist) argue, in the precise terms of Boswell's discussion, that "categories of sexual preference and behaviour are created by humans and human societies. Whatever reality they have is the consequence of the power they exert in those societies and the socialization processes which make them seem real to persons influenced by them" (Boswell, p. 91). The debate over the "construction of homosexuality" illustrates strikingly a general level of insufficiency in the social-constructionist model.

33   David F. Greenberg, p. 486. Having sorted essentialists and social constructionists into the paradigm of realists (conservatives) and nominalists (radicals), Boswell concludes that they should both "lower their voices" (p. 113). Although most scholars who have studied disgust phenomena would deny that they are "essentialists" (not even moralists would willingly seek to invoke that nasty rap), it will be obvious that many do yearn, however secretly, to speak universally. Even while denying it, they will be seeking a universal, or essential, "disgust-object." Experimental psychologists strike me as yearning for universal disgust-objects, even while proclaiming their value-free methodologies; philosophers yearn for universality and essentialism, even while denying it. (Some, such as Kekes, hardly seem to deny it.) One philosopher, even while arguing that we "can and often do expand our tastes," asserts that both "the conservatism of taste and the reactive feature of revulsion probably contribute to the idea that tastes are brute facts and thus not disputable" (Korshmeyer, p. 93). It might make sense to divide social constructionist into the genuine relativists (who mostly take the beatings in the right-wing press and at the hands of the moralists) and the trans-historicists who find always-recurring elements in both family and society.

34   During a series of lectures on the theory of disgust that I gave in Melbourne, Australia in August 1994, under the auspices of Deakin University Literary Society, I was told several times by members of the audience that small children do not feel disgust. This seems to be the common experience of parents, but I had never heard it expressed so colourfully or with such wealth of anecdote. Freud observes, "The excreta arouse no disgust in children" (*Civilization and Its Discontents*, p. 54 n. 1).

35   Angyal, p. 394. I think it is clear that Angyal writes as if his conclusions applied to all persons whether or not they had been subjects in an experiment. He supports the generalizing tendencies of the argument by citing from secondary materials, in partic- ular the ethnographic (but hardly anthropologic) nineteenth-century study by John Gregory Bourke. Though remarkably Casaubonic in scope, Bourke is still worth reading. He examines a wide range of customs, including medicine as well as cuisine, that involve the ingestion of excrement, both feces and urine. Lewin, writing more than a century later, finds that Bourke "has provided some interesting documentation" (p. 146). Greenblatt has written on Bourke's "dissertation." He looks for evidence in Bourke to help clarify the "complex shaping of a sense of social decency and social horror" (p. 61). It is worth observing that Greenblatt comments on only the opening pages of *Scatalogic Rites* and that he consistently misspells Bourke's title. A similar, if truncated, desire to touch on a wide range of human experience may be seen in Laporte.

36   Fallon and Rozin, p. 28. Angyal claims that "disgust from true wastes is rather universal whereas disgust from other substances varies greatly with the culture" (p. 396). He also asserts, even more emphatically, that in spite of "certain cultural variations, disgust can be regarded as a phenomenon which is universal in the human race" (p. 402). I suspect that many people reflecting upon the nature of disgust, psychologists as well as philosophers, *want* disgust to be universal and are willing to extrapolate athletically to make it so. In a bizarre move in his argument, William Ian Miller claims that a human hair is more disgusting than feces. "Long before the smell of feces, the feel of a hair in the mouth elicits an expression of disgust" (p. 55). This seems to show that Miller thinks, whether well or badly, in terms of essential or universal disgust-objects.

37   Coprophagy is a known human perversion. The history of western literature provides a number of extremely explicit representations of excrement-eating. This literary tradition may show that eating excrement is shocking, but it also shows that the act is known and imaginable. Martin Pops discusses the extravagant coprophagy in the Marquis de Sade's *The Hundred and Twenty Days of Sodom* (pp. 39-41). However, de Sade is outrageously theatrical. Out of sight, most coprophagous acts probably involve both less theatre and more psychological tension. (For what is perhaps the most brilliant representation of coprophagy in contemporary literature, see Pynchon, *Gravity's Rainbow*, pp. 235-36; quoted and discussed in Chapter 3.) All the theatre exists in the narrator's voice which is, as always in Pynchon, at once sly and intricate. Bourke cites a large number of instances of excrement-eating, from many cultures, in which the moti- vation is either culinary or medicinable. Ralph Lewin observes that human excrement retains considerable nutritional value, at least eight percent of the digested food's original calorific content (p. 79). Discussions of coprophagy need to bear in mind that excrement may be eaten for other than reasons of sexual excitement: it can be a food.

If you have eaten tripe and they have not been thoroughly washed, then you have eaten excrement. For many species of animals, coprophagy is a normal act. Lewin discusses animal coprophagy, or refection, at some length (pp. 92–97). Lewin's provocative study is observant and empirical; Laporte's "history" is, by contrast, almost silly in its unempirical speculations.

38   Miller, p. 51. Had Miller glanced, in even an inattentive way, through the source materials on paraphilia and sexual aberrations generally, he would have learned that coprophagy is not that uncommon. Had he searched the topic on the Internet, he might have been shocked, but he would also so have been instructed.

39   It is worth noting that psychoanalytic versions of social formation can draw upon the social constructionist model, but the latter has little or no use for psychoanalysis. Social construction offers a general explanation of why people respond to experience as they do. It provides an excellent account of why people have the toilet habits that they do. It would probably always seem insufficient to account for such core affects as disgust and shame or, for that matter, sexual appetency. From the social constructionist position, there is no reason why any response should occur at the unconscious level or even why the idea of an Unconscious should be invoked at all.

40   Wollheim, p. 113.

41   Juni, p. 203.

42   Letter 75, November 14, 1897; *Works,* vol. 2, p. 269.

43   Bourke was writing largely from second-hand experience, in the nineteenth-century manner. However, even if you assume the worst, that he misunderstood what he had seen and trusted too easily in what he had not, the sheer accumulation of detail supports the proposition that bodily wastes, excreta and effluvia, have been imagined very differently in different cultures. From that proposition it is a safe jump to the corollary that such wastes have been (actually) treated quite differently. It takes only a single contradictory instance to defeat an argument's universalizing trajectory. Citing Bourke in support of my argument may not be as hazardous as it might seem. Even if you suppose, following Greenblatt, that Bourke misunderstood what he witnessed among the Zuñi (which is, after all, only the first incident in his study) and confused theatre with actual enjoyment, there remain the thousands of other examples.

44   Neu, p. 181.

45   Freud, "The Paths to The Formation of Symptoms," pp. 412–13. Freud does not seem to have wavered in an insistence upon disgust as a key reaction-formation in the mechanism of repression. In his early *The Interpretation of Dreams* (1900), he observes that the problem of repression raises the question of what "motive forces" are at work in this transformation. "It is enough for us to be clear," he writes, "that a transformation of this kind does occur in the course of development—we have only to recall the way in which disgust emerges in childhood after having been absent to begin with—and that it is related to the activity of the secondary system" (*Works,* vols. 4–5, p. 764). The image of the skin forming upon the surface of milk, though difficult to imagine in an age of pasteurized milk, standard distribution procedures and refrigeration, is still striking. Kristeva employs it to illustrate the force of the abject as "an item of food." "I experience a gagging sensation," she writes, "and, still further down, spasms in the stomach, the belly; and all the organs shrivel up the body, provoke tears and bile, increase the heartbeat, cause forehead and hands to perspire" (pp. 2-3). The milk skin would also, I think, exemplify the fourth model which analyses disgust as the experience of transformation, of deliquescence and slime. Nonetheless, it is obvious that many people *like* the skin that forms over milk and milk puddings. They may even actively seek it out, asking for the "skin" at table.

46 Freud's concept of repression, as well as that of the unconscious itself, has been attacked by both scientists and philosophers. It has little empirical evidence (only the evidence of how neurotic people act and how they may be, in therapeutic situations, cured) and it strikes many philosophers as incoherent. The concept of a repressive force that works during waking hours but becomes entirely inept during sleep and which, insofar as it requires a "censor," both knows and cannot know the material that it represses does not win high marks for consistency and logical coherence. The argument is acutely stated by Colin McGinn in a review of several recent books on Freudian psychoanalysis. From the point of view of this book, the presumed incoherence of Freud's concept of repression, and its enforcing agents, the reaction-formations, does not matter. The logical inadequacies of the social constructionist model have also been frequently observed. What matters is that it does constitute an explanatory model which has had immense acceptance. Even if Freudian psychoanalysis ceased to be a viable therapeutic, it would remain a provocative theory of human nature and, above all, a historical model that anyone interested in twentieth-century art and literature would need to know, rather as anyone interested in the Renaissance must understand Ptolemaic astronomy.

47 Lukacher, p. ix. David-Ménard discusses the function of disgust within a hysterical person. It is an addition, a supplement. "Disgust can be conceptualized only as a modification—a rejection—of an experience of *jouissance* that can be conceptualized only within a body" (p. 71). Similarly, Lukacher writes in his foreword that the "hysterogenic body is a kind of prosthesis for the lack of an erotogenic body" (p. xiv). The notion of a learned affect as a prosthesis leads into the discussion of the "technologies of the body." I shall return to this topic, and the existence of cyber(body)parts that are both actual and metaphoric, in Chapter 4.

48 Freud, *Civilization and Its Discontents*, p. 60.

49 Žižek, *The Metastases of Enjoyment*, p. 91.

50 This bleak reflection is hardly unique to Freudian psychoanalysis. In a similar vein, Nietzsche observes, "Ah, reason, seriousness, mastery over the affects, the whole somber thing called reflection, all these prerogatives and showpieces of man: how dearly they have been bought" (p. 62).

51 Douglas acknowledges her debt to Sartre (p. 38). Sartre's primary term is *visqueux*; his translator renders this as "slimy"; Douglas uses "stickiness." It might seem that Douglas chooses a term that mistranslates in order to gain the extra impact of a physical degradation from which it is difficult to disentangle oneself. However, Sartre's point is that there are states between liquid and solid, aberrant and melting. Sartre's translator, Hazel Barnes, remarks that she prefers "slimy" over "sticky" as a translation

for *visqueux* because "slimy" captures the figurative meaning of the French term. However, Moi observes that while slimy is in "some cases an excellent translation, in others it comes across as far too repulsive" (*Simone de Beauvoir*, p. 269 n. 5). Moi elects to translate *visqueux* as "sticky" while admitting that it does not always work well. Part of the difficulty arises because Sartre's examples are often extremely figurative. In images such as the root of the chestnut tree before which Roquentin feels nauseous or the portrait gallery of former mayors of Bouville, each brimming with pretentiousness and bad faith, Sartre's novel *Nausea* embodies much of the theory of disgust in *Being and Nothingness*. The chestnut root may be slimy, but the posing dignitaries of Bouville are simply sticky.

52   Sartre, *Being and Nothingness*, p. 604.

53   Sartre, *Being and Nothingness*, p. 607.

54   Sartre, *Nausea*, pp. 88–89.

55   Leak, p. 63. Later in his essay, Leak argues that, in several passages throughout *La Nausée*, what is at stake is the "jeopardizing of the masculine attitude, the loss of gender-identity, and, ultimately, castration" (p. 65). Roquentin experiences the world as *visqueux*, as slime, but he also experiences himself, for ontological not moral reasons, as flowing towards dissolution.

56   A similar scene takes place in Buñuel's and Salvador Dali's 1928 film, *Un Chien Andalou*, in which a man's armpit dissolves into a nest of scurrying ants. Proliferation, multiplicity, pullulation, fecundity itself, are all possible occasions for disgust. For this reason, they often appear as motifs in horror fiction and, perhaps especially, films. I discuss the uses of insect swarms and armies in creating disgust-horror later in Chapter 4. It should be obvious that my early encounter with the peach would have been, in Sartrean terms, a brute contact with a disgusting semi-object, a slimy suggestion of my own fragile physical boundaries but also of the world's irremediable deliquescence. However, my perception of the peach could also have been influenced by the experience with the swarm of spiderlings which, though each in itself whole and enclosed, would have seemed, in their multitude, fluid (life flowing in slime). That swarm, through the normal mechanism of condensation, might have been identified in my mind with my fascinated sight of the neighbourhood girl's genitalia.

57   At least considered as something to ingest, pus would surely strike most people as being unspeakably nauseous and vomit-making. Kekes would seem to have chosen a powerful motif for his argument. Still, as with every other in-the-world disgusting thing, pus can function as an object of desire. Saint Catherine of Sienna is said to have drunk pus in order to humble herself (a *desideratum* for a potential saint). Some versions of her story insist that she collected a bowl of pus from the infected abscesses of a nun whom she particularly disliked. You can imagine situations in which you might willingly, if not happily, drink pus. Travelling in a remote place, you might find yourself sucking a loved one's abscess, or perhaps an infected snake-bite wound, as a matter of life or death. The example of pus simply indicates how unlikely it is that there exist fundamentally invariant disgust-objects.

58   Paglia, *Sexual Personae*, p. 257.

59 Sartre, *Being and Nothingness*, p. 610.

60 Moi, *Simone de Beauvoir*, p. 102. Moi observes that Sartre's analysis of slimy in-between states of being seems contaminated by misogynist metaphors. When Sartre describes *le visqueux* as a "soft yielding action, a moist and feminine sucking," he has chosen a metaphor more narrow (by half) than his target. Such contaminated metaphors reveal "the way in which sexist prejudice tends to insinuate itself into the most unexpected philosophical contexts" (p. 102).

61 Douglas, *Purity and Danger*, p. 35.

62 Rozin and Fallon link contamination to the experience of disgust. In every culture, they argue, there "are some substances that can generate psychological contamination by physical contact." Disgust can be evoked by "an object associated with a disgusting item. More commonly, disgust is elicited by objects that have contacted a disgusting item or by objects that physically resemble a disgusting item" (pp. 29–30). They then introduce the notion of contagion and the theory of sympathetic magic. They believe that they have been able to demonstrate, through laboratory studies and questionnaires, that "the phenomena of sympathetic magic operate in the domain of disgust." An experiment in which they dropped a "dead, sterilized cockroach into a glass of palatable juice" and then removed it, showed, they assert, that their subjects found this juice less desirable than a juice in which no cockroach had ever been. To the non-psychologist this experiment may only demonstrate the obvious, but it does support (since the subjects' refusal may be irrational) the general proposition that links the "domain of disgust" with the concepts of contamination, contagion and sympathetic magic (pp. 30–1; see also Paul Rozin et al., "Operation of the Laws of Sympathetic Magic in Disgust and Other Domains").

63 Lars-Henrik Schmidt had this experience during a trip to Mexico. Hence the anecdote is his and I have borrowed it (with permission) to illustrate the problem of "dirt out of place." His anecdote emerged during a discussion of disgust and hidden symbolic systems at the Center for Kulturforskning at Aarhus University in 1995. Schmidt was asked why he had not attempted to help the woman or at least to turn his head away. Someone suggested that the situation was like that in which you come upon a man defecating in the woods and, knowing that only bodily exigency has forced him to semi-public defecation, you look away. However, the mini-van was crowded, the situation was novel and, for a philosopher, sufficiently problematic to observe intently. Could he have helped? Should he have offered his own hands to the woman? His cap? A woman in the audience rather startlingly recounted an experience in which she had stumbled upon a man, obviously caught short, who was relieving himself a few steps back from a path in the woods near Aarhus. She had stopped to give him tissues with which to wipe himself and then, using a stick to dig, had helped him to bury his feces. Could not Schmidt have given this poor woman his own cap? Once dirt is actually "out of place," it becomes uncertain, ambiguous and open to conflicting interpretations.

64 Douglas, *Purity and Danger*, p. 55.

65 Douglas, *Purity and Danger*, p. 40. In her article on "Pollution" for the *International Encyclopedia of the Social Sciences*, Douglas observes that "pollution beliefs protect the most vulnerable domains, where ambiguity would most weaken the fragile structure" ("Pollution;" rpt. in *Implicit Meanings*, pp. 47–59).

66 Edmund Spenser, *The Faerie Queene*, II, 9, 32–33. Observing the Port Esquiline of Alma's Castle where everything "that noyous was" is, after traveling "by secret ways," secretly thrown out and "avoided quite," the two knights, Sir Guyon and Prince Arthur, experience "rare delight, / And gazing wonder they their minds did fill; / For never had they seene so straunge a sight" (II, 33: 3–4). Visiting in the allegorical castle that represents the human body, Spenser's knights are watching the anus function. I discuss the anus, as a source of both self-disgust and abjection, in Chapter 7.

67 Sartre, *Being and Nothingness*, p. 605.

68 Deleuze and Guattari, *A Thousand Plateaus*, p. 16–7. An arborescent space is one that has been segmented by a conceptual root-system and will "impose on us the striations of a homogenous space." Even an unsegmented space, one that follows the pattern of rhizomes rather than taproots, that opens up "lines of flight" may arborify into a fixed and repressive system. The "lines of flight" themselves always "risk abandoning their creative potentialities and turning into a line of death, being turned into a line of destruction pure and simple (fascism)" (p. 506). The vision of human life that Deleuze and Guattari hold out as a model for ideal behaviour defines itself as the exact opposition to a "normal," encoded and striated society. The ideal society that they envision would be smooth and make possible all manner of lines of flight. For a collection of recent essays on the problems raised in the work of Deleuze and Guattari, see Massumi.

69 In North America, the argument against repression has been fierce, but also sporadic. A massively repressed culture, in which arguments for all manner of repressions are conducted fiercely and under the aegis of divine sanction, might seem to have no room for explorations beyond established boundaries. Part of the attraction of the '60s lay in the various efforts made to blast people through, or else sneak them around, the cultural boundaries. No doubt, the dark side of the 1960s, the use of drugs to achieve border-crossings, would in the minds of some people cancel out the positive agenda of the time while for others it would only confirm their worst suspicions. Camille Paglia points out the "pure romanticism" of the period, much of which could be found in the varied attempts, not only with drugs, to free the person from habitual repression (*Sex, Art, and American Culture*, p. 130). The Human Potential Movement has carried on the revolutionary tendencies of the period, urging (in various ways) the discovery of happiness beyond repression. The key ideological texts of the '60s seemed to be Norman O. Brown's *Life Against Death* and *Love's Body*. Both books argue for the discovery of happiness through pleasure and envision a culture, free of repression, in which people might become happy. In Deleuze and Guattari's terms, they might, in such an open society, become nomads.

70 Beginning with Prometheus allows Shattuck to impose spiritual/religious perspective upon his argument: transgression is always against an established order, or against a set of social rules, but if you believe that society has been founded upon, or otherwise mirrors, a transcendent order, then transgression, crossing boundaries or breaking taboos, takes on an entirely different cast. A more favourable consideration of significant modern manifestations of the Promethean tradition, at least in its negative and mocking dimension, can be found in Marcus. For an intellectual history of the "Kynical" tradition in philosophy, which includes Menippean, and is thus both Promethean and de Sadean in some sense, see Sloterdijk.

71 Sherbert, p. 2. Sloterdijk includes Menippean (in the person of Menippus' follower, Lucian) within the Kynical tradition. (For Sloterdijk, a "cynic" is someone quite distinct from a Kynic.) The Kynic, he observes, "farts, shits, pisses, masturbates on the street, before the eyes of the Athenian market. He shows contempt for fame, ridicules the architecture, refuses respect, parodies the stories of the gods and heroes ..." (pp. 103–04).

72 Frye, p. 233.

73 The limitations of Marcus' historiography can be seen in his treatment of Bataille. Marcus finds a place for Bataille only insofar as he figures as a commentator upon Marcel Mauss' study of exchange, The Gift (1925). Although Bataille stands out as an exponent of de Sade and as a theorist of transgression and social reversal, he has no standing in Marcus' study of twentieth-century anarchism, transgression and social disturbance (pp. 394–95).

74 Bakhtin traces the history of the novel to its precursors, the polyglot writers of the Roman Empire, who created, within the urban spaces in which diverse peoples gathered, a hybrid discourse. One major dimension of this linguistic diversity was Menippean satire, the "heteroglossia of the clown" (Dialogic Imagination, p. 273). The use of "bodily grotesque" and other modes of scatology, extreme physical distortion and caricature play a central role in Menippean discourse and flow directly from that discourse into the novel. Like Menippean, the novel is "saturated with marketplace elements" (Rabelais, pp. 186–87). The diverse languages of the novel can not be laid out on a single plane nor stretched along a single line; rather, the novel is a "system of intersecting planes" (Dialogic Imagination, p. 48). Menippean, or different elements of it in different novels, constitutes one such plane. Not all historians of the novel accept Bakhtin's model of a precursive hybridity located in Menippean satire. Yet it should be clear, to all but the most rigid genre-formalist, that whatever the first novelists had read, it could not have been other novels.

75 The lower bodily stratum is "always laughing" (Rabelais, p. 22).

76 Carter, The Sadeian Woman, p. 17. Carter seems to have had de Sade often on her mind prior to completing The Sadeian Woman. He shows up, as a motif and as a "originary" for certain characters, in her fiction from The Infernal Desire Machines of Doctor Hoffman (1972) to Nights at The Circus (1984). For Carter, de Sade was much more than a "savage sideshow." She finds in de Sade what Bataille also finds: a program, if not an actual inventory of techniques (not yet a fully constructed war-machine), for smashing arbitrary boundaries and social fetters. For a wide-ranging discussion of Carter's work, paying close attention to her understanding of de Sade, see Olchowy.

77 Žižek, The Indivisible Remainder, p. 173. Žižek must have in mind Kant's proposition that the will to action should be conducted as if it were an instance of universal legislation. The Sadean will-to-enjoy could be considered as coming within the Kantian dictum: everyone should will to act so as to maximize enjoyment. However, it is also clear that Žižek is not thinking about Kant's other fundamental moral law that you must never treat another human being as a means, but only as an end. That is, in the Kantian moral system each person must be a subject, an end in himself, not an object, a simple means to your enjoyment. In the Sadean realm, as The 120 Days of Sodom, with its kidnappings, rapes, violations and abuse, makes plain, the other person is always a

means, a mere object, of the transgressor's pleasure. For a discussion of de Sadean libertinage, see Frappier-Mazur.

78 Bataille, "Letter to René Char," p. 37.

79 For an overview of de Sade, or for the "theory" of de Sade, see Bataille's 1929 essay "The Use Value of D.A.F. de Sade," in *Visions of Excess*, pp. 91–102.

80 Carter, *Expletives*, p. 37. Carter thinks that French intellectuals find blasphemy exhilarating, while English intellectuals find it only "silly." I shall discuss attitudes towards blasphemy, certainly a disgusting act in some eyes, in Chapter 6 within the context of the *fatwa* against Salman Rushdie.

81 Yve-Alain Bois in Lauren Sedofsky, "Formless: Down and Dirty (Interview with Curators Rosalind Krauss and Yve-Alain Bois)," www.phreebyrd.com/˜sisyphus/ bataille/gbsedofsky.html. The phreebyrd Bataille website contains a bibliography and several valuable essays on Bataille's thought. See Alexander Nehamas, "The Attraction of Repulsion: The deep and ugly thought of Georges Bataille," www.phreebyrd.com/ ˜sisyphus/bataille/gbnehamas.html. In an essay on "cleanliness prohibitions" in *The Accursed Share*, Bataille refers to his program for transgression and personal revolution as a "reversal of alliances." This depends upon a twofold erotic movement: rejection of an experience followed by its reintegration into a whole "when that which was denied to the point of nausea, which held an ambiguous value, is remembered as desirable" (pp. 76–78).

82 Bataille, *Visions of Excess*, pp. 20–23.

83 Literature is "an assemblage. It has nothing to do with ideology. There is no ideology and never has been" (Deleuze and Guttari, *A Thousand Plateaus*, p. 4). Perhaps they have Althusser in mind, or the narrow ferocity of neo-Althusserians, but they have highlighted one problem of a (complex) theory of disgust. Ideology is like a "tap-root" that runs through all the social strata and reinforces their power of being obstacles to desire. If you take "ideology" to indicate a set of ideas held by many people (the "majority"), and not as an unconscious structure that it is impossible to escape (the Althusserian model), then their point about literature may become clear. Literature does not reinforce the obstacles to desire, but rather provides a vehicle for driving through them, for re-establishing your life beyond all the obstacles. In the theory of disgust, the role of literature, and of all art, is illustrative, paradigmatic and also exploratory. Literature is a source of images and, hence, an "imagistic" tool. Everyone, I assume, possesses a culture-specific imaginary, the sum of the mind's visual resources (its archive, in effect) for interpreting reality. The constituents of this Imaginary derive from cultural stereotypes and other scripts, the unexamined mental boilerplate in a culture, but they may also come from literature. They serve repression, of course, but they may also be retooled as new parts in an anti-repressive war-machine.

84 For the discussion of machines, see *A Thousand Plateaus*, throughout. See also Deleuze and Guttari, *Anti-Oedipus*, pp. 322–39.

85 I confess that I am a pluralist. I like to see things open up to very different questions. Most theory these days in literature departments is hyper-deductive, top-down and as slenderly cast as a Toledo rapier. (That is, it is top-down when it is anything; often it is

nothing: a citational, or ornamental, fret work.) I leave still-open the question of whether an array of models should be serial, a number of sequential problems to be taken up in turn, or synchronic, a number of questions that can be shuffled about to meet the exigencies of the problem. Gass observes that "the war for reality is ... a struggle between data and design" (*Habitations*, p. 95). Those who love the data are Thicks; those who love design, Thins. A Pluralist, however, must tend to take a rather plump, Thickish, stance towards theory: let there be much of it; let it not be exclusionary (or top-down). A student, wholly dedicated to de Man (I think it was) and his version of deconstruction, once told me that she had finally grasped that there was "no way out or around" deconstruction. Clearly, I thought, she had become a true believer as Gass observes Thins have a tendency to become. She received with considerable reserve my remark that all global models work in similar ways: peremptory, dominating, masterful, but poorly equipped with escape hatches. She appeared to experience a slight twinge of disgust at the sight of a professor whom a foxy pluralism had, evidently, corrupted. She was even more hostile when I suggested that one version of theory has sometimes been called "measuring the Mandarin's fingernails." (The theorist with the longest fingernails [de Man, say] commands the most respect, the greatest and most marketable esteem, and ends up dominating, if neither for very long nor very steadily, a disciplinary field.) Measuring the Mandarin's fingernails implies the effort to establish one theorist, and a single way of investigating phenomena, or one theoretical model ascribed to a person or (more likely) a person's name, as superior, the last word, the unexamined skyhook. This is the version of theory that lumps texts together, flattens out problems, and then refines its rather pancake-ish lump into dazzlingly Thin models. Such excessively Thin models will privilege one person over another, convert thinkers into gurus and will become just about as hermetic as they are argumentative (contaminated by ill-will, animosities and rivalry). It seemed to me that my student had succumbed to the practice of measuring fingernails. Not long after that encounter, she packed her PhD work off to another supervisor. I have discussed the issue of pluralism in several places, including *Shakespearean Narrative*. See also "Literary Theory's Edginess," "Seeing With A Fly's Eye" and "Hyperplay: Playing The Sly Man at Theory."

86 These worlds are often painful or nauseous to imagine. Hence a theory of disgust
   . requires models not only to account for the formation of powerful affects and their roles in the maintenance of cultural boundaries, but also to explain the capacity of the imagination to experience disgust-worlds which ought to be so disturbingly aversive as to be unviewable. I will take up this problem in Chapters 3 and 4. The compound, dialectical theory of disgust that I am presenting in this book involves a definite theory of the imagination, largely but not exclusively Sartrean in spirit.

87 Stereotypes are what, in a social constructionist model at least, human beings learn to think with. Stereotypes are a received, or a borrowed, discourse, a number of already-marked paths that lead to recognizable destinations. They constitute a technology for transforming human individuals into fictional characters. A stereotype abstracts a person into another person's private fictional world. More narrowly yet, a stereotype is like a tiny theatre in which the Other is compelled to play a part. One way of looking at the problem of disgust (a simple way, of course) would be to say that, like desire, disgust functions according to a discourse of stereotypes. Re-cognition, when it

supplants recognition, occurs when it has become possible to see beyond, under or through, the culturally routinized stereotypes. At that point another person whom you have learned to find disgusting may begin to seem desirable. For a literary-theoretical study of stereotypes, see Castillo Durante. For a recent analysis of the formation of stereotypes, deriving their power from their very abstractness in the face of the manifold of experience (its "abundance") from which they are derived, see Feyerabend's posthumous *Conquest of Abundance*.

Chapter 3 ❊ Its Lair

1   Paglia, *Sexual Personae*, p. 21. Havelock Ellis remarks that the "almost complete absence from statuary art of the posture of urination in women" may be explained by the "fact" that the "humble squatting attitude ... seldom lends itself easily to art" (p. 392). Like "earthbound," "humble" reflects the superego rather than the viscera. Later, Ellis cites a wide range of evidence to show that in many cultures women stand erect to urinate while men squat.

2   In a letter to René Char, published in *Botthege Oscure* (May, 1950), Bataille takes up Char's claim that human beings are two parts Ariel but only one part Caliban. (If Ariel resigns, Char had written, "a sickness of flies" will follow.) Bataille urges the importance of a life without measure. "I am speaking by and large of what, beyond productive activity, and, in our disorder, is the analogue of holiness." Humanity, he adds, is "most touching in its inanity when night grows filthier, when the horror of night turns its creatures into a vast heap of rubbish" ("Letter to René Char," p. 35).

3   Although racism is not a specific topic of this study, it is certainly possible to see how it falls within the general model of the imagination that I have been developing. One person observes another, different with respect to physical appearance, and begins to incorporate him/her into a negative fictional world which draws upon the observer's ingrained imaginary of stereotypes and physiognomic clichés. A vast amount has been written on the subject of racism, although nearly always proceeding from a potted definition in a top-down method of argument. In his recent study of Joseph Conrad, Peter Edgerly Firchow summarizes the most common definitions of racism and sorts through the tangled distinctions between racism, ethnicity and nationality (Firchow, p. 1-17). Having examined the spectrum of definitions, Firchow concludes that some theorists of racism seem to be on missionary projects of their own. Firchow also sorts ably through the varied definitions of colonialism and imperialism.

4   Edmund White, p. 63. The consequences of power, such as genocide, torture, execution or the more diffuse miseries of ethnic cleansing, are (in many eyes, if not those of the power-holders) disgusting. The question is whether power, as a source of corruption or (ironic) diminishment, is, in itself, disgusting. White thinks that, because it is the condition of human indifference, power is an active cause of disgust. On the topic of "administrative ecstasy" (the delight in arbitrary exercises of power), see Chapter 1, note 6.

5   de Sade, pp. 328-9.

6   Even if universalists were correct in claiming that some single in-the-world disgust-object, such as mammalian feces, was always and everywhere disgusting, the manner in which human beings relate to (handle, manage, dispose of) that object would vary greatly from culture to culture, sub-group to sub-group, within a culture. For example, as I have already argued, the manner and context for defecation matters a great deal. Many cultures would frown, or worse, on public dumping, but certainly not all. Still, the temptation towards universalism among experts on disgust seems very strong. Although mammalian feces is the usual choice for a universal disgust-object, it is not the only one. William Ian Miller thinks that human hair is more disgusting than feces (p. 55). Robertson argues that Miller's revulsion at human hair, though evidently bizarre, correlates to his quite personal sexual disgust and revulsion at the penis which is unmistakably present in *The Anatomy of Disgust*. Miller refers to the penis as a "slug," and one that spits "ooze" at that, and expresses commiseration for women in their sexual encounters with men. "Structurally, allowing for the differences in corporeality, hairs and slugs have much in common" (Robertson, p. 215 n. 5). Robertson also observes that Miller could find a little support for his revulsion in Peter Greenaway's 1997 film *Pillow Book*, in which "the film's calligraphy-obsessed heroine compares the penis to a 'green sea-slug'. *Green* is a move beyond Miller's sexual disgust and very personal *horror genitalium*" (p. 214 n. 4).

7   Some time ago, I invented a fictional character, inhabiting parables and cautionary tales, whom I call the Sly Man. The Sly Man is very successful at theory, but he also creates obstacles. He is the embodiment of the success of theory which is also its failure. The Sly Man proposes answers to questions he has asked only to show how the answers work. He inhabits circles. Circles surround him. Trickster, master of illusions, he can pull discourse out of a word, like rabbits out of hats, and then find the same word, like a hat secretly within the rabbit, nested within the discourse. Because the Sly Man seeks knowledge, seeks to be correct and (thus) hegemonic, he also desires conclusions. He likes to show others how to solve problems. The conclusions are always handy. His theoretical model, functioning always as a template, makes them ready to hand, ready to pluck from the system, like tools.

If you point towards some textual or cultural fact that bothers you, the Sly Man will explain it for you. He may refer to its context, citing its material conditions, or he may refer to the inescapable nature of textuality or culture. He will point to the general account of all textual and cultural facts that will explain the one that interests you. The fact that bothers you will illustrate the model of culture, or of history, or of text, or of speech act. Each particular fact exemplifies the general account; the account will (seem to) have been learned from the particulars. The Sly Man likes to prove the inevitability of the model from the particulars, giving it an historical authenticity, and then use it to explain each particular in succession. The Sly Man has cultivated a masterful skill in framing the issues within debate, and he strives to win arguments in advance in order to achieve a socio-historical account of highly general applicability. (I am not associating the Sly Man fallacy with any single contextual model. The Sly Man gets about.) As the Sly Man argues, a cultural fact, a custom or a convention (say) will receive the same account as will its textual representation. The Sly Man claims exclusiveness. Much of the Sly Man's cleverness lies in constricting the scope of the questions to be asked. The Sly Man fallacy arises when he persuades you to substitute a delimited set for a more extensive one, urging a narrow response where a broad one had been possible. Hence it is possible to see the Sly Man as representative of a certain mode of fallacious thinking. The central issue in the debate with the Sly Man concerns the nature of textual facts or, to put the problem more vigorously, the nature of the questions, or sets of questions, that can be asked about representations. For the Sly Man, disgust would always be explained on the level of cultural fact. The distinction between in-the-world phenomenon and representation would not be allowed to exist. Much of what I have to say in this chapter and in Chapter 4 can be construed as personal combat with the Sly Man.

8　Miller, p. 111.

9　Kristeva, pp. 10, 1.

10　Grosz, *Volatile Bodies*, p. 36. It would be a mistake to suppose that Kristeva herself discovered the complex interwindings between body and mind, physical spatiality and mythology. Bataille had crossed much the same territory, and with a similar arsenal of images, a generation previously. Furthermore, there have always been many appropriate metaphors for this twisting, braided Möbius effect.

11　The mouth has more than one possible action in disgust. At first it may narrow, like the nares, the upper lip raised, as if it were screwing away from a sight or odour, but then, as the saliva begins to flow, it may purse and open slightly in preparation for vomiting. Rozin, Lowery and Ebert argue that the face varies according to the "elicitors." They conclude that the facework involved in the expression of disgust is both functional and communicative; that is, it responds to the "strong stimulation of a particular sensory modality" but it also "takes on moral tones" and may "share some properties of anger … the upper lip raise, a component of the expression of anger, may become a salient part of the disgust expression under such conditions." The authors provide a page of photos showing *posed* varieties of facial expressions that register different kinds and degrees of disgust (Rozin et al., "Varieties of Disgust Faces," pp. 871–72). The fact that the authors use posed expressions to illustrate their conclusions suggests the theatrical and easily acted facework of disgust.

12　Gass, *Habitations,* p. 135. Ceremonial retching, or ritual gagging, in which one person pretends to vomit over another or at another's actions or ideas, is intended both as a measure of distance and as a powerful insult. Students sometimes call the process by which another person's ideas or behaviour registers as disgusting, eliciting ceremonial retching, "barfogenesis." If someone did actually vomit over you in order to insult, it would be more degrading, stronger than either spitting or urinating.

13　Kekes, p. 445.

14　Goffman, *Interaction Ritual*, p. 13.

15　Even today, Chaney's repertory of faces, the sheer range of his cinematic facework (the "thousand faces"), seems amazing (see Robert G. Anderson). It might be argued that facework developed for film or theatre is inauthentic and cannot truly show how a human face might look during an actual-world experience. However, as already noted, psychologists, such as Paul Rozin, employ *posed* facework to exemplify the range of facial expressions correlative to a designated affect. On the other hand, all of Chaney's films, except for the 1930 *The Unholy Three*, were silent films using the stylized expressive conventions of that tradition. In Tod Browning's 1928 film *West of Zanzibar*, Chaney played a freak, a human chicken (thus anticipating Browning's 1932 *Freaks*), who both feels and causes disgust. The facework in this film is still impressive (Anderson, p. 204).

16 Positivistic social sciences, such as physical anthropology and empirical psychology, showed early interests in cataloguing the varieties of human expressions. Nineteenth-century photographers, such as Guillaume-Benjamin Duchenne, created inventories of expressions (Ewing, pp. 109, 116). Charles Darwin studied faces and expressions, animal as well as human, extensively. The nineteenth-century interest in faces as "evidence" from which conclusions might be inferred with regard to psychological type and intellectual capacity was only an aspect, or a positivistic science that simplified both the problem of evidence and that of inference. Creating inventories of faces was related to such other investigations as Cesare Lombroso's anthropology of criminal types and the "science" of craniometry. Gould discusses both Lombroso and craniometry. The use of posed facial expressions in psychological studies of affects, such as Rozin on disgust, does not reflect an analogous positivism since they use photographs only to illustrate conclusions that the researchers have reached by other methods of empirical research.

17 Usually a person can not pretend a blush (though I have met those who claim this ability), but many other features of shame are easy enough to mimic, such as downcast eyes or a fist striking the breast in a mock *mea culpa*. By contrast, the face of hate is more closely linked to disgust and its facial manifestations. In hate, the face is deformed by pent-up energy. It is like the entrance to a furnace. The teeth, which in conventional cliché are said to "gnash," are bared as if in preparation for biting and tearing. The nose, because the teeth are exposed, will also crinkle. The face of contempt is, moving to the opposite extreme, a stylized version of the disgust face, as far from hate as ice from fire. Alphonso Lingis puts the problem of faces neatly: "A face faces to express meaning. A face faces to express subjective feelings" (p. 43).

18 Scheff, p. 74. Scheff observes that when "we are accepted as we present ourselves, we usually feel rewarded by the pleasant emotion of pride and fellow feeling" (p. 75). Rejection, and even more powerfully disgust, are prima facie evidence that you have not been taken as you would have wished to present yourself. Having realized that sad state of affairs, you may readily feel shame. Still, both shame and disgust involve more than self-presentation. I take an "ego ideal" to constitute a more powerful concept than self-presentation. And, like disgust, shame inescapably involves transgression(s) on some level.

19 Scheff puts considerable emphasis upon interaction (drawing, in part, upon Goffman), and hence upon shame-dealing. He calls the spiral of shame-rage a "feeling trap" (pp. 102–06; cf. pp. 18–19) . In Chapter 7, I argue that self-disgust and abjection arise from diverse actual-world experience that may be widely distributed over a long period of life. Of course, specific acts of shame-dealing do occur, perhaps often, and will contribute to the personal awareness of having fallen beneath your personal ego-ideal.

20 People who have undergone colostomies will not lose control of their bowels (since that control has been removed). However, a prosthetic anus may fail, beginning to leak or spill. TV ads for adult diapers, often pushed by former film stars, suggest that the

possibilities for embarrassment are actually quite common. Once riding a train from Melbourne to Geelong, I sat opposite a middle-aged man who was reading the single volume edition of Isaac Asimov's *Foundation Trilogy*. Suddenly, he exclaimed, "Oh, shit!" and ran to the toilet at the end of the coach. The air was abruptly filled with a strong feculent odour. The man didn't return, but later I saw him lurking by the door, obviously hoping to be the first person off the train. I assumed that he had undergone a colostomy and now wore a bag which had begun to leak. He might simply have had an unexpected bowel movement. In either case, his embarrassment was visibly acute. Later, when he recalled the incident on the train, he may well have felt shame.

21 Goffman, *Interaction Ritual*, p. 99.

22 Goffman, *Interaction Ritual*, p. 97.

23 The image is Katherine Dunn's.

24 Roman Polanski fully understood the symbolic import of spitting in another person's face when he directed *Rosemary's Baby* (1968). Rosemary (Mia Farrow) enters the living room of the Satanist coven who have (it appears) mated her with Satan. She is carrying a large kitchen knife. The audience expects her to kill someone, either Roman the Satanist leader or her husband who has sold her body in a Faustian compact to achieve success in his acting career. Holding the knife, she finds her husband who tries to explain that he hadn't thought it would matter since giving a child to Satan would not be much different from losing a child in a miscarriage. Rather than stabbing him, Rosemary spits copiously and directly into her husband's face.

25 In Polanski's 1993 film *Bitter Moon*, there is a long narrative analepsis in which Oskar tells Nigel about his meeting with Mimi and their subsequent passion. Their affair had involved ritual sado-masochism. Oscar describes a golden shower in which he crawls under Mimi while she is urinating and drinks her urine. He describes her urine splattering (or eddying) up his nostrils. The experience had led him to have a powerful, responsive orgasm.

26 Bob Gallagher, a great fantasist, who worked as a tutor at the University of Melbourne in the middle 1970s, once went with me to see Ashton's Circus. I said something about a rather boring act involving camels being interesting to watch because (if nothing else) it was difficult to do. Bob exploded with laughter. "Well," he said, "many things are difficult, but you wouldn't want to watch. It's pretty difficult to shit green, but no one wants to see it done." That seemed to put things into perspective.

27 Sutherland, p. 465. Magnus Hirschfeld remarks that *urolagnia* denotes the urge to witness urination and to have "warm urine thrown over one's body" (Haire, p. 427). The notion that anyone might want to have urine "thrown" over his or her body seems to evoke the practices of Nordic saunas, a collective bucket rather than a personal stream, but the basic sensation of wetness, stench and (possibly) warmth would remain unchanged. The underlying motivations for urolagnia must be complex and must include both temporary as well as permanent causes. Hirschfeld assumes that the only motivation must be masochism. Havelock Ellis, who prefers the term "Undinism" (invoking a Teutonic motif), thinks that urolagnia is "specially frequent" among women (whereas coprolagnia is, he thinks, more common among men), encouraged, he

argues, "by the close and obvious connection of the urinary function with the sexual organs" (p. 164). Although Ellis thinks that women are more likely than men to enjoy urinary, or urethral, eroticism, there is evidence that he himself enjoyed having women urinate upon him. Ellis is said to have asked the American poet H.D. to urinate upon him (how often or under what conditions does not appear to be known) and she complied (Guest, p. 121). Cookie Mueller's title for her story about a man who loves urine, "The One Percent," probably catches the social distribution of the phenomenon more or less accurately. I have treated the phenomenon of the golden shower as a heterosexual experience, but it is clearly a gay sexual modality as well (or even more so). For a stunning account of golden showering as a gay experience, see Glück's moving "Sex Story." Despite Ellis' dictum, the golden shower does not seem to play an important (or much discussed) role in lesbian eroticism. However, see Califia's *Macho Sluts* where *urolagnia* appears, in passing as it were, as an aspect of ritualized S/M encounters.

28 *Antony and Cleopatra* 1.4.60–63; *The Riverside Shakespeare*, p. 1353.

29 Scheff, p. 18, and passim.

30 Why didn't I try to see Georgia Lee again? My work often brought me back to San Francisco and I knew exactly where she lived. I could easily have found her. The answer is quite simple: I was ashamed and, when shamed, it is hard to know what to say. Furthermore, there is another question which I haven't asked until this moment. Did I enjoy urinating upon her? Did I derive pleasure from watching my urine strike her? (And that would have been a transgression *beyond* that of actually urinating upon her.) I was aware that, despite my disgust at the act, I might still have taken pleasure from it. I may have had Georgia Lee on my mind, but I could not comfortably have spoken to her.

31 Luis Buñuel, *The Phantom of Liberty*. Martin Pops discusses this scene but seems to have it all wrong. He thinks that a young woman participates in a shit-together in a dining room and then eats alone in a lavatory, feeling silent shame. Actually, she does register shame, but only for having disturbed the police lecturer while he is eating. The final shot in the scene shows her standing outside the eating cubicle, looking flustered and ashamed. Pops also discusses a parallel scene in Günter Grass's *The Flounder*. In such scenes, there is an "ironic inversion between shitting (social and convivial) and eating (private and silent)" (p. 45). Such an inversion will seem ironic if, and only if, the division of functions has already been explicitly established and if the inversion can convey more than descriptive significance. The divisions are social and customary (we do not, and as children are not encouraged to, eat and excrete in the same places), but they are also fragile, far less solid than our ideology of social conditioning claims. The actual manoeuvres of excretion are also customary. Which hand should one use to wipe oneself? Does it matter? (You bet it does! Don't eat with your left hand in Arab cultures, don't even point with a left finger in some.) Europeans, North Americans and Australians typically sit upon toilets, flush or dry, but other human beings squat over holes. (In southern Europe it is still common to encounter Turkish holes. The initial adaptation of posture may be difficult, or even embarrassing, but it is simple to learn.) In a story aptly entitled "Squatter," Indo-Canadian writer Rohinton Mistry recounts the troubles of a man from Bombay who, having immigrated to Toronto, finds that

sitting upon western toilets constipates him. He spends ten years squatting on the seats of toilets, occasionally with the embarrassment of being seen doing this in public lavatories. In India, people squat and, following ancient custom, use water to clean themselves, not paper. Even to ask a Hindu host for paper might be like hitting him in the face with a vision of excrement, something too disgusting to look squarely upon. As Salahuddin Chamchawala, a Muslim boy from Bombay, prepares to leave for school in England, his mother warns him, "Don't go dirty like those English." The dirty English, she explains, "wipe their bee tee ems with paper only" (Rushdie, *The Satanic Verses*, p. 39). In *Midnight's Children*, Amina Sinai, another mother, complains about the toilet practices of "Britishers": "You've looked in the bathrooms? No water near the pot. I never believed, but it's true, my God, they wipe their bottoms with paper only!" (p. 110). In India, tourist hotels will have paper, but they will also supply a small plastic cup, something that resembles a beaker, so you can carry water from the sink. Toilet paper is, as everyone who uses the stuff knows, both messy and awkward. What will you say to someone, a stranger, who has left a public toilet with paper dangling from skirt or pants? Should you point it out? Or discreetly turn away? Would it make any difference to you if the trailing paper was obviously soiled? Would a human sympathy with another person's mortification urge you to intrude? What response would you expect? Questionnaires on this topic have revealed that more women than men would point out the dangling embarrassment, especially for another woman, but also that there are plenty of people of either gender who would prefer to turn away or, coldly, to laugh.

32   Kekes, p. 433.

33   Sex, the most corporeal of psychological functions, is as regulated by boundaries as either vomiting and defecation. No doubt, it is a weakness in the social constructionist model that it becomes difficult to distinguish one voluntary, or conscious, bodily function from another. Gilman observes cogently that sex, "with its implied risk for the male and its focus on the corrosive nature of female genitalia, is as marked in early modern culture by disgust as excretion is—if not more" (p. 18). Miller links sex to human disgust as a visceral revulsion. However, unlike Gilman, he sees it as primarily a problem for women who must endure the "ugliness" of the male sexual organ, an organ "reminiscent of a slug that emits viscous ooze" (p. 128).

34   Jameson, p. 56.

35   Joyce, *Ulysses*, p. 56.

36   Woolsey, "United States of America v. One Book Called 'Ulysses' Random House, Inc." (rpt. in *Ulysses*, Random House-Modern Library, pp. ix–xiv).

37   Bakhtin, *Rabelais*. p. 22. Anticipating Kristeva (who first introduced him to French theory), Bakhtin also refers to the "ambivalent lower stratum" (p. 83).

38   Joyce, p. 45.

39   Ellmann, p. 49 n.

40   Joyce, p. 655.

41   Joyce, p. 656.

42   Buzzi, pp. 60–61

43   Radford, p. 82.

44   I should note that my father, who was certainly an intelligent and educated man, refused to distinguish between loathsome representations and loathsome things. He saw things more or less as Kekes and Miller do: representations pollute, contaminate the mind, and they must be judged exactly as actual objects or acts should be. He would not have admitted that representations were disgusting only when there was a deliberate intention to offend . I remember quarrelling with him over the interpretation of the grand inquisitor passage in Dostoevsky's *The Brothers Karamazov*. He saw the passage as an affront to Christianity and the principles of a well-ordered western society. He would not agree that it served primarily to characterize the narrator who tells the story, Ivan Karamazov. He insisted, obdurately (I thought), that the passage must directly reveal Dostoevsky's own thinking. No doubt, a psychoanalyst, or someone holding to the third model I discussed in the previous chapter, would want to insist that my own insistence upon distinguishing representations from their actual world counterpart reflects an on-going Oedipal quarrel with my father.

45   As an object, perhaps more than as an act, vomit is particularly marked in western cultures as a source of disgust. Every point that I have argued concerning disgust in general could be made with respect to vomit alone, except for one: there is no evidence that there are secret groups of vomit-eaters, or any indications that private compulsions drive anyone to eat or lick vomit. Occasionally, a person may be forced to eat vomit (as an insult or a punishment) or, compelled by circumstances as is the Mexican woman in Lars-Henrik Schmidt's anecdote, to ingest vomit in order to hide it. However, there does not appear to be any recognized desire to consume vomit willingly, or any perversion to correspond to either urolagnia or to coprolagnia. Although Kristeva thinks that vomit is not perceived as abject in the same manner that feces and menstrual blood are, slang and popular lore generally tell a different tale. Keith Allan and Kate Burridge reproduce a questionnaire that they administered on the topic of "Bodily Effluvia, Sex, and Tabooed Body-Parts." Participants were asked to rate "SUBSTANCES as produced by an adult stranger using a scale of RRR for the most revolting, RR for less revolting, R for even less revolting." Female participants produced a sixty-two percent RRR for vomit, but only twenty-nine percent result for menstrual blood. Male participants gave vomit and menstrual blood equally a sixty percent RRR rating. The averaged results showed vomit to be the single most revolting substance (just under sixty-two percent, more even than feces at slightly less than sixty-one percent). Menstrual blood produced an averaged RRR result of thirty-six percent (pp. 69–74). Allan and Burridge cite only a handful of synonyms for vomit, but they demonstrate that the words for vomit occupy a scale that runs from the neutral to the strongly dysphemistic (p. 77). A "Giant Vomit Synonym List" is available on the Internet. It lists 224 synonyms. Many of these might seem sufficiently puerile to be ignored but some (such as "liquid laugh," "pavement pizza" or "Technicolor yawn") are noteworthy and might be usable in ordinary vulgar speech.

46   Kristeva, p. 3.

47　Grosz, "Language and The Limits of The Body," p. 108. In *Sexual Subversions*, Grosz observes that waste products can never be fully obliterated, but hover "at the borders of our existence, threatening the apparently settled unity of the subject with disruption and possible dissolution" (p. 71). In her *Volatile Bodies*, Grosz compares the cultural phenomenon of bodily inscription to Franz Kafka's punishment machine in his short fiction "The Penal Colony" in which a machine "with an entire legal system, that openly acknowledges the body of the prisoner as its target and objective and clearly positions consciousness and conscience as the by-products, effects, or results of corporeal inscriptions in a theater of cruelty" (p. 135).

48　Many modern novelists, as Kristeva points out, have "traversed" the territory of the disgusting and the abject. However, Patrick White stands out for the range and diversity of his disgust motifs and for the complexity with which he treats disgust thematically. His novel *The Twyborn Affair* follows the cross-dressing hero, Eddie, through three distinct life-stages in each of which disgust possesses different functions. In the first episode, where Eddie lives as a woman, Eudoxia, in pre-World War One France, disgust marks the Other, the contrasting condition of those who are not, themselves, happily in love. In the second stage, Eddie has returned to Australia to attempt living as a man. In this section of the novel, disgust figures as the condition of Eddie's own existence which is profoundly ambiguous, even a "mistake." In the third episode, Eddie is living in London, once again cross-dressed as a woman but now a brothel-madam, not a young lover. In this final stage of his/her life, disgust has been integrated into Eadith's (or Eddie's) life and no longer appears as recognizable repugnant objects. Disgust has been re-cognized, in effect, as part of the shadow side of human life, worked seamlessly into the individuated life of a mature person.

49　Findley, p. 125.

50　*The Winter's Tale* 2.1.36–45; *The Riverside Shakespeare*, p. 1576.

51　I have cited from Allen Tate's translation, "A Carrion." It is a smooth translation, but it seeks effects that Baudelaire did not need. For example, Tate translates Baudelaire's phrase "comme une femme lubrique" as "courtesan" and his "sur ce ventre putride" as "the putrid vulva." (It is clear that this is what Baudelaire meant since he writes the adverbial phrase "D'où sortaient" to indicate that the "noir bataillons" tumble, as Tate puts it, from within the woman.) I have always thought that the effect of a disgusting image within a beautiful poem was even more forceful in Baudelaire than in Tate. However, Tate's translation seems to have carried the day for anglophones. Gass' comments are evidently written with Tate, not Baudelaire, in mind. See Baudelaire, pp. 38–39, 264–65. Needless to say, I can never read this poem without vividly imagining swarming maggots and spiderlings.

52　Gass, *Habitations*, p. 136.

53　I have discussed the immense range of narrative conventions in *Hamlet* elsewhere. See *Shakespearean Narrative*, Chapter 6.

54　Mack, pp. 30–58.

55 The splatter of images evoking disease, deformity, corruption and poison pervades *Hamlet*. You are constantly being forced to consider the interplay between words and disgusting things. How does the ghost enter into Hamlet's ear? How does the prince internalize the ghost's words? What is the relation between Hamlet's reflections upon the efficacy of a "vicious mole of nature" and his subsequent epithet "old mole" to describe the ghost? It is a verbal link that identifies this ghost with the polluting blot that stains rationality: corrupting, destructive, and monstrous. Calling the ghost "old mole" establishes a verbal link rather like that between Bloom's anality and his bar of soap. Actual disgust does not generate verbal links other than, transformed into a mental image, in the imagination.

56 Mack, p. 33.

57 Barthes, pp. 17, 19, 84-86.

58 On three occasions in 1997, I stood before Gustave Moreau's painting of *Hercule et L'Hydre de Lerne* (1876) in the Art Institute, Chicago, trying to imagine what Moreau had already imagined: how the hero must have felt. Each time, I noticed that the painting was extremely popular. In a room that also contained paintings by Caillebotte, Manet and Pissaro, Moreau's vision of Herakles' encounter with the Hydra commanded the most attention. Small groups of people gathered around it and many of them remained for long periods. I do not think it was only the lurid, horrific aspects of the painting that drew them. Even more, it was the hero's gaze: his steady look, lips slightly pursed but tight, across a short space into the monster's fecund nest of heads. That gaze touched something familiar. Furthermore, it told me that Moreau belonged to the tradition within French art that includes de Sade, Huysmans, Proust, Céline and Bataille.

59 *Hamlet*, 2.2.461-64; *The Riverside Shakespeare*, p. 1158.

60 Sophocles, p. 4.

61 The Hydra is also a chaos monster. Like many other hybrid or multi-partite monsters, such as Typhon whom Zeus kills or Leviathan whose heads God breaks into pieces (Psalms 74:14), the Hydra represents the forces that human beings must learn to control if they are to possess civilization. Chaos monsters typically live in mountains or otherwise beneath the ground (from whence their rumblings and struggles to free themselves can be heard) where a hero has chained or imprisoned them. Many cultures have tales about chaos monsters and Greek mythology contains several such monsters. My own interests in the Hydra are rather different: I want her to stand for both the overwhelming power of disgust and for its multiplicity, but I also want to put the emphasis upon the monster's mythological and fictional status. The kinds of connections that entwine Philoctetes with the Hydra are textual. In this book, she embodies disgust, but she also represents the distinction between actual and textual disgust. Wilk points out that when Perseus killed her grandmother, Medusa, he viewed her in a mirror in order to "attenuate her petrifying powers" (p. 21). The wan ("attenuated") image of Medusa in the polished surface of Perseus' shield may stand as an emblem of the difference between actual things and their representations. The Medusa in the reflection is not the Medusa who, were he to turn around, would transform Perseus into stone.

62 Wilk, pp. 28–29, 241.

63 I draw these inferences from Philoctetes' wound even while bearing in mind G.S. Kirk's admonition that I probably should not make too much of my reading. Noting the connections between the Centaur's blood in Herakles' death and his earlier involvement with water (Hydra, hot springs, Nessus and the river), Kirk comments that it would be both easy and "superficially attractive" to build a theory about Herakles' death out of these materials. "It is not hard," Kirk writes, "to build apparent systems out of the diverse materials and manifold variants of classical Greek myths, and Heracles provides more opportunities for this sort of thing than any other mythical figure" (p. 201). However, I write as a parabolist, not as a mythographer, seeking only to understand the concept of disgust.

64 Douglas, *Purity and Danger*, p. 151; *Implicit Meanings*, p. 55.

65 Douglas, *Purity and Danger*, p. 147. Denise L. Lawrence observes that ethnographic discussions of menstruation, such as Douglas', have traditionally focussed on "men's reactions of fear" (p. 117). Lawrence discusses the behaviour of women in rural Portugal during the annual pig-killing (a "menstruating woman is believed to be able to cause the pork to spoil simply by looking at it") in terms of their "conscious choice of modes of behavior reflecting strategic goals important to their own perceived self-interest" (pp. 125, 117). Douglas discusses menstruation as a social problem requiring the situational negotiations of both men and women (*Implicit Meanings*, pp. 60–72). See also Thomas Buckley and Alma Gottlieb; Anne E. Clarke and Diane N. Ruble; J. Brooks-Gunn and Diane N. Ruble; Janice Delaney, Mary Jane Lupton and Emily Toth; Patricia McKeever. For a unremittingly positive view of menstruation, see Muscio (pp. 28–52). For a discussion of the male perception of the female body as disgusting, see Claire Kahane; David Hellerstein; William C. Manson. Natalie Angier notes that the history of male thinking, "west to east, up to down," on the topic of menstrual blood holds it to be toxic, "as dirty, much filthier than blood from a cut on the arm." This is a view, she adds (with Camille Paglia in mind), that many "modern women" share (p. 96–97). She also contrasts the reputation of menstrual blood in popular lore to the "reputed purity of ... breast milk" (p. 145). For a summary of the "vile attitudes" towards women in ancient (both pagan and Jewish) and medieval writing, see Wills (pp. 104–21).

66 Anonymous fifteenth-century English poet (Crawley, p. 77). Keith Allan and Kate Burridge cite these lines at the beginning of their discussion of menstruation taboos and euphemisms. However, in counterpoint they also cite Dale Spender that menstruation would have been "the locus for glorification" if it had been a male experience (p. 63).

67 Lessing, p. 303. Suzette Henke thinks that patriarchal discourse has so pervaded female consciousness, even including Doris Lessing's, that women writers "rarely tell the truth about their own experiences as women." Lessing, Henke writes, may have introduced the "first Tampax" [in fact, Lessing does not use brand names] but "*not* the first Durex." Women writers have been, Henke thinks, unwilling to discuss frankly the problems of birth control and sexual pleasure ("Sexuality and Silence," pp. 45–62). In her *Shattered Subjects*, Henke refers to the "uncanny world of excremental anxiety, the translinguistic spoor of psychological abjection" (p. 123). I shall return to Henke's analysis of female abjection in Chapter 7.

68 Faulkner, p. 137. Indeed, it is the "smell" of the black girl that incites Joe's fury. "But he could not move at once, standing there, smelling the woman, smelling the Negro all at once; enclosed by the womanshenegro and the haste, driven, having to wait until she spoke: a guiding sound that was no particular word and completely unaware. Then it seemed to him that he could see her--something, prone, abject; her eyes perhaps." Then Joe begins kicking her hard. Faulkner has craftily fused racial and gender disgust in Joe's mind.

69 Faulkner, p. 161. On the traditional "lexicon" for menstruation, see Allan and Burridge (pp. 81–85). Jane Mills traces the same ground, but adds the positive focus of ascribing to menstruation, and inversely to the phobias/taboos associated with it, the sense of female magic. Nonetheless, the customary taboos have been transformed into weapons "against woman's self-assertion" and act as a "constant confirmation of a negative self-image" (pp. 155–58). For a very interesting discussion of women's use of formally taboo terms, see Casey Miller and Kate Swift (pp. 105–23). Miller and Swift conclude that, in the United States at least, "our most obscene verbal weapons also reveal the deep-seated, violent anger many men feel toward women" (p. 122). This is precisely the territory that Faulkner explores.

70 Grosz, *Volatile Bodies*, pp. 205, 206. Mary Daly remarks that the "menstruating woman is called filthy, sick, unbalanced, ritually impure. In patriarchy her bloodshed is made into a badge of shame, a sign of her radical ontological impurity. It is consistent with the logic of woman loathers' doublethink that the cessation of menstruation is also horrifying" (p. 248). Grosz links the male revulsion at female menstruation to Freud's analysis of the origins of disgust, along with shame and morality, in the child's toilet training, and finds it "unsurprising" that "women's menstrual flow is regarded not only with shame and embarrassment but with disgust" (p. 206). Freud may symbolize the problem of male loathing, but he can not be said to have originated it. Anthropological studies trace the cultural taboos, the systems of repression and prohibition, associated with menstruation through many human societies. Daly bases much of her discussion on this point upon Culpepper. See also Wills; Crawford; Manson; Brooks-Gunn and Ruble.

71 The use of the *pileta* was not limited to Chile. A vivid description of its use in Argentina during the "dirty war" can be found in Horacio Vázquez Rial's *Triste's History*: "[T]he treatment he was subjected to was ferocious: three or four hours of electric shocks, an incalculable length of time with his head submerged in the tank, forced to swallow the sea of excrement, his nostrils filling with a stench that he would never be able to rid himself of ... (pp. 202–03). Labanyi's English translation does not use the word *pileta*, though that is what (rendered as "tank") it describes (although also signifying a baptismal font). The word appears in the original Spanish (p. 204).

72 Lewin, p. 96. Lewin dismisses coprophagy because it does not seem to have a necessary, or biological, basis. He sees it as a practice of small infants and, like Miller, of "certain mentally deranged adults." However, many practices are followed not for biological necessity but rather for cultural or psychological purposes. The culinary uses of excrement, including human, are catalogued in Bourke's *Scatalogic Rites of All Nations*. Laporte discusses some of the more extravagant uses of human excrement in medicine and cosmetics. He claims that feces have been used as a cosmetic to "preserve a youthful complexion" (p. 102). However, all of his claims, though putatively founded in classical texts, seem to turn upon his rather obtuse chiasm that the pearl always "requires" mud (p. 17). It is worth noting that human excrement is commonly used as a fertilizer, particularly for vegetables, in many countries. Even in North America, there are many people who compost human excrement for gardening. It is even possible to buy instructions for this purpose (Jenkins). Its use as fertilizer or "humanure," if nothing more, gives human excrement an indirect connection to human diet. Bourke's compendium reveals a large number of culture-specific, but apparently bizarre, uses for excrement. In his study of Haitian "voodoos, zombis, and magic," Wade Davis observes that in many parts of West Africa, "women breed beetles and feed them on a species of [*Datura stramonium*], and in turn use the feces to kill unfaithful lovers" (p. 40).

73   In Rushdie's *The Satanic Verses*, Saladin Chamcha, having begun to metamorphose into a goat-like figure of Satan, is forced, by English immigration police, to eat his droppings in the back of a Black Maria. This suggests a hazing practice, not a kind of torture. It easily becomes torture in the penal practices of "unevolved" states.

74   Freud, *Three Essays* p. 21 n.

75   de Sade, p. 328.

76   Sartre, *Being and Nothingness*, p. 607.

77   Laporte argues for the historical importance of human feces in cosmetics and cultivation, even citing the high nitrogen content of human, as opposed to animal, feces (p. 125), but he has little to say about coprophagy. He does observe, almost in passing (as it were), that the feces of priests was traditionally considered to be pure enough to eat (pp. 109–12).

78   Doležel, "Towards a Typology of Fictional Worlds," pp. 261–76. This line of analysis is expanded in Doležel's most recent work (see *Heterocosmica*). In *Fictional Worlds*, Thomas Pavel discusses the issue briefly and cites Félix Martínez-Bonati's quadri-partite classification into homogeneous versus heterogeneous, pure versus contaminated, realistic versus fantastic, and stable versus unstable. He calls this the most "complete and suggestive" classification of fictional worlds (p. 155 n. 5). He does not seem to have read Doležel's essay on the topic. Pavel remarks that the "notion of world as an ontological metaphor for fiction remains too appealing to be dismissed" (p. 50). For a general discussion of the problem of fictional worlds, see Maitre. See also Wilson, *In Palamedes' Shadow*, pp. 176–208.

79   King, *Stephen King's Danse Macabre*, pp. xiv, 4. King also refers to the "melodies of the horror tale," which he thinks are simple and repetitive. King's metaphors, rhythm and melody, have been expanded into a narrative model. Michael MacDowell writes of King's use of "interconnecting and intersecting rhythms" (p. 95).

80   Quoted in Ozick, p. 79.

81   Rushdie, *The Satanic Verses*, p. 81.

82 Rushdie, "Chekov and Zulu," pp. 170–71. Always interesting, Rushdie is especially so on the question of terrorism. At the conclusion of "Chekov and Zulu," the secret service agent, "Chekov," experiences time as having stopped. In the final instant of his life, he experiences an alternative world, based upon the first *Star Trek* series (from which he has also taken his *nom de guerre*), in which he is standing upon the deck of the *Enterprise*, without shields or weapons, watching a Klingon Bird of Prey uncloak and prepare to strike. Rushdie employs a literary convention familiar from Ambrose Bierce's fiction ("An Incident at Owl Creek") and from the work of many modern writers (Conrad Aiken, Jorge Luis Borges, William Golding, D.M. Thomas, among others) in which a character experiences an alternative world, with dazzling clarity, even at the moment of death. The abruptness of a terror-world demands that embedded fictional worlds be experienced with corresponding suddenness.

83 Ozick, p. 79.

84 It does not matter at this stage in the argument whether you think of the actions of a terror state or of the terrorism of a resistance. They both act against their enemies suddenly, using surprise and unexpectedness, and both employ violent means. Early in George Roy Hill's 1984 film *The Little Drummer Girl* (based on the John Le Carré novel), a Palestinian terrorist, wearing a bright-red blazer and a knitted mask, tells an audience that he and his comrades are called terrorists because "we must deliver our bombs with our hands. We have no American planes." The distinction between state terror and political terrorism is made to seem no more than one of weapons and the means of delivery. They are the dance and counter-dance of perverse geometries.

85 Stephen King thinks of terror as a higher narrative effect than horror. "So: terror on top, horror below it, and lowest of all, the gag reflex." King adds, "I will try to terrorize the reader. But if I find I cannot terrify him/her, I will try to horrify; and if I find I cannot horrify, I'll go for the gross-out. I'm not proud"(*Stephen King's Danse Macabre*, p. 25).

86 "[T]his latest mutation in space—postmodern hyperspace—has finally succeeded in transcending the capacities of the individual human body to locate itself, to organize its immediate surroundings perceptually, and cognitively to map its position in a mappable external world" (Jameson, p. 44). Jameson likes to call this unimaginable spatial complexity the "postmodern or technological sublime" (p. 37). It generates the fused affects of awe and dread. Pynchon, of course, had already attempted to imagine something like this complexity in *Gravity's Rainbow*. Although Jameson acknowledges Pynchon, he seems to think that very contemporary fiction with a tradition outside literature in electronic writing, such as hypertext, comes closest to being able to imagine the complex synchronicity of postmodern space. Cyberpunk, Jameson writes, "determines an orgy of language and representation" (p. 321). Something like an word-orgy, or else the baroque architecture of a computer chip, will be needed to provide images of the unimaginable.

87 Pynchon, p. 235.

88 Edwards, p. 100. The coprophagy in *Gravity's Rainbow* decentres ordering and totalitarian systems, of which the Rocket-state contains many and is itself one. Edwards thinks of this textual decentring as a form of resistance, "a tactic merry with the possibilities of evasion and self-assertion" (p. 95).

89 Pynchon, p. 566. The City Dactylic is only one of Pynchon's metaphors for civilization, the future city, anticipated by the *racketenstadt*, in which a computer technology will structure everything. Nonetheless, it rises upon the (repressed) knowledge of shit. Colonization, a synecdoche in *Gravity's Rainbow* for the aggressive projection of technology, builds upon the colonial masters' desire to shit. "Colonies are the outhouses of the European soul, where a fellow can let his pants down and relax, enjoy the smell of his own shit" (p. 317).

90 Fowles, p. 129.

91 Fussell, pp. 330, 333. Fussell's analysis of the coprographic scene in *Gravity's Rainbow* offers support, I think, for my early argument concerning the existence of compound affects in literature. No reader, certainly not an experienced reader, could feel only disgust (whereas witnessing a similar in-the-world scene might well produce only disgust). The effect would be more like revulsion-nostalgia or even sympathy-disgust. It may be the case that the disgust experienced in reading such scenes is (in some ways) greater than in seeing in-the-world coprophagy because it is more vivid and less blurred. Textual disgust is never straightforward.

92 This evocative phrase belongs to Ian McEwan (p. 165).

93 Imagination is always the wild card in cultural and semiotic analyses. How does it work? Within what limitations and under what constraints? What is the relation of imagination to reason? Is it a necessary condition of constructing fictional worlds? I find phenomenological accounts of the imagination, as in Sartre and Casey, most satisfying. However, I would also like to appeal to models of play, such as that found in Edwards' *Theories of Play and Postmodern Fiction*, and models of fictional worlds. I take up the problem of the imagination in Chapter 5.

94 Representations differ from their in-the-world counterparts (if they have any at all) both in bearing a distinct appearance ("wan" or "attenuated") and also in functioning differently. You must ask very different questions of a representation and the answers to these will lead you into surprising connections. The obvious simile would be that of a hyperlink. Although Stephen R. Wilk does not discuss the Hydra (and seems mostly to forget her descent from Medusa), focussed as he is upon Medusa's encounter with Perseus and the long-unfolding consequences of that battle, his method illustrates my argument. Touch at any point in a complex representation, ask the questions that assert themselves, and you will end up in some very different context. And there will be many of these linked contexts. Actual things connect to each other in more immediate ways.

95 White, *Voss*, p. 447.

Chapter 4 ✳ Its Body

1 Scarry, pp. 4, 6.

2 Miller finds few things "more unnerving and disgust evoking than our partibility." His prime example of this bodily "partibility" or "severability" is castration (p. 27). It is certainly the case that, for men at least, castration is a particularly horrible example of severing a body part. However, I think that it is important to include the entire human race within the hypothesis. No one, male or female, wishes to have body parts severed or his or her sense of wholeness and integrity decomposed. Although castration has been, as Miller remarks, "fetishized in psychoanalysis," I imagine that women feel an equal horror about, and sense of loss over, the severance of their breasts and labia.

3 Ed Gein is also said to have inspired Hitchcock's *Psycho*. Since Gein enjoyed keeping and wearing the body parts of his victims, particularly female parts (he kept a skinned-out "vest," complete with breasts), he must be considered to have been the inspiration of Thomas Harris' character "Buffalo Bill" in his *The Silence of the Lambs*. "The remains of Mary Hogan were found in a house which was like an abattoir. In the basement parts of human bodies hung from hooks on the walls and the floor was thick with dried blood and tissue. In the kitchen, four human noses were found in a cup and a pair of human lips dangled from a string like a grisly mobile toy. Decorating the walls were ten female heads, all sawn off above the eyebrows, some with traces of lipstick on the cold, hard lips." After his arrest, his Wisconsin neighbours are said to have "shuddered with sickened disgust to remember that Gein had sometimes given them gifts of 'venison'." Gein is supposed to have danced about his house wearing his skinned "vest" in the throes of a personal exuberance (Davis, p. 163). It is easy to suppose that Gein, and perhaps all serial murders (but not heat-of-the-moment killers), was using his imagination: his ghastly exhibits must have had the status of props. No doubt, all serial killers "look ahead" (in their imaginations) to the actual moment of the crime (Martingale, pp. 80–81; see also Newton, pp. 133–36). As Tithecott notes the "serial killer is a paradoxical figure." Like Ed Gein (or Ted Bundy or the exemplary Hannibal Lector), they can be polite, fastidious, extremely private, but outgoing in their violence. A serial killer belongs to a myth of popular American culture as someone who is "maintained with the help of fantasies that we ascribe to the serial killer being inextricably implicated in and interpenetrated by the dreams of 'normal' society" (Tithecott, pp. 179, 178). Ed Gein seems to have set a standard by which other serial killers can be measured. Patrick Bateman, the first-person narrator of *American Psycho*, refers to Gein and even quotes him (p. 92).

4 *USA Today* (October 15, 1992), cited in Henke, "Toward a Feminist Semiotics of Revulsion," p. 96. Henke describes Chikatilo's mutilations as "acts of linguaphagia" and specifically compares them to Hannibal Lecter's similar appetites in *The Silence of the Lambs* (p. 97). Unlike Hannibal Lecter, Chikatilo fantasised his acts of cannibalism. A Soviet psychologist, Alexsandr Bukhanovsky, who first interviewed him in 1990 in an effort to construct a psychological portrait, remarked that Chikatilo's "internal world is a thousand times richer than the surface expression of that world" (Martingale, p. 142).

He also justified his murders with the eugenic claim that his victims were inferior, morally corrupt and "fallen." "He was disgusted by the squalor and the promiscuity of the women, the alcoholism, the shabbiness and the dirtiness of these fallen people" (Martingale, p. 133). By contrast, Hannibal Lecter is conceived in the purely literary tradition of the Nietzschean *übermensch*, or de Sadean libertine, transgressive for the sheer playful joy of transgression.

5   Carroll, p. 46.

6   *Morphing* suggests a better metaphor than time-lapse photography since it is "edgeless." However, old habits die hard. Morphing is a technique for transforming digitalized information in which reference frames "numerically cross-dissolve into the next frame using pixel point-to-point interpolation." It has become a stand-by in making rock music videos, in advertising (a powerful car, for instance, may be shown morphing gracefully into a powerful animal) and, most recently, in political ads. In the latter case, the thrust is normally negative: the local politician changes swiftly, and seamlessly, into a hated national politician (Benson, pp. 691–96). When you view a face morphed into something quite different, you might well think of Ovid's characters meta*morph*osing into strange, unforseen shapes. On the other hand, the time-lapse metaphor explicitly calls attention to the body's passage through time, its actual-world existential placement. For a discussion of hyper-photographic techniques, see Ritchin. Ades discusses techniques of photomontage. However, even the revised edition ignores the possibilities of digitalization in photography. A brief history of photo-collage and montage is provided under the title "Metamorphosis," in Ewing, pp. 354–85. There is a fundamental distinction between the photography of, say, Man Ray and that of Joel-Peter Witkin which may be located more in the absence or presence of digitalized information in the processes by which the photograph comes into existence than in the photographer's imagination.

7   In writing about the imagination of execution, I do not intend to suggest that the condemned person's victims are somehow less pathetic, less shocking or less human. Of course, human sympathy should turn towards the victims and their families. However, I am writing about the imagination of horror and the kinds of small fictional worlds that the imagination may create when creating the scene of death. The obvious theatricality of executions in the United States makes a comment upon the imagination and disgust, but not upon the course of justice.

8   The bill providing for the execution of murderers by electricity was signed into law on June 4, 1889.

9   In her *Pictures at an Execution*, Wendy Lesser, discussing the San Francisco lawsuit brought to force the TV coverage of Robert Alton Harris' execution, uses the phrase the "condemned man," but she makes it clear that she has in mind (as well) the "generic person who is threatened with execution." She thinks that the gender-free phrases, "condemned person" or simply the "condemned," help "to deprive the person who is dying of some of the individuality, some of the claim to specific character, that the execution and its accompanying procedures are designed to obliterate." She declines to collaborate with the "process of bureaucratic depersonalization" and for that reason chooses "man" over "person." After all, she remarks, the vast majority of people on

death row "are and have always been men" (p. 31 n). Her intention may be admirable (let us all fight "bureaucratic depersonalization" whenever possible!), but it is also sexist. Many women currently inhabit death row cells and several have been executed since Lesser's book was published. Women have often been executed in American prisons, and by all the diverse methods in use. In the United Kingdom, the execution of Edith Thompson on January 9, 1923 became a notorious horror-show. Charged as an accomplice in the murder of her husband, Mrs. Thompson was widely felt to have been executed for her adultery more than for her (possible) complicity in murder. The evidence was thin and circumstantial and she always vehemently denied her guilt. The trial judge, Sir Montague Shearman, made no secret of his dislike for her adultery and summed up against her. She was carried semi-conscious to the scaffold whimpering, "Will it hurt?" Her hair was said to have turned completely grey during her last days. Twenty-five years later in an debate in Parliament, it was alleged that her "insides" had fallen out when she was hanged. The Home Office has never revealed what actually took place. It is known that the executioner, John Ellis, never recovered from the experience. He resigned his position as hangman in 1924 and, "in a sudden frenzy of madness," cut his throat in 1932. His wife told the inquest that it was because of having had to hang Edith Thompson. Carl Sandburg's lines, "What does the hangman think about / When he goes home at night from work?" are disturbingly pertinent. None of the bureaucratic protocols, the turn-ourselves-into-a-machine defences, probably work altogether successfully. All the accounts of the time indicate that everyone associated with the execution of Edith Thompson, including the governor and participating warders of Holloway prison, had been sickened, appalled and utterly disgusted. Whatever the allegation that Edith Thompson's "insides fell out" means (and, given Home Office secrecy, you will never know), it does indicate that something ghastly happened to the condemned woman involving (at least) psychic disintegration (Potter, pp. 180–84). Lesser's insistence on a generic "condemned man" is well intended, since anti-bureaucratic, but both misleading and sexist.

10   "How Kemmler Died," p. 4.

11   Kemmler's brain was removed during the autopsy. "In the longitudinal sinus corresponding with the region of contact the blood was carbonised. There were decided changes in the consistency and color of the brain corresponding with point of contact. Destructive changes of the blood corpuscles were noted" ("Far Worse Than Hanging," p. 2). Describing the execution of Ted Bundy, also by electrocution, David Von Drehle remarks that the prisoner is "heated like the coils of an electric stove" (p. 399). In 1999, after the execution of Allen Lee "Tiny" Davis, the Florida Supreme Court posted photos of his executed body on its webpage (www.firn.edu/supct/death-warrents). Blood had poured from his nose, staining his shirt, and his face, in death, was seen to have turned purple. This led to a petition before the Florida Supreme Court to abolish the electric chair as "cruel" (Pressley, p. A3). Soon afterwards, Florida moved to the use of lethal injection as its chosen mode of execution.

12   "Far Worse than Hanging," p. 2. Nearly all the witnesses called the execution a failure. Only Dr. A.P. Southwick (the "Father of the Electrical Execution Bill") called the execution a "success." He claimed that he was "one of the happiest men in the State of New York." Other doctors, with less professional investment in the execution, freely

expressed their revulsion. Dr. W.I. Jenkins, the deputy coroner of New York, remarked that he "would rather see ten hangings than one such execution as this. In fact I never care to witness such a scene again. It was fearful. No humane man could witness it without the keenest agony." Another medical witness compared death by electrocution unfavourably to the guillotine. A reporter for the New York *World* observed that, when Kemmler was seen to be still alive after the initial surge (and the only one actually planned), "warden, physicians, everybody, lost their wits. There was a startled cry for the current to be turned on again. Signals, only half understood, were given ... " (quoted in Nash, p. 98). The second electrocution at Auburn Prison, that of William G. Taylor on August 23, 1893, was even more horrifying. The condemned man kicked loose from his chair, a box was placed beneath the chair for support, the generator in the prison powerhouse burned out and the current failed. Taylor was removed from the chair and given drugs to "ease whatever pain he may have had" and, the current restored from the city's grid, he was restrapped into the chair (though he seemed already to have died) and given a gratuitous thirty-second surge of electricity (Nash, pp. 98–99).

13 "How Kemmler Died," p. 4. The *Los Angeles Times* article contains drawings of the "death chair" and of the helmet.

14 "Doomed Killer," p. 1. The *New York Times* reported that he ate his meals "with heartiness" and that he spoke with his keeper "about his approaching end without breaking down." Just before noon on the day before the execution, another condemned murderer, a man named Fish, was removed from the "cage" next to that of Kemmler and "taken elsewhere." He took Kemmler by the hand and said, "Keep your courage up." Kemmler replied, "I guess I will behave all right. It can't come too soon for me. Being so near the end is as bad as the actual going" ("Kemmler's Last Night," p. 1). Although it seems that Kemmler did "behave well" and that he conducted himself more bravely than most, the opinion-makers of the time tried to rob him of his courage by attributing it to his criminal mentality. The New York *Times* commented in passing that Kemmler is "incapable of thinking and feeling as other men feel" (p. 1).

15 Lesser, p. 55.

16 Trombley, p. 36. Proponents of capital punishment frequently assert that, in electrocution, the condemned person becomes unconscious instantly and that the jerking, straining and extending of fingers are only involuntary muscle spasms. (Leuchter estimates that unconsciousness occurs within 4.16 milliseconds, or within the 1/240 part of a second (Trombley, p. 34). However, speed of death makes little difference with respect to the disgusting, horrific and/or morally repugnant aspects of capital punishment. The point of Trombley's book is the desire of prison officials to protect the execution teams from trauma by creating "protocols" that will provide machine-like routinization. In his study of executions and execution processes in Florida, Von Drehle also considers the bureaucratic creation of routinizing machine-like procedures. "The rhythm of 'the procedure'," he writes, "is like a truck coming along a flat, straight highway" (p. 396).

17 Potter, pp. 162–63.

18 Masur discusses the rituals of public execution during the first seventy-five years of the United States. He points out how deeply religion had been woven into the public performance of an execution. The condemned person was often made into an *exemplum* for sermons. However, a religious fervour does not imply a lack of pleasure. It is simply one mode for the expression, and realization, of pleasure. The movement towards private executions inside the prison walls hardly made them less spectacular, only more elite. "In principle, private executions were supposed to protect the sensibilities of all citizens, eliminate a scene of public chaos and confusion, and permit the prisoner to die quietly penitent; in practice, they became a theatrical event for an assembly of elite men who attended the execution by invitation while the community at large was excluded" (p. 11).

19 The *New York Times* (April 22, 1992): p. A22.

20 Since the KQED suit, there has been at least one further attempt to compel a video record of an execution. Talk show host Phil Donahue sought to record the execution by gas of David Lawson in North Carolina. Donahue petitioned the United States Supreme Court directly. The Court denied the request without comment. The day before Lawson's execution, Donahue conducted an hour-long death row interview. Lawson had asked Donahue to televise the execution "to serve as an example to others of the effects of child abuse, clinical depression and the dangers inherent in a life of crime" ("The TV Column," p. C6). During his execution on June 15, 1994, Lawson "screamed for five minutes through a leather mask and thrashed against straps binding him to a wooden chair as he died in the gas chamber" ("Around The Nation," p. A17). Eventually, I suspect, a suit will go in favour of a TV station and executions in the United States will once again become public. At that time the psychological issues of participation in death that Lesser discusses will become central to American national life. Other issues that she fails to discuss will move into the foreground. There will certainly be anthologies of executions. Will these have laugh-tracks added?

21 Lesser, p. 25. Sleaze, like slime, is a subjective category. Would it be sleazy to watch another person in any situation? Would reading a shameful, or shockingly frank, autobiography be sleazy? Would it be as sleazy as would, say, watching the disgusting accusations and confessions of a typical Jerry Springer show? Isn't the vastly popular "Reality TV," such as CBS's nauseous "Big Brother," nearly as sleazy as you could find? Would reading an unauthorized biography be sleazy? What about those instances when biography has truly become a "blood sport"? How would that differ from reading someone's private mail or cached e-mail? Are any of these possibilities much different than peaking through a secret hole while another person makes love or uses the toilet? On biography as a blood sport, and the indignities of being an unwilling subject, see Eakin, pp. 159–72.

22 Lesser, p. 32.

23 Lesser, p. 37.

24 Lesser, p. 47.

25 Lesser, p. 41. This proves to be Lesser's chief preoccupation.

26 Lesser, p. 39. An execution, Lesser thinks, is very different from a murder, and certainly very different from a simulated death in fiction or drama, in that it is so excruciatingly planned. Hence seeing Robert Alton Harris gassed to death would not be the same as seeing, for instance, Lee Harvey Oswald shot on TV. A more important difference would be, as Dostoevsky emphasizes in *The Idiot*, that the condemned person would be fully conscious of all this planning. There would be no surprise, or abrupt realization, for him or her.

27 Lesser, pp. 39–40.

28 Foucault, pp. 3–31. Commenting upon the changes in the "mechanisms" of punishment in the decades immediately after the public, and highly ritualized, execution of Damiens, Foucault observes that punishment "had gradually ceased to be a spectacle. And whatever theatrical elements it still retained were now downgraded, as if the functions of the penal ceremony were gradually ceasing to be understood, as if this rite that 'concluded the crime' was suspected of being in some undesirable way linked with it." Throughout the eighteenth century, changing attitudes towards public execution now caused people eventually to see public execution as "a hearth in which violence bursts again into flame" (p. 9).

29 Lesser, p. 64. Trombley studies the "protocols" designed to protect the execution team at the Missouri State Penitentiary at Jefferson City. This involves training and a set of rigorous procedures so that the execution will take place with machine-like precision and (hence) keep each member of the execution team at a great psychological distance from the condemned person. "Every second of everyone's time is accounted for," Trombley writes, and then gives the step-by-step protocol (pp. 110-12). In the United Kingdom, the 1949-53 Royal Commission Inquiry on capital punishment established "three criteria that any method of execution must satisfy: humanity, certainty, decency" (p. 72). Trombley keeps these in mind as motivations behind such bureaucratic machines as that Missouri has invented, but it is more likely that the actual motivation is merely to protect the execution team against revulsion and self-disgust. The effect of an execution upon the entire prison population, including guards and wardens (who may have come to know the condemned person over a period of years), "can be deeply disturbing" (*When the State Kills*, p. 6).

30 Lesser, p. 49. Lesser's book has a small, but fascinating, portfolio of photographs. One, also reproduced on the dust-jacket, is entitled "Balcony Seats at a Murder." It was taken by the photojournalist Weegee and was printed in his book *Naked City*. It shows a scene from a Little Italy tenement in the 1940s in which a number of people, both adults and children, are watching a murder taking place (or one that has just taken place) with a variety of expressions ranging from glee to dismay. In the centre of the photo a small girl with dark hair and a chubby face leans forward, eyes bulging, in an intense effort to see as much as she can. For Weegee, Lesser writes, "murder in New York is always about spectatorship" (p. 177). Reflections such as this reinforce my contention that fictional worlds can be, and are, imagined within actual-world situations, taking bits of the world (such as tattoos or the "mechanisms" of death) as props.

31 Lesser, p. 51.

32 Lesser, pp. 52, 55.

33 Henke, "Toward a Feminist Semiotics of Revulsion," p. 107. "Hannibal's perverted authority is articulated to the symbolic order insofar as it asserts the law and the word of the Father but upends collective social fantasies of patriarchal benevolence" (p. 97).

34 Lesser, p. 67. Lesser cites Clover to support the point. "Clover extensively documents the ways in which male audience members identify with female characters in horror movies, showing that gender boundaries are more permeable than most film theorists have supposed" (pp. 264–65 n. 52). Similarly, it might be argued (against Henke) that extreme, and very explicit, depictions of violence against women, many far more violently so than *The Silence of the Lambs*, such as *American Psycho*, force their male readers to identify with the female victims and to distance themselves from the psychotic male narrator.

35 Lesser, p. 83.

36 Lesser, p. 145.

37 Lesser, p. 183.

38 Lesser, p. 93. One KQED employee remarked that Judge Schnacke acted "as if we shouldn't even be bringing the suit in the first place" (p. 93). Even authors who write about murder and execution, such as Norman Mailer, Ann Rule or Janet Malcolm (and even Lesser herself), can be charged with "sleazy amusement-seeking and voyeurism," even with exploitation (p. 103). Sleaze "rubs off, even on the slightest contact" (p. 110). Nutshelled for popular consumption, this is simply the normal argument of moral philosophers.

39 Public execution, or else murder, as a form of popular TV entertainment constitutes a common science-fiction theme. It is a measure of a future dystopia's imaginatively diminished and routinized condition. See, for example, Stephen King's *The Running Man* (pp. 533–692). In King's dystopian narrative, poor men volunteer to be hunted on TV ("Free-Vee") and to be killed publicly. Paul Michael Glasner's 1987 film version of King's novel changes nearly everything, but keeps the motif of a man or woman being hunted to death. In Glasner's film, the hunted are always criminals so that the stalking-killing motif is seen as a mode of future justice. The film also makes much of King's original motif of cheering crowds and audience participation. The implication seems to be that a future society that allowed executions to become public entertainment would be degraded and lessened (in terms of some ideal of human behaviour), more or less as moral philosophers claim would have to be the case. It is worth observing that the Paul Bernardo trial, which took place in Toronto in 1995, confronted the issue of televising court proceedings in a peculiarly dramatic way. Bernardo was accused of having, with the assistance of his wife, Karla Homolka, kidnapped, sexually assaulted and strangled two teenage girls, Leslie Mahaffy and Kristen French. Bernardo had kept a video record of his abuse of the girls. Legal controversy battled for a year over the right of the court to show the film. Eventually, the trial judge, Mr. Justice Patrick LeSage, determined that only the jury, the accused, the lawyers involved and members of court could see the videos. The TV monitors were turned away from the public while tapes of the rape and humiliation of the two girls were shown to the jury, but the audio portion of the tapes was allowed. The families of the girls went to the Supreme Court of Canada in an effort to block playing the audio in open court, but

were denied. The jury has been described as stunned and traumatized by what they had to watch, but the public audience, hearing only the audio, also responded with disgust and horror. The pattern developed in which the court began to empty during the day as individual members of the audience lost their capacity to withstand the mental images which the audio alone generated. The tapes have been described as "almost unbearable" and worse than the "worst porn." (However, the videos are not true snuff films since they do not, it is said, actually film the murder of the girls.) One CBC reporter, covering the trial, described going into the court to listen to the final tapes showing Kristen French as "returning to the pit." A disproportionate number of the public seeking admission (people begin to line up for the available seats early in the morning) were "under 30, female and willing to go to great lengths to see Paul Bernardo, a self-declared king" (Grange, p. A5). The young women listening to the audio and imagining the violent scenes of degradation may have been trying to exorcize their own fears. What the Bernardo trial showed was the nearly unlimited human capacity to inflict hurt and the willingness to imagine that hurt for some individual purpose (pleasure or education, say). Leaving Bernado and Holmoka aside, would the jurors who saw the videos or the reporters who wanted to see them (but couldn't) be lessened or diminished? That was part of the argument that the girls' families brought before the court in an effort to suppress the tapes and it seems to have motivated the trial judge in his decision to prevent the public from seeing the visual portion of the tapes. However, all accounts of the audience in the courtroom have suggested that the people listening to the tapes were in control of their feelings (they got up and left when they felt too disturbed) and knew what they were doing. Subsequent to the trail, Bernardo's original lawyer was charged (in 1999) with having kept the tapes in his possession for more than a year before turning them over to the police. An author who had written on the case was charged with having seen them.

40   Lesser, p. 123. "Horrific news photos or obscenely violent pieces of silent news footage can disgust or terrify us when we first see them," Lesser writes, but unless there is some kind of narrative, either historical or personal or both, the power of those images to move "may drain away in time; they may cease to upset us in the same way" (p. 171).

41   Lesser, perhaps not surprisingly given her narrow focus, seems not to know that executions, from third-world countries, have played on TV for at least thirty years. Some of the executions that followed the Cuban Revolution in 1959 were shown, in squalid detail, on American TV. Executions from African countries have shown up quite commonly on western television in news programs. (What *Faces of Death* shows in its anthology of necrophilliac thrills had already appeared on network TV.) Long ago, Margaret Atwood wrote poems about watching executions on TV.

42   Judge Schnacke ruled against KQED. Robert Alton Harris was executed privately before the usual small audience of invited witnesses. The execution was, outside the death-chamber, a confused, high-strung event in which different courts intervened and overruled each other. Harris was taken to the gas chamber and strapped in and then reprieved and returned to the holding cell. Two hours later, looking less steady than before, he was returned to the execution chamber and restrapped into the chair. The invited witnesses were still there, waiting. Ironically, a video film *was* made of Harris' execution but it was for Judge Schnacke and the appeals court (if it were called upon).

It was never shown. Lesser suspects that "a television station *will* be permitted to broadcast an American execution" (p. 248). No doubt, she is right.

43 It is this form of execution that fascinates Georges Bataille. He seems to have been particularly drawn to a version of lopping practised in China under the Manchu Dynasty (1644-1911), the Death by A Hundred Bites (or Death of The Hundred Pieces), in which the condemned person is slowly cut into small bits. Contemplating a photograph of the death of Fou-Tchou-Li on April 10, 1905, Bataille (who was drawn to the facework of torture, both the victim's and the audience's) writes that the "world evoked by this straightforward image of a tortured man, photographed several times during the torture, in Peking, is, to my knowledge, the most anguishing of worlds accessible to us through images captured on film." It is, Bataille, adds "an example of *horripilation*: when one's hair stands on end!" (*The Tears of Eros*, pp. 204-06). Death by a Hundred Bites may have ceased, as a formal punishment, with the end of the Manchu Dynasty, but André Malraux clearly ascribes a version of it to the Kuomintang forces under Chang Kai Shek during the suppression of communist cadres in 1927. The captured communists are burnt alive in a locomotive firebox, but not before they have their fingers chopped off, their eyes gouged out and their stomachs slit (pp. 278-92). For commentary on the current uses of torture in the Chinese judicial system, see Chiu.

44 Ingersoll, p. 144. For probing reflections upon the uses of torture and the "culture of torture," see Michael Taussig. Taussig observes that it is difficult, if not impossible, to penetrate "the hallucinatory veil of the heart of darkness" without succumbing to his hallucinatory quality or else losing that quality (p. 496). It is the power of the "hallucinatory veil" that may, perhaps, keep you from becoming hardened, say, or diminished. Much the same might be said about watching executions or even the abuse and degradation of others (as in the Paul Bernardo tapes).

45 Morris, p. 185. For a discussion of punishment and pain in *The Duchess of Malfi*, see Bowers. Of course, representations of torture, reflecting the juridical procedures of the existing culture, occur long before Webster, but they seldom dwell upon these scenes in the same intense manner. At the conclusion of Shakespeare's *Othello*, Lodovico exclaims, "For this slave, / If there be any cunning cruelty / That can torment him much, and hold him long, / It shall be his" (5.2.332-35). In the play's final words, Lodovico adds (speaking to Cassio, now the governor), "to you Lord Governor, / Remains the censure of this hellish villain, / The time, the place, the torture, O, enforce it!" (5.2.367-69; *The Riverside Shakespeare*, pp. 1239-40). For a good example of torture as a sexual stimulus from the period of the Decadence, see Mirabeau's *The Torture Garden*. The use of torture situations and motifs in recent American fiction is widespread. Harris' *Red Dragon* (at least insofar as it is a terror narrative) invokes several scenes of appalling mutilation and pain. The central example should be Bret Easton Ellis' *American Psycho*. Ellis' novel dwells coolly on many scenes of dismemberment and mutilation, evoking the other's pain both as sexual stimulus and psychic retribution (but leaves the narrative open with respect to the actual occurence of any of the acts described). Morris links the spectacle of torture to juridical proceedings (the Inquisition, the Nazi medical experiments) and illustrates it by reference to Kafka's narrative, "In The Penal Colony," in which the condemned person is executed by a machine that inscribes his crime into his flesh. In *Discipline and Punish*, Foucault

discusses the juridical uses of torture in the eighteenth century as an aspect of the public ritual through which the majesty and power of the monarchy was forced home upon the populace. Scarry's analysis of the relation of the human body in pain to imagination raises an issue that any discussion of torture needs to treat: how is pain to be imagined? Does the torturer create a small private world in which he or she exults in the other's pain? How can pain be re-imagined, recreated in narrative, once it is past? The imagination, Scarry writes, is "bound up with compassion" and is massive, continuous and ongoing "like a watchman patrolling the dykes of culture by day and by night" (p. 325). But the torturer cannot be denied imagination. Pain is not merely a problem for the powers of narrative to recuperate, but a condition of the torturer's private world-building. (Conroy turns repeatedly the problem of the torturer's split consciousness.) The personal anecdote with which I began this chapter assumes that pain is, as Nietzsche argued, a mnemotechnic.

46 Morris, p. 184.

47 I shall discuss the problem of prosthetics, or cyber(body)parts, in greater detail in Chapter 7.

48 Eakin discusses the problem of personhood in writing autobiography in considerable depth in his first two chapters. Does a story of the self, whether autobiography or bio-fictography, assume a firmly established self, with definite boundaries, or a merely relational self?

49 Clynes and Kline, p. 27. Patrick Clancy remarks that cyborgs "occupy the space between technology and nature, and science and culture" (p. 218). Generally, the initial optimistic view remains popular (though not in science fiction, normally dystopian), only more utopian than ever. The popular view might be along the order of believing that cyborg technology would constitute a true, viable prosthetic, an unconscious extension of your own agency. Optimism concerning cyborgs is not the same as optimism about androids, but they do tend to proceed hand in hand. One kind of technological euphoria seems to blend into others. For the current optimistic view of androids, or robots, see Moravec. For a reprise of his conclusions, see Moravec's "Rise of the Robots." An advanced android would not, I suppose, experience a split consciousness, except insofar as it might develop a "Pinocchio Complex" as so many androids (and even holographs), including Commander Data, in various *Star Trek* episodes have done.

50 Halacy, p. 9. This shows the original '60s optimism (still alive and well in the AI community) concerning cyborgs and hybrid body forms, but it also indicates a definite confusion since no such beings existed then, or even now, in any significant sense. What Halacy seems to have had in mind are "mechanical aids" as artificial bodily supplements such as, to cite two of his more risible examples, bustles and cosmetics. Persons of the future may well be hybrid, integrating organic and technological systems, but they have no actual forerunners other than in imagination. Most mechanical aids are not, I think, actually sufficiently consolidated into the "natural" human systems to constitute trans-human cyborgs. Viewers of *Star Trek—The Next Generation* and *Voyager* will understand that it is the "Borg," not Commander Data, who are the future embodiments of the cyborg hypothesis. In the minds of many viewers it would be "Seven of Nine" from the *Voyager* series, with her very human form but serviceable

Borg implants, who most convincingly represents the future of humanity. Though apparently born as other humanoids, the Borg have highly sophisticated non-organic parts, including a magnifying right eye and neural net programmes, integrated into their bodily systems. And the Borg are, notoriously, hostile and inimical. The distinction between cyborgs and androids is made razor-fine, pushed nearly to aporetic undecidability, in James Cameron's 1984 film *The Terminator* and in his 1991 *Terminator 2*. In both films, the terminator is called a "cyborg" but its only organic part is an integument of organic skin and a layer of flesh. (It also has hair and even "bad breath.") In the final sequence of *The Terminator*, its external skin and flesh having been burnt away, the "cyborg" is reduced to its internal metal structure and cybernetic systems. At that point, moving relentlessly ahead, it seems to be fully an android. This characterization inverts the normal sense of cyborg (a human body with synthetic parts rather than an artificial body with organic parts), but still maintains a distance, until the final scenes, from usual concept of an android.

51 *The Six Million Dollar Man* premiered on October 20, 1973 and *The Bionic Woman* on January 14, 1976. (The main character in *The Bionic Woman*, Jamie Sommers, was actually imagined as the girlfriend of Colonel Steve Austin, the hero of the antecedent series.) This schlock played well for '70s audiences enthralled by the prospects of body-part replacements, whether by transplants or by beyond-the-horizon technology. The excitement of the "Bionic Woman" as a role model evidently persists. Stacey Young, a student at the University of Toronto, writes that, "As a child I always wanted to be the Bionic Woman. I was a member of the fan club. I had the doll and the dome house. I was a fanatic. With long light brown hair, I felt an affinity for the Strong One ... Jamie Somers represented all the potentials that I admired in adult womanhood" (p. 8).

52 In *eXisTenZ*, the characters have "bio-ports" installed in their lower spines. Once they have a bio-port, they may then link together, by umbilical-like cords, in complex games in which different players play separate characters. Cronenberg imagines the world of the games as completely organic; that is, the game pods themselves are organic, subject even to disease (spoor invasions, in particular). The brain-shaped game pods are alive in some sense; a character repairing one is described as looking like a veterinarian operating upon an animal. The world of *eXisTenZ* is filled, appropriately, with disgusting images of rot and decay. The characters observe their cognitive dissonance, the weird and (almost) unimaginable schizophrenia that a prosthetic imagination would entail.

53 Gibson, *Neuromancer*. Gibson's novel concerns a hacker (the real-world analogue of the "console cowboys" of cyberpunk fiction) operating in cyberspace, a cybernetically enhanced bodyguard/mercenary, and a pair of mysterious AIs. It started the hard disk spinning as far as cyberpunk is concerned. It won the Hugo, Nebula, P.K. Dick, and Ditmar awards, something no other science-fiction work has done. Gibson also wrote two sequels in the same setting, *Count Zero* and *Mona Lisa Overdrive*. Gibson also wrote a collection of short stories, *Burning Chrome*, which contains three stories in *Neuromancer*'s setting, as well as several others. Gibson's *Virtual Light* has a near-future setting and somewhat more toned-down technology, but it deals with the familiar cyberpunk thematic concerns. Robert Longo's 1995 film *Johnny Mnemonic* is based upon a Gibson short story originally published in *Burning Chrome*. For a discussion of Gibson's fiction, see Bukatman (pp. 146–53 and *passim*).

54 Spivak, p. 169.

55 Haraway, "The Promises of Monsters."

56 Haraway, "A Manifesto for Cyborgs," p. 191. I have no doubt that Haraway intends her "we" to signify women only. I have taken it to include both women and men because that is, as I understand it, the actual direction of the analogy. We are all, women and men, sufficiently artifactual to justify the cyborg *analogy*. If you think that the subtext of the argument is "power," not simply the construction of consciousness, then I ask that you reflect upon Jonathan Goldberg's discussion of the distinction between "voice" and "voicing" in Shakespeare. "Authority in the Shakespearean text," he writes, "is a matter not of having a voice but of voicing" (Goldberg, p. 119). Neither women nor men, whatever voice they may think they possess, have the power, or only seldom, to "voice" (anything). Power "entails a disturbing heterogeneity, owned by no one voice—a voicing, as Luce Irigaray might say, that is not one" (Goldberg, p. 135).

57 Haraway, "A Manifesto for Cyborgs," p. 212. The solution to the condition of being a (discursive) cyborg is not to turn your back upon technology, but rather to understand it well enough to use it for your own constructive purposes. "I would rather be a cyborg," Haraway concludes, "than a goddess" (p. 223). The normal ambivalence about prostheses, whether hybrid body parts or cyborgian enhancements, carries over even to the level of metaphor. It is possible both to yearn for technological amplification and to feel disgust at the prospect.

58 It is not clear which body part most easily lends itself to cyborgization. In Cameron's *Terminator* films, the entire body, other than the skin and flesh, is non-organic. However, in many science-fiction novels, and in some films (including Cameron's own 1986 *Aliens*), it is the skin, conceived of as an exoskeleton or else as powered armor, that defines the cyborg. (In *Aliens*, Ripley enters a external cargo-moving frame and employs it, as if it were a skeleton or an armored frame designed for combat, to defeat the alien mother, who already possesses a silicon-based exoskeleton.) Steve Wang's 1991 film *The Guyver* and his 1994 *Guyver 2: Dark Hero* (both derived from Japanese *manga* stories) employ powered-armor motifs. The exoskeleton is a motif in Robert Heinlein's *Starship Troopers*, Joe Haldeman's *The Forever War* and John Steakley's *Armor*. The cyborgian exoskeleton occurs frequently in comic books, such as Marvel Comics' *Iron Man*. It is a key element in Japanese *manga* and in innumerable animated films. Shinya Tsukamoto's 1989 film *Tetsuo: The Iron Man*, which seems to take off from *manga* themes, varies the exoskeleton motif: an iron fetishist contaminates a young businessman (a salaryman) who begins to grow an outer integument of iron, his penis metamorphoses into a power drill, complete with a spinning auger at the tip, and his hair begins to look like a Medusa-head of scrap metal. Bukatman calls *Tetsuo* "techno-surrealism" (p. 308).

59 Haraway, "A Manifesto for Cyborgs," p. 191.

60 There may still be scholars, troglodytes or mere luddites, who prefer to write with pens (inherited, it may be, from their fathers) and who make the disgust face over computers. Seeing a young colleague clutching a new Mac Powerbook or IBM ThinkPad notebook, such scholars will crinkle their noses and twist their lips up and outwards. It will be a judgement upon their colleagues, but also upon technology and, in particular, upon electronic writing. You may say that such judgements are hypocritical, but (in a world unevenly split between luddites and ludites) they are also inevitable.

61   Bukatman, p. 296. The surrealist perspective upon machines has been developed in many provocative (as well as crazy, clumsy and stultifying) ways in modern art. For examples, see K.G. Pontus Hultén's catalogue to "The Machine" exhibition at the Museum of Modern Art which ran from November 25, 1968 until February 9, 1969 (and then was shown at the University of St. Thomas and the San Francisco Museum of Art).

62   In October 1996, David Cronenberg's film *Crash*, based on J.G. Ballard's 1973 novel, was released. It seemed to de-eroticize the fictional world even more than the novel had done. In interviews, Cronenberg repeatedly expressed his amusement that critics had found the car crashes "unrealistic" because they were not seen in slow motion, did not involve explosions and did not unfold through multiple camera angles. Cronenberg aims for an even greater deal of artifactuality in the desire/machine interface than Ballard.

63   Ballard, *Crash*, p. 138. Ballard's fascination with machines, both with their capacity to hurt and their power to stimulate desire, is also evident in *The Atrocity Exhibition*. The Re/Search edition provides the author's annotations in the form of marginalia, illustrations and appendices. It is another proto-hypertext format constructed under linear constraints. Perhaps even more than *Crash*, *The Atrocity Exhibition* constitutes a fantasy of contemporary technology, extravagantly imagining the near-future's techno-landscape.

64   Bukatman, p. 292.

65   Pynchon, *V.*, p. 389.

66   Pynchon, *V.*, pp. 285–86. Pynchon's interest in synthetic human objects and in the transformations of the body by surgery and prostheses continues in *Gravity's Rainbow*. "In and out of all the vibrant flesh moves the mad scavenger Tchicherine, who is more metal than anything else. Steel teeth wink as he talks. Under his pompadour is a silver plate. Gold wirework threads in three-dimensional tattoo among the fine wreckage of cartilage and bone inside his right knee-joint, the shape of it always felt, pain's handfashioned seal, and his proudest battle decoration, because it is invisible, and only he can feel it. A four-hour operation, and in the dark. It was the Eastern Front: there were no sulfa drugs, no anaesthesia. Of course he's proud" (p. 337).

67   Jameson, p. 28. Jameson identifies this fragmentation as the "fundamental aesthetic" of certain schools of postmodernism poetry. It makes more sense to say that it pervades, both as an aesthetic concept and as a structure of desire, all contemporary life. Ballard's *The Atrocity Exhibition* is a particularly forceful instance of the general theme of schizophrenic fragmentation. For example, the conventional notion of "character" is completely unmade. The character obsessed with creating "alternate death" scenarios is identified as Travis (section 1), Talbot (2), Traven (3 and 11), Tallis (4, 10 and 12), Trabert (5), Talbert (6), Travers (8), and is not named at all in some sections. Critics have read Ballard's fragmentary characterization in very distinct ways. Brian McHale understands the different sections as stories that recombine the same "fixed repertoire of modules" and the "T" character as a "mentally unbalanced researcher" (p. 70). On the other hand, Robert L. Platzner claims that "he" (the "T" character) might be "a doctor impersonating an ex-bomber-pilot, or a would-be assassin, or the amnesiac victim of a car-crash, or a psychopathic murderer, or a spy, or quite possibly none of the above" (p. 215).

Ballard's interest in fragmentation strikes me as similar to Pynchon's and both writers derive much of their schizophrenia (of fragments) from their unblinking look at the human and machine dance.

68   Androids, or at least robots, have had a long history in film. Though probably not the first film to envision an android, Fritz Lang's 1926 film *Metropolis* would provide an enthralling *terminus a quo* for that history. The history of cyborgs is both shorter and less certain. Michael Crichton's 1973 *Westworld* has seemed to some critics to be the first cyborg film (Strauss, pp. 35–36). However, the humanoids in that film are clearly robotic. Mike Hodges' 1974 techno-thriller, *The Terminal Man*, based upon Crichton's novel of the same name, does concern a cyborg in the sense that the scientist has a computer in his brain (but keeps his brain). Jud Taylor's 1976 *Future Cop*, a made-for-TV film, may have been *Robocop*'s actual progenitor (though the Future Cop was entirely robotic with a human appearance). Irvin Kershner's *Robocop 2* continues the story of Murphy's transformation. Albert Pyun's 1989 *Cyborg*, despite the promising title, basically has little to do with cyborgs and mostly explores *Mad Max/Road Warrior* territory. On the other hand, Pyun's 1992 *Nemesis*, though essentially a B-movie, has struck some viewers as a genuine cyborg film. It shows significant linkage to William Gibson's novels. James Cameron's two *Terminator* films (since the films call the Terminator a "cyborg," they must be cited in the cyborg category, even if that seems like a dubious rubric) would be fundamental to any discussion of cyborgs. Cyborgs have become a cliché in B-flicks with multifarious titles (rather like a massified insect swarm) such as *American Cyborg*, *Terminator Woman*, *Cyborg Cop*, *TC2000* and *Mandroid* filling out the cheap rentals.

69   Actually, it would make no significant difference to my argument if I *were* to claim that the loathing, and/or trepidation, people feel about machines was archetypal. If, as C.G. Jung so often argues, the idea of a whole or individuated self is an archetype (represented in fantasies, dreams and art by the mandala), then it might make sense to see the machine as falling within the archetype of the Shadow, or of a chaos monster perhaps, as a physical embodiment of dismemberment and de-individuation. I prefer to think about these matters along the lines set by Jerome Bruner: there are certain basic, but limited ways, in which the mind organizes the world. "The subjective reality that constitutes an individual's sense of his world is roughly divided into a natural and a human one" (Bruner, p. 88). The first takes shape in terms of logic; the latter, in narrative.

70   Insect films mark off a specific area of horror: an unending, implacable bio-machine composed of infinite separate entities. The prototype of this sub-genere would have to be Byron Haskin's 1954 *Naked Jungle*, based upon Carl Stephenson's story "Leiningen versus the Ants," which depicts an unceasing army of foraging ants that seem to possess a collective intelligence. Noël Carroll refers to insect hordes as monsters "of the magnified phobia variety" (p. 49). Insect films flourished during the 1970s. Freddie Francis' 1967 *The Deadly Bees* begins a list that contains a large number of titles. For example: Saul Bass' 1973 *Phase IV* (ants with collective intelligence); Curtis Harrington's 1974 *Killer Bees*; Bill Rebane's 1975 *The Giant Spider Invasion*; Bruce Geller's 1976 *The Savage Bees*; Bert I. Gordon's 1977 *Empire of The Ants*; John Bud Cardos' 1977 *Kingdom of the Spiders*; Robert Scheerer's 1977 *Ants!*; Irwin Allen's 1978 *The Swarm*. The possibilities for insect films are, like the insects themselves, countless. Jeff Lieberman's 1976 film

Squirm concerns worms. All four *Alien* films build upon the movie tradition of insect swarms, implacableness and fecundity. They show, as do all insect films, what Carroll analyses as instances of "massification." He claims that this process only works to create horror when the creatures "grouped into horrific hordes" are of the kind than an audience would already find repugnant. "Massing mountains of already disgusting creatures," he writes, "unified and guided by unfriendly purposes, generates art-horror by augmenting the threat posed by these antecedently phobic objects" (p. 50). The peak experience in viewing massified insect films would have to be Paul Verhoeven's 1997 film *Starship Troopers*. Sketchily based upon Robert Anson Heinlein's novel, the film recounts futuristic human battles with a planet of insects (called the "Arachnids") who mass and swarm in exceptionally deadly ways. There is even a high degree of the differentiation of labour among these insects, with some acting as flame-throwing tanks, others as tactical fighter-bombers and still others as intelligence officers (they suck the brains out of the skull before "reading" them). However, the present argument is that implacability and composition out of multiple parts would generate disgust even if the parts were unknown or known only as benign. An army of ladybugs, if only it crawled forward and could not be turned back, would probably be disgusting. (Carroll supposes that ladybugs, as butterflies, could not work in a horror film [p. 172]. Presumably there would be too many positive associations in play. But ladybugs, too, would be subject to Carroll's principle of massification.) For one thing (never taken into account by insect films), how would you react to all that frass?

71 Sloterdijk, p. 441.

72 The phrase "nameless metahuman" strikes me as vastly superior to "monster" and one which could be used cogently to describe how hybrid assemblages, techno-human constructions, are actually read in much recent art-horror and science-fiction (see Fiedler, *Freaks*, p. 22).

73 Wells, *The Island of Dr. Moreau*, p. 60.

74 Maslin, p. 103.

75 Nash and Ross, pp. 250–51. The convention of showing a cyborg's perception of the world through a screen striated with coded data is commonplace. Cameron's Terminator also perceives the world in this manner. In the Australian literary magazine *HEAT*, I discuss the problem of the cyborg's eye in an essay dealing with a number of encounters with wild animals that I have had ("In a Condor's Eye").

76 Strauss, p. 36.

77 Like all spatial metaphors, Freud's narrow tower can be reconfigured. Taking the flowchart of a commercial office as his model, Gass respatializes Freud's tower as a horizontal series of desks (*Habitations*, pp. 126–40). Each of the kinds of metaphor that I have mentioned has had scores of variations.

Chapter 5 ❀ Its Many Eyes

1   Pynchon, *Gravity's Rainbow*, p. 17.

2   "Sexual words and pictures, delivered in context, work the way pornography works: they do not merely describe sexuality or represent it. In a sense, they have sex. When a man sends a note ending, 'I'm going to fuck you even if I have to *rape* you', he is getting off on writing and sending the note and envisioning the recipient reading it. The recipient feels sexually violated as well as terrified of rape." A sexual insult would be a "sexual invasion, an act of sexual aggression, a violation of sexual boundaries, a sex act in itself" (MacKinnon, p. 58). It is worth noting that MacKinnon supposes the impetus behind sexual aggression lies in the aggressor's desire to create a private fictional world ("he is getting off on writing and sending the note and envisioning the recipient reading it") in which he may enjoy a certain fantasized scenario. The victim would have been a prop.

3   In this book, I am interested in neither the history of the art/craft nor in its most striking expression, full-body tattooing. Illustrated men and women, tattooed people with their bodies entirely covered, or nearly so, by their tattoos, entered circus exhibitions as early as 1840. The first full-bodied tattooed people to exhibit themselves enhanced the negative effect of tattoos by inventing stories of having been tattooed against their wills, either in primitive cultures or else as a punishment for having participated, and been captured, in foreign wars. Barnum's Captain Costentenus ("The Tattooed Greek Prince") claimed to have been given his tattoos against his will as a punishment by "Yakoob Beg, Khan of Kashagar" (see Bogdan, pp. 241-56; DeMello, pp. 44-96). Nor will I discuss communal tattoos. Tattoos which are given to each member of a community, usually in stages to mark various passages into adulthood, such as Maori and other Polynesian tattoos, while fascinating from an ethnographic standpoint, and often aesthetically pleasing as well, do not demonstrate the disgust factor. If you are supposed to do something, or commit a certain act once you reach a specified age, your community will likely not find it disgusting. They might even find it disgusting if you did not do it. I am primarily interested in individual tattoos that have been chosen to generate specific, quite often disturbing, effects. However, there is a category of tattoo known as "tribalism." A person with a tribal tattoo will have borrowed a design from Maori or other Polynesian cultures or from Borneo or even Japan, but will have done so for complex personal reasons (DeMello, pp. 86-89). DeMello observes that, for a time, the tribal tattoo "stood with the Japanese tattoo as the ultimate middle-class adornment" (p. 91). Appropriated within western society, the tribal tattoo does interest me.

4   I am following Ross Chambers' distinction between culture as the body of discourse that allows sense to be made and individual acts as moves made within the rules for sense-making that culture establishes. It is also the case that context is important. If you see a violent tattoo in an exhibition of *tatouage*, it should not disturb you any more than the tattooed people in Barnum's American Museum would have caused the audience genuine fear and dread. Twice, once in Australia, once in the United States, I have

seen men with spiders tattooed in the inside corner of the right eye and webs descending downwards across the cheek to disappear beneath the shirt collar. The social effect in both cases, but especially in Australia when I was drinking with members of the University of Melbourne's English Department in a pub near the University, was instantly startling and intensely disturbing. It was as if the man who bore the image of a spider were himself a spider; as if those who saw him had looked, with Leontes, into the cup and hung poised, pierced by loathing and (perhaps) dread, upon the edge of overwhelming disgust. We contemplated him, without appearing to look, imagining what he would do if he took note of us or if he came towards us. The reverse image (which I have never seen) of a spider beneath the collar with its web ascending to the eye would be, I suspect, equally off-putting. In such cases, you may easily feel that you are in the presence of a stigma personality: a self-stigmatizing and potentially dangerous individual, who might at any moment erupt upon you.

5   O'Connor, p. 514.

6   Goffman, pp. 43, 8–9.

7   I am not assuming that a verbal description of a tattoo in fiction does the same work, or is essentially equivalent to, a film representation of a tattoo. What I am assuming, and actually arguing for, is that, taken as a problem in interpretation (in reading or processing), there is less difference than one might suppose. This follows from the obvious (if not wholly self-evident) proposition that one's associations with a representation are deeply linked to the conceptual, not the manifest, content. The boundaries that a representation demands its readers/viewers cross are conceptual, though capable of being manifested in different forms, and persist from one image to another. Think about a spider and you will likely engage some of the associations always already available: in Ovid's account of Arachne, Shakespeare's characterization of Leontes' psychological violence when he imagines a drowned spider, the young man with the tattooed spider whom Guy Trebay describes or my parable of the young academic who has tried to self-inscribe himself as a genius, all draw upon (and play against) the cultural imaginary of prior associations with spiders.

8   I discuss exphrases and other minimal narrative forms in *In Palamedes' Shadow* (pp. 223–31) and in *Shakespearean Narrative* (passim). See also Donnelly and Becker.

9   "Path" may seem, rather too enthusiastically perhaps, to buy into the technicolmetaphoric lexicon of narratology. No doubt it raises difficulties similar to those that metaphors such as "boundary" or "map" pose (terms which Thomas Pavel employs extensively and which are, generally, dear to the hearts of narratologists). Each theoretical perspective possesses a number of privileged metaphors which are largely inseparable from its major preoccupations. Narratology borrows most of the formalist-structuralist metaphors (small units, machine parts, devices, concinnity and so forth), but adds significant images of borders, boundaries, domains, zones and maps.

10   Derrida, *The Post Card*, p. 179. Derrida plays upon the homophonic pun, playing across the different etymologies, between *cheminée*, chimney and *cheminé*, to have walked (slowly) along the path. His translator, Alan Bass, felicitously translates Derrida's *acheminer* as "to send something on its *a-way*." The wordplay across distinctions, giving typically poststructuralist metaphors, serves Derrida's purposes in *The Post Card*, but it also serves my own. The path-in-play moves towards a destination prescribed by a lusory goal and governed by rules, both constitutive and regulatory, but it is often, even within these limitations, open and free. It often does not reach its destination (and hence the usefulness of Derrida's neologism, *adestination*) and it often goes up in smoke, chemnified, or ends up *acheminé*, sent on its *a-way*. As seems always true of playfulness, the genuine excitement lies in play itself, the playing or the having played. It is always the case that "play exceeds the game" (Edwards, p. 7).

11   Suits argues that the presence of a (at least one) constitutive rule transforms play into game. Rules impose purposeful obstacles upon ordinary actions and the process of playing a game requires that you accept the "inefficiencies" of the rules in order to enjoy playing (it). There would be no fun (and no game) in simply walking across the green to drop the ball into the hole or in sweeping the board clean of your opponent's pieces to effect the most direct and efficient checkmate. When the game-player accepts the rules he acts within the voluntary confines of a "lusory" attitude (in a "pre-lusory" attitude you *would* walk the ball to the hole and drop it in). Suits would argue that, even in aleatory games, it is a lusory attitude that allows you willingly to choose chance as a basis, and hence a constitutive rule, for play. In his discussion of Suits' theory of play, Edwards observes that "play is an attitude of mind, a perspective on life or on being in the world, together with actions manifesting this attitude" (p. 17). There would be no need for rules if there were no prior life; no forms of life if there were no (possibility of) rules.

12   Chambers, "Rules and Moves," p. 96. Chambers formulates clearly an apparent paradox that you might suppose to be obvious (but isn't). One recurring theme of Macy's novel *The Fundamentals of Play* is precisely that while no one ever explains society's rules, you can't play its games unless you know them.

13   Chambers, p. 100.

14   Spariosu, *Dionysus Reborn*, p. 32. This seems like the abstract, philosophical equivalent of Kathy Acker's notion that play is personal, exploratory and sexual. Patricia Yaeger argues that women need a playful (and heuristic) discourse in order to discover their own values and ways of self-expression.

15   Spariosu, p. 165. Spariosu's notion of play recalls Félix Martínez-Bonati's idea that "contemplative play" lies behind the experience of literature (p. 92). My own view is that literature and art are playful in several respects: both as products of creative play and as texts that can only be grasped by acts of interpretation that constitute a number (perhaps many) of steps in a process of heuristic play. Diane Ackerman puts it sharply when she notes that much of "human life unfolds as play" (*Deep Play*, p. 11). Alas, she has in mind only the self-contained, "magic turf" dimension of play that Huizinga first analysed. Granted Huizinga's premise, it follows that everything self-contained, including all texts, is play. I think that it is much less obvious that literary texts are games, but they are obviously playful.

16 Walton's discussion of make-believe is excellent and I shall refer to it on several occasions for technical illustration and support. Of course, Walton is not the first thinker to analyze make-believe as a form of play. Caillois' discussion of play in *Man, Play and Games* precedes him, as does Suits' *The Grasshopper*. I do not accept Walton's final position that fictional worlds are *only* make-believe. My argument is, in part, that disgusting in-the-world things, objects and acts, can be transformed into props for the imagination. When that happens they reappear as elements in a private fictional world and/or as motifs in literature and art. I discuss fictional worlds and worldhood in several places, especially *Shakespearean Narrative*. Penetrating analyses of the concept may be found in Doleẑel, Maitre, Margolin and Pavel.

17 Casey, *Imagining*, p. 177. Casey's argument maintains both the independence and autonomy of the imagination, its unreducibility to any other mental act, and also that it is only a mental act, not necessarily the most autonomous nor the most important. I want to claim that imagination comes into play, building make-believe scenarios, in response to objects and acts that are perceived: its "props," in effect.

18 I accept Casey's argument that imagination is one kind of mental act among many. And with Casey, I would wish to avoid the "harmful consequences of thinking in exclusively hierarchical terms." It is only, he observes, within "the mind's multiplex structure that imagination's autonomy has its place." In this study of disgust, I have tried to avoid the "restrictiveness of scalariform thinking." In Chapter 2, I argued for for a pluralistic use of an array of models rather than a scalar and against the top-down application of any single model to the complex phenomena at hand. Hence I agree with Casey that only in terms of a non-scalar model can the "teeming pluralism of psychical phenomena can best be acknowledged and accommodated" (*Imagining*, p. 178).

19 Sanders, p. 75.

20 AFFA stands for "Angels forever, forever Angels." A member of Hell's Angels might have these letters tattooed on his or her fingers in order to demonstrate authenticity and lifetime commitment (Grognard, p. 32). JFFJ is a common variant among the Gypsy Jokers. Like the well-known set of "Hard" and "Luck," both AFFA and JFFJ are also FTW ("fuck the world") tattoos. "Grasshopper," a prison tattooist, neatly captures the impetus behind FTW tatttoos: "Life is a bitch, then we die" (DeMello, p. 134; on deviance, pp. 67–68). In any case, the clearest vantage for reading such tattoos would be while looking at the person's closed fists immediately before being struck.

21 Gray, p. 30. I have already argued that conformity is comforting and that one of the purposes of shock art, indeed of the avant-garde in general, is to puncture social conformity's protective balloon. Gray's observation that conformity is also "sensuous" strikes me as a valuable insight. How wonderfully warm and full-bodied it must seem to conform!

22 Vale and Juno, p. 77.

23 William Schipper, Memorial University, told me the following story out of his experience of teaching for seven years in Japan. In a small Tokyo tavern the customers were kept in terror for many hours by a local *yakuza*, perhaps a thug or more likely only a petty criminal, who did nothing more aggressive than sit in their presence and drink. He was covered by full-body tattoos. The striking aspect of the story was that the

yakuza was clothed and did not have tattoos on any public skin. The people in the tavern knew that he was tattooed because his light summer shirt disclosed, though quite indistinctly, the presence of his tattoos. In this situation, as in the other story of the men with spiders in the corner of the right eye, the challenge of reading a tattoo seems to fold into the theory of horror. In a horror tale, a monster does not need to be fully disclosed to generate the effects of horror. Anyone who has read even one of H.P. Lovecraft's tales knows that an absent monster may be more frightening than a present one: minimal disclosure may have more powerful effects than full. Of course the young man in the parable is not horrible, nor should he be horror-inspiring. He seems to have had an ideal purpose to lay claim to, and a desire to manifest his intellectual interests to the world at large. Yet his fate, at the hands of the selection committee, may well be the same as if he had actually intended to inspire horror. On the theory of horror, see Carroll; on Japanese *irezumi*, see Richie and Buruma, and Fellman. D.M. Thomas, writing in his introduction to Fellman's book, remarks that he would not be able to make love to a Japanese woman with back tattoos without also making love to the tattoo. He adds that the "deepest relationship" for a person with *irezumi* would be with the master who had worked his designs, "so tirelessly penetrating," into the skin (p. 9). Thomas precisely captures the erotic dimension of Japanese tattooing, also made evident in Bob Brooks' film *Tattoo*.

24 MacDonald, p. 204.

25 In *The Last Temptation of Christ*, tattoos of abstract design, upon the hands, arms and face, are given to some of the women, including Mary Magdalene, but they are orna-mental, in more senses than one, and not presented as problematic. Or, at least, this is my reading of the tattoos in Scorsese's film. However, Lynn Weinlos, a friend and former student, has told me emphatically that the tattoos in *The Last Temptation of Christ* were among the most disgusting things she had ever seen in a film. This clash of opinion seems to mark the difference between growing up in an Orthodox Jewish home, where Leviticus would be taken seriously as a primary guide to living, and growing up in a cultural context in which that same text would be seen as "deep" background, an ancient and "primitive" catalogue of prohibitions.

26 Back tattoos are especially striking. The area of skin to be covered is larger than any other part of the body and permits more detailed, integrated images. A back "piece" will take more time, cause more pain and cost more. It is also a part of the body that the tattooed person cannot normally see. Hence a back piece is intentionally designed for others to see. For a photo of the tattoo on Acker's back, see "Interview" (with Andrea Juno) in *Angry Women* (pp. 177–85, especially p. 181). Back tattoos embody a special panache. Acker's fascination with tattoos for her body seeps into her fiction. On Acker's use of tattoos in her fiction, see Burke.

27 Vale and Juno, *Angry Women*, p. 181. In *Modern Primitives*, Vale and Juno include an inter-view with the Canadian artist, ManWoman, whose full-body tattoos suggest thematic, but not narrative, unity. They possess what he claims to be "bilateral symmetry" (pp. 40–49). ManWoman also has a flaming third eye tattooed on his forehead. (As does Michael Wilson [pp. 37–39].) A third eye has quite different associations than a spider, but it also, tattooed upon the forehead, also suggests, as a deeply transgressive act,

many boundaries to be crossed. ManWoman observes that his tattooist, Fat Rick, made him wait a year before drawing it in order to test his determination (p. 42). This accords with the point often made by sociologists, such as Sanders, that professional tattooists do not like to work on public skin.

28   The term *imaginary* was introduced by Sartre in his *The Psychology of the Imagination*. It is now normally associated with Lacan. In any of several definitions, including Lacan's, the imaginary signifies the body, fund or archive of images in terms of which experience, the self or the world are to be represented. Thus it exists within an interplay between two poles: consciousness and the world (or the core self and the specular self). Sartre thought that the imaginary came into play by a conscious act, a voluntary mental act intended to make the world representable. I use the term to include the archive of cultural scripts, including stereotypes, clichés and other boilerplate. The fictional worlds that accompany human experience, and which replay it (with advantages) in the mind, are built up out of both the raw materials of perception and the learned modes of interpretation. Disgust can rather ferociously prompt the construction of worlds, but it does so through the mediation of a cultural imaginary. As an affect, it is so metamorphic precisely because the imaginary which shapes it can be so plastic. Wolfgang Iser discusses both the history of the term and several meanings that it has been given. For a discussion of Sartre's theory of the imagination, see Warnock (pp. 160–81).

29   Iser, p. 470.

30   The image of disgust's "falling glissando" is Ian McEwan's. He also provides an example of how a single bit of spoiled food can pollute the entire sense of being. In *Amsterdam*, Clive Linley rides a train to the Lake District where he hopes to find the solitude that will allow him to complete a symphony he is composing (under a deadline). He finds a "flattened black mass" of chewing gum on the sole of his shoe, deeply embedded into its tread. It is still pink, "like flesh," beneath the grime and gives off a faint "smell of peppermint." As he tries to pick and scrape it away with his pocket knife, his upper "lip arched in disgust," he reflects on how appalling it is to have "intimate contact with the contents of a stranger's mouth" (p. 63). You will remember that Freud puzzled over the disgust you might experience in having contact with the contents of your lover's mouth (in using his/her toothbrush). Even McEwan's weaker instance is richly illustrative.

31   The reverse experience may work differently in the sense that the memory of having polluted something, having crossed a definite boundary into a taboo space, may come back to haunt you with shameful imagery. (This, I think, happens less commonly than moralists like to suppose. But it does sometimes occur in the dim reaches of a contrite memory.) Suppose that when you were a young rebel, a blooming de Sadean perhaps, but still serving as an acolyte, you took a pious neighbourhood girl into the sacristy one Saturday night. It may even be, in an access of Huysmansesque bravado against repression (and the sacred), you took her out onto the altar. The accomplishment of having deflowered your pious girlfriend within the sacred precincts of the church may have thrilled you with the exhilaration of transgression, but it is likely to prove a harsh, even a shameful, memory in the on-flow of time.

32 I spent the summer that I turned twenty on the beach in Long Beach, California. I had given up sailing with the intention of returning to university and I had accepted an old friend's invitation to visit him in Long Beach where he was the night bellhop at the Villa Riviera hotel. (It may no longer exist, but at that time it was directly on the beach, about half a mile south of the Pike, Long Beach's seafront amusement park.) My friend changed the lock on a first-floor room so that the housemaids would leave me alone. This plan entailed some very dirty linen by the end of the summer, but it worked perfectly in its intention to provide me with free accommodation. Late in the summer, my friend quit his job and left for the east coast. I thought that it would be wise to leave myself. It would be true to say that friend had never offered me protection, but he had been a source of reassurance. (I had long since come to understand that the Villa Riviera was owned by a famous gangster. He had been, we believed, a close henchman of Bugsy Siegel.) A man I had come to know, Tony (I shall call him), owned a popular pizza shop in an old wooden house directly on the beach between the Villa Riviera and the Pike. It was a place where my friend and I had often hung out. Tony said that I could use an empty room on the second floor and stay as long as I liked. The room he gave me looked out over the sea and so I fell in love with it at first sight. I even contemplated staying for several more months, giving up my plans to go back to university. The first time that I took a shower, I discovered that there was a narrow room parallel to the bath/shower combination. When I looked into it I was surprised to see a single stool at the farther end. When I sat on the stool I saw that there was a tiny pinhole in the wall that looked directly into the women's toilet. The stool was obviously intended for a man to sit upon while he watched (and, I would guess, masturbate) women urinate. The next day, I stepped into this secret cubicle, sat down on the stool and looked through the tiny peephole. I saw a lithe brunette drop the one-piece swimming suit of that era and urinate. I stared at her while she semi-squatted a few inches above the toilet seat, making an uncomfortable muscular effort to avoid bringing her buttocks into a polluting contact with the seat, and went about her business. Suddenly, I felt overcome with a powerful sensation of sleaze. It was not, I think, the sense of actual pollution, but it was a definite sense that I was diminishing myself by spying in this way. I experienced a moment of Sartrean intensity. In fact, all that would have been necessary to saturate the moment with this intensity would have been for me to discover that there was another peephole at the other end of the cubicle through which someone was observing me spy upon the young woman. The sleaziness of the situation had "rubbed off" (Lesser, p. 110) on me and I felt it acutely. I never looked through the peephole again and when, two weeks later, I left, I moved the stool away from the viewing spot and covered the peephole with chewed gum. When he next checked his room, Tony may have felt my judgement upon him (but upon us both, really), but he may also have simply removed the gum while thinking of me as an unmanly, disgusting momma's boy. Since I had spied on girls urinating before, why did I experience the feeling of sleaze? I suspect that it must have been the disturbing experience with Georgie that had given me the ready sense of being sleazy. After that adventure had settled into my memory (and entered into my imaginary), I became much more sensitive to the threats of being shamed, and hence to sleaze, than I had ever been previously.

33 Consider, for example, the "paradox of the puppet show" from the episode in the
    second part of Cervantes' *Don Quijote* in which the Knight and Sancho watch a travel-
    ling puppet show representing the action of a story from a medieval romance. The
    Knight knows that it is a puppet show and offers a running commentary in which he
    criticizes the puppet master's technical abilities in staging the show. Nonetheless, at a
    certain moment, he rises and with his sword attacks the villains. The "paradox of the
    puppet show" states an obvious fact about all theatre and, indeed, most literature:
    it is possible to know the conventions, to be familiar with the story, to grasp the entire
    mechanism of the production (its technologies laid bare), yet still become absorbed in
    the action, carried away within the illusion of representation. I discuss this paradox
    more fully in *In Palamedes' Shadow*, pp. 197–99.

34 It is worth noting that the term *imagination* nowhere appears in Miller's *The Anatomy of
    Disgust*. My own understanding of the imagination and how "worlds" are imagined
    (visited, explored, even inhabited) owes much to Jean-Paul Sartre. I am endebted
    throughout to Casey's *Imagining* and to his *Remembering*. Casey's analysis of worldhood
    and his specific concept of a "mini-world" have influenced my own notion of small,
    even ephemeral fictional worlds prompted by various in-the-world items (such as
    tattoos). The scholarly discussion of fictional worldhood, in Maitre and Pavel for
    example, is also relevant. The most recent full-scale discussion of the problem is
    Lubomír Doleẑel's *Heterocosmica*. It contains a good bibliography, but it is rather
    restricted by Doleẑel's obsession with taxonomy and his (perhaps) slavish cap-touching
    in the direction of analytic philosophy. The title reveals the largest problem with
    Doleẑel's discussion: "possible" is a term used in analytic philosophy to indicate worlds
    different from the actual one in at least a single significant detail, but fictional worlds
    are often quite impossible and presuppose universal laws that do not, and could not,
    be the case in the actual world. Narratologists are usually happiest in dealing with
    novels in the tradition of realism. They tend to find fantasy perplexing.

35 Pavel glosses Walton's account as follows: "now when a group of children play with
    mud, they simultaneously touch globs of mud—in the really real world—*and* offer one
    another tasty pies in the world of make-believe, which is real within the game. Running
    away from tree stumps in the real world becomes, for the same children, a flight from
    dangerous bears in the world of make-believe" (p. 56). In the real world, Max Cady has
    crude jailhouse tattoos upon his back; in his make-believe world, huge phantasmagoric
    shapes struggle in an archetypal battle for personal justice.

36 See Landow.

37 Kolb, p. 334. Later, Kolb remarks that we "need forms of hypertext writing that are
    neither standard linear hierarchical unities nor the cloying shocks of simple juxta-
    position" (p. 339). The possibilities for hypertext, whether in scholarship or in fiction,
    lie in the links, not in the whole texts that could be keyboarded into the hypertext, and
    in the potential for individual readers, following these links (like paths), to create
    heuristic categories.

38 Landow, *Hypertext*, p. 12 (see also Landow, "What's a Critic to Do? Critical Theory in
    the Age of Hypertext"). Landow notes that one "great advantage of digitalization lies in
    the ease with which that form permits manipulation, searching, and (to use the new

jargon) re-purposing" ("What's A Critic to Do?" p. 27). Thus hypertext provides a model for new writing, but it also suggests a model for pure exploration. For many people, their access to the Internet proceeds through the World Wide Web, effectively a single hypertext document that continuously expands and changes (as individual documents, such as homepages, are deleted, modified or added) while maintaining its manifold of links. What I have called "paths" are recognizably the links and categories of an imagined hypertext environment.

39 Nabokov, p. 310.

40 Christopher Nash, p. 190. The problem that Nash invokes—the reality-status of characters whose names are mentioned but who never appear "in the text"—restates the earlier problem of the minimalist shard. Lolita does not appear in *Pale Fire*, neither as an inhabitant nor as an immigrant, but her name can cause a very complex fictional world (with a vast accretion of critical commentary) to intersect *Pale Fire*'s world and to occupy a shadowy other dimensionality within it.

41 Alter, p. 187.

42 Ingarden, p. 218.

43 Harry Levin, p. 146.

44 Terence Parsons distinguishes between "native" and "immigrant" objects. For example, Sherlock Holmes is native within Conan Doyle's stories, but London is immigrant in the sense that it is already familiar and crosses the boundary into the text at many points. I employ the distinction to indicate the difference between characters "at home" in a certain narrative, such as Priam, Pyrrhus and Hecuba in "Aeneas's Tale to Dido," and those, crossing in from a larger fictional world (or fictional world-matrix), which cannot be excluded once the process of signification has been engaged (Parsons, pp. 51-52). The vast world of the Matter of Troy immigrates into the more narrow world of Aeneas' tale. If Hamlet were to enter that world he would do so as an immigrant, though he is native to the containing world, *Hamlet*.

45 Pavel, pp. 94-105. "I would call *narrative* or *dramatic orchestration* the relationship between the number of domains and that of the corresponding characters" (p. 103).

46 Maitre, p. 119.

47 Pavel, p. 94.

48 Although "brand-name realism" is usually associated with Bobbie Ann Mason's fiction, it is a relatively common minimalist convention. (Carver himself uses it sparingly.) In *American Psycho*, Bret Easton Ellis employs brand names in what some readers have taken to be a monotonous drone. To a much lesser degree, he also uses brand names for narrative effect in his two earlier novels, *Less Than Zero* (1985) and *The Rules of Attraction* (1987). His characters seem always to know where articles of clothing have been purchased. They also know the titles of popular songs and who is singing at any given moment. What is the narrative effect? The convention of citing brand names helps to establish, but also to delimit, a character's perspective. Shared out between several characters, the convention defines a narrow fictional world, circumscribed by consumerist interests and the dialectic between advertising and consumption. *American*

Psycho evokes a split fictional world, though still quite minimalist, in which clean, precise product-consumption (associated with gold or platinum American Express cards) frames, and counterpoints, the deranged serial killer's sexual mutilations and murders (or his fantasies of them). A minimalist narrative ("dirty realism") is not the same as a "minimal world." It may seem problematic to use *minimal* in two sense (or else a good joke), but the two senses do bear upon each other and each calls attention to the imagination's power to maximalize the minimal.

49 Buford, "Observations," pp. 4–5. The American origins, and deeply ingrained properties, of dirty realism suggest several analogies. Dirty realism belongs to the current US pattern of backlash and rejection. In a culture given to internal mythologizing, there is only a little room for self-examination. (Assumptions do their deductive work without criticism.) Similarly, much recent American painting makes semiotic homogeneity into a constitutive feature. Super realism (or neorealism), a dominant American mode, takes the ordinary "belly-side" of American life as its special province. Writers, such as Raymond Carver, Richard Ford, Bobbie Ann Mason, Bret Easton Ellis and David Foster Wallace, recreate underbellies. Many of Shakespeare's embedded fictional worlds, such as the afterlife-world that the Ghost creates (but even the garden-world that he creates next), are essentially minimalist.

50 Carver, p. 223.

51 Carver, p. 213.

52 Carver, p. 218.

53 Carver, p. 237.

54 Carver, p. 220.

55 Carver, p. 236.

56 Carver, pp. 232–33.

57 The problem of coherence and relevant "coherence criteria" might seem to arise primarily with regard to long, diverse narratives. Issues of coherence arise from the internal structure of a narrative, from the tension between diverse semiotic domains, not from mere length or number of words. A truly incoherent narrative (an effect which might reflect full authorial deliberation) would probably best be thought of as one in which semiotic domains clash and do not either overlap or reach a resolution. Thus even minimal narratives raise issues of (possible) internal contradiction and the failure of coherence. In the parable of the young man with the spider tattoo, the academic (fictional) world is split by the multiple significance of the young man's tattoo. The questions of his intention and the ways in which a spider tattoo (on the forehead) might be read divide the narrative and strain, but do not destroy, the possibilities for coherence. On coherence criteria, see Maitre, pp. 29–34.

58 Altman's revision of the story does add complexity—it alludes to all manner of tales, *I Pagliacci* or Angela Carter's *Nights at The Circus* for instance, in which the sad personal lives of clowns are in counterpoint to their professionally simulated happiness—but it does so at the expense of the implicit male view of events in Carver, that view which must be inferred from the antagonistic female narrative voice.

59 Casey observes that single imagined objects can be, and perhaps usually are, imagined within a "nexus of relations," within a ongoing state of affairs (p. 42). He also argues that such complex states may be imagined in either sensuous or nonsensuous ways. In the latter case, the imagined events do not "come clothed in sensuous detail" (p. 43). I suspect that his distinction makes sense, but I have not called upon it. From my standpoint, analysing how in-the-world experience may lead to the building of imaginary worlds that may further be transformed into representations as art, literature or film, imagination is most lucidly viewed as operating in sensuous ways. (Thinkers from Sartre to Jameson have argued that imagination creates only "wan" experience.) This is not to say that very abstract mental construction of experience cannot be disgusting. In the next chapter, I call disgusting abstractions "perverse geometries."

60 Fictional worlds relate to the actual world in several ways: as descriptions, explanations, hypotheses, alternatives and exaggerations. For example, Menippean characters and worlds grossly exaggerate features of the actual world, but they also instruct readers in that world's hypocrisies and self-deceptiveness. Philosophers like to deny relevance to fictional worlds or, in the Humean manner, to assert their lack of cognitive engagement and purpose. Catherine Wilson examines several positions with respect to what can be learned from fiction. She concludes (while granting more sense to the traditional philosophical views than I would) that a bond of "cognitive reciprocity" exists between writers and readers. She observes the "pang of recognition" that readers often experience in fiction.

Chapter 6 ⁕ Its Heads

1 I discussed this scene in Chapter 3.

2 With great lucidity, Ross Chambers distinguishes between resistance and opposition. Opposition "is generated within a system of power even as it works against it" and functions as a mode of "survival tactics" within the circumstances set up by the system of power "for purposes the power may ignore or deny" (*Room For Maneuver*, pp. xvii, 1). It operates within the "play" that the system of power permits, reading the system for significance that it has never claimed, and projects into the system (or into the world as delimited by that system) a "technology of the self" that makes possible (some) expression and personal definition (pp. xvii, 252). Opposition enables the "transformation of alienation into self-education" (p. 174). Considered only as a way of reading, a *techné* or set of skills, opposition reads out (other *stories*) that the system does not recognize. In Chambers' study, oppositionality is, typically, the "know-how" that enables you to read the textual production of a dictatorial regime as irony rather than, untransformed by skilled (or playful) reading, as allegory (p. 250). I discuss Chambers' argument at length in "Terror Becomes Graffiti."

3 Chambers, *Room For Maneuver*, p. 188.

4   Deleuze and Guattari, *A Thousand Plateaus*, pp. 105–06. I have equated "majoritarian" with ideology only in the sense of there being a dominant set of ideas, a solid "*arbre-racine*," a tap-root, and corresponding consciousness in both. No doubt thinking of Althusser, and the ferocity of neo-Althusserians everywhere, Deleuze and Guattari hold that "ideology is a most execrable concept obscuring all of the effectively operating social machines." Literature, they also observe, has "nothing to do with ideology. There is no ideology and never has been" (pp. 68, 4). Although Chambers does not dwell upon the concept, he accepts the normal signifying work of "ideology." He writes, for example, of the "ideology of gender" which may be said to exercise "a dictation of its own" (p. 175). If you take "ideology" to indicate a set of ideas held by many people (the "majority"), and not as an unconscious structure that it is impossible to escape, then the equivalence will be apparent.

5   Theroux, "Letter," in *The Rushdie Letters*, pp. 32–33. Mario Vargas Llosa sees Rushdie's predicament as marking a line that "divides the rational from the irrational, the just from the unjust, the barbarous from the civilized" (p. 96). Not all the authors who contribute to *The Rushdie Letters* write with such fury and scorn, but the sense of outrage is always implicit. Bafflement and amazement are also present as is, always, sympathy and fellow feeling. The most effective letters are those that reveal that the authors have read *The Satanic Verses*. The idea behind *The Rushdie Letters* developed in early 1992 when the German newspaper *Die Tageszeitung* published a series of letters from important writers in several countries to Rushdie. The letters are intended to express solidarity with Rushdie, but they do so from dissimilar backgrounds, in terms of different assumptions and with a fascinating variety of perspectives. Rushdie's 1991 *apologia*, "One Thousand Days in a Balloon," is printed first and the letters follow as replies or as independent reflections upon his predicament. Rushdie responds to the letters, noting how the case of *The Satanic Verses* has become "the symbol and the archetype of all the other cases of repression" in the world, which several of the writers had mentioned (p. 122). Finally, Carmel Bedford, of Article 19 and Secretary of the International Committee for the Defence of Salman Rushdie, contributes "Fiction, fact and the *fatwa*," a sixty-page chronology of events between February 14, 1989, the day upon which Ayatollah Ruhollah Khomeini pronounced the religious edict, the *fatwa*, in which he sentenced to death both Rushdie and all others who had been "involved in its publication who were aware of its content" (p. 130), and November 27, 1992 (Day 1372) at which time "Salman Rushdie remains in deep hiding, under armed guard" (p. 183). The chronology, as a record of smarmy, pompous and plain murderous nastiness in the name of religion, makes grim, but enlightening, reading. Not only are different Muslim spokesmen revealed making inflammatory statements, speaking with stunning disrespect for the laws of the nations where they live, or speaking equivocally in uncertain future tenses, but western spiritual leaders, such as the Archbishop of Canterbury, are overheard uttering foolish propositions. "Tolerance is achieved," the archbishop says, "when people hold their religion as so important that to part from it is to die," ignoring, as one English newspaper pointed out editorially, that it was the Ayatollah who had condemned Rushdie to death, not the other way round. "If the archbishop lacks the intellect to distinguish between freedom of conscience and freedom to commit crimes he should keep quiet" (pp. 167–68). Other leaders, such as the pope and former US president Jimmy Carter, are observed, in their passion to defend religion, falling into similar confusions. Today, Rushdie, though still living under the *fatwa*, seems on much safer ground, the government sanction of the edict having been, it seems, withdrawn. The issue remains and will do so, far into the future, long after the particulars of the situation, such as the novel or the author himself, have all been absorbed into the vastness of past events. It is an allegorical issue, a "case."

6   Keeping Chambers' distinction between opposition and resistance, it seems that Rushdie, in writing the Mahound sections of *The Satanic Verses*, had been engaged in opposition. The Ayatollah responded as if Rushdie had been fomenting resistance. The problem then arises whether majoritarian religions, or theocratic states, have the conceptual means to make the distinction themselves.

7   Martin Amis, p. 172.

8   Levy, p. 569. To the shock of many western people, the Rushdie affair has shown that Islam has no tradition of creating literature out of its revealed texts, still less of writing secular fiction out of its sacred code. As Rushdie observes, Islam makes "literalism a weapon and redescriptions a crime" (*The Rushdie Letters*, p. 22).

9   Appignanesi and Maitland, p. 88–89.

10   *For Rushdie*, p. 74. *For Rushdie* was initially published in French in 1993 as *Pour Rushdie: Cent intellectuals et musulmans pour la liberté d'expression.* (Neither text names its editors.) A collection of essays and fictions (and music) by Arab and Muslim intellectuals, *For Rushdie* contains many statements that not only support Rushdie, but also attack Khomeini's *fatwa* as either illegal or un-Islamic in intent. It is a fascinating book that could be read rewardingly in conjunction with *The Rushdie Letters*. Rushdie is not without support in the world, even among Muslims. One of the contributors to *The Rushdie Letters* is the Iranian writer Fahimeh Farsaie, the author of *The Glass Home Country*, herself like Rushdie and Taslima Nasrin an exile. Farsaie, who lives in Germany, tells Rushdie that she can "very well imagine this dreadful, terrifying" situation in which he finds himself. Many writers, even poets, have been tortured and executed in Iran. Rushdie may have an international profile, but his situation is scarcely unique. Farsaie points out that PEN has identified 739 writers who have been persecuted in seventy-five countries (pp. 56–57). In his reply, Rushdie thanks Farsaie for having shown that the attack against him "is only one battle in a larger war" (p. 121). That war (fanaticism against freedom, totalitarianism against social openness, repression against play, literalism against fiction, spirituality against materialism, Islamic triumphalism against the west) is being fought in many places and takes many shapes: religious denunciations, censorship, demonstrations, *fatwas*, terrorism. Reflecting upon the interdependence of fundamentalist Islam and politically repressive states ruled by "Machiavellian" dictators driven by "ambitious fury," Jamel Eddine Bencheikh observes that, once in place, "such a system as the one we have now never lets go of its prey" (*For Rushdie*, p. 75).

11   Lawton, p. 182. Westerners may suspect that Muslims, fiercely closed within their own communities and "shared tradition," take offence too furiously and show too little tolerance for the imagination.

12   Lawton, p. 180. The case of Taslima Nasrin, a Bangladesh writer, indicates that the Rushdie affair has hardly constituted a singular event. However, Nasrin's novel does not seem to involve redescriptions, either of Islamic doctrine nor the pious tradition of telling the Prophet's life in exemplary terms. The animosity towards Nasrin by her fellow Muslims seems actually to have arisen from her treatment of Hindu characters in her novel *Lajia* (Shame), not from a supposed transgression of doctrine nor from having broken the limits fixed upon "writing about" the Prophet. The "redescription" under attack is simply a cultural, and quite local, attempt to show a Bangladesh religious minority in a fresh perspective: Nasrin's attempt to represent the suffering of persecuted Hindus in Bangladesh. What western writers (and readers) might take to be a novel's first order of business, to show sympathy and understanding for the Other, has been in Muslim Bangladesh an occasion for offence and the accusation of blasphemy. It would be difficult to find an instance of the charge of blasphemy being brought that more explicitly illustrates Lawton's argument (that blasphemy directly indicates an offence to a community) to the discourse of a community (the way it talks to itself and about itself) as it has been received and is accepted, but only indirectly (if at all) to a supreme being. The religious community, the men in the mosques and clamouring on the streets, seem genuinely to hate her, and ready, as always in such moments, to believe the worst. As in the case of Rushdie, a writer who is believed to have transgressed doctrine may actually only have become offensive to a cultural community and progressively a symbol of many things that community finds disturbing, unsettling and hateful. Viswanathan observes that Nasrin's case, like that of Rushdie, demonstrates the "continuing force of blasphemy as a functional concept in Islamic societies underlies the reading of efforts at internal social reform as a generalized form of apostasy, with effects not only on those societies themselves but on how Islam is represented and understood in non-Islamic countries" (p. 241.) Nasrin comments that "the mullahs who would murder me will kill everything progressive in Bangladesh if they are allowed to prevail" (Nasrin).

13   Rushdie, *The Satanic Verses*, pp. 318–19.

14   Tazi, *For Rushdie*, p. 289.

15   Lawton, p. 21.

16   Levy observes that many Muslims have seemed "overeager to be offended" (p. 559). Lawton's argument identifies the offense as a blow to their very sense of community, to their (varied) culture and discourse.

17   Rushdie, *The Rushdie Letters*, p. 24.

18   Some questions, such as how to respect the religious sensibilities of immigrants within a pluralistic democracy, elicit answers that are both problematic and various. Others, such as how students, teachers and other writers should treat Rushdie, are simpler: read him; defend him. Writing movingly of his experience of reading *The Satanic Verses*, Kazuo Ishiguro points to "the exuberance and noise, [and the] profound sense of loneliness" at the heart of the novel and tells Rushdie that "novels like yours have helped me learn a little more of what it means to be human" *(The Rushdie Letters*, pp. 79–80). Actually reading *The Satanic Verses* might make evident how magnificently it possesses what Graham Swift calls its "life: energy, invention, colour, animation, intelligence,

humour, questions, doubts, passion, quickness: life" (*The Rushdie Letters*, pp. 63–64). The enraged Muslims who condemn Rushdie have not read *The Satanic Verses*, and for the most part never will do so. For them it will remain a perverse geometry in the most abstract possible sense: unread, unseen, a rumour.

19   On the whole, it does not seem to have been a luminous moment for western principles of free speech and expression. Outside of the UK, the response was occasionally more clear-headed. Speaking vatically, François Mitterrand linked the moral and spiritual progress of humanity to "the recoil of all fanaticisms" (Appignanesi and Maitland, p. 105).

20   Barnes, p. 99.

21   Appignanesi and Maitland, p. 195. In an interview in *Der Spiegel*, Naguib Mahfouz, the Egyptian novelist and Nobel laureate, called Khomeini a "terrorist." Islam, he comments, "authorizes no one, not even spiritual leaders who meddle in politics, to impose a death sentence on other people" (p. 141). *The Satanic Verses* has shown that terrorism, like blasphemy, is a two-faced charge. Many of the Muslims who would like to see Rushdie executed, by whatever means, feel themselves to have been the victims of a terroristic act. They might say that they feel struck, directly in the heart perhaps, by something too disgusting to contemplate.

22   Said, *For Rushdie*, p. 261. During the 1993 meeting of the Modern Language Association in Toronto, buttons were distributed which carried the war-cry, "We are Salman Rushdie." I wore one, discovering that many colleagues looked at me askance or with trepidation as if a religious zealot were about to bomb me at the very moment. A friend, who teaches postcolonial literature, let me know that he disagreed with the "offence" I was giving to wounded Muslims. Clearly, I did not agree with him. Terrorism (like bad argument in general), even if it has religious or third-world sanction, should be resisted. Julian Barnes puts it neatly: "words count" (p. 105).

23   Lawton, pp. 134–36; Levy, pp. 508–11.

24   Ingersoll, p. 151.

25   Ingersoll, p. 213.

26   How will western pluralistic democracies persuade patriarchal, and deeply self-assured, monocultural immigrants in their midst that "intellectual hospitality" is a good? Though difficult at best, never easy, not always possible, talk is what the world needs. For a sustained effort to distinguish belief from the repression of (various) ortho-doxies, see Stephen L. Carter.

27   Tazi, *For Rushdie*, p. 295.

28   A major problem for any pluralistic democracy, Canada and Australia as well as the United States, will be that many of its immigrants will have economic motivations only. Only refugees fleeing tyranny can be expected to have minds open to the new demo-cratic belief-system. And even then, not always. An economic immigrant may actually continue to see the dominant belief system as perverse. In many ways, the theory of disgust confronts the possibility that people will engage in disgusting behaviour even while experiencing it as disgusting. This includes even the possibility that a person

might immigrate, for other than idealistic motivations, to a country that he or she has found, and will continue to find, disgusting. "We have to accept, however reluctantly," Leszek Kolakowski writes, "the simple fact that we live in an age of refugees, of migrants, vagrants, nomads roaming about the continents and warming their souls with the memory of their—spiritual or ethnic, divine or geographical, real or imaginary—homes" (p. 59).

29 Viswanathan analyses the use made of religious conversion in colonial societies in order to bring "modernity" to (what were seen as) backward, primitive cultures. Thus modernity became "relocated not in the capacity for change but in the authority of institutions to establish criteria for membership" (p. 77). It was at once a universalizing, if Euro-centred, schemata of ideas and a source of chaos in producing "multitudinous responses" to the comparative openness of the updated society (p. 243).

30 Gordon, pp. 42–43.

31 Gordon, pp. 43–44.

32 Gordon, p. 44.

33 Gordon, p. 48.

34 Amartya Sen points out that there has developed a "fashionable chorus of attacks on the Enlightenment" (p. 33). He is especially puzzled that philosophers, such as Jonathan Glover, willingly join this chorus. The tendency within Enlightenment thinkers to believe in the perfectability of human nature has led critics to blame the Enlightenment for the worst excesses in twentieth-century totalitarian ideology. On the other hand, the chorus largely overlooks, or underplays, the Enlightenment exploration of the power and reach of reason (Sen, p. 34). Outside this chorus of moralizing philosophers, many might suppose that the distinctive contribution of the Enlightenment was the development of critique as a method of discovery. On critique, see Sloterdijk, pp. 15–75.

35 Kolakowski, p. 5.

36 Wills, p. 40.

37 Leo XIII had more than one sense of "Americanism" in mind. Carefully excluding the legitimate patriotism of American citizens, he dwelt upon the secular nature of American life, the openness to liberal thinking and, in general, "the effects of new world conditions on the doctrines and practices of the Catholic faith" (McAvoy, p. 135.) The latter led both to an unacceptable tolerance of other religious views and to an emphasis upon natural "virtues" (such as making money). Father Cyprian rejects both tolerance and natural virtue and seems to hold a deep sense of "the effects of new world conditions" when he mentors Felicitas, who (predictably) becomes eventually what he has feared.

38 *New Catholic Encyclopedia*, p. 995.

39 Gordon, p. 45. Schleiermacher was a Protestant systematic theologian of the early nineteenth century whose thinking "marked the points of the compass" for most subsequent theology (see Niebuhr).

40   The author of a potted definition of modernism in a Catholic dictionary of doctrine makes this reductive claim. The same author also announces confidently that Pius X (in *Pascendi Dominici Gregis*) had exposed the falsity of modernism and "sounded its death knell" (Nevins). Kolakowski's epithet "endless" captures the problem more accurately.

41   There were eighty propositions in the first publication of the *Syllabus*. Many of the "errors," such as the idea that people should be permitted the free exercise of their "own peculiar worship," now seem fundamental to the normal functioning of a democracy. Other "errors," such as the proposition that the church should reconcile itself to "modern civilization," seem only ludicrous. All, as Wills argues, had the definition and maintenance of papal authority as their hidden purpose (Wills, pp. 239–45).

42   Heaney, pp. 994–95.

43   Kerlin, p. 239. Kerlin observes that the "Modernist crisis of the early 1900s supposed that all sides in the controversy took the work of the theologians and the authority of the Pope and the bishops with high seriousness" (p. 242). This agreement over first principles has become increasingly unlikely. Kerlin's observation also indicates that the analogy between the Catholic reaction to modernism and fundamentalist Islam's virulent reaction to secularism is only accurate in part. The Islamic phenomenon is exceptionally horizontal, founded in a traditional way of reading the Qu'ran, not upon a hierarchical authority ruling universally on many matters of doctrine. For a catascopic perspective on the modernist controversy within the Catholic church, see Holmes.

44   The philosophical background of modernism is thoroughly traversed in Heaney's article in the *New Catholic Encyclopedia*.

45   McAvoy, p. 152.

46   Appignanesi and Maitland, p. 47.

47   Levy, p. 559. Still, Muslim outrage has been deep and, it seems, often sincere. The savage reactions to Rushdie may not display western standards of tolerance, pluralism or even literary criticism, but they seem truly (in many instances) to have been *felt*.

48   *The Rushdie File* makes a good starting point. The editors have collected newspaper articles, commentary and interviews from the first few days of the *fatwa* that reveal something of the furious exchanges between infuriated Muslims and defenders of free speech. The chronology given in *The Rushdie File* ends in August 1989, six months after the *fatwa*, and its final contribution, an argument for the "value of toleration" by Michael Ignatieff reprinted from the London *Observer*, is dated April 2. From its chronicle, one may learn both the text of Khomeini's *fatwa* and some of the fiercely condemnatory Iranian commentary that surrounded its pronouncement at the time (Asspignanesi and Maitland, pp. 69–76). Even though a great deal of blood has flowed under the bridge since then, *The Rushdie File* remains the place (after having read *The Satanic Verses*) to begin.

49   Appignanesi and Maitland, p. 75.

50   Appignanesi and Maitland, p. 90.

51   Cherif, *For Rushdie*, p. 102.

52 Al-Azmeh, *For Rushdie*, p. 25.

53 Chamsi, *For Rushdie*, pp. 97–98.

54 Bencheikh, *For Rushdie*, p. 78.

55 Levy shows how the *fatwa* came in the wake of a 1976 blasphemy case against the *Gay News* for having published an erotic poem in which a Roman centurion lusts for Christ and performs various sex acts with him: after the prosecution had won the appeal, the question arose, in judicial review and in parliament, whether to abolish the law or extend it to other religions (pp. 534–50). Anglicans, having a stake in keeping the blasphemy law in effect, were happy to support the proposal to extend it. Although there have been no charges of blasphemy in the United Kingdom since the *Gay News* case, parliament has not amended the law which now "ticks away as if it were a bomb that no longer detonates" (p. 550).

56 It might seem odd to suppose the then-Archbishop of Canterbury, Robert Runcie, to have been a religious fundamentalist, but his response to the *fatwa*, a strongly expressed sympathy with Muslim outrage, suggests that fundamentalism lurks as a possible mental disposition in all religious thinking. The Vatican also expressed its "solidarity with people who have been injured in their faith" (*The Rushdie Letters*, p. 140). Jimmy Carter, in so many respects a reasonable and humanitarian man, found the voices within "the furor caused by Salman Rushdie's book" to be "obviously sincere." Carter did not support the condemnation to death, of course, but, speaking from his own religious conviction, he did sympathize with Muslim outrage, accepting the charge that *The Satanic Verses* vilified the Prophet and defamed the Qu'ran (Appignanesi and Maitland, pp. 236–37). Christians seemed compelled to offer support to the *fatwa* merely because it (appeared to have) emerged from a religious mind-set. John Harriot, writing in the *Independent* on March 8, 1989, described an unsigned (but authoritative) article in the Vatican newspaper, *Osservatore Romano*, condemning Rushdie for blaspheming, as being "at least intelligible" however "ignoble it may be thought, smacking more of institutional calculation than religious principle" (Appignanesi and Maitland, pp. 116–18). This is perhaps the best that can be said of the Christian religious leaders who gave support to the *fatwa*: they spoke out of religious calculation, but not from principle.

57 Lawton, p. 202.

58 Lawton adds, "Sexual deviance as well as sexual excess is therefore a signifier of blasphemy" (p. 29). The sexual passages in *The Satanic Verses*, though tame by contemporary western norms, strike many Muslims as signifying the greater "filth" of blasphemy. That the brothel in the city of Jahila is called the "Hijab" (the curtain, or veil) and that the whores there deliberately take the names of the Prophet's wives torments Muslims. They see this description as an attack upon Islam's most sacred traditions, the piety of the Prophet and his family. (It has also been read, foolishly, as Rushdie's assertion that all "faithful Muslim women" are whores.) Lawton argues that Rushdie is actually "tabling, in the most provocative manner, passionate questions about freedom" (p. 182). It seems possible that religious law enslaves women as utterly, if differently, as does prostitution. Like Ranter excess (or the tattoo of Christ on O.B. Parker's back), such deviations may seem, to the religiously orthodox person, nearly unviewable. Lawton notes that Rushdie "takes as his starting-point what he sees as a religious and cultural refusal—a violent and masculine refusal—to license the feminine" (p. 181). In that sense the act of the whores in the Hijab is a revolutionary gesture against patriarchal dominance (and thus doubly offensive in patriarchal Islamic societies). In Rushdie's terms, "fundamentalism is the biggest blasphemy around" (p. 188) because it represses the imagination and denies so much that is integral to human experience. More terribly perhaps, fundamentalism, by a monologic insistence upon its own singularity, denies the possibilities of human community. For that reason, as Lawton argues, Rushdie treats "the issues of community and blasphemy" as simultaneous (p. 181). Fundamentalists, such as the Imam in *The Satanic Verses*, deny the basis for a human community that could incorporate difference and change. The Imam would break all clocks once his revolution has succeeded.

59 Levy, p. 579.

60 Even if you accept that Khomeini acted duplicitously, transforming personal pique and domestic troubles into an international scandal, you might still acknowledge that Muslim anger has usually been unfeigned. The mobs in Dhaka baying for Taslima Nasrin's death were, no doubt, guileless enough. The problem that westerners experience does not stem from the private conscience of individual Muslims, but from the nature of the *fatwa* itself as a quasi-legal, transnational document: *that* is what stinks so feculently.

61 Levy, p. 565.

62 Lawton, p. 187.

63 It is not, I think, entirely clear what the psychological component of disgust would look like without its more evident visceral manifestation. The work of psychologists, such as Paul Rozin, on disgust concentrates upon the visceral dimension. All the experiments with sterilized cockroaches and imitation dog turds made from peanut butter are designed to capture the visceral reaction, though transferred to an apprehension of contamination and pollution. However, the fear of pollution (which enters centrally into the experiments just mentioned) is certainly psychic and intellectual. In what follows, I assume that the psychological component must be close to horror (from which disgust can never be fully split off), a chill sensation, a quickened heartbeat, a narrowing of perception so that nothing else can be experienced, and perhaps a few minor physical signs such as shallow breathing and droplets of sweat trickling from the armpits coldly down the ribcage. If Mughram Al-Ghamdi were to tell me that he vomited every time that he thought about *The Satanic Verses*, I might not believe him. If he told me that he felt his heart race and sweat drip from his armpits, I could easily believe him.

64 Wallace, p. 88. The narrator in this "interview" recalls his father who spent his working life as an attendant in a men's room at an expensive hotel.

65 Samuels, p. 152. The disgust motifs suffuse the film. The opening shot shows Henry Spencer resting while a huge tumour, or perhaps a wart, pulsates from his right temple. It seems as if it should explode, but instead it floats away from Henry's head. It establishes the *mise-en-scène* as a film in which disgusting things will happen, but it also provides the suggestion that everything that happens may take place "only" in Henry's mind.

66　Samuels, p. 159. Paul Sammon calls the landscape "suffocating and terrifying expressionism" represented in "seething, sooty imagery" (p. 219).

67　Sammon, p. 219 n. 9.

68　Samuels, p. 162. As I argued in Chapter 2, disintegration, imagined as slime, constitutes a fundamental category for the theory of disgust, even (it may be) a necessary condition, but it does not necessarily lead to the feeling of horror. Disintegration is a path, a direction in reading, that may lead to alienation, to the feeling of being apart, deracinated in a world, like Roquentin's, that has become unbearably strange.

69　"Lynch spent five months building this 'thing'. It rivals other man-made monsters in its ability to evoke horror in us" (Samuels, p. 162). Evidently, Lynch was obsessed with "maintaining a veil of secrecy" about his "thing" during the making of *Eraserhead*. He has, fifteen years later, still not revealed how it was made (Sammon, p. 219fn. 9). I think that it creates an impression of monstrousness without the danger, though certainly with the interstitial uncertainty, of horror monsters. It evokes affects of sympathy and pity more readily, I would suppose, than dread or horror.

70　Pynchon, *Gravity's Rainbow*, p. 688.

71　Pynchon, *Gravity's Rainbow*, pp. 715-17.

72　Standard surveys of horror films tend to treat *Repulsion* as a horror film or as an extremely "well-handled psycho-drama with moments of genuine shock" (Maxford, p. 229; for an older view that treats *Repulsion* as a psychological thriller in which the characters verge on "battiness," see Ross, p. 154).

73　A straight razor, left by the boyfriend of Carol's sister, has an important role in the film. Carol picks it up and stares at it intently. Later she uses it to slash the landlord to death.

74　Monsters, Noël Carroll argues, are always threatening, impure (often hybrid), and they cause anxiety in part by triggering "certain enduring infantile fears, such as those of being eaten or dismembered, or sexual fears, concerning rape and incest"(Carroll, p. 43). Later in his book, Carroll discusses the role of the monster in art-horror in terms of Freudian psychoanalysis and the concept of repressed memory (pp. 168–78). Following that analysis, the uncle in *Repulsion* would be a condensed figure, over-determined in several respects, who represents the anxieties of Carol's childhood whether or not he has actually raped her.

75　There have been many fewer alienation films than horror films. The archive is far more narrow. Yet some of these, such as the two I have discussed, stand out as major film classics. Mike Leigh's 1993 film *Naked* strikes me as one of the most penetrating studies of dissociation, alienation and anomie that has ever been made. *Naked* should rank with Beckett's bleakest novels, those in the "Trilogy" (which, at several places, it seems to quote), *Molloy, Malone Dies* and *The Unnamable*. In the last scene of *Naked*, Johnny (played by David Thewlis) hops down the centre of a street on one foot (the other unusable from a beating he has received), having rejected the illusion of love, his great-coat flapping about him. The final words of Beckett's *The Unnamable* are, "I can't go on, I'll go on." Mary Harron's 2000 film *American Psycho* brilliantly depicts a sterile, constricted world in which "greed and disgust" seem to be the only affects the characters experience.

76 Miller, p. 26.

77 See Graves, vol. 2, pp. 107–10. Of course, the Hydra may have stunk so badly, miasmally as it were, because she inhabited the "unfathomable Learnean swamp" (p. 108). In this case, the swamp and the monster are related as metonymies, but the stench is a synecdoche (a part that indicates either the monster or its dwelling). In either case, like all literary monsters, the Hydra is a monstrously plurisignificant creature. As my analysis of her relationship to Philoctetes (in Chapter 3) indicates, she also represents femaleness (in male narrative) and the threat (so often present in male-written literature) of feminisation, the softening and attenuation of the hero's masculinity.

78 Many monsters look human. Their appearance hides their lack of human affects, human desire and even human virtues (such as mercy, compassion or pity). Above all, their human form disguises an inhuman intention. For this reason, it is easy enough to call certain actual-world killers "monsters," and to do so without the epithet "moral" in mind. The analogy leads to a metaphor that can pass as natural. In Spanish popular mythology, there is a being called the *sacamantecas* (literally, a sucker of fat) who kidnaps small children and sucks their flesh. He is a kind of vampire, but the popular stories do not attribute any peculiar marks to the *sacamantecas*, no pointed teeth, no thin web of disease-like purple veins. He is simply an incarnation of purely natural evil carried to a loathsome extreme. In this sense, the *sacamantecas* is a terror monster more than a horror monster (such as literary vampires from Bram Stoker to Anne Rice) since it strikes suddenly without warning. However, it does possess some conventional signs: it is said to have red eyes (if you have the chance to see them), to be immensely thin, ravenously hungry, to dress in black and to wear a slouch hat. It haunts back lanes and remote country paths. A literary narrative that turned upon the existence of a *sacamantecas* would probably be written as a horror tale, but from the character's point of view it might easily seem like a terror tale. Stephen King's splendid retelling of Hawthorne's "Young Goodman Brown," a short narrative called "The Man in The Black Suit," centres upon a thin, famished figure with red eyes that, although the narrator remembers it as the "Devil," more closely resembles the Spanish *sacamantecas*, both in appearance and in behaviour, than any other monster (that I recall) in English fiction.

79 This may be taken as a narrative dilemma for all horror fiction and film: either the monster is shown or it is not. Given the second strategy, the audience may feel disappointed or even cheated. Moreover, if the monster is revealed, it will inevitably be less scary than it was initially suggested to be. Occasionally, there are horror films in which the monster is revealed, as in the *Alien* films, with great success. There the monster is revealed many times, breaking the films down into a sequence of separate horror plots.

80 Does Herakles see both the Hydra's monstrosity and her humanity? The hero must hate the deformity he has been called upon to extinguish, but he cannot hate her fully if he has not also seen the humanity that underlies and has made her deformity recognizable. I imagine the hero as he faces the monster: thoughts run through his mind, memories of love or dreams of heroic comfort, the vision (perhaps) of a bee-hive tomb, but most of all a deep hatred for the deformation of human form before his eyes (and a gut-churning, gorge-cracking revulsion as those eyes fill with disgust), but there is also an awareness that behind the deformity other possibilities lie hidden, an original form or undeformed human shape. And so, dancing momentarily in the hero's mind in the instant before he commits himself, there may also be a vision of love. As Judith Halberstam observes, a monster possesses a remarkable mobile, permeable and infinitely interpretable body that becomes a "primary focus of interpretation and its monstrosity becomes available for any number of meanings" (p. 2). André Gide imagines that, seeing the Minotaur for the first time, Theseus experiences the monster as beautiful, a "harmonious blending of man and beast ." And so Theseus recalls his victory as having been "on the whole somewhat voluptuous" (p. 87). Fairly quivering with its sharp Baudelairian echo, voluptuousness strikes me as precisely the right word. In my mind's eye, I see Theseus drawn to the Minotaur (whom Pasiphaë has already identified as her son), feeling a brief, sharp sympathy, a longing to understand, before he kills him. Would that have amounted to love? Perhaps.

81   Creed, p. 2. Reviewing Creed's book, Frances Devlin-Glass comments that the "logic of her argument suggests that the outcome, even when the films are created by women directors (a rare phenomenon, judging by the filmography) as profoundly conservative of the patriarchal *status quo*. The ultimate feminist challenge, it seems to me, would be to construct films which celebrate menstrual blood or the aging process, and which critically interrogate the taboos to do with excreta, and the relations between human beings and animals. However, by definition such films could not be horror films, because such a politics would deprive the genre of its semiotic vocabulary" (p. 262). Wilk summarizes Freud's view and mentions a number of others (pp. 97–98).

82   In the story I told at the beginning of Chapter 2, the little boy has his first experience of female nudity with a playmate, not his mother. When this is coupled with his subsequent experience of being pushed from his tricycle by the same girls, and having his nose broken, you might suspect that he always thereafter feared castration and looked upon women as the source of this fear. In that reading, he may have loathed the cut peach his mother gave him because it reminded him directly of the girls' genitalia, but indirectly of his own mutilated member. Introspection reveals nothing to support this. The little boy (me) seems to have grown up without deeply rooted castration fears.

83   Creed, p. 111.

84   I have discussed Obeyesekere's reaction to the dancing woman in Chapter 1.

85   Lovecraft, "The Call of Cthulhu." The recreation of the monster in retrospect by a narrator who was not present only slightly varies the Lovecraftian rule that the monster should not be seen, the "closet door" left unopened. In "The Call of Cthulhu," the monster is, in any event, described only vaguely: "Everyone listened, and everyone was listening still when It lumbered slobberingly into sight and gropingly squeezed Its gelatinous green immensity through the black doorway into the tainted outside air of that poison city of madness" (p. 156).

86   A Lovecraftian world is also sticky and slimy. The monsters, even when they are not seen, are characterized by sliminess (wetness and stench, say) and by their power to arouse disgust. For example, from "The Colour Out Of Space": "The men sniffed in disgust at the fluid, and toward the last held their noses against the foetor they were uncovering" (*Crawling Chaos*, p. 174). The echo of Herakles' battle with the Hydra should be apparent.

87   Borges, "There are More Things," in *Collected Fiction*.

88   King, *Danse Macabre*, pp. 110–11. King also claims that it is H.P. Lovecraft's "shadow, so long and gaunt, and his eyes, so dark and puritanical, which overlie almost all of the important horror fiction that has come since" (p. 97).

89   I discuss the range of these false narrative worlds and how they function, as evil deceptions, trials of characters or as playful (though deadly serious) godgames, in *Shakespearean Narrative*, especially Chapter 4.

90   On rumours and the pandemonium of noise in *Hamlet*, see Gross. It important to add that the rumours and lies are told in darkness or poorly lit rooms. They are reinforced by deceptive faces (rather like those of TV newsreaders) and misleading facework. In *Hamlet* as much, or more, as in *Macbeth*, it is true that "There's no art / To find the mind's construction in the face" (1.4.11–12; *Riverside Shakespeare*, p. 1315).

91   King's hotel is called "The Overlook." Its name indicates its spatial location in the mountains, but not its mode of being. Every reader will see quite quickly that it looks in, not out.

92   Price, p. 71. Allende, who writes eloquently about torture in *The House of The Spirits*, continues to observe that terror is a "capacity" which is present in the world. No one should believe that his or her community could *never* become a Northern Ireland, a Lebanon, a Chile under Pinochet, or worse. This is a point that Conroy makes both emphatically and convincingly: terror, in the shape of torture, occurs where you might least expect it (in Chicago, say).

93   Robin Morgan traces the continuity between political and sexual acts of terrorism. Patriarchy may seem to make up a system, like any other ideology, in terms of which, and out of which, sudden acts of violence erupt. See Morgan, *The Demon Lover*. Morgan provides an excellent survey of definitions of political terrorism (see especially Chapter 2, pp. 23–50).

94   Carroll, p. 23.

95   Bataille, "Letter to René Char," p. 35.

96   It is important to remember that the boiler is not in the film and the tide of blood is not in the novel.

97   Fiedler, "Fantasy as Commodity and Myth," p. 51. However, as Fiedler ought to have known, the ingredients of blood and water are commonplaces in King's writing, not merely in the film versions. It is important that Carrie enter the menarche during the film in order to identify her as an adolescent (and, in a ritual gesture to mark her passage from pubescence, her schoolmates bombard her with tampons), but the onset of her menstrual period while showering permits the introduction of a conventional motif of art-horror. Creed observes that Carrie's blood signifies maternal blood, and hence a kind of power, but that it is also "a source of abjection." The film version, Creed argues, "redeploys ancient blood taboos and misogynistic myths" (p. 83).

98 Creed, p. 45. Looked at from another perspective, Cronenberg's characterization of Nola anticipates his emphasis upon bodily functions (and dysfunctions) in all of subsequent films. This can be seen in all of his films, though his 1996 *Crash*, in which bodily disfigurement from car accidents are taken to be erotic, stands out. The 1999 *eXisTenZ*, which takes the physicality of the prosthetic imagination as a basic theme, foregrounds organic decay. The "pods" grow sick, appear diseased, look like animals and, when healthy, seem to be detached body parts. They do everything an organic being does except excrete.

99 Fan magazines, such as *Gorezone* and *Fangoria*, devoted to horror films carry many articles explaining how certain special effects have been achieved. This seems to indicate that experienced fans of horror films can assume psychical distance, taking a technical interest in how things are being done, and yet enjoy the thrills of suspense and voyeurism, or even more powerful affects such as disgust-anxiety. The history of drama provides much evidence for the capacity of an experienced viewer to play make-believe, as a participant-observer within a fictional world, and still exercise critical observation. Shakespeare turns often to this paradox of split perception, as in the fifth act of *A Midsummer Night's Dream*.

100 For an excellent analysis of King's "rhythms" and his use of steady but alternating build-ups, see McDowell.

101 Harvey R. Greenberg, p. 94. The xenomorph resembles a wasp, but not in an exact way. During its larval stage, it chooses another creature for pupation. This makes it especially horrible (a better monster) since it is the imago, or adult form, not the larva, that tears through the abdomen of the host-incubator. The xenomorph is also a machine, a digestive and reproductive machine, possessing, as Greenberg observes, a "metalloid skullbrow." This is made particularly evident in David Fincher's *Aliens 3* where the xenomorph turns out to be a "new model," even more metallic, its skullbrow resembling a nacelle on a motorcycle or a spacecraft. Ironically, it also resembles a dog, reflecting the physiognomy of its host.

102 The thick, milky android "blood" resembles nothing so much as semen. This creates an unpleasant juxtaposition (of the kind important to overdetermined, allusive horror films) between human procreativity and android sterility.

103 This is not to say that the other models which I discussed in Chapter 2 could not be illustrated from the *Alien* films, but the Sartre model fits them, as it were, like wet latex.

104 The alien creatures' intelligence is never in doubt, but it is always left open whether this is instinctual or cultivated. In *Alien Resurrection*, the creatures do communicate, but sub-linguistically. They may be a race of telepaths, a point that future *Alien* films may make clear.

105 In a CBC *Prime Time Live* magazine program on Belfast, broadcast on December 13, 1993, the Catholic novelist Robert Wilson noted that life in Belfast, subject to unexpected violence from the police, the British army, the IRA, the UDF and other Ulster paramilitary formations, was "degrading." It was not merely the pervasive violence that disturbed him, but its random, unpredictable and abrupt nature.

106 The term "godgame" belongs to John Fowles (pp. 5–10). For a discussion of the godgame as a narrative structure, see Chapter 4, "The Archetype of Bamboozlement: Godgames and Labyrinths," in *In Palamedes' Shadow*, pp. 105–66.

107 There are a few moments in which Dolarhyde is shown looking strangely gangling and forlorn. In one scene he is shown watching from his car as the blind woman with whom he has made love seems to flirt with another man. (He is actually picking a bug from her clothes.) Dolarhyde's face is lost in shadows and the impression of distance and apartness is very strong. However, Mann does nothing to suggest either Dolarhyde's physical impediment nor his personal drive to transcend himself. In the novel, Dolarhyde sees that with work, if he cultivates his inspirations as they truly are, "he could Become" (Harris, p. 224). In the film, the red dragon motif is nearly entirely excised from the plot. Dolarhyde's trip to Brooklyn where he steals and then *eats* the William Blake drawing of the *The Great Red Dragon and the Woman Clothed with the Sun* is cut. Dolarhyde's ordinary efforts at self-transcendence, such as weight-lifting, which deepen his characterization, are also eliminated. Significantly, Mann even cuts Dolarhyde's red dragon tattoo. Harris' Dolarhyde has powerful, if perverse, motivations; Mann's, a mere sequence of paracinematic acts. The upshot is that Mann creates a standard horror film, complete with final shoot-out in which the monster falls dead, after many shots, in an outstretched, crucifixion-like posture. Harris had written a terror novel in which the horror perspective (that of the FBI agents tracking the killer) is also possible.

108 Harris' *Black Sunday* also navigates a course between horror and terror. It establishes the sense of injustice and outrage that permeates Black September, the Palestinian terrorist gang, which gives them an ideology, a conceptual framework from which their acts spring. However, it ties the action to a single big event, bombing the Superbowl, which is methodically exposed and prevented. John Frakenheimer's 1976 film version, *Black Sunday*, flattens out the terrorist ideology considerably, though it does allow the dedication and meticulous planning to remain. Like Mann in making *Manhunter*, Frankenheimer opts for the horror side of Harris' narrative. Bloody finality is more appropriate to the narrative closure of a horror tale than a terror tale (where the ideology will live on). Of course, Dolarhyde *does* die in *Red Dragon* (though much differently than in the film), but the ideology of the serial killer lives on in Hannibal Lector and in all other killers who kill in order to discover self-transcendence or to remake themselves in the image of God.

109 Rushdie, *The Satanic Verses*, p. 207. A reader of *Gravity's Rainbow* must bear in mind the "complexities of connection that Pynchon invokes in the term 'paranoia'" (Edwards, p. 101).

110 In *The Satanic Verses*, Rushdie does not specifically link his terrorists to the Sikh movement for an independent Kalistan, but the inference is clear. He also gives the female leader of the commando group, Tavleen ("whose eyes turned inwards"), a Canadian accent: "Tavleen spoke with a Canadian accent, smooth-edged, with those give-away rounded O's" (p. 78). This is an instance of Rushdie's sly humor. Canada has a large Sikh population and has long been suspect, as a source of funds for the Sikh independence movement, in the eyes of the Indian government. In 1987, travelling extensively throughout India, I found myself subjected to time-consuming security checks at every airport. Later that year, before I was permitted to serve as an outside examiner on a PhD committee at an Indian university, I was required to swear an affidavit that I had never been an Indian citizen. Clearly, bearded Canadians cut an uncertain figure in India.

111 Rushdie, *The Satanic Verses*, pp. 214–15.

112 Rushdie shows an unfailing awareness of the adamantine certainties that make terrorism possible. I would choose André Malraux's Tchen in *Man's Estate* as the most moving characterization of a terrorist in literature. Tchen behaves as if he were dead, or at least as if his life had ended, and springs eagerly forward (fruitlessly, it turns out) with a bomb to kill Chang Kai Shek, no doubt smiling.

113 Chambers, *Room For Maneuver*, p. 174. Chambers discusses the concept of dictation throughout Chapter 4 with special reference to three Latin American novels: Miguel Ángel Asturias' *El señor presidente*, Gabriel García Márquez' *El otoño del patriarcha* and Manuel Puig's *El beso del mujer araña*. Chambers cites these novels as instances of opposition, not resistance. There is no counter-terror that acts against the Terror State in these novels. (However, in the case of García Márquez' novel, there is ineffective resistance and in Puig's novel there are references to the resistance movement to which Valentín belongs.)

114 Saladin is said to appear as "some kind of Elephant Man illness, a thing to feel disgusted by but not necessarily to fear." His ugliness is most strikingly apparent to white British natives, but much less so, easily accepted in fact, among his fellow Indian immigrants (Rushdie, *The Satanic Verses*, p. 275).

115 Rushdie, *The Satanic Verses*, pp. 158–60.

116 Rushdie, *The Satanic Verses*, p. 163.

117 Rushdie, *The Satanic Verses*, p. 168.

118 Rushdie, *The Satanic Verses*, p. 171. As they escape, the immigrants go their separate ways, "without hope, but also without shame." Reading passages such as this, the reader ought to observe the significance of Rushdie's often-repeated comment that he wrote the novel to celebrate the lives of immigrants to the United Kingdom from the Indian subcontinent, not to mock Islam.

119 Chambers distinguishes between opposition and resistance. The latter may adopt terror as one of its weapons, but the former seeks only sufficient space within the system for its own expression. It seeks modification through persuasion, not total destruction. Opposition is a way of (mis)reading within whatever play the system makes possible; resistance, the acceptance of the Terror State's own methods.

120 Once travelling in Peru, I fell into conversation with a beautiful Quechua woman who, I quickly learned, belonged to an evangelical faith. She asked me directly about my belief in God and, to avoid giving her pain, I said that I did believe, but only in a very abstract form of deity. I actually saw her disgust spasm, like a tiny quiver of loathing, through her mind (or soul). In seeking to avoid giving offence, I had instead chosen the words that would most deeply hurt a woman with a strongly felt conviction about a personal deity.

Chapter 7 ❊ *Its Venom*

1   Hocquenghem, p. 96. Sublimation, Hocquenghem adds, is "exercised on the anus as on no other organ ... anality is the very movement of sublimation itself."

2   William Ian Miller discusses the human anus at several places in his study of disgust. He thinks that while a "multitude of taboos" encompass the mouth and "rank" the substances that enter the mouth, the anus, as an "endpoint in the reductive digestive process," is significantly more democratic. I suspect that a little reflection would show that the anus is massively over-determined with multiple taboos regulating the places, methods and conditions of excretion as well as the possibilities for sexual excitement. Like the eye or, indeed, the phallus, it is a mythological part. On the other hand, Miller strikes me as spot on when he argues that the "female anus may not bear the surcharge of significance the male one does." Women, he adds, "expect a certain amount of penetration as coming with the territory of femaleness." During anal intercourse, the male is feminized, but "penetrating a woman's [anus] does more than brutally drive home her penetrability as a woman; it shows rather that she is penetrable as a man ... Her anus is an anus being used as if she were a he being used as a she" (pp. 99–101).

3   "Dags" are the feces-encrusted strands of wool around a sheep's anus that must be cut away during shearing. A person who is a dag typically dresses down and tries to make himself appear much rougher and more lower-class than he or she actually is. The boy on the bus was not a dag because, however badly he stank and poor his manners, he dressed well.

4   *Theme*, it will be objected, is the wrong term in this context. It makes the body seem too much like a literary text, not enough like a cultural text. But theme is the word I have used throughout this book to indicate the concepts that writing (or other art) signifies and which run, paracursively, through a text. It has become commonplace in the scholarly discourse of the humanities to use the term "inscription" with reference to the coded messages that the body bears in, from and through culture like habits, or coded memories, burnt into the flesh. The usage, with its attractive suggestions of writing *into* or cutting through the surface (revivifying the concept of a stylus as an instrument for writing), derives, at least in part, from Derrida's use of the term in *Of Grammatology* to account for the origins of the concept of space. As a concept, space begins from the possibility of multiple inscriptions upon the same site. Elizabeth Grosz enhances the "problematic of inscription" by her allusion to Kafka's tale, "The Penal Colony," in which the juridical machine inscribes the name of the crime upon the convict's body. The body may be considered as a "surface of erotogenic intensity," but it must also be seen as a surface of punishment, pain and all manner of cultural sanctions (*Volatile Bodies*, p. 138). "All the effects of depth and interiority," Grosz writes, "can be explained in terms of the inscriptions and transformations of the subject's corporeal surface" (p. vii). However, though provocative, this formulation seems more like one metaphor (the inscribed body) displacing another metaphor (consciousness), or one analogy forced to do the work of another. Even modes of freedom, of escape through transgression, such as tattooing, scarification and branding, are messages

"written" upon the body only in consciousness, as deliberate acts of awareness. Taken a step or two further, the notion of inscription leads to the concept of body "technologies" and, finally, the body as a cyborg. The cover to the Allen & Unwin edition of *Volatile Bodies* shows a nude female body, the upper half of which, beginning at the pubic region, metamorphoses into a semi-opaque plastic mannikin. In feminist analyses of the body as inscripted surface, the female body is always already a cyborg. Despite reservations, I have used "inscription" to indicate cultural messages, themes that appear and reappear in human life as functions of how the body has been constructed through the inevitable processes of socio-cultural formation.

5 "Your body is a battleground" is reproduced in Ewing (p. 337; the Annie Sprinkle photo is on p. 336). Reading *The Body* constitutes both a delightful corrective and a source of corroborative evidence for highly theoretical (and often rigid) discussions of the body, such as Judith Butler's *Bodies That Matter* or even Grosz's more flexible *Volatile Bodies*. Looking at human bodies complements the conceptual systems that are required for thinking about them. I learned a great deal about the nature of tattoos from seeing the man in Melbourne with the spider tattooed into the corner of his right eye.

6 People who have tattoos like to point out that piercings can be obliterated. Once you cease to wear a ring or pin, new skin begins to close the hole. Even scars will fade and can be hidden by cosmetics or surgery. A tattoo resists surgical eradication: even laser surgery leaves a scar-like discolouration. Thus a tattoo is said to show a permanent sense of commitment, even a more profound sense of personal worth and purpose.

7 Some tattoos are so startling that the problem of interpretation may actually precede the recognition that the body has been marked, divided and split into fragments. The two men with spiders tattooed in the corners of their right eyes whom I mentioned earlier were so shocking to see that the question of meaning was immediate and quite brutal. Only later was it possible to discuss the re-cognition that these men had split their faces, the most public of "public skin," into zones, arachnida/human, or art/nature. A few years ago I had an unforgettable experience of first seeing a tattoo as a recognizable zone of difference. I had gone to a South American restaurant with a friend from Morocco. As we were being served, the waitress bent over the table and her blouse fell open. Quite inadvertently, I saw that she had something blue tattooed upon her right breast. Of course, I was interested, but I found myself in the predicament that, far from being able to ask *what* she had tattooed on her breast, I could not even admit that I had glanced (however unplanned or accidentally) into her open blouse. I explained this situation to Aicha and she asked the waitress very directly to show us the tattoo. The waitress then undid her blouse further and revealed a long, blue dragon, the head of which was hidden within the cup of her bra while the tail stretched upwards towards her neck. She then explained that she had chosen the tattoo to commemorate her twenty-fifth birthday. She had spent four months deciding upon an image. I asked her why the dragon was in blue only. She replied that her research had informed her that other colours would fade more quickly and she wanted her tattoo to remain as fresh as her memory of her birthday. This encounter showed me how seriously a person may choose a tattoo (not everyone who has a tattoo is, or has been, a drunken seaman at the end of a pier) and with what intelligent consideration. It also showed that a viewer may easily see the tattoo as a division of the body, a zone of purposeful differ-

ence, prior to entering into the problem of interpretation. Such personal tattoos reveal a numinous attraction similar to that of the sacred: they both mark the body *off* and they mark the body *as* (an inviolate and distinct zone).

8 Elias, *The Loneliness of The Dying*, p. 3. It is the living who worry about disposing of the corpse, what to do with it, what ceremonies (if any) to award it, how to demonstrate grief. Elias writes about the embarrassment that a corpse causes family and friends and the inevitable "screening off," putting both dying and death out of sight, that occurs (p. 23). In modern western culture, there is always a great deal of what Elias calls "hygienic suppression" (p. 30). What he calls the "process of decay," often long, seldom pretty, inspires many strategies of aversion and repression. Generational cruelty alone (in his phrase) insures that the dying, unavoidably more a problem for the living than for themselves, enter into the field of the disgusting (pp. 71-73). The dying approach the condition of the abject and, once dead, have become abject.

9 Beckett's fictional worlds are bleak and (from the outside) swarming with disgusting objects. However, there are seldom even hints of internal boundaries: the world as a. whole is disgusting or, from within, neutral and indifferent: "Labyrinthine torment that can't be grasped, or limited, or felt, or suffered, no, not even suffered, I suffer all wrong too, even that I do all wrong too, like an old turkey-hen dying on her feet, her back covered with chickens and the rats spying on her" (*Three Novels*, p. 314). I have not discussed Beckett's fiction extensively in this book, but his presence looms over any study of the representation of disgust.

10 Jameson, p. 12.

11 It is probably appropriate that a book dealing with the theory of disgust should return so often to "cult" films. Typical Hollywood shlock always assumes Apollonian boundaries, even if it shows them being transgressed, and hence the real presence of disgust. Films such as *Eraserhead* and *King of Hearts* do not make such naïve assumptions and hence played, in the 1970s and '80s, to large audiences of young people who had been influenced by punk values. No one who had listened to the Sex Pistols in 1977 (the year in which *Eraserhead* was made) would fail to see that Henry's world, stripped of Apollonian carapace, is the *real* world. De Broca's *King of Hearts* sees the Great War very much as Paul Fussell sees it: stench, death, unforgivable waste. *King of Hearts* holds the record for consecutive performances at a single theatre in the United States. It showed, twice a night, for six and a half years at the Central Square Cinema 1 in Cambridge, Massachusetts (Samuels, *Midnight Movies*, p. 200).

12 *Voss*, p. 447.

13 *The Twyborn Affair*, p. 429.

14 "Letter to René Char," p. 36.

15 *Hamlet* 2.2.585; *The Riverside Shakespeare*, p. 1159.

16 Habib, p. 113.

17 *Sexual Personae*, pp. 93-94.

18 "The horrors in Swift's writing are not the men and women who have bowels and fart but those who can work out how long a two year old baby carcass would feed a family, or who, like Judge Whitshed, bent on sending a printer to jail, sought a guilty verdict by sending a jury back nine times, and who turned up to the court in a coach bearing a personal motto declaring how much he cherished liberty and patriotism in the abstract. The horror and the disgust are always directed at those who exempt themselves from the discourse of the body, for it is the body which is the sign both of our commonality, a shared eschatology, the same universal origin and destination" (Probyn, p. 41).

19 Fiedler, *Freaks*, p. 24. The mystique of the freak has not disappeared simply because the travelling sideshow is now uncommon in most parts of North America. Extreme punk styles amount to temporary transformation into a freak (sometimes term of affection in punk circles since "freak" can be used to describe the person's appearance, not his or her actuality, in a straight, non-punk world). To "freak out," whether because of drugs or emotional stress, is not necessarily a bad thing, certainly not a condition to be despised. The Jim Rose Circus, which I discussed in Chapter 1, calls itself a "sideshow" to signify its marginal social position and to call attention to the status of certain acts. (As I said earlier, it is an excellent circus, with classical acts, masquerading as a marginal, disgusting experience. It is, like gothic rock and grunge, a complex performance that stimulates the disgusting behaviour of true punk.) When I saw the Jim Rose Circus, one member of the troupe was known as "Mr. Enigma." He was heavily clothed through most of the performance, but eventually revealed himself as massively tattooed in abstract, blue patterns (which might have been bodypaint). He turned out to be a sword-swallower and glass-eater. In some performances (including that on the commercial tape), he eats bugs and maggots. In effect, Mr. Enigma is a geek, a voluntary or self-fashioned freak. His freak-status is registered from the very moment that the performance begins. (For a photo of Mr. Enigma swallowing a sword, see Swerdlow, p. 11.) In his final chapter, Fiedler examines the image of the mutant in western culture to show the ways in which desire enters into the ambivalent image of the freak. The mutant illustrates how a person might become a freak in the endpoint of metamorphosis. Reading Fiedler together with Robert Bogdan, providing both recognition (Bogdan) and re-cognition (Fiedler), makes available a very thorough survey of the social problem, now more historical than contemporary, of freaks.

20 Browning employed genuine freaks, each with a career independently of the film, and this was, no doubt, one reason that the film evoked such averse reactions. Browning's performers include several pinheads, such as Koo-Koo the "Bird Girl" Randian the "human torso" (also known as "The Caterpillar Man"), the Hilton Sisters (Siamese twins joined at the hips who each accept offers of marriage during the film, thus introducing an erotic note), a legless man, played by Johnny Eck, who walks on his hands, and an armless woman, played by Frances O'Connor, and a hermaphroditic boy-girl, Joseph-Josephine. Many of these freaks are mentioned in Mannix. This is a weak book, but one with many photos (for photos, see also Drimmer). Bogdan's study, though rich in photos has only a few photos of the freaks who star in Browning's film, but these include a delightful poster of the Hilton Sisters dating from the 1920s. There are four photographs of the Hilton Sisters in Ewing (pp. 262–63). Both Mannix and Drimmer adopt righteous, patronizing attitudes (the latter's title indicates the tone). Browning's much-reviled film does much more to register the humanity of the quite genuine freaks who performed for him. Fiedler discusses Browning at several points (pp. 288–98). Fiedler remarks that his book "represents a belated tribute to that great director [Browning] and his truly astonishing film" (p. 18).

21 Browning's film emphasizes the humanity, and the genuine community, of the circus freaks set against the "freakish" behaviour of the "norms." The freaks follow what the film calls "the code of the freaks." This is said dramatically in the film to indicate the impending act of revenge. However, it does have an important thematic import: normal people act freakishly; freaks act lovingly and well. The possibility of feeling disgust over the freaks is transmuted by their gentle and mutually respectful behaviour. The pinheads are especially childlike and loveable. The film's plot revolves around the beautiful Cleopatra marrying the circus' midget for his money and then trying to poison him slowly (all the while making love to the strong man). The freaks learn about this and decide to punish Cleopatra. She is chased through the circus grounds and under wagons while a storm rages. (Browning was a master of horror conventions and had, in 1931, directed the original *Dracula* with Bela Lugosi.) The freaks, each over-coming his or her handicap to join the chase (Randian slithers through the mud with a knife clenched in his mouth), close in upon the deviant aerialist and execute an appropriate punishment. In the film's final scene, the audience learns what had been hidden from sight in the opening scene: Cleopatra has been transformed into a speech-less, gabbling Chicken Woman. The dramatic irony involved in having the immoral Cleopatra transformed into an obviously disgusting "freak" has struck some viewers as undercutting the film's main theme that there is no natural connection between physical appearance and moral character.

22 Fiedler, *Freaks*, p. 295. Fiedler remarks that audiences sometimes laugh at Browning's ending, but sometimes scream. It is deeply disturbing, in the extremity of the freaks' sense of justice, and unresolvably ambiguous. More than most films it must be seen in order to be "seen." Browning's ending has inspired variants in horror writing. Ray Bradbury's "The Jar" explores similar territory in transforming an Evil Woman into an embryo-like object (still possessing the woman's eyes) in a jar.

23 Pynchon, *V.*, p. 237.

24 Synthetic voices have become ever-more commonplace. Hawking's stands out because he uses it in such a complete manner, answering questions and expounding difficult abstractions. *What* it replaces can never be out of mind. One of the most striking instances of a prosthetic voice can be found in Gerard Corbiau's 1995 film, *Farinelli*. Corbiau's film is based upon the life of the famous eighteenth-century castrato, Carlo Broschi ("Farinelli" was his stage-name). To recreate the (unknown) tone of a castrato's voice, Corbiau had the voice digitally processed from the actual voices of a counter-tenor (Derek Lee Ragin) and a coloratura (Ewa Godlewska). Presumably, Stephen Hawking's rather shrill American accent could be replaced by a similar digital fusion if he thought it worth the trouble.

25   "Phantasmatic" is Judith Butler's term (*Bodies That Matter*, pp. 88–9). The penis is
"phantasmatic" because it bears a vast weight of mythological associations. Using
William Ian Miller's more direct term, you could simply say that it is, like the mouth
(but unlike, in Miller's view, the anus), mythological. So much has been said about the
penis in myth and legend, so much has been expected of it (in myth, in legend, in ordinary life) that it can hardly be reduced to mere nature, to a wrinkled fleshy appendage
with a bio-hydraulic pumping mechanism to effect tumescence. It exists in a zone
created by the intersection of memory and anticipation. Hence the distinction between
penis and phallus, like that between nature and culture (or between history and
legend), seems important. Writing of the opposition between phallus and castration
(the male/female polarity in, she claims, Freud's view), Elizabeth Grosz remarks that
there is no natural body to return to, no pure sexual difference one could gain access if
only the distortions and deformations of patriarchy could be removed or transformed.
The phallus "binarizes the differences between sexes, dividing up a sexual-corporeal
continuum into two mutually exclusive categories which in fact belie the multiplicity
of bodies and body types" (*Volatile Bodies*, p. 58). If the penis is as phantasmatic as
Butler argues (and it probably is), the hardships that it effects fall upon men as well as
upon women. (It is hard, indeed, to live up to a standard set by Zeus.) My argument is
that all prostheses have a double impact upon consciousness, as well as upon the body,
in that they both enhance performance but remain mere machines designed to supplement failing performance (of eye, or knee, or penis), reminders of a personal Fall. This
is especially the case when the cyber(body)part replaces, or supplements, a phantasmatic part such as the penis.

26   A "neovagina" is also possible, both in transsexual surgery and in reconstructive plastic
surgery after disease or mutilation, but neovaginoplasty does not involve the use of
prostheses as does neophalloplasty. (In some cases, it appears that a mould is used as an
aid in constructing the vaginal cavity. However, it would be removed in a postoperative
procedure. This may, or may not, constitute a prosthesis.) Since stenosis is a possible
complication in neovaginoplasty, it may eventually call for a prosthetic solution (see
Martine-Mora et al.; Eldh; and van Noort). I write as a male, and the split consciousness
that I invoke in this chapter is a personalized (but hardly universalized) male consciousness. I would not wish even to suppose how the possession of a neovagina might play
out in a female consciousness. Nonetheless, there is evidence to indicate that many
women, possessing healthy and fully functional genitalia, do seek to have their vaginas
modified and surgically enhanced. See Debra Ollivier's on "Designer Vaginas."

27   Govier et al.

28   A large body of material exists concerning penile implants. Medical journals publish
dozens of articles each year on reconstructive phalloplasty in which the surgeon builds
a "neophallus" to replace a penis that has been lost because of accident, gunshot
wound or disease. The same surgical techniques are used to construct a neophallus
where, in the case of transsexuals, it had never existed. Much less is written with respect
to cosmetic phalloplasty. For articles on penile implants see Irwin Goldstein et al. and
Levine et al (see also Francesco Montrosi et al.). Considerable information, as well as a
discussion of problems inherent in implant therapy, can be found in Findlay.

29 Heidegger, p. 103 .

30 Porush, p. 8.

31 Halacy, Jr., p. 25.

32 Lawrence Douglas, p. 13.

33 Plotinsky, p. 297.

34 Plotinsky, p. 298. Both science-fiction and art-horror employ the motif of a machine that develops its own identity and consciousness and then begins to take over. A hyper-complex machine, such as the starship *Enterprise*, may decide to run itself, or else a computer, such as HAL in Kubrick's *2001*, may attempt to take over (having developed a consciousness that reveals to itself its own superior intelligence but inferior role as a server). In art-horror, Stephen King's *Christine*, in which a car comes to life, stands out. (King had experimented with this theme ten years earlier in his 1973 short story "Trucks" in which interstate rigs acquire an evil life.)

35 As I suggested in Chapter 4, I think that James Cameron's *Terminator* films actually pose this metafictional problem. Although the Terminator is called a "cyborg," it is actually an android with prosthetic organic skin and flesh. Hence the Terminator inverts the paradigm I have been discussing in this chapter: an android with an organic prosthesis may experience itself as diminished, less than a machine. A memorably loathsome variant occurs in Gregory Benford's *Great Sky River*. Benford's narrative is set far into the future on an interstellar human colony in which the Mechs, a hyper-advanced machine civilization that has displaced human, grow body parts to act as prostheses. Disembodied parts, legs, hearts or other parts, are sustained in a battery by an organic gruel-like substance to produce more efficient "motors." This is an image that has now spread through science-fiction films. The Borg in the *Star Trek* TV series or the failed versions of the Riply clone in *Alien Resurrection* come strikingly to mind.

36 De Nooy, p. 183.

37 They have been colonized but not (at the time of telling this story) subjected to genocide. Victims of genocide, especially if they are living within an ongoing genocidal project, must experience abjection. You could hardly be more cast out, or discarded, by your society than when it tries to kill you. Firchow points out that the sense that genocide is the worst of all possible crimes reflects a very modern sensibility. It has not always been so. There has been a great deal of loose talk about genocide. Inadvertent and non-purposeful deaths, even if they are in considerable numbers, probably should not be classified as genocide (Firchow, pp. 148–52).

38 Ignatieff, *Blood and Belonging*, p. 6. Ignatieff identifies himself as a "civic nationalist," someone who believes in multinational states which provide homes for different nations, with a definite fear of ethnic nationalism (p. 249). Ignatieff probes the ambiguities of nationalism, and of being a "nation," with great intelligence. He would probably agree with English novelist Penelope Lively that for "a nation, it is a great historical convenience to have edges" (p. 134). However, even the clearest, most precisely demarcated edges (such as the United States possesses, say) will not keep a nation, once it is moving in a collective action against its minorities or against an alien "enemy," from appearing disgusting from the outside.

39 De-individuation is another common science-fiction and horror theme. Both Don Siegel's 1956 film *Invasion of the Body Snatchers* and Philip Kaufman's 1978 re-make memorably explore this territory. Ira Levin's *The Stepford Wives* suggests a classic example, on the borders between horror and science-fiction, in which de-individuation functions as a gender-specific manipulation (the male characters methodically de-individuate the female). Disgust arises only upon the consideration of the slippage, the fall from a human ideal of individual personhood. Human beings will seem disgusting when they slip into a trans-entity existence such as that which the women in Levin's novel share once they have been given a reprogrammed femininity that excludes personal identity.

40 Rushdie, *The Satanic Verses*, pp. 212–15. Rushdie has in mind the unswerving ferocity of the Iranian mobs, under the religious leadership of the Ayatollah Khomeini, that marched against the Shah's army in 1978. As Gibreel flies over the land of Desh, observing the insurrection, he carries the Imam, a simulacrum of Khomeini, on his back.

41 Klinkenborg draws attention to the sense of being persecuted among anti-abortion protesters at a Milwaukee clinic. "There is a community, a bond, in opposition. Persecution is election, even when it is self-persecution, a martyrdom in the parking lot" (p. 43). Rushdie attributes a sense of persecution, which is largely "self-persecution," to the Imam and his followers.

42 Canetti, p. 29.

43 Buford, p. 193. I cite Buford's fascinating book in absence of any intimate experience of my own. I have on three occasions observed riots or (at least) mass actions in which the participants appeared to be de-individuated. On one of these occasions, in Nicaragua, which was perhaps more like a large rumble than a riot, I stood as far to one side, though unable to escape, as I could move while the young men involved threatened each other with multiple rich variations upon the Spanish verb *matar* (kill). On another occasion, during a major sporting event in Vancouver, I was so interested in the police use of dogs that I foolishly got too close (trying to overhear the whispered commands) and abruptly found myself grabbed in a police armlock. I spent a grim night in the Vancouver jail. However, I have never actually participated in a riot and, thus, I have never experienced, at first hand, de-individuation of that kind. Buford's vivid first-hand account of participation may stand in for my own lack.

44 Buford, p. 205.

45 Buford, p. 299.

46 Grosz, *Volatile Bodies*, p. 192. Writing of her "Möbius strip model," Grosz observes that it has "the advantage of showing that there can be a relation between two 'things'—mind and body—which presumes neither their identity nor their radical disjunction, a model which shows that while there are disparate 'things' being related, they have the capacity to twist one into the other" (pp. 209–10). The abject is the primary, and exemplary, fact subsumed by the Möbius strip. Discussing Kristeva's analysis of the abject, de Nooy observes that the "abject, explored in *Powers of Horror*, is a form of otherness that never quite constitutes a definable Other. It never accedes to the status of object, in that—although heterogeneous—it can never be completely expelled from the subject.

It disrupts the neat organization into inside and outside, self and other, as an inaccessible otherness within" (pp. 24–25 n. 27). There seems to be no simple (non-Möbius) way to think about the abject.

47   Kristeva, p. 15. I have never felt certain that I understand the reasons for insisting upon the menses as a fundamental category of the abject. Pre- and post-menstrual women should not experience abjection. Neither should women who, either through ignorance or education, do not feel shame over the public inconvenience of menstruation. In Chapter 3, I discussed the results of one survey showing that menstrual blood actually ranked low, among both male and female respondents, as a source of disgust. Blood suggests its own Möbius strip, at once life-giving and a life poisoning, a complete pharmacy of positive and negative powers (see Camporesi, esp. pp. 101–21). Muscio, taking a robustly positive view of menstruation, describes the flowering in the United States of menarche parties (pp. 32–33). Of course, Kristeva and her followers, such as Henke, may have ideological reasons for their cock-eyed insistence.

48   Henke, *Shattered Subjects*, p. 86. In her earlier study of the idea of desire in the writings of James Joyce, Henke had explicitly adopted Kristeva's analysis of the female condition as a heuristic tool. In that book, she was more concerned with Kristeva's theory of "semiosis," the fluid proto-language beneath linguistic articulation, the "mysterious and polymorphous iterations of a woman's psyche" (*James Joyce*, p. 127). The common marker in both Kristeva's and Henke's analysis of female psychology is fluidity, or flow. The female proto-language (the pre-male inarticulation of semiosis) and the abjection of menstrual blood are both, private and public, manifestations of flow.

49   In the more than thirty years since it was written, *The Golden Notebook* has become a key text for many different scholarly interests. It has been seen as a glass held up to the shifting tides of modern European history: the collapse of empires and the rise of distinct postcolonial voices; the disillusionment with the Communist party after 1956; the critique of American political values particularly as manifested in the House Un-American Activities Committee whose many victims helped to create one of "the classic, already archetypal stories of our time" (p. 490); the rise of popular culture and entertainment as a dominating force throughout western civilization; the evolution of postmodernism as both a register of cultural phenomena (the novel's interest in both popular and marginal culture) and as a repertory of narrative conventions (the novel's overtly metafictional strategies). Above all, *The Golden Notebook* has been seen as focussing a brilliant light upon the condition of women "in our time" and as providing both an analysis of this condition and range of possible solutions. I do not wish to deny the validity of any of these interests. *The Golden Notebook* is, rightly I think, a textual lens for the study of the political background to recent British fiction, the emergence of a self-reflexive postcolonial discourse, and the evolution of postmodernism (it was published in 1962, the same year as Nabokov's *Pale Fire*). Along the way, the novel examines a wide spectrum of political issues, such as the developing hegemony of American anti-communist ideology and its impact upon European thinking. Most importantly perhaps, *The Golden Notebook* records the conceptual structure of an unfolding feminism both as an historical movement and as a continuing area for discussion. What I want to argue in this chapter is that the novel also helps to focus the concepts of disgust and abjection. This is not, as I shall show, a minor excrescence

of a complex narrative that derives its significance from other, more transcendental if not more fundamental, preoccupations. Disgust plays a central role in the novel just as it does in the western society that the novel reflects. I also want to argue that grasping the role of disgust in the novel helps to see the other issues (for which it is famous) even more clearly.

50   The word *disgust* is used twenty-six times in the novel. *Self-disgust* is used seven times; *disgusted*, six times; *disgusting*, three times. In addition, words such as *repulsion, revulsion, loathing, self-abasement* and *abject* are used frequently.

51   Lessing, p. 368. Massified and swarming insects are not the exclusive property of horror films.

52   Lessing, p. 419. A similar (if not identical) figure ("some malicious creature, sarcastic and 'rational'" who appears in "various guises with different traits") haunts the dreams and waking hallucinations of Nicholai Vsevolodovich Stavrogin in Dostoevsky's *Devils* (p. 455). It is the figure of nihilism but also the embodiment of self-disgust and despair. It is also a familiar figure, in "various guises," throughout modern European literature. Compare the character of the malign (but highly intelligent) dwarf in Pär Lagerkvist's *The Dwarf*. Viewers of David Lynch's films will recall how often dancing dwarfs figure in his work, especially the "hieratic dwarf" in the aborted TV series *Twin Peaks* (Wallace, *A Supposedly Fun Thing*, p. 148).

53   Lessing, p. 532.

54   Lessing, p. 358. Although feminists seem to think that menstrual blood lies at the core of male misogyny, other factors may play equal, or more important, roles. Myth, fable, anecdote and tale, all suggest that men fear female fecundity (for which the Hydra is the outstanding image) and softness. Male jokes about the normal absence of female muscle-tone ("gravity lends definition to the female body") tell at least as clear a story as do those about menstruation. Lingis, drawing upon the fiction of Marguerite Duras, sees this thorny issue very sharply. Certain female nudity (that of a "temple maiden," say) is "obscene": it "invites strangulation, rape, ill usage, insults, shouts of hatred, the unleashing of deadly and unmitigated passions ... [men may] "feel a vertiginous attraction for the muck and stench of the disordered organs and suppurating orifices that her soft forms and delicate skin hold so weakly. Voluptuousness plunges all that is infantile, feral, violent in oneself into another, seeking all that is frenzied, predatory, bloodthirsty in the other" (p. 147). Wills cites Albert the Great in the thirteenth century for the proposition that the "woman contains more liquid than the man, and it is a property of liquid to take things up easily and to hold them poorly" (p. 109).

55   Henke, *Shattered Subjects*, p. 95.

56   Paglia, *Sexual Personae*, p. 94.

57   Grosz, *Volatile Bodies*, p. 203. Grosz' diction, especially her use of "viscosity," suggests that she, like Paglia, is thinking of Sartre. However, it also displays an obvious congruence with Henke (and Kristeva) in insisting upon female fluidity, and/or wetness, as the distinctive gender-marker. Reading Lynda Goldstein's essay, "Raging in Tongues: Confession and Performance Art," on the expression of rage in female performance art, I was struck by the description of Karen Finley's act: [Finley] "works

into a screaming rage. Stripping off her dress in a nonerotic fashion, she tosses stuffed animals and raw, coloured Easter eggs into a large, clear garbage bag, repeatedly smashing it on the floor until the gooey yolks coast everything inside. Pulling the yellow-slimed stuffed animals from the bag, she uses them to sponge the eggs over her body." This gesture, charged with archetypal as well as cultural significance, is said to create an "interplay" between battering and subjection.

58 Paglia, *Sexual Personae*, p. 93. Although Paglia seems to support Henke and Grosz, her discourse is several degrees more flamboyant than theirs. Her philosophical guide is Sartre (and the world of imagination and fiction), not Kristeva. There are no references to Kristeva in *Sexual Personae*.

59 Paglia does not mean the same thing by "Dionysian" as Bataille does. She seeks a radical polarity in framing Dionysus as Apollo's "antagonist and rival." Dionysus represents "obliteration" of seeing (whereas Apollo is an "eye-god"), the dark underside of human experience (*Sexual Personae*, p. 88). For Bataille, the Dionysian is transgressive, life lived excessively and against Apollonian constraints, but it does not exclude either intelligence or intellectual expression. It is, rather, an active, exploratory mode. It is the source of human creativity (whereas Paglia associates creativity with Apollo, with order and light). Bataille and Paglia would seem to agree that, whatever its ends, the Dionysian inhabits a fluid, dissolving world that mocks both constraints and categories.

60 Shakespeare, *Richard III*, 1.1.106; *The Riverside Shakespeare*, p. 714.

61 Shakespeare, *Troilus and Cressida*, 3.3.127-28; *The Riverside Shakespeare*, p. 472. *Abject* appears only in the *Folio* text.

62 Shakespeare, *2 Henry VI*, 4.1.104-05; *The Riverside Shakespeare*, p. 654.

63 Grosz, *Sexual Subversions*, p. 71.

64 Kristeva, p. 71.

65 Grosz, *Sexual Subversions*, p. 73.

66 King's phrase crisply sums up the role of death in horror fiction and points unmistakably to the role that necrophilia plays in contemporary American culture (*Kingdom of Fear*, p. 97).

67 Grosz distinguishes neatly between essentialism and biologism as the "postulation of a fixed essence" and the "postulation of a biological universality" (*Volatile Bodies*, p. 212 n. 15). Many psychologists would probably wish to deny that they sought a biological universality, but their conclusions, as I argued previously, exhibit their desire.

68 Self, p. 18.

69 Kristeva, p. 18.

70 Although feces, menstrual blood and corpse rot are the central examples of the abject, there are many other candidates (Miller, as I noted previously, suggests hair). In fact, any boundary that is involved in, or constitutes an aspect of, your human individuality might seem to function both as a marker of the abject and as a first step towards

creativity. De Nooy lucidly discusses the role of the abject in defining femininity. You are defined by, but also against, your mother. "No longer one with the child but not yet separate," she writes, " the mother is 'abjected': halfway between same and other, unnamable, she seems repulsive, something to be expelled like excrement, like unwanted food" (p. 45).

71   I am taking a shortcut here. Saul may be either a "real" character (i.e., an inhabitant of the same fictional world that Anna Wulf inhabits) or he may be a creation of Anna's imagination (and hence an inhabitant of an embedded world), a projection of her animus. Many of Lessing's critics have taken the further step of identifying Saul with one of Lessing's in-the-world lovers, Clancy Sigal. Lessing, Pierpont writes, calls her character Saul Green, but he is "identifiable as the American writer Clancy Sigal, 'already pretty ill when he arrived in London', according to Lessing's memoir" (Pierpont, p. 242). I am not arguing the point, and both of the opposing interpretive positions can certainly be argued; rather, I am merely assuming that Saul Green is a creation, a fictional embodiment of Anna's archetypal animus, that will lead her, in the section called "The Golden Notebook," to individuation. Even though Lessing herself describes Saul as if he were a real character, and the inner "Golden Notebook" as if it had been written by both of them, I find my "fictional" reading consistent with Lessing's Jungianism in the novel. "In the inner Golden Notebook, which is written by both of them," Lessing writes, "you can no longer distinguish between what is Saul and what is Anna, and between them an the other people in the book" (p. 8). There is considerable internal evidence that Saul is best understood as a projection of Anna's animus. For one thing, Anna seems to know about him, or at least how he writes, before she meets him. In section 19 of the Yellow Notebook, she writes a pastiche called "The Romantic Tough School of Writing" in which Saul's style and emotional affiliations are already made plain. (Compare his unlikely "American" stance of standing, "his thumbs hitched through his belt, fingers loose, but pointing as it were to his genitals" [p. 484], the "mensch-pose" [p. 487], or Anna's insight that Saul's strongest emotions are reserved for his "group of buddies" [p. 542].) In the numbered sections of the final entry in the Blue Notebook, the passage in which Anna notes that she sees Saul clearly, "the slum kid, member of a gang of slum kids, lifting something from a shop counter, or running from the police," is also a number 19. Clue or snare? Finally, Saul's fictionality (within the fictional world that Anna inhabits) supports a Kristevean reading of Anna's feelings as abjection (since that is a potentially creative experience), but if he is read as "real," then Anna's "fug of stale disgust" is simply self-loathing, negative and deadend. (For a recent analysis, interesting if trendy, of fragmentation in The Golden Notebook which accepts Saul's "reality," while arguing that "Anna-the-editor" elides the distinction, see Hayles, pp. 236–64). In order to see the Jungian reading in a deeper perspective, compare Theodora Goodman's creation of "Holstius," out of a similar need for male companionship in the third section of Patrick White's The Aunt's Story.

72   Lessing, "Preface," p. 7.

73   Saul gives Anna the first sentence of the "Free Women" novella. Anna gives Saul a first sentence, "On a dry hillside in Algeria, a soldier watched the moonlight glinting on his rifle," that simply could not have led to a novel, certainly not one that "did rather well"

(pp. 556–57). It is pastiche, very much a part of the final section from the Yellow Notebook, and defies all that Anna represents as a writer: write out of your own experience, write what you know.

74 Lessing, p. 299.

75 Lessing, p. 298.

76 Lessing, p. 303.

77 Carter, p. 39.

78 Pierpont seems to find Anna's response to the on-set of her period excessive. She "does more frantic blood-washing than Lady Macbeth" (Pierpont, p. 240). I would hardly dare comment on this judgement as referring to an actual-world situation. However, Lessing has written the episode of Anna's menstrual period as a symbolic exploration of a typical, or representative, experience.

79 Calasso, p. 175. Thought of another way (Northrop Frye's way), myths are the boilerplate of the imagination, a culturally-inscribed imaginary. They function in the building of fictional worlds as a high-order fund of stereotypes and thematic allusions.

80 I do not think that the penis is more mythological (or phantasmatic) than the vagina, though it is probably the case, things being as they are, that more has been written about it. When I was four and watched my mother cut a peach open, feeling strong aversion at the sight, it may be that the open concavity where the pit had been, so pink and shaggy, may have reminded me of an open vagina. Of course, I had only seen one vagina at that point in my life, my playmate's, and it been neither open nor shaggy. So that account of my instantaneous disgust has to appeal to such difficult mental phenomena as archetypes and collective memory. Once I begin to entertain that hypothesis, I can move on to ask whether the slit-open peach had reminded me of a *vagina dentata*. I could not have had such a concept, but, according to the hypothesis, I might have had the archetype hidden within some intellectual node, waiting actualization.

81 Ovid, p. 82.

82 Calasso, p. 291.

83 Ovid, p. 82.

84 Butler, *Bodies That Matter*, p. 75.

85 Mindich, p. 72. Cosmetic phalloplasty lays claim to many success tales (measured by the mythological yardstick), but it also seems to have had many failures (p. 74). Reconstructive phalloplasty, having smaller objectives but more distance to cover, seems to have good success rates (see J. Joris Hage et al.). The possibilities for disappointment in attempting to enhance the penis are, evidently, great. Even the dangers and potential failures of penile prostheses, which are strictly corrective within the natural limitations of an individual penis, are considerable (see Findlay). It is easy to suppose that a man who seeks to have his penis enhanced has been thinking mythologically. He will have been building private fictional worlds in which, mythologically enhanced, he brilliantly flares, thrusting across the heavens like an elongated flash of lightening.

86   See Malloy. Adam Parfrey observes that postmodern "penises seem positively naked without ornate tattoos, and a stud, ring or chain piercing the glans and the urethra" (*Apocalypse Culture*, p. 98).

87   Malloy, p. 25. I write this as a male, open to contradiction. There is a vaginal piercing known as the Princess Albertina. Whether this imitates, precedes or is entirely independent of the male Prince Albert, I do not know. Anne Greenblatt describes the Princess Albertina as another "relatively new and experimental piercing, this piercing passes through the back wall of the urethra. In the piercing documented by *Piercing World* magazine, a captive bead ring was used." Greenblatt's enthusiasm for labial and clitoral piercings, always identifying an appropriate piece of jewellery for each local piercing, suggests that I may be wrong in claiming a greater mythic, or phantasmatic, aura for the penis than for the vagina. Anne Greenblatt, *rec.arts.bodyart* (1995).

88   I cannot say whether a tampon is a prosthetic. Clearly, it both enhances the vagina, making it more socially flexible, and acts as a mnemotechnic. In the entry in the blue notebook that I discussed above, Anna Wulf experiences her vagina during menstruation as mythological.

89   The mythological dimension of all body parts, including both cyberparts and transplants, can be seen clearly in the contemporary ethical debates concerning commercial transplants. While transplants from the bodies of those who have died in accidents (and signed the appropriate release forms before dying or, if children, have had relatives give permission) are a triumph of medical science, the commercial traffic in body parts is ethically suspect and, in many places, illegal. A forty-nine-year-old real-estate agent from British Columbia named Robert Kinnee exemplifies the problem. His kidneys failed in 1992 and he had been on dialysis while waiting for transplant kidneys. If someone had died, even in a grisly accident, whose kidneys could have been transplanted into Kinnee's body, it would have been a normal medical procedure. However, Kinnee grew tired of waiting and, taking matters into his own hand, travelled to Madras, India, where he *bought* a kidney from a seventeen-year-old construction worker. The young man is said to have received about two thousand dollars for giving up one kidney. Buying organs for transplantation has become relatively commonplace. (A great deal of business is done in China with the organs of executed criminals.) This example of aggressive self-preservation, or of successful market capitalism, causes furious ethical debate. The director of the British Columbia Transplant Society, Bill Barrable, was quoted as finding the act "deplorable." The British Columbia Minister of Health, Paul Ramsey, said that the practice was "unethical." Kinnee's act, Ramsey said, "sent a chill up my spine" (McInnes). While the temptation might be to call Kinnee an ethical monster, or else Ramsey a hypocrite, a more detached view would be only to note the confusion in this contemporary debate. The potential ferocity of the argument, one side or the other, for the commercialization of human body parts turns largely upon the mythological encrustations of the body. Two other current debates, whether to use animals, such as pigs, as incubators to grow organs for human use and whether to employ stem cells (or even to do research on the problem) from fetuses to grow new organs, arouse intense anger and dismay. In both cases, heated reference is made to the mythological status of the human body. It is, we are told, sacred. Even its most secret parts are sacrosanct, inviolable to casual, or monetary, invasion. However, many of the people who make these arguments happily support the death penalty (or would, in Canada, if only the politicians would bring it back). One person's Apollonian order turns out to be another's disgusting experience of a perverse geometry.

90 Mythology does not show up only in fables and tales. Jokes are a fundamental vehicle for mythology. And they are also, as Freud observes, a form of rape. For a recent analysis of male jokes designed to degrade, and to exercise dominance over, women, see Murphy.

91 The failure to consider the workings of disgust (and abjection) in modern literature constitutes the single most glaring weakness in Miller's occasionally brilliant study of disgust. I found this absence to be a frustrating and infuriating shortcoming. Robertson observes that when he told a colleague in Sydney that Miller had written a study of disgust that ignored the twentieth century, his colleague replied that "such an endeavor would be like writing a study of mass destruction but dismissing everything that has occurred since *The Charge of The Light Brigade*" (Robertson, p. 223 n. 10).

Bibliography

Ackerman, Dianne. *A Natural History of the Senses*. New York: Random House-Vintage, 1991.

———. *Deep Play*. New York: Random House, 1999.

Ades, Dawn. *Photomontage*. Rev. ed. London: Thames and Hudson, 1993 [1976].

Allan, Keith and Kate Burridge. *Euphemism and Dysphemism: Language Used as Shield and Weapon*. New York: Oxford University Press, 1991.

Alter, Robert. *Partial Magic: The Novel as a Self-Conscious Genre*. Berkeley: University of California Press, 1975.

Amis, Martin. "Salman Rushdie." In *Visiting Mrs. Nabokov and Other Excursions*. Toronto: Knopf, 1993.

Angyal, A[ndras]. "Disgust and Related Aversions." *Journal of Abnormal and Social Psychology* 36 (1941): 393-412.

Anderson, Kevin and Kenneth Whitehead, trans. *For Rushdie: Essays by Arab and Muslim Writers in Defense of Free Speech*. New York: Braziller, 1994 [1993].

Anderson, Robert G. *Faces, Forms, Films: The Artistry of Lon Chaney*. New York: Castle Books, 1971.

Angier, Natalie. *Woman: An Intimate Geography*. Boston: Houghton Mifflin, 1999.

Anspaugh, Kelly. "'Bung Goes the Enemay': Wyndham Lewis and the Uses of Disgust." *Mattoid* 48 (1994): 225-40.

———. "Powers of Ordure: James Joyce and the Excremental Vision(s)." *Mosaic* 27 (March 1994): 73-100.

Appignanesi, Lisa and Sara Maitland, eds. *The Rushdie File*. Syracuse: Syracuse University Press, 1990.

"Around the Nation." *Washington Post*. 16 June 1994, A17.

Bakhtin, M.M. *Rabelais and His World*. Trans. Hélène Iswolsky. Cambridge: MIT Press, 1968.

———. *Problems of Dostoevsky's Poetics*. Trans. Caryl Emerson. Minneapolis: University of Minnesota Press, 1984.

———. *The Diologic Imagination: Four Essays*. Trans. Caryl Emerson and Michael Holquist. Austin: University of Texas Press, 1981.

Ballard, J.G. *Crash*. New York: Vintage, 1995 [1973].

———. *The Atrocity Exhibition*. San Francisco: Re/Search, 1990.

Barnes, Julian. "Letter From London: Staying Alive." *New Yorker*, 21 February 1994, 97-105.

Barron, Stephanie et al., eds. *Degenerate Art: The Fate of the Avant-Garde in Nazi Germany*. New York and Los Angeles: Los Angeles County Museum of Art and Abrams, 1993.

Barth, Frederick. "On Responsibility and Humanity: Calling a Colleague to Account." *Current Anthropology* 15 (March 1974): 99-103.

Barthes, Roland. *S/Z: An Essay*. Trans. Richard Miller. New York: Hill and Wang, 1974 [1970].

Bataille, Georges. *Story of the Eye, by Lord Auch*. Trans. Joachim Neugroschal. London: Penguin Books, 1982 [1928].

——. "The Big Toe." In *Visions of Excess: Selected Writings, 1927–1939*. Trans. Allan Stoekl et al. Minneapolis: University of Minnesota Press, 1985.

——. *The Tears of Eros*. Trans. Peter Connor. San Francisco: City Lights Books, 1992 [1989].

——. "Letter to René Char on the Incompatibilities of the Writer [1929]." Trans. Christopher Carsten. *Yale French Review*, 78 (1990): 31–43.

——. *The Impossible*. Trans. Robert Hurley. San Francisco: City Lights Books, 1991 [1962].

——. "Cleanliness Prohibitions and Self-Creation." In *The Accursed Share: An Essay on General Economy*. Vols. II and III. Trans. Robert Hurley. New York: Zone Books, 1993.

Baudelaire, Charles. *The Flowers of Evil*. Eds. Marthiel and Jackson Mathews. New York: New Directions, 1955.

Becker, Andrew Sprague. *The Shield of Achilles and the Poetics of Ekphrasis*. Lanham, MD: Rowman and Littlefield, 1995.

Beckett, Samuel. *Three Novels By Samuel Beckett: Molloy, Malone Dies, The Unnamable*. Trans. Patrick Bowles and Samuel Beckett. New York: Grove Press, 1955.

——. *Waiting for Godot*. Trans. Samuel Beckett. New York: Grove Press, 1956.

Belsey, Catherine. *Desire: Love Stories in Western Culture*. Oxford: Blackwell, 1994.

——. *Shakespeare and the Loss of Eden: The Construction of Family Values in Early Modern Culture*. New Brunswick, NJ: Rutgers, 1999.

Bendeich, Mark. "Found: Someone Who Can Shock Australians." *Globe and Mail*, 11 February 1995, D2.

Benford, Gregory. *Great Sky River*. New York: Bantam, 1987.

Benson, Philip J. "Morph Transformation of the Facial Image." *Image and Vision Computing* 12 (December 1994): 691–96.

Berger, Peter L. and Thomas Luckmann. *The Social Construction of Reality: A Treatise in the Sociology of Knowledge*. Garden City, NY: Doubleday, 1966.

Bergmann, Martin S. *In the Shadow of Moloch: The Sacrifice of Children and Its Impact on Western Religions*. New York: Columbia University Press, 1993.

Black, Max. *Models and Metaphors: Studies in Language and Philosophy*. Ithaca: Cornell University Press, 1962.

Blishen, Edward. *A Cackhanded War*. London: Thames and Hudson, 1972.

Blount, Jeb. "The Railway Ties That Bind." *Globe and Mail*, 9 August 1991, A14.

Bogdan, Robert. *Freak Show: Presenting Human Oddities for Amusement and Profit*. Chicago: University of Chicago Press, 1988.

Boon, James A. "Paradox and Limits in the History of Ethnology." *Daedalus* 109 (1980): 73–91.

Borges, Jorge Luis. "There Are More Things." In *Collected Fiction: Jorge Luis Borges*. Trans. Andrew Hurley. New York: Penguin, 1998 [1975].

Borgman, Albert. *Crossing the Postmodern Divide*. Chicago: University of Chicago Press, 1992.

Boswell, John. "Revolutions, Universals, Sexual Categories." *Salmagundi* 58–59 (Fall 1982–Winter 1983): 89–113.

Bourke, John G. *Scatalogic Rites of All Nations: A Dissertation upon the Employment of Excrementitious Remedial Agents in Religion, Therapeutics, Divination, Witchcraft, Love-Philters, etc., in all Parts of the Globe*. Washington, DC: W.H. Lowdermilk & Co., 1891 ; rpt. Johnson Reprint Corp., 1968.

Bowers, Rick. "The Cruel Mathematics of *The Duchess of Malfi*." *English Studies in Canada* 16 (December 1990): 369–83.

Bradbury, Ray. "The Jar." In *The October Country*. New York: Ballantine, 1956.

Branham, R. Bracht and Daniel Kinney, eds. and trans. *Petronius' Satyrica*. Berkeley: University of California Press, 1996.

Brooks-Gunn, J. and Diane N. Ruble. "Men's and Women's Attitudes and Beliefs about the Menstrual Cycle." *Sex Roles* 14 (March 1986): 287–99.

Brown, Donald E. *Human Universals*. Philadelphia: Temple University Press, 1991.

Brown, Norman O. *Life Against Death: The Psychoanalytic Meaning of History*. New York: Vintage Books, 1959.

——. *Love's Body*. Berkeley: University of California Press, 1990 [1966].

Bruner, Jerome. *Actual Minds, Possible Worlds*. Cambridge: Harvard University Press, 1986.

Buckley, Thomas and Alma Gottlieb, eds. *Blood Magic: The Anthropology of Menstruation*. Berkeley: University of California Press, 1988.

Buford, Bill. "Observations." *Dirty Realism: New Writing from America*. Special issue of *Granta* 8 (1983): 4–5.

——. *Among the Thugs*. New York: Random House-Vintage, 1993 [1990].

Bukatman, Scott. *Terminal Identity: The Virtual Subject in Postmodern Science Fiction*. Durham: Duke University Press, 1993.

Bürger, Peter. *Theory of the Avant-Garde*. Trans. Michael Shaw. Minneapolis: University of Minnesota Press, 1984.

Burke, Victoria. "Writing Violence: Kathy Acker's Tattoos." *Canadian Journal of Political and Social Theory* 13,1–2 (1989): 162–66.

Burston, Paul and Dave Swindells. "Friends and Enemas." *Time Out*, 11 January 1995, 21.

Butler, Judith. "The Body Politics of Julia Kristeva." *Hypatia* 3,3 (Winter 1989): 104–18.

——. *Gender Trouble: Feminism and the Subversion of Identity*. New York and London: Routledge, 1990.

——. *Bodies That Matter: On the Discursive Limits of 'Sex'*. New York and London: Routledge, 1993.

Buzzi, Aldo. "Journey to Gorgonzola." Trans. Ann Goldstein. *New York Review of Books*, 16 December 1993, 60–61.

Cailois, Roger. *Man, Play, and Games*. Trans. Meyer Barash. New York: Schocken Books, 1979 [1958].

Calasso, Roberto. *The Marriage of Cadmus and Harmony*. Trans. Tim Parks. New York: Alfred J. Knopf, 1993 [1984].

Camporesi, Piero. *Juices of Life: The Symbolic and Magical Significance of Blood*. Trans. Robert R. Barr. New York: Continuum, 1995.

Canetti, Elias. *Crowds and Power*. Trans. Carol Stewart. New York: Continuum, 1978.

Carroll, Noël. *The Philosophy of Horror, or Paradoxes of the Heart*. New York: Routledge, 1990.

Carter, Angela. *The Sadeian Woman: An Exercise in Cultural History*. London: Virago, 1979.

——. *Nights at the Circus*. London: Picador, 1993 [1984].

——. *Expletives Deleted: Selected Writings*. London: Chatto & Windus, 1992.

Carter, Stephen L. *The Culture of Disbelief*. New York: Basic Books, 1993.

Carver, Raymond. "So Much Water So Close to Home." In *Where I'm Calling From: New and Selected Stories*. New York: Vintage, 1989. Pp. 213–37.

Casey, Edward S. *Imagining: A Phenomenological Study*. Bloomington: Indiana University Press, 1984.

——. *Remembering: A Phenomenological Study*. Bloomington: Indiana University Press, 1987.

Castillo Durante, Daniel. *Du Stéréotype à la littérature*. Montréal: XYZ, 1994.

Chambers, Ross. *Room For Maneuver: Reading (the) Oppositional (in) Narrative*. Chicago: University of Chicago Press, 1991.

——. "Rules and Moves." *Canadian Review of Comparative Literature* 19,1–2 (March/June 1992): 95–100.

Chapman, Graham et al. *Monty Python's Flying Circus: Just the Words*. Vol. 2 London: Methuen, 1989.

Chatman, Seymour. *Story and Discourse: Narrative Structures in Fiction and Film*. Ithaca: Cornell University Press, 1978.

——. "What Novels Can Do That Films Can't (and Vice Versa)." *Critical Inquiry* 7 (Autumn 1980): 121–40.

Chavalier, Jean and Alain Gheerbrant, ed. *Dictionnaire des Symboles*. 2nd ed. Paris: R. Laffont, 1982.

Chiu, Hungdah. "China's Changing Criminal Justice System." *Current History* 87 (1988): 265–72.

Clancy, Patrick. "Telefigures and Cyberspace." In *Rethinking Technologies*. Verena Andermatt Conley, ed. Minneapolis: University of Minnesota Press, 1993.

Clarke, Anne E. and Diane N. Ruble. "Young Adolescents' Beliefs Concerning Menstruation." *Child Development* 49 (March 1978): 231–34.

Clerc, Charles, ed. *Approaches to "Gravity's Rainbow"*. Columbus: Ohio University Press, 1983.

Clover, Carol. *Men, Women, and Chainsaws*. Princeton: Princeton University Press, 1992.

Clynes, Manfred and Nathan S. Kline. "Cyborgs and Space." *Astronautics* 5,9 (September 1960): 26–27, 74–76.

Colombo, John Robert. *Worlds in Small*. Vancouver: Cacanadaddada Press, 1992.

Conroy, John. *Unspeakable Acts, Ordinary People: The Dynamics of Torture*. New York: Alfred A. Knopf, 2000.

Corbin, Alain. *The Foul and the Fragrant: Odor and the French Social Imagination*. Trans. Meriam L. Kochan, Roy Porter and Christopher Prendergast. Cambridge: Harvard University Press, 1986 [1982].

Crawford, Patricia. "Attitudes to Menstruation in Seventeenth-Century England." *Past and Present* 91 (May 1981): 47–73.

Crawley, Ernest. *The Mystic Rose: A Study of Primitives and of Primitive Thought Bearing on Marriage*. New York: Meridian Books, 1960 [1927].

Creed, Barbara. *The Monstrous-Feminine: Film, Feminism, Psychoanalysis*. London and New York: Routledge, 1993.

Culpepper, Emily. "Zoroastrian Menstruation Taboos: A Women's Studies Perspective." *Women and Religion, 1973 Proceedings*. Ed. Joan Arnold Romero. Tallahassee: Florida State University Press, 1973.

Daly, Mary. *Gyn/Ecology: The Metaethics of Radical Feminism.* Boston: Beacon, 1978.

Darwin, Charles. *The Expression of the Emotions in Man and Animals.* Chicago: University of Chicago Press, 1965 [1872].

Davis, Don. *The Milwaukee Murders.* New York: St. Martin's Press, 1991.

Davis, Wade. *The Serpent and the Rainbow.* New York: Simon & Schuster-Touchstone, 1997 [1985].

de Lauretis, Teresa. *Technologies of Gender: Essays on Theory, Film, and Fiction.* Bloomington: University of Indiana Press, 1987.

De Nooy, Juliana. *Derrida, Kristeva, And the Dividing Line: An Articulation of Two Theories of Difference.* New York: Garland Publishing, 1998.

De Sade, Marquis [Donatien Alphonse François]. *The 120 Days of Sodom and Other Writings.* Trans. Austryn Wainhouse and Richard Seaver. New York: Grove Press, 1966.

de Waal, Alex. "In the Disaster Zone." *Times Literary Supplement* 4711 (July 16, 1993): 5–6.

Delaney, Janice, Mary Jane Lupton and Emily Toth. *The Curse: A Cultural History of Menstruation.* Rev. ed. Urbana: University of Illinois Press, 1988.

Deleuze, Gilles and Félix Guattari. *Anti-Oedipus: Capitalism and Schizophrenia.* Trans. Robert Hurley, Mark Seem and Helen L. Lane. Minneapolis: University of Minnesota Press, 1983 [1977].

———. *A Thousand Plateaus: Capitalism and Schizophrenia.* Trans. Brian Massumi. Minneapolis: University of Minnesota Press, 1987 [1980].

DeMello, Margo. *Bodies of Inscription: A Cultural History of the Modern Tattoo Community.* Durham: Duke University Press, 2000.

Deming, Robert H., ed. *James Joyce: The Critical Heritage.* New York: Barnes, 1970.

Derrida, Jacques. "Economimesis." *Diacritics* 11 (1981): 3–25.

———. *The Post Card: From Socrates to Freud and Beyond.* Trans. Alan Bass. Chicago: University of Chicago Press, 1987 [1980].

Devlin, Patrick. *The Enforcement of Morals.* London: Oxford University Press, 1968 [1965]).

Devlin-Glass, Frances. "Vaginal Teeth That Gnash." *Mattoid* 48 (1994): 261–65.

Didion, Joan. "Letter from California: Trouble in Lakewood." *New Yorker,* 26 July 1993, 46–65.

Diesing, Paul. *Patterns of Discovery in the Social Sciences.* Chicago: Aldine-Atherton, 1971.

Doležel, Lubomír. "Towards a Typology of Fictional Worlds." *Tamking Review* 14 (1984–1985): 261–76.

———. *Heterocosmica: Fiction and Possible Worlds.* Baltimore: Johns Hopkins University Press, 1998.

Doniger, Wendy. "Why God Changed His Mind About Isaac." *New York Times Book Review,* 1 August 1993, 17.

Donnelly, Michael L. "Ecphrasis." In *The Spenser Encyclopedia.*

"Doomed Killer." *Los Angeles Times,* August 6, 1890, 1.

Dostoevsky, Fyodor. *Devils.* Trans. Michael R. Katz. Oxford and New York: Oxford University Press, 1992.

Douglas, Lawrence. "Last Bus From Auschwitz." *Massachusetts Review* 25 (Spring 1994).

Douglas, Mary. *Purity and Danger: An Analysis of Concepts of Pollution and Taboo.* New York: Praeger, 1966.

———. *Implicit Meanings: Essays in Anthropology.* London and New York: Routledge, 1991 [Routledge & Kegan Paul, 1975]

Drimmer, Frederick. *Very Special People: The Struggles, Loves and Triumphs of Human Oddities.* New York: Bantam, 1976 [1973].

Dunn, Katherine. *Geek Love.* New York: Warner Books, 1983.

Eakin, Paul John. *How Our Lives Become Stories: Making Selves.* Ithaca: Cornell University Press, 1999.

Eco, Umberto. *The Role of the Reader: Explorations in the Semiotics of Texts.* Bloomington: Indiana University Press, 1976.

Edwards, Brian. *Theories of Play and Postmodern Fiction.* New York: Garland Publishing, 1998.

Eldh, Jan. "Construction of a Neovagina with Preservation of the Glans Penis as a Clitoris in Male Transsexuals." *Plastic and Reconstructive Surgery* 91 (April 1993): 895-900

Elias, Norbert. *The Civilizing Process.* Trans. Edmond Jephcott. New York: Urizen Books, 1978 [1939].

———. *The Loneliness of the Dying.* Trans. Edmund Jephcott. Oxford: Basil Blackwell, 1985.

Ellis, Bret Easton. *American Psycho.* New York: Vintage, 1991.

Ellis, Havelock. *Studies in the Psychology of Sex.* New York: Random House, 1936 [1900].

Ellmann, James. *James Joyce.* New York: Oxford University Press, 1982 [1959].

Ewing, William A. *The Body: Photographs of the Human Form.* San Francisco: Chronicle Books, 1994.

Faulkner, William. *Light in August.* New York: Random House-Modern Library, 1950 [1932].

Fallon, April E. and Paul Rozin. "The Child's Conception of Food: the Development of Food Rejections with Special Reference to Disgust and Contamination Sensitivity." *Child Development* 55 (1984): 567-75.

"Far Worse Than Hanging: Kemmler's Death Proves an Awful Spectacle." *New York Times,* 7 August 1890, 2.

Feitlowitz, Marguerite. *A Lexicon of Terror: Argentina and the Legacies of Torture.* New York: Oxford University Press, 1998.

Fellman, Sandi. *The Japanese Tattoo.* New York: Abbeville Press, 1986.

Feyerabend, Paul. *Conquest of Abundance: A Tale of Abstraction Versus the Richness of Being.* Ed. Bert Terpstra. Chicago: University of Chicago Press, 2000.

Fiedler, Leslie. *Freaks: Myths and Images of the Secret Self.* New York: Simon and Schuster, 1978.

———. "Fantasy as Commodity and Myth." In *Kingdom of Fear: The World of Stephen King.* Eds. Tim Underwood and Chuck Miller. New York: Plume, 1986.

Findlay, Steven et al. "Danger: Implants." *U.S. News & World Report,* 24 August 1992, 62-67.

Findley, Timothy. *The Wars.* Harmondsworth: Penguin, 1978.

Finn, Peter. "Intolerance Threatens to Consume Kosovo." *Washington Post,* 13 October 1999, A1.

Finney, Charles G. *The Circus of Dr. Lao.* New York: Avon, 1976 [1935].

Firchow, Peter Edgerly. *Envisioning Africa: Racism and Imperialism.* Lexington: University Press of Kentucky, 2000.

Foster, Hal. *The Return of the Real: The Avant-Garde at the End of the Century.* Cambridge: MIT Press, 1996.

Fowles, John. *The Magus.* Rev. ed. Boston: Little Brown, 1977 [1965].

Foucault, Michel. *Discipline and Punish: The Birth of the Prison.* Trans. Alan Sheridan. New York: Vintage, 1979 [1975].

Frappier-Mazur, Lucienne. "Sadean Libertinage and the Esthetics of Violence." *Yale French Studies* 94 (1998): 184-98.

Freud, Sigmund. "The Most Prevalent Form of Degradation in Erotic Life [1912]." In *Collected Papers*. Ed. Joan Riviere. 5 vols. New York: Basic Books, 1959 [1924–50]. 4: 203–16.

——. *The Interpretation of Dreams*, vols. 4–5.

——. "The Sexual Aberrations." In *Three Essays on Sexuality, Works*, vol. 5.

——. "The Paths to the Formation of Symptoms." In *Introductory Lectures on Psychoanalysis, Works*, vols. 15–16.

——. *Civilization and Its Discontents*. Trans. James Strachey. New York: W.W. Norton, 1989 [1961].

Friedman, Alan J. "Science and Technology." In *Approaches to "Gravity's Rainbow."* Ed. Charles Clerc. Columbus: Ohio State University Press. 1983.

Frye, Northrop. *The Anatomy of Criticism: Four Essays*. Princeton: Princeton University Press, 1957.

Fussell, Paul. *The Great War and Modern Memory*. New York: Oxford University Press, 1977.

——. *Wartime: Understanding and Behavior in the Second World War*. New York: Oxford University Press, 1989.

Gass, William. *On Being Blue: A Philosophical Inquiry*. Boston: Godine, 1979 [1976].

——. "The Soul Inside the Sentence." *Salmagundi* 56 (Spring 1982): 65–86; rpt. in *Habitations of the Word: Essays*. New York: Simon & Schuster-Touchstone, 1985.

Geertz, Clifford. *The Interpretation of Culture*. New York: Harper Collins, 1973.

——. "The Uses of Diversity." *Michigan Quarterly Review* 25 (1986): 105–23.

——. *Works and Lives: The Anthropologist as Author*. Stanford: Stanford University Press, 1988.

Genette, Gérard. *Narrative Discourse: An Essay in Method*. Trans. Jane E. Lewin. Ithaca: Cornell University Press, 1980 [1972].

Georgieff, Anthony. "Death Regained." *Katalog* 7 (March 1995): 15–21.

Gibson, William. *Neuromancer*. New York: Ace, 1984.

——. *Count Zero*. New York: Ace, 1986.

——. *Burning Chrome*. New York: Ace, 1987.

——. *Mona Lisa Overdrive*. New York: Bantam, 1988.

Gide, André. *Two Legends: Oedipus and Theseus*. Trans. John Russell. New York: Random House-Vintage, 1950 [1946].

Gilman, Sander L. *Love Marriage = Death: And Other Essays on Representing Difference*. Stanford: Stanford University Press, 1998

Glover, Jonathan. *Humanity: A Moral History of the Twentieth-Century*. New Haven: Yale University Press, 2000 [1999].

Glück, Robert. "Sex Story." In *Elements of a Coffee Service*. San Francisco: Four Seasons Foundation, 1982.

Goffman, Erving. *Stigma: Notes on the Management of Spoiled Identity*. Englewood Cliffs: Prentice-Hall, 1963.

——. *Interaction Ritual: Essays on Face-To-Face Behavior*. New York: Pantheon Books, 1967.

Goldberg, Jonathan. "Shakespearean Inscriptions: The Voicing of Power." In *Shakespeare and the Question of Theory*. Eds. Patricia Parker and Geoffrey Hartman. New York and London: Methuen. 1985.

Goldstein, Irwin et al. "Early Experience With the First Pre- Connected 3-Piece Inflatable Penile Prosthesis: The Mentor Alpha-1." *The Journal of Urology* 150 (1993): 1814–18.

Goldstein, Lynda. "Raging in Tongues: Confession and Performance Art." In *Confessional Politics: Women's Sexual Self-Representations in Life Writing and Popular Media*. Ed. Irene Gammel. Carbondale and Edwardsville: Southern Illinois University Press, 1999.

Gordon, Mary. *The Company of Women*. New York: Ballantine, 1989 [1980].

Gould, Stephen Jay. *The Mismeasure of Man*. New York: W.W. Norton, 1981.

Govier, Fred E., R. Dale McClure, Robert M. Weissman, Robert P. Gibbons, Thomas R. Pritchett and Denise Kramer-Levien. "Experience With Triple-Drug Therapy in a Pharmacological Erection Program." *Journal of Urology* 150 (1993): 1822–24.

Grange, Michael. "'The crimes break so many boundaries'." *Globe and Mail*, 3 June 1995, A5.

Gray, John. *I Love Mom: An Irreverent History of the Tattoo*. Toronto: Key Porter, 1994.

Graves, Robert. *The Greek Myths*. 2 Vols. Baltimore: Penguin, 1955.

Greenberg, David F. *The Construction of Homosexuality*. Chicago: University of Chicago Press, 1988.

Greenberg, Harvey R. "Reimagining the Gargoyle: Psychoanalytic Notes on *Alien*." *Camera Obscura: A Journal of Feminism and Film Theory* 15 (Fall 1986): 87–107.

Greenberg, Jeff and Tom Pyszczynski. "The Effect of an Overheard Ethnic Slur on Evaluations of the Target: How to Spread a Social Disease." *Journal of Experimental and Social Psychology* 21 (1985): 61–72.

Greenblatt, Stephen J. "Filthy Rites." *Learning to Curse: Essays in Early Modern Culture*. New York: Routledge, 1990.

Grognard, Catherine and Cloddy Lazi. *The Tattoo: Graffiti for the Soul*. N.p.: Promotional Reprint, 1994.

Gross, Kenneth. "The Rumor of *Hamlet*." *Raritan* 14,2 (Fall 1994): 43–67.

Grosz, E[lizabeth]. A. "Language and the Limits of the Body: Kristeva and Abjection." In *Futur*Fall: Excursions into Post-Modernity*. Ed. E.A. Grosz et al. Sydney: Power Institute, 1986.

——. *Sexual Subversions: Three French Feminists*. Sydney: Allen & Unwin, 1989.

——. *Volatile Bodies: Toward A Corporeal Feminism*. Bloomington: University of Indiana Press, 1994; Sydney: Allen & Unwin, 1994.

Gubar, Susan. *Critical Condition: Feminism at the Turn of the Century*. New York: Columbia University Press, 2000.

Guest, Barbara. *Herself Defined: The Poet H.D. and Her World*. London: Collins, 1985.

Gwyther, Matthew. "Skin Pics." *Observer Magazine*, 8 December 1991, 48–53.

Habib, Imtiaz. *Shakespeare's Pluralistic Concepts of Character: A Study in Dramatic Anamorphism*. Cranbury, NJ: Associated University Press, 1993.

Haidt, Jonathan et al. "Individual Differences in Sensitivity to Disgust: A Scale Sampling Seven Domains of Disgust Elicitors." *Personality and Individual Differences* 16,5 (1994): 701–13.

Haire, Norman, ed. *Sexual Anomalies and Perversions*. London: Encyclopedia Press, 1938.

Hage, J. Joris et al. "Sculpturing the Glans in Phalloplasty." *Plastic and Reconstructive Surgery* 92 (1993): 157–62.

Halacy, Jr., D.S. *Cyborg—Evolution of the Superman*. New York: Harper & Row, 1965.

Halberstam, Judith. *Skin Shows: Gothic Horror and the Technology of Monsters*. Durham: Duke University Press, 1995.

Haldeman, Joe. *The Forever War*. New York: Avon, 1991 [1974].

Hamilton, A.C. et al., eds. *The Spenser Encyclopedia*. Toronto: University of Toronto Press, 1990.

Haraway, Donna, "A Manifesto for Cyborgs: Science, Technology, and Socialist Feminism in the 1980s." In Linda J. Nicholson, ed., *Feminism/Postmodernism*. New York and London: Routledge, 1990.

———. "The Promises of Monsters: A Regenerative Politics for Inappropriate(d) Others." In Lawrence Grossberg, Cary Nelson and Paula A. Treichler, eds., *Cultural Studies*. New York and London: Routledge, 1992. Pp. 295–337.

Harris, Thomas. *Black Sunday*. New York: Dell-Bantam, 1975.

———. *Red Dragon*. New York: Dell, 1981.

———. *The Silence of the Lambs*. New York: St. Martin's, 1988.

Hayles, N. Katherine. *Chaos Bound: Orderly Disorder in Contemporary Literature and Science*. Ithaca: Cornell University Press, 1990.

Hayman, Ronald. *K: A Biography of Kafka*. London: Weidenfeld and Nicolson, 1981.

Heaney, J.J. "Modernism." In *The New Catholic Encyclopedia*. Vol. 9. 1967.

Heidegger, Martin. *Being and Time*. Trans. John Macquarie and Edward Robinson. New York: Harper & Row, 1962.

Heinlein, Robert. *Starship Troopers*. New York: Ace, 1987 [1968].

Hellerstein, David. "The Training of a Gynecologist—How the 'Old Boys' Talk about Women's Bodies." *MS* 13 (November 1984): 136–37.

Henke, Suzette A. "Sexuality and Silence in Women's Literature." *Power, Gender, Values*. Ed. Judith Genova. Edmonton: Academic, 1987.

———. *James Joyce and the Politics of Desire*. New York and London: Routledge, 1990.

———. *Shattered Subjects: Trauma and Testimony in Women's Life- Writing*. New York: St. Martin's Press, 1998.

Hesse, Carla and Robert Post, eds. *Human Rights in Political Transitions: Gettysburg to Bosnia*. New York: Zone Books, 1999.

Hirschfeld, Magnus. *Sexual Anomalies and Perversions*. Ed. Norman Haire. London: Encyclopedia Press, 1938.

Hocquenghem, Guy. *Homosexual Desire*. Trans. Daniella Dangoor. Durham: Duke University Press, 1993 [1972].

Holmes, J. Derek. "Some Notes on Liberal Catholicism and Catholic Modernism." *The Irish Theological Quarterly* 38 (October 1971): 348–57.

"How Kemmler Died." *Los Angeles Times*, 7 August 1890, 4.

Hughes, Robert. *The Shock of the New: Art and the Century of Change*. London: Thames and Hudson, 1991 [1980].

———. *Culture of Complaint: The Fraying of America*. New York: New York Public Library and Oxford University Press, 1993.

Huizinga, Johan. *Homo Ludens: A Study of the Play-Element in Culture*. New York: Roy Publishers, 1950; rpt. Boston: Beacon Press, 1955.

Hultén, K.G. Pontus. *The Machine: As Seen at the End of the Mechanical Age*. New York: Museum of Modern Art, 1968.

Ignatieff, Michael. *Blood and Belonging: Journeys into the New Nationalism*. Toronto: Penguin, 1993.

————. "The Seductiveness of Moral Disgust." In *The Warrior's Honour: Ethnic War and the Modern Conscience*. Toronto: Penguin Books, 1999 [1998].

————. "Human Rights." In *Human Rights in Political Transitions*.

Ingarden, Roman. *The Literary Work of Art: An Investigation on the Borderlines of Ontology, Logic, and Theory of Literature*. Trans. George G. Grabowicz. Evanston: Northwestern University Press, 1973 [1965].

Ingersoll, Robert. G. *The Gods and Other Lectures*. New York: Willey, 1938.

Iser, Wolfgang. "The Imaginary." In *Encyclopedia of Aesthetics*. Vol. 2.

Jameson, Fredric. *Postmodernism, or, the Cultural Logic of Late Capitalism*. Durham: Duke University Press, 1991.

Jenkins, Joseph. *The Humanure Handbook: A Guide to Composting Human Manure*. 2nd ed. White River, VT: Chelsea Green Publishing, 1998.

Johnson, Samuel. *The Works of Samuel Johnson, L.L.D. in Nine Volumes*. London: 1825.

Joyce, James. *Ulysses*. London: Penguin, 1986.

————. *Ulysses*. New York: Modern Library, 1934.

Juni, Samuel. "The Psychodynamics of Disgust." *Journal of Genetic Psychology* 144 (1984): 203–08.

Kahane, Claire. "Freud's Sublimation: Disgust, Desire and the Female Body." *American Imago* 49 (1992): 411–25.

Kant, Immanuel. *The Critique of Judgement*. Trans. James Creed Meredith. Oxford: Oxford University Press, 1952.

Kapalka, Jason. "Anthropologists on Disgust—Three Interviews." *Mattoid* 48 (1994): pp. 165–86.

Kaufman, Marc. "Scientists Probe Origin of Emotions." *Washington Post*, 2 November 1999, H12.

Kekes, John. "Disgust and Moral Taboos." *Philosophy* 67 (1992): 431–46.

Kelly, Deirdre. "Banned Art Work Takes to the Street." *Globe and Mail*, 30 September 1999, C1.

Kelly, Michael, ed. *Encyclopedia of Aesthetics*. 4 vols. New York and Oxford: Oxford University Press, 1998.

Kerlin, Michael J. "A New Modernist Crisis? Hardly." *America* 129 (October 6, 1973): 239–42.

King, Stephen. *Christine*. New York: Signet, 1983.

————. *Stephen King's Danse Macabre*. New York: Berkeley Books, 1983 [1981].

————. [Richard Bachman] *The Running Man*. In *The Bachman Books: Four Early Novels by Stephen King*. New York: NAL-Plume, 1985 [1982].

————. "The Man in the Black Suit." *New Yorker*, 31 October 1994, 92–103.

Kirchner, Helmut. "Orgies Mysteries Theater." *Formations* 2,1 (Spring 1985): 73–80.

Kingwell, Mark. *Better Living: In Pursuit of Happiness from Plato to Prozac*. Toronto: Viking, 1998.

Kirk, Eugene P. *Menippean Satire: An Annotated Catalogue of Texts and Criticism*. New York: Garland, 1980.

Kirk, G.S. *The Nature of Greek Myths*. London: Penguin, 1974.

Klinkenborg, Verlyn. "Violent Certainties." *Harper's* (January 1995): 37–52.

Kolb, David. "Socrates in the Labyrinth." In *Hyper/Text/Theory*.

Kolakowski, Lesek. *Modernity on Endless Trial*. Chicago: University of Chicago Press, 1990.

Kolker, Claudia. "The Art of Execution, Texas Style." *Los Angeles Times*, 11 April 2000, A1, A9.

Korsmeyer, Carolyn. *Making Sense of Taste: Food and Philosophy*. Ithaca: Cornell University Press, 1999.

Kristeva, Julia. *Powers of Horror: An Essay on Abjection*. Trans. Leon S. Roudiez. New York: Columbia University Press, 1982.

Kumar, Amitava. *Passport Photos*. Berkeley: University of California Press, 2000.

Landow, George P. *Hypertext: The Convergence of Contemporary Critical Theory and Technology*. Baltimore: Johns Hopkins University Press, 1992.

——. Ed. *Hyper/Text/Theory*. Baltimore: Johns Hopkins University Press, 1994.

——. "What's a Critic to Do? Critical Theory in the Age of Hypertext." In *Hyper/Text/Theory*.

——. "Hypertext." In *Encyclopedia of Aesthetics*. Vol. 2.

Lane, Anthony. "To the Limit." *New Yorker*, 17 April 2000, 124–25.

Lagerkvist, Pär. *The Dwarf*. Trans. Alexandra Dick. London: Quartet, 1986 [1944].

Laporte, Dominique. *History of Shit*. Trans. Nadia Benabid and Rodolphe El-Khoury. Cambridge: MIT Press, 2000 [1978].

Lawrence, Denise L. "Menstrual Politics: Women and Pigs in rural Portugal." In *Blood Magic: The Anthropology of Menstruation*. Pp. 117–36, 266–68.

Lawton, David. *Blasphemy*. Philadelphia: University of Pennsylvania Press, 1993.

Leak, Andy. "Nausea and Desire in Sartre's *La Nausée*." *French Studies* 43 (1989): 61–72.

Lesser, Wendy. *Pictures at An Execution: An Inquiry into the Subject of Murder*. Cambridge: Harvard University Press, 1993.

Lessing, Doris. *The Golden Notebook*. London: Paladin, 1989 [1962].

Levin, Harry. *The Question of Hamlet*. New York: St. Martin's, 1959.

Levin, Ira. *The Stepford Wives*. London: Pan Books, 1973 [1972].

Levine, Laurence A. et al. "Prosthesis Placement After Total Phallic Reconstruction." *Journal of Urology* 149 (1993): 593–98.

Levy, Leonard W. *Blasphemy: Verbal Offense Against the Sacred, From Moses to Salman Rushdie*. New York: Alfred A. Knopf, 1993.

Lewin, Ralph A. *Merde: Excursions in Scientific, Cultural, and Sociohistorical Coprology*. New York: Random House, 1999.

Lingis, Alphonso. *Dangerous Emotions*. Berkeley: University of California Press, 2000.

Lively, Penelope. *Moon Tiger*. London: Penguin, 1987.

Lovecraft, H.P. "The Call of Cthulhu." In *Crawling Chaos: Selected Works 1920–1935*. Ed. James Havoc. London: Creation Press, 1992.

Lukacher, Ned. "The Epistemology of Disgust." Foreword to *Hysteria From Freud to Lacan*. Monique David-Ménard. Trans. Catherine Porter. Ithaca: Cornell University Press, 1989.

MacDonald, John D. *Cape Fear*. New York: Fawcett, 1991 [1957].

MacDonogh, Steve, in association with Article 19, ed. *The Rushdie Letters: Freedom to Speak, Freedom to Write*. Lincoln: University of Nebraska Press, 1993.

Macy, Caitlin. *The Fundamentals of Play*. New York: Random House, 2000.

Mack, Maynard. "The World of *Hamlet*." *Tragic Themes in Western Literature*. Ed. Cleanth Brooks. New Haven: Yale University Press, 1955.

MacKinnon, Catherine A. *Only Words*. Cambridge: Harvard University Press, 1993.

Maitre, Doreen. *Literature and Possible Worlds*. London: Middlesex Polytechnic Press, 1983.

Malinowski, Bronislaw. *The Sexual Lives of Savages in North-Western Melanesia*. New York: Harcourt Brace & World, 1929.

Malloy, Doug. "Body Piercings." In *Modern Primitives: An Investigation of Contemporary Adornment and Ritual.*

Malraux, André. *Man's Estate.* Trans. Alastair MacDonald. Hammondsworth: Penguin, 1961 [1933].

Mannix, Daniel P. *Freaks: We Who Are Not As Others.* Re/Search, 1976; 2nd edition, 1990 [1976].

Manson, William C. "Desire and Danger: A Reconsideration of Menstrual Taboos." *Journal of Psychoanalytic Anthropology* 7 (Summer 1984): 241–55.

Marcus, Greil. *Lipstick Traces: A Secret History of the Twentieth Century.* Cambridge: Harvard University Press, 1989.

Margolin, Uri. "Characterization in Narrative: Some Theoretical Prolegomena." *Neophilologus* 67 (1983): 1–14.

———. "Dealing with the Non-Actual: Conception, Reception, Description." *Poetics Today* 9 (Winter 1988): 863–78.

———. "Individuals in Narrative Worlds: An Ontological Perspective." *Poetics Today* 11 (Winter 1990): 843–71.

Martine-Mora, J.R., A. Castellvi Insard and P. López-Ortiz, "Neovagina in Vaginal Agenesis: Surgical Methods and Long-Term Results." *Journal of Pediatric Surgery* 27 (January 1992): 10–14.

Martínez-Bonati, Félix. *Fictive Discourse and the Structure of Literature: A Phenomenological Approach.* Ithaca: Cornell University Press, 1981.

Martingale, Moira. *Cannibal Killers: The Impossible Monsters.* London: Robert Hale, 1993.

Maslin, Janet. "Summer Serves Up Its Sleepers." *New York Times,* 2 August 1987, 103.

Massumi, ed. "Deleuze, Guattari and the Philosophy of Expression." *Canadian Review of Comparative Literature* 24, 3 (September/septembre 1997).

Masur, Louis P. *Rites of Execution: Capital Punishment and the Transformation of American Culture, 1776–1865.* New York: Oxford University Press, 1989.

Maxford, Howard. *The A–Z of Horror Film.* Bloomington: Indiana University Press, 1997.

McAvoy, Thomas T. "Americanism, Fact and Fiction." *Catholic Historical Review* 31 (July 1945): 133–53.

McDowell, Michael. "The Unexpected and the Inevitable." In *Kingdom of Fear: The World of Stephen King.* Eds. Tim Underwood and Chuck Miller. New York: Plume, 1986.

McEvilley, Thomas. "Art in the Dark." In *Apocalypse Culture.*

McEwan, Ian. *Amsterdam.* Toronto: Knopf, 1998.

McGinn, Colin. "Freud Under Analysis." *New York Review of Books,* 4 November 1999, 20–24.

McHale, Brian. *Postmodernist Fiction.* New York: Methuen, 1987.

McInnes, Craig. "B.C. Deplores Man's Purchase of Kidney." *Globe and Mail,* 7 January 1995, A1, A6.

McKenna, Andrew. "After Bakhtin: On the Future of Laughter and Its History in France." *University of Ottawa Quarterly* 53 (January–March 1983): 67–82.

McKeever, Patricia. "The Perception of Menstrual Shame: Implications and Directions." *Women and Health* 9 (Winter 1984): 33–47.

Mindich, Jeremy. "A Game of Inches: The Penis Enlargement Operation." *Details* 12 (May 1994).

Miller, Casey and Kate Swift. *Words and Women.* New York: Anchor- Doubleday, 1976.

Miller, William Ian. *The Anatomy of Disgust.* Cambridge: Harvard University Press, 1997.

Mills, Jane. *Womanwords: A Vocabulary of Culture and Patriarchal Society.* London: Longman, 1989.

Milowicki, Edward J. "The Quest for Genre: Menippean Satire, Romance, and the Novel." *Canadian Review of Comparative Literature* 23,4 (December 1996): 1213-25.

Mirabeau, Octave. *The Torture Garden.* Trans. Alvah C. Bessie. San Francisco: Re/Search, 1989 [1899].

Mistry, Rohinton. "Squatter." In *Tales From Firozsha Baag.* Toronto: McClelland & Stewart, 1992.

Mitchell, Basil. *Law, Morality and Religion in a Secular Society.* London: Oxford University Press, 1970.

"Modernism." In Albert J. Nevins, M.M., ed. *The Maryknoll Catholic Dictionary.* Wilkes-Barre, PA: Dimension Books, 1965.

Moi, Toril. *Sexual/Textual Politics: Feminist Literary Theory.* London: Methuen, 1985.

———. *Simone De Beauvoir: The Making of an Intellectual Woman.* Oxford: Blackwell, 1999.

Montrosi, Francesco et al. "Patient-Partner Satisfaction With Semirigid Penile Prostheses for Peyronie's Disease: A 5-Year Followup Study." *Journal of Urology* 150 (1993): 1819-21.

Moravec. Hans. *Robot: Mere Machine to Transcendent Mind.* New York: Oxford University Press, 1999.

———. "Rise of the Robots." *Scientific American* (December 1999): 124-35.

Morgan, Robin. *The Demon Lover: On the Sexuality of Terrorism.* New York: Norton, 1989.

Morris, David B. *The Culture of Pain.* Berkeley: University of California Press, 1991.

Morton, Jim, ed. *Incredibly Strange Films.* San Francisco: Re/Search, 1986.

Mueller, Cookie. "The One Percent." In *High Risk: An Anthology of Forbidden Writings.*

Murphy, Peter. "Insidious Humour and the Construction of Masculinity." *Mattoid* 54. Special Issue on "Examining/Experiencing Masculinities" (1999): 61-73.

Muscio, Inga. *CUNT: A Declaration of Independence.* Seattle: Seal Press, 1998.

Nabokov, Vladimir. *Pale Fire.* New York: Perigee-Putnam, 1980 [1962].

Namias, June. *White Captives: Gender and Ethnicity on the American Frontier.* Chapel Hill: University of North Carolina Press, 1993.

Nash, Christopher. *World-Games: The Tradition of Anti-Realist Revolt.* London: Methuen, 1987.

Nash, Jay Robert. *Almanac of World Crime.* New York: Anchor, 1981.

Nash, Jay Robert and Stanley Ralph Ross, eds. "Robocop." In *The Motion Picture Guide Annual.* Evanston: Cinebooks, 1988.

Nasrin, Taslima. "Sentenced to Death." *New York Times.* 30 November 1993, A25.

Neher, Jacques. "France Amazed, Amused by Disney Dress Code." *International Herald Tribune,* 26 December 1991.

Neu, Jerome, ed. *The Cambridge Companion to Freud.* Cambridge: Cambridge University Press, 1991.

Neumann, Erich. *The Great Mother: An Analysis of the Archetype.* 2nd ed. New York: Bollingen, 1963.

New Catholic Encyclopedia. Ed. Catholic University of America. 19 vols. New York: McGraw Hill, 1967.

Newton, Michael. *Hunting Humans: The Encyclopedia of Serial Killers,* Vol. I. New York: Avon, 1990.

Niebuhr, Richard R. "Schleiermacher, Friedrich Daniel Ernst." In *The Encyclopedia of Philosophy,* Vol. 7. Ed. Paul Edwards. New York: Collier-Macmillan, 1972 [1967].

Nietzsche, Friedrich. *On the Genealogy of Morals*. Trans. Walter Kaufmann and R.J. Hollingdale. New York: Vintage, 1967.

Obeyesekere, Gananath. *Medusa's Hair: An Essay on Personal Symbols and Religious Experience*. Chicago: University of Chicago Press, 1981.

O'Connor, Flannery. *The Complete Stories*. New York: Farrer, Strauss and Giroux, 1979.

Olchowy, James Richard. "Eluding 'Mind-forg'd Manacles': Revisiting Oppression in the Fiction of Angela Carter." Unpublished Dissertation. Dalhousie University. 1994.

Ollivier, Debra. "Designer Vaginas." *Salon.com*, 14 November 2000.

Otto, Rudolf. *The Idea of the Holy: An Inquiry into the Non- Rational Factor in the Idea of the Divine and Its Relation to the Rational*. Trans. John W. Harvey. London: Oxford University Press, 1925.

Ozick, Cynthia. "Rushdie in the Louvre." *New Yorker*, 13 December 1993.

Paglia, Camille. *Sexual Personae: Art and Decadence from Nefertiti to Emily Dickinson*. New York: Vintage, 1990.

———. *Sex, Art, and American Culture*. New York: Vintage, 1992.

Parfrey, Adam, ed. *Apocalypse Culture*. Rev. ed. New York: Feral House, 1990 [1987].

———. "G.G. Allin: Portrait of the Enemy." In *Apocalypse Culture*.

Parsons, Terence. *Nonexistent Objects*. New Haven: Yale University Press, 1980.

Pavel, Thomas. *Fictional Worlds*. Cambridge: Harvard University Press, 1986.

Perniola, Mario. *Disgusti: Le nouve tendenze estetiche*. Milano: Costa & Nolan, 1998.

Peto, Peter. *Modern Satire: Four Studies*. Berlin: Mouton, 1982.

"Photograph of Young Man Outside San Quentin Prison." *New York Times*. 22 April 1992, A22.

Pierpont, Claudia Roth. *Passionate Minds: Women Rewriting the World*. New York: Albert A. Knopf, 2000.

Platzner, Robert L. "The Metamorphic Vision of J.G. Ballard." *Essays in Literature* 10 (1983).

Plotinsky, Arkady. *Reconfigurations: Critical Theory and General Economy*. Gainsville: University Press of Florida, 1993.

Pops, Martin. "The Metamorphosis of Shit." *Salmagundi* 56 (Spring 1982): 26–61.

Porush, David. *The Soft Machine: Cybernetic Fiction*. New York and London: Methuen, 1985.

Potter, John Deanne. *The Fatal Gallows Tree*. London: Elek Books, 1965.

Pressley, Sue Anne. "New Debate About an Old Killer." *Washington Post*, 26 August 1999, A3.

Price, Greg. "Interview with Isabel Allende." In *Latin America: The Writer's Journey*. London: Hamish Hamilton, 1990.

Probyn, Clive. "Surfacing and Falling into Matter: Johnson, Swift, Disgust, and Beyond." *Mattoid* 48 (1994): 37–43.

Pynchon, Thomas. *V.* New York: Modern Library, 1966 [1961].

———. *Gravity's Rainbow*. New York: Viking, 1973.

Rabinowitz, Peter J. *Before Reading: Narrative Conventions and the Politics of Interpretation*. Ithaca: Cornell University Press, 1987.

Radford, Fred. "'Cloacal Obsession': Hugo, Joyce and the Sewer Museum of Paris." *Mattoid* 48 (1994): 66–85.

Rice, Boyd. "Mondo Films." In *Incredibly Strange Films*.

Richie, Donald and Ian Buruma. *The Japanese Tattoo*. New York: Weatherhill, 1980.

Ritchin, Fred. *In Our Own Image: The Coming Revolution in Photography*. New York: Aperture, 1990.

Robertson, W.R. "Disgust: Being's Sludgewards Fall." *Canadian Review of Comparative Literature* 25,1–2 (March–June/Mars–Juin 1998): 210–24.

Ross, T.J. "Polanski, *Repulsion*, and the New Mythology." In *Focus on the Horror Film.* Roy Huss and T. J. Ross, eds. Englewood Cliffs: Prentice-Hall, 1972.

Rozin, Paul et al. "The Child's Conception of Food: The Development of Contamination Sensitivity to 'Disgusting' Substances." *Developmental Psychology* 21,6 (1985): 1075–79.

Rozin, Paul et al. "Operation of the Laws of Sympathetic Magic in Disgust and Other Domains." *Journal of Personality and Social Psychology* 50, 4 (1986): 703–12.

Rozin, Paul and April E. Fallon. "A Perspective on Disgust." *Psychological Review* 94 (1987): 23–41.

Rozin, Paul and Carol Nemeroff. "The Laws of Sympathetic Magic: A Psychological Analysis of Similarity and Contagion." In *Cultural Psychology: Essays on Comparative Human Development.* Eds. James W. Stigler et al. New York: Cambridge University Press, 1990.

Rozin, Paul et al. "Varieties of Disgust Faces and the Structure of Disgust." *Journal of Personality and Social Psychology* 66 (1994): 870–81.

Rushdie, Salman. "Chekov and Zulu." In *East, West.* New York: Pantheon Books, 1994.

———. *Midnight's Children.* New York: Penguin, 1991 [1980].

———. *Shame.* London: Jonathan Cape, 1981.

———. *The Satanic Verses.* New York: Viking, 1988.

Rushdy, Ashraf H.A. "A New Emetics of Interpretation: Swift, His Critics and the Alimentary Canal." *Mosaic* 24 (1991): 1–32.

Sallot, Jeff. "Airborne 'Initiation' Rite Probed." *Globe and Mail,* January 29, 1995.

Sammon, Paul M. "The Salacious Gaze: Sex, the Erotic Trilogy and the Decline of David Lynch." In *Cut! Horror Writers on Horror Film.* Ed. Christopher Golden. Grantham, NH: Borderlands Press, 1992.

Samuels, David. "Notes From Underground: Among the Radicals of the Pacific Northwest." *Harper's,* May 2000, 35–47.

Samuels, Stuart. *Midnight Movies.* New York: Collier Books, 1983.

Sanders, Clinton R. *Customizing the Body: The Art and Culture of Tattooing.* Philadelphia: Temple University Press, 1989.

Sartre, Jean-Paul. *Being and Nothingness.* Trans. Hazel Barnes. New York: Washington Square Press, 1969 [1943].

———. "The Childhood of a Leader" and "Erostratus." In *Intimacy.* Trans. Lloyd Alexander. London: Panther Books, 1960.

———. *Imagination: A Psychological Critique.* Trans. Forrest Williams. Ann Arbor: University of Michigan Press, 1962.

———. *The Psychology of Imagination.* Trans. Bernard Frechtman. New York: Citadel Press, 1963 [1948].

———. *Nausea.* Trans. Robert Baldick. Harmondsworth: Penguin, 1965.

Scarry, Elaine. *The Body in Pain: The Making and Unmaking of the World.* New York: Oxford University Press, 1985.

———. "The Difficulty of Imagining Other Persons." In *Human Rights in Political Transitions.*

Scheff, Thomas J. *Microsociology: Discourse, Emotion, and Social Structure.* Chicago: University of Chicago Press, 1990.

Schiller, Friedrich. *On the Aesthetic Education of Man in a Series of Letters*. Trans. E.M. Wilkinson and L.A. Willoughby. Oxford: Clarendon, 1967.

Schjedahl, Peter. "Those Nasty Brits." *New Yorker*, 11 October 1999, 104–05.

Scholder, Amy and Ira Silverberg, eds. *High Risk: An Anthology of Forbidden Writings*. New York: Penguin-Plume, 1991.

Self, Will. *The Quantity Theory of Insanity*. London: Penguin, 1991.

Seltzer, Mark. *Bodies and Machines*. New York and London: Routledge, 1992.

Sen, Amartya. "East and West: The Reach of Reason." *The New York Review of Books* 47,12: 33–38.

Shakespeare, William. *The Riverside Shakespeare*. Ed. G. Blakemore Evans. Boston: Houghton Mifflin, 1974.

Shattuck, Roger. *Forbidden Knowledge: From Prometheus to Pornography*. New York: St. Martin's Press, 1996.

Sherbert, Garry. *Menippean Satire and the Poetics of Wit: Ideologies of Self-Consciousness in Dunton, D'Urfey, and Sterne*. New York: Peter Lang, 1996.

Shklovsky, Victor. "Art as Technique." In *Russian Formalist Criticism*. L.T. Lemon and M.J. Reis, eds. Lincoln: University of Nebraska Press, 1965.

Simeons, Albert T. *Man's Presumptuous Brain*. New York: Dutton, 1962.

Sloterdijk, Peter. *Critique of Cynical Reason*. Trans. Michael Eldred. Minneapolis: University of Minnesota Press, 1987 [1983].

Slemon, Stephen. "Bones of Contention: Post-Colonial Writing and the 'Cannibal' Question." *Literature and the Body*. Ed. Anthony Purdy. Amsterdam: Rodopi, 1992.

Sobieszek, Robert A., ed. *Photography and the Human soul, 1850– 2000: Essays on Camera Portraiture*. Los Angeles: Los Angeles County Museum of Art; Cambridge, MIT Press, 2000.

Sophocles. *Philoctetes*. Trans. Kenneth Cavender. San Francisco: Chandler, 1965.

Soren, David, Aicha Ben Abed Ben Khader and Hedi Slim. *Carthage: Uncovering the Mysteries and Splendors of Ancient Tunisia*. New York: Simon and Schuster, 1990.

Spariosu, Mihai I. *Dionysus Reborn: Play and the Aesthetic Dimension in Modern Philosophical and Scientific Discourse*. Ithaca: Cornell University Press, 1989.

——. *The Wreath of Wild Olive: Play, Liminality, and the Study of Literature*. Albany: SUNY Press, 1997.

Spinrad, Paul. *The Re/Search Guide to Bodily Fluids*. San Francisco: Re/Search Publications, 1994.

Spivak, Gayatri Chakravorty. "Displacement and the Discourse of Woman." In *Displacement: Derrida and After*. Ed. Mark Krupnick. Blomington: Indiana University Press, 1983.

Stager, Lawrence and Samuel Wolff, "Child Sacrifice at Carthage—Religious Rite or Population Control?" *Biblical Archeology Review* 10,1 (1984): 30–51.

Steakley, John. *Armor*. New York: DAW, 1984.

Stern, Jane and Michael Stern, eds. *The Encyclopedia of Bad Taste*. New York: HarperCollins, 1990.

Strauss, Philip. "Robocop." *Monthly Film Bulletin* 55 (February 1988): 35–36.

Stoekl, Allan, ed. "On Bataille" (special issue). *Yale French Studies* 78 (1990).

Suits, Bernard. *The Grasshopper: Games, Life and Utopia*. Toronto: University of Toronto Press, 1978.

Sulloway, Frank J. *Freud, Biologist of the Mind: Beyond the Psychoanalytic Legend.* New York: Basic Books, 1979.

Sutherland, Stuart, ed. *International Dictionary of Psychology.* New York: Continuum, 1990.

Swerdlow, Joel L. "Quiet Miracles of the Brain." *National Geographic* 187,6 (June 1995).

Tanner, Laura E. *Intimate Violence: Reading Rape and Torture in Twentieth-Century Fiction.* Bloomington: Indiana University Press, 1994.

Taussig, Michael. "Culture of Terror—Space of Death: Roger Casement's Putumayo Report and the Explanation of Torture." *Comparative Studies in Society and History* 26 (1984): 467–97.

Theroux, Paul. "Letter." In *The Rushdie Letters: Freedom to Speak, Freedom to Write.*

Timerman, Jacobo. *Prisoner Without a Name, Cell Without a Number.* Trans. Toby Talbot. New York: Vintage, 1981.

Tisdale, Sallie. *Talk Dirty To Me: An Intimate Philosophy of Sex.* New York: Doubleday, 1994.

Trebay, Guy. "Primitive Culture." *Village Voice,* 12 November 1991, 38

Tithecott, Richard. *Of Mice and Monsters: Jeffrey Dahmer and the Construction of the Serial Killer.* Madison: University of Wisconsin Press, 1997.

Trombley, Stephen. *The Execution Protocol: Inside America's Capital Punishment Industry.* New York: Anchor, 1993 [1992].

Turnbull, Colin M. *The Mountain People.* New York: Simon & Schuster-Touchstone, 1987 [1972].

"The TV Column." *Washington Post,* 14 June 1994, C6.

Underwood, Tim and Chuck Miller, eds. *Kingdom of Fear: The World of Stephen King.* New York: New American Library-Plume, 1986.

van Noort, Dirk E. and Jean-Phillippe A. Nicolai, "Comparison of Two Methods of Vagina Construction in Transsexuals." *Plastic and Reconstructive Surgery* 91 (June 1993): 1308–15.

Vale, V. and Andrea Juno, eds. *Modern Primitives: An Investigation of Contemporary Adornment and Ritual.* San Francisco: Re/Search Publications, 1989.

———. *Angry Women.* San Francisco: Re/Search Publications, 1991.

Viswanathan, Gauri. *Outside the Fold: Conversion, Modernity, and Belief.* Princeton: Princeton University Press, 1998.

Vázquez Rial, Horacio. *Historia del Triste.* Barcelona: Ediciones Destino, 1987.

———. *Triste's History.* Trans. Jo Labanyi. London: Readers International, 1990 [1987].

Von Drehle, David. *Among the Lowest of the Dead: The Culture of Death Row.* New York: Random House, 1995.

Wallace, David Foster. *A Supposedly Fun Thing I'll Never Do Again: Essays and Arguments.* Boston: Little, Brown and Company, 1997.

———. *Brief Interviews With Hideous Men.* Boston: Little, Brown and Company, 2000 [1999].

Walton, Kendall L. *Mimesis as Make-Believe: On the Foundations of the Representational Arts.* Cambridge: Harvard University Press, 1990.

Warnock, Mary. *Imagination.* London: Faber and Faber, 1976.

Wear, Delese. "Medical Students' Encounters with the Cadaver: A Poetic Response." *Death Studies* 11 (1987): 123–30.

———. "Cadaver Talk: Medical Students' Accounts of Their Year-Long Experience." *Death Studies* 13 (1989): 379–91.

Weedon, Chris. *Feminist Practice and Poststructuralist Theory.* Oxford: Basil Blackwell, 1987.

Weegee. *Naked City*. New York: Da Capo Press, 1985 [1945].

Wells, H.G. *The Island of Dr. Moreau*. New York: Signet, 1988 [1896].

——. "Review of James Joyce's *A Portrait of the Artist as a Young Man*." *The Nation*, February 24, 1917; rpt. *James Joyce: The Critical Heritage*. Ed. Robert H. Deming. New York: Barnes, 1970. Pp. 86-88.

When the State Kills: The Death Penalty v. Human Rights. London: Amnesty International Publications, 1989.

White, Patrick. *Voss*. Ringwood: Penguin Books, 1960 [1957].

——. *The Twyborn Affair*. London: Jonathan Cape, 1979.

White, Edmund. *The Burning Library: Writings on Art, Politics and Sexuality 1969–1993*. Ed. David Bergman. London: Picador in association with Chato & Windus, 1995 [1994].

Wilk, Stephen R. *Medusa: Solving the Mystery of the Gorgon*. New York: Oxford University Press, 2000.

Wills, David. *Prosthesis*. Stanford: Stanford University Press, 1995.

Wills, Garry. *Papal Sin: Structures of Deceit*. New York: Doubleday, 2000.

Wilson, Catherine. "Epistemology of Fiction." In *Encyclopedia of Aesthetics*. Vol. 2.

Wilson, Peter J., Grant McCall, W.R. Geddes, A.K. Mark, John E. Pfeiffer and James B. Boskey, with Colin M. Turnbull's Reply. "More Thoughts on the Ik and Anthropology." *Current Anthropology* 16 (September 1975): 343-58.

Wilson, R[obert] Rawdon. *In Palamedes' Shadow: Explorations in Play, Game, and Narrative Theory*. Boston: Northeastern University Press, 1990.

——. "Literary Theory's Edginess: Texts, Problems, And the Array of Questions." *English Studies in Canada* 23,1 (March 1992): 19-41.

——. "Seeing With a Fly's Eye: Comparative Perspectives on Commonwealth Literature." *Open Letter* 8,2 (Winter 1992): 5-27.

——. "Graffiti Become Terror: The Idea of Resistance." *Canadian Review of Comparative Literature* 22,2 (June 1995): 267-85.

——. *Shakespearean Narrative*. Newark: University of Delaware Press, 1995.

——. "Hyperplay: Playing the Sly Man at Theory." *Mattoid* 51 (1997): 42-68.

——. "In a Condor's Eye." *HEAT* 13 (1999): 125-36.

Wilson, Robert Rawdon and Edward Milowicki, "*Troilus and Cressida*: Voices in the Darkness of Troy." In *Reading the Renaissance: Culture, Poetics, and Drama*. Ed. Jonathan Hart. New York: Garland Publishing, 1996. Pp. 129-44, 234-40.

Wollheim, Richard. *Freud*. Glasgow: Fontana/Collins, 1971.

Woolsey, John M. "United States of America v. One Book Called '*Ulysses*' Random House, Inc." Rpt. in *Ulysses*. New York: Modern Library, 1934. Pp. ix-xiv.

Yaeger, Patricia. *Honey-Mad Women: Emancipatory Strategies in Women's Writing*. New York: Columbia University Press, 1988.

Young, Stacey. "If You Could Be Anyone on Television, Who Would It Be?" *University of Toronto Varsity*, 12 January 1995, 8.

Žižek, Slavoj. *The Metastases of Enjoyment: Six Essays on Woman and Causality*. London: Verso, 1994.

——. *The Indivisible Remainder: An Essay on Schelling and Related Matters*. London: Verso, 1996.

Index

abjection, 241–86. *See also* self disgust
and death, 254, 394 n.8
experience of, 33, 108, 251, 252, 339 n.19
friendship with abused man, 241–45,
249, 263, 265, 270, 284–86
importance of feces and menstrual
blood, 107, 116, 146, 269, 270,
276–78, 343 n.45, 400 n.47, 402
n.70, 403 n.70
literary examples, 250–52, 251, 256, 344
n.48, 388 n.97
Shakespeare, 253, 275
Lessing *Golden Notebook*, 270–76,
279–81, 319 n.83, 400 n.49
relationship to self-disgust, 265, 266, 269
viewed by Grosz, 399 n.46, 400 n.46
viewed by Henke, 270, 346 n.67, 400 n.48
viewed by Kristeva, 33, 93, 275–78, 285,
286, 328 n.48, 329 n.48, 399 n.46
academic with spider tattoo story, 34–36,
126, 163, 183, 184, 370 n.23, 375 n.57
Acker, Kathy, 169, 317 n.75, 368 n.14, 370 n.26
Ackerman, Diane, 319 n.81, 368 n.15
aesthetics, 22, 54, 127–29, 186. *See also* art
historical aspects, 21, 304 n.4, 308 n.29
and Shakespeare, 110
and shock, 123, 308 n.28
tattoos, 168, 366 n.3
Al-Azmeh, Aziz, 208
Al-Ghamdi, Mughram, 207, 210, 384 n.63
Albert the Great, 401 n.54
alienation, 17, 205, 212–16, 251, 279, 385 n.75,
313 n.53
Alien films, 234, 364 n.70, 362 n.58, 386 n.79,
389 n.101, 389 n.103, 389 n.104. *See
also* Cameron, James; Fincher,

David; Jeunet, Jean-Pierre; Scott,
Ridley.
Allais, Alphonse, 319 n.85
Allan, Keith, 343 n.45, 346 n.66, 347 n.69
Allen, Irwin, 364 n.70
Allende, Isabel, 224, 237, 388 n.92
Allin, G.G., xix, 25, 26, 57, 162, 250, 308 n.28,
313 n.51, 313 n.52, 314 n.56
Althusser, Louis, 334 n.86, 377 n.4
Altman, Robert, 183, 375 n.58
Angyal, A., 59, 60, 327 n.38, 327 n.39
androids. *See* machines
anger. *See* mental states and disorders
animals
animal sacrifices, 23
ants, 330 n.59, 364 n.70
bees, 364 n.70
cockroaches, 45, 331 n.65
dogs, 108, 177, 178, 229, 290, 389 n.101
flies, 110
horses, 108, 219, 254
insects. *See also* insect eating
as disgust objects, 47, 65, 226
in food, 1, 2, 170
literary and film depictions,
228–31, 270, 271, 364 n.70, 365 n.70,
389 n.101, 401 n.51
maggots, xii, xiii, 110, 170, 314 n.57, 344
n.51
pigs, 316 n.64, 354 n.65, 405 n.89
rabbits, 214
rats, 145
scorpions, 312 n.44
sharks, 169
snakes, 113–15, 117, 219, 220
spiders

academic with spider tattoo story,
34–36, 126, 163, 183, 184, 370 n.23,
375 n.57
author's experiences, 45, 330 n.59,
344 n.51
facial tattoos, 187, 367 n.4, 370 n.23
Lessing *Golden Notebook*, 38, 272,
274, 280
literary depictions, 364 n.70, 367
n.7
Shakespeare, 35, 36, 38, 69, 367 n.7
symbolism, 38
tattoos, 167, 316 n.68, 367 n.7
wasps, 389 n.101
worms, 111
anomie, 212, 385 n.75
Anselm, Saint, 105
Anspaugh, Kelly, 15, 308 n.25, 310 n.38
anthropologist experiences, 13, 14, 32, 33, 54,
306 n.19, 307 n.19, 315 n.64, 316
n.64
anus, 68, 213, 244, 263, 277, 284, 285, 332 n.69,
392 n.1–3, 397 n.25
anxiety, 26, 217–21, 224
aphrodisiacs, 167
Apollo, 115, 282
Apollonian actions, 64, 87, 105, 107, 252, 394
n.11, 406 n.89
feminist views, 275–78, 402 n.59
viewed by Bataille, 76, 77, 253, 402 n.59
Aristophanes, 33
Arp, Jean, 308 n.29, 309 n.29
art. *See also* aesthetics; Dada
the arts, xv, 54, 72, 74, 75, 186, 205
Nitsch performances, 23, 24, 312 n.44
rage, 401 n.57, 402 n.57
Shakespeare, 27
shock performance art, 18, 19, 27, 28, 166,
294, 308 n.27, 311 n.39, 313 n.50, 369
n.21
and transgression, 71, 74, 92, 162, 308
n.28, 311 n.42
visual art, xv, 26, 106, 313 n.50, 363 n.61
Ashton's Circus, 340 n.26
Asturias, Miguel Angel, 391 n.113

author's experiences. *See* experiences of
author
Atwood, Margaret, 293, 358 n.41

Bakhtin, M.M., 21, 74, 92, 104, 311 n.39, 333
n.77 342 n.37
Ballard, J.G., 150, 251, 363 n.62, 363 n.63, 363
n.67, 364 n.67
Barnes, Hazel, 329 n.54
Barnes, Julian, 201, 380 n.22
Barnum, P.T., 255, 366 n.3, 366 n.4
Barrable, Bill, 405 n.89
Barth, Frederick, 307 n.19
Barthes, Roland, 39, 112, 148, 175, 319 n.84
Bass, Alan, 368 n.10
Bass, Saul, 364 n.70
Bataille, George
disgust as means to self-knowledge, 40,
70, 262, 278, 280
and transgression, xxi–xxiii, 308 n.29, 333
n.76, 333 n.79, 334 n.84, 402 n.59
transgression model of disgust, 31, 48,
75–77
views about execution, 359 n.43
views about humanity, 47, 225, 252, 253,
336 n.2, 338 n.10
views about de Sade, 334 n.82
Bateson, Gregory, 57
Baudelaire, Charles, 66, 110, 344 n.51
Beckett, Samuel, 211, 212, 250, 252
The Unnamable, 17, 216, 385 n.75, 394 n.9
Bedford, Carmel, 377 n.5
Bencheikh, Jamel Eddine, 199, 209, 378 n.10
Benford, Gregory, 398 n.35
Berger, Chief Justice, 141
Berger, Peter L., 55, 324 n.24, 325 n.28
Berlin, Isaiah, 246
Bernardo, Paul, 357 n.39, 358 n.39
Bible, 140, 201, 306 n.18. *See also* religious
aspects
Leviticus, 35, 67, 228, 370 n.25
Bierce, Ambrose, 349 n.82
Black, Max, 47, 320 n.5
Blake, William, 390 n.107
blasphemy

sweat, 384 n.63
toe jam, 89, 93, 213, 276, 278, 285
urine, 44, 104, 108, 109, 290, 291, 312 n.49,
313 n.50
El-Khoury, Rodolphe, 303 n.2
electrocution. See killing and torture
Elias, Norbert, 28, 249, 394 n.8
Eliot, George, *Middlemarch*, 9
Ellis, Bret Easton, 215, 313 n.53, 359 n.45, 374
n.48, 375 n.48
Ellis, Havelock, 336 n.1, 341 n.27
Ellis, John, 353 n.9, 375 n.49
Ellman, Richard, 104, 310 n.38
emblems, tattoos, 166–68
emotional states. See mental states
execution. See killing and torture
executioner experiences, 144, 353 n.9, 354
n.16, 356 n.29
experiencing vs participating in disgusting
acts, 54, 72
experiences of author
animal encounters, 365 n.75
beautiful, stinking man, 245–48, 266
beggar eating snot, 247, 248
colostomy accident, 340
cooking maggot-infested meat, xii, xiii
father eating insects in food, 1, 2
female genitalia childhood, 43–47, 387
n.82
food aversions, 43–46, 62, 79, 80, 83, 170,
330 n.59, 404 n.80
friendship with abject man, 241–45, 249,
263, 265, 270, 284–86
Georgia Lee, 83–90, 99–101, 106, 108, 127,
129, 170, 291, 292, 341 n.30, 372 n.32
international travels, 316 n.65, 391 n.110,
391 n.120
motorcycle accident, 131–33, 157, 162, 258
riot observations, 399 n.41
seeing spider tattoo, 367 n.4, 393 n.5
sports bore conversation, 159–61, 172, 184,
245
spying on woman's bathroom, 372 n.32
strip club visit, 191, 192
visits to bars with friends, 189–94
waitress tattoo of dragon, 393 n.7

wearing Rushdie button, 380 n.22
woman on Paris bus, 289–92
externalization, 55, 58
eyes, 248, 370 n.27
Polanski *Repulsion*, 214, 215
prosthetic eyes, 257, 258, 282, 283
symbolism, 282, 283

facial expressions. *See also* visceral reactions
acting, 96, 338 n.15
disgust, 11, 13, 15, 24, 90, 92–95, 102, 217,
221, 222, 226, 248, 305 n.14, 338 n.11
embarrassment, 97
facial tattoos and markings, 19, 316 n.68
necessity for horror, 217, 223
scholarly interest in, 339 n.16
Shakespeare, 222, 223
shame, 97, 339 n.17
shock, 24
viewed by others 307 n.23, 323 n.21, 305
n.14
Fallon, April E., 60, 331 n.65
Farsaie, Fahimeh, 378 n.10
Fat Rick, 371 n.27
fatwa, 199, 201, 207–09, 378 n.10, 377 n.5, 378
n.5, 382 n.48, 383 n.56, 384 n.60
Faulkner, William, 116, 274, 347 n.68, 347
n.69
fear, 132, 133, 194, 216, 217, 221, 223, 261, 316
n.66
feet, 77
Feitlowitz, Marguerite, 323 n.20
feminine hygiene products, 116, 314 n.58, 405
n.88
feminism, 317 n.75, 325 n.29, 326 n.29, 393
n.4, 397 n.25, 400 n.49. *See also*
gender aspects
Feyerabend, Paul, 311 n.41, 336 n.90
fictional worlds, 176–83. *See also* imagination
actual world relationship, 161, 293, 366
n.2, 376 n.60, 404 n.85
conventions and theories, 318 n.78, 320
n.5, 348 n.78, 373 n.34
disgust-worlds, 128, 162, 186, 205, 211–15,
270

Ingarden, Roman, 175
Ingersoll, Robert G., 145, 202
Inquisition, 359 n.45
insanity. *See* mental states and disorders
insect eating, 14, 314 n.57, 395 n.19. *See also*
    animals, insects
internalization, 55, 58
Irigaray, Luce, 362 n.56
Iser, Wolfgang, 371 n.28
Ishiguro, Kazuo, 379 n.18
Islam. *See* religious aspects

Jameson, Fredric, 124, 148, 151, 363 n.67, 349
    n.86
Japan, 168, 169, 369 n.23, 370 n.23
Jenkins, Dr. W. I., 354 n.12
Jesus Christ, 164, 168, 383 n.58
Jeunet, Jean-Pierre, 230, 231, 398 n.35. *See also*
    Alien films
Jim Rose Circus Sideshow, 26, 314 n.56, 395
    n.19
Johnson, Dr. Samuel, 9, 305 n.13
Joyce, James, 310 n.38, 400 n.48
    Portrait of the Artist as a Young Man, 104,
        310 n.38
    Ulysses, xxiii, 14, 57, 97, 103-06, 118, 198,
        205, 345 n.55
Jung, C.G., 364 n.69
jokes. *See* humour and satire
Juno, Andrea, 370 n.26, 370 n.27
juror experiences, 54, 358 n.39

Kafka, Franz, 312 n.43, 344 n.47, 359 n.45, 392
    n.4
Kant, Immanuel, xix, 37, 304 n.4, 316 n.68,
    322 n.18, 323 n.21, 333 n.80
Kapalka, Jason, 306 n.19, 307 n.19, 307 n.21,
    316 n.64
Katz, Michael R., 304 n.6
Kaufman, Paul, 305 n.14, 399 n.39
Keats, John, 318 n.78
Kekes, John
    moral-legal model of disgust, 53, 54, 91

influence of disgusting acts, 54, 70, 91,
    143, 322 n.17
moral taboos, 50, 94
universality inclinations, 323 n.21, 326
    n.36
views about disgust, 70, 71, 91, 103, 321
    n.15, 322 n.18, 330 n.60, 343 n.44
Kemmler, William, 136-38, 145, 353 n.11, 354
    n.12, 354 n.13, 354 n.14
Kerlin, Michael J., 382 n.43
Kershner, Irvin, 364 n.68
Khomeini, Ayatollah Ruhollah, 199, 207-09,
    377 n.5, 378 n.10, 378 n.6, 380 n.21,
    382 n.48, 384 n.60, 399 n.40
kidneys, 405 n.89
killing and torture. *See also* wounds
    assassination, 6
    cannibalism, xviii, 135, 351 n.4
    castration, 220, 227, 235, 351 n.2
    electrocution, 136-38, 145, 352 n.8, 353
        n.11, 353 n.12, 354 n.12, 354 n.13, 354
        n.14, 354 n.16
    excrement immersion, 118, 119
    execution, 143-45, 157, 352 n.7, 355 n.18,
        356 n.26, 357 n.38, 358 n.42
    execution celebrating, 134-36, 143, 184
    execution methods, 136-40, 196, 356 n.28,
        356 n.29, 359 n.43
    execution watching, 139-45, 171, 358 n.41,
        359 n.42
    gassing, 138, 140, 145, 355 n.20, 356 n.26,
        358 n.42
    genocide, 321 n.13
    hanging, 137, 139, 353 n.9
    infanticide, 212, 250
    lethal injection, 353 n.11
    murder, 111, 243, 356 n.30, 375 n.48
    mutilation, 359 n.45
    serial killers, xviii, 135, 224, 232, 233, 351
        n.3, 375 n.48, 390 n.108
    torture, 53, 54, 323 n.20, 347 n.71, 359
        n.43, 359 n.44, 359 n.45, 360 n.45,
        388 n.92
    torture methods, 53, 145, 146
Kinbote, Charles, 173, 174
King, Stephen

Levy, Leonard, 201, 207, 208, 209, 210, 306
  n.18, 379 n.16, 383 n.55
Lewin, Ralph A., 14, 72, 119, 327 n.38, 327
  n.40, 328 n.40, 347 n.72
Leyton, Elliott, xviii
Lieberman, Jeff, 364 n.70
Lingis, Alphonso, 305 n.14, 339 n.17, 401 n.54
lips, 234
Lively, Penelope, 398 n.38
Llosa, Mario Vargas, 377 n.5
Lombroso, Cesare Gould, 339 n.16
Longo, Robert, 361 n.53
Lovecraft, H.P., xxix, 197, 221, 234, 227, 370
  n.23, 387 n.85, 387 n.86, 388 n.88
Lowery, 338 n.11
Lucian of Samosata, 74
Luckmann, Thomas, 55, 324 n.24, 325 n.28
Lukacher, Ned, 62, 329 n.50
Luxemburg, Rosa, 309 n.32
Lydon, John, 18
Lynch, David, 17, 211, 212, 215, 216, 250, 385
  n.69, 394 n.11, 401 n.52

Márquez, Gabriel García, 391 n.113
Marxism. See political aspects
MacDonald, John D., 164, 168
MacDowell, Michael, 348 n.79
Machen, Arthur, 225
machines
  androids, 228, 229, 360 n.49, 364 n.68, 389
    n.102, 398 n.35
  consciousness development, 398 n.34
  cyborgs, 326 n.29, 360 n.49, 360 n.50, 361
    n.50, 361 n.52, 362n n.56-58, 364
    n.68, 365 n.75, 398 n.35
  machine-animal similarities, 228, 389
    n.101
  machine-human interaction, 146-57, 251,
    257-62, 362 n.57, 362 n.58, 363 n.61,
    363 n.63, 363 n.66, 363 n.67, 363n
    n.67-69
Mack, Maynard, 111, 112
MacKinnon, Catherine A., 366 n.2
Macy, Caitlin, 368 n.12
Mahaffy, Leslie, 357 n.39, 358 n.39

Mahfouz, Naguib, 380 n.21
Mailer, Norman, 144, 357 n.38
Maitre, Doreen, 176, 369 n.16, 373 n.34
majoritarian, 195, 377, 378 n.6
Malcolm, Janet, 357 n.38
Malraux, André, 359 n.43, 391
Mann, Michael, 142, 233, 234, 235, 390 n.107,
  390 n.108
Manning, Frederick, 139,144
Manning, Marie, 139, 144
Mannix, Daniel P., 395 n.20, 396 n.20
ManWoman, 370 n.27, 371 n.27
Manzoni, Piero, 25, 312 n.50
Marcus, Greil, 18, 19, 24, 25, 74, 308 n.27, 309
  n.31, 309 n.32, 310 n.36, 332 n.73, 333
  n.76
Margolin, Uri, 369 n.16
Martinez-Bonati, Félix, 348 n.78, 368 n.15
Martingale, Moira, 351 n.3
masochism, 119, 341 n.27
Mason, Bobbie Ann, 4 n.48, 375 n.49
Massumi, Brian, 332 n.71
Masur, Louis P., 355 n.18
Mauss, Marcel, 333 n.76
McEwan, Ian, 350 n.92, 371 n.30
McGinn, Colin, 329 n.49
McHale, Brian, 363 n.67
Medusa. See monsters
Menippean satire. See humour and satire
menstruation. See also blood
  cultural sanctions and taboos, 115, 116,
    270, 346 n.66, 347 n.69
  literary depictions, 226, 281, 404 n.78
  male reactions, 115, 346 n.65, 347
    n.70, 401 n.54
  menarche, 388 n.97
  menstrual blood, 226, 285
    viewed by Kristeva, 107, 116, 146,
      269, 270, 276-78, 343 n.45, 400 n.47
    viewed by others, 346 n.65, 387
      n.81, 400 n.47, 400 n.48, 402 n.70,
      403 n.70
mental states and disorders. See also misanthropy; misogyny
  anger, 185, 280, 281
  coprolalia, 307 n.22

text and plot, 267, 342 n.31, 348
n.73, 391 n.118

de Sade, Donatien Alphonse François
advocate of toe-jam licking, 89, 119, 120
influence on others, 333 n.79, 334 n.82
The 120 Days of Sodom, 93, 125, 327 n.40,
333 n.80
and transgression model of disgust,
70–77
views about transgression, 31, 90, 333
n.76
sado-masochism, 340 n.25
Said, Edward W., 201
Sammon, Paul M., 212, 385 n.66
Samuels, David, 310 n.36
Samuels, Stuart, 211
Sanowar-Makhan, Tamara Zeta, 314 n.58
Sartre, Jean-Paul
Being and Nothingness, xxi, 40, 64, 229, 330
n.54
Childhood of a Leader, xxii, 309 n.29
language issues, 329 n.54, 330 n.54, 331
n.63, 371 n.28
Nausea, 3, 4, 117, 161, 181, 211, 212, 251, 271,
330 n.54
phenomenological model of disgust,
64–70, 121, 279, 320 n.5, 350 n.93,
335 n.89, 389 n.103
Psychology of the Imagination, 371 n.28
views about disgust, 40, 44, 64, 68–70,
90, 121, 170, 181
views about imagination, 282
viewed by others, 373 n.34, 402 n.58
Satanism 340 n.24
satire. *See* humour and satire
Scarry, Elaine, 133, 162, 360 n.45
Scheerer, Robert, 364 n.70
Scheff, Thomas J., 8, 55, 339 n.18, 339 n.19,
325 n.27
Schiller, Friedrich, 308 n.29
Schleiermacher, Friedrich, 206, 381 n.39
Schmidt, Lars-Henrik, 312 n.46, 331 n.66, 343
n.45

Schnacke, Judge Robert, 140, 357 n.38, 358
n.42
scientific method, 324 n.24, 326 n.33
Scilingo, Adolfo, 323 n.20
Scorsese, Martin, 164, 168, 169, 171, 172, 318
n.78, 370 n.25, 373 n.35, 249
Scott, Ridley, 154, 155, 261, 227, 228. *See also*
Aliens films
self-disgust. *See also* abjection
and abjection, 265, 266, 269–80, 285, 339
n.19
author's experiences, 87, 88, 242–45, 249,
285
characteristics, 239, 249, 251–54
feminist views, 277–81
object transferral to self, 33
Lessing *Golden Notebook*, 270–74, 276,
279–81, 401 n.50, 401 n.52
literary depictions, 252, 254
Shakespeare, 253, 254
and shame, 90, 96
self-inflicted mutilation and wounds, 24, 25,
226, 241–43
self-knowledge, 252, 280
Sen, Amartya, 381 n.34
serial killers. *See* killing and torture
Serrano, Andres, 313 n.50
sewers, 315 n.59
Sex Pistols 18, 309 n.31
sexism. *See* mental states and disorders
sexual abuse, 76, 243, 244
sexual activities
adultery, 111, 353 n.9
and aggression, 366 n.2
anus, 392 n.2
in church, 371 n.31
coprophagy, 119
desire and pleasure, 278, 315 n.61
deviance, 383 n.58
golden showers, 91, 341 n.27,
author's experience, 86–88, 100,
108, 127–29, 292, 341 n.30
descriptions, 99–101, 340 n.25
as deviant act, 55, 56, 72
role of context 108, 109, 325 n.28

homosexual vs heterosexual
classification, 320 n.6
infidelity, 69
kissing, 315 n.61
necrophilia, 26, 50, 61, 402 n.66
oral sex, 29, 46, 61, 315 n.61
orgasm, 340 n.25
perversion, 68, 315 n.61
repression, 62, 63
sexual openness and excess, 209, 383 n.58
social and cultural aspects, 29, 325 n.28,
342 n.33
sodomy, 243, 244
techno-sex, 251
as terrorism act, 388 n.93
Shade, John, 173, 174
Shakespeare, William, 27, 359 n.45, 362 n.56,
375 n.49
and disgust 6, 7, 251
language usage, 4, 8, 10, 35, 275, 276, 362
n.56
Menippean elements, 308 n.26
use of term "abject", 275, 276, 402 n.61
Antony and Cleopatra, 100
Hamlet, 20, 22
fictional worlds, 253, 254, 285
language employed, 7, 8, 112, 219
Menippean elements, 308 n.26
Pyrrhus character, 113, 117
representation of filth, 112, 345
n.55
role of surprise and deception, 27,
222, 223, 388 n.90
role of Troy myth, 174, 175, 374
n.44
Yorick's skull passage, 9, 16, 111,
251
2 Henry VI, 275
Julius Caesar, 6
King Lear, 8, 20,   304 n.9, 305 n.9
Macbeth, 388 n.90
Measure for Measure, 20, 308 n.26
A Midsummer's Night Dream, 389
Much Ado About Nothing, 27
Othello, 95, 222, 358 n.45
The Rape of Lucrece, 222, 318 n.78

Richard III, 275
Timon of Athens, 20, 308 n.26
Titus Andronicus, 7, 22, 27, 275
Troilus and Cressida, 17, 18, 20, 22, 73, 74,
275, 307 n.23, 308 n.26
Winter's Tale, 7, 35, 36, 38, 39, 69, 251, 367
n.7
shame
antecedents, 33
author experiences, 87–89, 101, 372 n.32
childhood experiences, 62
and disgust, 185, 281, 285, 317 n.71, 339
n.18, 339 n.19
facial expression of, 96, 97
Shakespeare, 7, 111
Shattuck, Roger, 72, 74, 332 n.73
Shearman, Sir Montague, 353 n.9
Shelley, Mary, 135
Sherbert, Garry, 73, 309 n.34, 316 n.68
shit. *See* effluvia and excreta, feces
Shklovsky, Victor, 309 n.30
shock, 16, 20, 21, 27, 73, 75, 123
sideshows. *See* circuses, carnivals and
sideshows
Siegal, Don, 399 n.39
Sigal, Clancy, 403 n.71
Simeons, Albert T. 316 n.66
skin, 163
sliminess
author's experiences, 44, 45, 58
characteristics, 128
fictional depictions, 225, 226, 228, 229, 387
n.86
viewed by Sartre, 64–68, 121, 329 n.54, 331
n.63, 330 n.58
Sloterdijk, Peter, 74, 333 n.74
Smith, Adam, 51
Smith, Robert, 26
social aspects, 50–53, 66, 325 n.28. *See also*
cultural aspects
sociocultural aspects, 92, 165, 166, 250,
269
law of oppositionality, 56, 57
social constructionist model of disgust. *See*
also models of disgust
overview, 54–60

terror. *See also* horror; terrorism
    fictional portrayals, 122, 124, 232–37, 388
        n.92,
        compared with horror, 98, 122, 194,
            195, 224, 225, 232, 262, 349 n.85, 390
            n.108
    ideological terror, 197, 210
    terror vs disgust, 211, 217
terrorism. *See also* terror
    fictional depictions, 390 n.108, 391 n.112
    political aspects, 380 n.22, 388 n.93
    Rushdie *Satanic Verses* 122, 123, 208, 349
        n.82, 378 n.10, 391 n.112
    viewed by others, 349 n.84, 380 n.21
testicles. *See* genitalia, male
theatre. *See* art
Theroux, Paul, 198, 199
Thomas, D.M., 370 n.23
Thompson, Edith, 353 n.9
Thucydides, 266
Tisdale, Sallie, 317 n.75
Tithecott, Richard, xviii, xxi, 351 n.3
Titian, 39
toe licking and sucking, 89, 93, 119, 120
toilet training, 57, 58, 60, 62, 66, 68, 278, 309
    n.33
Tokyo Shock Boys, 312 n.44
torso, 226
torture. *See* killing and torture
transgression, 3, 92, 121, 165
    aesthetics, 22, 23, 321 n.15
    and disgust, 12, 30, 79, 185, 270,
    and self-knowledge 308 n.29, 310 n.35, 312
        n.44, 334 n.84, 402 n.59
    and sex, 88, 108, 251
    and shame, 339 n.18, 371 n.31,
    shock art, 162, 311 n.42, 312 n.44,
    social aspects, 55, 101–03, 246, 248, 332
        n.73, 333 n.76
    tattoos, 163, 168, 319 n.81, 370 n.27, 371
        n.27
transgression model of disgust, 70–77, 79,
    275. *See also* models of disgust
Trebay, Guy, 316 n.68, 367 n.7
Trofimovich, Stepan, 304 n.6
Trombley, Stephen, 354 n.16, 356 n.29

Tropmann, 143
Tsukamoto, Shinya, 362 n.58
Tunnell, Gary, 307 n.21
Turgenev, Ivan Sergeyvich, 143
Turnbull, Colin M., 307 n.19, 306 n.19

urination, 85, 90, 99, 100, 108, 109, 124, 137,
    336 n.1, 325 n.28
urine drinking, 124, 325 n.28, 327 n.38, 340
    n.25,
urolagnia, 56, 85, 86, 340 n.27, 341 n.27
uterus. *See* genitalia, female

vagina. *See* genitalia, female
Vázquez, Horacio, 347 n.71
Vaihinger, Hans, 311 n.41
Vale, V., 370 n.27
vampires. *See* monsters
Vasquez, Daniel, 140, 141
Verhoeven, Paul, 151–55, 365 n.70
Vicious, Sid, 162
violence, 190, 192–94, 128, 224, 266–68, 389
    n.105
visceral reactions to disgust. *See also* facial
    expressions
    disgust as psycho-visceral affect 15, 40,
        186, 304 n.5, 325 n.26, 384 n.63
    gagging, 87, 89, 91, 100, 103, 108, 329 n.48,
        338 n.12,
    nausea, 59, 61, 67, 91, 103
    viewed by others, 3, 98, 342 n.33
    vomiting, 61, 204, 210
Viswanathan, Gauri, 379 n.12, 381 n.29
vomit, xviii, 49, 65, 67, 93, 213, 312 n.49, 343
    n.45
vomit eating, 67, 325 n.28, 331 n.66, 343 n.45
vomiting, 8, 19, 91, 144, 273, 274, 315 n.61, 338
    n.12
Von Drehle, David, 353 n.11, 354 n.16
voyeurism, 372 n.32
vulva. *See* genitalia, female

Waal, Alex de, 307 n.19
Wallace, David Foster, xi, 104, 211, 375 n.49